DATE DUE

PRINTED IN U.S.A.

Notable
Twentieth-Century
Pianists

Notable Twentieth-Century Pianists

A Bio-Critical Sourcebook
Volume 1, A–J

John Gillespie
and Anna Gillespie

Bio-Critical Sourcebooks on Musical Performance

Greenwood Press
Westport, Connecticut • London

Library of Congress Cataloging-in-Publication Data

Gillespie, John.
    Notable twentieth-century pianists : a bio-critical sourcebook /
John Gillespie and Anna Gillespie.
        p.   cm.—(Bio-critical sourcebooks on musical performance,
    ISSN 1069-5230)
    Includes bibliographical references and index.
    ISBN 0–313–25660–8 (set : alk. paper).—ISBN 0–313–29695–2 (vol.
1 : alk. paper).—ISBN 0–313–29696–0 (vol. 2 : alk. paper)
    1. Pianists—Biography. I. Gillespie, Anna. II. Title.
III. Series.
ML397.G45   1995
786.2′092′2—dc20
    [B]   95–9757

British Library Cataloguing in Publication Data is available.

Library of Congress Catalog Card Number: 95–9757
ISBN: 0–313–25660–8(set); 0–313–29695–2(v.1); 0–313–29696–0(v.2)
ISSN: 1069–5230

First published in 1995

Greenwood Press, 88 Post Road West, Westport, CT 06881
An imprint of Greenwood Publishing Group, Inc.

Printed in the United States of America

The paper used in this book complies with the
Permanent Paper Standard issued by the National
Information Standards Organization (Z39.48–1984).

10 9 8 7 6 5 4 3 2 1

Copyright Acknowledgment

For our children . . .

And their children . . .

Contents

Photo Essay follows General Bibliography

Preface_____

This source book of notable pianists contains biographical data; style analyses (culled from reviews, recordings, articles, essays); pedagogical history and methods, when applicable; lists of selected references and reviews; and a representative discography.

Recordings, or lack of recordings, basically set the perimeters of the study. With few exceptions, some recordings are available by which to evaluate each pianist's performance; and, with careful, sensible listening, even the early acoustic discs, many of which have been reissued in CD format, will reveal characteristics of a pianist's style.

How were the pianists selected? A preliminary list was compiled from a questionnaire sent in 1986 to pianists and pedagogues in music conservatories and colleges throughout the United States. Each respondent supplied names of pianists that he or she would include among the 100 most significant pianists who have performed and recorded in the 20th century. We tabulated the results, including our own choices, then throughout eight years of library research and reams of correspondence, we added and deleted names.

We have tried to be as impartial and as "scientific" (if that word may be used in this context) as possible, but of course the final list of 100 pianists will not, could not possibly, please everyone. We excuse the omission of names from the current crop of impressive young pianists on the grounds that they have not been around long enough to acquire "notable" status.

Listening (recordings, recitals, concerts) has been a major part of the study from the very beginning, and we concentrated on trying to listen objectively. But it soon became evident that if we were to give a fair, objective appraisal of each pianist, we had to study reviews of performances throughout all the stages of a career and from as many diverse sources and as many different critics as possible. The process of first finding reviews, interviews and articles for each pianist, then weighing the contents (an ongoing project all through the study) was absolutely fascinating—and addictive! The diverse, highly individual, often eccentric personalities among these 100 pianists make for interesting reading. But the fascinating part has been discovering and comparing individual musical styles, musical approaches, practice methods, repertoire choices and attitudes toward the piano itself. Some pianists first work on technique and technical problems; others prefer to study the qualities of the music first. One will practice eight hours or more at a time, another only one or two hours. Some never practice on the day of a performance; others practice in the dressing room right up to the moment of walking onstage.

There are pianists who will play only works they feel very strongly about; others try to acquire as large a repertoire as possible. Some try to develop a personal "sound" that audiences will recognize as theirs every time they play; others avoid a recognizable sound. Some performers obviously have a wonderful time onstage; others are terrified. Some pianists refuse to play if the piano is not exactly right; other pianists take in stride whatever piano comes along on a tour.

Perhaps most fascinating of all was realizing that digesting so many reviews spread across a century inevitably created a naturally evolving critical process based on the critic's subjectivity (personal likes and dislikes, expectations, comments on past performances); the critic's qualifications (education, experience, writing skill); and how his or her critique compares with others of the same performance.

Working with so much material uncovered a multitude of conflicting facts. One example: In *Gramophone* of January 1991 we read that "the Chopin Etudes were not part of Bolet's repertoire." But in the May 1991 issue of *Gramophone* another writer says that Bolet played the Etudes regularly and programmed the complete Opus 25 set on a number of occasions. That discrepancy is but one of hundreds encountered during this project. By checking, rechecking, sifting and comparing data, we have done our best to uncover true facts and correct dates (nearly impossible) among all the myths and flowery prose surrounding many pianists, especially those from the past. All told, the results, we believe, are fair.

We have carefully noted sources and dates for all quoted reviews and have for the most part omitted the names of the critics. One reason for this omission was to avoid having the fame of the critic influence the reader. Another reason was that in such a large book there would be just too much name-dropping. (Sometimes, however, an important concert or record review will appear in the Selected Reference section to each entry.) Selected reviews and sources for quoted reviews are identified by abbreviations explained in the Periodical and Newspaper Abbreviations list at the front of the book. Text references to items in the General Bibliography are likewise identified by abbreviations given for each bibliographical item. Orchestras in the discographies are frequently abbreviated: i. e., SO (Symphony Orchestra), PO (Philadelphia Orchestra), CO (Chamber Orchestra); FO (Festival Orchestra), RAI (Italian Radio Orchestra).

Compiling discographies has been difficult and frustrating. Record labels appear and disappear, seemingly almost from one month to another. Discs can change from one label to another. For example, Rosalyn Tureck's Bach

CDs, originally issued under the Albany label, are now distributed under the VAIA label. Since many companies will issue only a restricted number of a certain CD, it may be out of print by the time the next record catalogue appears.

By the time this work is published, many listed recordings may no longer be available through regular record outlets. However, often they can be obtained through stores specializing in hard-to-find items. To locate such items and also foreign releases not distributed in the United States, try the following sources:

USA releases:

Parnassus Records (914) 246-3332
56 Parnassus Lane
Saugerties, NY 12477

H & B Records Direct (800) 222-6872
2186 Jackson Keller-Dept. F
San Antonio, TX 78213

Rose Records (800) 955-7673
214 South Wabash Avenue
Chicago, IL 60604

Europe/Great Britain:

Harold Moores Records & Video
2 Great Marlborough St.
London W1V 1DE, Great Britain

MDT Mail Order
6 Old Blacksmiths Yard, Sadler Gate
Derby DE1 3PD, Great Britain

Tandy's Records, Ltd.
24 Islington Row, Birmingham
B15 1LJ, Great Britain

Another possibility is to locate an out-of-print item at libraries or at special archives such as:

Historical Sound Recordings Program
226 Sterling Morton Library
1603A Yale Station
New Haven, CT 06520

Library of Congress
Recorded Sound Division
Music Division, Library of Congress
Washington, D. C., 20540

Phonograph Record Library
Woolworth Center of Musical Studies
Princeton University
Princeton, NJ 08540

Rodgers and Hammerstein
Archives of Recorded Sound
The New York Public Library
111 Amsterdam Avenue
New York, NY 10023

International Piano Archives at Maryland
Music Library, Hornbake 3210
University of Maryland
College Park, MD 20740

Stanford Archive of Recorded Sound
Stanford University, The Knoll
Stanford, CA 94305

Discography listings and numbers come primarily from the Schwann Opus catalogue, Musical Heritage Society (a private record label with recordings not listed in Schwann) and the Gustafson Piano Library. Cassettes from the latter may be obtained on loan. Write to:

>Gustafson Piano Library
>Interlibrary Loans Officer
>John Bassett Memorial Library
>Bishop's University
>Lennoxville, Quebec, Canada J1M 1Z7

We have used principally the following record guides: *Fanfare*, *Gramophone*, *American Record Guide*, plus selected reviews from other sources. Most listings are CDs, identified by the number 2 appended to the record number (i.e., 6257-2) or the use of the letters CD. When a significant performance is available only in cassette or LP format, we have included it in our discography.

We have restricted most of our reference materials and reviews to articles in English, and have used hundreds of sources, principally *The New York Times* and *The Times* (London) and the periodical *Performing Arts* (1978–present, see Bibliog.), available in many libraries.

Some pianists have had societies established in their names:

Fondation Cziffra, 1 Place Saint-Pierre, 60300 Senlis, France
Emil Gilels Society, P. O. Box 22124, Carmel, CA 93922
The Glenn Gould Society, c/o Moesstraat 9f, 9717 JT Groningen, The Netherlands
International Percy Grainger Society, 7 Cromwell Place, White Plains, NY 10601
Association Clara Haskil, Case postale 234, CH-1800 Vevey 1, Switzerland
Société Paderewski, Centre Culturel, Place du Casino 1, CH-1110 Morges, Switzerland
Friends of Sviatoslav Richter, Low Warden Barns, Hexham NE46 4SN, Great Britain
Rachmaninoff Society, 5215 West 64th Terrace, Prairie Village, KS 66208

We did the research, writing and "word-processing" ourselves, none of which would have been nearly as complete without the efficient help of the many librarians who kindly responded to inquiries, pianists' agents who generously supplied information, and others who assisted in so many ways. We are very grateful to the pianists who graciously responded to our inquiries and to Mr. James Methuen-Campbell, whose books and articles have proven invaluable to our research. Also, special thanks must be given to the following:

Edwin Alan (Appian Publications
  & Recordings)
John Berrie (Friends of Sviatoslav
  Richter)

Bryan Crimp
Mrs. Gwendolyn Cutner
Michael Rolland Davis (Chesky
  Recordings)

Allan Evans
Richard Fisher
Shirley Freeman
Mrs. Bice Horszowski
Mrs. Griselda Kentner
Wynfred Lyddane

Fred Maroth (Music & Arts
    Programs of America)
Mrs. Fergus Pope
Pro Arte Productions
Dr. Raymond Warner
Lou Waryncia

And, finally, we are grateful to *all* of the reviewers and critics, past and present, for their keen observations and analyses. In particular, we have greatly enjoyed reading and comparing the writings of Paula Adamick, Mark Adamo, Richard Aldrich, John Amis, Carl Apone, John Ardoin, Joseph Banowetz, Melinda Bargreen, Greta Beigel, Byron Belt, Gregor Benko, Karen Berger, Martin Bernheimer, Louis Biancolli, Alan Blyth, Hugh Canning, Scott Cantrell, Neville Cardus, Daniel Cariaga, Claudia Cassidy, Peter Catalano, Abram Chasins, Olin Chism, Joan Chissell, Robert Commanday, James Francis Cooke, Bryan Crimp, Will Crutchfield, Peter G. Davis, Wynne Delacoma, Olin Downes, David Dubal, Bob Doerschuk, Paul Driver, Jessica Duchen, Richard Dyer, Thor Eckert, Jr., Dean Elder, Susan Elliott, Raymond Ericson, Allan Evans, Hilary Finch, Henry Finck, Robert Finn, Josiah Fisk, Shirley Fleming, Alfred Frankenstein, Richard Freed, Rena Fruchter, Leslie Gerber, Harris Goldsmith, Noel Goodwin, Channing Gray, Albert Goldberg, Peter Goodman, Edward Greenfield, Paul Griffiths, John Gruen, Philip Hale, Max Harrison, A. M. Henderson, Donal Henehan, Derrick Henry, Paul Hertelendy, Maurice Hinson, Jan Holcman, Bernard Holland, Joseph Horowitz, Paul Hume, James Huneker, Stuart Isacoff, Speight Jenkins, Barbara Jepson, Rafael Kammerer, Nicholas Kenyon, Michael Kimmelmann, Irving Kolodin, Allan Kozinn, Herbert Kupferberg, Theodore W. Libbey, Jr., Joseph McLellan, Nancy Malitz, Donald Manildi, Robert C. Marsh, Lisa Marum, Robert Matthew-Walker, James Methuen-Campbell, Karen Monson, Carol Montparker, Bryce Morrison, James R. Oestreich, Robert Offergeld, Ates Orga, Richard Osborne, Tim Page, Malince Peris, Donna Perlmutter, Stephen Pettitt, Andrew L. Pincus, Andrew Porter, Michael Redmond, Howard Reich, John von Rhein, Alan Rich, Trevor Richardson, Kate Rivers, John Rockwell, John Rosenfield, Edward Rothstein, Peter Runkel, Harvey Sachs, Harold C. Schonberg, Marc Shulgold, Robert J. Silverman, Larry Sitsky, David Patrick Stearns, Mark Swed, Howard Taubman, Virgil Thomson, Anthony Tommasini, Marilyn Tucker, Lesley Valdes, Michael Walsh, Daniel Webster and Stephen Wigler.

Periodical and Newspaper Abbreviations_____

AA	Adelaide (Australia) Advertiser	ARSC	Association for Recorded Sound Collections Journal
ABJ	Akron (OH) Beacon Journal	AT	Anchorage (AK) Times
AC	Ashville (NC) Citizen		
ADN	Anchorage (AK) Daily News	BaS	Baltimore (MD) Sun
		BDG	Berkeley (CA) Daily Gazette
AEE	Aberdeen (Scotland) Evening Express	BDN	Bangor (ME) Daily News
AG	Arkansas Gazette (Little Rock)	BE	Berkshire Eagle (Pittsfield, MA)
AJ	Atlanta (GA) Journal (-Constitution)	BEE	Bournemouth Evening Echo (England)
AJL	American Jewish Ledger	BEN	Buffalo (Evening) News (NY)
ALJ	Albuquerque (NM) Journal	BET	Boston (MA) Evening Transcript
AM	Asia Magazine	BG	Boston (MA) Globe
AMICA	Automatic Musical Instrument Collectors' Assn.	BH	Boston (MA) Herald
		BJ	Beacon Journal (Cleveland, OH)
AmM	American Music		
APP	Asbury Park Press (Neptune, NJ)	BP	Boston (MA) Post
		BPh	The Bulletin (Philadelphia)
AR	Arizona Republic (Phoenix)	BS	Boston (MA) Sentinal
ARG	American Record Guide	BT	Belfast Telegraph (Ireland)

CA	Commercial Appeal (Memphis, TN)	CT	Chicago (IL) Tribune
CaT	Capitol Times (Madison, WI)	DC	Daily Camera (Boulder, CO)
CCC-T	Corpus Christi (TX) Caller-Times	DDN	Dayton (OH) Daily News
CD	Columbus (OH) Dispatch	DeDN	Detroit (MI) Daily News
		DeT	Detroit (MI) Times
CDJ	Chicago (IL) Daily Journal	DFP	Detroit (MI) Free Press
		DMN	Dallas (TX) Morning News
CDM	Charleston (SC) Daily Mail	DMR	Des Moines (IA) Register
CDN	Chicago (IL) Daily News	DN	Deseret News (Salt Lake City, UT)
CDR	CD Review		
CE	Cincinnati (OH) Enquirer	DNH	Daily News (Halifax, Nova Scotia)
CEA	Chicago (IL) Evening American	DNL	Daily News (Lebanon, PA)
CED	Columbus (Ohio) Evening Dispatch	DNLA	Daily News (Los Angeles)
CEP	Chicago (IL) Evening Post	DO	(Daily) Oklahoman (Oklahoma City)
CG	Charleston (SC) Gazette	DP	Denver (CO) Post
CH	Chronicle Herald (Halifax, Nova Scotia)	DT	Daily Telegraph (London)
CHE	Chicago (IL) Herald Examiner	DTH	Dallas (TX) Times Herald
CiP	Cincinnati Post		
C-J	Courier-Journal (Louisville, KY)	EP	Evening Post (Charleston, SC)
CL	Clavier	EPNZ	Evening Post (New Zealand)
C-L	Clarion-Ledger (Jackson, MS)	ES	Evening Sun (Baltimore, MD)
CLA	Classic (CD)	ESQ	Esquire
CNC	Charleston (SC) News & Courier	ET	Evening Times (Glasgow, Scotland)
CO	Charlotte (NC) Observer	Etude	Etude
CoP	Connecticut Post (Bridgeport)		
CP	Classical Pulse	Fan	Fanfare
CPD	Cleveland (OH) Plain Dealer	FB	Fresno (CA) Bee
		FJ	Flint (MI) Journal
CS	Columbia (SC) State	FLSS	Fort Lauderdale (FL) Sun/Sentinel
CSM	Christian Science Monitor	FT	Financial Times (London)
CST	Chicago (IL) Sun-Times		

FTU	Florida Times-Union (Jacksonville)
FWJG	(Fort Wayne) Journal-Gazette (IN)
GBPG	Green Bay (WI) Press-Gazette
GH	Glasgow Herald (Scotland)
GloM	The Globe and Mail (Toronto, Canada)
GM	Guardian (Manchester, England)
G-M	Gazette (Montreal)
Gram	Gramophone
GRP	Grand Rapids (MI) Press
GT	Gazette Telegraph (Colorado Springs, CO)
GWN	Garnett Westchester Newspapers
HA	Herald American (Boston, MA)
HaC	Hartford (CT) Courant
HB	Honolulu (Star-) Bulletin (HI)
HC	Houston (TX) Chronicle
HF	High Fidelity
HF-MA	Hi Fi/Musical America
HKS	Hong Kong Stardard
HP	Houston (TX) Post
HR	Hudson Revue
IHT	International Herald Tribune
IN	Indianapolis (IN) News
IND	The Independent (London)
IrT	Irish Times (Belfast)
IS	Indianapolis (IN) Star
IT	Indianapolis (IN) Times
JS	Journal & Star (Lincoln, NE)
KCS	Kansas City (MO) Star

KCT	Kansas City (MO) Times
KeCl	Keyboard Classics
KeM	Keyboard Magazine
Key	Keynote (Magazine for the Musical Arts Including the Program Guide for WNCN 104 FM)
KJ	Knoxville (TN) Journal
LADN	Los Angeles (CA) Daily News
LAHE	Los Angeles (CA) Herald Examiner
LAM	L.A. Magazine
LAT	Los Angeles (CA) Times
LDN	London Daily News
LF	*Le Figaro* (Paris)
LI	The Listener
LIN	Long Island (NY) Newsday
LM	*Le Monde* (Paris)
LMP	London Morning Post
MA	Musical America
MABR	Morning Advocate (Baton Rouge, LA)
MC	Musical Courier
MD	Michigan Daily
MG	Montreal Gazette (Canada)
MH	Miami (FL) Herald
MiT	Minneapolis (Star and) Tribune (MN)
MJ	Milwaukee (WI) Journal
MJA	Montgomery (Journal &) Advertiser (AL)
MM	Music and Musicians
MO	Musical Opinion
MoC	Morning Call (Allentown, PA)
MoT	Montclair (NJ) Times
MQ	Musical Quarterly
MS	Milwaukee (WI) Sentinel
M-SH	Mail-Star (Halifax)

MT	Musical Times	OT	Oakland (CA) Tribune
MuJ	Music Journal	OV	Ovation
MuM	Music Magazine	OWH	Omaha (NE) World Herald
NAO	News and Observer (Raleigh NC)	PEB	Philadelphia (PA) Evening Bulletin
Nat	The Nation		
ND	Newsday (New York, NY)	PI	Philadelphia (PA) Inquirer
NDN	Newport (RI) Daily News	PJ	Providence (RI) Journal (-Bulletin)
NewY	New York	PL	Patriot Ledger
NHR	New Haven (CT) Register		(Pittsburgh, PA)
		PM	People Magazine
NM	New Mexican	PoJ	Poughkeepsie (NY) Journal
NO	National Observer		
NR	New Republic	PP	Pittsburgh (PA) Press
NW	Newsweek	PPG	(Pittsburgh) Post-Gazette (PA)
NY	New Yorker		
NYA	New York American	PPH	Portland (ME) Press Herald
NYCT	New York City Tribune		
NYDN	New York Daily News	PQ	Piano Quarterly
NYEM	New York Evening Mail	PS	Press-Scimitar (Memphis)
NYEP	New York Evening Post		
NYHT	New York Herald Tribune	P-S	Post-Standard (Syracuse, NY)
NYJA	New York Journal American		
		RDC	(Rochester) Democrat & Chronicle (NY)
NYP	New York Post		
NYS	New York Sun	RE	Reading (PA) Eagle/Times
NYT	New York Times		
NYTr	New York Tribune	RIR	Records in Review
NYW	New York World	RMN	Rocky Mountain News (Denver, CO)
NYWT	New York World-Telegram and Sun		
		RNL	Richmond (VA) News Leader
NZZ	Neue Züriche Zeitung		
		RR	Records and Recordings
OaR	Oak Ridger (TN)	R-S	Register-Star (Rockford, IL)
OC	Ottowa Citizen (Canada)		
OCR	Orange County Register (Santa Ana, CA)	RT	Richmond (VA) Times (Dispatch)
OP	Opus	RTU	(Rochester) Times-Union (NY)
ORE	The Oregonian (Portland)		
OrS	Orlando (FL) Sentinel	RTW-N	Roanoke (VA) Times & World-News
OS	Oregon Statesman (Salem)		

SBNP	Santa Barbara (CA) News-Press	TC	Tucson (AZ) Citizen
SCMP	South China Morning Post	TEN	Tennessean (Nashville)
		TET	Toronto Evening Telegram (Canada)
SDU	San Diego (CA) Union	Time	Time
S-E	Star-Eagle (Newark, NJ)	TL	The Times (London)
SFC	San Francisco (CA) Chronicle	TP	Times Picayune (New Orleans, LA)
SFE	San Francisco (CA) Examiner	TS	Toronto Star (Canada)
		TT	Toronto Telegram (Canada)
SFR	Santa Fe (NM) Reporter		
SH-J	Syracuse (NY) Herald-Journal	TU	Times Union (Rochester, NY)
SJM	San Jose (CA) Mercury	TUA	Times-Union (Albany, NY)
SJS	San Juan Star (Puerto Rico)	TWaI	The World and I
SL	Standard (London)		
S-L	Star-Ledger (Newark, NJ)	USA	USA Today
SLGD	St. Louis (MO) Globe-Democrat	V-P	Virginian-Pilot (Norfolk)
SLPD	St Louis (MO) Post Dispatch	VV	Village Voice (New York, NY)
SLT	(Salt Lake) Tribune (UT)	WDT	Worcester (MA) Daily Telegram (and Gazette)
SM	Scotsman (Edinburgh)		
SMH	Sydney Morning Herald	WE	Wichita (KS) Eagle (-Beacon)
SMU	Springfield (MA) Morning Union	WEJ	Wilmington (DE) Evening Journal
SN	Sunday News (New York, NY))	WEP	Worcester (MA) Evening Post
SP	Spectator (Raleigh, NC)	WG	Westminister Gazette
SPI	Seattle (OR) Post Intelligencer	WP	Washington (DC) Post
		WS	Washington (DC) Star
SPPP	Saint Paul (MN) Pioneer Press Dispatch	WSJ	Wall Street Journal (New York, NY)
SPT	St. Petersburg (FL) Times	W-SJ	Winston-Salem Journal (NC)
SR	Saturday Review	WS-N	Washington Star-News
ST	Seattle (WA) Times	WT	Washington (DC) Times
STL	Sunday Times (London)	W-T	World Telegram
StR	Stereo Review	WWD	Women's Wear Daily
SU	Sacramento (CA) Union		
T-A	Times-Argus (Montpellier, VT)	YO	Yorkshire Observer (England)
TB	Toledo (OH) Blade		

General Bibliography———————

A. BOOKS

Abd/Bla   Abdul, Raoul. *Blacks In Classical Music*. New York: Dodd, Mead and Company, 1977.

Ald/Con   Aldrich, Richard. *Concert Life in New York 1902–1923*. Freeport, New York: Books for Libraries Press, 1971(1941).

Ali/Pia   Alink, Gustav A. *Piano Competitions: A Comprehensive Directory of National and International Piano Competitions*. Den Haag: CIP-Gegevens Koninklijke Bibliotheek, 1990.

Bac/Pia   Bacon, Ernst. "Pianists Then and Now." *Clavier*, Nov 1981, pp. 22–25. Brief recollections of Paderewski, Carreño, d'Albert, Grainger, Gabrilowitsch, Bauer, Hofmann, de Pachmann, Godowsky, Lhévinne, Backhaus, Rachmaninoff.

Bak/Bio   *Baker's Biographical Dictionary of Musicians*. Seventh Edition, rev. Nicolas Slonimsky. New York: Schirmer Books. 1984.

Ben/For   Bennett, Joseph. *Forty Years of Music*. London: Methuen and Co., 1908.

Bie/His   Bie, Oscar. *A History of the Pianoforte and Pianoforte Players*, trans. E. E. Kellett and E. W. Naylor. New York: Da Capo Press, 1966 (1899).

Bla/Gra   Blaukopf, Kurt. *Les Grands Virtuoses*, traduit de l'Allemand par Jean–Claude Salel. Paris: Editions Corrêa, 1955.

Bro/Mas   Brook, Donald. *Masters of the Keyboard*. London: Rockliff, 1947.

Bro/Mod   Brower, Harriette. *Modern Masters of the Keyboard*. New York: Books for Libraries Press, 1969 (1926).

Bro/Par   Brody, Elaine. *Paris: The Musical Kaleidoscope 1870–1925*. New York: George Braziller, 1987.

Bro/Pia   Brower, Harriette. *Piano Mastery*. New York: Frederick A. Stokes Company, 1915.

Bro/PiS   Brower, Harriette. *Piano Mastery*. Second Series. New York:
             Frederick A. Stokes Company, 1917.
Bül/Br   Bülow, Hans von. *Briefe*. Leipzig: Druck und Verlag von
             Breitkopf und Härtel, 1908, 7 volumes.
Bül/Let   Bülow, Hans von. *Letters*, New York: Vienna House, 1972.
Cal/MG   Calvocoressi, M. D. *Musicians Gallery*. London: Faber and Faber
             Limited, 1933.
Cal/Mus   Calvocoressi, M. D. *Music and Ballet*. London: Faber and Faber,
             1934.
Car/Del   Cardus, Neville. *The Delights of Music*. London: Victor Gollancz
             Ltd., 1966.
Car/Ful   Cardus, Neville. *Full Score*. London: Cassell, 1970.
Car/Tal   Cardus, Neville. *Talking Of Music*. London: Collins, 1957.
Cat/Mus   *Catalog of Music-Rolls for the Duo-Art Reproducing Piano*. New
             York: The Aeolian Company, 1924.
Cen/Lib   *Century Library of Music*, ed. Ignace Jan Paderewski. New York:
             The Century Co., 1900. 20 vols.
Cha/Gia   Chapin, Victor. *Giants of the Keyboard*. Philadelphia: J. G.
             Lippincott Co., 1967.
Cha/Spe   Chasins, Abram. *Speaking of Pianists*. New York: Alfred A.
             Knopf, 1958.
Coh/Rec   Cohn, Arthur. *Recorded Classical Music*. New York: Schirmer
             Books, 1982.
Con/Bak   *The Concise Baker's Biographical Dictionary of Musicians*. Eighth
             Edition. New York: Schirmer Books, 1994.
Coo/Gre   Cooke, James Francis. *Great Men and Famous Musicians on The
             Art of Music*. Philadelphia: Theo. Presser Co., 1925.
Coo/GrP   Cooke, James Francis. *Great Pianists on Piano Playing*. New
             York: AMS Press, Inc., 1976 (1917).
Cur/Bio   *Current Biography*. New York: H. W. Wilson, 1940–.
Dan/Con   Daniels, Robin. *Conversations With Cardus*. Foreword by Yehudi
             Menuhin. London: Victor Gollancz Ltd., 1976.
Dic/Am   *Dictionary of American Biography*. New York: Charles Scribner's
             Sons, 1928–1936. 20 volumes, 2 supplementary volumes.
Doe/Tra   Doerschuk, Bob. "Tradition & Innovation in Bach Keyboard
             Performance." *Keyboard*, March 1985, pp. 13–16, 78–84.
Dow/Oli   Downes, Olin. *Olin Downes on Music*. New York: Simon &
             Schuster, 1957.
Dub/Eve   Dubal, David. *Evenings with Horowitz*. New York: Birch Lane
             Press, 1991.
Dub/Ref   Dubal, David. *Reflections from the Keyboard*. New York:
             Summit Books, 1984.
Eld/Pia   Elder, Dean. *Pianists at Play*. Evanston: The Instrumentalist
             Company, 1982.
Ewe/Li   Ewen, David. *Living Musicians*. New York: The H. W. Wilson
             Co., 1940.

Ewe/Li2   Ewen, David. *Living Musicians*, First Supplement. New York: The H. W. Wilson Co., 1957.

Ewe/Me   Ewen, David. *Men and Women Who Make Music.* New York: Merlin Press, 1949.

Ewe/Mu   Ewen, David. *Musicians Since 1900.* New York: The H. W. Wilson Co., 1978.

Ffr/Mus   Ffrench, Florence. *Music and Musicians in Chicago.* New York: Da Capo Press, 1979 (c. 1899).

Fin/My   Finck, Henry T. *My Adventures in the Golden Age of Music.* New York: Funk and Wagnalls Company, 1926.

Fin/Suc   Finck, Henry T. *Success in Music and How it is Won.* New York: Charles Scribners's Sons, 1909.

Ful/Doo   Fuller-Maitland, J. A. *A Door-Keeper of Music.* London: John Murray, 1929.

Gai/Liv   Gaines, James R. *The Lives of the Piano.* New York: Harper Colophon, 1983.

Gai/Mus   Gaisberg, F. W. *The Music Goes Round.* New York: The Macmillan Company, 1942.

Gav/Vin   Gavoty, Bernard. *Vingt Grands Interprètes.* Lausanne: Les Editions Rencontre, 1966.

Gel/Mus   Gelatt, Roland. *Music-Makers.* New York: Alfred A. Knopf, 1953.

Ger/Fam   Gerig, Reginald. *Famous Pianists and Their Technique.* Washington, New York: Robert B. Luce, Inc., 1974.

Gil/Boo   Gill, Dominic, ed. *The Book of the Piano.* Ithaca, New York: Cornell University Press, 1981.

Gol/Jou   Gollancz, Victor. *Journey Towards Music.* New York: E. P. Dutton and Company, Inc., 1965.

Gra/Bib   Gray, Michael and Gerald D. Gibson. *Bibliography of Discographies*, Vol. 1. New York: R. R. Bowker Company, 1977.

Gra/Cla   Gray, Michael. *Classical Music Discographies. 1976–1988.* Westport, CT: Greenwood Press, 1989.

Gra/Goo   *The Gramophone Good CD Guide.* Harrow: General Gramophone Publications Limited, 1994, 1995.

Gra/Jub   *Gramophone Jubilee Book*, ed. Roger Wimbush. Harrow: Gramophone Publications Limited, 1973.

Gui/Com   *Guide to Competitions.* New York: Concert Artists Guild, 1989.

Hag/Dec   Haggin, B. H. *A Decade of Music.* New York: Horizon Press, 1973.

Hag/Mus   Haggin, B. H. *Music in the Nation.* New York: William Sloane Associates, Inc., 1949.

Hag/Thi   Haggin, B. H. *Thirty-Five Years of Music.* New York: Horizon Press, 1974.

Ham/Lis   Hamilton, David. *The Listener's Guide to Great Instrumentalists.* New York: Facts on File, Inc., 1982.

Han/Vie   Hanslick, Edouard. *Vienna's Golden Years of Music 1850–1900*, trans. Henry Pleasants III. London: Victor Gollancz, 1951.

Hei/Rhy   Heiles, William. *Rhythmic Nuance in Chopin Performances Recorded by Moriz Rosenthal, Ignaz Friedman, and Ignaz Jan Paderewski*. D.M.A. diss., University of Illinois, 1964.

Hen/Pre   Henderson, W. J. *Preludes and Studies*. New York: Longmans, Green & Co., 1891.

Her/Cla   Herring, Peter. *Classical Music on Compact Disc*. New York: Harmony Books, 1986.

Hor/Ivo   Horowitz, Joseph. *The Ivory Trade: Piano Competitions and the Business of Music*. Boston: Northeastern University Press, 1991.

Hun/Old   Huneker, James. *Old Fogy*. Philadelphia: Theodore Presser Co., 1913.

Hun/Ste   Huneker, James. *Steeplejack*. New York: Charles Scribner's Sons, 1918, 1920 (2 volumes in 1).

Hun/Uni   Huneker, James. *Unicorns*. New York: Charles Scribners's Sons, 1917.

Hun/Var   Huneker, James. *Variations*. New York: Charles Scribner's Sons, 1921.

IWWM   *International Who's Who in Music and Musician's Directory*, Eleventh edition. Cambridge, England: International Who's Who in Music, 1988.

Jac/Rev   Jacobson, Robert. *Reverberations*. New York: William Morrow and Co., 1974.

Kai/Gre   Kaiser, Joachim. *Great Pianists of our Time*, trans. D. Woodridge and George Unwin. London: George Allen and Unwin, Ltd., 1971.

Kau/Art   Kaufmann, Helen, and Eva vB. Hansl. *Artists in Music of Today*. New York: Grosset and Dunlap, 1933.

Keh/Pia   Kehler, George. *The Piano in Concert*. Metuchen, N.J.: The Scarecrow Press, Inc., 1982. 2 volumes.

Kir/Pab   Kirk, H. L. *Pablo Casals*, New York: Holt, Rinehart and Winston, 1974.

Kol/Que   Kolodin, Irving. *In Quest of Music*. New York: Doubleday and Co., Inc., 1980.

Lah/Fam   Lahee, Henry C. *Famous Pianists of Today and Yesterday*, Boston: L. C. Page and Co., 1900.

Lan/Mus   Langford, Samuel. *Musical Criticisms*, ed. Neville Cardus. London: Oxford University Press, 1929.

Lam/Mem   Lamond, Frederic. *The Memoirs of Frederic Lamond*. Foreword by Ernest Newman, Introduction and Postscript by I. T. Lamond. Glasgow: William MacLellan,1949.

Loe/Men   Loesser, Arthur. *Men, Women and Pianos*. New York: Simon & Schuster, 1954.

Lyl/Dic   Lyle, Wilson. *A Dictionary of Pianists*. New York: Schirmer Books, 1984.

Mac/Gre   Mach, Elyse. *Great Pianists Speak for Themselves*. New York: Dodd, Mead and Co., 1980.

Mac/Gr2   Mach, Elyse. *Great Pianists Speak for Themselves*. Volume 2. New York: Dodd, Mead and Co., 1988. Both Mach volumes are available together in a Dover (1991) paperback.

Mar/Gre   Marcus, Adele. *Great Pianists Speak*. New Jersey: Paganiniana, 1979.

Met/Cat   Methuen-Campbell, James. *Catalogue of Recordings by Classical Pianists*. Volume I (Pianists born to 1871). Chipping Norton: Disco Epsom Limited, 1984.

Met/Cho   Methuen-Campbell, James. *Chopin Playing*. From the Composer to the Present Day. New York: Taplinger Publishing Company, 1981.

MGG   *Die Musik in Geschichte und Gegenwart*. Kassel und Basel: Bärenreiter Verlag, 1949-68. 14 volumes plus supplement.

Moh/My   Mohr, Franz (with Edith Schaeffer). *My Life with the Great Pianists*. Grand Rapids: Baker Book House, 1992.

Moo/Am   Moore, Gerald. *Am I Too Loud?: A Musical Autobiography*. New York: The Macmillan Company, 1962.

Neu/Art   Neuhaus, Heinrich. *The Art of Piano Playing*, trans. K. A. Leibovitch. London: Barrie and Jenkins, 1973.

New/GrA   *The New Grove Dictionary of American Music*, ed. H. Wiley Hitchcock and Stanley Sadie. London: Macmillan Press Limited, 1986. 4 volumes.

New/Gro   *The New Grove Dictionary of Music and Musicians*, ed. Stanley Sadie. London: Macmillan Publishers Limited, 1980. 20 volumes.

Nie/Mei   Niemann, Walter. *Meister des Klaviers*. Berlin: Schuster & Loeffler, 1921.

Noy/Pia   Noyle, Linda. *Pianists on Playing*. Metuchen, N. J.: The Scarecrow Press, 1987.

O'N/Gra   O'Neil, Thomas. *The Grammys for the Record*. New York: Penguin Books, 1993.

Pau/Dic   Pauer, E. *A Dictionary of Pianists and Composers for the Pianoforte*. London: Novello, Ewer and Co., 1895.

Pay/Cel   Payne, Albert (pseud. A. Ehrlich). *Celebrated Pianists Past and Present*. London: Harold Reeves, n.d.

Pen/Gui   *The Penguin Guide To Compact Discs*. London: Penguin Books. Published variously as *The Complete Penguin Stereo Record and Cassette Guide, New Penguin Guide to Compact Discs and Cassettes, Penguin Guide to Compact Discs, Penguin Guide to Compact Discs, Cassettes and LPs*. 1984, 1986, 1988, 1990.

Per/Art   *Performing Arts Index* (Review of the Arts). NewsBank, Inc., 1975–.

Ran/Kon   Range, Hans-Peter. *Die Konzertpianiste der Gegenwart*. Lahr/ Schwarzwald: Moritz Schauenburg Verlag, 1966.

Rat/Cle   Rattalino, Piero. *Da Clementi a Pollini*. Duecento anni con i grandi pianisti. Milano: Ricordi/Giunti Martello, 1983.

Reu/Gre   Reuter, Florizel von. *Great People I Have Known*. Waukesha: Freeman Printing Co., 1961.

Rub/MyM   Rubinstein, Arthur. *My Many Years*. New York: Alfred A. Knopf, 1980.

Rub/MyY   Rubinstein, Arthur. *My Young Years*. New York: Alfred A. Knopf, 1973.

Sac/Vir   Sachs, Harvey. *Virtuoso*. New York: Thames and Hudson, Inc., 1982.

Sah/Not   Sahling, Herbert. *Notate zur Pianistik*. Aufsätze sowjetischer Klavierpädagogen und Interpreten. Leipzig: VEB Deutscher Verlag für Musik, 1976.

Sal/Fam   Saleski, Gdal. *Famous Musicians of Jewish Origin*. New York: Bloch Publishing Company, 1949.

Sch/Fac   Schonberg, Harold C. *Facing the Music*. New York: Summit Books, 1981.

Sch/Glo   Schonberg, Harold. C. *The Glorious Ones*. New York: Times Books, 1985.

Sch/Gre   Schonberg, Harold C. *The Great Pianists* (revised and updated). New York: Simon & Schuster, Inc., 1987.

Sch/My   Schnabel, Artur. *My Life And Music*. New York: St. Martin's Press, 1961.

Sha/Lon   Shaw, Bernard. *London Music in 1888–89 As Heard by Corno Di Bassetto*. London: Constable and Company Limited, 1937.

Sha/Mus   Shaw, Bernard. *Music In London 1890–94*. London: Constable and Company Limited, 1932. 3 volumes.

Sit/Cla   Sitsky, Larry. *The Classical Reproducing Piano Roll*. A Catalogue-Index. Westport, Connecticut: Greenwood Press, 1990. 2 volumes.

Sor/Aro   Sorabji, Kaikhosru. *Around Music*. London: The Unicorn Press, 1932.

Tho/MRL   Thomson, Virgil. *Music Right and Left*. New York: Henry Holt and Company, 1951.

Tho/Mus   Thomson, Virgil. *Music Reviewed 1940–1954*. New York: Vintage Books, 1967.

Tho/MuS   Thomson, Virgil. *The Musical Scene*. New York: Alfred A. Knopf, 1947.

Tho/Pia   Thompson, Wendy, with Fanny Waterman. *Piano Competition: The Story of the Leeds*. London: Faber and Faber, 1991.

Ung/Key   Unger-Hamilton, Clive. *Keyboard Instruments*. Minneapolis: Central Data Publishing, 1981.

Wal/The   Walter, Bruno. *Theme and Variations*, trans. James A. Galston. New York: Alfred A. Knopf, 1959.

Wod/Evi   Wodehouse, Artis S. *Evidence of 19th Century Piano Performance Practice Found in Recordings of Chopin's Nocturne, op. 15,*

	no. 2, Made by Pianists born before 1910. D.M.A. diss., Stanford, 1977.
Woo/My	Wood, Sir Henry. *My Life of Music.* London: Victor Gollancz Ltd., 1938.
WW	*Who's Who.* New York: St. Martin's Press, 1994.
WWAM	*Who's Who in American Music.* Classical Second Edition. New York: R. R. Bowker Company, 1985.
WWF	*Who's Who in France.* Paris: Editions Jacques Lafitte, 1990.
WWM	*Who's Who in Music and Musicians' Directory.* Cambridge: Melrose Press, 1992–93.
Zil/Rus	Zilberquit, Mark, Dr. *Russia's Great Modern Pianists.* Neptune, New Jersey: Paganiniana Publications, 1983.

B. ARTICLES

Bacon, Ernst. "Pianists Then and Now." *Clavier*, Nov 1981, pp. 22–25.

Brower, Harriette. "American Women Pianists: Their Views and Achievements." *Musical America*, 26 Oct 1918, pp. 18–19.

————. "Golden Age of Piano Playing." *Musical America*, 5 May 1917, p. 23.

————. "How The Master's Touch Transforms." *Musical America*, 12 July 1919, p. 10. (Bauer, Paderewski, Novaes).

————. "Principles of Piano Study: Laying the Right Foundation—Finger Action—The Best Sort of Music for Study Purposes—Questions of Memorizing." *Musical America*, 29 July 1916, p. 23.

————. "Recovering The Greater Chopin." *Musical America*, 23 Nov 1918, pp. 44–45.

————. "Vital Points in Piano Playing: Authoritative Views on Rhythm and Tone Color." *Musical America*, 26 Sept 1914, p. 11.

————. "Vital Points in Piano Playing: An Epitome of Expert Opinions on 'How to Memorize'." *Musical America*, 1 Aug 1914, p. 9.

————. "Vital Points in Piano Playing: Hints from Leading Authorities on Hand Position, Finger Action and Artistic Touch. *Musical America*, 18 July 1914, p. 9.

————. "Vital Points in Piano Playing: Noted Performers and Teachers Supply Advice on 'How to Practice'." *Musical America*, 25 July 1914, p. 9.

Chase, Gilbert. "Five Volumes of Memoirs Make Absorbing Reading." *Musical America*, 10 Nov 1938, pp. 13, 25. (Paderewski, Busoni, Clara Clemens Gabrilowitsch.)

Chasins, Abram. "The Grand Manner." *Saturday Review*, 24 Sept 1955, pp. 40, 42.

Clark, Sedgwick. "Who Wants To Be Another Horowitz?" *Village Voice*, 20 March 1978, pp. 36–37. (Argerich, Ax, Kovacevich, Lupu, Pollini, Serkin)

Crutchfield, Will. "The Lure of History and Interpretive Power." *New York Times*, 25 March 1990, sec. 2, p. 81. A suggested basic library of historic recordings on compact discs from instrumental masters of the past.

Doerschuk, Bob. "Tradition & Innovation In Bach Keyboard Performance." *Keyboard*, March 1985, pp. 13–16, 78–84. (Busoni, E. Fischer, Gould, Tureck.)

Downes, Olin. "Pianists Past and Present—Changes in Public Taste." *New York Times*, 16 May 1926, sec 8, p. 6.

Ericson, Raymond. "Many and Good." *New York Times*, 7 June 1964, sec. 10, p. 18. (Ashkenazy, Badura-Skoda, Brailowsky, Ogdon, Richter, Rosen, Rubinstein.)

"Famous Russian Pianists on the Art of Piano Study." *Etude*, March 1913, p. 171.

Goldberg, Albert. "Pianists: Victories, Vagaries." *Los Angeles Times*, 8 April 1979, pp. 72–73. (Hofmann, Rubinstein, J. Lhévinne.)

Goldsmith, Harris. "Record Reviews." *ARSC Journal*, Vol. 17, nos. 1–3, 1985, pp. 142–155. (Backhaus, Cortot, Ed. Fischer, Gieseking, Haskil.)

Hart, Philip. "The Pianist of Now and Then." *Musical Courier*, July 1961, pp. 48–51.

"Has the Art of the Piano Reached Its Zenith or Is It Capable of Further Development." *Etude*, Feb 1919, pp. 79–80; March 1919, pp. 139–140. Conference with Bauer, Grainger, Jonas, Gabrilowitsch, Hofmann, Lambert, Ganz, Hutcheson, Stojowski.

Henahan, Donal. "First the Lucky Break—and Then?" *New York Times*, 24 Jan 1988, sec. 2, p. 21. (Cliburn, Feltsman, Watts.)

Holland, Bernard, and Michael Kimmelman. "Critics Select Favorites from 87's Classical Crop." *New York Times*, 6 Dec 1987, sec. 8, pp. 29-30. (Horszowski, Kapell, Schiff.)

Husarik, Stephen. "Piano Rolls: Untapped Technical Resources." *Clavier*, April 1986, pp. 14–16.

Kammerer, Rafael. "Golden Age of Pianists Preserved on Old Records." *Musical America*, Feb 1957, pp. 28–29, 122, 172–173.

———. "Rosenthal, Cortot, and other old masters." *American Record Guide*, Nov 1957, pp. 80–81, 120.

Methuen-Campbell, James. "Leschetizky pupils on record." *Records and Recording*, Aug 1980, pp. 21–22.

———. "Polish pianists on record." Records and Recording, Jan 1979, pp. 42–45.

Michener, Charles. "Pianists—A Golden Age." *Newsweek*, 23 Jan 1978, pp. 70–72.

Morrison, Bryce. "The Russian Piano School." *Gramophone*, Feb 1993, pp. 31–32.

"Piano Concertos from Mozart to Prokofiev." *Gramophone*, 15 July 1961, p. 11. (Arrau, Cliburn, Cortot, Rubinstein.)

Schonberg, Harold C. "Great Pianists From the Past Re-Emerge." *New York Times*, 17 June 1990, pp. 23, 26. (Hess, Moiseiwitsch.)

Thompson, Oscar. "Where Are the Prodigies of Yesteryear." *Musical America*, 3 Jan 1920, pp. 5–6.

Claudio Arrau (ICM Artists)

Vladimir Ashkenazy (Harrison/Parrott Ltd.)

Daniel Barenboim (Harold Holt Ltd.)

Jorge Bolet

John Browning (Christian Steiner)

Teresa Carreño (Photo Courtesy of Aimé Dupont)

Aldo Ciccolini

Alfred Cortot

Misha Dichter (ICM Artists)

Philippe Entremont (ICM Artists)

Annie Fischer

Malcolm Frager

Nelson Freire (Columbia Artists Management)

Ossip Gabrilowitsch (Portrait Bust by Brenda Putnam)

Walter Gieseking

Percy Grainger

Horacio Gutiérrez

Clara Haskil (Courtesy Archives de l'Association Clara Haskil)

Josef Hofmann

Mieczyslaw Horszowski (Courtesy Colbert Artists Management Inc.)

Grant Johannesen (ICM Artists)

Notable
Twentieth-Century
Pianists

$\mathcal{A}$

ALBERT, EUGEN d' (Eugène Francis Charles): b. Glasgow, Scotland, 10 April 1864; d. Riga, Latvia, 3 March 1932.

> One of the most illusive, variable, unaccountable and surprising musical personalities before the public.
>
> (*Musical Courier*, Berlin, 21 March 1914)

Eugen d' Albert had a phenomenal reputation. Intelligent, temperamental and greatly gifted, he was known not only as the greatest Beethoven interpreter but as the greatest all-around pianist of his day, and he had an immeasurable effect on his own generation.

D'Albert was born in Scotland and given his early musical training in London, yet for years he repudiated everything about Great Britain, especially its musical institutions and standards. He lived in Germany for decades, changed Eugène to Eugen and professed to be German to the core. He had in fact a very mixed ancestry. His d'Albert forebears were Italian and included the composers Giuseppe Matteo Alberti (1685–1751) and Domenico Alberti (1710–ca.1740); his father Charles Louis Napoleon d'Albert (1809–86) was the son of a French army captain and a German woman of Russian descent; his mother was Annie Rowell, an English girl from Newcastle-on-Tyne. In about 1863 d'Albert's parents settled in Glasgow, where his father had an enormous success both as a dancing master—his classes held at the Queen's Rooms became highly fashionable—and as a composer of dance music.

Eugen d'Albert's musical talent appeared very early. His father became his teacher, intending to make him a composer, and years later d'Albert told

Frederic Lamond that without his father's early instruction he might have come to nothing. That training included a thorough grounding in Bach, Beethoven and Brahms and months and months of writing contrapuntal exercises and fugues. D'Albert was about eight years old when he began to assist his father, either taking a dancer's place to complete a set or playing the piano for the class.

At age 12 he won the Newcastle-on-Tyne Scholarship at London's newly opened (1876) National Training School for Music, forerunner of the Royal College of Music, and there he studied piano with Ernst Pauer, theory with Ebenezer Prout, harmony with John Stainer and composition with Arthur Sullivan, the first principal of the National Training School for Music. At the students' first public concert (23 June 1879), d'Albert starred as both pianist and composer. He played the Schumann Concerto in A Minor, op. 54, and the orchestra performed d'Albert's Concert Overture in C Major. At the next important student concert (25 May 1880), given to show London's officials what the Training School had accomplished, he played a movement from Schumann's Sonata in F-sharp Minor, op. 11, and Chopin's Etude in A Minor, op. 25, no. 11.

"The piano solos by d'Albert," reported one critic, "were, without doubt, the most successful instrumental performances. This young gentleman needs no apology on the score of brevity of years, for he plays with all the certainty, expression and fire of a practised artist." (*MT*, June 1880) This was high praise for a student pianist but d'Albert wanted to be a composer, not a pianist, and felt that he had little support from Sullivan even though Sullivan had entrusted him—d'Albert was only 16—with making a piano arrangement of his sacred music drama *The Martyr of Antioch.* Disappointment at school may partially account for d'Albert's long-standing, outspoken hatred of British music and culture.

Meanwhile, his exciting student performances paved the way for important piano engagements. At a Monday Popular Concert (22 Nov 1880), d'Albert played Schumann's Symphonic Etudes, op. 13, and (with Alfredo Piatti) Beethoven's Sonata in A Major, op. 69, for violoncello and piano. In 1881 he played the Schumann Concerto at a Crystal Palace Saturday Concert (5 Feb) and again at a Philharmonic Concert (10 March), and later that year performed (24 Oct) his own First Piano Concerto at one of Hans Richter's prestigious Orchestral Festival Concerts, later known as the Richter Concerts.

When d'Albert was elected (25 Nov 1881) Mendelssohn Scholar, entitling him to a year abroad, he followed Richter's advice and chose Vienna for further study. Early the following spring d'Albert created a sensation performing his own Piano Concerto with the Vienna Philharmonic Orchestra, being at that time the youngest pianist ever to play with that organization. These were spectacular achievements for an 18-year-old pianist, yet d'Albert still considered himself primarily a composer.

It was Richter who, in April 1882, took d'Albert to Liszt, and it was Liszt who turned him to the piano. After hearing d'Albert play a Suite (D Minor) he had composed, Liszt remarked that for a composer d'Albert played exceptionally well. That prompted d'Albert to ask Liszt if he thought d'Albert could become a pianist, and Liszt replied, "Most certainly I do—I never heard a better pianist." (Lam/Mem, see Bibliog.) D'Albert immediately joined the Liszt circle at Weimar, and under Liszt's guidance his technique and musicianship matured rapidly.

D'Albert played his first Berlin concert (10 Jan 1883) at the *Singakademie*, eliciting warm applause from the critical Berliners for his "stupendous mechanism, beautiful and expressive touch, and original taste." (*MT*, 1 Nov 1904) He had found a sympathetic home in Germany. Eventually d'Albert became more German than some Germans, and he greatly offended his British countrymen with his derogatory statements about almost everything British, especially his own musical training. After a decade's absence from London, d'Albert played (28 April 1896) the Beethoven Concerto No. 5 in E-flat Major, op. 74, at a Mottl Concert, and the English critics denounced both the man and his talent. But after five recitals performed within two months, d'Albert had recaptured his British audience, "a most striking proof of his ability and of the power of real genius such as he undoubtedly possesses." (*TL*, 10 June 1896)

From about 1885 d'Albert reigned for 20 years as one of the world's greatest virtuosos, touring Europe from Spain to Russia and performing abroad in England and America. He created a sensation at his American debut (18 Nov 1889) in a joint concert with the violinist Pablo Sarasate at the Metropolitan Opera House. D'Albert's imposing program included the Chopin Concerto No. 1 in E Minor, op. 11 (with the New York Symphony Society Orchestra, conducted by Walter Damrosch); Grieg's Humoresque, op. 6, no. 2; Anton Rubinstein's Barcarolle No. 5 in E Minor; and Tausig's transcription of a Strauss waltz.

At the peak of his concert career d'Albert returned to composition, his first love, and allowed his piano technique to deteriorate. He became careless, often playing inaccurately. Unfortunately his compositions (MGG, vol. I, see Bibliog.) show little personal style, and it was said that he borrowed from almost every famous composer. After the long absence largely devoted to composing, d'Albert returned to the concert stage with a Berlin recital (15 Feb 1912) hailed by *Musical America* as an "epochal event." His renowned "perfect mechanism" was rusty, but within a year he was again playing "with tremendous power and élan and with fire and impetuosity not seen since Rubinstein." (*MC*, 7 Feb 1913) After World War I d'Albert appeared only infrequently on the concert platform, but he composed until the end of his life.

Contemporary writers describe an unattractive d'Albert, small and feisty with a high-pitched boyish voice. Yet he married six times, fathered eight children and usually was the partner who sued for divorce. His second wife, the majestic Teresa Carreño, was ten years his senior and equally temperamental and talented. During their stormy marriage (1892–95), they occasionally played two-piano recitals, and it was said that d'Albert taught Carreño how to control her overwhelming technique and how to play in the Liszt manner.

Wilhelm Backhaus, Ernst von Dohnányi and others spoke of themselves as d'Albert's students. These were mostly coaching sessions, for d'Albert's daughter Desiderata Ehrlich-d'Albert claimed that her father "detested teaching, he did not have pupils. Various people played for him, he always encouraged them but they never had lessons." (Symposium CD 1046, liner notes)

Without a doubt, d'Albert was one of the keyboard giants of his age, greatly admired by his peers and by Liszt, who in a letter (24 Nov 1882) speaks of "an extraordinary pianist, by the name of d'Albert. . . . Among the young virtuosi, from the time of Tausig . . . I know of none of a more gifted as well as of a more dazzling talent than d'Albert." (Liszt)

Likened to Anton Rubinstein because of the elemental force in his playing, d'Albert's greatest fame lies in his interpretations of the three mighty Germans—Bach, Beethoven and Brahms. Although a Beethoven specialist, a rarity among Liszt pupils, his repertoire also included the two Brahms concertos and the Chopin Concerto in E Minor, and he played them many times. When he played (9 May 1890) the Brahms Concerto No. 2 in B-flat Major, op. 83, at the Metropolitan Opera House with Hans von Bülow as conductor, "his marvelous range of tonal power from the most subtle *pianissimo* to the most sonorous *forte* was never displayed to finer advantage. Together with Dr. von Bülow he gave a remarkably clear and intelligible reading of the entire work, whose manifold beauties have never before seemed to us to be so conspicuously exhibited." (*NYT*, 10 May 1890)

Brahms, an admirer of d'Albert's playing, often conducted when d'Albert performed Brahms's concertos. Arthur Abell once asked Brahms what he thought of the uncanny skill with which d'Albert played Brahms's exceedingly difficult Paganini Variations. "It is a mystery to me how he does it," confessed Brahms. "I devised those variations in the Sixties with the help of Tausig as technical studies for the piano. . . . I practiced those particular variations very hard, but if I lived to be as old as Methuselah and practiced every minute, I never could play them as d'Albert does." (*NYT*, 14 Nov 1937)

Paradoxically, d'Albert the avowed Germanophile liked Chopin's music, especially some of the large-scale works. At his American debut (18 Nov 1889) his performance of Chopin's Concerto in E Minor drew exceptional praise. "D'Albert is not only a great pianist, but also a great musician. . . . It is doing no injustice to the other pianists to say that d'Albert's performance of the work was in conception and in execution the greatest ever heard in this city." (*NYT*, 19 Nov 1889) D'Albert received an equally extravagant review for his performance (7 Jan 1890) of Chopin's Sonata No. 3. "In the Chopin B minor sonata, the wonderful extent of his dynamic scale and the astonishing variety of his tone color were fully exhibited. The extreme finish and accuracy of his technique were displayed in a most advantageous manner in the delicious scherzo. The finale was played with magnificent vigor and a white heat of feeling." (*NYT*, 8 Jan 1890)

Pianist and conductor Hans von Bülow's letters reveal his unqualified admiration for d'Albert's playing. "Hear d'Albert when you can, a phenomenon among giants." (Bül/Br, see Bibliog.) "D'Albert played delightfully in Berlin the day before yesterday. It was an ideal, an intrinsically finished performance. . . . A phenomenal fellow. There is indeed no one worth listening to besides himself and occasionally Joachim." (Bül/Let, see Bibliog.)

It was d'Albert's playing of Beethoven that brought him awesome fame and ardent followers. Bruno Walter tells of hearing d'Albert in Berlin in the early

1890s. "I shall never forget the titanic force in his rendition of Beethoven's Concerto in E-flat Major. I am almost tempted to say he didn't play it, that he personified it. In his intimate contact with his instrument he appeared to me like a new centaur, half piano and half man." (Wal/The, see Bibliog.) Indeed, d'Albert was famous throughout his lifetime for his "Emperor" Concerto. "I very much doubt whether we have heard anything greater, from the musical point of view, than d'Albert's performance of Beethoven's 'Emperor' Concerto. . . . It was an all but perfect interpretation of such a kind that it needs an effort of memory to recall that others find problems in the work." (*MA*, London Bureau, 23 Nov 1912)

On 3 January 1890 d'Albert played a long New York recital which included two Beethoven sonatas. One review reads: "D'Albert is a very great Beethoven player—the greatest now living, so far as we know. His reading of the opus 109, with the wonderful performance of the double trills and the amazingly shaded diminuendo at the close, would alone have sufficed to give him a high place. But this, together with his beautiful performance of the Waldstein sonata and what he has done in this city heretofore, makes his calling and election sure." (*NYT*, 4 Jan 1890) Artur Rubinstein wrote of hearing d'Albert play Beethoven's Concerto No. 4 "with a nobility and tenderness which has remained in my mind as the model performance of this work." (Rub/MyY, see Bibliog.)

D'Albert's shining reputation has dimmed in the half-century following his death, yet the old-time piano titan still earned high marks from another legendary pianist, Claudio Arrau. "I myself heard d'Albert when he was no longer at his best—too preoccupied with composing—but how he played! The chordal command was orchestral, in the Liszt manner, and the passages, arpeggios, trills—everything—were played with the expressive points in mind. No mere note spinning anywhere." (*PQ*, Spring 1975)

D'Albert made a number of reproducing piano rolls for Hupfeld and Welte, including performances of Liszt's B Minor Sonata and many smaller works (Sit/Cla, see Bibliog.). He also made acoustic records for three companies, probably recording first for *Odéon* around 1910. From about 1916 to 1923 he made discs for *Deutsche Grammophon Gesellschaft*, then he changed to Vox. By the time d'Albert began to make recordings, he was giving most of his time to composition and neglecting his piano technique. Even at their best, the piano rolls seldom reveal his great talent. The disc recordings, despite the primitive sound quality, are more indicative of his keyboard mastery. Most of them, piano rolls and original recordings, are difficult to find.

His Beethoven recordings, particularly the sonata movements, are his finest. Here his careful phrasing, precisely articulated left hand and grand style are well in evidence, firmly upholding his wondrous reputation as a Beethoven interpreter. Some d'Albert recordings (i.e., Beethoven's Concerto No. 5, Symposium CD 1046) contain erratic passages, noticeably in his rhythms and use of *rubato*, but much of this is typical of late 19th-century playing style.

In view of d'Albert's close association with Brahms, his recording (ca.1910–12) of Brahms's Capriccio in B Minor, op. 76, no. 2, is very important and historic. More than that, it clearly reveals d'Albert's superb technique, emotional depth and dramatic power (Symposium CD 1046).

D'Albert made only one disc recording of Liszt's music, the scintillating *Au bord d'une source*. There are two versions, one made for *Odéon* around 1911 and a later DG pressing (see Discog.). The earliest version is superior; here the brook sparkles, beautifully displaying d'Albert's legendary technique.

Also noteworthy are his recordings of Schubert's Impromptus, D. 935, nos. 3 and 4. The F-minor Impromptu (no. 4), in particular, is as fine an example of masterly piano playing as one is likely to experience. In the lightness and glittering brilliance of the runs, the delicate shading, the fiery abandon, the poised phrasing that permits the melody to soar, in all this we hear a supreme master of the keyboard who was also a true Schubertian.

SELECTED REFERENCES

Abell, Arthur M. "A Picture of Brahms: Discovery of Old Photograph Recalls Memories of Composer and Friends." *New York Times*, 14 Nov 1937, sec. 11, p. 9.

Albert, Eugène d'. "The Glory of Beethoven," trans. F. S. Law. *Etude*, Dec 1911, pp. 809–10.

————. "The Interpretation of Beethoven's Piano Masterpieces," trans. F. S. Law. *Etude*, Jan 1912, pp. 13–14.

————. "Ludwig van Beethoven." In *Century Library of Music*, ed. Ignace Jan Paderewski, vol. 14. New York: The Century Co., 1900.

Benko, Gregor, and John Hall. "Eugen d'Albert: A Discography." *Antique Records*, Sept 1972, pp. 8–11.

"Eugen d'Albert: A Biographical Sketch." *Musical Times*, 1 Nov 1904, pp. 697–700.

"Eugène d'Albert." *The British Musician and Musical News*, May 1932, pp. 99–100.

Henderson, A. M. "Eugène d'Albert Reveals How Liszt Prepared for Scales." *Etude*, Sept 1955, pp. 12, 50–51.

Liszt, Franz. *The Letters of Franz Liszt to Marie zu Sayn-Wittgenstein*, trans. Howard E. Hugo. Cambridge: Harvard University Press, 1953.

Obituary. *Musical America*, 10 March 1932, p. 11. *New York Herald-Tribune*, 4 March 1932, p. 13. *New York Times*, 4 March 1932, p. 19.

Schonberg, Harold C. "Your Children, My Children, Our Children." *New York Times*, 6 April 1969, sec. 2, p. 17.

Walter, Bruno. *Theme and Variations*, trans. James A. Galston. New York: Alfred A. Knopf, 1959.

Wilhelm, Paul. "D'Albert On Playing Beethoven." *Musical America*, 15 Feb 1913, p. 27.

See also Bibliography: Ald/Con; Ful/Doo; Hen/Pre; Hun/Old; Hun/Uni; Lah/Fam; Pay/Cel; Rat/Cle; Rub/MyM; Rub/MyY; Sch/Gre; Sha/Mus.

SELECTED REVIEWS

MA: 9 March 1912; 7 Dec 1912; Berlin, 15 Jan 1916. *MC*: 22 Nov 1912; 7 Feb 1913; 1 March 1913; Berlin, 21 March 1914. *NYT*: 19 Nov 1889; 23 Nov 1889; 24 Nov 1889; 3 Dec 1889; 6 Dec 1889; 4 Jan 1890; 8 Jan 1890; 14 Jan 1890; 6 April 1890; 10 May 1890; 26 Nov 1890; 6 April 1892; 3 May 1892. *TL*: 12 June 1885; 30 April 1896; 2 May 1896; 3 June 1896; 10 June 1896; 9 Nov 1896; 25 Nov 1896; 15 May 1897; 11 June 1898; 6 June 1913.

SELECTED DISCOGRAPHY

D'Albert. D'Albert: Myrtocle's Aria from *Die Toten Augen*; *Tiefland*: "*Schau her, das ist ein Taler*" and *Zwischenspiel*. Beethoven: "Emperor" Concerto (1st movt.). Beethoven-d'Albert: *Ecossaises* in E Flat. Brahms: Capriccio in B Minor, op. 76, no. 2. Chopin: Etude in F Minor, op. 25, no. 2; Etude in G-flat Major, op. 25, no. 9; Nocturne in F-sharp Major, op. 15, no. 2; Waltz in A-flat Major, op. 42. Liszt: *Au bord d'une source*. Schubert: Impromptu in B-flat Major, D. 935, no. 3; Impromptu in F Minor, D. 935, no. 4. Schubert-Tausig: *Marche militaire*. Weber: Invitation to the Dance, op. 65. Symposium CD 1046.

Eugen d'Albert Piano Recital. D'Albert: *Capriolen*, op. 32, nos. 2, 4, 5; Gavotte and Minuet, op. 1; Myrtocle's Aria from *Die Toten Augen*. Arnold Bax: Mediterranean. Beethoven: *Andante favori* in F Major; *Rondo a capriccio*, op. 129; Scherzo (Sonata, op. 31, no. 3); Rondo ("*Waldstein*" Sonata, op. 53). Beethoven-d'Albert: *Ecossaises*. Teresa Carreño: *Kleiner Walzer*. Chopin: Nocturne in F-sharp Major, op. 15, no. 2. Liszt: *Au bord d'une source*. Mozart: *Rondo alla Turca* (Sonata, K. 331). Concert Artist/Fidelio cassette CH4-TC-4013.

The Pupils of Liszt. D'Albert: Myrtocle's Aria from *Die Toten Augen*. Brahms: Capriccio in B Minor, op. 76, no. 2. Chopin: Nocturne in F-sharp Major, op. 15, no. 2. Liszt: *Au bord d'une source*. Pearl Opal LP 824/5.

The Pupils of Liszt. D'Albert: Gavotte and Minuet; Scherzo in F-sharp Major, op.16, no. 2. Beethoven: *Andante favori* in F Major. Brahms: Capriccio in B Minor, op. 76, no. 2. Carreño: Little Waltz. Liszt: *Au bord d'une source*. Pearl GEMM CDS 9972 (2 CDs).

ANDA, GÉZA: b. Budapest, Hungary, 19 November 1921; d. Zurich, Switzerland, 14 June 1976.

> If there is one thing I can't bear it's the musical or unmusical pedantry of today . . . that has too much to do with musicology and too little to do with music.
>
> Géza Anda (*Music and Musicians*, June 1975)

Géza Anda's untimely death at age 54 moved some of his grieving colleagues to publish a memorial tribute that portrays Anda as a genial man with an inquiring mind and a musician internationally recognized as pianist, teacher and conductor. (Götze)

Anda's schoolmaster father, who played the violin as a hobby, intended to make him a teacher, but Anda's mother, an amateur pianist, started him with piano lessons. At age 13 he was accepted at the Franz Liszt Academy of Music (so named in 1925, formerly the National Hungarian Royal Academy of Music, founded 1875), where he studied with Imre Stefániai and Imre Keéri-Szántó, and spent the last two years in Ernst von Dohnányi's select piano master class. Throughout his life Anda consistently voiced his appreciation for the thorough musical grounding he felt he had received at the Academy. During his school years he helped with expenses by teaching elementary piano lessons and playing the harmonium in salon and radio orchestras. At age 19 he won the coveted Franz Liszt Prize, and as a result made his professional debut, playing the Brahms Concerto No. 2 in B-flat Major with the Budapest Philharmonic Orchestra under Willem Mengelberg. Wilhelm Furtwängler, director of the Berlin Philharmonic Orchestra and a frequent visitor to Budapest, spotted Anda's talent ("a troubadour of the piano," said Furtwängler) and urged him to have further training in Berlin.

Anda graduated from the Academy in June 1941 and, supported by a State scholarship (Kodály served on the deciding committee), took up residence at the *Collegium Hungaricum* in Berlin in December. The following year he made his Berlin debut, playing the César Franck Symphonic Variations with Furtwängler and the BPO. A career in Berlin looked promising but Germany, critically involved in World War II, forced Hungary to mobilize, and Anda was eligible for the Hungarian army. Aided by friends at the Swiss Embassy, he escaped (1942), using a doctor's certificate falsely claiming that he had tuberculosis and must live in Switzerland. He made his way to Zurich, became a Swiss citizen (1955) and married (1964) Hortense Bührle, member of a prominent Swiss manufacturing family. Their one child, Gratian Béla Anda, was six when Anda died.

After the war Anda treated himself to a nine-month sojourn in Paris, studying French music and culture. Pierre Souvchinsky, Stravinsky's longtime friend and confidant, became Anda's musical mentor; Swiss friends arranged Paris concert dates for him. A year before his death Anda told an interviewer that there had been several great influences in his life: Dohnányi and Stefániai in Budapest,

Pierre Souvchinsky in Paris *and* opera—a lifelong passion with Anda. (Morrison)

As Europe recovered and travel restrictions eased, Anda toured on the Continent and in Scandinavia, England and Israel, quietly and steadily gaining in both stature and recognition. Preceded by his European reputation and the acclaim of his many Angel recordings, he made his American orchestral debut (1 Nov 1955) at Carnegie Hall, playing the Brahms Second Piano Concerto with the Philadelphia Orchestra under Eugene Ormandy. He made his American recital debut (14 Nov 1955) at Town Hall, and that same season played four additional engagements with the Philadelphia Orchestra and also appeared with the Chicago, San Francisco, Cleveland, Minneapolis and Vancouver orchestras. Thereafter he toured regularly in the United States and Canada.

Anda, one of the most frequent and popular performers at the Salzburg Festival (he first appeared there in 1952), missed only five years over a 23-year period, performing 19 times with orchestra and playing 8 solo recitals. It was in Salzburg that he developed a productive association with Bernhard Paumgartner, director of the Salzburg *Mozarteum* (1917–38; 1945–59) and founder (1952) of the *Camerata Academica*, an orchestra made up of teachers, students and graduates of the *Mozarteum*. Anda and the *Camerata Academica* formed a very successful performing-recording team. With Anda conducting from the piano, they toured Austria, Germany, Switzerland and France in the 1960s, and over a nine-year period recorded all the Mozart concertos for *Deutsche Grammophon*, frequently using Anda's own cadenzas. He made his American debut as conductor-pianist (21 Aug 1970) with the New York Chamber Orchestra in the Mostly Mozart Festival at Philharmonic Hall.

Anda battled cancer for two years, but he continued to perform. In one of his last concerts, on 9 April 1975, at London's Festival Hall, Anda appeared as pianist-conductor with the English Chamber Orchestra, playing Mozart's Concerto in G Major, K. 453, and Beethoven's Concerto No. 3. For one critic, "the Mozart hummed along like a well-oiled machine, a bit insouciant about dramatic shifts of harmony, unmindful of the potential liveliness of wind dialogue in the first movement's exposition." He admired Anda's "lovely, caressing, subtly differentiated tone," and felt that the Finale received many pleasant and refined touches, "alas, none of them particularly witty." The "rough and ready" approach to Beethoven was disturbing as was the lack of attention to orchestral nuance. (*TL*, 10 April 1975)

Géza Anda, a highly successful, respected teacher, conducted a summer class at the International Summer Academy of the Salzburg *Mozarteum* from 1953 to 1955. In 1960 he took over Edwin Fischer's famed master class at Lucerne, returning each year until 1969. That year Anda began a new series of piano workshops in Zurich, having been appointed head of the piano course of the International Music Institute for Master Classes. He also taught occasionally at the Royal Academy of Music in London (he became an honorary member in 1969) and at the Paris Conservatory.

Egil Harder of Copenhagen, an early Anda pupil, having been referred to Anda in Berlin in 1942, became a close friend and colleague, and for 14 years

(1962–76) assisted at Anda's master classes. Harder's explanation of Anda's teaching credo brings to mind Furtwängler's early description of Anda as "a troubadour of the piano." Anda wanted his pupils to "sing" through the piano, to understand that music ultimately derives from the human voice. When his students played for him, he would caution them to make the line clear. If they were unable to imagine the phrasing of a passage, he told them to try to sing it. Anda was very strict, said Harder, but he was an excellent and much-loved teacher.

Géza Anda was not a *wunderkind*, but he had a splendid pianistic talent. All his life he worked at the piano, developing and refining that talent. His preparations were complete, intelligent and sensitive. Without playing a note, he would work for hours analyzing a concerto score in order to discover the motivating force behind each movement, the expressive intent and the conveyed artistic message. His goal, at all times: to achieve a synthesis of intellect and temperament, always keeping emotions securely in hand. Anda's strict analytical intellect prevailed until he began to play. Then intellect melded with temperament—in his case those inborn Hungarian qualities of warmth, color and beauty—to create a "magic and unique touch of sound." (Stettler, *Ein Erinnerungsbild*) Having an innate sense of style, Anda could be dramatic but not showy, lyrical but not sentimental, bringing just the right emphasis to each melody and phrase.

Anda's wide-ranging repertoire ended with Bartók, for, as he said, "there is nothing I would call real piano music after Bartók." Although he refused to be called a specialist, inevitably he has become closely associated with the music of Mozart and of Bartók. He played Bartók's Piano Concerto No. 2 with the Radio Cologne Orchestra under Ferenc Fricsay at the International Society For Contemporary Music Festival held in Salzburg in June 1952, a time when not many pianists played—and fewer understood—this Bartók Concerto. Anda softened the percussive character, emphasizing instead the expressive and lyrical aspects of the music. The audience applauded so enthusiastically that Anda and the orchestra finally repeated the last movement.

Five years later Anda played all three Bartók piano concertos in one evening (26 April 1957) for *Musica Viva*, a society Karl Amadeus Hartmann had organized after World War II to promote the performance of contemporary music. Herculean and stunning performances, they not only affirmed Anda's technical prowess, but also revealed the extraordinary vitality and beauty of the concertos. The physical effort alone was enormous. And Anda's ability to understand the music of his great compatriot and bring to it "the fire, the color, the rhythmic audacities and, in the slow parts, the latent magic of its tone qualities, all this bespeaks genius." (Ruppel, *Ein Erinnerungsbild*)

Géza Anda had many admirers. Others had reservations about his playing. At his American debut recital (14 Nov 1955), one critic characterized Anda's performance of Beethoven's Sonata, op. 101, as "erratic." He also disagreed wholeheartedly with Anda's interpretation of the Schumann *Carnaval*, and considered Anda's playing of Brahms's Paganini Variations mannered but acceptable. However, "the sum total of the concert left the impression of an exceedingly talented young pianist who is not yet a mature artist, but who has a superb potential." (*NYT*, 15 Nov 1955) Fourteen years later the same critic still had misgivings. Anda's recital on 19 February 1969 was, in his view, not successful. More specifically, he complained that the essence of Schumann's *Davids-bündlertänze* seemed to escape the pianist, that Anda attempted a series of devices in the Chopin Etudes, op. 25, that did not come off, and that his performance of the Mozart Sonata, K. 576, lacked character. (*NYT*, 20 Feb 1969)

    At the other extreme, an equally noted critic greatly admired Anda. In a glowing account of Anda's Los Angeles recital debut (28 Nov 1956), this critic describes Anda as an interpreter of impressive ability and impeccable taste, equally at home in many styles of music and in command of a wide tonal scope that gives constant interest to his playing. And, "if there is anything in the range of technical feats he cannot accomplish with the utmost ease, his taxing and comprehensive program [Beethoven, Brahms, Schumann, Bártok] failed to give a clue as to what it might be." (*LAT*, 29 Nov 1956)

    Anda had at his command a colorful keyboard sonority and an exciting dynamism, but he never abused his instrument. Even in blatantly bravura passages his tone carried weight without percussiveness. And in passages like the *Adagio religioso* of Bartók's Concerto No. 3, he proved his mastery of the subtler colorations with a cantabile line that could soften to a whisper. Anda's stylish playing, derived from a well-mannered, orderly musicianship, always avoided extremes.

    The Anda discography embraces a repertoire ranging from Bach to Bartók. The available recordings show this stylish artist at his best. He recorded the complete Mozart concertos in the 1960s and 1970s, conducting the Salzburg *Mozarteum* Orchestra from the keyboard. A project hailed as unique at the time, presently Anda's set of 25 concertos (see Discog.) must compete with others made by Vladimir Ashkenazy, Daniel Barenboim, Murray Perahia and Mitsuko Uchida. Allowing for more modern recording techniques and a resultant improved sound, Anda's set holds its own remarkably well. The piano and smallish orchestra are well-balanced, the piano tone is good. Overall, Anda manifests beautifully poised concepts and a grand feeling for style. The deft, sparkling allegro movements and the poetic phrasing of the inner movements are especially appealing.

    Anda's Bartók readings confirm his classic approach to interpretation. He can be refined but urgent, incisive but red-blooded when necessary. In 1960–61 Anda recorded the three Bartók concertos with Ferenc Fricsay and the Radio Berlin Symphony Orchestra. Arthur Cohn, writing of the 20th-century elements of structural development, rhythmic thrust, instrumentational vitality and percussive quality inherent to Bartók's Concerto No. 2, states that "it is the secure balance of these properties that makes Géza Anda's discourse practically perfect. Others tend to stress either the color contrasts or the basal flavor. Fine but not enough. Anda's forthright conception also provides a lesson in the difference between a forceful realization of the score's contents and mere forceful piano playing." (Coh/Rec, see Bibliog.) Anda and conductor Fricsay won the 1961 *Grand Prix du Disque* for their recording of the Bartók Second and Third Concertos.

Anda's Bartók performances are still eminently valuable. A 1991 CD reissue elicited a comparison with several other available sets (Kovacevich, Ashkenazy, Sándor): "Anda unfailingly projects the music's grotesqueries, its motor rhythms and knife-edged thrusts. But he can spin out the snippets of folksong with beguiling simplicity and can convey Bartók's whimsy . . . in a manner none of the other pianists here quite matches." (*MA*, July 1991) The three Concertos are now in their second CD reissue (see Discog.).

In 1962 Anda won another *Grand Prix du Disque* for his recording of the 24 Chopin Preludes, op. 28, and received it again for his recording, with the *Camerata Academica*, of two Mozart concertos (K. 453 and K. 467, see Discog.). This last record remained at the top of the American classical music charts for 50 weeks (1968–69) because the Andante of Concerto in C Major, K. 467, had been chosen as background "love music" for the Swedish film *Elvira Madigan*.

SELECTED REFERENCES

Anda, Géza. *Kadenzen zu Klavierkonzerten von Wolfgang A. Mozart*. Berlin: Bote & Bock, 1973.
Blyth, Alan. "Géza Anda's Bartók." *The Times* (London), 5 Dec 1973, p. 11.
Brozen, Michael. "Géza Anda: Open Horizons." *Musical America*, March 1962, p. 18.
Götze, Willibald, Max Kaindl-Hönig, Egil Harder, Karl Heinrich Ruppel, Karl Schumann and Michael Stettler. *Géza Anda: Ein Erinnerungsbild*. Zurich: Artemis, 1977.
Hodgson, Antony. "The Keyboard Mozart." *Records and Recording*, Nov 1971, pp. 62–65.
Hughes, Allen. "'Elvira' and Her 24 Sisters." *New York Times*, 29 Aug 1971, pp. 19, 23.
Morrison, Bryce. "Géza Anda Interviewed by Bryce Morrison." *Music and Musicians*, June 1975, pp. 18–19.
Obituary. *Neue Züriche Zeitung*, 15 June 1976, p. 31. *New York Times*, 15 June 1976, p. 40. *The Times* (London), 15 June 1976, p. 4.
Offergeld, Robert. "Stereo Review Talks to Géza Anda." *Stereo Review*, Sept 1969, p. 81.
Salzburg Festival Programs 1952–74.
See also Bibliography: Ewe/Li2; Kai/Gre; New/Gro; Ran/Kon; Rat/Cle.

SELECTED REVIEWS

LAT: 29 Nov 1956; 24 Nov 1961. *NYT*: 2 Nov 1955; 15 Nov 1955; 20 Feb 1969; 23 Aug 1970. *SR*: 14 Nov 1964. *TL*: 24 April 1956; 11 June 1963; 30 Nov 1973; 5 Dec 1973; 17 Dec 1973; 10 April 1975.

SELECTED DISCOGRAPHY

Bartók: Piano Concertos Nos. 1-3. DG 447 398-2. (2 CDs). Fricsay/Radio Berlin SO.

Beethoven: Concerto No. 1 in C Major, op. 15. Bach: Concerto for 2 pianos
    and orchestra in C Major, BWV 1061 (with Clara Haskil). Mozart:
    Concerto for 2 pianos and orchestra in E-flat Major, K. 365 (with Clara
    Haskil). EMI *Références* CDH 7 63492-2. Galliera/PO.
Brahms: Concerto No. 2 in B-flat Major, op. 83. Hunt 733 (CD). Klemperer/
    Cologne RSO. Also Fleisher with Beethoven: Concerto No. 4, op. 58.
Brahms: Concerto No. 2 in B-flat Major, op. 83. DG 431 162-2. Karajan/Berlin
    PO. Also Kempff with Op. 118.
Chopin: 12 Etudes, op. 10; 24 Preludes, op. 28. *Fonit Cetra* CDE 1018.
Chopin: 14 Waltzes. RCA Victrola 7744-2-RV. CD.
Mozart: Piano Concertos (27). DG 429-001-2. (10 CDs). Anda/*Camerata
    Academica.*
Mozart: Concerto in G Major, K. 453; Concerto in C Major, K. 467. DG
    Musikfest 429522-2. Anda/*Camerata Academica.*
Schumann: Piano Concerto in A Minor, op. 54. Grieg: Piano Concerto in A
    Minor, op. 16. DG 415 850-2. Kubelík/Berlin SO.
Schumann: *Davidsbündlertänze*, op. 6; *Kreisleriana*, op. 16. DG (Privilege)
    Stereo 2535 145-10.
Schumann: Fantasia in C, op. 17; Symphonic Etudes, op. 13. DG (Privilege)
    Stereo 2535 364-10.
Schumann: *Carnaval*, op. 9; *Kreisleriana*, op. 16; Symphonic Etudes, op. 13.
    Orfeo C295921B.

⚜ ⚜ ⚜

ARGERICH, MARTHA: b. Buenos Aires, Argentina, 5 June 1941.

> I love to play the piano but I don't want to be a pianist. I have a con-
> flict.
>
> Martha Argerich (*People*, 31 March 1980)

Martha Argerich's love for the piano shines through in her playing; yet, as
Argerich has consistently told interviewers, she never wanted to be a concert pianist. This old conflict apparently took root in childhood when Argerich, a child
prodigy, dreaded playing in public. Although the piano has always been incredibly easy for her, she was an extremely shy little girl, forever seeking ways to
avoid performing for an audience. Prodded to practice by her parents and her
teacher—who would remind her that Myra Hess looked on the piano as her fi-
ancé—Argerich learned to hate practicing, and she longed for childhood freedom.
The shy little girl became a fiercely independent woman, the reluctant prodigy a
ravishing performer, but the conflict continues.

At about age three Argerich began piano lessons with Ernestine C. de
Kussrow, who taught small children to play by ear, and from age five until ten
she studied with Vincent Scaramuzza. She made her orchestral debut in Buenos
Aires in 1949, playing the Mozart Concerto in D Minor, K. 466, Beethoven's
Concerto No. 1, op. 15, and the Bach French Suite No. 5. She also played (the

last movement of the Beethoven Sonata in E-flat Major, op. 31, no. 3) for Walter Gieseking and he, perhaps realizing how much the eight-year-old disliked performing, advised her parents to leave her in peace.

Argerich's astonishing piano skills prompted Argentina's dictator Juan Perón to assign her parents, both foreign service professionals, to the Argentine embassy in Vienna in order to give Argerich the opportunity for further music study. In 1955 she began lessons there with Friedrich Gulda, who would prove to be a special influence in her life. Years later Argerich told an interviewer that working with Gulda—she studied with him for about a year and a half—had been fascinating. (Kozinn) A simpatico sense of communication arose between the two, and Argerich believes that she learned a great deal from Gulda. Apparently so, for in 1957 the 16-year-old Argerich stunned the musical world by winning two important competitions, the F. Busoni International Piano Competition in Bolzano, Italy, and the *Concours International d'Exécution Musicale* in Geneva, Switzerland.

For the next few years she concertized in Western Europe and Poland. Although young and inexperienced, Argerich traveled alone, going from town to town by train and finding her own accommodations. Since she was not at all prepared for the boredom of that kind of traveling or the pressures of concertizing, it was only a matter of time before her playing "began to show signs of confusion and lack of concentration." (Kai/Gre, see Bibliog.) At age 20, lonely and depleted, she stopped performing because she had lost all pleasure in the concert life, both as a pianist and as a person. Hoping to overcome her problems, Argerich went to study with Arturo Benedetti Michelangeli in Montcalieri, Italy, a venture that failed completely. She shared a large house with a lot of people and mostly passed her time going to movies and restaurants, watching television, playing table tennis or listening to records. In a year and a half she had only about four lessons with Michelangeli and learned one piece. She next tried living in New York, which was not much help, for she stayed away from the piano for another year.

At age 22 Argerich married composer-conductor Robert Chen, a brief marriage ending in 1964, just before the birth of their daughter Lyda. About a month after Lyda's birth, Argerich's mother impetuously entered her in the 1964 Queen Elisabeth of Belgium Competition in Brussels. It was a foolhardy gesture. Argerich had no confidence and she knew she could not play, but for some reason she went to Brussels, and there had the good fortune to meet jury member Stefan Askenase, a pianist she had known as a child. Askenase convinced her to play for him and invited her to stay at his home. He also gave her lessons, but it was his wife who fully restored Argerich's self-confidence. As Argerich explained years later, she had been absolutely fascinated with Mrs. Askenase, who "had something very special, like a sun." Argerich began to believe in herself again and little by little started to play, as she described it, "very bad, wrong notes all over the place."

That autumn, with both facility and confidence restored, Argerich played in Zurich, made a smashing London debut (16 Nov 1964), and early in 1965 mustered the courage to enter the seventh International Frédéric Chopin Piano Competition at Warsaw. Press reports describe her as moody, dressed in black, smoking incessantly and suffering so badly from insomnia and exhaustion that at one point a doctor had to treat her backstage. If true, none of it mattered. Argerich overwhelmed the competition, winning both first prize and the Polish Radio Prize for the best interpretation of the Chopin mazurkas. She won, she said, only because of Mrs. Askenase: "Otherwise I couldn't have done it."

Argerich's spectacular success at the Chopin competition ignited her concert career. She gave her American recital debut (16 Jan 1966) in New York at Philharmonic Hall and made her New York orchestral debut on 19 February 1970, playing Prokofiev's Third Piano Concerto with the New York Philharmonic Orchestra under Claudio Abbado. The *New York Times* reviewer spoke of her big technique, extraordinary power and sensitive musical mind. What impressed him most was her rare ability to let the notes shine through the clatter of Prokofiev's orchestration.

Argerich has toured in Europe, the Americas, the Soviet Union, Israel and Japan. Most of her early performances were in Europe, within commuting distance of Geneva, where she raised her three daughters. (Anne, her second child, is the daughter of Swiss conductor Charles Dutoit, to whom she was married for five years; Stephanie, her youngest child, is the daughter of pianist Stephen Kovacevich.)

The unconventional, unpredictable Argerich seems to make her own rules, professionally as well as personally. Despite a reputation for canceling engagements, she always has offers. Shy in public, she is the opposite with family and friends. (Talking, she says, is a vice with her, and most important in her life.) A natural pianist, she is endowed with perfect pitch, a prodigious memory and a wonderful gift for musical parody that enables her to create devastating takeoffs on many of the great pianists.

Martha Argerich ranks among the most remarkable of all pianists. Her magnificent talent, however, has ever been subject to her nervous, capricious temperament. To illustrate, at a performance (19 March 1981) of the Chopin F Minor Concerto with the Los Angeles Philharmonic Orchestra, Myung-Whun Chung conducting, Argerich played "with exquisite poetry, rowdy bombast, swooning introspection, explosive violence, pearly clarity, feathery finesse, technical wizardry and perfunctory prose." Everything hinged on how the spirit or the music moved her, and as a result, "it was wonderful and it was awful, depending on the given moment." (*LAT*, 21 March 1981) The Argerich temperament is also responsible for her sometimes unaccountable lapses of confidence and concentration; her sudden cancellations and program changes; and her small number of solo recitals. It seems as though she has gradually lost interest in solo performances. In fact, the Argerich reviews from the 1980s and 1990s make it patently clear that she played very few solo recitals anywhere. For whatever reason—nerves, boredom, necessity, temperament or a renewal of her lifetime conflict with the piano—Argerich mostly performs with orchestra or with other instrumentalists.

She has a substantial concerto repertoire to offer an orchestra. Reviews spanning two decades show that Argerich has played, among others, the Beethoven Concertos Nos. 1 and 2; Chopin Concertos Nos. 1 and 2; Haydn D

Major Concerto, Hob. XVIII/11; Liszt No. 1 in E Flat; Mozart in C Major, K. 503; the Prokofiev Piano Concerto No. 3; the Ravel Concerto in G; the Schumann Concerto; Tchaikovsky's Concerto No. 1. On her infrequent solo recitals over this same period Argerich has performed works by Bach, Bartók, Beethoven, Chopin, Debussy, Liszt, Mozart, Prokofiev, Ravel and Schumann. How she prepares her repertoire is not clear. She learns fast and has a fabulous memory. Her practicing seems variable and, as everything seems to be with Martha Argerich, is spontaneous.

Her individuality stamps every review and interview. "In a time when so many of her peers are indistinguishable, Argerich is a throwback to titans like Rachmaninoff and Rubinstein, with her dazzling ability to charge notes with raw passion." (PM, 31 March 1980) Just not knowing how Argerich's mood will affect her adds special excitement to her performances. Besides, she has the effortless, natural technique of (to use a much overused phrase) "the born pianist." It is a grand and agile technique, perfectly suited to her Romantic playing style. Even at age 23, at her London debut (16 Nov 1964), Argerich displayed "the kind of technique, plus the vitality to go with it, of which legends are made; indeed in so far as sheer pianism is concerned it is difficult to recall any more auspicious debut recital in this hall [Wigmore] since the war." (TL, 17 Nov 1964) Her playing at her American debut (16 Jan 1966) revealed a complete mastery of the Romantic style: "tone quality that makes the Philharmonic Hall sound like an acoustical marvel, technique that makes the playing of Schumann's intricacies seem like the easiest thing in the world and interpretative instincts that make the ebb and flow of the music seem altogether natural and spontaneous." (NYT, 17 Jan 1966)

It was Argerich's wondrous pianism that conquered the Chopin Piano Competition. "Though a slight, delicate girl, she played with an almost masculine power and assertiveness. For more introspective passages, she tempered her mercurial attack with a limpid, poetic tone and subtlety of phrasing." (Time, 26 March 1965) According to Chopin specialist James Methuen-Campbell, one of the most telling features of an Argerich performance is that she always manages to preserve her musical taste and judgment even when playing fiendishly difficult music. "I have never heard the C major Etude, op. 10, no. 1, for extended arpeggios in the right hand, played with the same speed and temperament. . . . Yet Argerich is in no sense a mechanical musician—her temperament always makes her playing exciting but above that, her insight and extreme subtlety and sensitivity make her genius unique." (Met/Cho, see Bibliog.)

A London performance (31 May 1985) of the Beethoven Concerto No. 2 with the Philharmonia Orchestra, Giuseppe Sinopoli conducting, revealed that Argerich's "vertiginous, fire-spitting bravura remains unaltered. For her, every note of early Beethoven crackles with revelatory life and this together with her rare delicacy in the Adagio seemed of special significance when one considers that Miss Argerich has not given a London recital for approximately 25 years." (MM, Aug 1985)

On 26 September 1985 Argerich played Ravel's Concerto in G in London's Festival Hall with the National Symphony Orchestra of Washington, D.C., Mstislav Rostropovich conducting. "I doubt," marveled one critic, "whether this concerto has often been given with a greater sense of magic, fluency and finesse in its entire history." (*MM*, Nov 1985)

On 11 October 1990 the versatile Argerich played Prokofiev's Piano Concerto No. 3 with the Boston Symphony Orchestra, Seiji Ozawa conducting. "Her playing was electrifying, if a bit unbridled. She can produce an immense sound, as well as a hushed, ghostly gray tone at the appropriate moment. None of Prokofiev's demanding virtuosity seems to daunt her." (*BH*, 13 Oct 1990) Indeed, there is more to Argerich's playing than the often-mentioned bravura. Again and again she has proved her skill in making the piano "sigh and whisper and croon with radiant introspection," as in Los Angeles, when her interpretation of Schumann's *Des Abends* "emerged as an exquisite study in pianissimo tenderness." (*LAT*, 23 Feb 1978)

Not all critics acknowledge Argerich's mastery. Her playing is too eccentric for some. For others, she gets so carried away that she tends to exaggerate. And there are those who complain that she sometimes rushes the tempo, forcing conductors and orchestras to keep her pace. But for the great majority Martha Argerich has become a legendary, charismatic performer. For most critics—and just about all audiences—an Argerich performance is a thrilling event.

Martha Argerich has made recordings since she was in her early twenties. It is a tribute to her high recording standards that so many of her LPs have recently been reissued as CDs. Reviewers wax ecstatic over her Chopin recordings. "Argerich's volatile and poetic playing of the Preludes (first issued 10 years ago) remains for me the best version of these ever-fresh pieces." (*Fan*, Jan/Feb 1988) And this: "Her discs of both Chopin sonatas are quite exceptional, as is that of the twenty-four Preludes, and her high-pitched tension is always controlled by her artistry and musical intelligence." (Met/Cho, see Bibliog.)

Argerich's 1986 recording of Beethoven's first two concertos competes successfully with the best of the existing versions. With the polished assistance of Giuseppe Sinopoli and the Philharmonia Orchestra, she gives a bravura performance of the Concerto No. 1 in C Major, op. 15, alternately lyrical and aggressive, tinged with surprises and stylistically consistent. "She is, of course, a brilliant technician; but there is also a fantastic streak in her make-up, a capacity for creative fantasy, which is needed if areas of these remarkable works are to be brought fully and vividly to life." (*Gram*, Sept 1986) Argerich has also recorded the Beethoven Concerto No. 2 with the London Sinfonietta, Argerich herself conducting at the piano. Issued on CD with the well-known Haydn Concerto in D Major, these performances have earned her exceptional praise (see Discog.). "Elegant passage work, natural phrasing, and tonal refinement characterize Argerich's Beethoven Second." (*Fan*, March/April 1991)

The Argerich readings of Ravel's Concerto in G and his *Gaspard de la nuit* are virtuoso masterpieces. "In 'Ondine' the piano almost disappears behind the splashing waters depicted by the composer." (*Fan*, Jan/Feb 1988) In an entirely different vein, Argerich has recorded two of Schumann's most romantic keyboard collections, *Kinderscenen*, op. 15, and *Kreisleriana*, op. 16 (see

Discog.). The *Kreisleriana*, by turns songlike and capricious, is beautifully suited to her innate impetuosity,

A recent CD reissue of several classic Argerich performances is a treasure. The 1972 recordings of the Liszt Sonata in B Minor and the Schumann
Sonata in G Minor (see Discog.) have seldom if ever been bettered. In the Liszt,
"her prodigious fluency unites with a trail-blazing temperament, and Valhalla itself never ignited to such effect as at the central *Andante's* central climax. . . .
This is a performance to make other pianists turn pale and ask, how is it possible to play like this?" As for the Schumann, it too "is among her most mete-
oric, headlong flights. In terms of sheer brilliance she leaves all others standing." (*Gram*, Feb 1993)

In her many concerto recordings—Chopin, Beethoven, Prokofiev,
Tchaikovsky, Schumann—each composer is beautifully served by Argerich, a
keyboard artist who transforms the challenge of concerted music into a stimulating musical experience.

SELECTED REFERENCES

"Dark Victor." *Time*, 26 March 1965, p. 64.
Elder, Dean. "The Mercurial Martha Argerich: an interview." *Clavier*, Sept
    1979, pp. 20–24.
Halberstam, David. "Argentine Wins Chopin Event." *New York Times*, 16
    March 1965, p. 44.
Hauptfuhrer, Fred, and Mary Vespa. "A Top Woman Pianist, Martha Argerich,
    Nearly Gave Up Her Steinway for Steno." *People*, 31 March 1980, pp. 67–
    68.
Kozinn, Allan. "Martha Argerich, Argentina's Enigmatic Classical Virtuosa."
    Keyboard, July 1981, pp. 34, 36, 38.
Morrison, Bryce. "One in a million." Gramophone, Jan 1995, pp. 12-13, 16.
Rockwell, John. "Who Says Modern Pianists Are Un-Romantic?" *New York
    Times*, 3 June 1984, sec. 2, p. 23.
"Scaling the Mountain." *Newsweek*, 18 Sept 1967, pp. 91–92.
Wigler, Stephen. "Women At The Keyboard." *Baltimore Sun*, 22 April 1990,
    sec. K, p. 1.
See also Bibliography: Eld/Pia; Kai/Gre; New/Gro; Ran/Kon; Rat/Cle.

SELECTED REVIEWS

AJ: 27 Feb 1976. *BH*: 13 Oct 1990. *DT*: 23 Feb 1989. *FT*: 23 Feb 1989. *IS*:
    12 Nov 1977. *LAHE*: 21 March 1981. *LAT*: 16 Dec 1967; 2 Sept 1972;
    23 Feb 1978; 21 March 1981; 22 March 1988. *MM*: July 1978; Aug
    1985; Nov 1985; April 1988. *NY*: 7 April 1980. *NYT*:17 Jan 1966; 20
    Feb 1970; 5 March 1972; 11 Feb 1974; 22 Feb 1974; 3 Feb 1978. *STL*:
    21 Feb 1988; 28 April 1991. *TL*: 17 Nov 1964; 23 June 1965; 8 Sept
    1966; 19 Sept 1966; 26 Oct 1966; 14 Feb 1977; 22 March 1977; 11 March
    1978; 3 Nov 1979; 3 Dec 1979; 26 Sept 1985; 13 Feb 1988; 14 Feb 1990;
    2 Dec 1991.

SELECTED DISCOGRAPHY

Beethoven: Concerto No. 1 in C Major, op. 15; Concerto No. 2 in B-flat Major, op. 19. DG 415 682-2. Sinopoli/PO.

Beethoven: Concerto No. 2 in B-flat Major, op. 19. Haydn: Concerto in D Major, Hob. XVIII/11. EMI Studio CDM 7 63575 2. Argerich/London Sinfonietta.

Chopin: Concerto No. 1 in E Minor, op. 11. Liszt: Concerto No. 1 in E-flat Major. DG 415061-2. Abbado/LSO.

Chopin: Concerto No. 1 in E Minor, op. 11; Barcarolle, op. 60; Etude in C-sharp Minor, op. 10, no. 4; Mazurkas, op. 24, no. 2, op. 59, nos. 1-2; Nocturnes, op. 15, no. 1, op. 55, no. 2; Scherzo in C-sharp Minor, op. 39. Liszt: *Etude de concert*. Prokofiev: Sonata No. 7. Arkadia 574 (CD). Orizio/Orchestra "Gasparo da Salò."

Chopin: Concerto No. 2 in F Minor, op. 21. Sonata No. 2 in B-flat Minor, op. 35. DG Sig. 413 976-2. Rostropovich/NSO.

Chopin: Mazurkas, op. 59, nos. 1-3; Polonaise in A-flat Major, op. 53; Polonaise-fantaisie in A-flat Major, op. 61; Sonata No. 3 in B Minor, op. 58. Musical Heritage Society MHS 419389Z (CD).

Chopin: 24 Preludes, op. 28; Prelude in C-sharp Minor, op. 45; Prelude in A-flat Major, op. posth.; Barcarolle in F-sharp Major, op. 60; Polonaise in A-flat Major, op. 53; Scherzo No. 2 in B-flat Minor, op. 31. DG (Galleria) 415 836-2.

Debussy: *Estampes*. Prokofiev: Sonata No. 7 in B-flat Major, op. 83. Ravel: Concerto in G. Exclusive EXL 65 (CD). Abbado/Rome RAI SO.

Haydn: Concerto in D Major, Hob. XVIII:11. Shostakovich: Concerto for Piano, Trumpet and Strings, op. 35. DG 439 864-2. Guy Touvron, trumpet, Faerber/Württemberg CO.

Liszt: Hungarian Rhapsody No. 6 in D-flat Major; Sonata in B Minor. Brahms: Two Rhapsodies, op. 79. Schumann: Sonata No. 2 in G Minor, op. 22. DG Galleria 437 252-2.

Prokofiev: Concerto No. 3 in C Major, op. 26 (Abbado/Berlin PO). Tchaikovsky: Concerto No. 1 in B-flat Minor, op. 23 (Dutoit/RPO). MHS 11201F (CD). The Prokofiev is also available on DG 439 413-2.

Rarities. Bach: English Suite No. 2, BWV 807. Beethoven: Sonata in A Major, op. 101. Schumann: *Kinderscenen*, op. 15. Artists FED 070 (CD).

Ravel: *Gaspard de la nuit*; *Sonatine*; Concerto in G Major. DG (Galleria) 419 062-2. Abbado/Berlin SO.

Schumann: Concerto in A Minor, op. 54. Teldec 4509-90696-2. Harnoncourt/CO of Europe.

Schumann: *Kinderscenen*, op. 15; *Kreisleriana*, op. 16. DG 410 653-2.

Stravinsky: *Les Noces*. DG 423 251-2. With pianists Cyprien Katsaris, Krystian Zimerman and Homero Francesch, Leonard Bernstein conducting.

Tchaikovsky: Concerto No. 1 in B-flat Minor, op. 23 (Kord/Warsaw NPO). Schumann: Concerto in A Minor, op. 54 (Celibidache/*Orchestre National de France*). Artists FED 012.

VIDEO

Scarlatti, Debussy, Ravel. Scarlatti: Sonata in D Minor, K. 141. Debussy: Sonata for Cello and Piano in D Minor. Ravel: *La Valse*; *Gaspard de la nuit.* Martha Argerich, assisted by Misha Maisky and Nelson Freire. Sony Video LP.

ARRAU, CLAUDIO: b. Chillán, Chile, 6 February 1903; d. Mürzzuschlag, Austria, 9 June 1991.

> I had this urge to play at four, and from then on it was the only thing I wanted to do.
>
> Claudio Arrau (*Musical America*, March 1988)

That mystical, inborn "urge to play" sustained Claudio Arrau through an incredible eight decades of concertizing and, perhaps even more incredible, more than 5,000 performances. From infant prodigy to elderly master, Arrau was inspired and guided by his great love for the piano. Lucrecia León de Arrau, already 43 when Arrau was born, became an impoverished widow a year later, her husband, Carlos, a popular but improvident Chillán occulist, having been thrown from a horse. Since she was a good amateur pianist, Doña Lucrecia supported her three children by giving lessons, usually with the infant Claudio playing nearby. No one could ever explain how he learned to read music before he could read words, but Arrau eventually concluded that his inherent curiosity about music must have been stimulated in infancy by hearing his mother play at practice and at lessons. According to Doña Lucrecia, at about age three her son could sketch out lines, clefs and notes. She would show him the notes on the piano, and by the time he reached four he could read music. Beyond that, Arrau was endowed with an exceptional sight-reading ability, a remarkable memory and hands that by age nine could easily span an octave and ultimately cover 11 notes between thumb and forefinger.

Arrau gave his first public recital (19 Sept 1908) at age five at Chillán's Municipal Theater, causing a sensation, as he did with his second Chillán recital in October of the following year. About two years later Doña Lucrecia moved the family to Santiago so that her son could study with Bindo Paoli, a well-known pedagogue, and she could lobby the Chilean Congress for funds for her son to study abroad. Arrau's youth and talent enchanted the capital. Thanks to broad press coverage, his mother was able to wangle appointments for him to play for each senator and deputy, and in due time Congress granted a renewable scholarship generous enough to support the entire Arrau family abroad for ten years. They moved to Berlin in 1911. Arrau remembered spending a useless year studying with Waldemar Lütschg and a better year with Paul Schramm, a teacher he liked and from whom he felt he learned a lot.

In 1913 the Chilean pianist Rosita Renard arranged an audition for Arrau with her teacher Martin Krause, and Krause accepted him as a pupil. At first the ten-year-old Arrau was afraid of "Herr Professor," the exacting master who had studied with Liszt, but ultimately Krause became his mentor and surrogate father. Every morning Arrau went to Krause's home to practice on an upright piano for seven or eight hours. Krause checked on him periodically and at day's end gave him a lesson. As with all his students, Krause insisted that Arrau develop more power, speed and endurance than he would ever need in performance, not for the sake of virtuosity but to create a technique that would convey a feeling of absolute mastery to an audience. Krause also taught him that achieving a sensitive interpretation of the music was even more important than technique. Arrau's lifelong concern with trills, tremolos and other decorative elements came from Krause, who had learned from Liszt that such elements must also be given meaning, that you do not, for example, play a Chopin trill the same way you play a Beethoven trill.

The authoritative Krause took no payment for the lessons, but he took over the boy's life, deciding what he should eat, choosing his tutors (Arrau had only a few months of formal schooling), taking him on daily walks and seeing to it that he visited museums, the opera and other musical events. If Krause intended to develop his little pupil into a cultured, well-rounded individual, he succeeded. Arrau became an inveterate reader (he spoke and read five languages), an art collector (notably pre-Columbian figurines) and a devotee of films, theater and dance.

Arrau's spectacular career as a prodigy was largely due to Krause's reputation and connections. Playing first in student recitals, where he was singled out for praise by the press, at age 11 Arrau made his formal debut (10 Dec 1914) in the Berlin *Künstlerhaus*, a performance causing such a stir that two months later his second recital at the *Künstlerhaus* drew an overflowing audience. Arrau was only 12 when he played the Liszt Concerto No. 1 under Arthur Nikisch in Dresden. Most seasons Krause arranged from 15 to 20 appearances, many before royalty who presented the young Arrau with gifts and jewels. This exciting, pampered existence (yet for a teenager isolated and lonely) ended abruptly when Krause died on 18 February 1918.

Fiercely loyal to Krause, who had taught him so much, the 15-year-old Arrau never sought another teacher. On his own, he continued through the classical piano literature, following the course set by Krause; but without Krause's social and professional contacts, Arrau's life changed drastically. He made a successful if not profitable tour through Norway, Finland, Bulgaria, Yugoslavia and Romania. He won the Liszt Prize in 1919 and again in 1920, the same year he made both his debut with the Berlin Philharmonic Orchestra, playing the Schubert-Liszt *Wanderer* Fantasy under Karl Muck, and his London debut, playing Bach's Goldberg Variations at Aeolian Hall. But these successes were not enough to prevent a painful period of self-doubt and depression induced by years of trying to please first his mother, then Krause. Melancholia interfered with his playing, he made errors and, to make matters worse, his long-running Chilean scholarship ended in 1921.

Arrau had 20 engagements promised in the United States for the 1923–24 season but only five dates materialized—three recitals (two in New York and one in Hackensack, New Jersey) and two orchestral concerts. Nothing went right. The American critics were not overly kind, and Arrau discovered that he had to pay all expenses. As a result, he and Doña Lucrecia were stranded in America until the Baldwin Piano Company generously paid their fare to Berlin.

Penniless and more depressed than ever, Arrau gave lessons to support his family, and his mother pawned ornaments and jewels given to him in better days. At this point Arrau turned to Dr. Hubert Abrahamson, a Düsseldorf psychoanalyst, and three months of almost daily treatments helped immensely. Slowly the shy Arrau began to mature. In 1926 he was appointed professor at the Stern Conservatory, where he taught for many years, and that same year he toured England with Richard Tauber, the eminent Austrian tenor. Winning first prize at the 1927 Geneva *Concours International d'Exécution Musicale* gave him a tremendous lift psychologically and brought him more invitations to play. He toured Russia in 1929 and again in 1930. (When Arrau returned in 1968, his Moscow and Leningrad concerts sold out in two hours.)

Arrau's fabulous repertoire, awesome in its range, depth and scope, had already begun to emerge. In Mexico City (11 Oct 1933–11 Jan 1934) he performed an heroic series of 15 recitals and 4 orchestral concerts, the wide-ranging programs including works by 25 composers representing 7 nationalities. In Berlin he began a stunning sequence of performances that completely recaptured his German audiences: a 12-recital (1935–36) survey of Bach's solo clavier works; five evenings (1936) devoted to the keyboard works of Mozart; and, in 1937, four evenings of Schubert and one of Weber. In 1938 he performed a cycle of the complete Beethoven sonatas in Mexico City. A peerless Beethoven interpreter, Arrau gained added fame for his huge repertoire, "always kept in perfect repair." (*STL*, 8 June 1975)

By 1940 Arrau had behind him a decade of successful concertizing in Europe, Mexico and South America. Meanwhile he had married (8 July 1937) Ruth Schneider, a mezzo-soprano from Frankfurt, who gave up her career after marriage. They lived in Germany until World War II, in 1940 moved to Santiago, Chile. From there, Arrau made a second attempt to win American audiences. His recital at Town Hall (25 Jan 1941) earned only lukewarm reviews, but a second one, played at Carnegie Hall (19 Feb 1941), was hugely successful. Rave reviews resulted in more than 50 bookings, and the following season he played over 100 concerts in the United States and Canada. Thereafter the wondrously energetic Arrau (he loved performing) pursued a marathon schedule. Crisscrossing the continents, he played all over the world, usually about 100—at one point as many as 130—concerts a season. Although with age he gradually reduced the number of appearances, even in his eighties Arrau was playing around 50 concerts a season.

His long life, overflowing with success and honors, is perhaps best described by Arrau's own favorite word: marvelous! On his 65th birthday the Berlin Philharmonic Orchestra honored him with a tribute written by Kurt

Westphal, who acknowledged Arrau as the heir to Busoni and Gieseking. In 1970 Arrau was awarded the *Bundesverdienstkreuz*, one of West Germany's highest honors. In 1980 the BPO awarded him the Hans von Bülow Medal, its highest honor, to commemorate the 60th anniversary of his debut with that orchestra. Throughout the 1982–83 season much of the musical world celebrated Arrau's 80th birthday. And Arrau garnered a new crop of honors and prizes: the International UNESCO Music Prize for 1983, National Arts Prize from Chile, Order of the Aztec Eagle from Mexico, title of *Commendatore* from the Academy of St. Cecilia in Rome and Commander of the French *Légion d'honneur*, France's highest tribute.

At age 81 Arrau, after a 17-year absence in protest against authoritarian regimes, returned (May 1984) to his homeland to play, as he said, for a new generation that had never heard of him. He avoided politics and donated his concert receipts to young Chilean artists. It was a triumphant passage. Though he had been an American citizen since 1979, Arrau remained a national hero in Chile, where streets have been named for him in Santiago and Chillán. People waited in line as long as 13 hours to buy tickets for his concerts, and sometimes the applause lasted 30 minutes.

Arrau stopped performing in June 1989 after the death of his wife. He was scheduled to give his first recital in two years on 7 June 1991 in Mürzzuschlag, Austria, to commemorate the opening of a renovated museum named after Johannes Brahms. He was also scheduled to play a week later at the Schumann Festival in Düsseldorf, where the baritone Dietrich Fischer-Dieskau was to have presented him with the Gold Medal of the Royal Philharmonic Society of London. Both events were canceled. Arrau became ill, underwent emergency surgery on 8 June and died the following day. The Chilean government proclaimed June 10 a national day of mourning.

On 7 March 1992 the London Symphony Orchestra and London Symphony Chorus, Sir Colin Davis conducting, presented the Verdi Requiem as a memorial tribute to Claudio Arrau. Before the performance Sir Yehudi Menuhin made a posthumous presentation of the Royal Philharmonic Society's Gold Medal to the pianist's daughter.

Arrau never regarded himself as a specialist in any composer, era or style, believing that musicians should have as wide a range of interests and knowledge as possible. A perfectionist and merciless self-critic, he achieved his intelligent, distinctive readings by studying the best possible edition of the particular work, reading about the composer's style and in general learning all he could about the composer's life and environment. He would memorize not only the entire work but all its parts, memorize it so well that if necessary he could put it together like a jigsaw puzzle. To accomplish this memorizing, Arrau visualized four stages: finger memory, visual memory, sound memory and, most important, structural memory.

Although he often said that hearing and watching Teresa Carreño and Ferruccio Busoni play had greatly influenced his own technique and playing style, essentially Arrau owed his renowned technique and accuracy to ingenuity and practice. Krause had never discussed technique much except for reminding him to keep relaxed and never get stiff. After Krause died, Arrau began to practice before a mirror. Watching himself play, he noted the rotation, vibration, use of arm weight, etc. In time he worked out a way of playing that emphasized keeping the shoulders relaxed, using the upper body weight and never striking the piano from the wrist.

Age did not diminish his seemingly insatiable intellectual curiosity either and that, together with his uncommon stamina and rare capacity for spiritual renewal, undoubtedly contributed to Arrau's long career. At age 83 he played four Beethoven sonatas at the Royal Festival Hall, a program (4 June 1986) said *The Times*, that "would have taxed a man half his age." At age 85, with about 50 concert appearances planned, Arrau took on a monster recording project for Philips and also began a five-part home video series for Video Artists International (see Discog. and Video).

Arrau has been pictured as a gentle, retiring man whose shyness and humility kept him somewhat isolated from the world, even from having many close colleagues within his own field. Unconcerned about modern conveniences, he never learned to drive a car or operate a phonograph (his wife Ruth did this for him), and he preferred that interviewers not use a tape recorder.

How does one describe, let alone understand, the art of Claudio Arrau? Like many other great performers, he was famous for his incredible memory and technique. But beyond that Arrau was a rare pianist, a "prince of players" equally acclaimed for that inquiring intellect that made him scrutinize every phrase and every musical motive for the most expressive delineation of the composer's intention. Labeling his art is truly difficult. Perhaps Arrau's greatness lay in his unique universality (his repertoire embraced the whole field of piano literature) and his splendid and seemingly inexhaustible creative energies.

Any study of Arrau will turn up hundreds (and hundreds!) of reviews, amassed over decades and impossible to summarize in any brief space, but their consistency testifies to the constancy of his art. A long ago review (1918) of a Berlin recital, reprinted in Joseph Horowitz's *Conversations with Arrau,* confirms Arrau's steadfast consistency. "He has a singular gift for the piano. He exhibits a healthy timbre which does not conform to the present preference for coquettish and rustling effects, and which in forte is capable of the greatest dynamic intensification with absolute clarity and assurance." This, said Horowitz, is a "description of Arrau's sound that could have as accurately been applied fifty years later." (Horowitz)

Compare the following review, written a half-century later: "Claudio Arrau is the complete pianist. He can revel in the keyboard for its own pianistic sake, presenting to us the instrument's range, its power to mingle song, percussion, depth of harmony and rhythmic fluency; but also he can go beyond piano-playing, taking us into the world of music, into the mind of a composer, so searchingly that we are free to forget his great technical scope; we take it for granted as we are led by his art to the secret chambers of creative imagination." (*TL*, 18 Jan 1975) Compare also this review written 67 years after that early Berlin recital: "If, at age 82, Claudio Arrau were no longer playing the piano, or if he were playing badly, it would certainly be understandable. After all, he has been on the concert stage longer than most of us have been anywhere. . . . But Arrau is still playing, and his performance . . . was, from beginning to end, nothing short of sublime. . . . What was missing was an occasional note, and not his control, which was as miraculous as ever. . . . Arrau's playing, truly, is as invincible as a law of nature, and as perfectly beautiful." (*BH,* 14 March 1985)

In the bulk, from earliest to latest, the Arrau reviews are a steady paean of praise for his pianism and musical integrity. But his playing puzzled some critics. While always admiring his pianism, they found his music emotionally unsatisfying and questioned his interpretations, particularly in the matter of tempos. One such critic found an Arrau performance "thoughtful, large and beautifully 'voiced'—satisfying, if not exactly exhilarating." But something was missing. Although there was nothing wrong, and actually much that was marvelous, this critic wondered, "Was it grit, a keener clash of harmonic incidents that I missed? I don't know. But I do know that Mr. Arrau . . . is still one of the world's greatest pianists." (*NY,* 3 March 1980)

The "puzzled" reviewers are overwhelmingly outnumbered by whole-hearted admirers. Less than a year before Arrau stopped performing in June 1989, he played (9 Sept 1988) the Beethoven Third Piano Concerto with the Dallas Symphony Orchestra, Eduardo Mata conducting. Still provocative at age 85, Arrau made no noticeable concessions to time in the fresh, free way he played. "While the sinuous style of his playing was a compelling feature, what one remembered most from the evening was the heightened sense of lyricism in which he couched the score, especially the radiance he brought to the concerto's deeply affecting slow movement." (*DMN,* 12 Sept 1988)

Two months later, for an 85th-birthday concert, Arrau played Beethoven's "Emperor" Concerto with the London Symphony Orchestra, Sir Colin Davis conducting. Though frail, Arrau still emerged as a phenomenal musician. Despite the outward failings, Arrau "allowed us to see far beyond the notes. . . . It was not simply the element of uncertainty that made his reading so much more compelling than Brendel's last Sunday. . . . The immense and majestic strength, for example, of those opening, rolling chords was both physical and deeply spiritual, and from the moment they sounded it was plain that this was to be a performance of implicit power and single-mindedness." (*TL,* 5 Nov 1988)

Half a century ago Arrau, ever articulate with the spoken and written word, described his personal approach to the art of pianism: "The ultimate problem of the pianist is one of interpretation. The goal of his studies may be simply stated: The comprehension and restatement of the thought of the composer." (*Etude,* Aug 1942) And later: "Know what each passage, each phrase, each motif means. Never play a work when you are in doubt as to the meaning of a single bar." (*Etude,* April 1948) Still guided by those precepts, the Arrau of later decades may have changed his interpretative approach to various works, but his basic concepts of piano playing remained constant.

Arrau began making discs in 1928 (he had already made a few piano rolls in 1922) and was still busily recording until almost the end of his life. During an awesome 60-year span, he recorded—sometimes rerecorded—a large quantity of the Beethoven, Chopin, Schumann, Mozart, Brahms and Liszt solo repertoires, plus all the major Romantic concertos. Many of his earlier recordings are still available. A retrospective album (3 CDs) in honor of his 80th birthday contains remastered discs from 1946 through 1952, among them some truly magisterial performances (see Discog.). Philips, his producer for the last 15 years, issued the Arrau Edition (6768 350 through 357), 58 LP records in eight boxed sets comprising works by Beethoven (concertos on 6 discs, sonatas and variations on 14 discs), Schubert (4 discs), Schumann (10 discs), Liszt (7 discs), Chopin (9 discs), Brahms (5 discs) and Debussy (3 discs). With the advent of the compact disc, Philips has reissued the Arrau Edition on CD (see Discog.).

This Arrau Edition is "bound to be regarded as one of the century's monumental recorded legacies. . . . The beauty of Arrau's playing on all these discs does not lie only in hearing definitive statements by a definitive pianist. The real musical excitement comes from the sense of a continuing adventure, the discoveries of an inquiring musical intelligence that has peered deeply, uncovered many secrets, and is still looking for more." (NewY, 14 March 1983)

Honoring Arrau's ongoing recording sessions at age 85, Philips reissued on CD over a dozen performances dating as far back as the late 1950s, among them earlier readings of Chopin, Debussy, Brahms and Tchaikovsky. And of course there are the newer recordings of the Beethoven and Mozart sonatas.

Arrau dedicated a large portion of his career to performing and recording the music of Beethoven, and one of his most famous recordings featured Beethoven's "Diabelli" Variations, op. 120. Made in 1952, it was out of print for some years, and a new version (1985) was eagerly anticipated. "Arrau's approach to the work has a strength of spirit and singularity of manner which you will encounter in no other version in or out of the current catalogues. . . . Arrau, ever the heroic individualist, occupies ground which is uniquely his own. The length of his experience, his massive technical command, and the posture he assumes in the presence of ageing, endlessly idiosyncratic Beethoven make their own ensemble, create a mode of address that is peculiarly revealing." (Gram, May 1987)

It is impossible here to consider even briefly the works of the many composers represented in Arrau's vast recorded repertoire, but one further example indicates the fantastic stylistic scope of Claudio Arrau's concepts. His recordings (1969) of the two Brahms concertos are among the finest he made. Other excellent recordings of these concertos are available, for example, those by Curzon, Barenboim and Serkin, but the Arrau version of these two masterpieces is very special.

Four of Arrau's recordings received Grammy awards: Chopin concert works for piano and orchestra (1974); Liszt Transcendental Etudes (1978); Chopin album of scherzos, etc. (1985); and the Beethoven Concerto No. 5 (1986).

SELECTED REFERENCES

Arrau, Claudio. "Creative Technic for the Pianist." *Etude,* Aug 1942, pp. 511–512, 562.

———. "Mozart: The Piano Music." *Musical America*, 15 Feb 1956, pp. 6–7, 124, 126.

———. "The Piano Sonatas: Performance Insights." (interview with Dean Elder on the Beethoven sonatas). *Clavier*, Jan 1970, pp. 18–23.

———. "Thoughts at 85." *Keynote*, Feb 1988, pp. 8–10.

———. "Training for Artistry." *Etude*, April 1948, pp. 209, 260, 276.

Arrau, Claudio, and Hilde Somer. "Two Artists Talk." *Piano Quarterly,* Fall 1973, pp. 6–14.

Banowetz, Joseph. "Arrau, Horowitz, Serkin: A Walk Among Giants." *Piano Quarterly*, Fall 1979, pp. 23–27, 30.

Cairns, David. "Keepers of the eternal flame." *The Sunday Times* (London), 7 July 1991, sec. 5, p. 5. Arrau, Kempff, Serkin.

Goodwin, Noel. "Tribute in Keeping." *The Times* (London), 11 March 1992.

Harden, Ingo. *Claudio Arrau: Ein Interpretenportrait.* Frankfurt, Berlin, Vienna: Ullstein, 1983. Contains a fine discography.

Harrison, Max. "Arrau at 80." *Music and Musicians*, Jan 1983, pp. 8–9.

Horowitz, Joseph. "Artistry Grows With Age, Says Arrau at 75." *New York Times*, 5 Feb 1978, sec. 3, pp. 1, 19.

———. *Conversations with Arrau.* New York: Alfred A. Knopf, 1982. Revised edition, Limelight Editions, 1992.

———. "The Last Days of Claudio Arrau." *Keyboard Classics*, Sept/Oct 1992, pp. 6–8.

———. "The Poet and the Ponderer." *New York Times*, 23 Aug 1992, sec. 8, p. 21.

Isacoff, Stuart. "I, Claudio." *Keyboard Classics*, Jan/Feb 1983, pp. 7–10.

Kerr, Russell. "Arrau as Beethoven Cyclist." *Music Magazine*, Sept 1962, pp. 12–13, 56.

Kimmelman, Michael. "Disks New and Old Salute Arrau at 85." *New York Times*, 17 April 1988, p. 35.

Kozinn, Allan. "Claudio Arrau: 75 Years on the Concert Circuit." *Keyboard*, July 1983, pp. 27–31.

Kupferberg, Herbert. "Claudio Arrau." *Musical America*, March 1988, pp. 5–7.

———. "Claudio Arrau: Gearing up for a busy 80th birthday year." *Ovation*, July 1982, pp. 12–15.

Matthew-Walker, Robert. "Claudio Arrau at 85." *Music and Musicians*, Feb 1988, pp. 11–12.

Morrison, Bryce. "Arrau at 75." *Music and Musicians*, April 1978, pp. 32–34.

Obituary. *Los Angeles Times*, 10 June 1991, sec. A, p. 22. *New York Times*, 10 June 1991, sec. 2, p. 11. *The Times* (London), 10 June 1991, pp. 1, 8.

Osborne, Richard. "Arrau's Brahms." *Records and Recording*, Oct 1970, pp. 34–35.

———. "Keyboard Oracle." *Records and Recording*, Oct 1972, pp. 26–29.

Riva, Douglas. "Claudio Arrau: Reflections at 85." *Keyboard Classics*, Sept/Oct 1988, pp. 4–6.
Selmon, Diane. "Remembering Claudio Arrau." *Clavier*, Feb 1994, pp. 24–26.
Silverman, Robert J. "Claudio Arrau." *Piano Quarterly*, Winter 1982–83, pp. 30–33.
———. "Conversations with Claudio Arrau on Liszt." *Piano Quarterly*, Spring 1975, pp. 7–11.
Taitte, W. L. "The Art of Claudio Arrau." *Texas Monthly*, Oct 1983, pp. 184–186.
Weaver, Mary. "Interview with Claudio Arrau." *Piano Quarterly*, Winter 1962–63, pp. 18–22.
Wiser, John D. "In His Eighth Decade: Claudio Arrau's Recordings, 1982–1985." *Fanfare*, Jan/Feb 1988, pp. 51–54.
See also Bibliography: Car/Del; Car/Ful; Dan/Con; Dub/Ref; Eld/Pia; Kai/Gre; Kol/Que; Mac/Gre; Nie/Mei; Ran/Kon; Rat/Cle; Rub/MyM; Sch/Gre; Tho/Mus.

SELECTED REVIEWS

BG: 14 March 1985; 16 Jan 1989. *BH*: 14 March 1985. *CST*: 19 Feb 1979; 24 March 1980. *CT*: 25 March 1980; 1 Dec 1980; 11 March 1985. *DMN*: 12 Sept 1988. *DT*: 5 Nov 1988. *GM*: 3 Sept 1954; 10 Sept 1958. *LAT*: 13 Feb 1948; 4 April 1952; 21 Nov 1959; 5 Feb 1968; 7 Dec 1971; 15 Feb 1977; 10 Jan 1978; 18 Dec 1987; 2 Feb 1988. *MM*: Aug 1965. *MT*: July 1978; Aug 1986. *NY*: 3 March 1980. *NYT*: 20 Feb 1941; 18 Jan 1979; 18 Feb 1980; 15 Feb 1981; 14 May 1984. *PI*: 3 Feb 1983; 30 Oct 1987. *PP*: 6 March 1982. *SFC*: 14 Feb 1984; 7 March 1986. *TL*: 25 March 1927; 23 Jan 1947; 12 Dec 1949; 12 May 1951; 29 May 1956; 5 Nov 1957; 4 June 1959; 17 June 1959; 15 Oct 1959; 8 June 1961; 21 June 1961; 7 June 1962; 18 Jan 1975; 5 June 1975; 5 June 1986; 5 Nov 1988. *TU*: 30 Jan 1981.

SELECTED DISCOGRAPHY

The Arrau Edition. An eight-volume set comprising 44 CDs. Philips 432301-432308.
Bach: Chromatic Fantasy and Fugue; Goldberg Variations; Inventions nos. 2, 6, 8; Sinfonias nos. 2, 6, 15. RCA 7841-2-RG (2 CDs).
Beethoven: The Five Piano Concerti. Philips 422149-2 (3 CDs). Davis/Dresden State Orchestra.
Beethoven: Sonata in C Minor, op. 10, no. 1; Sonata in C Minor, op. 111. Philips 420154-2.
Beethoven: Sonata in C Minor, op. 13 ("*Pathétique*"); Sonata in C-sharp Minor, op. 27, no. 2 ("Moonlight"); Sonata in F Minor, op. 57 ("*Appassionata*"). Philips 422 970-2.
Beethoven: Sonata in C Minor, op. 13; Sonata in E-flat Major, op. 7. Philips 416820-2.

Beethoven: Sonata in E-flat Major, op. 27, no. 1; Sonata in F Minor, op. 57; Sonata in E-flat Major, op. 81a. Philips 416146-2.

Beethoven: Sonata in C Major, op. 53; Sonata in E Major, op. 109; *Andante favori.* Philips 416145-2.

Beethoven: 32 Variations on a Waltz by Diabelli, op. 120. Philips 416295-2, rec. 1985.

Brahms: Concerto No. 1 in D Minor, op. 15. Philips 420702-2. Haitink/*Concertgebouw.*

Brahms: Concerto No. 2 in B-flat Major, op. 83. Philips 420885-2. Haitink/ *Concertgebouw.*

Chopin: *Andante spianato* and *Grande Polonaise Brillante*, op. 22; Ballade No. 3 in A-flat Major, op. 47; Barcarolle, op. 60; Concert Rondo in F Major, op. 14; Concerto No. 1 in E Minor, op. 11; Concerto No. 2 in F Minor, op. 21; Fantasy in F Minor, op. 49; Impromptu in C-sharp Minor, op. 66; Nocturne, op. 9, no. 2; Nocturne, op. 15, no. 2; Waltz, op. 64, no. 2; Waltz, op. 69, no. 1; Variations, op. 2. Musical Heritage Society MHS 533049F (3 CDs). Inbal/LPO.

Chopin: Études, op. 10 and op. 25; *Trois nouvelles études.* Angel CDH-61016.

Chopin: The Nocturnes. MHS 523422A (2 CDs).

Claudio Arrau: A Retrospective (In Honor of His 80th Birthday). Chopin: *Andante spianato* and *Grande Polonaise*, op. 22 (Scherman/Little OS). Debussy: *Estampes*; *Pour le piano.* Liszt: Concerto No. 1 (Ormandy/PO); Hungarian Fantasy (Ormandy/PO); Hungarian Rhapsodies Nos. 8, 9, 10, 11, 13. Schumann: *Arabesque*, op. 18; *Kreisleriana*, op. 16. Ravel: *Ondine, Le Gibet* (*Gaspard de la nuit*). CBS Masterworks CB293 (3 LPs).

Claudio Arrau in Performance. Chopin: Concerto No. 1 in E Minor, op. 11 (Klemperer/Cologne RO, 1954). Liszt: Concerto No. 2 in A Major (Cantelli/PSO, 1953). Music and Arts CD 625.

Claudio Arrau: The 1968 Santiago Concert. Beethoven: Sonata in E-flat Major, op. 81a (*"Les Adieux"*). Liszt: *Après une Lecture du Dante*; Sonata in B Minor. Music and Arts CD-282.

Debussy: Preludes Book 1; *Images* Book 1. Philips 420393-2.

Debussy: Preludes Book 2; *Images* Book 2. Philips 420394-2.

Grieg: Concerto in A Minor, op. 16. Schumann: Concerto in A Minor, op. 54. Musical Heritage Society MHS 512860Y (CD). Davis/Boston SO.

Liszt: *La Chapelle de Guillaume Tell* (*Années de pèlerinage*); *Liebestraum* No. 3; Mephisto Waltz No. 1; Sonata in B Minor. Philips 422060 (CD).

Liszt: Transcendental Etudes. Philips 416458-2.

Mozart: Sonata in A Minor, K. 310; Sonata in C Major, K. 330. Philips 416648-2.

Schubert: Allegretto in C Minor; Impromptus, D. 899; Sonata in C Minor, D. 958; Sonata in A Major, D. 959; Sonata in B-flat Major, D. 960. Philips 432307 (3 CDs).

Schubert: *Moments musicaux*, D. 780; Sonata in G Major, D. 894. Philips 432 987-2.

VIDEO

Arrau and Brahms: The Two Romantics. Brahms: Sonata No. 3 in F Minor, op.
  5; Concerto No. 1 in D Minor, op. 15. KULTUR VHS 1192. Izquierdo/
  Santiago PO.
Beethoven. Concerto No. 4 in G Major, op. 58 (Muti/PO). Concerto No. 5 in
  E-flat Major, op. 67 (Davis/LSO). Philips 070 222-3.
Claudio Arrau : *The 80th Birthday Recital*. Beethoven: Sonata, op. 53; Sonata,
  op. 57. Chopin: Scherzo No. 1, op. 20. Debussy: *Reflets dans l'eau*
  (*Images* Book I). Liszt: Ballade No. 2 in B Minor; *Les Jeux d'eaux à la
  Villa d'Este* (*Années de pèlerinage*). (Signature Performance Series).
  KULTUR 1190, 1983.
Claudio Arrau: *The Emperor*. Beethoven: Concerto No. 5 in E-flat Major, op.
  73. KULTUR 1191, 1987. Tevah/U. of Chile SO.
Claudio Arrau: The Maestro and The Masters. Beethoven: Concerto No. 4 in G
  Major, op. 58; Sonata in D Major, op. 10, no. 3. Chopin: Ballade in A-flat
  Major, op. 47. Debussy: *L'Isle joyeuse*. Liszt: *Sonetto del Petrarca* No.
  104. Schubert: *Klavierstück* No. 1 in E-flat Minor, D. 946. KULTUR
  1193. Recorded live on the Historic Tour (1984) of Chile. Tevah/U. of
  Chile SO.

ASHKENAZY, VLADIMIR: b. Gorky, USSR, 6 July 1937.

> People can be talented . . . but lacking in the intuitive, irrational, gut
> feeling which is the *first* musical impulse. . . . Often I think I have it,
> and then I am grateful, then at other times, I don't know.
>   Vladimir Ashkenazy (*Piano Quarterly*, Fall 1978)

Strong, contradictory bloodlines—father a pure Jew, mother a pure Russian—and
the decidedly opposite natures of his parents inevitably influenced Ashkenazy's
early development. His father David Ashkenazy was a lively showbusiness personality employed as a piano accompanist for *Estrada*, the Soviet concert organization providing people with every kind of popular entertainment, whether
worker celebrations, military events or official affairs. Playing the piano mostly
by ear, David Ashkenazy's amazing gift for improvising exactly the right accompaniment for every kind of variety act made him a very popular entertainer,
and he spent most of his time on the road with *Estrada* touring companies.
Vladimir saw very little of his father and learned absolutely nothing about his
Jewish heritage. His mother (Evstolia) had him baptized in an Orthodox church
and raised him in a strictly Russian environment. (Ashkenazy was a grown
schoolboy before he realized that he was part Jewish.) She poured all the love
and attention she might have bestowed on her absent husband on her small son,

especially when at about age three the youngster showed his musical talent by singing, and singing correctly, some of the songs he heard his father play.

In 1940 the Ashkenazys moved to Moscow, only to be evacuated the next year when Hitler invaded Russia. For months they lived on the road with a troupe of *Estrada* families, traveling even as far as Siberia. Sometime in 1943 they returned to Moscow, where they lived in one room in a communal apartment. It was unbearably crowded, even more so after the Ashkenazys' daughter Elena was born in 1949. Neighbors complained when Vladimir practiced on his father's upright piano, but his protective mother, hoping his musical talent would take him to the top of the Soviet elite system, treated him, as he remembered, like "crystal glass."

His mother arranged private music lessons with a good teacher from a local district school. Though just turning six, within a few months he was allowed to enroll in the school itself, and there his talent caught the attention of Anaida Sumbatian, an Armenian music teacher known for her ability to teach young children. At age eight he was enrolled at the Central Music School, automatically became Sumbatian's pupil and studied with her for ten years. From the age of ten Ashkenazy was permitted to play in six or seven school concerts each year, concerts open to the public and often attended by professors of the Moscow Conservatory. With this good exposure, he soon became known as a prodigy and often performed at events arranged by the Moscow *Estrada* and other district organizations.

A fast learner, young Ashkenazy quickly became bored with practice. To challenge him and hold his interest, his parents provided him with piano reductions of operas and orchestral works. It worked like a miracle. He learned to enjoy practicing, improved his already fine sight-reading skills, and discovered a repertoire that he might otherwise never have explored. At age 17 he placed second in the fifth International Frédéric Chopin Piano Competition (1955) in Warsaw, after which he took final exams at the Central Music School and entrance examinations for the Moscow Conservatory. Ashkenazy was accepted for Professor Lev Oborin's class, but Oborin preferred performing to teaching, so Ashkenazy actually studied with Oborin's assistant, Boris Zemlyansky, who, he said, "really made music my life. For him, it was always a matter of life and death." (Parrott)

Ashkenazy made his first visit to the West in 1956 to compete in the Queen Elisabeth of Belgium Competition at Brussels. The jury (Artur Rubinstein, Emil Gilels and Robert Casadesus were members) unanimously awarded him first prize, a victory practically guaranteeing him a brilliant career in Russia *if* he used his gifts "for the good of the State" and never challenged authority. At year's end the State rewarded his family with a two-room apartment.

With his name now beginning to circulate in the musical world, Ashkenazy toured in Belgium, Holland, East and West Germany, and Poland. Then American impresario Sol Hurok signed him to a contract for a ten-week North American tour (Oct–Dec 1958). Ashkenazy had no say in the arrangements. Hurok dealt solely with *Goskoncert*, a Ministry of Culture agency handling all foreign engagements for Soviet artists and those of foreign artists appearing in Russia. This labyrinthine bureaucratic department released Ashkenazy's passport and ticket just one day before he was due in Washington, D.C., to play his first concert. He arrived tired from jet lag and nervous under the watchful eye of the "companion" sent along by the State, yet his performance (12 Oct 1958) of Chopin's Second Piano Concerto with the National Symphony Orchestra under Howard Mitchell received "a prolonged ovation from the brilliant first-night assemblage." (*MA*, 1 Nov 1958) On the whole, Ashkenazy felt terribly isolated on this tour. He spoke very little English, and his companion was not much help.

On the bright side, he had a "terrific" response at Carnegie Hall (24 Oct 1958); he was thrilled with American record shops; and he found a new friend in Malcolm Frager, the American pianist. Introduced at a New York party, the two later exchanged quantities of letters, mostly about music, and eventually played two-piano recitals. But once home in Moscow, the tour companion filed a negative report concerning Ashkenazy's attitude and behavior in America. A mock trial held at the Ministry of Culture found him guilty and banned him from making further trips abroad. It was a mild punishment, the authorities no doubt realizing that Ashkenazy now had international fame and could be a valuable propaganda asset. He was allowed to continue his studies, and in 1960 was graduated from the Conservatory and accepted for the *Aspirantura*, a two-and-a-half-year postgraduate course open only to the topmost students.

Meanwhile, the first International Tchaikovsky Piano Competition, held in Moscow in 1958, greatly affected Ashkenazy's life even though he did not participate. One of the contestants was Thorunn (Dody) Johannsdottir, born in Iceland and raised in London, where she studied with Harold Craxton at the Royal Academy of Music. She and Ashkenazy met only briefly during the 1958 competition, renewed the acquaintance when she returned in 1960 to attend the Moscow Conservatory, and a year later they married (Feb 1961) and moved into one room of his parents' two-room apartment.

Russian officials, devastated by Van Cliburn's sensational accomplishment at that 1958 Tchaikovsky Competition, began at once to screen pianists to be groomed for the next Tchaikovsky, due in 1962, and Ashkenazy emerged as the State's brightest hope. He had not even wanted to be considered, the competition being intended primarily for young, unknown talent; yet he knew how foolish it would be to resist official pressure. Besides, entering the Tchaikovsky might remove the travel ban still blocking his career. He made the right decision. In May 1962 Ashkenazy and John Ogdon shared first prize at the second Tchaikovsky Competition, and the government promptly removed his travel ban. Taking full advantage of his new prestige, Ashkenazy requested separate living quarters for his wife, son and himself, and in January 1963 they moved into a two-room apartment with a small kitchen and bath. Their piano, purchased with money earned on his 1958 American tour plus a $500 loan from friend Malcolm Frager, took up most of the space.

With the travel ban removed, Hurok immediately signed with *Goskoncert* for a second Ashkenazy tour of the United States. Delayed once again by bureaucratic inefficiency, he arrived in Washington, D.C., just the day before his first concert. This tour was not at all like the first, when he had felt lonely and isolated. This time his wife accompanied him and, thanks to the

American State Department somehow delaying the necessary visa, the watchful State "companion" got left behind in Russia. This time also Ashkenazy understood the language, his English having improved considerably since his marriage. This long, successful tour (Oct–Dec 1962) established his reputation in America. When it ended, both Ashkenazys were allowed to visit Mrs. Ashkenazy's parents in London, but when they returned to Moscow in January, they found life as difficult as ever.

Ashkenazy's first tour of England was scheduled to begin in March. At departure time, he was cleared but his wife and son were detained. Only by threatening to contact the Icelandic Embassy and cause an international incident was she finally allowed to join Ashkenazy in London, where she immediately applied to the British Home Office for a resident's permit. In April both Ashkenazys received resident permits, thereby provoking the Soviets into issuing them multiple exit and re-entry visas valid for six months.

Ashkenazy's highly successful British tour included a memorable London debut (7 March 1963), at which he played Beethoven's C Major Concerto and Brahms's Concerto in B Flat with the London Symphony Orchestra under George Hurst. At the end of the tour, the Ashkenazys returned (May 1963) to Moscow for a short visit, wisely leaving their son in London with his maternal grandparents. It was a tense time. Not wanting to lose their famous musician, the authorities delayed him in Russia on one pretext or another. Ashkenazy, fearful of repercussions for his parents, agreed to play some concerts, including a series of two-piano performances with Malcolm Frager (*Time*, 21 June 1963). In July the Ashkenazys finally fled the country by pretending they were off to London merely to fetch their son. Leaving their apartment as it was, they packed just enough for a brief stay and even purchased round-trip tickets. When they arrived in London, they knew they would not return, although Ashkenazy retained his passport.

In November 1989 Ashkenazy ended his 26-year exile. Invited back by the Soviet Cultural Foundation, he conducted the Royal Philharmonic Orchestra in two charity concerts and appeared as soloist in Beethoven's Concerto No. 3. He returned to his homeland, not as a traitorous defector but, in the new environment of *perestroika* and *glasnost*, as a famous and honored Russian artist. It was a joyful return.

But in 1963 the transition had been extremely difficult. Predicting a defection, the Western press hounded the Ashkenazys, who kept a low profile, fearing to offend Soviet authorities and cause trouble for his Moscow family. Fortunately, Ashkenazy's career soared in the West. That first year he played 54 concerts; for each of the next two years he played more than 90; in 1966 he played 107; in 1967 he played 114; and in 1968 he had 129 engagements, a level he maintained for some years.

After five years in the heady London environment, the Ashkenazys lived for 10 years (1968–78) in Reykjavík, Iceland, where they found quiet and privacy. Ashkenazy developed such a rewarding kinship with the Icelanders that in 1972, when he applied for Icelandic citizenship, the parliament voted a special dispensation allowing him to keep his own name (Icelandic law requires newly naturalized citizens to assume Icelandic names) because it was so famous. For his part, Ashkenazy served as artistic advisor for the Reykjavík Music Festival, and cajoled some of his famous colleagues into making the long journey north to participate. The difficulty of arranging airline connections for his many tours finally forced the Ashkenazys to leave Iceland. They chose Lucerne, Switzerland, only an hour from Zurich's international airport and within driving distance of many of the European cities on his regular itinerary, which meant that they had much more time at home. As always, whenever possible, Mrs. Ashkenazy (sometimes the whole family) accompanied him on his tours. Her constant companionship and wise counsel have been the mainstays of Ashkenazy's life and career.

Ashkenazy made his first attempts at conducting while in Iceland, between 1969 and 1976 developing a most satisfying arrangement with the Iceland Symphony Orchestra. He attracted distinguished soloists; in turn, the orchestra gave Ashkenazy an opportunity to test his conducting skills free from pressure. He next conducted small orchestras like the Northern Sinfonia in Newcastle and the Lancaster University Symphony, and later conducted the Royal Liverpool Philharmonic and the Swedish Radio Orchestra. Between 1978 and 1982 he worked mostly with the Philharmonia Orchestra, honing his techniques with concerts in and out of London. The Philharmonia also benefited, his name and fame attracting recording contracts, television appearances and tours in Europe, Japan, North America and Australia. In 1993 Ashkenazy was music director of London's Royal Philharmonic (resigned 1994), principal guest conductor with the Cleveland Orchestra and chief conductor of the Berlin Radio Symphony Orchestra.

Although conducting engagements now fill at least one-third of his schedule, Ashkenazy is still a very active pianist, performing and recording solo recitals and chamber music, sometimes with violinist Itzhak Perlman and often with his longtime partner, cellist Lynn Harrell. He has made solo tours in Europe, England, North America, Japan, Australia and South Africa. On his first visit to China in 1979, under the auspices of the BBC, he rehearsed the Shanghai Symphony Orchestra, gave a recital and conducted several master classes at the Shanghai Conservatory.

His early, traditional keyboard repertoire (Beethoven, Chopin, Mozart, Brahms, Schubert, Schumann) later expanded with the works of his many favorites, including Richard Strauss, Ravel and Debussy. His programs include a great deal of Russian music but rarely Liszt and never contemporary music. He usually requires only three hours a day of practice.

The public Ashkenazy appears shy and retiring. The private man has been described as warm and charming. He was awarded the Icelandic Order of the Falcon (1971) and made an honorary member of the Royal Academy of Music in London (1972).

Through three decades reviewers have, with remarkable consistency, praised Ashkenazy's artistry: his instinctive feeling for music; his ability to combine spontaneous poetry with a dramatic drive and intellectual sturdiness; his sensitivity to style and the means to achieve and sustain it, whether it is the classicism of Mozart, the late romanticism of Brahms, or the classical impressionism of Ravel. For example, Ashkenazy has a style "of an elegance and scope that has few peers among contemporary pianists . . . a style of limpid sound and prismatic color effect, impressionistic, microscopically detailed, never vague, always unerringly exact. Ashkenazy is . . . one of the supreme colorists of the keyboard." (*LAT*, 15 March 1977)

Ashkenazy's long list of fine American reviews began at his American debut (12 Oct 1958) with his sensitive interpretation of the Chopin Concerto No. 2: "This work requires poetry, restraint, finesse, delicacy, and a technique that permits exposition of the many subtle beauties in the score. The young pianist was master of all these qualities. . . . Here was Chopin in the old tradition, almost understated, yet so exquisitely proportioned and perfectly paced that the capacity audience in the vast hall seemed caught in the spell of finely wrought chamber music." (*MA*, 1 Nov 1958)

Ashkenazy played a formidable program for his Los Angeles recital debut (6 Dec 1958): Bach's Partita No. 6 in E Minor, the Brahms Variations and Fugue on a Theme by Handel, Ravel's *Gaspard de la nuit* and Prokofiev's Sonata No. 7. And even though his program did not show what he could do with, say, major Beethoven, Mozart or Chopin, "it told enough to prove that he is an extraordinary virtuoso and a remarkably sensitive and poetic interpreter of the music he chose to play." The Partita "was played with great refinement and clarity." The Brahms-Handel Variations "had an enormous range of contrasts and they progressed with a firm sense of form and continuity." The difficult Ravel triptych was "exquisitely played," and for the Prokofiev Sonata Ashkenazy "produced the percussive style of playing essential to the idiom and made it into a tour de force." (*LAT*, 8 Dec 1958)

A New York Philharmonic Hall recital (28 Oct 1962) included Mozart's Sonata in D Major, K. 311, the Prokofiev Sonata No. 6 in A Major, op. 82, *and* the entire set of Chopin Etudes, op. 25. "Lyricism rather than heroism is at the core of Mr. Ashkenazy's playing. He uses his enormous technique in a subtle manner, never over-stressing. . . . There is strength to Mr. Ashkenazy's playing, to be sure, but it is a tensile strength, tempered steel rather than concrete." (*NYT*, 29 Oct 1962)

Just as the recitals garnered plaudits wherever Ashkenazy played, so did his appearances with orchestra. He played the Schumann Concerto in A Minor on 1 August 1967 at the Hollywood Bowl with the Los Angeles Philharmonic Orchestra, Lawrence Foster conducting. "His playing of the Schumann was of the type that first stamped him as a pianist of extraordinary gifts—a pianist of a delicacy of tone and artful nuance scarcely equaled since the late Walter Gieseking. . . . It was an acutely sensitive performance, lyrical, joyous, touched with sentiment but never by sentimentality." (*LAT*, 3 Aug 1967)

The critic who, at Ashkenazy's 1958 Los Angeles recital, wished to hear what Ashkenazy would do "with major Beethoven, Mozart or Chopin," was amply satisfied with the pianist's UCLA (Royce Hall) program (20 May 1973) of just those composers' music—Mozart Sonata in C Minor, K. 457, Beethoven's Sonata in E Major, op. 109, and four Chopin pieces. "Refined sensitivity reigned supreme; there was never the slightest forcing for effect, and the intensity and concentration of his perceptions made for an emotional communicativeness the pianist has never achieved before." (*LAT*, 22 May 1973)

Ashkenazy's Minneapolis recital on 10 February 1980 included the Rachmaninoff Sonata No. 2 in B-flat Minor. This work, with its dense sonorities and interpretative complexities, presents problems for both audience and pianist. But what could have been "an unbearably cloying experience for the listener turned out to be an edifying one. Clarifying the diffuse strands of the piece, keeping its structure and melodic lines carefully pointed . . . Ashkenazy charged through it, as though riding an elephant through the jungle. Dynamic contrasts were wide, and at appropriate points there was some lovely soft playing." (*MiT*, 12 Feb 1980)

Even with his present interests divided between playing and conducting, Ashkenazy maintains his high performance standards at the piano. A 1990 solo recital in Toronto, Canada, featuring one work by Schumann (*Kreisleriana*) and two by Brahms (Piano Pieces, op. 119; Sonata, op. 5) received an enthusiastic review. Brahms's Four Piano Pieces "were given poised, thoughtful performances" and "Ashkenazy's expressive use of color and texture [in *Kreisleriana*] throughout were especially memorable." However, it was the Brahms Sonata that found the pianist "at the height of his interpretive powers." (*GloM*, 29 March 1990)

When the reviews are not so overwhelmingly praiseful, one usually finds not definite criticisms, but merely objective statements. A reviewer admiring Ashkenazy's technique ("without peer on the concert stage today"), his "smooth and expressive" phrasing and his dynamics ("he understands the use of dynamics perhaps as well as any pianist alive"), confessed that despite Ashkenazy's exceptional ability, "he plays with an odd detachment, seldom permitting himself to be totally involved in the emotional content of the music." (*MABR*, 1 March 1978)

One of the best and most succinct appraisals of Ashkenazy's playing appears in a review of a recital (Beethoven and Schumann) at the 1986 Strasbourg Music Festival. "Vladimir Ashkenazy does not interpret music; he exudes it—breathes it. His creative process is not guided by absolute or personal theories. What motivates him is simply a profound love for composers. He serves them reverently and zealously. The most diverse, subtle forms of music are to him a part of everyday life; yet, he plays them with a constant sense of wonder." (*TWaI*, Aug 1986)

Ashkenazy is unquestionably one of the 20th century's finest pianists.

Ashkenazy has recorded most of the major works of Beethoven, Chopin, Scriabin and Rachmaninoff and a good many works by Brahms, Schumann and Mozart. The earlier recordings (many remastered to CD) have basically the same superb qualities found in the latest recordings. It is no surprise, then, that two Schubert sonatas (D. 784 in A Minor and D. 894 in G Major), originally recorded in 1967 and 1973, have been reissued on CD (see Discog.). Both have much to recommend them, "both are played with a freshness and immediacy of imaginative response." The Sonata in G Major is particularly fine. "There is a raptness, an inner spiritual glow, in the playing which together with the boldness of the dynamic contrasts, somehow holds you spellbound until the eventual relief of the lightfingered, dancing finale." (*Gram*, Aug 1990)

Not all Ashkenazy CD reissues have received the same warm praise. A recent reissue of his 1969 recording of the Brahms Concerto No. 2 under the baton of Otto Klemperer was found to be, at least for one reviewer, "just plain dull." (*Fan*, Sept/Oct 1990)

In his role of pianist-conductor, Ashkenazy has recorded all of the Mozart piano concertos with the Philharmonia Orchestra. Issued as single CDs and together as a 12-CD set, these performances have met with broad critical approval. For example, "Ashkenazy's performances [K. 413 in F Major, K. 449 in E-flat Major] are superb. His playing is fluent and stylistically apt." (*CPD*, 25 Dec 1988) Compared with other complete sets of Mozart concertos, notably those of Anda and Barenboim, "this Decca [London] series offers an aristocratic quality that is very appealing. . . . Ashkenazy's has the most stylistically convincing playing overall." (*Gram*, June 1990)

He has recorded the five Beethoven concertos twice: with the Vienna Philharmonic Orchestra under Zubin Mehta, and with the Cleveland Orchestra, Ashkenazy himself conducting. Against enormous competition (there are over twenty recorded versions of the complete Beethoven concertos now available), Ashkenazy's performances have drawn mixed reactions. "While he is a thoughtful and intelligent musician as well as an excellent technician, Ashkenazy is not the most poetic of pianists; for that reason, some movements of some of the concertos are more convincing than others." (*Fan*, July/Aug 1989) On the other hand, "the definitive cycle is as elusive as the philosopher's stone and in his latest cycle Ashkenazy and his Cleveland musicians give us some wonderful, absorbingly articulate music-making, expertly and lovingly recorded." (*Gram*, March 1989)

Ashkenazy is a great devotee of Schumann, and obviously there is a splendid Schumann-Ashkenazy affinity. In his CD recording of the *Humoreske*, op. 20, and *Carnaval*, op. 9, "Ashkenazy can still muster that silky, soft-edged tone that has always been one of his most powerful assets." (*OrS*, 31 July 1988) For another reviewer, Ashkenazy's playing of *Carnaval* recalls the great 1919 recording by Rachmaninoff: "The conception is gigantic, the tempos are considerably faster than one is accustomed to nowadays and the power in climaxes is astonishing." The same review covers Ashkenazy's recorded performance of Schumann's Sonata No. 1 in F-sharp Minor. "This is one of Schumann's most difficult pieces. In most hands, its quick changes in mood and tempo can make the music sound sentimental and downright stupid. Ashkenazy makes it a noble, coherent experience and his sheer command of the notes is amazing." (*BaS*, 14 May 1989)

In 1959–60 Ashkenazy recorded both books of Chopin Etudes for *Melodiya*; he made a later version in stereo for London Records. A CD reissue of the early sets may be one of the finest of its kind. "With awesome technical control, with melting tone, and with overwhelming penetration to the music's core, Ashkenazy . . . never sounded better." (*Fan*, May/June 1993) Another critic praised this reissue for "its fleet, effortless pianism and freshness. For its extraordinary level of Chopin playing, this is a top choice." (*ARG*, May/June 1993)

From 1963 through 1985 Ashkenazy received nine Grammy awards for his solo discs—Chopin Ballades (1965); recital with Malcolm Frager (1965); Chopin Etudes (1975); Rachmaninoff Preludes (1982); Ravel recital (1985)—and concerto performances—Rachmaninoff No. 3 (1963); Beethoven Concertos (1975); Prokofiev Concertos (1982); Mozart K. 482 (1982).

SELECTED REFERENCES

Bowers, Faubion. "Russia's Ashkenazy: He Can't (Won't?) Go Home Again." *New York Times*, 23 Jan 1972, sec. 3, pp. 15, 28.
Commanday, Robert. "Ashkenazy on Music—Mum's the Word." *San Francisco Chronicle*, 6 Jan 1993, sec. E, pp. 1, 3.
Grant, Nancy S. "Vladimir Ashkenazy: The Lifelong Process of Music." *Keyboard*, March 1987, pp. 42–48.
Henken, John. "Vladimir Ashkenazy's Long Voyage Home." *Los Angeles Times*, 16 Dec 1970, CAL, pp. 7, 73.
Jenkins, Speight. "Vladimir Ashkenazy: Searching for New Vistas." *Ovation*, Aug 1981, pp. 12–15.
Longfellow, Pauline, and Daniel Burgart. "Vladimir Ashkenazy: 'Nothing by Halves'." *The World & I*, Aug 1986, pp. 294–300.
Mertens, Susan. "New Career Begins for Vladimir Ashkenazy." *Music Magazine*, May/June 1979, pp. 6–9.
Montparker, Carol. "Conversation with Vladimir Ashkenazy." *Clavier*, Nov 1986, pp. 22–25.
———. "Vladimir Ashkenazy: Impulse and Intellect." *Piano Quarterly*, Fall 1978, pp. 3–5.
Parks, Michael. "Pianist Finds He Can Go Home Again—a Hero." *Los Angeles Times*, 13 Nov 1989, sec. F, pp. 1, 6.
Parrott, Jasper, with Vladimir Ashkenazy. *Beyond Frontiers*. London: Hamish Hamilton Ltd., 1985. Also New York: Atheneum, 1985.
Rockwell, John. "Ashkenazy Puts Precision Over Showmanship." *New York Times*, 14 May 1978, pp. 19, 39.
Sachs, Harvey. "Seriously Great." *Atlantic Monthly*, Dec 1990, pp. 116–119.
Schonberg, Harold C. "Ashkenazy Says 'Da'." *New York Times*, 23 Nov 1958, sec. 2, p. 11.
See also Bibliography: Dub/Ref; Ewe/Mu; Kol/Que; Mac/Gre; New/Gro; Noy/Pia; Ran/Kon; Rat/Cle; Sch/Gre.

SELECTED REVIEWS

BG: 13 Dec 1990. *CPD*: 23 Feb 1981; 10 Feb 1986. *CSM*: 16 Nov 1965; 1 March 1988. *CST*: 22 Jan 1979. *CT:* 22 Jan 1979; 30 April 1984. *FT*: 29 Oct 1987; 13 Sept 1989. *GloM:* 29 March 1990. *LAT*: 8 Dec 1958; 3 Dec 1962; 3 Aug 1967; 18 Nov 1967; 8 Dec 1970; 22 Feb 1971; 22 May 1973; 3 March 1976; 15 March 1977; 17 April 1980; 5 May 1988; 7 Feb

1994. *MA*: 1 Nov 1958. *MABR*: 1 March 1978. *MiT*: 21 March 1977; 12 Feb 1980. *MM*: Aug 1966; May 1985. *MT*: May 1963; Dec 1974; April 1980. *NYP*: 17 Dec 1990. *NYT*: 29 Nov 1958; 29 Oct 1962; 15 Jan 1966; 26 Nov 1967; 18 March 1969; 15 Nov 1969; 28 Jan 1972; 17 Dec 1990. *PEB*: 14 March 1978. *PP*: 15 Jan 1985. *SFE*: 9 Feb 1979. *TB*: 7 Dec 1990. *WP*: 12 May 1988; 26 March 1990.

SELECTED DISCOGRAPHY

Bartók: Concerto No. 3. Prokofiev: Concerto No. 3. London 411 969-2. Scolti/LPO.

Beethoven: The Five Piano Concertos; Fantasy, op. 80. London 421 718-2 (3 CDs). Ashkenazy/Cleveland Orchestra.

Beethoven: Sonata in C Minor, op. 13; Sonata in C-sharp Minor, op. 27, no. 2; Sonata in F Minor, op. 57. London 410260-2. Also Musical Heritage Society MHS 513120A (CD).

Beethoven: Sonata in E-flat Major, op. 31, no. 3. Chopin: Ballades (4). Debussy: *Clair de lune*; *l'Isle joyeuse*; *Sérénade interrompue*. Russian Disc RD CD 11208. Recorded live 1963.

Beethoven: Piano Sonatas (complete). London 425 590-2 (10 CDs).

Brahms: Concerto No. 1 in D Minor, op. 15. London 410009-2. Haitink/ *Concertgebouw*.

Brahms: Concerto No. 2 in B-flat Major, op. 83. London 410 199 (CD). Haitink/Vienna PO.

Chopin: Ballades; Scherzos. London 417 474-2.

Chopin: Concerto No. 2, op. 21. Tchaikovsky: Concerto No. 1 in B-flat Minor, op. 23. London 417750-2. Zinman/LPO.

Chopin: Etudes (complete). *Melodiya* SUCD 10-00511. Recorded in 1959–1960.

Chopin: Nocturnes (21). London 414 564-2.

Chopin: Sonata No. 2 in B-flat Minor, op. 35; Sonata No. 3 in B Minor, op. 58; Fantasy in F Minor, op. 49. London 417 475-2.

Mozart: Concertos (complete). London 425557-2 (12 CDs). Ashkenazy/PO.

Mozart: Concerto in C Major, K. 246; Concerto in E-flat Major, K. 271; Rondo in A Major K. 386. Decca 443 576-2. Kertéz/ London SO.

Rachmaninoff: The Four Piano Concertos. London 421 590-2 (2 CDs). Haitink/*Concertgebouw*.

Rachmaninoff: *Etudes-Tableaux*, op. 33; Variations, op. 42. London 417 671-2.

Rachmaninoff: Sonata No. 2 in B-flat Minor, op. 36; Preludes, op. 23. 2-London 414 417-2.

Ravel: *Gaspard de la nuit; Pavane*; *Valses nobles et sentimentales*. London 410 255-2.

Schubert: Sonata in A Major, D. 664; Sonata in A Minor, D. 784; *Ungarische Melodie*; 12 Waltzes, D. 145. Decca 443 579-2.

Schubert: Sonata in A Minor, D. 784; Sonata in G Major, D. 894. London 425 017-2.

Schumann: *Carnaval*, op. 9; *Humoreske*, op. 20; *Noveletten*, op. 21. London 421 010-2.

Schumann: Fantasy in C Major, op. 17; *Faschingsschwank aus Wien*, op. 26; Theme and Variations on the name "Abegg," op. 1. Decca 443 322-2.

Schumann: *Kreisleriana*, op. 16; *Noveletten*, op. 21; Sonata No. 2 in F-sharp Minor, op. 22. London 425940 (CD).

Schumann: Sonata No. 1 in F-sharp Minor, op. 11; *Kinderscenen*, op. 15; *Waldscenen*, op. 82. London 421290-2.

Scriabin: Piano Sonatas. London 425579-2 (2 CDs).

Stravinsky: *Le Sacre du printemps*; Concerto for 2 pianos; Sonata for 2 pianos. London 433 829-2. With Andrei Gavrilov.

The Young Ashkenazy. Chopin: Barcarolle, op. 60; Concerto No. 2 in F Minor, op. 21; Etude in C Major, op. 10, no. 1; Etude in F Major, op. 25, no. 3; Sonata No. 3 in B Minor, op. 58; Scherzo No. 4 in E Major, op. 54. Testament SBT 1045 (CD). Gorzynski/Warsaw PO.

VIDEO

Ashkenazy Observed. (Episodes From The Life Of A Wandering Musician) Teldec Video 9031-70772-3.

Ashkenazy plays Beethoven. The Late Piano Sonatas: ops. 101, 106, 109, 110, 111. Films for the Humanities, FH 899A.

Ashkenazy plays Chopin. Preludes, op. 28; Nocturnes, op. 9, nos. 1, 3; Nocturnes, op. 27, nos. 1-2; Sonata in B Minor, op. 58; Polonaise in F-sharp Minor, op. 44; Impromptu in F-sharp Major, op. 32; Scherzo No. 3 in C-sharp Minor, op. 39. Films for the Humanities, FH 898A.

AX, EMANUEL: b. L'vov, USSR, 8 June 1949.

> There's great value in having good taste, but it's not the only thing that makes an artist. . . . I would rather hear an emotional, overindulgent performance than a restrained, tasteful one anytime."
>
> Emanuel Ax (Dubal, *Reflections from the Keyboard*)

When Emanuel Ax's father Joachim was born in L'vov, it was part of the Austro-Hungarian Empire. When his mother Hellen was born there, it belonged to Poland. By the time Ax was born, L'vov had become part of the Soviet Union. However, his parents (both Nazi concentration camp survivors, each had lost a first spouse during the Holocaust) never considered themselves anything but Polish and always spoke Polish at home.

At age six Ax began music lessons with his father, a speech and voice therapist who also coached singers (he had once studied singing in Vienna) at the L'vov Opera. Ax was eight when his family moved to Warsaw, and he was ten when they emigrated to Winnipeg, Canada. Two years later, hoping to find better music teachers for Ax and better job opportunities for his father, they moved to New York City, where the 12-year-old Ax was accepted in the pre-college division of the Juilliard School.

To be off the city streets and also get some exercise, he joined the Kips Bay Boys' Club. Once aware of young Ax's talent, local club officials sought financial help for him through the parent organization, the Boys' Clubs of America, and the response was generous and recurrent, the Boys' Clubs, in effect, supporting Ax through his musical studies and at Columbia University. In 1963 the Boy's Clubs, through the Steven David Epstein Memorial Fund, provided a five-year scholarship for Ax's studies at Juilliard, and from 1968 renewed the scholarship on a yearly basis. When Ax was 20, the Epstein Foundation cosponsored, with the State Department's People-to-People Program, a five-country concert tour of South America, a tour that netted Ax invitations to play with the national symphonies in Peru and Bolivia. The Boys' Clubs of America also paid for Ax's New York debut recital (Alice Tully Hall, 12 March 1973).

At Juilliard he became a pupil of Mieczyslaw Munz, a Polish pianist who had studied with Ferruccio Busoni in Berlin and, before signing on at Juilliard, had taught at the Curtis Institute of Music. In 1970 (the year Ax became a U.S. citizen) he received a B.A. in French at Columbia University and, guided by Munz, began to enter international piano competitions. He placed seventh in the Chopin Competition in Warsaw in 1970, finished third (no first prize awarded) in the Vianna da Motta contest in Lisbon in 1971 and placed seventh in the Queen Elisabeth Competition in Brussels in 1972. Not spectacular results but, as Ax said later, he always made it to the finals, and that got his name in the papers. There were other benefits. Being a finalist in the 1970 Warsaw competition earned him a 20-concert tour of Poland. And in 1972–73 he performed at Chopin festivals held in Portugal and Czechoslovakia.

Ax made his New York solo debut on 12 March 1973, a recital with "the stamp of quality," reported the *New York Times*, and playing that showed "well-schooled fluency and power" and "considerable grace and elegance when he felt the music called for it." Later that year Ax auditioned for the Young Concert Artists, a nonprofit, privately funded organization, and secured a place on their roster. Under their auspices he played several recitals in the Young Concert Artists Series and also gave what he called mini-residencies, spending from one to three days at various schools to present informal lecture-recitals.

Although performing often and successfully, Ax was not well-known until he won the first Artur Rubinstein International Piano Master Competition, held in Tel Aviv, Israel. On 13 September 1974 the jury, which included Rubinstein himself, presented Ax with a very generous first prize: a cash stipend, a management contract with Sol Hurok Concerts, a recording contract with RCA, two appearances at Carnegie Hall and engagements with several major orchestras (Berlin, Vienna, Israel, Cleveland, the BBC). In 1975 the Young Concert Artists presented Ax with its Michaels Award in recognition of his outstanding achievements as a concert performer—an honor bringing yet more orchestral engagements.

The important concert appearances engendered by the Rubinstein and Michaels awards mark a turning point in Ax's career. At this same time (1975) Mieczyslaw Munz, Ax's teacher for 14 years, left New York to teach in Tokyo, and Ax decided not to take on another teacher. He gave up piano competitions and began concertizing, and since then Ax has become one of the busiest, most popular pianists on the concert stage, making from 80 to 90 appearances each year, many of them concerto performances with the world's finest orchestras. On 10 May 1979 another honor—the prestigious Avery Fisher Prize, awarded yearly to an American instrumentalist in recognition of outstanding achievement—gave Ax engagements with the New York Philharmonic Orchestra (during its regular season), the Great Performer Series at Avery Fisher Hall, the Mostly Mozart Festival and the Chamber Music Society of Lincoln Center.

Ax loves to play chamber music. He began studying the chamber literature at Juilliard when he was only 13, and for about 12 years worked very intensely with violinist Felix Galimir. During his student years Ax earned money accompanying Leonard Rose's cello pupils. Later he accompanied the great violinist Nathan Milstein and that, he found, was an immensely valuable learning experience, a matter of his "soaking up" everything Milstein had to say about music. Playing with fine instrumentalists became—and remains—an integral part of Ax's musical experience. He has performed and recorded with a wide variety of ensembles, including the Cleveland, Guarnieri and Tokyo Quartets, the Los Angeles Chamber Music Society, the Orpheus Ensemble and the Chamber Music Society of Lincoln Center.

Ax occasionally performs with individual colleagues, among them Isaac Stern, Jaime Laredo, Young Uck Kim, Lynn Harrell, and Pinchas and Eugenia Zuckerman. His most notable collaboration is the duo formed more than a decade ago with his close friend, cellist Yo-Yo Ma. In a typical season they play about 15 joint performances, sometimes including trio performances with Young Uck Kim or Isaac Stern. Ax and Ma make a splendid duo. Each is a star soloist, yet together they instinctively play off, and with, one another; and they have earned a reputation as masterful interpreters of cello-piano literature.

More than once Ax has remarked that he would like to play in the style of Artur Rubinstein, to Ax the most complete, most powerful, most emotional and most aristocratic pianist. After the Tel Aviv competition, Rubinstein gave Ax some coaching on Chopin's F Minor Concerto and Ravel's *Valses nobles et sentimentales*. Contrary to the prevalent notion about Rubinstein, that the music simply flowed out without any thought on his part, Ax discovered that Rubinstein knew precisely what he wanted to do with every note: "He'd stop me every second note and tell me what he did there." (*NYT*, 28 Feb 1988)

Ax's playing style, primarily influenced by his longtime teacher Munz, is, according to Ax, "very much Hofmann, Lhévinne, Rosenthal, Friedman." Ax built his reputation on the traditional repertoire—Beethoven, Brahms, Chopin, Haydn, Mozart. In the 1980s he began to add more and more contemporary music. Although still performing mostly standard works onstage and still best known as an interpreter of Romantic composers, at the same time he tried to make it his policy to learn a new 20th-century concerto every year. Ax also believes that today's recital programs should include something besides the traditional repertoire.

For his own programs, even when playing standard repertoire, Ax tries to find works not currently being played too often on the concert circuit. For example, he will program Schumann's *Humoreske* rather than the *Carnaval*, and Liszt's Petrarch Sonnet No. 123 rather than No. 104. While he continues to search for less-familiar works in the repertoire, he plays only those he really likes. And with new music, he will play only that which is, in his view, pianistically accessible. His interest in contemporary music is not new. Ax played Schoenberg's Three Pieces, op. 11, at his Young Concert Artists recital in 1974; and in 1975 he played Schoenberg's Six Piano Pieces, op. 19, at Alice Tully Hall, making those pieces very much his own: "Suddenly, the atonal Schoenberg sounded Debussyian. And gorgeous." (*NYT*, 24 April 1975) In 1976 Ax gave the New York premiere of Ned Rorem's Eight Etudes in a recital (6 May) at the McMillin Theater, and he "played the set flawlessly." (*NYT*, 9 May 1976)

Ax also played the premiere performance (31 May 1984) of Hans Werner Henze's 45-minute work *Tristan* (for piano, orchestra and tape, written 1974), with the New York Philharmonic Orchestra, Henze conducting (*Key*, July 1984). On 8 July 1988 Ax played the world premiere of Joseph Schwanter's Piano Concerto with the St. Louis Symphony Orchestra, Leonard Slatkin conducting, at Avery Fisher Hall in Lincoln Center. Programs since 1988 show that Ax has also played William Bolcom's Piano Concerto, Anton Webern's Variations, op. 27, Aaron Copland's Piano Variations and André Previn's Variations on a Theme of Haydn.

The self-effacing, modest Ax says that his profession has three major components: 5 percent talent, 5 percent very hard work and 90 percent luck. Invariably, interviewers mention his engaging personality and gentle sense of humor. He is one of today's most popular performers. After playing from 80 to 90 concerts a season for some years, he tried to reduce his appearances to around 60, which would allow more time with his wife, the pianist Yoko Nozaki (m. 1974) and children. But his heavy schedule persists, for Emanuel Ax is much in demand; besides, there are so many benefits he wants to do, so many hoped-for performances with Ma and always new works to introduce.

Some 80 reviews spanning the busy Ax's entire career list countless, sometimes extravagant accolades and very few negative criticisms. His playing is fresh, sensitive and beautifully lyric. His fine musical insights guide his virtuoso talent, thus he downplays bravura displays. That Ax is not a grandstand performer occasionally bothers critics who miss the kind of spine-tingling pyrotechnics found, for instance, in an Earl Wild performance. But in his own way the dedicated, enthusiastic Ax always makes the music come alive.

His preconceived ideas concerning interpretative matters show in his performances. "An interpreter must also be an academic to some degree. The more knowledge he has about a score, about the time in which it was written, about how it was performed, how it has been edited, the more creative he can actually be." (*Key*, Nov 1988)

Ax's beautiful tone, careful pedaling, marvelous dynamic control and rhythmic clarity give his Mozart interpretations a convincing authenticity. His performance (19 Jan 1984) of the Mozart Concerto in G Major, K. 453, with the Los Angeles Philharmonic Orchestra, Erich Leinsdorf conducting, was "music making of the purest sort. . . . Both pianist and conductor were masters of the most exquisitely refined delicacy and the subtlest manipulation of phrase. . . . It is hard to think of any pianist who could surpass his velvet smoothness of technique, his floating, singing tone, his style and perception of Mozart." (*LAT*, 20 Jan 1984)

The way Ax plays Chopin is not far removed from that of his idol, Artur Rubinstein. Ax's talent for projecting a mood, his superb command of linear lyrical elements and his ability to fathom the innermost meaning of the written notes result in some of the finest Chopin playing to be heard today. His Santa Barbara performance (25 Jan 1988) of the *Polonaise-Fantasie*, op. 61, the *Andante spianato* and *Grande Polonaise*, op. 22, and some mazurkas left the impression that Chopin's music could be played in no other way. Yet success with one composer does not always ensure success with another. At a Chicago recital (10 April 1988), "Ax's account of Brahms's Variations and Fugue on a Theme by Handel (Op. 24) suffered because of the pianist's arch-romantic approach. . . . Without complete textural clarity and an unmistakable rhythmic pulse—features that link Brahms's music to 18th Century traditions—the piece becomes a dull wash of notes." (*CT*, 11 April 1988)

Ax's pleasure in playing with orchestra is mirrored in the reviews. On 18 March 1993 he played Mozart's Concert Rondo, K. 382, and the Strauss *Burleske* with the Boston Symphony Orchestra, Bernard Haitink conducting. "In both Mozart and Strauss, Ax brought great beauty of tone, pellucid passagework and a sense of fun to his playing. He also took obvious pleasure in what the orchestra was doing." (*BH*, 20 March 1993)

Amid today's many talented pianists equipped with fearful techniques, extraordinary memories and huge repertoires, Ax has managed to project an identity all his own. His playing is distinguished and distinctive, every detail so carefully articulated that interest is continuously stimulated. Above all, Ax is a poet of the piano, a pianist of elegance and grace, known especially for his refined and subtle interpretations, a gift for rhapsody, a shimmering tone and a velvety, iridescent touch.

Ax, seemingly not too enthusiastic about recording, says, "It's so easy to make a boring record, everything ship-shape and Bristol fashion, as trim as a well-ordered garden, but. . . ." (*Gram*, Dec 1989) Nevertheless, his affiliation with RCA produced over 20 LPs, including both Chopin concertos, each of which won a Grammy award (No. 1 in 1981, No. 2 in 1978). Early in 1987 he became an exclusive CBS Masterworks (now Sony Classical) recording artist, with a debut album featuring a collection of Chopin scherzos and mazurkas.

Ax's recording of four Haydn sonatas (see Discog.) is revealing and rewarding. "He approaches Haydn from the Beethoven end, making his readings a touch weightier and more serious than most other pianists." However, Ax does not lose sight of Haydn's less profound moods. "His playing of the F-Major

Sonata [Hob. XVI:23] is light and graceful, its Adagio pure bliss." (*Fan, Sept/Oct* 1989) In Ax's recording of Haydn's C Minor Sonata (Hob. XVI:20), his "wide but disciplined range of colour and expression, his delicacy and compelling sense of purpose combine to give a performance of unusual beauty and grandeur." (*Gram,* Dec 1989)

Although frequently described as a "romantic" pianist, Ax obviously has great skill in performing Classic repertoire. Like his Haydn recordings, his recording of two Mozart concertos (K. 453, K. 456) elicited high praise. "The soloist is a superb Mozartean—rhythmically and tonally supple and able to convince us at all times that he knows exactly why each note is there." (*CT,* 16 Dec 1982)

His reading of the Brahms Concerto No. 1 (see Discog.), a reading that garnered a Grammy award in 1984, brings that romantic masterpiece to vibrant life. Despite the outwardly emotion-charged passages dominating this monumental work, Ax is always aware of the classic form holding it together. His all-pervading sensitivity, the balance between hands and between pianist and orchestra, the subtle *rubato* between piano and orchestra, all make this a notable addition to the Brahms discography. Ax's recording of Brahms's Sonata in F Minor, op. 5, and Intermezzos, op. 117, was listed as one of the "Best Recordings of the Month" by *Stereo Review* (Jan 1991): "Ax's enlivening way with this music . . . suggests an intuitive response in its natural flow. . . . The entire sequence of movements is, as it should be, a grand, sweeping whole, greater than the sum of its wonderful parts, bespeaking the very deepest conviction and projected with the most direct, at times almost heart-stopping impact." More recently, a Brahms disc featuring the Handel Variations, op. 24, won the 1993 Edison Prize.

Ax's recording of two of Schumann's finest collections (*Humoreske,* op. 20, and *Fantasiestücke,* op. 12, see Discog.) give ample proof that he is a romantic lyricist, a master of tenderness. The fleeting moods, the exploration of the fantastic, varied hues and colors, the sometimes quiet nostalgia, all are captured with sensitivity and masterful musicianship. This disc received a Grammy award in 1982.

A recent CD on the Sony Classical label couples the Liszt Concertos Nos. 1 and 2 with the Schoenberg Concerto, op. 42 (see Discog.), an admittedly unusual combination—but it works: "In Ax's hands the Schoenberg Concerto discloses something of its essential geniality—a quality which is always clear in the lilting opening and in the ghost-of-a-gavotte finale. . . . And he shows that Liszt's concertos so abound in musical strength that there is no need to inflate or glamorize them." (*Gram,* Dec 1993)

SELECTED REFERENCES

Ax, Emanuel. "Artist's Life." *Keynote,* Nov 1988, p. 18.
"Boys' Clubs Promote Pianist." *Music Journal,* April 1971, pp. 37, 61.
Elliott, Susan. "To Emanuel Ax, the Future Is Increasingly the Present." *New York Times,* 28 Feb 1988, pp. 25, 32.

Henahan, Donal. "Emanuel Ax Prefers Concerts to Contests." *New York Times*, 14 Aug 1977, p. 13.

Kozinn, Allan. "Emanuel Ax: Blazing New Trails Through the Forest of Classical Piano Repertoire." *Keyboard*, Sept 1984, pp. 22–27.

———. "Emanuel Ax Goes 20th Century." *Keynote*, July 1984, pp. 18–22.

Malitz, Nancy. "Pianism's razor-sharp Ax." *Detroit News*, 17 March 1985, sec. K, pp. 1, 6.

Monson, Karen. "Pianist Emanuel Ax: An Adventurous Virtuoso." *Ovation*, April 1985, pp. 8–12.

Seckerson, Edward. "Living For The Moment." *Gramophone*, Dec 1993, pp. 16–17, 19.

Yost, Lee Prater. "Time off with Emanuel Ax." *Clavier*, Jan 1980, pp. 12–15.

See also Bibliography: Cur/Bio (1984); Dub/Ref; Kol/Que; Rub/MyM.

SELECTED REVIEWS

BE: 5 Aug 1991. *BH*: 21 Nov 1983; 20 March 1993; 14 Nov 1994. *CoP*: 17 Nov 1994. *CST*: 30 Jan 1978; 11 April 1988; 25 Feb 1991. *CT*: 22 May 1976; 30 Jan 1978; 11 April 1988; 26 Feb 1991. *DMR*: 12 May 1982. *LAHE*: 13 May 1980. *LAT*: 6 March 1975; 20 Jan 1984; 28 Jan 1988. *NYP*: 15 April 1980; 9 May 1989; 15 Oct 1991. *NYT*: 14 March 1973; 24 April 1975; 9 May 1976; 12 Dec 1977; 14 May 1979; 3 Feb 1983; 14 Feb 1985; 10 July 1988; 10 Oct 1989; 26 Feb 1991. *PEB*: 18 Oct 1980; 3 Nov 1981. *PI*: 30 March 1984; 16 Nov 1991; 14 Nov 1994. *PJ*: 18 Jan 1993. *SFC*: 8 Jan 1994. *S-L*: 20 July 1991. *ST*: 30 Nov 1990. *TL*: 25 June 1977. *WP*: 10 Dec 1983; 16 July 1986; 13 April 1993. *WT*: 7 March 1993.

SELECTED DISCOGRAPHY

Beethoven: Concerto No. 1 in C Major, op. 15; Concerto No. 2 in B-flat Major, op. 19. RCA RCD1-7199. Previn/Royal PO.

Beethoven: Concerto No. 3 in C Minor, op. 37; Concerto No. 4 in G Major, op. 58. RCA 60476-2. Previn/Royal PO.

Beethoven: Concerto No. 5 in E-flat Major, op. 73. RCA 09026-61213-2. Previn/Royal PO.

Brahms: Concerto No. 1 in D Minor, op. 15. RCA RCD1-4962. Levine/Chicago SO.

Brahms: Piano Pieces, op. 118; Rhapsodies, op. 79; Variations and Fugue on a Theme by Handel, op. 24. Sony 48046 (CD).

Brahms: Sonata No. 3 in F Minor, op. 5; Intermezzos op. 117. Sony Classical SK-45933 (CD).

Chopin: Ballades (4); Sonata No. 2 in B-flat Minor, op. 35. RCA Victor RCD1-7069.

Chopin: Concerto No. 1 in E Minor, op. 11; Concerto No. 2 in F Minor, op. 21. RCA (Silver Seal) 60789-2. Ormandy/PO.

Chopin: Mazurkas (6); Scherzos (4). CBS CD MK-44544.

Haydn: Concerto in F Major, Hob. XVIII:3; Concerto in G Major, Hob. XVIII:4; Concerto in D Major, Hob. XVIII:11. Sony Classical SK 48383 (CD).

Haydn: Sonata No. 33 in C Minor, Hob. XVI:20; Sonata No. 38 in F Major, Hob. XVI:23; Sonata No. 58 in C Major, Hob. XVI:48; Sonata No. 60 in C Major, Hob. XVI:50. CBS CD MK-44918.

Liszt: Concert paraphrases on *Aida*, *Rigoletto*; Sonata in B Minor; *Vallée d'Obermann*. Sony Classical SK 48484 (CD).

Liszt: Concerto No. 1 in E-flat Major; Concerto No. 2 in A Major. Schoenberg: Concerto, op. 42. Sony Classical SK 53289 (CD). Salonen/PO.

Mozart: Concerto No. 17 in G Major, K. 453; Concerto No.18 in B-flat Major, K. 456. RCA 60136-2. Zukerman/St. Paul CO.

Schumann: *Humoreske*, op. 20; *Fantasiestücke*, op. 12. RCA RCD1-4275.

B

BACHAUER, GINA: b. Athens, Greece, 21 May 1913; d. Athens, 22 August 1976.

> Here was pianism in the grand manner, played by an artist who was mistress of both her music and her keyboard.
>
> *Newsweek* (5 February 1951)

Gina Bachauer—that "glorious Greek"—enchanted her audiences. A woman of endless vitality and warmth, Bachauer loved people, just as she loved to swim and to cook, but above all she loved the piano. Beyond her tremendous technique, she played with a grand and joyful spirit that sent tingles of excitement through her audience.

She was by no means an infant prodigy. Both her parents (Jean Bachauer, her Austrian father, owned a foreign car dealership in Athens; her mother Ersilia was Greek and Italian) enjoyed music but apparently noticed nothing special in their daughter. Bachauer's father took her to an Emil von Sauer recital when she was five years old. She liked it so much that she began agitating for a piano, meanwhile endlessly playing a toy piano, usually tunes from songs she heard her mother sing. Her parents finally succumbed to her entreaties, providing not only a real piano but also private lessons with Ariadne Casasis, who taught elementary piano at the Athens Conservatory.

At age eight Bachauer gave her first recital, an Athens charity performance for wounded soldiers. At age 11 she enrolled at the Conservatory to study with Woldemar Freeman (a Polish pianist and close friend of Rachmaninoff). At age 16 she graduated from the Conservatory with a gold medal in performance, and Freeman, who had given her a thorough grounding in the German classics, advised her to go to Paris in order to hear French music and study with Alfred Cortot, the great specialist in French music. But to please her father, who considered a concert career inappropriate for a woman, Bachauer began law studies at the University of Athens, keeping up her music on her own.

She finally got to Paris in 1931 and began studies with Cortot at the *École Normale de Musique*. At lessons Cortot talked more than he played (although when he played Schumann for her, Bachauer thought it was the most beautiful Schumann she had ever heard), and he had a gift for creating wonderful pictures of what a piece was about and what was in the composer's mind as he wrote it. She completed her studies at the *École Normale* in 1933.

Freeman had sent her a letter of introduction to Rachmaninoff, but it took her many weeks to summon the courage to approach him. When finally she presented the letter in London, Rachmaninoff accepted her as a pupil; and for three years she studied with him intermittently as his schedule permitted, following him to Paris, Rome, London, wherever necessary. Bachauer always cherished her memories of their discussions, as she preferred to call the Rachmaninoff lessons, and carefully preserved the scores he had marked (fingerings, phrasings, pedalings) for her. Rachmaninoff rarely dealt with technique (his own came so easily, so naturally, that he had no idea how to explain it to others), but his thoughts on musical interpretation and the design and architecture of a work were absolutely invaluable to Bachauer. For Rachmaninoff, sound ("color, color, color!") took precedence over everything else, even technique. He often worked with her on concertos, she playing on one piano, Rachmaninoff playing on another and making suggestions as they went along. The suggestions would be different each time they played a work, but Bachauer found it wonderful that the music could be so fresh to him.

In 1933 Bachauer won a gold medal at the Vienna Competition for Piano and Song. Primed and eager for a professional career, she postponed it to help her father recover from business losses. She found a job teaching piano at the Athens Conservatory, practiced long hours at night to maintain her own piano technique and gained valuable experience performing with the Conservatory orchestra. In 1935 she made her formal debut in Athens, playing the Tchaikovsky Concerto No. 1 with Dimitri Mitropoulos and the Athens Symphony Orchestra. By 1937 she was able to return to Paris, where she gave her first important professional recital, at the *Salle Pleyel*, and also appeared with Pierre Monteux and the Paris Symphony Orchestra. Tours of Italy, France, Yugoslavia, Austria, Greece and Egypt followed, and her career seemed well launched; but in the midst of her third tour of Italy, World War II erupted, once again dashing her career hopes.

Bachauer spent the war years in Alexandria, Egypt, performing (more than 600 times) for the British, American, Australian, New Zealand and South African forces passing through that area. This second career setback crushed her, but the irrepressible Bachauer quickly rebounded. She learned to play whatever the soldiers requested ("a lot of Home Sweet Home and the Warsaw Concerto") and on all sorts of pianos ("uprights, grands, in tune, out of tune").

After the war Bachauer made a third attempt at establishing a concert career, this time in London. It was difficult. She had very little money, and few engagements turned up for an unknown female pianist. Her breakthrough came via a prominent Englishwoman, who heard her play at a private gathering and insisted that Alec Sherman, conductor of the New London Orchestra, feature Bachauer in a forthcoming Albert Hall concert. At that performance (21 Jan 1946) Bachauer's playing of the Grieg Concerto in A Minor mesmerized just about everyone who heard it. Tours in England, France, Holland and Italy firmly established her as a front-rank pianist, and because of her majestic vitality and technical brilliancy, critics began comparing her with Teresa Carreño, known in her day as the "Valkyrie of the piano."

Americans generally had not heard of Bachauer. Only about 35 people attended her American debut recital (29 Oct 1950) at New York's Town Hall, but pianists Myra Hess and Simon Barere were there. Wonderful reviews in the *New York Times* ("in the grand tradition of pianists, male or female") and the *New York Herald Tribune* ("a truly phenomenal pianist having few peers among pianists of either sex") quickly caught public attention, and word traveled fast. Bachauer's second New York recital (26 Jan 1951), also at Town Hall, drew a full house. Her American career rocketed, and suddenly it seemed that the whole world wanted to hear Gina Bachauer. She toured extensively (Europe, the Americas, Australia, New Zealand, the Orient), became a regular guest with the New York Philharmonic Orchestra and just about every year made an extensive tour of the United States.

Bachauer, first married (1937) to John Christodoulo, who died in 1950, married Alec Sherman, conductor at her London debut, in New York City in 1951. They made their home in London but regularly spent 10 or 11 months touring, four or five of them in the United States. Sherman gave up his own career in order to tour with his wife.

Gina Bachauer was engaged to perform at the 1976 Athens Festival with the National Symphony Orchestra of Washington, D.C., Antal Dorati conducting. She rehearsed with the orchestra on 20 August and the next day attended the orchestra's first concert of the festival. Taken suddenly ill, Bachauer died of a heart attack on the day she was due to play. After announcing her death to the audience waiting in the ancient Herod Atticus amphitheater at the foot of the Acropolis, Dorati led the orchestra in the dirgelike *Marcia funebre* (2nd movement) from Beethoven's Symphony No. 3.

A "special friend of the State," Bachauer was made an honorary citizen of Utah and awarded an honorary Doctor of Humanities degree from the University of Utah. After her death, the Gina Bachauer International Piano Competition was founded in 1976 in Salt Lake City, Utah.

Gina Bachauer's approach to the piano, described in detail in a 1955 interview, involved two stages. Before taking a work to the piano, she spent days reading it through, as she said, "like a book." She first made a rough analysis of the work (general concept and style, noting indications, melodic continuity, harmonic development, orchestral color, etc.); next she analyzed musical and technical problems (phrasings, fingerings, dynamics, emphasis of voices, etc.);

and finally she practiced the work mentally, fitting her analysis of it to her own way of expressing it. Bachauer believed that this work done away from the piano helped her to gain musical understanding and made memorizing easier.

When she began the second stage of preparation, at the piano, Bachauer was already thoroughly familiar with the work. In her practice sessions she played slowly, playing the work at tempo only once or twice and playing each hand separately. She never practiced mechanically, always being aware of what she was playing, how she was playing it and why she was playing it that particular way. Finally, she listened, really listened, to herself playing, making herself hear what was coming out of the piano, not what she wanted to hear.

A rare mixture of personal magnetism and instinctive pianism made Bachauer's playing exciting, colorful and immensely satisfying. Her style was romantic but strictly her own: "One does not have to see her to recognize her playing. Ten measures should be enough for any trained listener to put his finger on what constitutes a Bachauer performance." (*NYT*, 9 March 1964) In some ways her explosive style is difficult to categorize, due to her startling but exciting originality. "Unlike most modern pianists she was a romantic with a virtuoso approach to the keyboard. Like Horowitz, she was a throwback. Unlike Horowitz, she played in an unmannered, unaffected way, never placing effect above substance." (Sch/Gre, see Bibliog.)

A stunning technique, a powerful drive and an overflowing joy in the music dominated a Bachauer performance. A severe self-critic never wholly pleased with her playing, she practiced five or six hours a day and at performances she even practiced in her dressing room until time to go onstage. Bachauer adored playing, and it never seemed difficult for her. Consider, for example, that at a Washington, D.C., recital she played the entire second book of the Brahms-Paganini Variations as an *encore*, tossing them off "with bravura ease and brilliance." (*WP*, 29 March 1976)

Her scintillating technique, elegant style and tonal control naturally suited large-scale works. Nothing in the piano repertoire seemed to faze her. For example, her New York debut recital (29 Oct 1950) included a Haydn Sonata, the Bach-Busoni Toccata in C Major, Book II of the Brahms-Paganini Variations, Liszt's *Funérailles* and, for a grand finale, Ravel's *Gaspard de la nuit*.

Never a specialist, Bachauer played some Bach (mostly in transcription); often programmed Mozart on her recitals; and from that point ran the gamut of the entire 19th century: Beethoven ("*Waldstein*" Sonata; Sonata, op. 109); Chopin (B-minor Sonata); Liszt (Spanish Rhapsody, Sonata in B Minor); Schumann (*Kinderscenen*); Brahms (Paganini Variations); Grieg (Concerto in A Minor); Rachmaninoff (Concertos Nos. 2 and 3). She had two 20th-century favorites, both fiendishly difficult: Ravel's *Gaspard de la nuit* and Stravinsky's *Trois Mouvements de Petrouchka*.

The fact is that Bachauer excelled in music from every era, music of every style. At her second Town Hall recital her interpretation of Beethoven's Sonata in E Major, op. 109, was most impressive in her "treatment of the march with its rhythmic energy and the ominous striding basses." (*NYT*, 27 Jan 1951) Famed for her performances of the Grieg Concerto, at one Los Angeles concert

(16 July 1959) she played it "poetically, which is the way it should be played. She restored its characteristic atmosphere with incisive rhythms, she colored its tender melodies with a persuasive singing tone." (*LAT*, 18 July 1959) In a performance (13 Feb 1976) of the Rachmaninoff Concerto No. 2 in C Minor with the Cincinnati Symphony Orchestra, François Huybrechts conducting, Bachauer made the music "breathe naturally, imparting a marvelously free sense of motion to the long musical lines." (*CE*, 15 Feb 1976) And after hearing Bachauer play the three Stravinsky *Petrouchka* arrangements in a Los Angeles recital (2 Dec 1960), one reviewer suggested that "she would be wise to exploit more of the modern repertoire, for they were played with iridescent color and tempestuous verve and they provided space for a pianistic display that surpassed anything else on the program." (*LAT*, 4 Dec 1960)

Sometimes Bachauer's phenomenal technique led to faster and faster tempos, which can be thrilling, as in Ravel's *Gaspard de la nuit* (*Scarbo*) and many overtly virtuosic pieces, but not with, say, Debussy's *Pour le piano* or Beethoven's elegant and noble "Emperor" Concerto. Although at times criticized for her fast tempos, or phrasing, or concept, Bachauer played as she felt at the moment, and almost always her playing gave great pleasure to the listener.

In many ways she was a female counterpart of Artur Rubinstein. Her playing, like his, had "a kind of *joie de vivre*, a sweet and controlled romanticism." Like Rubinstein, she had a very large technique, capable of handling with ease such things as the Rachmaninoff Piano Concerto No. 3 and Brahms's Concerto No. 2, and her tone was large and penetrating.

Bachauer made comparatively few recordings (her constant self-criticism may have prevented her from committing her performances to permanency); however, the available recordings stand as a fitting memorial to this exceptional artist. Listening to her Grieg Concerto (see Discog.), one can imagine the excitement she created with her first London performance. In the CD reissue of her recordings of Beethoven's Concertos Nos. 4 and 5 (see Discog.) with Stanislaw Skrowaczewski and the London Symphony Orchestra, made respectively in 1963 and 1962, "one feels the unerring sense of a consummate artist shaping her phrases, interpreting the music with a strong but sympathetic personal vision, and making *music*." (*ARG*, March/April 1992)

Bachauer's 1967 recording of the Brahms Concerto No. 2 with Antal Dorati and the London Symphony Orchestra reveals her heroic-dramatic propensities. On the CD reissue (see Discog.), "one is struck immediately by the larger-than-life sound, the rich orchestral texture and Bachauer's powerful playing. . . . This is the Grand Romantic Style; and we should be very grateful that it was captured in such a great recording." (*ARG*, July/Aug 1990) Bachauer had recorded the same concerto in 1962 with Stanislaw Skrowaczewski conducting the London Symphony Orchestra. This reading, equally as exciting as the later one, appears in recent CD reissue with some solo items, including a superb performance of one of Bachauer's favorites, the Brahms Variations on a Theme by Paganini, op. 35 (Book II).

The album *Gina Bachauer Plays French Music* gives ample proof that Bachauer's studies with Alfred Cortot gave her an insight into French pianism

and French repertoire.   Bachauer plays the Saint-Saëns Concerto No. 2 with the
requisite energy, verve, even wit.   Three Debussy Preludes and his earlier *Pour le
piano* are in turn charming and revelatory, and *Ravel's Gaspard de la nuit* positively sparkles.

Bachauer's interpretation of the Rachmaninoff Concerto No. 2, overplayed though that work may be, still reveals hidden beauties under her skillful
hands (see Discog.).   And on a second Bachauer recording of Ravel's very difficult triptych *Gaspard de la nuit*, Sir John Gielgud prefaces each movement with
a reading of the corresponding Aloysius Bertrand poem in a translation by British
playwright Christopher Fry (see Discog.).   This is a successful and highly stimulating collaboration.

SELECTED REFERENCES

Bachauer, Gina. "The Education of a Pianist." (interview with Burton Paige).
    Etude, June 1955, pp. 9, 47.
———. "My Study with Rachmaninoff." *Clavier*, Oct 1973, pp. 12–14, 16.
Fleming, Shirley. "Gina Bachauer." *High Fidelity Magazine*, Nov 1963, p. 46.
Kammerer, Rafael. "Gina Bachauer." *Musical America*, Oct 1961, pp. 12–13.
"Keyboard Mistress." *Newsweek*, 5 Feb 1951, p. 78.
Lawrence, Harold.   "Gina Bachauer Remembered." *High Fidelity/Musical
    America*, Feb 1977, pp. MA 18–19.
Lyons, James. "Perseverance Pays." *Musical America*, 1 Feb 1954, pp. 8–9.
Obituary. *New York Times*, 23 Aug 1976, p. 26. *Washington Post*, 23 Aug
    1976, sec. B, pp. 1, 5.
Russell, Frank. "Gina Bachauer." *Piano Quarterly*, Fall 1965, pp. 13–18.
Schonberg, Harold C.   "A Pianist with Power." *New York Times*, 23 Aug
    1976, p. 6.
See also Bibliography: Cur/Bio (1954); Eld/Pia; Ewe/Mu; Mar/Gre; Sch/Gre.

SELECTED REVIEWS

CE: 15 Feb 1976. *CSM*: 4 March 1964. *LAT*: 10 March 1954; 18 July 1959;
    4 Dec 1960; 6 April 1963; 31 March 1970; 1 Feb 1972; 12 March 1974; 2
    Feb 1976. *NY*: 3 Feb 1951. *NYT*: 30 Oct 1950; 27 Jan 1951; 7 Feb
    1952; 24 Jan 1953; 25 Feb 1954; 4 Jan 1955; 27 Jan 1958; 23 Nov 1959;
    30 Nov 1962; 9 March 1964; 19 Feb 1965; 10 March 1966; 13 Jan 1969;
    25 April 1969; 27 Feb 1970; 30 April 1971; 22 March 1974. *SFC*: 8 Feb
    1960. *Time*: 5 Feb 1951. *TL*: 23 April 1951; 22 April 1960. *WP*: 29
    March 1976.

SELECTED DISCOGRAPHY

Beethoven: Concerto No. 4 in G Major, op. 58; Concerto No. 5 in E-flat Major,
    op. 73. Mercury 432 018-2. Skrowaczewski/London SO.
Brahms: Concerto No. 2 in B-flat Major, op. 83. Chesky CD 36. Dorati/
    London SO, rec. 1967.

Brahms: Concerto No. 2 in B-flat Major, op. 83; Variations on a Theme by
Paganini, op. 35 (Book II). Beethoven: Sonata in E Major, op. 14, no. 1.
Liszt: Hungarian Rhapsody No. 12. Mercury 434 340-2. Skrowaczewski/
London SO, rec. 1962.
Gina Bachauer Plays French Music. Couperin: *Le Bavolet flottant*; *La Fleurie*;
Soeur Monique. Debussy: *Bruyères*; *Danseuses de Delphes*; *La Fille aux
cheveux de lin*; *Pour le piano.* Ravel: *Gaspard de la nuit.* Saint-Saëns:
Concerto No. 2 in G Minor, op. 22. IPAM 1202 (CD). Sherman/New
London Orchestra.
Grieg: Concerto in A Minor, op. 16. Seraphim S-60032. Weldon/Royal PO.
Rachmaninoff: Concerto No. 2 in C Minor, op. 18; Preludes in C-sharp Minor,
op. 3, no. 2; G Minor, op. 23, no. 5; B Minor, op. 32, no. 10. Erato
Success/RCA ECD-40009. Lombard/*Orchestre Philharmonique de Stras-
bourg.*
Ravel: *Gaspard de la nuit.* Debussy: *Pour le piano*; Three Preludes. Mercury
Golden Imports SRI 75139. Each of the Ravel pieces is prefaced with an
English translation of the original Bertrand poem by Christopher Fry, re-
cited by Sir John Gielgud.

BACKHAUS, WILHELM: b. Leipzig, Germany, 26 March 1884; d.
Villach, Austria, 5 July 1969.

> He was his generation's greatest surviving exponent of the classical
> German musical tradition fostered in the Conservatoire of his native
> Leipzig.
>
> *The Times*, London (7 July 1969)

Wilhelm Backhaus, the fifth of eight children born to Guido and Clara Backhaus,
began life in near poverty. It was only because his mother liked music that he
was exposed to it as an infant. From age seven Backhaus had four years of private piano lessons with Alois Reckendorf, a Moravian pedagogue who for many
years taught at the Leipzig Conservatory, and another four years with him at the
Conservatory on a scholarship arranged by Reckendorf. Backhaus also studied
composition with Salomon Jadassohn.

In 1898–99 Backhaus had about 25 lessons (i.e., coaching sessions)
with Eugen d'Albert at Frankfurt-am-Main. His memories of those sessions varied. In one interview (*MA*, 6 Jan 1912) Backhaus recalled d'Albert as being a
poor teacher, too nervous and excitable to settle down to the details of explaining
the elementary principles of piano playing. But a year later Backhaus is quoted
in the same magazine (15 Nov 1913) as being grateful to d'Albert, and undoubtedly d'Albert was partly responsible for Backhaus's fine interpretations of
Beethoven's music. Those meetings with d'Albert completed Backhaus's formal
musical training. From age 16 he was wholly self-taught, depending on his own

self-criticism to improve both technically and artistically. Teaching himself meant hard, persistent effort. Years later, when asked if he had ever taken students, the laconic and witty Backhaus replied, "Yes, me."

Backhaus gave several concerts in England during the 1900–1901 season, his first performances outside of Germany. They were so successful that he was immediately engaged to return to England. In the spring of 1901 he substituted for an ailing Alexander Siloti in Manchester, where he played Beethoven's Concerto No. 4 with Hans Richter and the Hallé Orchestra. Richter, overwhelmed with the 17-year-old pianist's skillful performance, invited him to play with the Hallé the following year and just about every season thereafter. That same year Backhaus made his first appearance (27 Aug 1901) at Henry Wood's Promenade Concerts, performing Mendelssohn's Concerto in G Minor, op. 25, and on 31 August 1901 played the Brahms-Paganini Variations. "We were still in early days," explained Henry Wood later, "and it was not an invariable rule that a pianist should play a concerto." (Woo/My, see Bibliog.)

Backhaus had been concertizing in Great Britain and Europe for about five years when in 1905 he won (Bartók placed second) the prestigious Rubinstein Prize offered in Paris. It gave his career an enormous thrust. For more than 50 years he was to live the life of a traveling virtuoso, touring extensively through Europe and Great Britain, where he was a great favorite, and also in North America. His first American tour (1912–13) took him through the northeastern and central states. He made an eminently successful American orchestral debut (5 Jan 1912) playing Beethoven's Concerto No. 5 ("Emperor") with the New York Symphony Society, conducted by Walter Damrosch. A week later he made his New York recital debut (12 Jan 1912) at Carnegie Hall before a small but discriminating audience (Josef Hoffman and Josef Lhévinne were present, enthusiastically applauding), and he toured North America again in 1913–14.

He served in the German army during World War I (apparently assigned garrison duty so as not to damage his hands in the field), and while in uniform periodically gave concerts in Berlin. After the war Backhaus immediately resumed his concert career, performing in many major European cities and returning to America for the 1921–22 season. His recital at Town Hall on 12 November 1921, his first American performance in eight years, drew an enormous, warmly appreciative audience. He toured the United States again in 1923–24, returned in 1926, then stayed away for 28 years. When he played at Carnegie Hall (30 March 1954) after that extraordinarily long absence, the 70-year-old Backhaus proved that he was still wholly in command of his technique and retained undiminished interpretative powers. For one critic, that Beethoven recital ranked as one of the greatest evenings of Beethoven's piano music that New Yorkers had heard in all those 28 years. (*NYT*, 31 March 1954)

The audience at his all-Beethoven recital at Carnegie Hall the following year "seemed to include at least one pianist every square yard" (*NYT*, 14 Feb 1955), on hand to study Backhaus's masterful Beethoven interpretations. Although he continued to perform in Europe up to the time of his death, during his last years Backhaus was known in America mostly through his numerous recordings.

About 1931 Backhaus and his Brazilian wife, the former Alma Herzberg, settled in Switzerland on the lake near Lugano, and he became a Swiss citizen. There were no children, and his wife always traveled with him. On 28 June 1969 he had a mild heart attack while performing at a church in Ossiach in southern Austria. A week later, as he was preparing for a concert in the nearby resort village of Villach, Backhaus suffered a second heart attack and died on 5 July 1969.

Many anecdotes survive concerning Backhaus's fabulous ability for instantaneous transposing. As a boy he had played for Grieg, proudly performing Grieg's Norwegian Wedding March in F Major, instead of in E. Amused and delighted, Grieg inscribed a few bars of the piece in Backhaus's always handy autograph album (all his life Backhaus collected autographs) and marked it "in F Major." (*MA*, 24 May 1913) In another anecdote, a Reminiscence published in *Musical America* (20 Jan 1912), Stanley Olmstead recalled a visit in Leipzig with the 10-year-old Backhaus and his father. The father proudly boasted that his son, who had just easily sight-read a Bach fugue, could play any fugue in any key. Olmstead named a fugue and a key, and the boy instantly transposed. Backhaus himself told the story of a 1909 concert with Sir Landon Ronald at Blackpool, England. At the afternoon rehearsal it was discovered that the piano was pitched one half-tone low. Undaunted, Backhaus transposed the piano score (Grieg's Concerto in A Minor) to B-flat Minor for the rehearsal; and that evening, with the piano retuned, played the concerto in the proper key of A Minor. (*MA*, 24 May 1913)

Backhaus taught (1905) at the Royal Manchester College of Music. He also gave master classes (1907–09) at the Conservatory of Music in Sondershausen, Germany, and later taught briefly (1925–26) at the Curtis Institute of Music in Philadelphia. Otherwise he mostly avoided teaching and never considered himself to be a teacher. Playing the piano came so naturally to him that he never had to think about how he did it. When it came to teaching, he felt he could not explain to someone else just how he accomplished what he did. Despite professing not to be a teacher, Backhaus wrote two articulate essays for *Etude*. His own approach to keyboard technique sounds very modern. "Personally, I practice scales in preference to all other forms of technical exercises when I am preparing for a concert. Add to this arpeggios and Bach, and you have the basis upon which my technical work stands." ("The Training of the Pianist of the Future.")

Backhaus eventually built an enormous repertoire based on the works of Beethoven, Brahms, Mozart and Schumann (he had little sympathy with contemporary music) and he played formidable, often very long programs. On the occasion of his twenty-fifth London recital (7 Oct 1911) the souvenir program listed all the compositions—more than 200—played by Backhaus at those 25 London recitals, and the audience was invited to choose the pieces for his next recital. That "plebiscite program" selected by the public and played by Backhaus on 2 November 1911 consisted of two Beethoven sonatas ("Moonlight" and "*Appassionata*"); works by Schumann (*Papillons*), Chopin (*Fantasie-Impromptu*, *Berceuse*, Ballade in A Flat), Liszt (*Liebestraum*, *La Campanella*,

Hungarian Rhapsody No. 2), Mendelssohn (*Rondo capriccioso*) and Rachmaninoff (Prelude in C-sharp Minor).

Backhaus practiced three or four hours a day when preparing his repertoire, only about an hour each day while on tour. But he worked all the time, even away from the piano. "Have you noticed," he asked A. E. Eichmann, "that throughout our conversation I have been playing a Haydn Sonata on the table? I read it this morning and, while you've been talking, I have been working out the fingering of a difficult passage." (Eichmann)

Backhaus was a towering pianist, one of the great exponents of the classical German-Austrian tradition. His musicianship—meticulous, cerebral, sober, strong—embodied the ideals of that tradition: classical restraint and strict textual fidelity. "His interpretations of the Classical repertory were broadly conceived: direct, magisterial and unfussy, revealing the structural strength of the great works that he most favoured, and marked by unfailing integrity of purpose." (New/Gro, see Bibliog.) Not a deeply emotional or profoundly poetic artist, for Backhaus it was the intention of the composer and the architectural contours of a work that mattered most. Even as a young man he showed little interest in dazzling virtuosity or tonal color, and basically he never changed.

From his first to his last performances, Backhaus received mixed critiques. Barely 18 when he first toured in Great Britain, he garnered amazing reviews: "The mastery which he possesses over his instrument is complete, his technique is perfect, and his touch is soft and beautiful." (*TL*, 29 June 1901) Yet, paradoxically, throughout his career almost every review mentions that his playing was uninteresting or cold or lifeless. For example, a reviewer admiring Backhaus's soft, rich and sympathetic touch also complains that it had little variety and that "his performances are apt to be rather monotonous." (*TL*, 8 April 1902)

Nearly a decade later reviewers express the same theme. There is praise for Backhaus's command of tone, his clear and clean attack and his accurate technique, but at the same time "there was an absence of warmth" and "the whole thing was, in fact, too articulate and too calculated." (*TL*, 12 June 1911) Later that year Backhaus's playing of Bach's Chromatic Fantasy and Fugue displayed his "extremely clear and neat technique and from the first bar to the last, not a note was played inaccurately." However, "the whole thing was almost entirely lacking in warmth or vitality; the Fugue was not rigid, but for all the *rubato* put into it and the skill with which the final entry of the theme in octaves in the left hand was given, it was not alive, and the Fantasy was astonishingly cold and deliberate considering the rhapsodic nature of the music." (*TL*, 9 Oct 1911)

At his New York solo recital debut (12 Jan 1912), Backhaus's playing, once again, was commended in general for "its virility, its boldness, solidity and breadth." In particular, his performance of Beethoven's "*Waldstein*" Sonata had "variety of dramatic feeling and great nobility of utterance." At the same time, the reviewer describes Backhaus as an artist of commanding intellect rather than profoundly emotional characteristics. "The secret of a true *rubato* is not Mr. Backhaus' and his Chopin, instead of being characterized by elasticity of rhythm, inclines toward the metronomic." (*MA*, 20 Jan 1912) Years later, when

Backhaus resumed his concert tours after World War I, his legendary technical powers remained intact. But the old nemesis still persisted: "He did not disclose himself yesterday as a deeply emotional or a profoundly poetic artist nor did there seem to have come about all the growth in those qualities that were reasonably to be expected from his performances as a young man." (*NYT*, 13 Nov 1921)

As early as 1919, Walter Niemann, the highly respected pianist and musicologist, correctly summed up the Backhaus style in terms which would be repeated throughout the pianist's career: "For the virtuoso Backhaus . . . there are no technical difficulties. Backhaus offers us the universally valid content of a work of art as a polished surface, perfect in form and technically crystal-clear. . . . The accomplishment of his enormous technique, the evenness of his touch, the energetic modelling of his wonderful, great and compact piano-tone, the strength, endurance and accuracy of his playing—all this is complete mastery. . . . But, however generous and natural all this may be . . . his capacity to shade his piano tone remains limited; as a result, the 'neutral' middle colors predominate to a tiring degree, and his piano is cold. . . . Backhaus is and remains the academic technician." (Nie/Mei, see Bibliog.)

Despite this persistent note of coldness, Backhaus enjoyed a fine reputation, particularly as a Beethoven specialist. Even in his later years he was greatly respected. "At an age when other pianists have to retire, there came with Backhaus, suddenly and increasingly, an added element of sweetness, of gentle movement and soft magic." (Kai/Gre, see Bibliog.) At age 70 he gave a program (30 March 1954) of five Beethoven sonatas at Carnegie Hall, and he played with amazing "virility, beauty of tone, and strength without hardness. . . . These are things that only come with the growth of a lifetime devoted to art on such a high level of thought and deed that every year that passes seems to heighten and deepen the beauty of the conception. Mr. Backhaus was young with Beethoven." (*NYT*, 31 March 1954)

Taken together, the criticisms are remarkably consistent in portraying Backhaus as a tasteful virtuoso with a well-nigh flawless technique, a pianist who never exaggerated, who might be cold at times but seldom without interest. Granted, his playing may never have radiated the passion or lyricism of a Rubinstein, but the Backhaus signature—integrity, control, insight, taste— stamped every performance.

Backhaus made his first recordings in the acoustical era, in 1909. In 1910 he made the first concerto recording (Grieg's Concerto in A Minor) in disc history. When he died at the age of 85, he was just about to complete his second set of the 32 Beethoven Sonatas—begun in 1964 when he was 80 years old. (Some of these have been reissued on CD, see Discog.) Only Opus 106, the "*Hammerklavier*," remained unrecorded. In comparing the mono and stereo performances, one reviewer observed that even in his eighties Backhaus could unfurl the flag of virtuosity when he chose: "In the wild chase of the finale to Op. 54, his stereo version is, if anything, cleaner, more controlled and more exciting than the mono performance. But the playing, early as well as late, impresses one most by its inexorable sweep, by its structural lucidity and its disdain for sentimentalities." (*NYT*, 22 March 1970)

Pianist Stephen Kovacevich, one of today's great Beethoven specialists, told an interviewer that Backhaus was the only person who ever truly understood Beethoven's "*Hammerklavier*" Sonata. "Listen to his recordings. It's true he may not be faithful to the text in every instance, but the wildness of what he's attempting to do is quite wonderful." (Dub/Ref, see Bibliog.) Backhaus recorded Beethoven's "Emperor" Concerto twice in the studio. There is also available a CD of a 1962 live performance together with a 1954 performance of Concerto No. 4 (see Discog.). They are all splendid examples of Backhaus doing what he did best. Although the later CD does not show the 78-year-old Backhaus's legendary technical prowess to best advantage, his reading of the G Major "has a light joyfulness that is thoroughly apt and ultimately more profound than the sleepy dreariness imposed on the music by more recent elder statesmen of the piano. The 'Emperor' too, its technical lapses notwithstanding, has a proud imperious grandeur that suits the music well." (*Fan*, March/April 1989)

Live performances, despite occasional wrong notes and momentary memory lapses, have much to recommend them. This is especially true concerning Backhaus. To quote *Fanfare*, "one has not heard Backhaus if one has heard only his studio recordings." A wonderful CD of three Beethoven sonatas (see Discog.) contains live performances from 1956 through 1964. "These live performances are a revelation. . . . There are the familiar strengths: sterling fingerwork, a large and satisfying authoritative tone, and an absence of vulgarity or striving after effect. Added in these live performances is an abundance of characterization and interior drama." (*Fan*, Jan/Feb 1990)

At age 11 Backhaus had met Brahms in Leipzig, an inspiring experience that he never forgot. Throughout his career he showed great sympathy for Brahms's music, and his "leonine, magisterial authority in this composer always attracted a great deal of admiration." (*ARG*, May/June 1990) The Pearl CD (see Discog.) offers a good sampling of Brahms's solo piano music. It is a treasure, a tribute to both composer and pianist. These works, recorded for HMV between 1933 and 1935, are very Germanic performances of great tonal and technical strength. "Backhaus brought a uniquely direct, virile approach to the sometimes elusive solo works. He seemed incapable of indulging in the sloppy sentiment that passes sometimes for 'profundity.' Within his avoidance of languor, there was a deft sense of proportion and an enlivening wealth of nuance." (*Fan*, March/April 1990)

One does not regularly associate the name of Backhaus with that of Chopin. But he played a great deal of Chopin's music during his early years and, in 1928, made the very first complete recording of the Etudes (see Discog.). From a purely technical standpoint, Backhaus had superlative qualifications but lacked "the elusive combination of subtlety, flexibility, and charm that defines an idiomatic Chopin style. . . . Nonetheless the Backhaus traversal is of much more than mere historical interest, and the authority with which he dispatches such pieces as Opus 10: 1, 9, and 10, or Opus 25: 6 is one of the factors that makes Backhaus still worthy of investigation." (*ARG*, Jan/Feb 1992)

SELECTED REFERENCES

Backhaus, Wilhelm. "The Hardest Things to Master in Music." *Etude*, July 1922, pp. 453–454. Also in Coo/Gre, see Bibliog.

———. "The Training of the Pianist of the Future." *Etude*, July 1912, pp. 465–466.

Brower, Harriette. "Backhaus Discusses His Technique." *Musical America*, 13 Dec 1913, p. 26.

Clough, F. F., and G. J. Cuming. "Wilhelm Backhaus: a Discography." *Gramophone Record Review*, June 1959, pp. 578–579.

Eichmann, A. H. *Wilhelm Backhaus*, trans. Barbara Wall. Geneva: René Kister, 1958 (series Great Concert Artists).

Foldes, Andor. "Mentor and Guide." *Music and Musicians*, Nov 1969, pp. 30–31.

Henahan, Donal. "At 85, Backhaus Was Still Creative." *New York Times*, 22 March 1970, sec. 2, p. 34.

Obituary. *New York Times*, 6 July 1969, p. 44. *The Times* (London), 7 July 1969, p. 10.

Olmsted, Stanley. "Bachaus, The Leipsic Wunderkind." *Musical America*, 20 Jan 1912, p. 32.

"Travelling Virtuoso." *The Times* (London), 11 April 1960, p. 14.

See also Bibliography: Ald/Con; Bro/Pia; Car/Del; Cha/Spe; Coo/Gre; Coo/GrP; Ewe/Li; Ewe/Li2; Kai/Gre; Kol/Que; Lan/Mus; Nie/Mei; Ran/Kon; Rat/Cle; Sch/Gre; Woo/My.

SELECTED REVIEWS

MA: 13 Jan 1912; 20 Jan 1912; 9 March 1912; 30 March 1912; 29 Nov 1913; 8 May 1914; 11 Dec 1916; 28 Nov 1925. *MT*: 1 Nov 1922. *NYT*: 6 Jan 1912; 13 Jan 1912; 20 Nov 1913; 13 Nov 1921; 11 Dec 1921; 13 Feb 1922; 14 Feb 1923; 7 March 1923; 16 April 1923; 18 Jan 1924; 28 Feb 1924; 22 Feb 1926; 31 March 1954; 14 Feb 1955; 13 Feb 1956. *TL*: 29 June 1901; 29 Aug 1901; 3 Sept 1901; 8 April 1902; 26 Nov 1908; 12 June 1911; 9 Oct 1911; 10 June 1912; 27 Nov 1912; 12 Feb 1913; 19 Nov 1929; 2 Feb 1931; 20 Oct 1948; 2 Nov 1948; 21 May 1956.

SELECTED DISCOGRAPHY

Backhaus at the Salzburg Festival. Beethoven: Sonata in E-flat Major, op. 7; Sonata in A Major, op. 101; Sonata in E Major, op. 109. Documents LV 964.

Backhaus plays Brahms, Vol. I. Concerto No. 1 in D Minor, op. 15; Scherzo in E-flat Minor, op. 4; Ballades, op. 10, nos. 1 and 2; Waltzes, op. 39, nos. 1-2, 15. Biddulph LHW 017. Boult/BBC SO.

Backhaus plays Brahms, Vol. II. Concerto No. 2 in B-flat Major, op. 83; Variations on an Original Theme, op. 21, no. 1; Variations on a Theme by Paganini, op. 35. Biddulph 018. Böhm/Saxon SO.

Backhaus plays Chopin. Berceuse, op. 57; Etudes (complete); Fantasy-Impromptu, op. 66; *Grande valse brillante*, op. 18; Valse in D Flat, op. 64, no. 1. Liszt: *Waldesrauschen*. Pearl GEMM CD 9902.

Beethoven: Concerto No. 4 in G Major, op. 58 (Knappertsbusch/Vienna PO); Concerto No. 5 in E-flat Major, op. 73 (Keilberth/Stuttgart RO). Recorded live in 1954 and 1962. Stradivarius STR 10002 CD.

Beethoven: Concerto No. 4 in G Major, op. 58 (rec. 1951); Concerto No. 5 in E-flat Major, op. 73 (rec. 1953). London 425 962-2. Krauss/Vienna PO.

Beethoven: Sonata in C Minor, op. 13; Sonata in C-sharp Minor, op. 27, no. 2; Sonata in C Major, op. 53; Sonata in F Minor, op. 57. Enterprise ENTBL 23 (CD). Recorded 1958–59.

Beethoven: Sonata in C-sharp Minor, op. 27, no. 2; Sonata in C Major, op. 53; Sonata in C Minor, op. 111. Mozart: Sonata in A Major, K. 331. Live performances: Besançon, 1959; Salzburg, 1959; Vienna, 1964; Salzburg, 1956. AS 303 (CD).

Beethoven: Sonata in F Major, op. 10, no. 2; Sonata in C Major, op. 53; Sonata in G Major, op. 79; Sonata in C Minor, op. 111. *Fonit-Cetra* CDE-1015 (rec. 1954, 1964); also Virtuoso CD 2697072.

Brahms: Concerto No. 2 in B-flat Major, op. 83. Böhm/Vienna PO. London 414142-2.

Brahms: Concerto No. 2 in B-flat Major, op. 83. Karajan/Berlin PO. Bellaphon 689-22-002 (CD).

Mozart: Sonata in C Major, K. 330; Sonata in A Major, K. 331; Sonata in C Minor, K. 457; Fantasia in C Minor, K. 475; Rondo in A Minor, K. 511. Recorded live from Salzburg Festival of 1956. *Frequenz* CMJ 1 or *Memoria* 991-009 (CD).

Wilhelm Backhaus Plays Brahms. Ballades, op. 10, nos. 1 and 2, op. 118, no. 3; Capriccio, op. 76, no. 8; Hungarian Dances, nos. 6 and 7; Intermezzos, op. 76, no. 7, op. 117, nos. 1 and 2, op. 118, nos. 1, 2, 4 and 6; Rhapsodies, op. 79; Romance, op. 118, no. 5; Scherzo, op. 4; Variations on an Original Theme, op. 21. Waltzes, op. 39, nos. 1, 2 and 15. Pearl GEMM CD 9385.

Wilhelm Backhaus plays Johannes Brahms. Ballades, op. 10, nos. 1 and 2; Concerto No. 2 in B-flat Major, op. 83; Hungarian Dances, nos. 6 and 7; Intermezzos, op. 117, nos. 1 and 2; Piano Pieces, op. 76, nos. 7 and 8; Piano Pieces, op. 118; Rhapsodies, op. 79; Scherzo, op. 4; Variations on an Original Theme, op. 21; Waltzes (7) from op. 39. Memories HR 4442/43 (2 CDs). Böhm/*Sächsische Staatskappelle*.

Wilhelm Backhaus plays Mozart. Fantasia and Sonata in C Minor, K. 475, 457; Sonata in C Major, K. 330; Sonata in A Major, K. 331; Rondo in A Minor, K. 511. *Memoria* 991-009.

BADURA-SKODA, PAUL: b. Vienna, Austria, 6 October 1927.

> To musicologists he is a scholar of keyboard style, to students he is a respected pianist-teacher on the master-class circuit, to audiences he is a specialist in the music of the Viennese classics—Mozart, Schubert and Beethoven.
>
> Nancy Malitz (*Cincinnati Enquirer*, 7 February 1978)

Paul Badura-Skoda, an equally good student in mathematics, science and music, intended to become an engineer but at about age 16 (he had begun piano studies at age six) he turned to music. He changed, he later said, because at that time Europe faced a great shortage of musicians (so many having fled during World War II), and conditions were exactly right for a career in music. Hearing an Edwin Fischer piano recital further influenced his decision. As he remembers it, Fischer's gorgeous playing enthralled him.

Paul Badura was an infant when his father died and still a child when his mother married a Viennese furniture dealer named Skoda. Out of appreciation and respect for his stepfather, who generously supported his decision to change careers, Paul Badura changed his name to Badura-Skoda. Having chosen a career in music, he enrolled at the Vienna Conservatory and for two years (1945–47) studied with Viola Thern, who gave him a solid musical foundation and earned his everlasting respect. Long after Badura-Skoda had begun his professional career, he would return to Thern for advice.

In 1947 he won the Austrian Music Competition, his prize being a scholarship for Edwin Fischer's master class in Lucerne. Enrolled that summer, he faithfully attended every Fischer performance, whether a piano recital, chamber-music performance or conducting performance. Fischer taught his students that the piano sings best when gently coaxed, that its singing quality deteriorates when one plays above a certain dynamic level; therefore, the pianist must calibrate the dynamic range so that *fortes* can be achieved without forcing. Fischer greatly influenced Badura-Skoda's playing style. A musician of taste and style, he is known for what critics have identified as his nonpercussive sound.

In June 1947 Badura-Skoda made his debut with the Vienna Symphony Orchestra, playing Liszt's Concerto in E Flat, Rudolf Moralt conducting. In 1948 he placed second in the Liszt Competition (from 1956 the Liszt-Bartók Competition) in Budapest. In 1949 he took third prize at the Marguerite Long Competition in Paris. Meanwhile, in 1948 he had also begun his professional career with a recital in Vienna and, in 1949, two performances with the Vienna Philharmonic Orchestra, once with Wilhelm Furtwängler conducting, later with Herbert von Karajan conducting. In 1950 he made his first appearance at the Salzburg Festival. These performances, all very successful, bolstered his career. He toured (1950–51) Italy and Scandinavia with the Vienna Chamber Orchestra; made his London debut in November 1951; toured (1952) Australia; and toured (1952–53) North America, making his debut (1 Nov 1952) in Toronto, Canada, and his first United States appearance (7 Nov 1952) in Cincinnati, Ohio, where he played Mozart's Concerto in B-flat Major, K. 595, with the Cincinnati

Symphony Orchestra under Thor Johnson. He toured regularly in the United States until 1957, thereafter only sporadically until he made another major American tour in 1978; and returned often during the 1980s. He performs mostly in Europe.

A well-known and highly respected teacher, Badura-Skoda assisted at Edwin Fischer's master classes during the last years of Fischer's illness, and he has continued to teach master classes around the world. He also holds an important post at the Vienna *Hochschule*. He and his wife Eva (married 1951) were visiting professors at the University of Wisconsin at Madison for the spring semester of 1964. During 1965–71 he was artist-in-residence at the Madison campus, and Eva Badura-Skoda taught musicology.

The very versatile Badura-Skoda pursues many diverse interests. He has attained a fine reputation for performing four-hand recitals with Jörg Demus, a team considered by many to have been the best since that of Rosina and Josef Lhévinne. After more than 30 years of playing what Badura-Skoda calls "the beautiful but limited" four-hand repertoire, they decided to dissolve the partnership. Besides pianist and teacher, he is also a composer, editor (Urtext scores and performing editions) and author (sometimes co-author with his wife) of scholarly books and articles.

Badura-Skoda has also acquired a fine collection of early pianos and, surprisingly, he can actually tune them himself, a skill he learned of necessity. When he began his music career right after World War II, there were very few playable pianos available in Europe and few competent tuners to maintain them. Having a natural technical bent, Badura-Skoda learned piano tuning rather easily. He began by asking questions of piano tuners and completed his training with a three-week tuning course at the Steinway factory in Hamburg. His piano collection (about 15 historical and 3 modern instruments) is reportedly one of the finest in the world. He has personally restored some of his early pianos and has used several of these in recitals and for recordings (Mozart, Haydn, Schubert, Beethoven). While early pianos certainly have a remarkable clarity, particularly in the lower registers, one misses the beautiful tone and the sustaining qualities of modern instruments.

Badura-Skoda's enormous repertoire includes about 30 concertos, other works with orchestra and nearly 200 solo compositions. It ranges from the great Austro-German composers to Chopin, Liszt, the Impressionists and such modern composers as Frank Martin and Alban Berg. In this vast repertoire Badura-Skoda's favorite composer, he says, is the one he is playing. Each work is meticulously prepared in a scholarly manner, without sentimentality. He will compare first editions and autographs, investigate text deviations and (most important in his view) look behind the scenes to understand the functioning and the impact of the music. Totally immersed in music, Badura-Skoda passionately searches for the artistic essence of the music he plays.

The reviews of Paul Badura-Skoda's performances in America during the 1950s are decidedly unlike those of his American performances since 1978. On his first U.S. tour, critics and audiences looked forward to hearing the pianist they had admired on his many Westminster recordings. Early reviews, however, disappointingly describe him as an honest, talented musician but with a small-scale playing style, not much depth or color, basically a pleasant but not very exciting pianist.

According to one reviewer from that early era, "The reason for his recording success is fairly clear, for his playing is generally of the small-scaled and lightly nuanced type most acceptable to the microphone; there is not much depth or range of color to his tone." (*LAT*, 26 March 1956) This was not the pianist expectant audiences had heard on the Westminster recordings. Badura-Skoda himself explains that in those early years he was not wholly self-confident on the concert stage. In a 1978 interview he claimed that his playing style had become very different from that of the 1950s and 1960s. The change, he believes, "lies in greater concentration, greater rhythmic impact, and particularly . . . a greater power of expression. It has to do with self-assurance, you know. I have not the slightest doubt about my artistic purpose." (Horowitz)

Critics mostly agree. Reviews since the late 1970s indicate that Badura-Skoda's playing has indeed become far more assured and virtuosic. "What is striking is a new found dynamism and sense of adventure. His *pianissimo*, which, 20 years ago, was more limp than it was soft, has acquired a real sense of mystery and instrumental luminousness. His coloristic sense is more acute than ever before." (*BG*, 7 Feb 1978) In a Washington recital he "turned in an electrifying performance of the [Mozart] Sonata in A Major, K. 331, the famous Alla Turca." (*WT*, 6 Feb 1984) And at Caramoor he gave a superlative performance of Beethoven's Sonata in C-sharp Minor, op. 27, no. 2 ("Moonlight"). "The sentiment of this work . . . offered the soloist the opportunity to express not only the 'sturm and drang' of Beethoven's psyche, but the interpretative genius of his own talent." (*GWN*, 23 Aug 1984)

The same themes continue to prevail. A performance of the Mozart Concerto in E-flat Major, K. 271, at SUNY-Stony Brook's Fine Arts Center was "just delicious. Badura-Skoda is a man who knows exactly how to make music. . . . He is a musician from an older school; his surfaces may have a nick in them occasionally, but the beauty of his playing is deeper than that." (*LIN*, Feb 1985)

On 18 July 1991, he played—and conducted—two Mozart Concertos (K. 459, K. 482) with the Australian Chamber Orchestra at Melbourne's Concert Hall. "Badura-Skoda's keyboard technique was flawless, as was the sense of ritual and order. In every phrase and bar, priority was given, honor paid, to Mozart. There was not a sign of personal indulgence. And the understanding that went with this humility was luminous." (*The Age*, 22 July 1991)

He earned a rave review ("a breathtaking performance at the piano") for his recital on 20 July 1991 in Adelaide's Festival Theatre. "Badura-Skoda is not only a fine pianist in the technical sense . . . he also possesses a profound intellectual grasp of the music as well. . . . The sprawling structure of Schubert's last sonata [B Flat, D. 960] was illuminated by his understanding of its structure and his ability to convey that understanding to the listener." And his performance of "the intricate variations which conclude Beethoven's final sonata [C Minor, op. 111] had a compelling logic which few other pianists can convey with such lucidity." (*AA*, 22 July 1991)

Badura-Skoda is brilliantly adept in combining teaching and performing into one experience.   On 8 February 1994 he gave a lecture-recital on Beethoven's Sonata in C Minor, op. 111, at the University of California, Santa Barbara.   During the first half, he analyzed the sonata with utmost clarity.   Then, after having disclosed the masterful construction and formidable logic, he put everything back into place with a sensational performance of that sonata.

Paul Badura-Skoda, not a born virtuoso with an infallible technique, has achieved success through unending hours of practice and study.   If at times he still has technical mishaps, displays an unpredictable sense of rhythm or sometimes the old emotional timidity, on the whole there is a "greatly revitalized Badura-Skoda, and a pianist of greatly increased stature." (*BG*, 7 Feb 1978) Badura-Skoda is, as he always has been, a master pianist and a scholar-performer but now, more often than not, a vivifying emotional (not sentimental) content offsets the scholarly earnestness.   The overused adage "a pianist's pianist" (or a "musician's musician") aptly applies to Paul Badura-Skoda.   His audiences know what to expect and invariably find his playing to be a moving musical experience.

Badura-Skoda began recording with Westminster Records in the early 1950s, and his recordings now number more than 100 LPs/CDs, including complete cycles of the sonatas of Mozart, Schubert and Beethoven.   Most of his Westminster recordings remain classics of refined, intelligent, highly musical performances.

His first great recording success—Schubert's Trout Quintet—spread his fame abroad because Westminster had worldwide distribution.   And it is with Schubert, Mozart, Beethoven and Brahms that Badura-Skoda established himself as a first-rate clavierist.   His Schubert CD for Music and Arts (rec. 1987, see Discog.) received very favorable comments.   The Fantasy is "uncompromising in tempo-choices, clear in texture," and the dance pieces are "done with real delicacy and swing."   (*Fan*, May/June 1988) And, "in the *Moments musicaux*, Badura-Skoda entirely comes into his element. . . . This will remain . . . a very special account of these masterpieces.   Nothing but the essentials of the music is conveyed and the pianist is quite forthright in conveying the message of each one." (*Gram*, Feb 1989)

Badura-Skoda has made numerous recordings on various instruments from his historical collection (see Discog.).   From a purely auditory point of view, the most successful of these recordings are those using the Conrad Graf, a Viennese piano dating from 1824.   His recordings using two other Viennese pianos, one made by Georg Hasska around 1815 and one by Johann Schantz dating from around 1790, have attractive qualities, as do the Schweighofer (ca.1846) and Schöfftos (ca.1810); however, the recording with the 1816 Broadwood does not have a very agreeable sound.   Badura-Skoda is presently recording a complete Schubert piano sonata cycle (9 CDs) for Arcana, using fortepianos from his collection.

Having previously recorded all the Beethoven sonatas on a modern piano, Badura-Skoda is rerecording them on instruments from his historic collection.   Some will find the thin tone and limited dynamic range of these instruments disquieting; others will appreciate the clarity and the distinctive tone color of the 19th-century fortepiano. Two Beethoven sonata CDs (Astrée 7738, 7741, see Discog.) in particular are outstanding of their kind: "Badura-Skoda brings his usual reliable musicianship to these readings, observing details of the score with scrupulous care. Phrasing, pedaling, and dynamics are followed faithfully, and his tempo choices always seem to serve the music beautifully. These are eminently satisfactory performances on musical grounds." (*Fan*, Sept/Oct 1988)

Badura-Skoda uses a modern piano for his recordings of two Mozart Concertos, K. 466 and K. 467 (see Discog.), and he also conducts the Prague Chamber Orchestra from the keyboard. The result is a revelation: "His playing is informed with a confluence of both approaches—the warmth of the old tradition and the linear clarity of the new—and here he produces two more than compelling performances. . . . Very few pianists before the public today can rival Badura-Skoda's uncanny ability to convert notes into music." (*Fan*, Jan/Feb 1993)

Badura-Skoda's Brahms recordings show the same admirable musicianship. He has recorded Brahms's Intermezzos, op. 117, and Piano Pieces, op. 119, on a 60-year-old Bösendorfer imperial grand. The tempos maintain a forward movement, his *rubato* does not distort the musical flow and the typical Brahmsian long phrases are admirably projected. The piano itself is a delight, and "Badura-Skoda plays it with technical mastery, producing a variety of touches and dynamic nuances." (*Fan*, July/Aug 1987)

In 1955 he recorded the six Bach Partitas on the piano and later performed them on the harpsichord (see Discog.). More recently—and most unusual for Badura-Skoda—he recorded a recital of selected Debussy compositions, played on his own 1923 Bösendorfer piano. This Debussy CD (see Discog.) is an interesting item, particularly to those staunch admirers of Badura-Skoda's art. Although many pianists specializing in Debussy have given us near definitive readings of these pieces, there is always room for yet another concept. Here, "in more impressionistic contexts there is much to enjoy in the atmospheric washes of sound and sensitive nuances of colour Badura-Skoda conjures from this mellow, albeit slightly 'covered'-toned instrument." (*Gram*, April 1991)

Badura-Skoda is a stylish Chopinist, as his recent CD on the Valois label testifies. Both the Sonata No. 2 in B-flat Minor and the Sonata No. 3 in B Minor are given simple, straightforward—and superb—performances. "Badura-Skoda emphasizes the sonatas' classical origins, offering readings of great clarity and lyric beauty. The drama is there but kept in the boundaries of classical propriety." (*ARG*, Sept/Oct 1993)

SELECTED REFERENCES

Badura-Skoda, Eva, and Paul Badura-Skoda. *Interpreting Mozart on the Keyboard* (trans. Leo Black). New York: St. Martin's Press, 1962.
Badura-Skoda, Paul. "Chopin's Influence." In *The Chopin Companion*, ed. Alan Walker. New York: W. W. Norton & Co., Inc., pp. 258–276.
———. "Concerning Interpretation." *Etude*, May 1954, pp. 9, 56.

————. *Interpreting Bach at the Keyboard* (trans. Alfred Clayton). New York: Oxford University Press, 1993.

————. "Interpreting Beethoven's Piano Sonatas." *Piano Quarterly*, Winter 1972–73, pp. 6–9.

————. "A Master Lesson on Mozart's Fantasy in C Minor, K. 475." *Piano Quarterly*, Spring 1984, pp. 36–39.

————. "Mozart's Rondo in A Minor, K. 511." *Piano Quarterly*, Fall 1976, pp. 29–32.

————. "On Ornamentation in Haydn." *Piano Quarterly*, Fall 1981, pp. 38–48.

————. "Textual Problems in Schubert—Discrepancies Between Text and Intention." *Piano Quarterly*, Winter 1978–79, pp. 49–55.

Badura-Skoda, Paul, and Jörg Demus. *Die Klaviersonaten von Ludwig van Beethoven.* Wiesbaden: F. A. Brockhaus, 1970.

Czerny, Karl. *On the Proper Performance of all Beethoven's Works for the Piano*, edited and with a commentary by Paul Badura-Skoda. Wien: Universal, 1970.

Goldsmith, Harris. "Schubert Explorations: Badura-Skoda's complete edition of the Piano Sonatas." *High-Fidelity Magazine*, Sept 1972, pp. 65–67.

Hertelendy, Paul. "Paul Badura-Skoda: Rediscovering The Virtues Of Mozart's Fortepiano." *Contemporary Keyboard*, Jan 1980, pp. 24–25.

Horowitz, Joseph. "A Second Debut for Paul Badura-Skoda." *New York Times*, 29 Jan 1978, pp. 19, 24.

"Pianist Badura-Skoda kicks off a major U. S. tour." *Capital Times* (Madison, WI), 4 Feb 1978, p. 10.

Reed, Christopher. "Paul Badura-Skoda." *Clavier*, Nov 1986, pp. 5–11.

Wagner, Denise. "An Interview with Paul Badura-Skoda." *Musical Heritage Review*, 26 May 1980, pp. 14–15, 19.

See also Bibliography: Dub/Ref; Eld/Pia; Kai/Gre; Kol/Que; Mac/Gr2; Ran/Kon; Rat/Cle; Sch/Gre.

SELECTED REVIEWS

AA: 22 July 1991. *BE*: 29 July 1991. *BG*: 7 Feb 1978; 29 July 1991. *CE*: 7 Feb 1978. *CPD*: 24 Feb 1976. *CSM*: 4 Feb 1953. *KCS*: 9 March 1980. *LAT*: 19 March 1954; 26 March 1956; 28 Feb 1984; 24 Feb 1987; 9 Feb 1993. *MC*: 1 Feb 1953. *MD*: 13 March 1985. *MM*: May 1983. *NYT*: 11 Jan 1953; 7 Feb 1954; 14 Jan 1955; 15 March 1956; 8 Jan 1959; 31 Jan 1984. *PI*: 12 Feb 1985. *SFC*: 17 Feb 1982. *SPI*: 2 March 1985. *ST*: 2 March 1985. *TL*: 20 Dec 1967. *WP*: 4 Feb 1984; 20 Feb 1985; 18 July 1987; 17 July 1992; 22 Feb 1994. *WS*: 25 July 1980. *WT*: 6 Feb 1984.

SELECTED DISCOGRAPHY

Bach, J. S.: Partitas (played on the harpsichord). Astrée E-7771 (2 CDs).

Bach, J. S.: Partitas (played on the piano). MCA Classics MCAD2-9840 (2 CDs).

Beethoven: Concerto No. 5 in E-flat Major, op. 73; Sonata in C Minor, op. 111. Music and Arts CD-241. Knappertsbusch/NDR Orchestra.

Beethoven: Sonatas in E-flat Major, op. 31, no. 3; F-sharp Major, op. 78; G Major, op. 79; E-flat Major, op. 81a; E Minor, op. 90. Astrée CD E-8696 (Hasska Hammer-flügel, ca. 1815).

Beethoven: Sonatas in B-flat Major, op. 106; A Major, op. 101. Astrée CD E 8698. (Graf Hammerflügel, ca. 1824).

Beethoven: Sonatas in E Major, op. 109; A-flat Major, op. 110; C Minor, op. 111. Astrée CD E 8699 (Graf Hammerflügel, ca. 1824).

Beethoven: Sonatas in C Major, op. 53; F-sharp Major, op. 78; G Minor, op. 49, no. 1; G Major, op. 49, no. 2; F Major, op. 54; F Minor, op. 57. Astrée CD E 8697 (Broadwood, ca. 1815).

Brahms: Intermezzi, op. 117; *Klavierstücke*, op. 118, op. 119. Auvidis AV-6115 (CD).

Chopin: Ballades (4); Barcarolle, op. 60; Fantasie in F Minor, op. 49; Nocturne in C-sharp Minor, op. posth. Auvidis Valois V 4672 (CD).

Chopin: Sonata No. 2 in B-flat Minor, op. 35; Sonata No. 3 in B Minor, op. 58. Valois V 4671 (CD).

Debussy: Piano Works. *Estampes*; *Préludes*, Book I: *Des pas sur la neige; La Fille aux cheveux de lin; La cathédrale engloutie. Suite bergamasque.* Harmonic/Target H/CD8505.

Martin: Concerto No. 2. Jecklin-Disco JD 632-2. Martin/Luxembourg RSO.

Mozart: Concerto in D Minor, K. 466; Concerto in C Major, K. 467. Valois V 4664 (CD). Badura-Skoda/Prague CO.

Mozart: Concerto in E-flat Major, K. 482; Concerto in B-flat Major, K. 595. Valois V 4669 (CD). Badura-Skoda/Prague CO.

Mozart: Sonatas (complete). Eurodisc 69169-2 (5 CDs).

Mozart: Sonatas in C Major, K. 330; A Major, K. 331; C Minor, K. 457; Fantasy in C Minor, K. 475; Rondo in A Minor, K. 511. Frequenz CMJ-1 (CD).

Mozart: Variations on "Ah vous dirai-je Maman"; Fantasia and Fugue in C Major, K. 394; Fantasia in D Minor, K. 397; Adagio, K. 540; Marche funèbre, K. 453a; Minuet in D Major, K. 355; Gigue in G Major, K. 574; Rondo in D Minor, K. 511. Astrée CD E-7710 (Schantz pianoforte, ca. 1790).

Schubert: Allegretto in C Minor, D. 915; Impromptus, D. 899 and D. 935; March in E Major, D. 606; *Moments musicaux*, D. 780; Sonata in A Major, D. 664; Two Scherzi, D. 593; Variation in C Minor, D. 718; *Valses nobles*. MCA Classics MCAD2-9844 (2 CDs). From 1958.

Schubert: Impromptus, D. 899, D. 935. Astrée CD E 7764 (Graf Hammerflügel, ca. 1824).

Schubert: Sonata in F-sharp Minor, D. 571/604/570; Sonata in D Major, D. 850. Arcana ACN 942015 (CD).

Schubert: Sonata in F Minor, D. 625/505; Sonata in C Minor, D. 958. Arcana ACN 942017 (CD).

Schubert: Sonata in A Minor, D. 784; Sonata in A Major, D. 959. Arcana ACN 942018 (CD).

Schubert: Sonata in A Major, D. 664; Sonata in B-flat Major, D. 960. Arcana ACN 942019 (CD).
Schubert: Wanderer Fantasia, D. 760; *Moments musicaux*, D. 780; *Lerchenwalzer* from *Ländler*, D. 145; Scherzo in B-flat Major, D. 593, no. 1; 13 Waltzes; *Abschiedswalzer*, op. posth. Music and Arts CD-267.

BARENBOIM, DANIEL: b. Buenos Aires, Argentina, 15 November 1942.

> Routine is the greatest enemy of music-making.
> Daniel Barenboim (*Records and Recording*, April 1978)

Routine rarely encroaches on the life of Daniel Barenboim. A man of bursting energy, the multitalented Barenboim (pianist, conductor, chamber player, festival organizer) has only occasionally settled into a single career. Throughout most of his life his multiple musical careers have taken him all over the globe, keeping him so busy that there have been periods when he has gone for years without a vacation. No matter to Barenboim, for making music is not just his career; it is his great joy.

Barenboim is a demanding, confident musician and an equally confident person. (Needless to say, nervousness, the bane of many performers, has never bothered him.) All told, his remarkable confidence is understandable. He has a protean talent, and his parents Enrique and Aida (Schuster) Barenboim, descendants of Russian Jews from Odessa, carefully nurtured that talent. They raised their only child in a wholly supportive musical environment. They took him to concerts and arranged for him to play at the musical evenings held in Buenos Aires. Martha Argerich, who also as a child performed at those soirees, is on record as hating the experience and remembering how very much the extroverted young Barenboim enjoyed playing for people (Eld/Pia, see Bibliog.).

Barenboim started piano lessons with his mother when he was five years old, learning so quickly that his father, who taught advanced students, soon took over his musical training. Thereafter, Barenboim studied only with his father and has never had another teacher. He made his first public appearance at age seven in Buenos Aires, and a few years later his parents decided to move to Israel, largely so that Daniel could be raised and educated in the one place in the world where he would be like everybody else and not part of a minority. En route to Israel the Barenboims stopped (summer 1952) at Salzburg, Austria, to visit their friend Igor Markevitch, then teaching a conducting class at the *Mozarteum*. Although not yet 10, Barenboim was allowed to observe Markevitch's conducting class and Edwin Fischer's piano class. He also created a sensation with two performances: He played Bach's D Minor Concerto (BWV 1052) and conducted a *Mozarteum* student orchestra in Brahms's Variations on a Theme by Haydn.

The Barenboims arrived in Israel later that year and eventually became Israeli citizens. Changing from their comfortable way of life in Argentina to the pioneer conditions of Israel caused a drastic difference in their way of living. It is interesting that Barenboim has said that much of his mature self-confidence stems from the egalitarianism of his early life in Israel, where everyone was zealously committed to building a new country and a new society. He attended public schools in Tel Aviv. Bright and ambitious, he was good at mathematics and the Talmud and excelled at history and languages. (He speaks Spanish, Hebrew, German, French, Italian and English.) Insofar as possible, he had a normal life for a prodigy. He had many nonmusical friends and, among other pursuits, collected stamps, and even took up boxing, his parents having agreed that he should not develop a complex about his hands.

As an Israeli citizen, Barenboim was eligible for the America-Israel Cultural Foundation's first scholarship for advanced musical studies in Europe. Thus supported, he was able to have three summers (1954–56) of study abroad. Though barely in his teens, he took Markevitch's conducting class at the *Mozarteum*; studied composition with Nadia Boulanger in Paris, studied violin, theory and composition at the Santa Cecilia Academy in Rome, where he graduated in 1956 as the youngest person up to that time to receive its diploma, and, also in 1956, studied conducting with Carlo Zecchi at the *Accademia Chigiana* in Siena, Italy.

Barenboim's parents wisely limited their young teenager to performing only about three months a year. He played in Israel, Europe (Vienna, Rome, Paris) and in England (Liverpool, Bournemouth) before making his London debut (17 Jan 1956) at Festival Hall, where he played Mozart's A Major Concerto, K. 488, with the Royal Philharmonic Orchestra, Josef Krips conducting. "His performance was well-nigh flawless. His tone was limpid, his rhythm buoyant, his passage-work beautifully disciplined, and the texture always transparent and clear. In the unruffled effortlessness of it all, he might have been a young Rubinstein." (*TL*, 18 Jan 1956)

Barenboim's American debut, another major step in his career, came about through Artur Rubinstein. While studying in Paris, Barenboim had been able to play privately for Rubinstein. As a result, Rubinstein arranged an audition with the impresario Sol Hurok, and Hurok signed Barenboim to a contract. Two years later he made his American orchestral debut (20 Jan 1957) at Carnegie Hall, with "an exhilarating performance" of Prokofiev's Piano Concerto No. 1 in D Flat, op. 10, with Leopold Stokowski conducting the Symphony of the Air. A year later Barenboim made his New York recital debut (17 Jan 1958) at Town Hall, playing three sonatas (Beethoven, op. 53; Brahms, op. 1; Prokofiev, op. 28) and Bach's Chromatic Fantasy and Fugue.

By 1959—he was only 17—Barenboim had finished his schooling and was concertizing full time. Even with his prodigious talents, he worked very hard and built his reputation slowly. Regular appearances with the Hallé Orchestra under Sir John Barbirolli, frequent appearances (1963–65) with the prestigious Berlin Philharmonic Orchestra, a debut (1964) with the New York Philharmonic Orchestra and a 20-week tour (1965) of the Soviet Union added immensely to his reputation. For nearly three decades Barenboim has ranked as one of the world's finest pianists.

He has also become an important conductor, not an overnight decision, for more than 20 years ago Barenboim told a *Saturday Evening Post* interviewer that from the time he was 10 he knew he wanted to be a conductor. (Kahn) He first conducted in 1957 in Haifa, in 1962 in Sydney and Melbourne. What firmly established him as a conductor was his mutually rewarding relationship with the English Chamber Orchestra—begun in 1964 and lasting for more than a decade. If Barenboim used the ECO as a stepping-stone, the orchestra also profited handsomely, commercially and artistically. Their performances of the complete Mozart concertos in London, Paris and New York were, according to Quintin Ballardie, a director of the ECO and also its principal violist, the "ECO's greatest achievement in more than 20 years." (*RR*, April 1976) Barenboim was Music Director of the *Orchestre de Paris* for about 15 years (appointed in 1975, resigned end of 1988–89 season). His appointment (1986) as musical and artistic director of the Bastille Opera ended in 1989 due to political problems. In September 1991, Barenboim succeeded Sir Georg Solti as music director of the Chicago Symphony Orchestra. And in August 1992 he became artistic director of the Berlin *Staatsoper*.

Like Stephen Kovacevich, Barenboim finds that conducting helps him as a pianist, especially with practicing, because, he says, he is able to hear things he is doing at the piano as if they were a section of the orchestra, outside himself. More than one critic agrees that Barenboim "has used his conducting experiences to enrich his pianism, drawing on the coloristic potential of the orchestra and the theatrical sweep of opera to invest his keyboard artistry with a higher level of intensity and drama." (*NYT*, 23 Feb 1990)

Barenboim dislikes practicing. Known among piano colleagues for his natural technique, he has never held himself to a fixed daily practice schedule. He practices, he says, to achieve physical comfort or out of musical necessity but not for self-confidence, and his practice sessions usually last only one or two hours. Rather than practice, he will study music for hours away from the piano. A dedicated musician—"I haven't played or conducted many uncommitted notes" (*RR*, April 1978)—Barenboim will memorize a work completely before ever playing a note of it, learning it in his mind rather than in his hands, an approach possible, of course, because he has been endowed with a fabulous memory.

Barenboim's active repertoire consists chiefly of Bach, Beethoven, Brahms, Chopin, Liszt, Mozart and some modern composers. His earlier repertoire was larger, consisting of all the Beethoven sonatas and concertos; the complete Mozart sonatas and concertos; the Berg *Kammerkonzert,* the Bartók concertos, the Alexander Goehr Piano Concerto, which he premiered in 1972. During the 1989–90 season Barenboim premiered two new piano concertos, one by Luciano Berio, the other by York Höller.

He has played a great deal of chamber music, mainly with his first wife, the English cellist Jacqueline du Pré. Married in 1967, they often played together in sonata recitals and in trio concerts with either Itzhak Perlman or Pinchas Zuckerman playing the violin. (Jacqueline du Pré, stricken with multiple sclerosis in the early 1970s, died in 1987. Barenboim and his second wife, the Russian pianist Elena Bashkirova, have two children.) As a lieder accompanist, Barenboim has performed extensively with Fischer-Dieskau. "In Lieder—Schubert or Schumann—there is no accompanying," says Barenboim, "but composed partnerships." (RR, April 1978)

He was awarded the Beethoven Medal in 1956, the Harriet Cohen Paderewski Centenary Prize in 1963 and the Beethoven Society Medal in 1982. Now at the half-century mark, the intelligent, witty Barenboim has three decades of an extremely active and successful musical life behind him, and he looks ahead to more of the same: piano recitals, conducting the Chicago Symphony Orchestra, playing concertos under other conductors and, undoubtedly, playing more chamber music, formally and informally.

It seems safe to assume that anyone who played all the Beethoven sonatas at age 14, as Barenboim did, is a born musician. Beyond his supreme self-confidence, he is a fiercely involved, dedicated musician with a constant need for making—and sharing—music. Throughout his long career as a concert pianist, his performances have been subjected to minute scrutiny; however, it is difficult to pinpoint the real Barenboim, for he is truly a creative performer. His performances are very personal, sometimes even eccentric. Though he follows the Romantic approach—expressive accents, flexibility in tempos and freedom in phrasing and nuance—each performance reflects his feelings and attitude at that given moment, thus no two performances of the same work are apt to be alike. The results, always somewhat unpredictable, can be exciting and moving. But at times this approach produces exceedingly controversial interpretations; for example, when Barenboim's ideas and feelings take over a performance, resulting, as critics have variously noted, in outrageous dynamics, unabashed virtuosity, exaggerated *rubato*, overstated dramatic passages or wide tempo variations.

His programs, past and present, and his current discography all reveal an unmistakable preference for Beethoven. Since the age of 17, when he played all 32 Beethoven sonatas in Tel Aviv, he has given numerous performances of the complete cycle of sonatas. He has also performed all five concertos with the world's finest orchestras. No matter his style, whether an intimate or heroic approach, Barenboim instinctively commands "that indefinable Beethoven sound which eludes so many pianists." (LAT, 25 May 1976) He clearly has become one of the great Beethoven specialists, and extravagant critical praise substantiates his mastery of the Beethoven repertoire.

A recital (5 Jan 1970) initiating a complete cycle (8 recitals) of the Beethoven sonatas at London's Queen Elizabeth Hall prompted one critic to name Barenboim as one of the foremost Beethoven interpreters of the younger generation. His reading of the great "*Hammerklavier*" Sonata was a profoundly moving experience, "so tightly bound together that nothing could slip into easy mannerism or cliché; one that compelled attention with every gesture and phrase, spoke of the music and not the notes, with its whole voice." (MT, March 1970)

Barenboim's performance (1 Feb 1973) of Beethoven's Third Piano Concerto, with Zubin Mehta and the Los Angeles Philharmonic Orchestra, was so spectacular that "it could well set a standard for a long time to come. . . . He discovered new depths, new dimensions, new perspectives. The things he disclosed have always been there of course, but few pianists in our experience have ever exposed them so perceptively or with such acute inwardness. It may sound trite, but he gave the feeling of being face to face with Beethoven." (*LAT*, 3 Feb 1973) In a memorable recital (26 Sept 1990) at Chicago's Orchestra Hall, Barenboim's performance of Beethoven's challenging Diabelli Variations drew exceptional praise: "Barenboim is the type of Beethoven interpreter who goes to the heart of the music and sets its ideas before us with clarity and force." (*CST*, 28 Sept 1990)

Such unequivocal praise does not usually extend to Barenboim's interpretations of some other repertoires, perhaps excepting those of Mozart and Brahms. (He usually receives high marks for his performances of the Mozart concertos and sonatas—he has played them all—and for his performances of the Brahms concertos.) His Chopin performances garner mixed reviews. At an all-Chopin program (13 Dec 1971) at Festival Hall in London, Barenboim was technically in excellent form, steely-fingered and confident. Yet as good as his playing was, it lacked heart. For one critic, this was an odd recital—cogent and brilliant yet lacking a sense of adventure and discovery. Barenboim communicated "admiration for and understanding of Chopin—but admiration without love." (*MT*, Feb 1972) Another all-Chopin program (19 Nov 1972, at Carnegie Hall) was criticized because Barenboim "took a Romantically personal, sometimes absolutely eccentric, approach to the music. . . . At such times, Mr. Barenboim seemed bent on reviving the sentimental Chopin style of maiden-aunt pianists of one's childhood." (*NYT*, 20 Nov 1972)

Barenboim's performances of Liszt and Bach usually elicit the same cautious admiration. His intensely personal interpretations of Bach's Goldberg Variations at New York's Avery Fisher Hall on 21 February 1990 and at Washington's Kennedy Center on 8 October 1990 "broke rules, raised eyebrows and touched hearts." Most important, however, is that on both occasions Barenboim thrilled his listeners with "a deeply personal statement of this masterpiece, one that owed interesting debts to the evolving performance tradition but that spoke eloquently with its own pianistic voice." (*NYT*, 23 Feb 1990) At the Washington performance "his solution was to embrace the possibilities of the grand piano and place them at the service of the spirit of Bach's score. . . . The demands Mr. Barenboim made on his audience were great indeed. The rewards of his playing were greater still." (*WT*, 10 Oct 1990)

No matter that Barenboim sometimes bends the rules, for his approach to music is always heartfelt and sincerely expressed. If at times controversial, his music, upheld by solid musicianship and a stunning technique, is invariably creative and compelling.

Barenboim is one pianist who does not mind recording. Playing before an audience in the concert hall and playing to microphones in the recording studio is all the same to him. In his impressive discography, preponderantly Beethoven and Mozart, it is difficult to select the best recordings because he has recorded many works more than once. However, the essence of Barenboim's artistry shines clearly in two Beethoven collections—the concertos and the sonatas.

The five concertos performed in collaboration with Otto Klemperer are magnificent (see Discog.). "The combination of Barenboim and Klemperer, recording together in 1967–68, is nothing if not stimulating, and for every willfulness of a measured Klemperer, there is a youthful spark from the spontaneously combusting Barenboim. . . . The concentration is formidable and especially compelling in the slow movements." (Pen/Gui, see Bibliog.)

Barenboim has twice recorded the cycle of 32 Beethoven sonatas (see Discog.). Both are available on CD, issued as a set and many of them separately. Barenboim was in his late twenties when he recorded the EMI set. The *Deutsche Grammophon* recordings, made later, are especially fine in matters of maturity, tempo concepts and simplicity when called for. All things considered, however, most critics prefer the earlier EMI set. Barenboim played them from memory, thus "his interpretations have a freedom and depth that players who use music never achieve. . . . In the middle-period sonatas, his performance of these works contains tremendous bursts of energy and rich forte chords. . . . The Appassionata's slow movement is a high point, deeply felt and technically impeccable. . . . In the Hammerklavier the tragedy of the Adagio and the unleashed comets of notes in the fugue are incredible." (Elder)

In the late 1960s and early 1970s Barenboim, conducting from the piano, recorded the complete Mozart solo concertos with the English Chamber Orchestra (see Discog.). His spontaneity gives an unusual air of freshness to these masterpieces, and he is well served by the orchestra. But despite the undeniably beautiful playing, there are occasions when mannerisms intrude, when "he is unconsciously telling us how exquisitely he can turn a phrase, rather than allowing Mozart to speak for himself." (*Gram*, June 1990)

On a later album containing Mozart's last eight piano concertos (see Discog.), performed with the Berlin Philharmonic Orchestra, Barenboim's playing "is, in the best sense, all of a kind. His artistic values are self-evident, among them being his inability to produce an ugly sound, a thoughtless phrase or a graceless texture. Add to this his sense of momentum at his chosen tempo and his rapport with the orchestra, and the results are very pleasing." (*Gram*, April 1991)

Barenboim has had notable success performing the Brahms concertos and has sometimes played both on the same program—a prodigious feat. Once more, it is his recordings made in the 1960s, particularly Concerto No. 1 in D Minor, op. 15, that are outstanding. His August 1967 recording of that concerto with Sir John Barbirolli and the Vienna Philharmonic Orchestra, now available on CD (see Discog.), may be one of the "finest renderings of the score ever committed to recording. . . . Barenboim's pianism is concentrated, intensely lyrical, delicately sensitive." The Adagio "is almost time in suspension for sixteen minutes." (*Fan*, March/April 1991)

Barenboim's recording of Bach's Goldberg Variations (see Discog.), a work he had studied for some 25 years before presenting it to the public, was made live (12 Oct 1989) at the *Teatro Colón* in Buenos Aires, a performance celebrating the 40th anniversary of his debut there. Even those who prefer hearing these variations on the harpsichord must admire Barenboim's mastery, maturity and dedication. Barenboim is playing the piano, and for him the Goldberg Variations are piano music. As such they must be judged. The reviews, even when tempered with understandable criticism, are remarkable. In this intensely probing performance, Barenboim "shows a unique grasp of the music and knows how to bring out the character of each variation and phrase without ever breaking the line or destroying the continuity." (*ARG*, Jan/Feb 1991) From another review: Barenboim's "quarter century of contemplation has yielded a wonderfully vivid and remarkably poetic vision of this endlessly fascinating work—not to mention a technical command that seems near-miraculous." (*MA*, July 1990)

On 21 and 22 December 1992, Barenboim gave two recitals in the Vienna *Musikverein* to celebrate the 40th anniversary of his debut in that city. Two of the live recorded performances—Schubert's Impromptus, D. 935, and the Sonata in B-flat Major, D. 960—are coupled on a recent disc (see Discog.). A reviewer who thoroughly enjoyed the Impromptus ("Barenboim plays them very much in the spirit of their title, that is to say, as if making new discoveries there and then.") was less impressed with the Sonata: "Though warmly experienced, Barenboim's point-making struck me as too overt in the intimately self-communing first movement. . . . Again in the slow movement I thought him too consciously striving to lay bare the composer's heart." (*Gram*, Feb 1994)

SELECTED REFERENCES

Barenboim, Daniel. *A Life in Music*. New York: Charles Scribners Sons, 1982.
———. "A Question of Rhythm." (in conversation with Jürgen Kesting). *Records and Recording*, April 1978, pp. 18–20.
Bennett, Catherine. "After the Bastille." *The Times* (London), 3 June 1989, p. 31.
"Beyond Dexterity." *Time*, 11 Aug 1967, p. 36.
Canning, Hugh. "Return of the Prodigy." *Sunday Times* (London), 3 March 1991, sec. 5, pp. 2–5.
Crutchfield, Will. "Daniel Barenboim Renews Link to Chopin." *New York Times*, 14 Dec 1986, sec. 1, p. 110.
Elder, Dean. "Beethoven's 32." *Clavier*, May–June 1991, pp. 45–47.
Franks, Alan. "Back To The Barricades at the Bastille." *The Times* (London), 17 Jan 1989, p. 14.
Griffiths, Paul. "Concentrated Musicianship." *The Times* (London), 17 Jan 1983, p. 9.
Holland, Bernard. "Barenboim's Beethoven Piano Series." *New York Times*, 21 Feb 1986, sec. 3, p. 3.
Horowitz, Joseph. "Daniel Barenboim's 'Unique' Dual Career." *New York Times*, 23 Nov 1980, sec. 2, pp. 19, 25.
Kahn, Roger. "They Shall Have Music." *Saturday Evening Post*, 7 Sept 1968, pp. 68–71.
Kozinn, Allan. "Daniel Barenboim on Bach, the Bastille and the Baton." *New York Times*, 20 Feb 1990, sec. 3, pp. 15, 19.

Kupferberg, Herbert. "Daniel Barenboim." *Stereo Review*, Sept 1991, pp. 50–52.

Lebrecht, Norman. "This very private boy wonder of music is 40 all of a sudden." *Sunday Times* (London), 21 Nov 1982, p. 5.

Mayer, Martin. "Always Looking for the Action." *New York Times*, 30 June 1968, sec. 2, p. 16.

Pitt, Charles. "A Storm at the Bastille." *Musical America*, May 1989, pp. 14–17.

Rhein, John von. "The Play of Daniel." *Musical America*, Sept–Oct 1991, pp. 26–31.

"Teen-Age Virtuoso." *Time*, 30 March 1962, p. 74.

Widdicombe, Gillian. "Wunderkind." *Records and Recording*, April 1976, pp. 24–26.

See also Bibliography: Cur/Bio (1969); Eld/Pia; Ewe/Mu; Hag/Dec; Kol/Que; Rat/Cle; Rub/MyM; Sch/Gre.

SELECTED REVIEWS

CPD: 2 Dec 1986. *CST*: 31 May 1975; 12 March 1986; 25 Oct 1988; 28 Sept 1990; 11 Jan 1993; 4 Feb 1993. *CT*: 27 Feb 1986; 3 Dec 1986; 27 Feb 1990; 11 Jan 1993. *DMN*: 5 Dec 1984. *GM*: 12 March 1991. *LAT*: 8 Dec 1962; 13 Dec 1967; 3 Feb 1973; 25 May 1976. *MM*: June 1984. *MT*: March 1970; Feb 1972; April 1985; April 1987. *NYP*: 1 Dec 1980; 6 Jan 1993. *NYT*: 21 Jan 1957; 18 Jan 1958; 1 March 1965; 30 March 1968; 21 Oct 1970; 20 Nov 1972; 6 May 1975; 28 Nov 1977; 21 Feb 1980; 1 Dec 1980; 22 Jan 1982; 26 Jan 1982; 27 Nov 1984; 21 Feb 1986; 23 Feb 1990; 5 Oct 1990; 12 Oct 1990; 6 Jan 1993. *TL*: 18 Jan 1956; 6 Feb 1959; 2 Oct 1961; 15 Nov 1976; 21 Feb 1978; 23 March 1978; 31 Oct 1979; 4 Feb 1980; 18 Feb 1980; 10 Feb 1981; 22 Feb 1983; 20 Nov 1989. *WP*: 11 Oct 1990. *WT*: 10 Oct 1990.

SELECTED DISCOGRAPHY

Bach, J. S: Goldberg Variations. Erato 2292-45468-2.

Bartók: Concerto No. 1; Concerto No. 3. EMI Classics CDC 7 54770-2. Boulez/New Philharmonia Orchestra.

Beethoven: The Complete Concerti. Angel CDMC-63360 (3 CDs). Klemperer/New PO.

Beethoven: Sonatas (32) (complete). EMI Classics CDZJ-62863 (10 CDs).

Beethoven: Sonatas (Nos. 1–15). DG 413759-2 GX6 (6 CDs).

Beethoven: Sonatas (Nos. 16–32). DG 413766-2 GX6 (6 CDs).

Beethoven: Variations on a waltz by Diabelli, op. 120. Erato 4509-94810-2.

Brahms: Concerto No. 1 in D Minor, op. 15. EMI CDM 63536. Barbirolli/Vienna PO.

Brahms: Concerto No. 2 in B-flat Major, op. 83. Odyssey MBK 42608 (CD). Mehta/ NYPO.

Chopin: Barcarolle, op. 60; *Berceuse*, op. 57; Fantasy, op. 49; Polonaise, op. 61; *Souvenir de Paganini*; *Variations brillantes*, op. 12. Laserlight Classics 16 211 (CD).
Liszt: *Années de Pèlerinage: Suisse*. DG 415 670-2.
Liszt: Sonata in B Minor; 3 Paraphrases (*Rigoletto, Il Trovatore, Aida*). Erato ECD 75477.
Mendelssohn: Songs Without Words (complete). DG (Galleria) 423931-2 (2 CDs).
Mozart: Concertos (25) (complete). EMI Classics CDZJ-62825 (10 CDs). Barenboim/ English CO.
Mozart: Concertos in D Minor, K. 466; C Major, K. 467; E-flat Major, K. 482; A Major, K. 488; C Minor, K. 491; C Major, K. 503; D Major, K. 537; B-flat Major, K. 595. Teldec/Warner Classics 9031-72024-2 (4 CDs). Barenboim/Berlin PO.
Mozart: Sonatas (17). Angel CDZE-67294 (5 CDs).
Schubert: Impromptus (complete). DG (Galleria) 415849-2.
Schubert: Impromptus, D. 935; Sonata in B-flat Major, D. 960. Erato 4509-91700-2.
Schumann: *Carnaval*, op. 9; *Kinderscenen*, op. 15; *Faschingsschwank aus Wien*, op. 26. DG (Musikfest) 431 167-2.

VIDEO

Mozart: Concerto in E-flat Major, K. 482; Concerto in A Major, K. 488; Concerto in C Minor, K. 491. Teldec 9031-73665-3. Barenboim/Berlin PO.
Mozart: Concerto in C Major, K. 503; Concerto in D Major, K. 537; Concerto in B-flat Major, K. 505. Teldec 9031-73668-3. Barenboim/Berlin PO.

BARERE, SIMON: b. Odessa, Russia, 1 September 1896; d. New York, New York, 2 April 1951.

> His tone, which invariably sang, was as enchanting in the most power-ful measures as in passages of the utmost delicacy of sound.
> Noel Straus (*New York Times*, 20 November 1945)

If we depend, as we must, on music writers and critics, Simon Barere was a glo-rious pianist in the rich tradition of Rachmaninoff, Godowsky, Hofmann and Lhévinne, yet his great reputation has so faded that currently Barere does not even rate an entry in *The New Grove Dictionary of Music and Musicians*. Granted that Barere was a modest musician who avoided publicity and that life dealt him one career setback after another, it is still difficult to explain why this brilliant virtuoso, who could enthrall the hard-to-please New York critics, has had so little attention.

Being the 11th of 13 children raised by poor Jewish parents in the Odessa ghetto, Barere's precocious musical gift had little opportunity for proper training. His two much older brothers, self-taught café musicians, started him on the piano, and a young neighbor gave him some elementary instruction in music principles. He was about nine years old when his father died, leaving the family destitute. Since his older brothers had long since left Odessa to work in the far reaches of Russia, Barere, though still a child, found work playing piano accompaniments—pop tunes and operetta scores—for silent movies. Mornings he attended a special public school that emphasized music (Benno Moiseiwitsch had gone there a few years earlier), and at night he played the piano at the movie house. He was so good at his job that he earned enough to support his mother and two younger sisters.

Playing long, hard hours in the darkened movie house, Barere developed an amazing technique, an equally astonishing sight-reading ability and a huge repertoire of popular and semiclassical pieces. As his skills developed, he was able to get better work, playing in restaurants and performing with all kinds of entertainment ensembles, including Jewish, Russian and Italian bands. At the same time, from about age 11, Barere studied at the Odessa Imperial Music Academy. By the time he reached 16 he was a seasoned, highly skilled popular entertainer, and this boyhood experience may account for his absolutely fearless playing. As a concert pianist, Barere was known for playing so effortlessly and automatically that he could achieve lightning speed without losing control or clarity.

At age 16 Barere's life changed completely. His mother died, and, faithful to her wishes, he placed his two younger sisters with friends and made plans to attend the St. Petersburg Conservatory. Ignoring the fact that Jews in czarist Russia needed a special police permit to enter St. Petersburg, Barere applied in person (Nov 1912) at the Conservatory. An impromptu audition so impressed Alexander Glazunov, director of the Conservatory, that he allowed Barere to enroll despite his unorthodox musical background. Recognizing Barere's already established talent, Glazunov also waived some of the required theoretical and historical studies, providing instead "an enlightened and encouraging environment within which the boy could reach musical and physical maturity." (Crimp)

Barere studied with Anna Essipoff, developing the gracefully effortless technique for which he later became so famous, and after her death he became a pupil of the virtuoso pianist Felix Blumenfeld. Since Barere was already 16 when he entered the Conservatory and was allowed to study for seven years, it may be that Glazunov (an obvious admirer who described Barere as Franz Liszt in one hand and Anton Rubinstein in the other) deliberately kept him a student in order for the young pianist to avoid compulsory military service. All through his Conservatory years Barere earned enough income playing in first-class restaurants to support himself and his two younger sisters. Consequently, there was little time for practice; but he graduated in 1919 with the Rubinstein Prize and was appointed professor of piano at the Kiev Conservatory.

In 1920 Barere married Helen Vlashek, also a piano student at the St. Petersburg Conservatory, and they both began concertizing. Neither one could tour abroad because of a ban on foreign travel, and even in Russia the disruptions in the wake of World War I restricted their tours. Within his limited concert sphere, Barere became known as a virtuoso pianist. He finally got out of Russia in 1928, having been assigned as cultural ambassador to the Baltic and Scandinavian countries, with Riga, Latvia, as his base. In due time, his wife and son Boris were permitted to join him.

In 1932 he gave a series of highly successful concerts in Berlin, but within a year his hopes for a career in Germany disappeared in the face of Hitler's ever expanding persecutions of Jews. Compounding misfortune, Barere's manager in London died suddenly, leaving Barere without funds and without bookings. Stranded, he supported his family working at a Hamburg theater, appearing (under an assumed name) four times daily, playing popular classics (such as the Liszt Hungarian Rhapsodies and Chopin Nocturnes) in between animal acts, jugglers and other vaudeville entertainers. In six weeks he earned enough money to get the family to Stockholm, but the strain of having his concert career in limbo and being reduced to playing with vaudeville acts caused a serious breakdown. For about a year Barere stayed away from the piano. To support the family, his wife taught advanced piano students and sometimes gave recitals. When Barere recovered, he did some teaching in Stockholm and gave a few recitals in Scandinavia.

There was finally a breakthrough in his frustrating career. A new manager arranged his British debut recital (16 Jan 1934) at London's Aeolian Hall, and it was a stunning success. "The most astonishing was Blumenfeld's Etude for the Left Hand Alone. . . . If the eye had not seen the right hand resting . . . the ear would have declared it was not possible to range over the whole compass of the keyboard with such consummate ease and unspoiled musical effect with the left hand alone." (*TL*, 19 Jan 1934) Immediately HMV signed Barere for a series of recordings, the first of ten sessions (1934–36) taking place on 30 January 1934. Later that year he made his British orchestral debut at the Queen's Hall, playing the Tchaikovsky Concerto No. 1 with the London Philharmonic Orchestra, conducted by Sir Thomas Beecham. An extensive tour of the British Isles followed.

Success brought more and more invitations to play, including one from the Baldwin Piano Company, which eventually took Barere to America. His American debut (9 Nov 1936) at Carnegie Hall proved an enormous success, and for the rest of his life Barere appeared in New York every year, sometimes twice a year, at either Carnegie Hall or Town Hall. (In 1939 the Bareres settled in the United States.) Touring in North and South America, Australia, and New Zealand, Barere acquired a phenomenal reputation, especially in New York. It seems likely that he was on the verge of a greater international fame when, at a Carnegie Hall concert (2 April 1951), just a few minutes after beginning the Grieg Piano Concerto (his first public performance of this work) with the Philadelphia Orchestra under Eugene Ormandy, Barere suffered a cerebral hemorrhage and died almost immediately.

Barere's boyhood jobs in the movie house and restaurants had allowed little time for practice, and possibly he had little need of practice. His practice habits confounded fellow musicians. Even before the Carnegie Hall recitals, usually his first performance each season, he stayed away from the piano for three or four weeks so as not to become, as he put it, "musically and emotionally stale." This unusual procedure was possible because Barere had an astonishing memory. Once he had a work in his memory and in his fingers, he never forgot it. His friend Fritz Kuttner remembered when Barere, vacationing in Massachusetts in the summer of 1946, was called one day and asked to substitute the following evening at the Brooklyn Academy of Music because Artur Rubinstein had to cancel due to family illness. Barere had not practiced for about three months, but the next night he played Rubinstein's planned program. (Kuttner)

Without question, Barere had an astounding technique: "His running technique is unparalleled, and his octaves might be duplicated by perhaps one or two of his colleagues, but no more." (*NYT*, 18 Nov 1950) Barere's two excellent articles, commissioned by *Etude,* explain his personal definition of technique and give suggestions for developing a strong technique. From *Etude,* November 1946: "Technique means control—of the fingers, the hands, the muscles, of the relationship between the notes to be played, of the dynamics; in short, control of everything that brings the printed page to life as music. Technique enters into the production of a fine singing tone quite as much as it does into the dashing off of fast passage work." From *Etude,* September 1950: "Correct technique means not only striking each note, but placing it—in the fingers, in its context; achieving just the right proportion between voices and in chords; balancing right and left hands for polyphonic emphasis; weighing and controlling musical values. It also means making all these elements so secure that the bridge between conscious and subconscious (one of the most important elements in public performance) may be safely spanned, without worries."

Barere's stupendous repertoire ("he had an unearthly ability to gobble up the hardest pieces in the repertory and then ask for more" [*NYT*, 3 Feb 1976]) consisted mostly of works by Liszt, Chopin and Schumann; some Bach, Scarlatti and Beethoven; several bravura Godowsky transcriptions; and works by his Russian compatriots, especially Scriabin.

Simon Barere was, in essence, a marvelous bravura performer whose playing most of the time was as remarkable for its superb control and dynamics as for its brilliant virtuosity. For about 15 years, from 1936 until his death, the New York critics had the opportunity to hear him every year. Some of their reviews border on the ecstatic. Even those critics who complained (often of Barere's unbelievable speed) invariably praised his wonderful pianism. For example, a reviewer deriding a performance that "abounded in erratic and contradictory features" (extreme tempos, failure to communicate the emotional substance, rhythmic mannerism) also had this to say: "The tone he produced in all dynamic grades and the range and beauty of nuance he encompassed had a soft magic which, in retrospect, became the most conspicuous virtue of his performance and continued to haunt the listener after the recital was over." (*MA,* 25 Dec 1943)

What we glean overall from these many reviews is that Barere may not have been as profound an interpreter as some pianists, but he possessed a rare combination—sensational technique and ravishing tone—that made his playing always a delight to hear. Such a technique led to formidable programs. His American debut recital (9 Nov 1936) included, among other works, the Liszt Sonata in B Minor, Blumenfeld's incredibly difficult Etude For The Left Hand and Balakirev's pyrotechnical fantasy *Islamey*. A year later, Barere's second Carnegie Hall recital (8 Nov 1937) drew an enormous audience and uniformly laudatory reviews: "Mr. Barere's terrific technic drove everything before it. His command of the keyboard is all-embracing. . . . There is another side to the man—the artist fashioning delicate cameos of sound with an uncanny sense of proportion." (*W-T*, 9 Nov 1937)

The critical raves continued through the years, with few negative reviews. After Barere's Town Hall recital on 4 December 1938, one critic flatly declared that, "the immensely gifted Russian pianist must be reckoned among the greatest of all exponents of the keyboard . . . with a technical equipment unrivaled among pianists of the day." (*NYT*, 5 Dec 1938) That same recital overwhelmed another reviewer: "Barere's mechanical equipment is without a peer among pianists at the present time. . . . He is a self-effacing musician of flawless taste, endowed with a kindling imagination and the sensibilities of a true poet." (*NYHT*, 5 Dec 1938)

Perhaps this says it best: "Barere had a prodigious repertory, a prodigious technique. It may be added that he was a prodigious musician, which is not necessarily the same thing. His knowledge was such that many pianists, great and small, sought his counsel as coach and teacher." (*NYT*, 3 April 1951)

Barere made comparatively few studio recordings. There are some *Parlophone/Odéon* 78 rpm discs made shortly after he left Russia and also three early LPs for Remington Records made in the United States (some performances taken from Carnegie Hall recitals). His most impressive discs date from 1934–36, a small selection recorded for HMV (see Discog.).

There are currently available three Appian CD collections of recordings made at Barere's various Carnegie Hall recitals during the years 1946–49 (see Discog.). His son Boris had the recitals recorded but not, of course, under studio conditions or supervision. The results vary but in general point up Barere's great strength and his equally great weakness, which are one and the same—his phenomenal technique. Unfortunately his remarkable facility often dominates. He played many pieces so fast that the entire musical concept is bypassed. Barere obviously stunned his live audiences, who seemingly adored his playing; however, a constant diet of excessive speed quickly bores the late 20th-century ear. At the same time, there are many performances here which show Barere as a consummate musician. "His Liszt Sonata, for example, has both infinite sweetness and an unparalleled daemonic fire. . . . His combination of bravura and delicacy is well exemplified in Liszt's Hungarian Rhapsody No. 12." (*Gram*, Nov 1989) Other fine examples include the Scriabin Etudes, some Godowsky transcriptions, Rachmaninoff's Preludes and Concerto No. 2, Liszt's Petrarch Sonnet No. 104

and also a lovely, remarkably restrained interpretation of Beethoven's Sonata in E Minor, op. 90.

The Complete HMV Recordings 1934–36 (see Discog.), recorded in a studio, reveal another Barere. Relieved of the tensions of live performance, he concentrated solely on his playing, polishing each piece until he was pleased with his performance. One review reads: "Simon Barere's playing is simply breathtaking in its unrestrained vigour and superb technical control, both laid at the feet of a unique and powerful musical insight. This 2-CD set is an essential memorial to one of the greatest, if unsung, heroes of the piano in this century." (Gra/Goo, see Bibliog.) This HMV album contains a good sampling of Liszt, Barere's specialty. The *Gnomenreigen*, recorded at the first session (30 Jan 1934) is a tour de force, confirming Barere's stupendous technique in all its bravura glory. On a larger scale, the Don Juan Fantasy and *Rapsodie espagnole*, both bristling with difficulties, are truly hair-raising performances. Other fine examples of Barere's best playing are heard in the glorious Chopin Scherzo No. 3, Balakirev's colorful *Islamey* and Blumenfeld's unbelievably virtuosic Etude For The Left Hand. These recordings "are of stunning brilliance and poetry, and at their best can seem all but incredible." (Shawe-Taylor)

SELECTED REFERENCES

Barere, Simon. "Developing Technique." *Etude,* Nov 1946, pp. 613–614.
———. "What is Technique?" *Etude*, Sept 1950, pp. 23, 57.
Crimp, Bryan. Liner Notes, Archive Piano Recordings, APR 7001.
Downes, Olin. "Barere Dies Giving Concert. . . ." *New York Times*, 3 April 1951, p. 1.
King, William C. "About Simon Barere." *New York Sun*, 20 Jan 1940, p. 28.
Kolodin, Irving. "Music to My Ears." *Saturday Review*, 14 April 1951, p. 49.
Kuttner, Fritz. "The Incredible Simon Barere." *HiFi-Stereo Review*, April 1966, pp. 52–56.
Rickenbacker, William F. "Simon Barere." *National Review*, 19 March 1990, pp. 58–59.
Schonberg, Harold C. "Some Legendary Playing from Barere." *New York Times*, 13 July 1986, sec. 2, p. 15.
Shawe-Taylor, Desmond. "Record of the Week." *Sunday Times* (London), 6 Oct 1991.
See also Bibliography: Ewe/Li; Ewe/Li2; Rat/Cle; Sal/Fam; Sch/Gre.

SELECTED REVIEWS

MA: 25 Nov 1936; 10 Dec 1940; 25 Dec 1941; 25 Dec 1943; 25 March 1944. *NYHT*: 9 Nov 1937; 5 Dec 1938. *NYT*: 10 Nov 1936; 9 Nov 1937; 5 Dec 1938; 26 Jan 1939; 26 Jan 1940; 25 Nov 1940; 3 Dec 1941; 9 Dec 1943; 2 Dec 1944; 20 Nov 1945; 18 May 1946; 19 Nov 1946; 20 June 1947; 12 Nov 1947; 8 Feb 1949; 19 Nov 1949; 18 Nov 1950. *NYWT*: 9 Nov 1937. *TL*: 19 Jan 1934.

SELECTED DISCOGRAPHY

Romantic Rarities, Volume Two: The 1929 *Odéon* and Off the air Recordings.
Chopin: Etude in F Major, op. 10, no. 8; Impromptu No. 1 in A-flat
Major, op. 29; Scherzo No. 3 in C-sharp Minor, op. 39; Waltz in A-flat
Major, op. 42. Liszt: *Gnomenreigen*; *La Leggierezza*. Rachmaninoff: *Polka
de W. R.* Scarlatti: Sonata in A Major, K. 113. Scriabin: Etude in D-
sharp Minor, op. 8, no. 12. CDAPR 7014.

Simon Barere: The Complete HMV Recordings 1934–36. Balakirev: *Islamey-*
Oriental fantasie. Blumenfeld: Etude for the Left Hand. Chopin: Mazurka
No. 38 in F-sharp Minor, op. 59, no. 3; Scherzo No. 3 in C-sharp Minor,
op. 39; Waltz No. 5 in A Flat, op. 42. Glazunov: Etude in C Major, op.
31, no. 1. Liszt: *Gnomenreigen*; *La Leggierezza*; Petrarch Sonnet No. 104;
Rapsodie espagnole; *Reminiscences de Don Juan*; *Valse oubliée* No. 1.
Loeillet-Godowsky: Gigue. Rameau-Godowsky: *Tambourin*. Schumann:
Toccata in C Major, op. 7. Scriabin: Etude in C-sharp Minor, op. 2, no. 1;
Etude in D-sharp Minor, op. 8, no. 12. Archive Piano Recordings,
CDAPR 7001.

Simon Barere at the Carnegie Hall, Volume One. Liszt: Concerto No. 1 in E-
flat Major; *Funérailles*; *Gnomenreigen*; Hungarian Rhapsody No. 12;
Petrarch Sonnet No. 104; *Rapsodie espagnole*, Sonata in B Minor; *Valse de
l'opéra Faust*. CDAPR 7007. Brockman/SO.

Simon Barere at the Carnegie Hall, Volume Two. Bach: Chromatic Fantasia and
Fugue in D Minor, BWV 903. Balakirev: *Islamey*. Blumenfeld: Etude for
the Left Hand. Corelli-Godowsky: Pastorale in G Major. Glazunov: Etude
in C Major, op. 31, no. 1. Loeillet-Godowsky: Gigue in E Major.
Rachmaninoff: Concerto No. 2 in C Minor, op. 18; *Polka de W.R.*; Prelude
in G Minor, op. 23, no. 5; Prelude in G-sharp Minor, op. 32, no. 12.
Rameau-Godowsky: *Tambourin* in E Minor. Schumann: Toccata in C
Major, op. 7; *Traumes Wirren*, op. 12, no. 7. Scriabin: Etude in D-flat
Major, op. 8, no. 10; Etude in D-sharp Minor, op. 8, no. 12. Weber:
Presto from Sonata No. 1 in C Major. CDAPR 7008.

Simon Barere at the Carnegie Hall, Volume Three. Beethoven: Sonata in E
Minor, op. 90. Chopin: *Andante spianato* and *Grande Polonaise*, op. 22;
Ballade in G Minor, op. 23; Etudes, op. 10, nos. 4, 5, 8; Fantasy in F
Minor, op. 49; Nocturne in D-flat Major, op. 27, no. 2; Scherzo in C-sharp
Minor, op. 39; Waltz in A-flat Major,op. 29. Liszt: *La leggierezza*, *Un
sospiro*. Schumann: *Carnaval*. Weber: Presto from Sonata No. 1 in C
Major. CDAPR 7009.

BAUER, HAROLD: b. New Malden, Surrey, England, 28 April 1873; d. Miami, Florida, 12 March 1951.

> It is for his ability to convey music in such human terms that he will
> be most lovingly remembered.
>   Edward Blickstein (IPA Album 112, Liner Notes)

Harold Bauer began his musical career as a professional violinist, but at age 22 he changed over to the piano. Remarkably, from that late start he proceeded to achieve international fame as a master pianist. Exactly how Bauer accomplished his piano skills has never been clearly explained.

He studied hard and worked hard to become a violinist. His piano training, on the other hand, was sketchy—some early piano lessons from a maternal aunt and, as a young man, more advanced piano instruction from Graham Moore, a Glasgow piano teacher and professor of piano at the Royal College of Music. Bauer also had some early, informal instruction in setting and correcting harmony and counterpoint exercises, apparently all the theory he ever studied, given to him by his father's business assistant, who played the organ. Perhaps more important to Bauer's piano training were the informal piano practice sessions he had with Ignace Paderewski. The fact remains, however, that there is no evidence of Bauer's ever studying with an important pedagogue or attending a conservatory. He was rare, a self-taught pianist who became a master pianist. And that may partly explain Bauer's "ability to convey music in such human terms."

His family was musical. His father Victor Bauer, of German ancestry, was a public accountant and also an excellent amateur violinist who often played piano quartets and quintets with family members and friends. Determined that his children would know music, Victor Bauer frequently took them to the Pops concerts held in London, thus from early childhood Bauer heard recitals by celebrated musicians, among them Anton Rubinstein, Clara Schumann, Paderewski, Joseph Joachim, Vladimir de Pachmann, Pablo de Sarasate, Hans von Bülow and Eugène Ysaÿe.

Bauer studied the violin with his father, and at age 10 played for Joachim, who offered to place him at the newly established National Training School for Music. For some reason, Bauer's father refused the offer. Instead, he sent his son to study with Adolf Pollitzer, the Hungarian violinist who at age 13 had played for Mendelssohn.

Bauer never attended school. His (English) mother Mary (Taylor) Bauer and her sister taught the children reading and writing. They studied arithmetic with their father and studied history, geography and languages with two tutors, one French and one German. The Bauer children often performed publicly, and two or three times a year Bauer and his sister Ethel, a fine pianist, gave concerts at Prince's Hall. They also played at the Crystal Palace under August Manns, Bauer on one occasion playing Henri Vieuxtemps's *Fantasia Appassionata* for violin, another time Vieuxtemps' Violin Concerto No. 4 in D Minor.

At age 12 Bauer gave a solo recital in London, playing both the violin and piano. Critic Louis Engel bluntly dismissed him for having more audacity

than talent. Undaunted, Bauer still would occasionally make a serious attempt at
the piano even though he disliked his tone and had endless problems with technique. He always returned gratefully to the violin. But his violin career moved
slowly. By age 19, convinced that his progress in England had come to a stand-
still, he wanted desperately to try his chances in Europe. Having no money, he
might never have left England had not two benefactors unexpectedly sent him
£50 "to be used to go abroad with."

Before he could leave England, Bauer had to fulfill violin engagements
in the provinces and in Scotland. It was in Glasgow that he met Graham Moore,
who took Bauer to a Paderewski recital and afterward introduced him to the
Polish pianist. Bauer played both the violin and the piano for Paderewski, and
was advised that he played the piano very nicely but had a lot to learn, and that
he should go to Paris to study violin with Paderewski's friend Wladyslaw
Górski. Paderewski proved to be a faithful, sympathetic patron. Daniel Mayer,
Paderewski's business manager, added Bauer to his list of clients, and in 1892
Mayer booked Bauer for a piano (not a violin) recital at the Erard building in
London. Despite his exceedingly difficult program, Bauer's recital attracted little
notice.

He finally made it to Paris in the spring of 1893. Paderewski was away
concertizing, but Bauer contacted the Górskis, who kindly invited him to their
musical receptions. (It is noteworthy that at this early period Górski considered
Bauer to be a better pianist than violinist, and that Górski invited Bauer to be his
accompanist at his annual concert.) Bauer practiced the violin intensively in
Paris and, although in those early years he had no intention of becoming a pianist, he often filled his free time practicing the piano. Giving violin lessons
and doing accompanist work helped to stretch his £50. Life was not easy, but
Bauer adored Paris, his home for more than 20 years.

Once returned to Paris, Paderewski drafted Bauer to help him to enlarge
his repertoire, specifically to play orchestral reductions on a second piano while
Paderewski worked on the concertos he needed to learn. Their meetings often
ended with Bauer consulting Paderewski about problems he was encountering as
a pianist, and Bauer always believed that from these sessions he learned a great
deal about the piano. He also managed to get some violin engagements, but
since Paris at that particular time had an oversupply of talented young violinists,
among them Jacques Thibaud and Henri Marteau, Bauer made little headway
against that competition. Searching for other ways to boost Bauer's income, the
kindly Paderewski in 1894 introduced Bauer to an elderly, wealthy Polish aristocrat (identified in *Harold Bauer: His Book* only as Marshal Théodore) who wanted
someone to play violin sonatas with him. The old gentleman was a dreadful
pianist, but he was kind and generous to Bauer, and their association lasted
several years.

Ultimately it was chance that turned Bauer from the violin to the piano.
He received an invitation to tour Russia with an American singer named Louise
Nikita (Nicholson) during the 1894–95 season, Bauer's job being to accompany
Nikita's songs and also to play violin numbers in the interludes. Nikita's uncle-
manager assured Bauer that in the large Russian cities it would be easy to find
pianists to play accompaniments for his violin solos. However, while they were

rehearsing in Berlin, the Emperor Alexander III died, and the Russian court canceled all public performances for a six-week mourning period. But Nikita's tour proceeded on schedule, her canny manager having quickly arranged bookings at private clubs in smaller Russian cities, where such clubs allowed the public to attend performances.

These changes affected Bauer's role for the entire tour. Since few small cities could provide the necessary pianist to accompany his violin solos, he was forced to play piano solos in the interludes. And, at the end of the mourning period, when the tour moved into the larger cities, Nikita's manager still refused to hire pianists to accompany Bauer's violin performances, declaring that he liked Bauer's piano playing and there was no need for additional expense. Bauer toured with Nikita for five months, strictly as a pianist. When he returned to Paris in the late spring of 1895, very few violin jobs were available, and increasingly he made his living from playing piano accompaniments, in the process becoming more and more experienced as a pianist. Some of his friends finally decided to pay the expenses for a piano recital at the *Salle Erard*, the start, Bauer often said, of his career as a pianist.

Unintentionally and circuitously, Bauer had become a professional pianist, but certainly a pianist facing horrendous problems. Never having attended a conservatory or studied with a special teacher, he had no proper technique and no idea as to how to acquire one. Problems of technique happened to be very much on his mind as he watched a young dancer (Isadora Duncan) entertain guests at a private party. As she danced to classical music that Bauer knew by heart, it struck him that her gestures illustrated all the dynamic variations of the musical phrase: vigorous gestures for loud tones, delicate gestures for soft tones. He wondered, as he watched, whether he might use his hands as she used her body. In his book and elsewhere in print, Bauer relates how he tried his idea at the piano, making a vigorous attack to achieve a loud tone, a gentle gesture for a soft tone. His practicing, he admitted, was awkward, angular and ridiculous, but he kept experimenting until he found the right gesture to produce the tone he wanted to hear. Somehow this unorthodox, purely physical approach to piano technique worked for Bauer. Created out of sheer necessity, it became an ingrained habit. With experience, he discovered that mental concentration away from the piano reduced his mechanical practice to a minimum.

At this early stage he had no grand ambitions about a career as a pianist. He merely hoped his piano playing would sound well enough to earn 50 francs at his next Saturday night performance. But that autumn (1895) Daniel Mayer booked Bauer for two piano engagements in Berlin, one with the Berlin Philharmonic Orchestra and one a solo recital. Bauer's highly successful performance with the BPO induced other symphony orchestras in some of the large German cities to invite him to play later that season. The Berlin solo recital was not as successful, mostly because Bauer played unfamiliar works. That same season three appearances with orchestras in Spain supplied him with funds to pay for two recitals in Amsterdam. By a stroke of good fortune, Willem Mengelberg, conductor of the *Concertgebouw* Orchestra, attended one of those recitals and invited Bauer to play at the next *Concertgebouw* concert. Thus began Bauer's enormously successful career in Holland, a country that for years afterward provided a major portion of his income.

Bauer now worked intensively at the piano, using his trial-and-error method but always guided by his innate musical taste. Performing often, he slowly built a reputation and eventually mastered a repertoire (as large as that of any pianist of his time) spanning four centuries. Known especially for his performances of Beethoven, Brahms and Schumann, Bauer also included some "modern" works in his repertoire. He played a great deal of Debussy (he gave the first performance of The Children's Corner) and Ravel (*Ondine* from *Gaspard de la nuit* is dedicated to Bauer).

In 1900 Sebastian Benson Schlesinger, a wealthy Boston businessman and amateur musician living in Paris, arranged for Bauer to play a pair of concerts with the Boston Symphony Orchestra, conducted by Wilhelm Gericke. For his Boston debut (30 Nov 1900) Bauer chose to play the Brahms Concerto No. 1 in D Minor, unaware that Boston audiences cared little for Brahms's music and that critic Philip Hale absolutely detested it. Hale's review (1 Dec 1900) of the first concert, while heartily condemning Brahms and his music, praised Bauer's playing, particularly his virtuosity and musicianship.

Within three months of his Boston debut, Bauer had made about 30 appearances in the United States. His reputation spread quickly, his prestige soared. Ever more in demand, he made extensive concert tours in both Europe and America right up to the beginning of the First World War. During that war Bauer raised funds (giving recitals and selling photographs and autographs) for needy musicians in France, for which wartime services the French government in 1927 awarded him the Cross of the *Légion d'honneur*. After the war Bauer resumed his career at full speed. From 1914 he lived in the United States, and in 1921 he became an American citizen. He gave concerts until just before World War II, playing his last formal New York recital at Town Hall on 15 January 1939.

A lifelong advocate of musical endeavors, in 1919 Bauer founded and became president (1919–39) of the Beethoven Association of New York to introduce music lovers to the seldom-played works of Beethoven and other composers. When the group disbanded in 1940, all assets, including its collection of books written on Beethoven, were given to the New York Public Library.

In retirement (he lived in Long Island, New York, and wintered in Miami), Bauer devoted himself to musical education, his goal being to elevate the standards of piano instruction in the United States. Under the auspices of the Association of American Colleges, he visited (over a six-year period) more than 100 campuses, where he talked with students about his own field of music and the importance of relating all branches of learning.

Bauer taught all his life, both private students and master classes. He lectured at the New England Conservatory, the Peabody Conservatory, Mills College, Texas State University, the University of Miami and Louisiana State University. He helped to organize the Manhattan School of Music in New York and for many years was joint head of its piano faculty. During his last 10 years Bauer gave annual master classes at the University of Miami and at Louisiana

State University. From 1945 until his death, he served as music counselor at the University of Miami's School of Music.

While living in Paris, Bauer had married (1906) a German woman named Marie Knapp, who died in 1940. His second wife was Winnie Pyle, a pianist. There were no children.

It is not surprising that Harold Bauer, whose earliest memories included the sounds of quartet music played by family and friends, had a rare sympathy for ensemble music. He played with many famous instrumentalists, among them Pablo Casals, Ossip Gabrilowitch, Jacques Thibaud, Fritz Kreisler, Efrem Zimbalist and Nathan Milstein. Should proof of his great devotion to ensemble playing be required, it lies in the fact that in one day (12 Dec 1911) he gave a long solo recital at Carnegie Hall in the afternoon and that evening played a program with the Kneisel Quartet at the ballroom of the Hotel Astor.

While still in his teens, he had founded a string quartet (Carl Engel was second violin) in London. Years later he enjoyed two great partnerships, one with Casals, the other with Gabrilowitch. For years Bauer and Casals played concerts together around the world whenever and wherever their respective schedules permitted. The joyous two-piano recitals he gave with Gabrilowitch, begun just before World War I, attracted much attention and spurred interest in the art. Because of the limited two-piano repertoire, Bauer made two-piano arrangements of works originally composed for four hands at one piano. Playing before packed houses, these two virtuoso pianists performed together until Gabrilowitch's untimely death in 1936. Even now their recording of the Arensky Waltz gets a rave notice: "A lovelier piano disc has never been made." (Sch/Gre, see Bibliog.)

Bauer claimed not to practice scales or exercises, maintaining that the pianist will find all the technical work required in the great piano works themselves. In his view, developing technique through mechanical exercises and scales would cause students to lose their individuality, which to Bauer was the keynote of all great playing. Despite his attitude toward technique and technical exercises, Bauer published two slender volumes of materials to aid the pianist's technique and facility: *The Pianist's Warming-Up Exercises* and *A Primer for Practical Keyboard Modulation.*

Pianists may attract their audiences with awesome virtuosity, a lovely tone, sheer personal magnetism, or a probing intellect. With Harold Bauer, it was his radiating warmth and deep musicality that captivated his audiences. He was a sincere musician who dearly loved to play the piano, and people loved to hear him because he made beautiful music. That was the essence of Bauer's cultivated, musicianly style.

Conveying the intent of the composer took precedence over displaying personal talent. He was always concerned with the style and historical perspective of the music; yet within this studied framework Bauer, with his wondrous tone and, when called for, moments of passion and virtuosity, could create a very special magic. His tonal command was always a source of amazement, and probably his early training as a violinist had a great deal to do with the sound he was able to evoke from the piano. Bauer's remarkable tone, said James Huneker, was "the warmest, mellow tone heard since Paderewski. His fingers always sing whether in velocity or cantabile passages . . . and at times a color sense becomes overpowering, suggesting Pachman in his most sensuous mood." (International Piano Archives LP 112, Liner Notes)

Bauer was noted for his concerto performances, particularly those of Schumann and Brahms. When he played the Brahms Concerto No. 1 in D Minor at his Boston debut, the eminent critic Philip Hale, despite loathing Brahms's music, liked Bauer's playing. "He was one of the orchestra in a sym-phonic work. His phrasing was thoughtful, intelligent; in a word, he played like a most accomplished pianist who is also an accomplished musician. . . . He played with unaffected ease with the authority of a master of his subject." (*MA*, 22 Nov 1913)

Bauer played (judging from the review) an absolutely spectacular all-Schumann recital (27 Feb 1925) at Aeolian Hall. "*He is the past master of Schumann's piano style.* . . . He played Schumann yesterday as if he were im-provising his own music and no other method of pianistic expression were com-prehensible to him. With Schumann he was wistful, confiding, impulsive or nobly prophetic, and always a poet. . . . The climax of the afternoon was the playing of the 'Fantasia.' This interpretation touched the heights and depths of music and accomplished this within as perfectly proportioned a scheme of dy-namics as ever we heard." (*NYT*, 28 Feb 1925)

The distinguished critic Richard Aldrich greatly admired Bauer's playing, and undoubtedly Aldrich's enthusiastic reviews furthered Bauer's career in America. "He stands apart from most of the virtuosos upon the piano in the profoundly artistic nature of what he does, in the high distinction of his playing, in the entire disregard of any personal display or any personal effect. . . . And while he is remarkably accomplished as a technician . . . there is that in his playing which is lifted above all considerations of technique, and technique is thereby put into its rightful place as a means to an end." (Ald/Con, see Bibliog.)

Three decades later at his last formal concert (15 Jan 1939), Bauer was still firmly in command, still delighting his audiences with his fabled velvety tone and innate musicianship. "His was the playing of one rich with memories of the past, communicating through tones consolatory and heartfelt messages for those ready to receive them. These he conveyed with an all-enveloping lyricism that purposely suppressed the exteriorly dramatic aspects of certain composi-tions, thereby investing them with new and more subtle meanings." (*NYT*, 16 Jan 1939)

In the 1920s Bauer recorded many piano rolls, mostly for the Duo-Art label (Sit/Cla, see Bibliog.). Some of them are now available on LP. Even those who downplay the idea of the player-piano must admit that these rolls are done to perfection and, particularly the Chopin album, are valuable testimonials to Bauer's talent. He often recorded in New York at the Aeolian Company's huge building on 42nd Street, which contained one of the most beautiful audito-riums of the time. He also spent innumerable hours in the office editing and correcting the paper rolls on which his performances had been mechanically recorded for the pianola, later electrified and renamed the Duo-Art.

Bauer believed that he was the first pianist to make a recording of a concerto (piano score only) for performance with a symphony orchestra. That Duo-Art roll of Saint-Saëns's Concerto in G Minor was performed (17 Nov 1917) at Aeolian Hall in New York City. The New York Symphony Society, conducted by Walter Damrosch, played a live onstage accompaniment to Bauer's piano roll of the Concerto. It was a sensational success—Bauer was in Chicago at the time!

Bauer also made many acoustic and electric discs which, discounting the faulty sound production, can be enjoyed and studied. His recording of the Liszt Etude in D-flat Major, with its shimmering arpeggios, is a lovely study in grace and a clear example of his control of tone and dynamics (see Discog.). The impressive general anthology (RCA, see Discog.) contains two Schumann pieces played in the manner for which Bauer was famous—passionate but intimate and lyrically dramatic. A trio of short compositions by Grieg and the Brahms Capriccio, op. 76, no. 2, substantiate Bauer's reputation as a master of the keyboard miniature.

Biddulph has initiated a complete edition (3 CDs) of Harold Bauer's recordings. The first CD (see Discog.) contains pressings from 1924–1928. "Bauer's eminently civilized pianism" is still highly enjoyable. This is playing of "flexibility, fluency, and unfailing good taste . . . refreshing for its unpretentiousness and absence of eccentricities." (*ARG*, March/April 1993) The second CD contains probably Bauer's finest solo recording—the Brahms Sonata No. 3 in F Minor, op. 5—made in 1939 when the pianist was in his mid-sixties. This massive work calls for the utmost tonal resources and digital dexterity as well as profound musicianship. Bauer's performance, mature and conditioned by time, is magnificent. A third and final Bauer album will include Schumann's *Fantasiestücke*, op. 12.

SELECTED REFERENCES

Bauer, Harold. "Artistic Aims in Pianoforte Playing." *Etude*, March 1912, pp. 163–164.

———. "Artistic Aspects of Piano Study." In Cooke, *Great Pianists on Piano Playing*, see Bibliog., pp. 64–78.

———. "Education as Emancipation." *Etude*, May 1948, pp. 287, 296.

———. *Harold Bauer: His Book.* New York: W. W. Norton, 1948; Greenwood Press, 1969.

———. "Leading the Pupil to Think While Practicing." *Etude*, March 1914, pp. 169–170.

———. "The Pianist's Palette." *Etude*, Nov 1921, pp. 703–704. Also see Bibliog. Coo/Gre.

———. *The Pianist's Warming-Up Exercises.* New York: G. Schirmer, Inc., 1950.

———. "The Present-Day Significance of Chopin." *Etude*, Feb 1926, pp. 99–100.

————. *A Primer for Practical Keyboard Modulation.* New York: G. Schirmer, Inc., n. d.

————. "Radical Methods in Modern Pianoforte Instruction." *Etude*, March 1916, pp. 171–172.

————. "The Road to Expression." *Etude*, April 1912, p. 253.

————. "Self-Portrait of the Artist as a Young Man." *Musical Quarterly*, April 1943, pp. 153–168.

Brower, Harriette. "Power and Velocity at the Piano." *Musical America*, 18 April 1914, p. 27.

————. "The Question of Piano Tone." *Musical America*, 16 Aug 1913, p. 11. Also see Bibliog. Bro/Pia.

"From the Correspondence of Harold Bauer and O. G. Sonneck." In *A Birthday Offering to Carl Engel.* New York: G. Schirmer, Inc., 1943, pp. 39–47.

Obituary. *The Miami Herald*, 13 March 1951, pp. 1, 4. *New York Times*, 13 March 1951, p. 31.

Russell, Alexander. "Harold Bauer as a Teacher." *Musical America*, 30 Oct 1915, pp. 9–10.

See also Bibliography: Bro/Pia; Coo/GrP; Ewe/Li; Ewe/Li2; Ewe/Mu; Ger/Fam; Kau/Art; Kir/Pab; New/Gro; Nie/Mei; Reu/Gre; Rub/MyM; Rub/MyY; Sal/Fam; Sch/Gre; Woo/My.

SELECTED REVIEWS

MA: 5 Jan 1907; 1 Feb 1907; 25 April 1908; 29 Jan 1910; 14 May 1910; 1 April 1911; 2 Dec 1911; 13 Jan 1912; 27 April 1912; 28 Dec 1912; 1 Nov 1913; 17 Jan 1914; 2 Jan 1915; 23 Jan 1915; 30 Jan 1915; 8 Jan 1916; 28 March 1916; 4 Nov 1916; 24 Nov 1917; 27 Oct 1928; 10 March 1929; 25 Jan 1939. *MT*: 1 July 1922; 1 Dec 1922; 1 Nov 1927; 1 July 1929. *NYHT*: 28 Feb 1925. *NYT*: 11 March 1906; 13 Dec 1911; 18 Jan 1912; 26 Oct 1913; 12 Jan 1914; 1 Jan 1919; 28 Feb 1925; 14 March 1927; 16 Feb 1930; 6 April 1930; 19 Oct 1930; 7 Dec 1930; 23 Dec 1930; 16 Jan 1939. *SFC*: 6 March 1912; 3 March 1926. *TL*: 13 March 1911.

SELECTED DISCOGRAPHY

Harold Bauer Concert. Chopin: *Fantaisie Impromptu*; Polonaise, op. 26, no. 1. Saint-Saëns: Concerto in G Minor. Schubert: Serenade; Swan Songs. Weber: *Rondo brillante.* Phonodisc Everest X 911, 1966. From piano rolls.

Harold Bauer plays Beethoven, Brahms and Liszt. Bach: Chorale from Cantata No. 147. Beethoven: Andante cantabile and Variations from Quartet, op. 18, no. 5. Boccherini: Minuet in A. Brahms: Intermezzo, op. 117, no. 1; Capriccio, op. 76, no. 5; Hungarian Dances nos. 5, 6, 8. Haydn: Gypsy Rondo. Liszt: *Eclogue*; Etude (Paganini) No. 2. Schubert-Liszt: Serenade (No. 4 of Swan Songs). Klavier KS-130. From piano rolls.

Harold Bauer plays Chopin. Sonata No. 3 in B Minor; Fantasy in F Minor, op. 49; Scherzo, op. 39; Polonaise, op. 26, no. 1. Klavier KS 113. From piano rolls.

Harold Bauer: The 1924–28 Victor Recordings. Bach-Bauer: Jesu, Joy of Man's Desiring. Bauer: Barberini's Minuet; Motley & Flourish. Beethoven: Sonata in C-sharp Minor, op. 27, no. 2; Sonata in F Minor, op. 57. Chopin: Impromptu in A-flat Major, op. 29; Fantaisie-Impromptu in C-sharp Minor, op. 66. Durand: Waltz in E-flat Major. Gluck-Saint-Saëns: Air de Ballet. Liszt: *Un Sospiro.* Rubinstein: *Kamennoi-Ostrow.* Schubert: Impromptu, D. 899, no. 4. Schumann: *In der Nacht.* Schütt: *A la bien aimée.* Biddulph LHW OO7 (CD). The first of three projected CDs.

Harold Bauer: The Schirmer Recordings. Bach: Prelude and Fugue in C-sharp Major. Brahms: Capriccio, op. 76, no. 2; Sonata No. 3 in F Minor, op. 5; Waltzes nos. 15 and 16. Chopin: *Berceuse.* Couperin: *Le Carillon de Cythère.* Debussy: *Clair de lune; Rêverie.* Grieg: *Albumblatt,* op. 28, no. 3. Handel: Harmonious Blacksmith. Mendelssohn: *Characterstück* in A Major, op. 7, no. 4.. Scarlatti: Sonata, K. 62. Schubert: *Moment musical* no. 3. Schumann: Novelette in D; Romance in B-flat Minor, op. 28, no. 1. Biddulph LHW 009. The second of three projected CDs.

Keyboard Giants of the Past. Arensky: Waltz from Suite, op. 15 (with O. Gabrilowitsch). RCA SP-33-143.

BOLET, JORGE: b. Havana, Cuba, 15 November 1914; d. Mountain View, California, 16 October 1990.

He played in his own way, and the world eventually caught up.
Harold C. Schonberg (*New York Times,* 17 October 1990)

Jorge Bolet (he pronounced it "George," and the final "t" is sounded) was a grand Romantic pianist, a throwback, if you will, to the age of superpianists like Sergei Rachmaninoff and Josef Hofmann. Like them, Bolet was an individualist. In the last half of the 20th century, decades largely dominated by a musicologically pure, very precise style of piano playing, Jorge Bolet gloried in music making that went beyond playing the correct notes to transforming those notes into musical tones that appealed, as he put it, to the heart and soul.

He was one of six children born to Antonio and Adelina (Tremoleda) Bolet, both of Catalan ancestry. There could not have been too much income from the minor position his father held in the Cuban army, yet the children had music lessons. Bolet's older sister Maria became a pianist, his brother Alberto a conductor. At a very young age Bolet began to sit beside Maria whenever she played or practiced. He learned to turn pages, in time became familiar with the repertoire she played and at about age seven began formal piano lessons with Maria. An excellent and devoted teacher, she even exercised his hands by flattening each palm and stretching the hand from one side to the other, especially the

spaces between fingers. She taught Bolet until 1927, the year he entered the
Curtis Institute of Music in Philadelphia, and meanwhile he also had about a
year of study with Hubert de Blanch, director of the National Conservatory in
Havana.

Bolet played his first public recital at age nine and at age twelve played
the Mozart Concerto in D Minor, K. 466, with the Havana Symphony
Orchestra, conducted by Gonzalo Roig. Sometimes he played at the monthly
soirees held by Mrs. Amelia Hoskinson, a Cuban married to an American and
one of Bolet's benefactors. She learned about the newly opened Curtis Institute
of Music, immediately sent for a catalogue and an application blank and organized a morning benefit concert (4 Sept 1927) to raise funds to send Bolet and his
sister to Philadelphia for the audition. Bolet passed, and that October began piano studies with David Saperton at Curtis.

Since Bolet was so young—he turned 13 a month after starting at
Curtis—his sister Maria stayed in Philadelphia to look after him. She devoted
herself to his career, even to the point of sitting with him as he practiced. Maria
had taught Bolet well. Saperton drilled him with heavy doses of scales in sixths
and thirds, exercises from Joseffy's *School of Advanced Piano Playing* and etudes
of Cramer, Clementi and Henselt; but he never altered Bolet's technique. Bolet
also had the advantage of having a wonderful memory, not a photographic memory but what he called a very strong ear memory. "My memory is 98 percent
ear." (*CL*, Oct 1983) At Curtis he could memorize any piece within a week.

As soon as Saperton (he was Leopold Godowsky's son-in-law) realized
the full degree of young Bolet's technical fluency, he assigned him some of
Godowsky's works, and had him play them for Godowsky. From time to time,
Bolet also played for Josef Hofmann, then director of Curtis. Under Saperton's
guidance, Bolet acquired a repertoire of about a dozen concertos and 10 recital
programs. While at Curtis, he also often accompanied singers and instrumentalists, especially Marcel Tabuteau, oboist with the Philadelphia Orchestra, and
thus learned a large chamber and vocal repertoire. All his life he enjoyed playing
chamber music, and though a thunderous virtuoso pianist, Bolet "played like a
born chamber musician, submerging his piano in accompanying sections, coming to the fore for his solos and always blending with the strings." (*NYT*, 17
Dec 1972)

In June 1934 Bolet graduated from both the Curtis Institute and the
Stony Brook Preparatory School in Long Island. "Those were the happy years,"
he told an interviewer in 1973, but some of his friends believe that the seven
years at Curtis were not all happiness. Curtis was a demanding school and
Saperton a hard master. Bryce Morrison, who is writing Bolet's biography for
Faber and Faber, describes Saperton as the kind of teacher who used bullying and
sarcasm as well as constructive criticism. Thus Bolet, young and virtually alone
in a strange country with an unfamiliar language, faced the added pressure of difficult studies and a strict teacher. Besides, he must have worried about proving
himself worthy to repay those who had spent time and money getting him to
Curtis and, most of all, he must have missed his way of life at home in Cuba.
Taken together, in Morrison's view the years at Curtis left their mark, creating
"a dark, disjunct and perverse" side to his nature. As a result, the adult Bolet

"cloaked his highly affectionate nature in an often awkward and impenetrable reserve." (*Gram*, Jan 1991)

The Republic of Cuba provided a monthly stipend and a special diplomatic passport to help Bolet in starting a concert career. He spent about nine months in Paris and another in London mostly practicing and listening to a great deal of music. He gave a recital in Amsterdam on 8 May 1935—according to Bolet, his professional recital debut—and other recitals at The Hague, Vienna, London, Paris, Milan, Berlin, Madrid and Oviedo.

In 1936 Bolet returned to Curtis to study conducting with Boris Goldovsky and Fritz Reiner. The next year he won the Naumburg Foundation Award, which made possible his "striking debut" at Town Hall on 26 October 1937. In 1939 he was appointed assistant to Rudolf Serkin, head of the piano department at Curtis. Whenever Serkin was away concertizing, Bolet took over his classes and he also had a few pupils of his own. He continued to teach all through his career. Not that he especially liked teaching, only that for many years he had to teach to support himself; and after he became successful, he still taught, believing it his duty to pass along the Romantic traditions. He taught at the Curtis Institute (1939–42) and at the University of Indiana at Bloomington (1968–77). In 1977 he succeeded Rudolf Serkin as head of the piano department at Curtis, resigning that position in May 1986 because of his extremely busy concert and recording schedules.

Honest and strict with his students, Bolet told them exactly where they stood and what they might expect, giving praise when due. "When a student does something really beautifully, I believe in letting him know." (Eld/Pia, see Bibliog.) He found modern students tended to overpractice and neglect their greater education, and urged his own students to study everything they possibly could to broaden their minds and not limit their lives to just the piano.

Having been ordered by President Batista to serve in the Cuban army, Bolet resigned from Curtis in 1942 and served as assistant military attaché at the Cuban Embassy in Washington, D.C. Two years later, when Batista lost reelection, Bolet resigned his post and enrolled as a private in the United States Army. Promoted to second lieutenant, he served with the army of occupation in Japan in a special services unit, mostly organizing entertainment for the troops. In August 1946 he conducted Gilbert and Sullivan's *The Mikado* with full orchestra (predominantly Japanese), the first performance of this work ever seen in Japan. He also played several times with the Nippon Philharmonic Orchestra.

Bolet returned to civilian life in 1946 and, as an American citizen, began his concert career. His progress was dishearteningly slow. Although he played often during the late 1940s and through the 1950s, he attracted little notice. Despite fine reviews, Bolet failed to find the right connections for success. During that long stretch of lean years, only the generosity of friends and his own self-confidence sustained him. Being chosen to play the piano for *Song Without End* (1960), a film based on the life of Franz Liszt, brought Bolet's name to public attention; but another decade passed (Bolet was then well into his fifties) before he became famous.

Why this late turnabout in his career even happened is really not clear. One explanation: "Bolet's performances, with their inimitable beauty of line and shimmering sonority, their poetic freedom within a basic pulse, were like some serene and final distillation of all he had learnt and known, the massive and legendary virtuosity of earlier days directed into an ever increasing concern with more durable musical truths." (*Gram*, Jan 1991) Or, according to Gregor Benko, president of the International Piano Archives (Bolet willed his personal papers to IPA), Bolet's performance at the multipianist (Alicia de Larrocha, Earl Wild, Guiomar Novaes, Rosalyn Tureck, among others) IPA benefit concert on 3 October 1970 gave the needed spark to his career. In this grand company, Bolet's "absolutely transcendental" performance eclipsed all others. Bolet himself wondered if audiences, perhaps tired of piano interpretations "bound to a rigid set of absolutes" and tired of pianists who had become "computerized mechanisms," had developed a new attitude about Romantic music and the way in which it was played. And Bolet, of course, was one of only a handful of veteran pianists (Shura Cherkassky and Earl Wild, for example) who could convincingly bring Romantic music to life. (Benko)

Whatever the reasons, suddenly Bolet's popularity soared. On 21 September 1971 he was a last-minute replacement for an ailing André Watts, performing the Liszt *Totentanz* with the New York Philharmonic Orchestra, conducted by Pierre Boulez. On 12 October he gave a spectacular performance of Prokofiev's Concerto No. 2 with the American Symphony Orchestra under Leopold Stokowski. On 12 November Bolet appeared again with the NYPO, performing Liszt's Fantasy on Beethoven's Ruins of Athens and Chopin's *Andante spianato* and *Grande Polonaise*, with Michael Tilson Thomas conducting. On 5 February 1972 Bolet played a solo recital at Alice Tully Hall, and that season he also signed a recording contract with RCA. From that dizzying point, Jorge Bolet never slowed down. Making whirlwind tours and repeated appearances with the world's great orchestras, at his peak he was giving about 150 concerts yearly. He became, essentially, the symbol of the Romantic revival in pianism, and he absolutely looked the part. Very tall and darkly handsome, at the piano his brooding air and reserve epitomized the image of a glamorous Romantic idol.

With his friends, however, Bolet remained warm and affectionate. A bachelor and (his own words) "a loner," he devoted his life to music. He was a good amateur photographer and loved racy sports cars. Health problems slowed his career in late 1988. In the summer of 1989 he underwent brain surgery, from which he apparently never fully recovered. He made his final New York appearance at Carnegie Hall on 16 April 1989 and gave his last solo recital at the West Berlin *Philharmonie* on 8 June 1989. Jorge Bolet died of heart failure on 16 October 1990.

From childhood on, Jorge Bolet had the good fortune to hear live performances of almost all the great pianists of this century. The idols of his youth—Godowsky, Lhévinne, Moiseiwitsch, Cortot, and especially Rachmaninoff and Hofmann—remained his lifelong inspiration. They flourished in an era when almost all great performers—pianists, violinists, cellists, even some conductors—were Romantics. Audiences attended concerts not only to hear the works of a certain composer but to hear what a specific performer had to say about that music. Like his idols, Bolet believed that freedom and spontaneity bring life to music making. He placed the performer on an equal, if not superior, footing with the composer. For his taste, modern pianists are far too subservient to the score—each one a carbon copy of all the others. Striving only for mechanical perfection, these "musical computers," as he called them, know how to play the piano but not how to make music.

Bolet had very decided ideas about how to perform Romantic music: It is stylistically wrong to play it in a musically correct but non-Romantic way, which does not mean, however, that the performer has an absolutely free hand. Not at all. Bolet insisted that in order to achieve the desired freedom and spontaneity, the pianist must adhere to the greatest rhythmic discipline possible. He therefore concentrated on the music, not giving particular attention to the process. For him, the mechanics came easily. Even as a child he had a natural facility at the keyboard, with the additional advantage of being a fast learner. Bolet never had to practice endless hours, being able to learn in about an hour what another pianist might take four hours to accomplish.

Since Bolet would not play a work if he did not really feel the music, he acquired his large repertoire very slowly. He loved the music of the 19th century, and that is what he played, especially Schumann, Chopin, Rachmaninoff and especially Liszt. He played a few contemporary works, for example, John LaMontaine's Piano Concerto, Norman Dello Joio's Third Sonata, and Joseph Marx's Romantic Concerto. He took great delight in playing transcriptions, and his typically outsize programs often included some of those devilishly difficult works. Unlike musical purists, Bolet thought that some transcriptions are both great piano pieces and great music and that most audiences greatly enjoy hearing them. (For an interesting article on transcriptions, see Schonberg's "Music: Old Wine in Lenox—Jorge Bolet Uncorks Some Vintage Liszt," *NYT*, 20 Aug 1966.)

Above all, Bolet is remembered as one of the great Liszt specialists of the century, "with the fingers of a Horowitz and the tone of a Lhévinne." (*NYT*, 23 Sept 1971) From the delicacy and lyricism of the Consolations to the dramatic intensity of the "Don Juan" Fantasy, Bolet's understanding and mastery of the Liszt idiom was complete. With the Fantasy, he "created the kind of edifice that Liszt certainly had in mind. This was piano playing that looked back to the great days of romanticism. It had style and aristocracy as well as blazing technique, and it put Mr. Bolet on a pretty exclusive pedestal as a Liszt pianist." (*NYT*, 5 May 1977)

At the very start of Bolet's career, a reviewer made a point of being "thankful that he did not use his really sensational technical gifts merely to dazzle, that musically he does beautiful things." (*Avondpost*, The Hague, 11 May 1935) Two years later, at his first New York recital (26 Oct 1937), Bolet again subordinated his enormous technique to the music, being aware even then "that music must have an emotional appeal and that it is not exclusively a finger or a cerebral exercise." (*NYT*, 27 Oct 1937) Bolet remained constant throughout his half-century career, never using his colossal technique for its own sake.

Decade after decade a remarkable consistency appears in the countless reviews encompassing Bolet's unique career: admiration for his awesome technique, his immense reserves of power rather than ostentatious display, his unwavering musical integrity and his radiant tone. These reviews also record the times when there were memory slips or lack of concentration, those times when Bolet disappointed listeners who, expecting a more pyrotechnical display of his incredible virtuosity, complained that he played with too much restraint and delicacy. But even when he played below his best, Jorge Bolet "could do more with the instrument than most other pianists around." (*WS*, 6 Aug 1976)

From within the large body of Bolet reviews there emerges a clear appraisal of his playing and artistry. At an early Richmond (Virginia) recital (26 Nov 1941) his playing of the great Brahms "Handel" Variations was "a gorgeous performance . . . a progress from outward exuberance to an increasingly deeper inner feeling, and then upward again to a culminating power, built on this deeper feeling." (*RT*, 27 Nov 1941) A Carnegie Hall recital (16 Oct 1957), a "rare and rewarding" program (Beethoven's 32 Variations in C Minor, the Schubert Sonata in B-flat Major, D. 960, and seven of Liszt's formidable Transcendental Etudes) established Bolet as a grand virtuoso and a great musician. The Liszt "gave an imposing demonstration of Mr. Bolet's well-used energy and thorough technical mastery. Mr. Bolet also captured and conveyed the studies' differing moods and their atmosphere of their period." (*NYHT*, 17 Oct 1957)

Bolet often planned unusual, imaginative programs. At one such recital (3 Nov 1973, at Washington's Kennedy Center) he played only Chopin in the first half and only Rachmaninoff transcriptions in the second half. One critic marveled at Bolet's phenomenal control and almost total mastery over all the diverse elements that go into the make-up of a great virtuoso: "His fingers give him just about everything and anything he asks for, and fortunately, he demands a lot from himself. . . . Bolet is a truly awe-inspiring pianist, master of some of the most finely nuanced playing you could possibly imagine." (*WS-N*, 5 Nov 1973) The same theme—kudos for Bolet's magnificent technique and beautiful tone—permeates a review of a Carnegie Hall recital (25 Feb 1974). "He is so at one with the instrument that it was hard to tell where he left off and the piano began. . . . He can make a sound that is rich, deep and thoughtful . . . or use a more extravagant display of color. . . . The point is he is an orchestra at the piano." (*NYP*, 26 Feb 1974)

A characteristically unhackneyed program (25 April 1984) in Los Angeles included Brahms's three Intermezzos, op. 117, and the monumental F Minor Sonata, op. 5; Rachmaninoff's Variations on a Theme of Chopin, op. 22; and two excerpts (*Gondoliera* and *Tarantella*) from Liszt's *Venezia e Napoli*. Once again, reviews emphasize Bolet's musical integrity and inimitable singing tone, his mighty yet restrained power. All told, it was "the kind of night when the critics stay for the encores." (*LAT*, 27 April 1984)

At age 72 Bolet's pianism "proved timeless, an absolute standard unto itself. . . . It is not simply a question of speed and accuracy, strength and stamina. Bolet's rare degree of control extends to coloring separate lines with their own distinct touch and articulations, simultaneously." (*LAT*, 12 Jan 1987) And at his final New York appearance at Carnegie Hall on 16 April 1989, Bolet, the keeper of a grand tradition and "one of the wonders of the musical world," still retained the "fire and artistry that first captured admirers half a century ago." (*NYCT*, 2 May 1989)

There is no doubt as to how Jorge Bolet felt about recording: "I hate recording," he would tell interviewers. "It is an artificial environment." Wanting to play for people, not to a battery of microphones, he found it frustrating not to have an audience.

The catalogue of Bolet's available recordings shows a preponderance of Liszt, the rest works by Chopin, Franck, Grieg, Schubert, Schumann, Rachmaninoff and Tchaikovsky. It is the Liszt recordings that show Bolet at his very finest. Working under contract for London (Decca) Records, he produced 10 albums (see Discog.) of consistently high quality. There is no greater testimony to Franz Liszt and his art than that bequeathed by Jorge Bolet and *his* art.

In his reading of the formidable Sonata in B Minor, Bolet "unravels Liszt's complexity with rare lucidity, a total absence of fuss or preening mannerisms. Such ease and naturalness suggest the most aristocratic of musical instincts." (*Gram*, April 1988) Bolet's recording of Liszt's *Années de pèlerinage* (Book 1, *Suisse*) won the 1984 Gramophone Award in the instrumental category, and its companion album (*Italie*) is equally compelling.

Bolet's glorious Carnegie Hall recital of 25 February 1974 was recorded by RCA Victor and issued as a two-record LP album. The program contains two classic repertoire items—the Bach-Busoni Chaconne and the Chopin Preludes, op. 28—and a fine sampling of what Bolet called "bonbons"—transcriptions by Tausig, Schulz-Evler and Liszt. The *New York Times* review of that concert, reproduced on the album, describes Bolet as a throwback to the romantic giants of the keyboard, capable of an evocation in the true grand manner; and extols his ravishing details and aristocracy of line, his total exploitation of tone, color, finger weightings, balances, sonorities and techniques. In 1988 RCA reissued the 1974 recital on CD (see Discog.), omitting the Tausig and Schulz-Evler. The Chaconne, perhaps more a tribute to Busoni than Bach, becomes a finely hewed architectural gem surrounded and enveloped by multitextured and multihued patterns of sound. Bolet's superb way with Chopin gives the Preludes an air of supreme authenticity, and the Wagner-Liszt transcription ("*Tannhäuser*" Overture) simply must be heard to be believed.

More recent recordings only sustain Bolet's reputation as one of this era's very finest keyboard artists. On a 1987 CD his performance of Schumann's *Carnaval*, op. 9, and Fantasia, op. 17, are true musical experiences, further testimony to Bolet's spiritual kinship with the 19th century. "Graceful, lyrical, fanciful, melancholy, passionate, wistful, and, above all, imbued with a strong but tender masculinity, this is one of the greatest Carnavals ever put on records. . . . In the sublime *Fantasie*, Bolet strikes the right blend of passion, melancholy, and elegance, always giving the music a spine, a feeling of continuous motion, without detracting from the music's spontaneity." (*Fan*, Sept/Oct 1987)

Bolet's CD collection of Encores, also dated 1987, provides delightful contrast. Besides a group of well-seasoned pieces by Mendelssohn (i.e., *Rondo capriccioso*), Chopin (i.e., "Minute" Waltz) and Debussy (The Girl with the

Flaxen Hair), Bolet offers an entirely different kind of repertoire—his special "bonbons." Two are by Moszkowski, including *La Jongleuse*; another is a flashy Etude by Paul de Schlözer; there is also an *Elegie* and four transcriptions by Leopold Godowsky, whose music is consistently of unbelievable difficulty. It is a delight to have these seldom-heard pieces preserved on disc.

A more recent disc comes from an Alabama recital performed on 14 April 1988. Of the three substantial works—Franck's Prelude Chorale and Fugue, Mendelssohn's Prelude and Fugue in E Minor, Liszt's *Réminiscences de Norma*—the Liszt is the most exciting. "Bolet plays the *Réminiscences de Norma* not only with a truly orchestral range of dynamics and colour but also with quite exceptional intensity—always knowing so well how to 'guard' secrets until the great moments of revelation arrive." (*Gram*, April 1994)

SELECTED REFERENCES

Benko, Gregor. "Jorge Bolet." *Stereo Review*, July 1972, pp. 56–57.

Bolet, Jorge. "Impersonating a Great Pianist." *Music Journal*, Oct 1959, pp. 16, 61.

———. "You need more than talent!" *Etude*, Nov 1951, pp. 23, 56.

Elder, Dean. "Jorge Bolet: Truth in Music." *Clavier*, Oct 1983, pp. 14–17.

Gruen, John. "Where Have You Been, Bolet?" *New York Times*, 28 Jan 1973, sec. 2, p. 17.

Kozinn, Allan. "Bolet—A Romantic at the Keyboard." *New York Times*, 25 April 1982, sec. 2, p. 17.

———. "Jorge Bolet: A Modern Keyboard Romantic." *Keyboard Classics*, Jan/Feb 1982, pp. 28–30.

Livingstone, William. "The Last Great Romantic." *Stereo Review*, Jan 1993, p. 112.

Morrison, Bryce. "Jorge Bolet." *Music and Musicians*, May 1977, pp. 16–20.

———. "Jorge Bolet." *Music and Musicians*, Dec 1984, pp. 10–11.

———. "A Path to Poetic Truth." *Gramophone*, Dec 1989, pp. 1082–1083.

Obituary. *The Times* (London), 18 Oct 1990, p. 16. *New York Times*, 17 Oct 1990, sec. 4, p. 24. *Washington Post*, 18 Oct 1990, sec. E, p. 6.

Scherer, Barrymore L. "Coping with the Demands of Liszt." *New York Times*, 19 April 1987, sec. 2, p. 27.

Silverman, Robert. "Jorge Bolet Talks to PQ's Editor." *Piano Quarterly*, Spring 1986, pp. 15–21.

Wadland, Peter, and Bryce Morrison. "Jorge Bolet (1914–1990)." *Gramophone*, Jan 1991, pp. 1365–1367. Includes CD discography.

See also Bibliography: Dub/Ref; Eld/Pia; Mac/Gr2; Noy/Pia; Ran/Kon; Rat/Cle; Sch/Gre.

SELECTED REVIEWS

CE: 10 Nov 1984. *DT*: 1 June 1935. *GM*: 26 Feb 1977. *LAT*: 27 April 1984; 12 Jan 1987. *MH*: 12 Jan 1979. *MM*: March 1985; Jan 1987. *MT*: Nov 1986. *NYHT*: 17 Oct 1957; 2 May 1989. *NYP*: 26 Feb 1974; 2 Dec

1986. *NYT*: 27 Oct 1937; 14 Oct 1947; 4 Dec 1948; 4 April 1951; 17 Oct 1957; 23 Oct 1958; 23 Oct 1965; 20 Aug 1966; 30 Oct 1967; 5 Oct 1970; 23 Sept 1971; 7 Feb 1972; 29 Jan 1973; 27 Feb 1974; 5 May 1977; 11 Jan 1982; 5 April 1986; 6 March 1988. *PI*: 27 March 1986. *RT*: 27 Nov 1941. *SFC*: 11 Jan 1988; 5 Oct 1988. *SFE*: 13 Dec 1986. *SLT*: 29 June 1980. *TL*: 4 June 1935; 14 March 1988; 8 Feb 1989. *WP*: 7 Aug 1976. *WS*: 6 Aug 1976; 30 March 1977; 8 Aug 1979. *WS-N*: 5 Nov 1973.

SELECTED DISCOGRAPHY

Bolet in Memoriam. Liszt: *Gnomenreigen*; Spanish Rhapsody; *Waldesrauschen.* Mendelssohn: *Variations sérieuses.* Rachmaninoff: Concerto No. 3 in D Minor, op. 30. Lyra House 1002 (CD). From live performances at Indiana University.

Brahms: Variations and Fugue on a Theme by Handel, op. 24. London 417 791-2.

Chopin: Ballades; Barcarolle, op. 60; Fantasy in F Minor, op. 49. London 417 651-2.

Chopin: Ballades. Liszt: Sonata in B Minor; Mendelssohn: *Rondo capriccioso.* AS 123. Recorded live, 1972.

Chopin: Piano Concertos. London 425 859-2. Dutoit/Montreal SO.

Franck: *Prélude, Choral et Fugue; Prélude, Aria et Finale*; Symphonic Variations. London 421 714-2.

Franck: *Prélude, Choral et Fugue.* Liszt: *Réminiscences de Norma.* Mendelssohn: Prelude and Fugue in E Minor, op. 35, no. 1. Decca 436 648-2. Recorded live, 1988.

Grieg: Concerto in A Minor, op. 16. Schumann: Concerto in A Minor, op. 54. London 430719-2. Chailly/Berlin RSO.

Jorge Bolet Live At Carnegie Hall. Bach-Busoni: Chaconne in D Minor. Chopin: Preludes, op. 28. Wagner-Liszt: "Tannhauser" Overture. RCA Victor CD 7710-2.

Jorge Bolet Encores. Albéniz-Godowsky: Tango, op. 165, no. 2. Bizet-Godowsky: *Adagietto* from *L'Arlésienne.* Chopin: Etudes, op. 25, nos. 1, 2, 11; Nocturne, op. 15, no. 2; Waltz, op. 64, no. 1; Waltz, op. posth. Debussy: *La Fille aux cheveux de lin.* Schlözer: Etude, op. 1, no. 2. Godowsky: *Elégie* (for left hand). Mendelssohn: *Jägerlied*, op. 19, no. 3; *Rondo capriccioso*, op. 14. Moszkowski: *En automne*, op. 36, no. 4; *La Jongleuse*, op. 52, no. 4. Schubert-Godowsky: Ballet Music from *Rosamunde.* London 417 361-2.

Liszt: Piano Music, Vol. 1. *La Campanella; Funérailles*; Hungarian Rhapsody No. 12; *Liebestraum* No. 3; Mephisto Waltz No. 1; Rigoletto Paraphrase. London 410 257-2.

Liszt: Piano Music, Vol. 2. Schubert Song Transcriptions. London 414 575-2.

Liszt: Piano Music, Vol. 3. *Grand galop chromatique; Liebesträume;* 3 Nocturnes; Sonata in B Minor; Valse impromptu. London 410 115-2.

Liszt: Piano Music, Vol. 4. *Années de Pèlerinage—Italie.* London 410 161-2.

Liszt: Piano Music, Vol. 5. *Années de Pèlerinage—Suisse*. London 410 160-2.
Liszt: Piano Music, Vol. 6. Ballade No. 2; *Benédiction de Dieu dans la solitude*;
    Les jeux d'eau à la Villa d'Este; *Venezia e Napoli* . London 411803-2.
Liszt: Piano Music, Vol. 7. Transcendental Studies. London 414 601-2.
Liszt: Piano Music, Vol. 8. Consolations; *Études de concert*; *Réminiscences de
    Don Juan*. London 417523-2.
Liszt: *Totentanz*; Hungarian Fantasy; *Malédiction*; *Totentanz*. London 414
    079-2. Fischer/London SO.
Liszt: *Totentanz*. Schubert-Liszt: *Wandererfantasie*. Rachmaninoff: Concerto
    No. 2 in C Minor, op. 18. London 430 736-2. Fischer/London SO.
Rachmaninoff: Variations on a Theme of Chopin, op. 22; Five Preludes, etc.
    London 421 061-2.
Schumann: *Carnaval*, op. 9; Fantasia, op. 17. London 417 401-2.

BRENDEL, ALFRED: b. Wiesenberg, Austria, 5 January 1931.

> I think of my function as being like that of a restorer of paintings who
> clears away the layers of old varnish. . . . I don't create the light, but I
> do what I can to let the light shine through.
>
>   Alfred Brendel (*Ovation*, March 1984)

Years of global tours and astonishing (more than a million) record sales document Alfred Brendel's high standing in the ranks of contemporary concert pianists. More difficult to ascertain is exactly where Brendel fits into those ranks.
Innately intelligent and resolutely independent, he is a pianist largely of his own
making, an uncompromising pianist intently seeking the meaning of the music.
That he is a master pianist has never been questioned. Disagreement arises concerning his sober, serious playing, a style that has attracted what amounts to a
very large, devoted Brendel cult on one hand and, on the other, a vocal body of
critics complaining that something is missing in his playing.

There is nothing musically auspicious in Alfred Brendel's background or
upbringing. His parents Albert and Ida (Wieltschnig) Brendel showed only a
passive interest in music and art, and their son certainly was not a child prodigy.
Brendel's first musical recollection is of playing operetta records on a wind-up
phonograph at the Adriatic resort hotel once owned by his parents. Most of the
time his family lived wherever his father found work, usually in the cultural
hinterlands of Yugoslavia and Austria.

While they were living in Zagreb, Yugoslavia (1937–42), Brendel, at
age six, started piano lessons with Sofia Dezelic. When they moved on to Graz,
Austria, he continued piano with Ludovika von Kaan at the Graz Conservatory
and studied composition privately with Artur Michl. The multitalented Brendel
also composed, wrote poetry and painted in watercolors. At age 17 his debut
recital (1948) in Graz consisted solely of fugues—he even titled it "The Fugue in

Music"—including one of his own compositions (a sonata with a double fugue) and more fugues for encores. Concurrently, a nearby art gallery exhibited some of Brendel's watercolors.

Brendel never studied privately with a famous teacher or at a great conservatory. His formal keyboard instruction ended about the time of his recital debut, so that from age 17 he was mostly self-taught and had to discover for himself how things went and worked. For instance, he had to learn the difference between playing in a room and playing in a large hall. He learned how to control his habit of making facial grimaces and swinging his arms about as he played (stage mannerisms he never knew he had until he saw himself on television) by practicing before a mirror. As Brendel has often explained, "Being self-taught, I learned to distrust anything I had not figured out for myself."

He found his artistic direction by studying the lives and works of the great composers; by listening to recordings by Edwin Fischer, Alfred Cortot and Artur Schnabel; and by attending Edwin Fischer's master classes at Lucerne, Switzerland, in the summers of 1949, 1950 and 1956. Brendel credits Fischer with teaching him to combine maximum sonority and force with maximum agility and speed, and to play passionately within the bounds of classicism. He has enormous admiration for Fischer, in his opinion a player of genius, "not a composer's genius but a true performer's genius. His playing is at the same time both absolutely *right* and *daring*. It has a particular freshness and intensity of communication which reaches you, more directly than from any other performer I know." (Richardson)

Brendel has worked hard for his success. From 1949, the year he was awarded third prize at the *Concorso Busoni* (Bolzano, Italy), into the early 1950s he had a moderately successful career in Europe, especially in Austria. He made his London debut on 11 January 1958, and as early as 1962 played all 32 Beethoven sonatas in eight recitals at Wigmore Hall. In 1962 he also began a four-year recording project for Vox-Turnabout: a six-volume set (36 LP discs) containing all of Beethoven's solo piano works. These recordings, awarded the *Grand Prix du Disque*, helped immensely in establishing Brendel's international reputation.

Still, he progressed slowly. Years later Brendel's agent admitted that his firm "went out on a limb" to promote Brendel, sometimes even badgering people to engage him. They had two problems. In the first place, Brendel was difficult to promote because he was not a stormy Rubinstein/Horowitz type of pianist; besides, he did not play the crowd-pleasing works of Chopin or Tchaikovsky. But Brendel eventually found his following, and for many years has made repeated international tours. He is in great demand in Europe and the Americas, and since 1973 has played almost every year at Carnegie Hall.

An excellent writer, Brendel often supplies the notes for his recordings and has published two collections of articles and lectures. *Musical Thoughts & After-thoughts* (1976) is basically a compilation of his essays and lectures, some dated as early as 1954, with particular emphasis on Beethoven, Schubert and Busoni. It also includes two brief articles on Edwin Fischer, the pianist Brendel acknowledges as having the greatest influence on him in his youth. This book is an important reference source. In the Preface of *Music Sounded Out* (1990),

Brendel explains that, "it continues where *Musical Thoughts and Afterthoughts* (1976) ended." This volume includes, among others, essays on Beethoven, Schubert, Liszt, Schumann and Busoni, all written in Brendel's intelligent, articulate, often highly persuasive manner.

Brendel enjoys avant-garde films, collects paintings and ceremonial masks, and is avid about architecture, especially the Baroque churches of Central Europe, on which subject he is considered to be an authority. He has received honorary degrees from London University (1978), Sussex University (1981) and Oxford University (1983). He has one daughter from his first marriage (1960–72) to Iris Heymann-Gonzala; and has a son and a daughter from his present marriage (1975) to Irene Semler. After 20 years in Vienna, Brendel in 1972 moved to London, his present home.

Alfred Brendel's repertoire reaches from Bach to Schoenberg, and he often devotes a single recital or a series of recitals to the works of just one composer. For example, as early as 1962 Brendel, recognized as one of this century's most renowned Beethoven interpreters, played cycles of the complete sonatas around the world. During the 1982–83 season he performed an eight-month Beethoven marathon, presenting the sonata cycle in 10 European cities and—in three weeks of May 1983—in New York at Carnegie Hall. A month later (June 1983) Brendel performed all five Beethoven piano concertos with the Chicago Symphony Orchestra, conducted by James Levine. Since 1992 he has been involved in a three-year, worldwide Beethoven project encompassing both the complete sonatas and the five concertos.

In 1978 Brendel commemorated the 150th anniversary of Schubert's death with all-Schubert recitals in Europe, Canada, the United States and Japan. A decade later, in January 1987, he began a globe-spanning (Great Britain, Europe, Israel, the USSR, Japan, the United States) tribute to Schubert—a series of four recitals presenting the solo piano works written between 1822 and 1828, in Brendel's view Schubert's most important, most dramatic music. Although the romantic, programmatic music of Liszt is a seeming anomaly in Brendel's thought-provoking repertoire, and indeed at one time Brendel virtually ignored Liszt's music, he has come to believe that the B Minor Sonata "can withstand any comparison" and that Liszt's music reflects the whole scope of possibilities of performance on the piano. During the 1985–86 season Brendel marked the 100th anniversary of the death of Liszt with all-Liszt recitals.

Early in his career Brendel played some Russian music, but now rarely performs works from the Russian (or French) repertoire. Although he enjoys listening to modern music, he has performed only a few contemporary compositions, such as the Berg Sonata, the Schoenberg Concerto and other Schoenberg pieces.

Among pianists, it would be difficult to find a greater champion of the composer than Alfred Brendel. His whole approach to music reflects his belief that the performer must always remember that his range of originality is limited, that he is there to serve the composer, not to draw attention to himself. To discover the composer's intention, Brendel approaches the music with, as he puts it, a combination of naïveté (the possibility of seeing things fresh, to him a most crucial quality of performance) and reason (because reason is a clarifying force, a filter for the emotions). He wants his listeners to forget about "good" or "beautiful" or "virtuosic" piano playing; that is, he eschews technique that reduces everything to pianistic terms. In other words, forget about the piano because the message is more important than the instrument.

Brendel first looks at how the composer constructed the work, how it holds together, and for the composer's special signatures and masterstrokes. Only then does he look at the composition as a pianist in terms of the technical problems it presents. When preparing a work—even one he has played many times—Brendel tries to blot out his earlier experiences with that work so that he can start afresh. For instance, before presenting the series of all-Schubert recitals, he spent three months going through the entire Schubert repertoire. He also listened to his earlier Schubert recordings. Then, using new scores, he made a new start, always "attempting to listen as naïvely as possible, and question everything I have done." (Fruchter)

Since Brendel does not have a photographic memory, he must constantly relearn everything—even the Beethoven works, the heart of his repertoire—and this, he believes, is good because there is always an element of re-creation. As for his technique, nearly 40 years ago a London reviewer noted (in a performance of the *"Hammerklavier"* Sonata) that Brendel's "quest for logical flow and structural clarity obliged him, because he is not a musical magician, to gloss over much felicitous detail." (*TL*, 13 Jan 1958) Brendel himself admits that missing a few notes does not bother him as long as the musical purpose is clear. "I know that I sometimes play wrong notes, but I am not a perfectionist. What I try to do is get it right, and I can only hope that sometimes I do." (Wigler) Considering his ranking among the world's finest pianists, Brendel obviously, more often than not, gets it right.

Alfred Brendel's straightforward, supremely intelligent musicianship suits this contemporary age to perfection. He insists that thinking—his approach to music is a mixture of emotion and intellect—does not exclude emotions but stimulates them. Those who feel that something is missing in his playing may disagree on the subject of emotions, but no one has ever questioned that he is a musician of indisputable probity, caring and deep respect for the music he plays. A discerning critic compares hearing a Brendel performance to watching a great surgeon at work: "His task is monumental; much of it is not even terribly pleasant, if nonetheless awesome. But when the job is completed, you have the feeling that you've traveled a lot of miles together—because you can appreciate the immense human qualities and discipline his achievement reveals." (*RMN*, 4 April 1975)

Brendel's impeccable, intensely personal playing has always aroused a mixed response. "Two Cult Figures," an essay about Brendel and Maurizio Pollini (the two play much of the same repertoire and are frequently compared), describes the playing style they both adhere to as "objective, literal, severe, impersonal, dedicated to an accurate blueprint of the architecture of the music," a style in which "color, charm and emotion mean much less than a stringent exposition of the form and relationship of a piece." (Sch/Gre, see Bibliog.) Brendel's critics contend that music needs more than an accurate blueprint, that it must also have tone color and emotion. Whatever the complaints, Brendel, as uncompromising as he is musicianly, has never changed his way of playing or chosen his programs just to please someone. Adverse comments aside, most modern concertgoers find that the intellectual and spiritual rewards in a Brendel performance far outweigh any loss of spontaneity or any display of artistic histrionics.

The mass of Brendel reviews generally divide into three categories: reviews written by ardent devotees who think Brendel can do no wrong; reviews by those who greatly esteem his approach and musicianship but feel that something is missing in his playing; and reviews by critics who find a Brendel performance irksome. These irritated critics—put together they make only a small shadow of a showing against the vast number of zealous Brendel followers—complain that his playing is either too correct, too abstemious, too immaculate, too dry, too finicky, too searching, too rarefied, or too infuriatingly objective. After hearing a series of Beethoven recitals, a critic wrote, "To my ears, Brendel's playing lacks charm of timbre—lacks warmth in cantabile melodies, lightness and ripple in quick figurations, and ethereal beauty of sound in the hushed trilling of the late sonatas." (*NY*, 1 Aug 1983) Whether or not any of the complaints are valid is ultimately irrelevant, for Brendel is a pianist who holds the attention even when causing disagreement.

Brendel devotees express themselves just as forcefully and colorfully as the disparagers. After a 16 February 1966 Wigmore Hall recital: "A more eloquent, masterly exponent of this music [Busoni and Liszt] could hardly be found in the world today." Busoni's transcription of the Bach D major prelude and fugue for organ was "brilliant, with a furious opening and vivid dramatic assaults on the bravura passages; but it was also clean and immensely dignified. . . . Mr. Brendel's moulding of Liszt's *Bénédiction de Dieu dans la solitude* was a musical experience in a million, exquisitely calculated, impeccably tasteful." (*TL*, 17 Feb 1966)

And this exuberant review from an all-Beethoven recital (15 Feb 1970) in London: "Not since Schnabel can any Beethoven interpreter have more powerfully suggested that he was creating on the spot. The *Hammerklavier* was the peak . . . an interpretation in a million, with its last 50 or so bars touching deeper springs of feeling than words can convey." (*TL*, 16 Feb 1970)

An all-Schubert performance (8 May 1988), one of a four-program cycle presented at Ravinia, received lavish praise. "In 50 years of concert-going I cannot recall performances any finer, either in style, execution, or content, than these. I went through the program in a state of cerebral ecstasy. Not many pianists can do that for you." (*CST*, 9 May 1988) When Brendel played that same four-recital Schubert cycle in Tel Aviv, Israel, an awestruck reviewer for the *Jerusalem Post* wrote, "There are not many cultural wonders in this world, but an Alfred Brendel concert performance must be considered one of these."

A review of Brendel's all-Schumann concert (7 Feb 1980) at Carnegie Hall comes as close as any in putting Brendel's artistry in true perspective. "He is a pianist who holds one's attention on everything he does. The 'Kinderscenen' pieces were shapely, sharply characterized, nervously alive. So were the

'Carnaval' pieces, and yet . . . there seemed to be too much brain and not enough simple feeling in their performance. 'Kreisleriana' was wonderful in its way, but one was aware of points that were being made, of problems that had been solved." (*NY*, 25 Feb 1980)

But after hearing Brendel's Beethoven cycle a London critic, granting that Brendel's touch was not finer, his tone more beautiful, or his pedaling more subtle than that of other pianists, concluded: "But his grasp of the issues at stake in the music is incomparable." (*TL*, 28 April 1983)

Brendel is currently involved with his ambitious Beethoven cycle covering the concertos and the sonatas, a series he is presenting in America, Great Britain and Europe. His second London program (the last one is scheduled for June 1995) featured Sonatas, op. 26, op. 27, op. 53 and op. 54, and "demonstrated exactly what one expected it to: that the man is a genius who combines magisterial technique with remarkable intellectual and emotional insight, communicating both with humility and warmth." (*TL*, 1 March 1993)

Alfred Brendel enjoys making recordings. Listening to a Brendel record is almost like hearing him in live performance. He has an enormous discography—mostly works by Beethoven, Haydn, Liszt, Mozart and Schubert—and in 1978 was presented with a gold record in recognition of his millionth record sale on the Philips label. His discs have received a fair share of Grammy awards—eight of them from 1973 through 1988. In 1973 and 1976 the awards were for Schubert sonatas; in 1977 and 1984 two separate cycles of the complete Beethoven concertos; the Brahms Concerto No. 2 in 1974; Mozart Concertos K. 456 and K. 595 in 1975; a Bach recital in 1978; and the Liszt *Années de pèlerinage* (Italy) in 1988.

Brendel's style has changed little over the decades. Although he frequently records two, sometimes three, different versions of a work, a disc made in the 1960s sounds surprisingly similar to one of the same work made 20 years later. Of course, given Brendel's searching intelligence, there are changes; however, they are subtle changes, perhaps revealing a new detail that he wishes to emphasize, or a slightly different way of phrasing a passage.

Brendel's Beethoven recordings, from the early (1950–60) Vox recordings of the complete (apart from some inconsequential early pieces) solo works to his much later (1990–91) discs, have made his name almost as synonymous with Beethoven (the same applies to his Schubert performances) as is that of the great Schnabel. One of the truly superb recordings of Beethoven's "Diabelli" Variations, op. 120, comes from Brendel, a Philips disc made in 1976 from a live performance (see Discog.). "From the first bars of the trivial waltz one is mesmerized by his confidence and his ability to get inside the work. One feels that this is *the* interpretation." (*Gram,* Jan 1987)

Brendel's recordings of the five Beethoven concertos (see Discog.) have also received high marks. Admirers of these recordings describe them as probing, musicianly and personal performances, particularly in the fast-moving tempos and dash of the outer movements. Those not quite so enthusiastic feel that the pianist strives for a special spontaneity which is foreign to his nature. He is currently rerecording the complete sonatas for Philips; he recorded them for the same label in the 1970s (see Discog.).

In recent years Brendel has recorded a good deal of Schubert—many of the sonatas and some of the sonata movements, including some rarely heard works. He has a profound understanding of this lovely, classically tinged Romantic music, and does much to dispel a commonly held opinion that Schubert was primarily a composer of lieder. He has made studio recordings of the composer's last three sonatas (C Minor, D. 958; A Major, D. 959; B-flat Major, D. 560) and has also made a video version, filmed in the Great Hall of the Honourable Society of the Middle Temple (1-3 January 1988). "Brendel's playing [on the video] took me by surprise," wrote one reviewer. "Here he performs with such depth and beauty that I found myself holding my breath. . . . On occasion I have called Brendel 'brittle Brendel,' but here the sound is the most beautiful I have ever heard from him. . . . Bravo!" (Elder, "Brendel Plays . . .")

SELECTED REFERENCES

Bargreen, Melinda. "Conversation with Alfred Brendel." *Clavier,* Feb 1979, pp. 25-26.

Brendel, Alfred. "Liszt's 'Bitterness of Heart'." *Musical Times*, April 1981, pp. 234-235.

———. *Musical Thoughts & After-Thoughts.* London: Robson Books, 1976.

———. *Music Sounded Out.* New York: Farrar Straus Giroux, 1990.

———. "The Playing of Schubert Sonatas is a new art." *Musical America,* Aug 1973, pp. MA 12–13.

Canning, Hugh. "Life in a Major Key." *Sunday Times* (London), 29 March 1992, sec. 6, pp. 12–13.

Elder, Dean. "Alfred Brendel talks about Beethoven." *Clavier,* Dec 1973, pp. 10–20.

———. "Brendel Plays Liszt and Schubert." *Clavier*, Oct 1993, pp. 37–39. An in-depth discussion of two Brendel videos.

Finch, Hilary. "Alfred Brendel." *Gramophone*, Nov 1987, p. 703.

Fruchter, Rena. "Pianist's Beethoven; A Festival's Celebration." *New York Times*, 1 May 1994, sec 2, p. 29.

———. "Seeing Schubert Whole." *New York Times*, 10 April 1988, sec. 2, p. 35.

Hoelteroff, Manuela. "Alfred Brendel: Today's Most Formidable Pianist?" *Wall Street Journal,* 26 Feb 1982, p. 31 (Leisure & The Arts).

Kozinn, Allan. "Alfred Brendel: The Impassioned Elegance of Liszt and Beethoven." *Keyboard,* May 1983, pp. 22, 24, 26, 28.

Levin, Bernard. "A passionate insight into the master's mind." *The Times* (London), 30 April 1983, p. 6.

Mann, William. "Brendel on Mozart." *The Times* (London), 5 March 1970, p. 9.

Montparker, Carol. "Alfred Brendel: The Search for Truth." *Clavier*, April 1989, pp. 10–15, 47.

Moor, Paul. "Alfred Brendel." *Musical America,* May 1988, pp. 6, 10–11.

Morrison, Bryce. "Alfred Brendel." *Music and Musicians*, Dec 1976, pp. 32–33.
Osborne, Richard. "Alfred Brendel." (interview) *Records and Recording*, June 1971, pp. 54–56.
Rhein, John von. "A Grand Piano Forte." *Chicago Tribune*, 21 April 1991, sec. 13, p. 14.
Richardson, Trevor. "Pilgrim Pianist." *Records and Recording,* March 1975, pp. 12–13.
Rockwell, John. "Brendel's Success Waxes on Records." *Los Angeles Times*, 18 Feb 1971, sec. IV, pp. 1, 12.
Shames, Laurence. "Alfred Brendel." *Ovation*, March 1984, pp. 9–11, 48.
Siepmann, Jeremy. "Talking to Brendel." *Music and Musicians*, Dec 1972, pp. 18–21.
Wigler, Stephen. "Brendel: Unlikely Superstar." *Baltimore Sun*, 8 April 1990, sec. J, pp. 1, 10.
Wolff, Konrad. "Alfred Brendel." (interview) *Piano Quarterly*, Fall 1979, pp. 12, 14–22.
See also Bibliography: Cur/Bio (1977); Dub/Ref; IWWM; Kai/Gre; Kol/Que; Mac/Gre; New/Gro; Ran/Kon; Rat/Cle; Rub/MyM; Sch/Gre.

SELECTED REVIEWS

BG: 10 April 1978. *CSM*: 18 Aug 1972. *CST:* 17 March 1975; 18 July 1979; 9 May 1988. *CT:* 15 July 1987; 25 May 1993. *LADN*: 20 April 1993. *LAT*: 27 Feb 1965; 1 Aug 1974; 20 March 1979; 18 April 1984; 20 April 1993; 28 April 1994. *MA*: April 1963; March 1964. *MiT*: 17 April 1978. *MM*: Feb 1974; Jan 1983; July 1983. *MT*: April 1966; Aug 1971; March 1977; May 1983; May 1986. *NY*: 25 Feb 1980; 22 March 1982; 1 Aug 1983. *NYDN*: 24 March 1984. *NYT*: 1 Feb 1971; 6 March 1972; 22 Jan 1973; 9 Feb 1980; 24 March 1984; 13 April 1988; 10 April 1991; 7 May 1993; 4 May 1994; 12 April 1995. *PP*: 14 Nov 1991. *RMN*: 4 April 1975. *SFC*: 17 April 1981; 22 April 1994. *STL*: 1 May 1983. *TL*: 13 Jan 1958; 12 Dec 1960; 18 Oct 1962; 1 Nov 1962; 3 Feb 1964; 17 Feb 1966; 6 Nov 1968; 31 Jan 1969; 10 Feb 1969; 16 Feb 1970; 17 Aug 1970; 16 Aug 1977; 3 Feb 1983; 28 April 1983; 1 March 1993. *WP*: 21 May 1993. *WS:* 19 Feb 1979. *WT*: 26 June 1991.

SELECTED DISCOGRAPHY

Alfred Brendel Recital. Bach (arr. Busoni): *Nun komm, der Heiden Heiland.* Beethoven: Sonata in A-flat Major, op. 110. Haydn: Sonata in C Minor, Hob.XVI:20; Sonata in G Minor, Hob.XVI:44. Philips 432 760-2.
Amnesty International Concert. Bach: Italian Concerto, BWV 971. Haydn: Andante and Variations, Hob.XVII:6. Beethoven: Sonata, op. 27, no. 2. Liszt: *Funérailles.* Berg: Sonata, op. 1. Busoni: Toccata. Philips 426 814-2.
The Art of Alfred Brendel, Vol. I. "Virtuoso Pieces" Chopin: Polonaise in A-flat Major, op. 53; Polonaise in F-Sharp Minor, op. 44; *Andante spianato*

and *Grande Polonaise*, op. 22; Liszt: Hungarian Rhapsodies Nos. 3, 8, 13, 15, 17; *Csardas obstiné*. Vanguard VCD 72007.

Beethoven: The Five Concertos for Piano. Philips 411189-2 (3 CDs). Also Musical Heritage Society MHS 532660M (3CDs). Haitink/LPO.

Beethoven: Sonatas op. 31, no. 1 in G Major; no. 2 in D Minor; no. 3 in E-flat Major. Philips 438 134-2. The first in Brendel's new cycle of the complete sonatas.

Beethoven: Sonata in C Major, op. 53; Sonata in F Major, op. 54; Sonata in A Major, op. 101. *Andante favori* in F Major. Philips 438 472-2. A further volume in Brendel's new Beethoven cycle.

Beethoven: Thirty-Two Sonatas. Philips 412575-2 (11 CDs).

Beethoven: Variations on a Theme by Diabelli, op. 120. Vox/Turnabout CD CT-4139, Philips 416 883-2.

Brahms: Concerto No. 1 in D Minor, op. 15. Philips 420071-2. Abbado/Berlin PO.

Haydn: Sonatas, Hob.XVI, nos. 20, 32, 34, 37, 40, 42, 48, 49, 50, 51, 52. Philips 416643-2 (4 CDs).

Liszt: *Années de Pèlerinage*, 1st Year; Wagner's *Liebestod* (transcription). Philips 420202-2.

Liszt: *Années de Pèlerinage*, 2nd Year. Philips 420169-2.

Mozart: Concertos. Philips 412856-2 (10 CDs). Marriner/ASMF.

Mozart: Sonatas in E-flat Major, K. 282; Sonata in F Major, K. 533/494; Fantasy in C Minor, K. 475; Rondo in A Minor, K. 511. Philips 434 663 (CD).

Schubert: Impromptus D. 899 and D. 935. Philips 411040-2.

Schubert: Sonata in B-flat, D. 960; Wanderer Fantasy. Philips 420644-2.

Schubert: Sonata in C Minor, D. 958; *Moments Musicaux*, D. 780. Philips 422076-2.

Schubert: Sonata in D Major, D. 850, Sonata in A Minor, D. 784. Philips 422063-2.

Theme and Variations (I). Mozart: Duport Variations, K. 573. Mendelssohn *Variations sérieuses*. Liszt: Variations on *Weinen, Klagen, Zorgen, Sagen*. Brahms: Theme and Variations in D Minor. Philips 426272-2.

Theme and Variations (II). Schumann: Symphonic Etudes, op. 34. Beethoven: 6 Variations, op. 34; 5 Variations WoO79 on Rule Britannia; 6 Variations WoO70 on *Nel cor più non mi sento*. Philips 432093-2.

VIDEO

Liszt: *Années de Pèlerinage*. I. *Suisse*. II. *Italie*. Philips 070 223-3.

Schubert: Sonata in C Minor, D. 958; Sonata in A Major, D. 959; Sonata in B-flat Major, D. 960. Philips 440 070 213-3.

BROWNING, JOHN: b. Denver, Colorado, 22 May 1933.

> By dint of unremitting application and a vast reserve of talent, he has
> built one of the most enduring careers of any American pianist solely
> on merit, with invariable dignity, without the slightest recourse to bal-
> lyhoo and banality.
>
> Albert Goldberg (*Los Angeles Times*, 18 August 1983)

At age 50 the enduring John Browning looked back on nearly three decades of relentless scheduling, years when he would be booked two seasons ahead and often
played more than 100 concerts a year. A sometime marathon performer,
Browning once played recitals in five different cities on five consecutive days;
another time played seven different concertos with four different orchestras (New
York, Los Angeles, Chicago, Denver), all within five weeks; and once appeared
on three different continents within the space of ten days. "I don't know what I
thought I was going to achieve," he told an interviewer in 1984, but he admits
that for him playing is a compulsion, that if not playing he is not happy.
Despite those hectic years, Browning at 50 could still say, "I'm more in love
with music than ever before. And I like performing more than ever." (*LAT*, 30
Sept 1984)

Even though he has cut back to about 90 appearances a year, Browning,
endowed with apparently unflagging energy, is still the most active American
pianist of his generation, the survivor who more than any other has fulfilled his
initial promise. His many return engagements with the world's finest orchestras
testify not only to his talent but to his musical integrity, taste, versatility and
dependability. He has made dozens of tours through Europe, the United States,
and Canada; and he has also performed in the Far East, South America and South
Africa.

Somehow he has managed to have time for teaching, including classes
at Tanglewood, Kent State University and Ravinia. An excellent teacher,
Browning has also conducted special master classes at Northwestern University,
the Manhattan School of Music (since 1980), and the Juilliard School (since
1986). He has received honorary doctorates from Occidental College and Ithaca
College, and an honorary membership in Pi Kappa Lambda, the honor society
for outstanding members of the musical profession.

The only child of John Browning, Sr., a former violinist with the
Denver Symphony Orchestra, and Esther (Green) Browning, a professional pianist, John Browning was only three years old when his mother started him on
the piano. At about age five he began studying with Edith Mills, and at age
nine he received a scholarship at the Lhévinnes's summer school in Denver, being the only child allowed to participate. He made his orchestral debut at age 10,
playing the Mozart "Coronation" Concerto at a special pops concert with members of the DSO, organized and conducted by his father. Despite the excitement
generated by his precocity, his parents refused all offered engagements and saw to
it that he had a normal childhood.

When the family moved to Los Angeles in 1945, Browning became a pupil of Lee Pattison, a Schnabel student. While attending the John Marshall High School (graduated 1951), Browning gave recitals, appeared as soloist at the Los Angeles Philharmonic Symphony Youth Concerts and won the KFI-Hollywood Bowl Young Artist Competition. After two years at Occidental College (he studied English literature and music), Browning received a scholarship to Juilliard, where he became a pupil of Rosina Lhévinne. He received the B.S. degree in 1955 and an M.M. in 1956.

Browning won the National Federation of Music Clubs' Steinway Centennial Award in 1954. In 1955 he won the Leventritt Award, which gave him, among other engagements, the chance to make his New York orchestral debut (5 Feb 1956) with the New York Philharmonic-Symphony. In 1956 he was the only American to reach the finals at the Queen Elisabeth of Belgium Competition, placing second behind Vladimir Ashkenazy. The engagements engendered by these achievements propelled Browning into the limelight. On 14 February 1957 he played the Beethoven Concerto No. 4 in G Major, op. 58, with the Los Angeles Philharmonic Orchestra under Eduard van Beinum. That same year (as an army private on furlough after basic training at Fort Ord, California) Browning was called upon to substitute for an ailing Glenn Gould at the Hollywood Bowl, where he played (27 Aug 1957) what Gould was scheduled to perform (again the same Beethoven Concerto No. 4) with the LAPO, conducted by William Steinberg. The following year Browning made his New York recital debut (5 Nov 1958) at Town Hall, and since these important appearances in the late 1950s, his career has never faltered.

In April 1965 he began an 11-week tour with the Cleveland Orchestra and conductor George Szell. (Browning, an ardent Szell admirer, once studied with him for a month in Switzerland, working on Beethoven, Mozart and Schubert; and it was Szell, claims Browning, who really made him understand the architecture in large-scale works.) Sponsored by the State Department, they toured in Russia, Sweden, Poland, Germany, France, Czechoslovakia and England. Russian audiences liked Browning so much that he was invited to tour Russia and Poland in the spring of 1967.

Browning enjoys playing chamber music. He has been a frequent guest with the Chamber Music Society at Lincoln Center, has played in Chicago with the Fine Arts Quartet and at Dumbarton Oaks with the Guarneri Quartet.

In a 1984 interview John Browning talked about nerves ("I have almost no nerves anymore. A lot of it is preparation"); and about sound ("the more individual the sound, the more singing the legato, the better"); and he ended the interview on a note of droll realism: "After all, getting up in public is an atavistic thing, the fear we have as animals of being attacked. It's like facing the lions in the arena." (Brokken) Browning need have no fear. His public is faithful, and critics (there are hundreds of Browning reviews) hold remarkably similar, favorable opinions of his playing. Repeatedly, the same words and phrases highlight his reviews: an eloquent pianist, a meticulous pianist, a satisfying pianist; nearly infallible control, innate musicality; verve, style, clarity, balance.

Browning's wide-ranging repertoire includes Classic, Romantic and contemporary works, and he keeps about 10 concertos current. The Browning programs of the 1970s and 1980s show that he played a great deal of Mozart, Beethoven, Debussy and Ravel; the Russians Rachmaninoff, Tchaikovsky, Mussorgsky and Prokofiev; also Chopin and, more recently, Liszt. In a 1988 interview Browning recalled that, except for the flamboyant Mephisto Waltz, which he programmed as a teenager, he really had not played any Liszt at all until the early 1980s when he became fascinated by the B Minor Sonata and decided to learn it. (Elliott) In 1985 he recorded it for the Delos label.

Browning maintains his large repertoire by practicing from six to seven hours a day. He has a marvelous memory and an assured technique. In his own view, his strongest areas of technique are "an evenness in my mechanism, an evenness in passagework." And he adds, "I also have a good left hand." (Dub/Ref, see Bibliog.)

Browning reviews separated by a quarter of a century express basically the same sentiments. For instance, in 1957 the 23-year-old Browning played (with the Los Angeles Philharmonic Orchestra, Eduard van Beinum conducting) Beethoven's G Major Piano Concerto "easily and with almost infallible accuracy; his passage work is extraordinarily smooth and clear; and he possesses a remarkable control of tonal gradations." (*LAT*, 1 Feb 1957) And in 1982 the veteran Browning played (with the Atlanta Symphony Orchestra, Louis Lane conducting) the Tchaikovsky Piano Concerto No. 1 "like a hungry young contestant. . . . The pleasure of listening to John Browning play Tchaikovsky is akin to pouring some bubbly into a squeaky clean glass and watching it effervesce. His passage work is so scrupulously transparent and each phrase has such propulsion that the music fairly sparkles." (*Atlanta Journal*, 12 Feb 1982. Reprinted by permission.)

Browning has a natural feeling for Mozart. At a performance (2 April 1982) with Yuval Zaliouk and the Toledo Symphony Orchestra, he played Mozart's Concerto in A Major, K. 488, "with elegant proportions and beautiful phrasing, yet also with the kind of virility which Mozart performances have lacked for so long. It was a very stylish, crystal-clear reading." (*TB*, 4 April 1982)

Very early in his career Browning's Carnegie Hall performance (14 Dec 1959) of the Beethoven Sonata, op. 57 ("*Appassionata*") predicted success. "Any pianist who can maintain his stride and pulse in this sonata in the spirit of its maker is already on the road to glory. Mr. Browning had everybody's attention riveted from first note to last." (*NYWT*, 15 Dec 1959) Twenty-five years later his performance (19 Nov 1984) of the Beethoven "Emperor" Concerto with Erich Bergel and the Seattle Symphony Orchestra was "brilliant without resorting to grandstanding; he was poignant and melancholy but never slipped into sentimentality. He knows how to be exuberant as well as reflective. He can be strong and stormy without ever pounding on the keyboard." (*SPI*, 20 Nov 1984)

Browning's aristocratic interpretations of the French musical repertoire draw like praise. When he played (27 Feb 1977) the Ravel Concerto in G with the Buffalo Philharmonic Orchestra, Michael Tilson Thomas conducting, "the high gloss, the elegant balance of crystal tones and mosaic figurations, above all the spell of that plagal slow movement were exceptional." (*BN*, 28 Feb 1977) At a London recital (22 April 1979) Browning's performances of Debussy's *Images, Estampes, Masques* and *Homage à Haydn* clearly revealed his mastery of the French idiom: "His fastidious, innate sense of keyboard elegance, his indolent, lazy *rubato*, playing like a gentle breeze throughout each phrase, made for magical experiences." (*DT*, 23 April 1979)

There are also extravagant kudos for his Liszt. At a Chicago recital (1 April 1984) he sped through the Mephisto Waltz "at such a tempo that one would never have expected such clarity of line and sparkle of figuration. . . . This was the kind of control in which a thunderous passage comes to a sudden halt, and the sound still buzzes throughout the hall. Browning relishes that sort of artistic effect and he achieved it time and again throughout the Liszt works." (*CT*, 2 April 1984)

Although he plays few large contemporary works, Browning has become indelibly affiliated with Samuel Barber's Piano Concerto ever since he played the premier performance (24 Sept 1962) with the Boston Symphony Orchestra, conducted by Erich Leinsdorf, at the gala opening week at Lincoln Center. (He now estimates that he has played this Pulitzer Prize–winning work more than 500 times.) This concerto is exactly right for Browning. "It demands a prodigious range in physical technique and artistic sensibility. Browning has both to spare and displays his formidable abilities in a cleanly energetic performance of the first rank." (*HB*, 3 March 1980)

To celebrate his 60th birthday, Browning scheduled three performances—25 October, 17 November, 8 December 1993—at Lincoln Center's Alice Tully Hall. At the first concert he played two concertos (Mozart, K. 488; Beethoven "Emperor") with the Juilliard Orchestra, conducted by Leonard Slatkin. "The playing was impressive throughout, at times quite masterly. . . . A more poetically concentrated pianist in recent years, [Browning] was at his best in the slow movements, particularly the Andante of the Mozart." (*NYT*, 28 Oct 1993) The principal works on the program of 17 November were Chopin's Sonata in B-flat Minor and the Barber Sonata. In the Chopin, the "middle of the Scherzo movement was very beautiful and the Funeral March appropriately grim. Few techniques are as suited to the finale's eerie scuttling as this one." In the Barber E-flat Minor Sonata, Browning "replicated its bleak, fierce language with the proper chiaroscuro, managing the technical horrors of the fugue quite well." (*NYT*, 20 Nov 1993) The third concert, with bass-baritone Thomas Hamson and the Ridge Ensemble, included the premiere performance of three of Barber's unpublished songs.

It is difficult, in perusing the many, many Browning reviews, to find a wholly negative critique; but of course not everyone is completely persuaded by his playing. His interpretations are not "profound" enough for some. He has at times been criticized for overuse of the pedal, slightly mannered rhythmic inflections, an element of literalism, a sometimes "too pat" perfection. And Harold Schonberg, in his revised (1987) edition of *The Great Pianists*, passes Browning by with only a brief mention. In essence, it is his masterful, dramatic technique

and his instinctive sense of what a piano can do that make a Browning performance a stylish, vivid musical statement.

For such an in-demand performer, Browning has relatively few current
recordings. His set of five Prokofiev Concertos has been unavailable for some
time (Nos. 1 and 2 won a Grammy award in 1966). But those recordings that are
available represent Browning at his best. On his 1986 CD of Rachmaninoff
compositions (see Discog.), Browning's dramatic, turbulent reading of the
Sonata No. 2 in B-flat Minor (original 1913 version) is electrifying, a magnificent work magnificently played. The shorter works (Preludes, *Etudes-tableaux*)
on this CD are "studies in rich tone colouring. The layered polyphonic life of
the music is immaculately done." (*Gram*, June 1987)

Those who find Liszt artificial and excessively flamboyant should listen
to Browning's CD devoted to that composer (see Discog.). "There is a great deal
of originality in his attention to both form and substance. The performances are
marked most of all, perhaps, by an emphatic but unlabored clarity that emphasizes the structural strength of the B Minor Sonata." (*StR*, May 1986)

Samuel Barber wrote his masterful Concerto, op. 38, for John Browning, who recorded it twice, first in 1964 with George Szell and the Cleveland Orchestra, more recently (1990) with Leonard Slatkin and the St. Louis Symphony
Orchestra. Both performances are superb—each won a Grammy award (1964,
1991)—but sonically the later version is preferable, a truly "fire-breathing performance."

Browning recently recorded Barber's complete solo piano music on the
MusicMasters label. His powerful reading of Barber's Sonata is a distinguished
one. The shorter works—Nocturne; Ballade; Excursions and Interlude—are
beautifully performed.

Recorded in April 1994, Browning's CD collection of 30 Scarlatti
sonatas (see Discog.) is a delight. The overtly virtuosic sonatas are played with
brilliance and stunning crystalline clarity. As one enthusiastic reviewer put it,
"His playing is lithe, agile and sharply chiseled; he respects a Baroque framework
in pedaling and articulation, but adds felicitous shadings of tempo and dynamics.
Deeply personal yet never mannered, these performances are among the finest
Scarlatti recorded on the piano." (*CP*, Feb 1995)

SELECTED REFERENCES

Beigel, Greta. "The Aches And Pains Of A Decade's Promising Pianists." *Los
    Angeles Times*, 30 Sept 1984, CAL, pp. 50–51. Browning, Fleisher,
    Janis.
Blyth, Alan. "John Browning." *Music and Musicians*, April 1970, pp. 44, 74.
Brokken, David. "Piano Master's Forte." *Minnesota Daily*, 10 Aug–16 Aug
    1984 (Arts and Entertainment), pp. 1, 8.
Browning, John. "Samuel Barber's Piano Concerto Turns Twenty-Five."
    Clavier, Sept 1987, pp. 24–27.
"The Busiest Fingers on the Keys." *Life*, 26 Nov 1965, pp. 87–90.
Coleman, Emily. "Golden Boys Have Their Troubles Too." *New York Times*,
    19 March 1967, sec. 2, p. 21.

Elliott, Susan. "Sustaining the Promise: John Browning at Mid-Career."
   Symphony Magazine, June–July 1988, pp. 30–32, 86.
Heylbut, Rose. "Once in a Century." *Etude*, Sept 1954, pp. 15, 48.
Jepson, Barbara. "Stepping Out Of the Shadow Of Cliburn." *New York Times*,
   24 Oct 1993, sec. 2, pp. 1, 30.
Mach, Elyse. "John Browning." (interview) *Piano Quarterly*, Fall 1975, pp. 32,
   34, 47.
Reese, Catherine. "How keyboard veteran keeps his edge." *Salt Lake City
   Tribune*, 3 Feb 1991, sec. E, p. 1.
Sweeney, Louise. "The real life of a concert pianist." *Christian Science
   Monitor*, 23 Aug 1989, p. 10.
"Veteran Prodigy." *Time*, 12 Jan 1962, p. 61.
See also Bibliography: Dub/Ref; Mac/Gre; Mar/Gre; New/GrA; Noy/Pia.

SELECTED REVIEWS

AJ: 12 Feb 1982. *BN*: 24 March 1975; 28 Feb 1977; 7 Nov 1987. *CPD*: 26
July 1975; 16 April 1982; 10 Jan 1986. *CST*: 31 March 1978. *CT*: 11
April 1960; 2 April 1984; 21 Oct 1986. *DMN*: 30 Jan 1986. *DMR*: 26
Sept 1993. *DP*: 19 Nov 19050; 26 July 1960; 19 Oct 1966. *DT*: 23 April
1979. *FT*: 24 April 1979. *HB*: 3 March 1980. *HP*: 20 Jan 1986. *LAT*: 1
Feb 1957; 28 Aug 1957; 26 April 1983; 18 Aug 1984. *MA*: April 1963.
MJ: 3 March 1986. *NYHT*: 15 Dec 1959. *NYT*: 6 Feb 1956; 6 Nov 1958;
25 Sept 1962; 17 April 1965; 21 Feb 1966; 10 Jan 1982; 23 March 1983;
7 Feb 1984; 28 Oct 1993; 20 Nov 1993. *NYWT*: 15 Dec 1959. *PEB*: 11
Oct 1976. *RMN*: 28 Dec 1957; 19 Oct 1966. *SPI*: 20 Nov 1984. *TB*: 4
April 1982. *TL*: 22 June 1965; 18 Feb 1975. *WP*: 13 May 1983; 26
March 1985; 4 Feb 1989; 20 Oct 1992.

SELECTED DISCOGRAPHY

Recital: Bach: Chromatic Fantasy and Fugue. Chopin: Nocturne in D-flat
   Major, op. 27, no. 2; *Grande valse brillante* in E-flat Major, op. 18.
   Debussy: Reflections in the Water. Liszt: Mephisto Waltz. Schubert:
   Impromptu in B-flat Major, D. 935, no. 3. Seraphim LP S-60099.
Barber: The Complete Solo Piano Music. Ballade, op. 46; Excursions, op. 20;
   Interlude No. 1; Nocturne; Sonata, op. 26. MusicMasters 01612-67122-2.
Barber: Concerto, op. 38. CBS Masterworks cassette MPT 39070. Szell/
   Cleveland SO, rec. 1964.
Barber: Concerto, op. 38; Souvenirs, op. 28 (with Slatkin); Symphony No. 1,
   op. 9. RCA 60732-2. Slatkin/St. Louis SO, rec. 1990.
Barber: Sonata for Piano. Cumming: Twenty-Four Preludes. Phoenix PHCD
   105.
Chopin: Etudes (complete). RCA CD 60131-2.
John Browning performs Domenico Scarlatti. 30 Keyboard Sonatas.
   MusicMasters 67146-2, also MHS 513732H.

Liszt: Sonata in B minor; *Après une lecture du Dante*; *Sonetti del Petrarca*, nos. 47, 104, 123. Delos DCD 3022.

Mussorgsky: Pictures at an Exhibition; Hopak; *Impromptu passioné*; Sonata. Delos DCD 1008.

Rachmaninoff: Daisies, op. 38, no. 3; *Etudes-Tableaux*, op. 33, nos. 2–3; op. 39, no. 5; *Moment musical*, op. 16, no. 5; Preludes, op. 23, nos. 4–6; op. 32, nos. 5, 12, 13; Sonata No. 2 in B-flat Minor, op. 36; Delos DCD 3044.

Ravel: *Gaspard de la nuit*; *Sonatine*; *Le Tombeau de Couperin*. RCA LP LSC-3028.

BUSONI, FERRUCCIO DANTE MICHELANGELO BENVENUTO
b. Empoli, Italy, 1 April 1866; d. Berlin, Germany, 27 July 1924.

> Busoni is a revolutionist, and in the piano-playing world, we have but one of his kind.
>
> August Spanuth (*Musical America*, 24 December 1910)

Edward Dent's detailed biography of Ferruccio Busoni makes one wonder what career Busoni might have followed had he been born into a different family. His parents were professional, but not successful, musicians. His father Ferdinando Busoni, an Italian from Tuscany with only a sketchy musical education, parlayed a natural talent for the clarinet into an extraordinary virtuoso style, but Ferdinando's willful, quick-tempered, troublemaking nature spoiled his chances for success. Busoni's mother, born Anna Weiss of a German-Jewish father and an Italian mother, was a fine pianist and already a local celebrity in Trieste when she met Ferdinando at a concert there in April 1865. Married within a few weeks—an unfortunate match for the educated, artistic Anna Weiss—they immediately began touring together, stopping just long enough for the birth of their only child, Ferruccio Busoni. The infant lived with his mother's family in Trieste until he was about two years old, then began touring with his parents. Meager concert earnings made for a mean, hard life, and about 1871 the parents separated. Anna and her son returned to her father's home in Trieste, Ferdinando continued touring.

Busoni's musical education began early with his mother. At age four he was, in her words, working at the piano like an angel, and by the time he reached six he was having an hour lesson and also taking violin lessons. All through his lonely childhood (Busoni claimed he never had a childhood, that until about age 20 he associated only with adults), his greatest comfort and best companion was his dog, the first of a lifelong succession of canine friends.

Busoni's father came back to his family early in 1873, very quickly realized that his son had a special musical talent and, although Anna Busoni was by far the better teacher, preempted the teaching duties. He knew little about the piano, was erratic in rhythm and taught more by bluster than basics. Four hours a day he sat by his son, keeping a stern watch on every note and every finger. Within a year of his father's taking over his instruction, Busoni—he was seven years old—appeared with his parents in a Trieste concert (24 Nov 1873) and on 26 March 1874 gave a concert of his own.

Busoni was also composing, though he had no proper training in composition. All he ever wanted to do was compose, but he was forced to play the piano. His father never let him forget that it was his duty to become a successful concert pianist so that he could support his parents in their old age. This "duty" undoubtedly changed the whole pattern of Busoni's life, yet he never questioned or rejected it. But wanting only to be a composer and being constantly pressured to become a pianist made for a life of frustration.

In the autumn of 1875 Ferdinando, with little money and without knowing German, took the nine-year-old Busoni to Vienna to show him off as pianist, composer and improviser. Busoni enrolled at the Vienna Conservatory, but he soon became disillusioned with his teachers and resumed his studies with his father. Despite his father's attitude and irritability, Busoni was always grateful to him. In the epilogue to his complete edition of Bach's clavier works, written in the last year of his life, Busoni thanked his father for keeping him strictly to the study of Bach in his childhood ("in a country where Bach was then rated little higher than a Carl Czerny") and for training him to be a "German" musician.

If the Vienna Conservatory proved disappointing, the Vienna stay otherwise was most rewarding in that Busoni met the Gomperz family, several sisters and brothers who became his longtime friends and benefactors. They provided a tutor to teach him German, helped generously with other expenses and, best of all, gave Busoni wise advice and affection. He was not quite 10, and his playing stunned Vienna. On 8 February 1876 he took part in a Haydn D Major Trio and played several solos—a rondo by Mozart, Hummel's Theme and Variations and five of his own compositions—amazing his audience with his technical mastery and enthralling them with his improvisations.

That summer (1876) at Gmunden, Austria, he studied counterpoint with Johannes Evangelista Hubert, organist of the cathedral, and had advice from composer Karl Goldmark. As always, living expenses had to be met, so that winter Busoni's father took him back to Vienna to look for concert engagements. Eventually, because of young Busoni's continuing poor health, his doctor ordered him to leave Vienna; but it took him about six months to earn enough to pay off board and lodging debts.

All through his peripatetic, unsettled and stressful childhood, Busoni kept composing. By age 13 he was already largely supporting his family. Wherever they settled, bills accumulated and, though not a strong child, he had to play concerts or find a patron to pay their debts before they could leave and try new towns. Poor health, an erratic life and the strain of early responsibilities seem overwhelming, especially for one so young, yet Busoni often managed his own affairs, arranging concerts and soliciting patronage. As he told friends many years later, "I was a wonder-child and everything turned on me." (Dent)

From the fall of 1879 until April 1881 Busoni lived a more stable life in Graz. For once, he had no need to earn money. A local committee sponsored his education and arranged for his parents to give piano lessons. Busoni studied with Dr. Wilhelm Mayer, completing Mayer's two-year composition course in 15 months. This interlude at Graz was one of the happy times of his young life. For the next two years he toured in Italy, where he gave five concerts in Bologna and received (March 1882) diplomas for composition and for piano from the *Accademia Filharmonica*, the first composer since Mozart to be admitted to that Academy at such a young age.

In the fall of 1883 Busoni and his father once again tried to conquer Vienna. The program of a concert (30 Nov 1883) there shows that even at age 17 Busoni already preferred gigantic programs like Rubinstein's: Beethoven's Sonata in C Minor, op. 111, Bach's Italian Concerto, Schumann's Symphonic Etudes, the Chopin *Andante spianato* and *Grande Polonaise*, op. 22, Liszt's transcription from Mendelssohn's Midsummer Night's Dream music and some compositions of his own. But Busoni's performance style annoyed the Viennese critics. They had admired him as a prodigy, but now he was 17, and they disliked the way he played. Since poor notices adversely influenced patronage, Busoni spent much of his time trying to talk his benefactors into continuing their support.

Vienna disappointed him again the next year. The Vienna Philharmonic Orchestra auditioned his Symphonic Suite and refused to perform it, a bitter rejection further aggravated by bad reviews of his playing. Viennese critics, thoroughly disapproving of his interpretation of Beethoven's *"Appassionata,"* advised him to moderate his *forte* and *fortissimo,* one cynically heading his review "a musical steeplechase." Some of them thought Busoni's almost orchestral effects on the piano completely strange, and most of them still disapproved of his free style, especially his use of the pedal.

Hating Vienna, tired of performing, even tired of people, Busoni begged funds from one of his most faithful supporters, and in February 1885 set off to try his chances in Berlin. The German critics—Busoni gave recitals in Leipzig and Berlin—were pleased that Busoni's own works were German in style, but they deplored his interpretations of Bach, Handel and Chopin. They also criticized his exuberant rhythms, liberal use of the pedal and lack of expression.

It was a bleak existence. He gave recitals whenever and wherever he could in order to support himself and his parents and, as usual, he had no close friends, only his dog. He wrote his father almost daily, carefully accounting for the money he earned from recitals, just how much he made and exactly how it was spent.

The musicologist Hugo Riemann recommended Busoni for a post at the conservatory in Helsingfors, Finland, beginning 15 September 1888. It meant steady income for a year, and Busoni accepted at once. The first term was lonely—his mother had refused to accompany him—and Helsingfors, for him, was a cultural wasteland. However, since he had only about a dozen students, he had plenty of time to compose and give recitals. At the holiday break he gave a concert (Jan 1889) in Hamburg, a program including the first of his transcriptions (Prelude and Fugue in D Major) from Bach's organ works. This time, pleased German critics thought he had acquired a greater variety of style and a deeper insight into the music, one reviewer even noting Busoni's wonderful reproduction of the full, soft organ tone on the piano. During the second term at Helsingfors, Busoni fell in love with Gerda Sjöstrand, daughter of a Swedish sculptor, and they married (27 Sept 1890) in Moscow, just as Busoni was to begin teaching at the Moscow Conservatory. Marriage brought him happiness and security, and every day Busoni made a point of thanking his wife for their time together.

Like Helsingfors, the Moscow position proved unsuitable. Busoni soon realized that his colleagues resented him as a foreigner. Even worse, he had so many pupils he had to teach about 35 hours a week. He felt completely cut off from European culture, and he made few friends. On the plus side, he began to study English while in Moscow, and his first concert there received thunderous applause, if little profit. Despite increased income and Gerda Busoni's managing skills, they lived frugally because money still had to be sent to his parents.

In late August 1891 the Busonis sailed for America with high hopes for his new position at the New England Conservatory of Music in Boston, Massachusetts. Once again he was disillusioned. The Conservatory, short of funds, indiscriminately accepted all pupils, with or without talent, and Busoni had to teach four lessons an hour. Only the birth of Benvenuto, their first son, in March 1892, brightened that intolerable year. (A second son, named Raffaello, was born in 1900; both became artists.) Resigning his post at the New England Conservatory, Busoni moved (summer 1892) to New York, hoping to start a successful concert career in America, but an initial flurry of engagements tapered off after about a year, and the Busonis returned (spring 1894) to Berlin, his home—except during World War I—for the rest of his life.

That autumn his Berlin concert (3 Nov 1894) received bitter criticism. The German reviewers disparaged his transcriptions and censured his additions to Weber's *Konzertstück*. At the same time, they admired his marvelous technique and tone color. A month later, Otto Lessman of the *Allgemeine Musikzeitung*, always a staunch Busoni supporter, wrote that although he had heard Liszt, Bülow and Rubinstein play Beethoven's Sonata in B-flat Major, op. 106, he thought Busoni's interpretation the greatest he had ever heard. It was, said Lessman, more than piano playing; it was orchestration.

By age 30 Busoni had become a pianist of amazing virtuosity, yet critics (many were bewildered by his playing) generally felt that he had not acquired full maturity in matters of interpretation. He gave more and more concerts and extended the range of his tours, playing from Spain to Russia, from Italy to Scandinavia. From 1897 he toured in Great Britain (where he initially faced small halls and cold critics), and during the first three months of 1904 he again toured in America. Busoni dreaded the traveling and playing, but he always needed money (both parents died in 1909 but he had his own family to support), and most years he toured from October, the beginning of the Continental season, to July, the end of the London season. Exhausting programs and the difficulties of constant travel drained his energies. When performing, however, he had extraordinary control and presence, a wonderful ability to overcome all weariness and nervous stress and concentrate mind and spirit on his playing. Now recognized as a great pianist, he hated the life.

Busoni started another, immensely successful American tour (about 35 recitals), in January 1910, and made an even more extensive American tour in 1911, during which he played the first American performance (13 Jan 1911) of his Concerto with the Theodore Thomas Orchestra in Chicago. Busoni's fifth (and last) American tour (Jan–Oct 1915) included recitals in the Western states. When he returned to New York, his agent announced he had no further bookings. New York, said the agent, was overrun with celebrated pianists. Disgusted with America but unable to return to his home in Berlin, Busoni spent the war years in Zurich, Switzerland, where he gave recitals and substituted for the conductor of the Zurich municipal orchestra. In the spring of 1919 he gave five concerts designed to illustrate the history of the piano concerto. In July 1919 the University of Zurich made him an honorary doctor of philosophy.

Although the older he grew the more he detested having to play the piano for a living, Busoni continued his tours of the Continent and Great Britain. His performance (29 May 1922) of the Beethoven Concerto in E-flat Major ("Emperor") with the Berlin Philharmonic Orchestra proved to be his last public appearance. Busoni had come to realize that although he was interested in the piano as an instrument, especially in what it could do, he was not interested in the music written for the piano. Believing that a new repertoire might help him, he asked his good friend Isidor Philipp for advice. Philipp suggested Alkan and Scriabin, but in the end Busoni abandoned the piano but not his composing or writing. His health, long neglected, steadily deteriorated. Two years after his final performance, Busoni died (27 July 1924) of heart and kidney complications.

Although Busoni's teaching methods were unorthodox and he taught only intermittently during his long, arduous career, he influenced a good number of musicians. Pianists Egon Petri, Rudolf Ganz, Eduard Steuermann and Dimitri Mitropoulous all studied with him. The composers Kurt Weill, Louis Gruenberg and Edgar Varèse benefited from Busoni's counsel. Arnold Schoenberg and Luigi Dallapiccola admitted to being inspired by Busoni, and Schoenberg even arranged Busoni's piano *Elegie* No. 7 for small chamber orchestra. Percy Grainger, Artur Rubinstein, Joseph Sigeti and Isidor Philipp also considered Busoni a major influence on their respective musical careers.

Petri, an ardent Busoni disciple, helped immeasurably in keeping Busoni's name alive after his death. In a 1940 interview for *Etude*, Petri explains that Busoni was not the kind of teacher who could guide a pupil through technical and artistic problems, but his ability to give the student a consummate understanding of art and the need for cultural and spiritual completion made him the most inspiring teacher of his time. Some evenings Busoni would play for his students in his candlelit studio and afterwards at dinner discuss the music he had played. In this way, said Petri, his students learned more than they ever could have learned in a dozen ordinary lessons. (Petri)

Busoni had one-year teaching posts at Helsingfors (1888–89), Moscow (1890–91) and Boston (1891–92). He taught advanced classes at Weimar in the summers of 1900 and 1901; a master class at the Vienna Conservatory (1907–

08); and a master class at Basel, Switzerland in 1909. In October 1913 he became director of the *Liceo Rossini* (later *Liceo G. B. Martini*) at Bologna, a provincial post he accepted only because of his devotion to his native Italy. He took leave from the *Liceo Rossini* to make his American tour in January 1915. Because of the war and problems with the *Liceo* council, he never returned to that position. In September 1920 Busoni began a class in advanced composition at the Berlin State (formerly Royal) Academy of Arts and Sciences.

Ferruccio Busoni had other talents. He drew clever pen sketches and cartoons. He spoke and read four languages. An avid reader whose favorite author was Charles Dickens, he often roamed London in search of Dickensian characters. A fluent writer, he wrote the librettos of his four operas. In 1907 he published his now famous essay "Sketch of a New Esthetic of Music" in which he attempted to justify his free transcriptions and free interpretations of other composers' music.

An unwilling piano virtuoso who wanted only to compose, Ferruccio Busoni now stands as one of history's great pianists; indeed, some connoisseurs rank Busoni as the greatest pianist of the century. Although the general public, and even some critics, sometimes found his playing too intellectual and too cold, Busoni was without a doubt one of the finest examples of the pianist-musician who used his phenomenal technique solely for musical ends. A "relentless" intellectual control, "unrivaled" technique, "wondrous" range of color, "unbelievable" tone—these, according to contemporary writers, were the hallmarks of Busoni's great playing. Eschewing the extroverted, romantic playing then in vogue, he offered his hearers interpretations dominated by a powerful intellect that seemingly controlled every note he played. He had no compunction about altering the written notes, infuriating critics who complained that he was modernizing the classics. Not modernizing, explained Busoni, but clearing away the dust of tradition and playing these classics as they must have sounded when first written down. Busoni's alterations—and his transcriptions—were designed with an overall aesthetic purpose and intelligently and skillfully worked out.

Critics, especially German writers, severely criticized his interpretations, but his biographer Edward Dent claimed there was a marvelous spiritual quality about them. And Claudio Arrau, who heard Busoni play many times, believed that Busoni's rich creativity and grand imagination shed new light on everything he played. Perhaps Busoni's "*Hammerklavier*" was not Beethoven, but it was gigantic and overwhelming. If Busoni's Mozart was not Mozart, it was something miraculously rewoven into something entirely new. That spiritual quality emerged only because of Busoni's consummate technique, a technique embodying perfect touch control, incredible finger rapidity, masterly pedaling, sparkling and always precise rhythms, crisp staccato, amazing leaps, a superb *forte* and *fortissimo* (the louder he played, the more beautiful the sonority of his tone).

Busoni achieved his technical perfection through tenacious practice, not practicing endless hours but rather with what he described as "a particular meticulousness." He would very slowly repeat a fragment of three or four bars (of Bach, of Beethoven or Liszt or Schumann, even one of his own works), and gradually play the fragment faster until he felt he had it right. As he practiced these fragments, he practiced the entire work in his brain. Most writers support Busoni's claim that he was self-taught, that he had created his own technique and developed the ideas and methods which guided him. However, as a boy Busoni had met Anton Rubinstein and had often heard Rubinstein play. Rubinstein greatly influenced Busoni's style, particularly his monumental conception of his art.

Busoni looked upon the piano as a kind of super orchestra, and his pedaling was largely responsible for producing the extraordinary range of color he drew from the instrument. According to Henry Wood, Busoni achieved remarkable effects with the sostenuto pedal, actually changing the tone of the entire instrument, at times with an almost orchestral effect. (Woo/My, see Bibliog.) And Edward Dent remembered vividly how Busoni could transform the most complicated passages of Beethoven or Liszt into "washes of color," yet play every single note accurately, with nothing smudged or blurred. (Dent) Busoni's unusual sound (some critics called his style "horizontal") came from tonal layers built up one upon the other to achieve great climaxes. This was especially noticeable with the classic fugal repertoire, such as the Beethoven fugues. As a matter of fact, Beethoven's great Sonata, op. 106, with its mighty fugue, was one of the touchstones of Busoni's art.

All through his mature career, Busoni had largely rave reviews, even from critics who could not fully understand his playing. When he played (6 Jan 1910) the "Emperor" Concerto with the New York Philharmonic Society, Gustav Mahler conducting, at Carnegie Hall, the *Musical America* critic, after duly reporting the great ovation rendered by the audience, noted his own surprise that Busoni, although an Italian, did not play with more warmth of tone. For this reviewer, Busoni's appeal lay in the "thorough-going artistic finish, which delights at every point of his work, and the limpid and lucid quality of his touch, which reveals itself with special charm in running passages." (*MA*, 15 Jan 1910)

A few weeks later Busoni's Carnegie Hall recital (10 Feb 1910) was, according to one reviewer, "one of the most marvelous exhibitions of piano playing ever heard in this city or ever likely to be heard anywhere else." Busoni's performance of the 24 Chopin Preludes won the most extravagant praise: "To rhapsodize over the flawless perfection of his technic were the sheerest impertinence, to parade forth all the pet adjectives of the music critic in praise of his tone, his touch, his apparently inexhaustible command of color, his intellect, his imaginative qualities, his temperament, and his personality, worse than futile. Yet all of these particularly wonderful qualities figured strongly in his interpretations." (*MA*, 19 Feb 1910)

Reviewing Busoni's Carnegie Hall recital of 4 February 1911, the erudite American composer Arthur Farwell wondered at the "tone marvels" in his playing. "Busoni has evidently studied out every possible kind of tone that can be extracted from a piano string by different methods of striking the keys and of pedaling. He has at his command everything from a tone sharp and cutting as a lightning flash to sounds the most delicate and gentle. By means of the alternation of these different effects, especially the very rapid alternation, he makes the piano seem to be several kinds of instruments at once." (*MA*, 11 Feb 1911)

A graphic, succinct summation of Busoni's pianism comes from the eminent English music critic Ferruccio Bonavia. "Busoni commanded a wider range of tone than any living pianist, although his preference for cold, unemotional shades might have caused some to doubt it. . . . It led him to a quality of tone which can only be called 'white,' a quality that was cold and almost inanimate. From this perfectly even basis he would start and build up a climax that reached the extreme limit of what is possible to a pianist, an avalanche of sound giving the impression of a red flame rising out of marble. His intellectual control was remorseless." (Bonavia)

Seventy years after his death, Busoni the composer remains in the background, and his music is infrequently performed. Busoni the pianist, however, still ranks among the great pianists of the century. "He was a formidable intellectual who could write almost as well as he could play. He was a personality whose mere presence raised the hair on a spectator's scalp. Above all, he was a pianist of fantastic splendor, acknowledged today as the mightiest technician of all time. His power was awesome, his speed almost beyond belief, his touch so delicately precise that he could transform the most complicated passages into washes of pure color. And yet technique was not an end in itself; Busoni invariably subordinated pianistic skill to musical meaning." ("A Bridge to the Future")

It is a pity that Busoni's active performing career took place before the phonograph was fully developed. He did make over 50 roll recordings for Duo-Art, Welte, Ampico and others. Some of these have been transferred to CD and give a general view of Busoni's incredible pianism (see Discog.). His Liszt performances in particular are spectacular and provide an opportunity for hearing some of Liszt's less frequently performed compositions. And a Symposium cassette gives a fascinating view of the great pianist playing his famous transcription of the Bach Chaconne in D Minor.

As to actual disc recordings, all that we have are nine brief compositions, including two versions of one of these. The extant acoustic recordings, originally preserved on four discs and now available on one CD, are listed below:

> Bach: Prelude and Fugue No. 1 (WTC I)
> Bach-Busoni: Chorale Prelude *Nun freut euch liebe Christen*
> Beethoven-Busoni: *Ecossaise*, WoO 83
> Chopin: Etude, op. 10, no 5
> Chopin: Etude, op. 25, no. 5
> Chopin: Nocturne, op. 15, no. 2
> Chopin: Prelude, op. 28, no. 7; Etude, op. 10, no. 5 (connected by an
> improvisatory-modulatory passage)
> Liszt: Hungarian Rhapsody No. 13 (abbreviated)

Busoni professed a great aversion to recording. In a letter to his wife, dated 20 November 1919, he speaks of suffering, of feeling battered and depressed, and refers to the recording apparatus as "this devilish machine." That attitude may account for the sometimes indeterminate performance quality of the piano rolls and the four disc recordings. But, in spite of the poor sound quality of these early discs, it is still possible to obtain a glimpse of the Busoni so admired by his contemporaries.

The Liszt Rhapsody probably has the best recorded piano tone. Some cuts were made in the original composition so it could be fitted to two sides of a 78 rpm record. Even so, the Rhapsody is beautifully projected with some dazzling cadenzas and the utmost clarity and regularity in the repeated notes of the Vivace section.

Some of the most beautiful playing is heard in the clear, unhurried Bach Prelude and Fugue. The Fugue in particular shows the carefully controlled part-playing for which Busoni was noted.

Some of the playing may strike the contemporary listener as strange, but Busoni was well-known for his liberal approach to the printed page. The Chopin Prelude, op. 28, no. 7, is cool, reserved and unsentimental. There is an improvised modulatory passage between the Prelude and the Etude, op. 10, no. 5, and the Etude has an added bar at the end. Busoni's performance of the Beethoven *Ecossaise* does not follow his own edition, and at the end he adds several cadential chords. In the Chopin Etude, op. 25, no. 5, he avoids romantic effusion, highlighting instead the extraordinary chromatic melody that runs in the inner part of the outer sections.

SELECTED REFERENCES

Agostini, Franco. "Introduction." *Piano Quarterly*, Winter 1979–80, pp. 16–20. Introduction to a special Busoni issue of *Piano Quarterly*.

Bonavia, F. "Giacomo Puccini and Ferruccio Busoni." *Music and Letters*, April 1925, pp. 105–109.

"A Bridge to the Future." *Time*, 18 Feb 1966, p. 44.

Busoni, Ferruccio. *The Essence of Music and Other Papers* (translated by Rosamond Ley). New York: Philosophical Library, 1957.

———. "Neglected Details in Pianoforte Study." *Etude,* April 1910, pp. 225–226; continued May 1910.

———. "Sketch of a New Esthetic of Music." In *Three Classics in the Aesthetic of Music*. New York: Dover Publications, 1962.

Chantavoine, Jean. "Busoni." *Musical Quarterly*, July 1921, pp. 331–343.

Collet, Robert. "Busoni and the Piano." *The Listener*, 3 July 1947, p. 36.

Creighton, Ursula. "Reminiscences of Busoni." *Recorded Sound*, Autumn 1962, pp. 249–255.

Dent, Edward. *Ferruccio Busoni*. Oxford: Clarendon Press, 1966.

Johansen, Gunnar. "Busoni the Pianist In Perspective." *Piano Quarterly*, Winter 1979–80, pp. 46–47.

Lauderdale-Hinds, Lynne A. *Four Organ Chorale Preludes of Johann Sebastian Bach (1685–1750) as Realized for the Piano by Ferruccio Busoni (1866–1924)*. DMA Thesis, North Texas State University, 1980.

Morris, Edmund. "The Romance of the Piano." *New Yorker*, 8 Jan 1990, pp. 94–99.

Paddack, Christopher. "The Piano Art of Ferruccio Busoni." *Etude*, Sept 1953, pp. 13, 51.

Petri, Egon. "How Ferruccio Busoni Taught." *Etude*, Oct 1940, pp. 657, 710. Interview with Friede F. Rothe.

Roberge, Marc-André. *Ferruccio Busoni*. Westport, Conn.: Greenwood Press, 1991.

Schonberg, Harold C. "Forgotten Man." *New York Times*, 2 Dec 1963, sec. 2, p. 13.

———. "Recalling Busoni." *New York Times*, 7 Oct 1951, sec. 2, p. 7. An interview with Busoni pupil Dimitri Mitropoulos.

Schwarz, K. Robert. "Busoni: The Contradictions Persist." *New York Times*, 1 Sept 1985, pp. 15, 18.

Sitsky, Larry. *Busoni and the Piano: The Works, the Writings, and the Recordings*. Westport, Conn.: Greenwood Press, 1986.

———. "Busoni: A Short Survey of the Piano Music." *Piano Quarterly*, Winter 1979–80, pp. 22–27.

Spanuth, August. "Busoni At The Keyboard." *Musical America*, 24 Dec 1910. A lengthy review of a Berlin recital reproduced from *Die Signale*.

Stevenson, Ronald. "Busoni and Mozart." *The Score*, Sept 1955, pp. 25–38.

———. "Busoni—The Legend of a Prodigal." *The Score*, March 1956, pp. 15–30.

Straus, Noel. "Carnegie Program Devoted to Busoni." *New York Times*, 29 Dec 1941, p. 21.

Stuckenschmidt, H. H. *Ferruccio Busoni: Chronicle of a European*. London: Calder & Boyers, 1970.

Weiss, Edward. "Ferruccio Busoni." *Music Journal*, Sept 1975, pp. 6, 46.

See also Bibliography: Ald/Con; Bro/Mas; Bro/Pia; Cal/Mus; Cha/Gia; Coo/GrP; Dow/Oli; Kol/Que; Lah/Fam; Lan/Mus; Nie/Mei; Rat/Cle; Rub/MyM; Sch/Gre; Woo/My.

SELECTED REVIEWS

CT: 3 April 1915. *MA*: 20 Feb 1909; 15 Jan 1910; 22 Jan 1910; 29 Jan 1910; 19 Feb 1910; 14 Jan 1911; 21 Jan 1911; 28 Jan 1911; 11 Feb 1911; 23 Jan 1915; 30 Jan 1915; 6 Feb 1915; 20 Feb 1915; 6 March 1915; 13 Mar 1915. *MT*: 1 March 1922. *NYT*: 26 Jan 1910. *TL*: 5 Nov 1897; 13 Nov 1897; 3 Dec 1897; 23 Nov 1899; 28 Nov 1900; 11 Dec 1901; 18 Oct 1909; 7 Feb 1913; 20 Feb 1913; 13 March 1913; 8 Dec 1919; 28 June 1920; 5 July 1920.

SELECTED DISCOGRAPHY

A. Recordings by Busoni (Piano Rolls)

Bach-Busoni: Chaconne from Violin Partita BWV 1004. Symposium cassette 1005. Duo-Art roll 6928.

Ferruccio Busoni performs Franz Liszt. Adelaide (Beethoven); *La Campanella*; Don Juan Fantasy; Hungarian March (Schubert); Norma Fantasy (Bellini);

Polonaise No. 2 in E Major; Rigoletto Paraphrase (Verdi); Ruins of Athens (Beethoven); Valse Caprice (Donizetti). Recorded Treasures. CD-1. (Welte Legacy of Piano Treasures)

Chopin: Preludes, op. 28. Klavier KD 136 (Duo-Art transfer).

Liszt: *Feux follets* (The Great Pianists of the Century). Vol. 4: Legendary Virtuosos). CBS Sony 25AC 244. Duo-Art roll.

B. Recordings by Busoni (Discs)

Busoni/Petri Play Busoni. The Complete Original Disc Recordings of Busoni plus the following Busoni compositions played by his pupil Petri: Sonatinas Nos. 3 and 6; Red Indian Diary (I); Fantasia after music by Bach; Elegy No. 2; Spanish Rhapsody (Liszt, arr. Busoni). Pearl GEMM CD 9347.

C. Recordings by others of Busoni's piano music

Complete Piano Music (Geoffrey Douglas Madge). Philips 420740-2 (6 CDs).

Sonatinas (Paul Jacobs). Elektra/Nonesuch H-71359.

C

CARREÑO, TERESA: b. Caracas, Venezuela, 22 December 1853; d. New York, New York, 12 June 1917.

> Oh, she was a goddess. She had this unbelievable drive, this power. .
> . . And her octaves were *fantastic*. I don't think there's anyone today
> who can play such octaves. The speed and the power!
>
> Claudio Arrau (Horowitz, *Conversations with Arrau*)

Teresa Carreño began life with music, for she was born into a family distinguished musically as well as politically. José Cayetano Carreño, her grandfather, was a composer; and Manuel Antonio Carreño, her father and Venezuela's minister of finance, was an excellent pianist. He started Carreño on piano lessons when she was about six, using his own method. He wrote out 580 technical exercises for his small daughter, some of them difficult passages from the works of great composers, some that he composed himself for one hand only, then arranged for two hands, so that both hands had an equal workout. Her father also made her learn to transpose Czerny and other Etudes, thus eventually anything Carreño could play, she could play in any key. Most important, her father taught her how to listen to her own playing and be self-critical.

Carreño was already a recognized child prodigy when, in July 1862, her family left Venezuela because of political upheaval and for the sake of her musical future. They settled in New York, where the nine-year-old Carreño played for Louis Moreau Gottschalk, one of the great pianists of the time. Her playing so astonished Gottschalk that he gave her occasional lessons and advised her father concerning her career. Though Carreño was only a child and knew Gottschalk only briefly, he became the model and inspiration of her early career, and she often included his works on her early concert programs. Gottschalk and her father introduced Carreño to the New York musical world in a private concert at Irving Hall on 7 November 1862, with Theodore Thomas, a young violinist at the outset of his conducting career, as assisting artist. Her playing caused a sensation. She made her New York public debut on 25 November 1862 and appeared in another concert four days later, both also at Irving Hall.

Even at this young age Carreño captivated audiences. During January and February of 1863 she played some 20 concerts in and around Boston, and the *Boston Globe* declared that, "this little child has created more excitement in musical circles, a more genuine furore than any artiste who has been in Boston since the visit of Jenny Lind." Incredibly, Carl Zerrahn, conductor of the Boston Philharmonic Society, invited the ten-year-old Carreño to play Mendelssohn's *Capriccio Brillant* at the Philharmonic Society concert (24 Jan 1863) held at the Boston Music Hall.

During the New York years (1862–66) Teresa studied English, practiced often and played in more concerts (Havana, New York, Baltimore, Philadelphia, and at the White House for President Lincoln in the fall of 1863). In the spring of 1866 her family moved to Paris. Almost immediately, the 12-year-old Teresa met and conquered the influential Mme. Erard, who not only sent a piano to the hotel but very quickly arranged for Teresa to make her Paris debut in a forthcoming Vivier Concert (14 May 1866) at the *Salle Erard.* Meanwhile, Teresa played (10 May) for Gioachino Rossini and so delighted the elderly composer that he attended her debut. The indefatigable Mme. Erard also managed an audition with Franz Liszt, held the morning of Carreño's debut. Liszt graciously played for her first, to put her at her ease, then Carreño played Gottschalk's The Last Hope for him. The fact that the child pianist had played for Liszt and Rossini assured a full house at her debut.

Carreño's father took her to London in June. Her matinee concert (23 July 1866) at St. James Minor Hall had a good review ("a proficiency that would become an artist twice or thrice her age"); but since the London season had ended, they returned to Paris. As a foreigner, Carreño could not enroll at the Paris Conservatory. Instead, she had piano lessons with Georges Matthias, a pupil of Chopin, and studied harmony and counterpoint with Emmanuel Bazin. For income, her father took private pupils, as did Carreño, most notably Blandine Ollivier, a daughter of Liszt, who took a lesson each week. Apart from the loss of her mother (Clorinda Carreño died of cholera in September 1866), the teenage Carreño must have found Paris exciting. She often played for Charles Gounod, and sometimes Gounod would play for her, showing her how Chopin had interpreted his own compositions. Through the connections of Mme. Erard, Gounod, the Princess Mathilde and her own father, Carreño met most of the important political and artistic people in Paris, including the music publisher M. Heugel, who began publishing her compositions.

Early in May 1868 Carreño and her father returned to London. Anton Rubinstein's presence at one of her concerts in July 1868 was by far the most exciting part of this London stay. Impressed by Carreño's playing, her beauty and her dazzling spirit, Rubinstein hurried backstage at the intermission to congratulate her. Ignoring the great difference in their ages, the two pianists became fast friends, and as Gottschalk had influenced the child prodigy, Rubinstein now guided the 15-year-old maturing artist. He gave her intermittent lessons whenever they happened to be in the same city, and advised her father on her career. Carreño adored Rubinstein and always believed that she had learned more from him than he was conscious of teaching her.

By the time she was 16, Carreño was receiving ever more invitations to join concert groups on tour, usually in Holland, the French provinces, Belgium and Great Britain. Between 1870 and 1874 she lived in London under the watchful eye of a chaperone. During 1871–74 she had a steady income as one of the regular artists with the Rivière Promenade Concerts, playing for both the Wednesday "classical" concerts conducted by Arthur Sullivan and for the Tuesday concerts devoted to opera. In 1872 Carreño also appeared in Arthur Chappel's fine Monday Popular Concerts, associating with quality performers such as Clara Schumann, Joseph Joachim and Charles Hallé. During January–March 1872 she toured the English provinces with a Mapleson opera company that included the great Therese Tietjens. In Edinburgh, Mapleson recruited Carreño to substitute for a defecting soprano who refused to sing the role of the Queen in *Les Huguenots*. Thus Carreño, not using her own name, made her singing debut (12 March 1872) in that role and earned passable reviews.

Carreño met Émile Sauret, a young French violinist, when both made a long Strakosch tour (Sept 1872–May 1873) through the United States. (The Strakosch brothers were leading late 19th-century impresarios.) Much to her father's distress, Carreño and Sauret married (June 1873) and established a home in London. Her first child, a daughter named Emilita, was born in March 1874. After her father's death in August of that year, Carreño realized that she was on her own, for the immature Sauret provided little support. Needing money, the Saurets signed with Strakosch for another long American tour, and left their daughter in the care of Mrs. Bischoff, Carreño's former chaperone. At the end of that tour, Sauret returned to London, leaving Carreño in America to await the arrival of their second child, who died at birth. The marriage steadily deteriorated, and the Saurets separated in the spring of 1875. Lacking regular means of support, Carreño allowed Mrs. Bischoff to adopt Emilita, giving up her maternal rights in order that the child might have a proper life. (Mrs. Bischoff died in 1902, but Emilita, raised to believe Carreño an uncaring, frivolous mother, waited three years before visiting her.)

Carreño decided to make a new start in Boston, where she had been so affectionately received as a child. But she was no longer an adorable prodigy. Ahead of her lay long, hard years of endless concerts, hordes of pupils and little relaxation. In Boston she supported herself working as an accompanist for a singing teacher. She also studied singing and made her American singing debut (25 Feb 1876) under her own name, singing the role of Zerlina in *Don Giovanni* with a Strakosch opera company at the New York Academy of Music.

At this low point in her life the Weber Piano Company engaged Carreño as its representative at a modest but fixed salary, an association that lasted 14 years. New York now being more convenient, she moved there in the fall of 1876, and shortly thereafter an old friend, the violinist Juan Buitrago, invited her to hear one of his pupils, a 15-year-old named Edward MacDowell. This meeting marked the beginning of a lifelong, intimate friendship (despite occasional misunderstandings) with the MacDowell family. Carreño greatly influenced MacDowell's formative years. She talked with him, practiced with him, gave him lessons and advised his parents concerning his career. At her urging, they sent him to Paris for study. MacDowell's early popularity was in great measure due to Carreño's unselfish efforts in playing his works. The mutual respect and affection between Carreño and MacDowell comes alive in his letter to her written 2 March 1899. It begins, "Respected Valkyrie and Grandmother."

In 1876 Carreño and Giovanni Tagliapietra, an Italian baritone on tour in America with a Strakosch opera company, entered into a common-law marriage, a relationship that endured for 14 years and produced three children. The marriage began happily. They lived in New Rochelle, New York, and both continued touring, sometimes appearing together. But once again Carreño had chosen the wrong husband. Tagliapietra, fond of drinking and gambling, proved irresponsible, and in time Carreño became the main support of the household. Apart from her joy in her children, these were depressing years. She toured whenever possible, taught private pupils and, to make more money, even played concerts at the New York Casino. In the spring of 1883 a grand, successful tour with Leopold Damrosch through the United States and Canada restored Carreño's status as a pianist.

In 1885 the president of Venezuela invited Carreño to give a series of concerts in Caracas and the provinces between October 1885 and September 1886. Her native land received her like a queen, and audiences responded with wild ovations. Unfortunately, when the Catholic Venezuelans learned of her common-law marriage, they shunned her. The Venezuelan government, however, invited her to organize an opera season in Caracas, for which the Tagliapietras created the Teresa Carreño Grand Opera Company. It performed in Caracas during February–May 1887, and from the start, it was a fiasco. Tagliapietra proved more troublesome than ever, and at one point Carreño even had to step in and conduct.

Carreño toured constantly, sometimes still with Tagliapietra, but his intemperance and temper had ruined the relationship. She finally left him in July 1889, taking her children first to London, then Paris, where she practiced six hours daily to prepare for her Berlin debut on 18 November 1889 at the *Singakademie*. She played the Grieg Concerto, Schumann's Symphonic Etudes and the Weber-Liszt *Polonaise Brillante*, and her electrifying, highly personal style absolutely stunned the Germans. Hans von Bülow, praising Carreño as an exotic phenomenon, invited her to repeat the Grieg Concerto at his Berlin Philharmonic concert on 31 January 1890. At her third Berlin concert (13 Feb 1890) Carreño played three concertos, one of which was MacDowell's Concerto No. 2 in D Minor.

Carreño made her home in Berlin for more than a quarter of a century (Oct 1889–Oct 1916). She performed every season, touring extensively in Europe and in the United States and Canada. A disciplined, strong woman, Carreño played no matter how she felt or what problems she faced. Critics called her the empress of the piano, the only pianist who could boast of a full house in a season overcrowded with concerts. She was, said Antwerp's *Le Précurseur*, "capable of thawing the North Pole."

Carreño and Eugen d'Albert met in April 1891, and they married in July 1892. From the beginning it seemed inevitable that this union of two highly artistic temperaments would fail. Between the births of their two daughters Carreño toured, sometimes playing d'Albert's compositions in her concerts. During 1893–94 the d'Alberts toured as a two-piano team, and under her husband's influence Carreño gradually discarded some of the bravura works once so prominent in her programs. She gained a new control, a new note of contemplation in her readings, and there were fewer occasions when she let herself go to wild extremes at the piano just for the joy of being able to do it. Some critics felt that she had acquired a new sense of musical values without spoiling her sparkling spontaneity. Others missed her "usually overflowing temperament," her famous signature.

Carreño divorced (Oct 1895) d'Albert on the grounds of willful desertion. Now the sole support of four children, she became a slave to her concert schedule, sometimes playing as many as 70 concerts a season. Through these years of stress and worry Arturo Tagliapietra, youngest brother of Carreño's second husband, had remained her friend. In time he became part of her household, an all-around manager, companion and secretary who helped with her tours, her children and her problems. Carreño and Arturo Tagliapietra married on 30 June 1902, and in this marriage Carreño was content. During the first five years of the marriage, she performed only in Europe. In 1907–08 she toured in Australia, New Zealand and the United States. In November 1909 she began an exhausting 18-month tour that included Europe, America, Australia, New Zealand, South Africa and Egypt.

Overwork, worry and years of overwhelming financial responsibilities began to take their toll. Carreño toured England in 1913 and the United States in 1914, but her old vigor had faded. The rest of her 1914 concerts were canceled because of World War II, but she made more than 40 appearances in 1915. In September 1916 she gave up her longtime residence in Berlin and moved to New York. She taught privately, held flourishing classes at the American Institute of Applied Music and went on tour. While in Cuba, Carreño apparently suffered a mild stroke, but she rallied to perform, giving her final concert in Havana on 21 March 1917. Teresa Carreño died in New York on 12 June 1917. In 1938 her ashes were returned to Caracas, and in honor of that event, Venezuela issued (14 Feb 1938) a special commemorative stamp. In 1983 the Teresa Carreño Foundation established the Teresa Carreño Arts Center in midtown Caracas.

Teresa Carreño's programs indicate that works by Beethoven, Chopin, Liszt, Schubert and Schumann predominated in her repertoire. She played some Bach, mostly in transcription, and faithfully promoted the works of Edward MacDowell. For her performances with orchestra, Carreño preferred large-scale dramatic works, usually concertos by Beethoven, Rubinstein, Liszt or Tchaikovsky.

Her very active, stressful life left little time for composing. Although a good composer (her compositions include a well-structured string quartet, some choral works and, above all, a fair number of solo piano compositions), she was not notably original. As might be expected, she wrote splendidly and idiomatically for the piano, incorporating into her works techniques—trills, passages in thirds and sixths—for which she was justly famous as a concert pianist. Most of her piano pieces are small-scale. Among the larger forms she attempted, the Ballade, op. 15, and Polonaise, op. 35, are works of substance and merit.

Carreño taught all her life, even as a teenage prodigy in Paris. She always took pupils when at home between tours, and regularly taught during summer vacations. In the 1890s literally armies of music students besieged Germany, and Carreño, the embodiment of their ideal pianist, acquired an impressive reputation as a teacher, often with a waiting list of 50 or more students. She said that she used her father's teaching method, but in practice the impetuous Carreño taught as the spirit moved her. She had three basic rules: Master the fundamentals, know what to do, do it. She rarely assigned pupils a fixed weekly lesson hour, and never timed the lessons. Typically she reacted spontaneously, offering a suggestion at one point, illustrating at the piano at another, or playing the orchestral part for a concerto on a second piano.

Every lesson began with Bach. In addition to the newly prepared material, the Bach prepared at the preceding lesson had to be smoothly transposed into a key remote from the original. Further, whatever composition the student brought to a lesson had to be memorized and worked up to the very best of that student's ability. Famous for her own remarkable power and endurance, Carreño taught that the secret lay in relaxation. For example, "For the heavy chords in the Tchaikovsky Concerto my arms are absolutely limp from the shoulder. . . . That is why I can play for hours without the slightest fatigue. It is mental relaxation, for one has to think it; it must be in the mind first before it can be worked out in arms and hands." (*MA*, 8 Nov 1913)

Perhaps above all else Carreño valued variety in interpretation, a color palette to be achieved by changes of tone rather than by rhythmic shiftings. Cultivating differences of touch in staccato and legato, increasing the dynamic range at both ends, this was as much her ambition for the student as keeping tone always within the margin of the beautiful. That she considered the pedal most important in achieving shading is proved by the fact that the only book she wrote deals with that subject (Carreño, *On the Possibilities . . .*).

Carreño obviously taught each pupil differently, "but not one would have exchanged that experience, unorganized as it was, for another. What after all is great teaching but bringing the student alive to the beautiful in music. . . . In that sense Carreño was a great teacher." (Milinowski)

Even as a child Teresa Carreño showed signs of the vividly personal playing style that would make her famous. Although only eight years old when she appeared in her second New York concert (29 Nov 1862), her remarkable playing caused a furore. "There are many performers who can boast of strength, and a few who have her execution, but it would be difficult to mention another who has her exquisite perception of musical thought, her delicate sensibility to form. These things, which come to her by nature and not by application, give her a position which no other juvenile performer on the piano has ever commanded." (*NYT*, 1 Dec 1862) At her Paris debut ("from beginning to end transcendently successful") on 14 May 1866, the critics raved that the 12-year-old was "a pianist with power, a Liszt in petticoats." Carreño never lost the magic power that swayed audiences and critics. Playing in Dresden a half-century later, she was "as great now as in her youth and, moreover, has added to her interpretations a deep emotional color, such as now and then nearly draws tears to one's eyes." (*MA*, 3 April 1915)

From the outset Carreño's amazing technique, memory and musicianship dazzled audiences. An 1889 reviewer neatly summed up her style in saying that it was in the music that approached the virtually impossible that Carreño was most completely at home. Essentially, it was not so much what she played as how she played it. If critics sometimes disagreed with her interpretations, most conceded that they were always carefully thought out and worthy of respect.

Nearly every review mentions Carreño's fiery temperament. In the words of contemporary writers, she was "a glorious lioness," "a pulsating embodiment of musical temperament," "a Sappho of the piano," "a Valkyrie of the keyboard." At the same time, she never stooped to the meretricious tricks of the mere virtuoso. "There is, possibly, nothing that is unplayable to Mme. Carreño; yet, as her technique is a means only to an artistic end, one might listen to her for hours without the fact being obtruded that her mechanical dexterity is enormous." (*TL*, 17 Feb 1902)

While obviously it was Carreño's unique personality and style that won her listeners, she never let her individuality get in the way of the music. At her Berlin debut (18 Nov 1889) the stern German critics marveled at her wondrous endurance and daring style; and this despite their feeling that Carreño's tone lacked richness and delicacy, that her tempos were too erratic, that she dealt in extremes. "With complete and blinding technical virtuosity, with strength sufficient for two pianists, and with an uncommonly and strongly sculptured sense of rhythm, Frau Carreño combines spiritual freedom and independence of interpretation, which lifts her far above mere pianism into the realm of true art." (*Allgemeine Musikzeitung*, 19 Nov 1889)

Carreño played the Tchaikovsky Concerto in B-flat Minor at her first appearance (1897) with Henry Wood's Promenade Concerts in London. "Her masculine vigor of tone and touch and her marvelous precision on executing octave passages carried everyone completely away. . . . It is difficult to express adequately what all musicians felt about this great woman who looked a queen among pianists and *played* like a goddess." (Woo/My, see Bibliog.)

The fact that at her London recital on 23 May 1898 Carreño "had lost none of her astounding virtuosity, but had gained much of the artistic charm of interpretation which was before lacking," may have been due to the influence of Eugen d'Albert. A critic who liked the "new Carreño" found that in her London Beethoven program (15 March 1900) her performance showed "admirable finish and musical intelligence, as well as the consummate virtuosity for which Mme. Carreño has long been famous. On the whole her playing this year seems far more artistic than it was formerly, her conception broader, and her means of realisation more matured." (*TL*, 16 March 1900) And again in 1900, when Carreño played in New York, the music editor of the *New York Times* remembered the time "when Carreño was temperament and nothing else. . . . But that day has gone by. She is now a ripe and thoughtful artist whose temperament blazes with unquenchable fire, but whose understanding holds sway on the throne of her art." (*NYT*, 18 Nov 1900)

Not all critics liked the change in Carreño's playing. An 1896 perform-ance of Beethoven's "Emperor" Concerto and Liszt's Hungarian Fantasy with the Berlin Philharmonic Orchestra under Arthur Nikisch showed impeccable tech-nique and understanding, but a writer for *Die neue Zeitschrift für Musik* "missed her usually overflowing temperament. This highly imaginative artist must not let herself be frightened by pedantic school teachers. Her fire, her passionateness are the very traits that differentiate her from the numberless hordes of pianists of both sexes who are technically capable but who do not stand out with any par-ticular artistic individuality. She should not take the trouble to repress these qualities, or else she will be robbed of her most beautiful jewel, her own person-ality."

Whatever the criticisms, through the years Carreño held her audiences. A dozen years later, a critic reviewing her program (7 May 1912) of Beethoven, Chopin, Schumann and Schubert offered a clear summary of her art: "Mme Carreño still takes her audience with her from the first moment and is always sure of them. . . . While difficulties are smiled away, passages generally held to be easy are treated just as carefully as if they were difficult. The tone is in a small scale; the absolute distance between extreme loud and soft is not so great as with many other good players; but there are a great many more gradations, and an instinctive and unerring command of them enables her to cover a greater range of feeling." (*TL*, 8 May 1912)

By 1913 Carreño showed the strain of her intense career and difficult life. She was "strangely subdued" at her Carnegie Hall recital on 4 November of that year, and at next year's Carnegie recital (9 Jan 1914) "there was less of the sweep and technical bravura that are associated with her name." But at her final Carnegie Hall recital (27 Oct 1916), played seven months before her death, Carreño showed a marvelous rejuvenation. "Immeasurably greater today than on her last American appearance. . . . Carreño remains the Valkyrie of the piano— but a Valkyrie as capable of the softest, most caressing and contemplative moods as of Amazonian stress and turbulence. Hers is the grand manner in its noblest exemplification." (*MA*, 4 Nov 1916)

James Huneker, an ardent Carreño admirer who loved her grand manner, has grandly described it: "When I wish to recall her I close my eyes and straightway as if in a scarlet mist I see her, hear her; for her playing has always been scarlet to me, as Rubinstein's is golden and Joseffy's silvery." (Hun/Uni, see Bibliog.)

It is difficult now to obtain a clear picture of Teresa Carreño's playing. She made no acoustic discs, but did record over 40 piano rolls for the Welte-Mignon, Duo-Art, Ampico and other companies (Sit/Cla, see Bibliog.). Despite the purely mechanistic results of this process and Carreño's great reluctance to record—for the first time in her life she was nervous about performing—the pi-ano rolls reveal a few characteristics of her artistry. Most noticeable is how

Carreño avoids using the pedal as a legato crutch and her use of it for the enhancement of tone. The piano rolls also show a clear articulation of inner voices, of contrapuntal lines; her use of *rubato*; her grand ritardandos at cadence points; and her playing of certain passages in a register different than that originally indicated.

Of the available piano-roll transfers, perhaps the finest is Carreño's playing of Beethoven's "*Waldstein*" Sonata, op. 53. There is no overt virtuosity or excess *rubato* here. The spirit of the composer prevails in a sincere, compassionate performance of this keyboard masterpiece. Another good example of Carreño's artistry can be heard in her version of Chopin's Nocturne in C Minor, op. 48, no. 1 (see Discog.).

SELECTED REFERENCES

Armstrong, William. "Teresa Carreño's Reminiscences." *Musical Courier*: Part I, 28 June 1917; Part 2, 6 July 1917.

Carreño, Teresa. "Early Technical Training." In Brower, *Piano Mastery* (see Bibliog.), pp. 160–167.

———. "Idealism in Music Study." *Etude*, June 1917, pp. 369–370.

———. "Individuality in Piano Playing." *Etude*, Dec 1909, p. 805, contd. Jan 1910. Also in Cooke, *Great Pianists on Piano Playing* (see Bibliog.), pp. 109–119.

———. *Obras de Teresa Carreño*, foreword by Rosario Marciano. Caracas: *Ediciones del Ministerio de Educacion*, 1974. Reprint by Da Capo Press (1985) as *Teresa Carreño: Selected Works*. Includes piano pieces ops. 9, 15, 17, 18, 25, 27, 28, 32, 33, 34 (two compositions), 35 (*Le Sommeil*), 38, 39, plus *Pequeño valse* and *Valse gayo*.

———. "Observation in Piano Playing." *Etude*, Feb 1914, pp. 89–90.

———. *On the Possibilities of Tone Color by Artistic Use of the Pedals.* Cincinnati: John Church Co., 1919.

Cooke, James Francis. "Musica Pan-America." *Etude*, Aug 1939, pp. 491-492.

Hinson, Maurice. "Teresa Carreño." *Clavier*, April 1988, pp. 16–23.

Horowitz, Joseph. *Conversations with Arrau.* New York: Alfred A. Knopf, 1982.

Kinscella, Hazel. "A Half Century of Piano Playing as Viewed Through Teresa Carreño's Eyes." *Musical America*, 30 Dec 1916, pp. 5–6.

Mann, Brian. "The Carreño Collection at Vassar College." *Notes*, June 1991, pp. 1064–1084.

Milinowski, Marta. *Teresa Carreno: "by the grace of God."* New Haven: Yale University Press, 1940. Reprint by Da Capo Press, 1977.

Nelson, Cordelia Hulburd. "The Queen of American Pianists." *Etude*, Aug 1938, pp. 497–498, 502.

Obituary. *Musical America*, 23 June 1917, pp. 13–14. *Musical Courier*, 21 June 1917, pp. 5, 17. *New York Times*, 13 June 1917, p. 13. *The Times* (London), 14 June 1917, p. 3.

Peña, Israel. *Teresa Carreño.* Caracas: *Ediciones de la "Fundacion Eugenio Mendoza,"* 1953.

See also Bibliography: Ald/Con; Bro/Pia; Cha/Gia; Coo/GrP; Ewe/Mu; Ger/Fam; Hun/Ste; Lah/Fam; MGG; New/Gro; Nie/Mei; Pay/Cel; Rat/Cle; Reu/Gre; Rub/MyY; Sch/Gre; Sha/Mus; Woo/My.

SELECTED REVIEWS

MA: 30 Nov 1907; 21 Dec 1907; 28 Dec 1907; 20 Nov 1909; 4 Dec 1909; 12 April 1913; 17 Jan 1914; 3 April 1915; 4 Nov 1916. *MT*: 1 June 1890; 1 July 1890. *NYT*: 1 Dec 1862; 9 Jan 1897; 16 April 1899; 18 Nov 1900; 28 Nov 1900; 5 Dec 1909; 5 Nov 1913; 10 Jan 1914; 28 Oct 1916. *TL*: 18 June 1890; 24 May 1898; 19 June 1899; 16 March 1900; 7 June 1901; 11 June 1901; 18 June 1901; 17 Feb 1902; 5 Oct 1908; 19 Oct 1908; 5 Oct 1911; 8 May 1912; 16 Dec 1912; 9 Oct 1913.

SELECTED DISCOGRAPHY

A. Played by Carreño (Long-play discs and CDs from piano rolls)

Teresa Carreño Performs In 1906. Beethoven: Sonata in C Major, op. 53. Chopin: Ballade No. 1 in G Minor, op. 23; Ballade No. 2 in A-flat Major, op. 47. Welte Legacy of Piano Treasures. S 670. (Side 2 is mislabeled.)

Carreño: *Kleiner Walzer.* Recorded Treasures.

Chopin: Nocturne, op. 37, no. 2. Classics Record Library.

The Compositions of Franz Liszt. Hungarian Rhapsody No. 6. The Welte Legacy.

The Definitive Piano. Schubert-Liszt: *Soirée de Vienne* No. 6. Telefunken TH 97013

Welte-Mignon 1905. Chopin: Nocturne in C Minor, op. 48, no. 1. Teldec CD 8.43930.

B. Carreño played by others.

Piano Works by Women Composers. Vox/Turnabout CT-4685.

String Quartet in B Minor. Vox Box CDX 5029.

CASADESUS, ROBERT: b. Paris, France, 7 April 1899; d. Paris, 19 September 1972.

> When all is said and done there is no true French style today. There is only good or bad international style. . . . One of the best Debussy players is Gieseking, a German. The best Bach I ever heard was by Casals, a Spaniard. You don't have to be born in New York to play Copland.
> Robert Casadesus (*Piano Quarterly*, Fall 1982)

In just two generations the family of Robert Casadesus (a Catalan name meaning "house of Jesus") produced a distinguished company of musicians. His own father, not a professional musician, became an actor, using the stage name of Robert Casa. But three of Casadesus's uncles became well-known musicians: François-Louis (Francis) founded the American Conservatory at Fontainebleau, Henri-Gustave established the Society of Ancient Instruments, Marius was a violinist. Their sister Rose, an accomplished pianist, had studied at the Paris Conservatory with Marmontel. In Casadesus's generation, Marcel, son of François-Louis, was a cellist.

Raised by his paternal grandparents—a matter of necessity because his Swedish mother died in childbirth and his father was so often away on theatrical tours—at about age five Casadesus began piano lessons with his Aunt Rose. (Even at age 30 he was still going to Normandy to play for her.) Casadesus first went to the Paris Conservatory at age 10 to study solfeggio. At age 12 he enrolled (Oct 1911) in the piano class of Louis Diémer, a pupil of Liszt; and in the spring of 1913 he received a first prize in piano at the Conservatory. At age 16 Casadesus began harmony instruction with his Uncle Francis, but after his father was called to active duty in World War I, he gave up his studies and found work playing celesta and percussion in the *Opéra-Comique* orchestra, an experience that later proved invaluable for his composing.

Casadesus fulfilled his own service obligation playing drums in the Corps of Engineers band, another experience later valuable to him as a composer. And in 1916 he returned to the Conservatory to complete his harmony studies, first with Xavier Leroux, a well-known composer and teacher, later with Noël Gallon. In 1917, at age 18, he made his debut in Paris with a recital at the *Salle des Agriculteurs*; in 1919 he received a first prize in harmony at the Conservatory; and in 1920 he was awarded the coveted Diémer Prize in piano, and he also toured Spain, playing chamber music with cellist Maurice Maréchal and violinist Marius Casadesus. The following year he married Gaby L'Hôte, one of Diémer's advanced pupils (of their three children, Jean became a professional pianist), and they lived in Fontainebleau while Casadesus taught (1921–24) at the American Conservatory founded by his Uncle Francis.

In 1922 Casadesus played Ravel's *Valses nobles et sentimentales* and *Gaspard de la nuit* in a concert of modern music at the *Vieux Columbier* in Paris, and Ravel, enchanted with the young pianist's interpretations of his music, asked Casadesus to accompany him to London to record some Ravel works for the Aeolian Company. As Mme. Casadesus recalled, "Ravel was too out of practice to make all the piano rolls himself. My husband played the *Miroirs* and *Gaspard*, and Ravel played the easier pieces." (Eld/Pia, see Bibliog.) Apparently these piano rolls were never issued commercially. In that same interview Mme. Casadesus stated that her husband was the first to record all of Ravel's piano music and the first to give an all-Ravel program in Paris, at the *Salle Pleyel* in 1922. Later that same year Ravel and Casadesus toured in Spain and Switzerland, always beginning their program with the original four-hand version of *Ma Mère l'Oye*, Ravel playing the top part, Casadesus playing the bass. As Mme. Casadesus remembered that tour, the program ended with Casadesus playing the Ravel Trio with his Uncle Marius and Maurice Maréchal.

Tours of Western Europe, Russia, Poland, the Baltic states, Romania, Greece, Turkey, North Africa and South America established Casadesus's reputation. For his American debut on 20 January 1935, he played the Mozart "Coronation" Concerto, K. 537, with the New York Philharmonic Society Orchestra, conducted by Hans Lange. Although critics generally agreed that his was a brilliant performance, some felt that Mozart was not the right choice for his debut. "In spite of the spirit of the performance, it led to the desire to hear Mr. Casadesus in another kind of concerto, one more modern and of fuller sonority than Mozart's." (*NYT*, 21 Jan 1935) However, Arturo Toscanini attended that concert and was so pleased that at intermission he asked Casadesus to play with him the following season. Thus, on 30 January 1936 Casadesus played the Brahms Concerto No. 2 with Toscanini and the NYPSO; and the following May, for a concert in Paris honoring Camile Saint-Saëns, Toscanini again chose Casadesus as soloist to play the Saint-Saëns Concerto No. 4 in C Minor. Thereafter, Casadesus made regular, very successful tours of the United States.

Forced to leave France because of the Nazi occupation, Casadesus and his family lived in Princeton, New Jersey, from 1940 through 1946. His career flourished in America. He toured, recorded and during the summers taught at the American Conservatory which, because of the war, had been transferred to the United States, first to St. George's School in Newport, Rhode Island, later to Great Barrington, Massachusetts, in the Berkshires. Casadesus put down deep roots in Princeton. Beginning in 1937, he performed seven times on the university concert series, more than any other pianist. And from 1946 to 1965 his name appeared on the Princeton University register as Honorary Lecturer; however, he apparently never taught at Princeton. The lectureship "was a symbol— the token of a relationship of mutual respect and admiration." (Cone)

Casadesus returned to France in 1947 to help reestablish the American Conservatory at Fontainebleau and to resume his European concert career, but for many years the Casadesus family spent winters in Princeton and the rest of the year in France. He resigned from the Conservatory in 1948 because of his enormously busy concert schedule and the desire for more time for composing. During a concert career spanning 55 years, Casadesus played about 3,000 concerts and never once canceled a performance because of illness.

Robert Casadesus's honors included the Order of Leopold of Belgium (1937); Officer of France's *Légion d'honneur* (1939); an honorary doctor of music from Lawrence University (Wisconsin) in 1944; Commander of the Order of Orange-Nassau, from the Queen of the Netherlands in 1958; the Brahms Medal from the City of Hamburg in 1958 (he was the only non-German up to that time to receive the medal); a gold medal from the City of Paris (1959). In 1969 Casadesus celebrated both his 70th birthday and the 35th anniversary of his American debut with a concert (26 Nov) honoring him as both pianist and composer. He played the same Mozart "Coronation" Concerto that he had played at his debut, and George Szell and the New York Philharmonic Orchestra played Casadesus's Suite No. 2 in B-flat Major.

Casadesus's son Jean, a successful pianist, died in an auto crash in Ontario, Canada, in January 1972. Eight months later Robert Casadesus died of cancer in Paris. On 17 July 1992 the International Piano Archives at the

University of Maryland formally accepted the Robert and Gaby Casadesus Collection as a gift from the Casadesus family. The papers and other materials are now available to scholars.

Robert Casadesus was that rare combination—master pianist and master teacher. In the early years of his career he taught a great deal—from 1921 to 1924 at the American Conservatory at Fontainebleau; in 1929–30 he gave classes in performance practice and interpretation at the Genoa Conservatory; in 1931–32 he taught at Lausanne. In 1934 he succeeded Isidor Philipp as head of the piano department at the American Conservatory at Fontainebleau. During World War II he gave summer classes at the American Conservatory, at the time temporarily established in the United States; from 1946 he was director; and he resigned in 1948. Thereafter he taught only private students, many of them Americans. Grant Johannesen, one of Casadesus's most notable students, says that Casadesus "was a wonderful teacher for those who could grasp what he was getting at. He had an enormous ability to show you what the structure of music was, for instance, in large works, such as the B minor Sonata of Chopin, or the Schumann Fantasia, or the Liszt Sonata. He had a way of describing this music which took you from beginning to end in a flash. He guided you." (Dub/Ref, see Bibliog.)

As a teacher, Casadesus had a gift for communicating the essence of the music itself in a very few words. His teaching, he said, was based on the two cornerstones of pianism—technique and musicianship. "The most fluent fingers are useless unless they have something to be fluent about; the most sensitive conceptions are valueless unless they find suitable outlet through the fingers." (*Etude*, May 1955) To acquire technique, Casadesus recommended the exercises of Czerny, Philipp and Brahms, advising his students to play scales and arpeggios 30 minutes a day, but only 10 minutes of the Philipp exercises (or the wrist may get stiff) and only 10 minutes of the Brahms (wonderful for extension). Casadesus advised only four hours a day practice; the important thing was to be consistent and practice every day.

To acquire musicianship, the other cornerstone of pianism, he urged his students to study good music and to faithfully reconstruct the composer's intentions, thus the choice of editions is most critical. "The basic creed is to follow the composer. He said what he meant to say in the key signature, the time signature, the notes, rests and indications. To tamper with any one of these is both unmusical and impertinent." (Eld/Pia, see Bibliog.) Of course Casadesus did not always follow all score indications. In Beethoven, for example, some of the pedal markings do not work on a modern piano. Casadesus, said his wife, came from the school that taught the pianist to listen to himself, that by listening and thinking with head and heart, the pianist will know which signs to observe and which ones need modification.

Casadesus instilled in his students his own sincere attitude towards making music. Although he rarely played for them, not wanting them to become mirror images of his own playing, he would sometimes demonstrate his ideas on the piano; for example, his illustration of how to play staccato was a "revelation" for one student, each note a polished entity in itself. Casadesus also would play the orchestra parts for a pupil working on a concerto; and he would demonstrate on the piano more often for pupils who spoke little French. He allowed students great freedom in how they played and in how they approached different compositions; encouraged them to find the overall design of a composition; and emphasized the value of rests, of silence as a psychological secret in music making. He stressed the importance of tempo and beat (pulse in music is the foundation of the structure) because, he said, it is impossible to have a beautiful and logical *rubato*, or any other adjustment of tempo and beat, if there is no thorough understanding and development of the beat itself.

A serious composer, Casadesus wrote his first work in 1916 and composed for the rest of his life. His compositions, many unpublished, include seven symphonies, concertos for one, two and three pianos with orchestra, chamber works, songs and piano pieces. Generally speaking, his works are seldom descriptive; modality and extreme dissonance prevail; in most of his works he manages some ingenious modification of classic form. (For further information on Casadesus as composer, see Stookes.)

Casadesus's repertoire, not huge by today's standards, was carefully selected from the classical, romantic and modern periods. A Frenchman, he played a large quantity of Debussy and Ravel, as well as works by other French composers—Fauré, Franck, Rameau, Saint-Saëns, Séverac. He especially liked Scarlatti, played some Bach, in general ignored Haydn. He played some Mozart sonatas and many of the Mozart concertos; and brought to Mozart's music "a sound and shape that revealed the strong sinews supporting its grace and elegance. Perhaps most of all he brought its joy." (Tolson) Over the span of his career Casadesus played about ten Beethoven sonatas in public, usually having two or three current at any one time. Chopin, especially the four Ballades and the Sonatas Nos. 2 and 3, appeared frequently on his programs.

Most of all, he played works by Schumann. His first teacher, his Aunt Rose, loved the music of Schumann and taught him, he said, just how to play it. He remembered that as a small boy put to bed after dinner he would hear his aunt's pupils working on *Waldscenen, Kinderscenen* and *Album für die Jugend.* "I was frightened when *Furchtenmachen* and *Verrufene Stelle* vibrated through the wall; I wanted to get up and play when I heard *Ritter von Steckenpferd* and *Hasche Mann*; and I closed my eyes at the sound of *Kind im Einschlummern.* But above all I was often moved to tears by the sadness of the music." (*SR*, 28 July 1956) In his performances of Schumann's solo works, "details never obtrude; impressionistic touches never take up too much room. He plays Schumann's Symphonic Studies as though in one breath—and this really few can do. . . . How wonderfully Gallic Schumann's piano works can turn out to be appears when Casadesus includes *Waldscenen* in his programme." (Kai/Gre, see Bibliog.)

What of Robert Casadesus's playing? What influences molded his approach to pianism? "Ravel's rather ineffectual piano playing influenced Casadesus little; Debussy's playing, on the other hand, created a deep impression." (Gel/Mus, see Bibliog.) Casadesus described Debussy as the most relaxed, supple, softly nuanced pianist he had ever heard, and listening to Debussy taught him the extraordinary importance of understatement as a means to musical expression. At the same time, Casadesus's playing reflects his own interpretative ideas. "Healthy vigor, strength and clarity of outline, even if occasionally at the expense of subjective mood, exemplify Casadesus' playing." (Banowetz)

Casadesus may not have admired Ravel's piano playing, but he loved Ravel's music, and his concern with precision, suavity and fastidiousness was ideally suited to that music, "whose equilibrium was of that order which posed clear-cut problems and admitted of no ambivalence. Casadesus is a skilled and authoritative interpreter of Ravel despite one of the severest handicaps that can befall an interpreter; he was a close friend of the composer." (Cha/Spe, see Bibliog.)

The reviews of Robert Casadesus's performances are incredibly alike, some even to the point of using identical descriptions of his playing. Overall, these critiques portray his playing as elegant, aristocratic, brilliant, sensitive, suave, impeccably artistic, crystal clear. More than anything, critics speak of Casadesus's wonderful clarity, his intelligence and his musical integrity. And Grant Johannesen, who studied formally with Casadesus for about five years, describes his teacher's playing as cool and elegant. His *rubato*, says Johannesen, "was so subtle, and yet there was lots of *rubato* in his playing, but it never had much to do with excesses of personality; it was solely based on his feeling for the music." (Dub/Ref)

Casadesus's first New York recital (16 Feb 1936) proved him to be a pianist of the first magnitude in works well suited to his native temperament: six Scarlatti Sonatas exquisitely played; the Mozart Sonata in F Major, K. 332, "a joy from start to finish. A more polished and sensitive reading is not easily imaginable. The slow movement in particular, conceived by the pianist in a mood of tender reverie, was enveloped in mystery under fingers that produced a veiled tone which sang forth in tones so tenuous one wondered at the carrying power they boasted. . . . [His] transcendent technique found full play in the Chopin Ballades . . . the Ravel group could hardly be improved upon, taken from any angle." (*NYT*, 17 Feb 1936)

"Transcendent" was used again by another reviewer when Casadesus played (28 Oct 1944) the Saint-Saëns Concerto No. 4 at Carnegie Hall with Artur Rodzinski conducting the Philharmonic-Symphony Orchestra. Casadesus played with the power, brilliance and virtuosity required, but also made "the most of the opportunities offered for sharply defined dynamic and color contrasts. . . . There was subtle poetry in the lyric episodes, and the dramatic intensity of the reading as a whole was brought to a climax with a breathtaking treatment of the peroration of the finale." (*NYT*, 29 Oct 1944)

London critics, great admirers of Casadesus's pianism, sometimes expressed their opinions quite colorfully. Casadesus's playing at a Festival Hall recital (Nov 1951) reminded one reviewer of another distinguished pianist: "If Mr. Gieseking (with whom from the viewpoint of repertory he may be compared) seems to touch velvet keys, Mr. Casadesus favours satin inlaid with a steel thread. Rhythmic vitality and a wooing imagination characterize his playing." (*TL*, 12 Nov 1951)

Fifty years ago, after hearing Casadesus play a recital (17 March 1943) at the Curran Theater in San Francisco, Alfred Frankenstein—music critic, art critic, university lecturer, author—concisely identified Casadesus as the ideal *musicien français*. Ever since, critics have borrowed freely from Frankenstein's near-perfect description of Casadesus's style:

"The French are traditionally logical, and there never has been a more crystal clear exposition of the logic of musical form than in Casadesus' playing of a Mozart sonata, Beethoven's 32 Variations in C Minor, and the Chopin sonata in B-flat Minor.

"The French are traditionally broad-minded, tolerant, and at home in the wide world. And Casadesus' musical temperament is obviously limited to no one style or group of styles, although one has heard a more romantically powerful Chopin than his.

"The French are traditionally masters of subtle refinement in sensuous effect. Debussy's preludes are one of the most important monuments of this aspect of the Gallic spirit, and Casadesus' playing of Debussy's preludes was incomparable in its delicacy, poetry and vividness of coloring.

"The French are traditionally economical, and Casadesus' performance was a miracle of perfect adjustment of line and phrase and dynamics, of magnificently controlled and sculptured shading, without a second's overstatement, without a hint or suggestion of the exaggerated or, at the opposite extreme, the underdeveloped.

"The French are traditionally large of heart, and Casadesus gave us everything he had, including a long string of encores. . . .

"One thing that is not sufficiently stressed above is the man's breathtaking technique, which encompasses every conceivable aspect of the mechanics of piano playing in the lordly manner that belongs to the transcendental virtuoso." (© *San Francisco Chronicle*, 8 March 1943, Reprinted by permission.)

Casadesus made his first recordings in the early 1930s, and he continued to record all through his career, mostly the same works he enjoyed playing for a live audience. Although there is a very substantial discography, a great many of the LPs are out of print, awaiting reissue on CD. (Kirby, "Discography")

To celebrate the 20th anniversary of Casadesus's American debut, Columbia issued an album (3 LPs) comprising a substantial number of Debussy's solo piano compositions. "Casadesus plays beautifully, in his cool and classic manner. He phrases with delicacy and understanding, and his flexible brand of pianism lovingly outlines the nuances of Debussy's music." (*NYT*, 15 May 1955) These Debussy recordings await reissue on CD, but the Ravel solo works (Casadesus was the first to record all the piano works of Ravel) have appeared on the Sony Classical CD label. There is also a delightful live recording (1952) of Ravel's Concerto for Left Hand (see Discog.).

Casadesus recorded the same Beethoven sonatas he used for his recitals, and his reading of the Concerto No. 5 ("Emperor") is truly a most telling performance. He recorded 13 of the Mozart concertos, and fortunately at least five have been reissued on CD (see Discog.). Here one can hear the exquisite clarity, the elegant phrasing, the carefully balanced dynamics that made Casadesus the legendary Mozart player. "There is a clear, cool logic in Casadesus' pianism, which harbours an unhurried, old-world charm all its own." (Gra/Goo, see Bibliog.)

Casadesus made a recording of his Concerto for Three Pianos and Orchestra, performing it with wife Gaby, son Jean and the *Orchestre des Concerts Colonne*, conducted by Pierre Dervaux. It is a fine example of Casadesus the composer, and on the same disc there are excellent Casadesus performances of Franck's Symphonic Variations and the d'Indy Symphony on a French Mountain Air.

SELECTED REFERENCES

"Anecdotes, Recollections and Tributes." *Piano Quarterly*, Fall 1982, pp. 33–41.

Banowetz, Joseph. "Reflections on Playing Debussy." *Piano Quarterly*, Fall 1982, pp. 42–46.

Casadesus, Robert. "Learning to Interpret Great Music." *Etude*, July 1939, pp. 429-430, 467.

———. "Memories of Ravel." *Musical America*, 10 Feb 1941, pp. 221, 225.

———. "Schumann and les musiciens français." *Saturday Review of Literature*, 28 July 1956, pp. 33–34.

Cone, Edward T. "The Years at Princeton." *Piano Quarterly*, Fall 1982, pp. 27–29.

Elder, Dean. "'Une Bavardage' with the French Pianist and Composer Robert Casadesus." *Clavier*, March 1971, pp. 10–17.

Feder, Edward. "Robert Casadesus: Composer, Performer, Pedagogue." *Ovation*, Aug 1983, pp. 12–15.

Heylbut, Rose. "The Development of Pianism." (interview) *Etude*, May 1955, pp. 12, 61–62.

———. "The Place of Technic in Music Study." (interview) *Etude*, May 1941, pp. 297–298.

———. "Teaching Music Means Teaching Taste." (interview) *Etude*, March 1946, pp. 125, 128.

Johannesen, Grant. "The Lesson." *Piano Quarterly*, Fall 1982, pp. 24–26.

Kirby, F. E. "Discography." *Piano Quarterly*, Fall 1982, pp. 47–53.

———. "Robert Casadesus, Pianist—Teacher—Composer." *Piano Quarterly*, Fall 1982, p. 15.

Obituary. *New York Times*, 20 Sept 1972, p. 50. *The Times* (London), 20 Sept 1972, p. 17.

Silverman, Robert J. "A Talk with Gaby Casadesus." *Piano Quarterly*, Fall 1982, pp. 17–19.

Stookes, Sacha. *The Art of Robert Casadesus*. London: The Fortune Press, 1960.

Sweeney, Louise. "Casadesus: piano's first family." *Christian Science Monitor*, 8 Feb 1967, p. 6.

Taubman, Howard. "20-Year Retrospect." *New York Times*, 16 Jan 1955, sec. 10, p. 9.

Tolson, Margaret. "Musicien Français." *Piano Quarterly*, Fall 1982, pp. 20–22.

Widhalm, Patrick. "A Conversation with Gaby Casadesus." *Piano Quarterly*, Summer 1992, pp. 32–37.
See also Bibliography: Bla/Gra; Cha/Spe; Cur/Bio (1945); Eld/Pia; Ewe/Li; Ewe/Mu; Gel/Mus; Kai/Gre; New/Gro; Rat/Cle; Rub/MyM; Sch/Gre.

SELECTED REVIEWS

LM: 2 July 1946. *MA*: 10 April 1941; 10 Nov 1941; 10 Nov 1944. *MT*: Dec 1951. *NYHT*: 4 Feb 1943. *NYT*: 20 Jan 1935; 21 Jan 1935; 17 Feb 1936; 9 Jan 1938; 2 Feb 1939; 8 March 1940; 6 Dec 1941; 15 Nov 1942; 4 Feb 1943; 17 Feb 1944; 29 Oct 1944; 10 April 1945; 21 Feb 1946; 19 April 1947; 26 Feb 1949; 1 March 1950; 28 Feb 1951; 22 Oct 1954; 17 Jan 1955; 2 Nov 1956; 18 Nov 1957; 27 Oct 1958; 14 Dec 1959; 12 Dec 1960; 23 Nov 1964; 22 Dec 1967; 23 Nov 1970. *SFC*: 8 March 1943. *TL*: 19 Nov 1929; 12 Nov 1951.

SELECTED DISCOGRAPHY

Beethoven: Concerto No. 5 in E-flat Major, op. 73 ("Emperor"); Sonata in A Major, op. 101. Philips 426 106-2. Rosbaud/*Concertgebouw*.
Beethoven: Sonatas in C-sharp Minor, op. 27, no. 2; F Minor, op. 57; F-sharp Major, op. 78; E-flat Major, op. 81a. Sony Classical CD SBK 46345.
Beethoven: Sonata in A-flat Major, op. 110. Schumann: Symphonic Etudes, op. 13. Columbia P 14165 (LP).
Casadesus: Concerto for Three Pianos and Strings (Dervaux/Colonne). D'Indy: Symphony on a French Mountain Air (Ormandy/PO). Franck: Symphonic Variations (Ormandy/PO). Sony Masterworks Portrait MPK 46730 (CD). With Gaby and Jean Casadesus.
Chopin: Sonata No. 3 in B Minor, op. 58. CBS LP ML6242/MS6842.
Fauré: Ballade in F-sharp Major, op. 19. Sony Classical SMK 47548 (CD). This "Bernstein Royal Edition" also contains music by Franck, Chausson and Ravel.
Fauré: Préludes (selected). CBS ML5777/MS6377.
Mémoires de l'Orchestre de la Suisse Romande. Falla: Nights in the Gardens of Spain. Liszt: Concerto No. 2 in A Major. Mozart: Concerto in D Major, K. 537. Cascavelle VEL 2008 (CD). Ansermet/OSR.
Mozart: Concerto in E-flat Major, K. 365 (with Gaby Casadeus); Concerto in C Major, K. 467; Concerto in E-flat Major, K. 482; Concerto in A Major, K. 488; Concerto in C Minor, K. 491; Concerto in D Major, K. 537. Sony Classical SM3K 46519 (3 CDs). Szell/Cleveland Orchestra, Ormandy/PO.
Ravel: *Concerto pour la main gauche. Nuova Era* 2318 (CD). Celibidache/RAI SO.
Ravel: Works (with Gaby Casadesus). *Gaspard de la nuit; Habanera; Jeux d'eau; Menuet antique; Ma Mère l'Oye; Miroirs; Pavane pour une infante défunte; Prélude* for Piano; *Le Tombeau de Couperin; Valses nobles et sentimentales.* Sony Classical Masterworks MPK 46733 (CD).

Saint-Saëns: Concerto No. 4 in C Minor, op. 44. Sony Classical SMK 47608 (CD). Bernstein/NYPO.

Scarlatti: Sonatas (11). *Melodiya* 27323-4.

Schumann: *Carnaval*, op. 9. CBS ML 5146.

CHERKASSKY, SHURA: b. Odessa, Ukraine, Russia, 7 October 1911.

> There is that aspect of revelry, that joy in the purely pianistic challenge that sets him apart from the moderns.
>
> Nancy Malitz (*Cincinnati Enquirer*, 28 October 1980)

A Shura Cherkassky performance is typically a happy event. Onstage at the piano Cherkassky gives the impression of having a wonderful time creating his truly idiosyncratic music; and out in the audience most listeners—purists and anti-Romantics excluded—find that Cherkassky's keyboard magic lifts the spirits and thrills the senses. Ample proof lies in the hundreds of reviews (Cherkassky has, after all, been playing before the public continuously for more than seven decades) liberally dotted with these telling words: joyous, mischievous, impudent, playful. Even at age 13 Cherkassky played "with a joyousness, a sensitiveness, frequently absent from more learned expositions." (*NYT*, 15 March 1925)

And he has never lost that heartwarming quality. Sixty years after that 1925 recital Cherkassky's playing was still the kind that "makes you smile, because ultimately he is putting one over on you by making you think the music is more important than it really is. That's the mark of a great artist, and that's what Cherkassky most definitely is." (*DFP*, 10 May 1986) For some reason (and is there a connection?), a remarkable number of the Cherkassky reviews make a point of picturing him as "a pixie," "a sprite," "an impish gnome" or, as in the 1990 *Current Biography*, "an endearingly gentle, leprechaunlike man." The final say lies with audiences. Most of them seem to be delighted with Shura Cherkassky's unique music making.

And Cherkassky delights in music, which is, and always has been, the most important thing in his life. Since his mother Lydia (Schlemenson) Cherkassky, a graduate of the St. Petersburg Conservatory and a pupil of Anna Essipoff, taught piano in Odessa, Cherkassky began life in a home filled with music, especially piano music. According to his parents, at age two he could pick out on the keyboard the lullabies sung to him. His mother quickly started him on piano lessons, and as soon as he learned to shape notes and bars, he began composing, not only filling notebooks but writing on walls, sometimes even on the furniture. He played his first public recital at age nine, and about two years later gave up composing to devote all his energies to the piano. He never attended school, but was taught at home by his father Isaac Cherkassky, a dentist.

Cherkassky's youthful talent might have been ruined had he continued to endure the cold and famine plaguing Russia after the Revolution of 1917. His family sold their possessions for food and burned their furniture to keep warm. Even so, he remembers often practicing in a bitterly cold room and living in fear that one day his piano would go for firewood. He escaped from this terrible existence only because a group of Odessa musicians pressured the government into allowing the Cherkasskys to leave Russia. Early in 1923 they joined Julius Bloom, a relative living in Baltimore, Maryland, and shortly after their arrival, Harold Randolph, director of the Peabody Conservatory of Music, had the 11-year-old Cherkassky play for him in his office. Overwhelmed by the boy's talent, Randolph immediately arranged a recital (3 March 1923) in the Little Lyric. Cherkassky's playing (he gave a second recital on 10 March 1923 in the Peabody Concert Hall) caused a sensation in all Baltimore.

Needing advice, Cherkassky's parents took him to New York to play for Rachmaninoff, who agreed to give the boy lessons if his parents would (1) keep him from concertizing for two years and (2) take him to Rosina Lhévinne to improve his technique. Uncertain about Rachmaninoff's conditions, the Cherkasskys sought a second opinion from Josef Hofmann, who not only agreed to take their son as a pupil but encouraged them to continue his public performances. Cherkassky was given a scholarship at the newly opened Curtis Institute of Music, where Hofmann was head of the piano department. Curtis Institute records reveal that Cherkassky studied with Hofmann for 11 years (1925–26 to 1927–28; 1930–38) and received his diploma (in absentia, because he was on tour) in May 1935.

True to his word, Hofmann allowed his young pupil to perform. From 1924, when he made his New York debut (12 Nov) at Aeolian Hall, Cherkassky played in New York almost every season, including a 1926 performance (6 Nov) of the Tchaikovsky Concerto in B-flat Minor with the New York Symphony Society, Walter Damrosch conducting. At age 16 Cherkassky began extensive touring abroad, in just two seasons (1928–29, 1929–30) playing a total of 120 concerts in Australia, New Zealand, South Africa, France and Great Britain. He made his English debut with a London recital on 31 January 1929, and that autumn began a long tour (15 Oct 1929–22 March 1930) through the provinces with the London Symphony Orchestra, conducted by Albert Coates. Reviews in the Curtis Institute files indicate that in every city Cherkassky more than justified his billing as "the phenomenal boy pianist." For example, in Christchurch, New Zealand, he played nine recitals on alternate days, yet captivated each audience with "his amazing demonstration of technical brilliance and musicianship." Although only age 18, he was, wrote a critic in Wellington, New Zealand, "a master of the keyboard in the same sense as Paderewski, Hofmann and Rachmaninoff."

Between foreign tours Cherkassky played in America and Canada and also studied with Hofmann, sometimes at Hofmann's summer home in Camden, Maine. After a New York recital (9 Feb 1935) that garnered brilliant reviews from the era's most eminent critics, Cherkassky made a tour of Russia, playing recitals in Moscow, Leningrad, Kharkov and Odessa and also performing with the Leningrad Philharmonic Symphony Orchestra. He spent that July working with Hofmann in Maine, and from August through December toured in the Orient: Tokyo, Osaka, Kyoto, Kobe and Shanghai. Not long after his return to New York, he was soloist (27 Jan 1936) with the National Orchestral Association under Leon Barzin in Carnegie Hall. Cherkassky returned to Europe in 1936 and stayed abroad for about four years, sometimes playing as many as four concerts a week.

Dozens of reviews from far-flung cities prove beyond any doubt that by the time he was 25 years old, Shura Cherkassky had become a star pianist on the international circuit. Conversely, his reputation in America began to fail. With World War II looming over Europe, he returned to the United States and played his first American recital (16 Oct 1940) in four years. Critics praised his speed, dexterity, power and finesse, yet feared "that Mr. Cherkassky too often sought to astonish his hearers than to move them by interpreting the works on his program from the composers' viewpoint." (*NYHT*, 17 Oct 1940)

Matters grew worse. Living in the United States during World War II, Cherkassky had few recital engagements, even fewer opportunities to play with orchestra. For one thing, his kind of unorthodox playing had apparently gone out of style in the United States. Compounding his problem was the fact that the American public had discovered Artur Rubinstein and Vladimir Horowitz. After the war Cherkassky returned to Europe, and to success. His first important postwar European tour (1946) laid the foundation for his great popularity in Germany and Austria. Cherkassky established a fame in Europe and Great Britain that has never diminished. Over a span of more than 40 years, he has received remarkably complimentary reviews from foreign critics.

Just as his fame steadily flourished abroad—there are dozens of London reviews from the 1950s and 1960s—at home in America Cherkassky's reputation steadily faded. After touring the United States in the 1960–61 season, he apparently stayed away for more than a decade, until a Hunter College recital on 13 March 1976. That performance restored his reputation with New York critics, and over the next few years other well-received performances revived his American reputation. American audiences by that time were once again ready for Cherkassky's kind of playing. In the ensuing years he has acquired a large and affectionate following in the United States. He plays some 60 concerts a year, touring in Great Britain, Europe, North America, the Far East, Australia, New Zealand and India.

Although a longtime American citizen who loves the musical camaraderie of New York City, he has for many years made his home in London, mostly living in hotels. A confirmed bachelor (his two-year marriage to Genia Ganz ended in 1948), Cherkassky actually enjoys hotel living, where he is unencumbered with housekeeping matters and served by competent staff. Where he once envied those with family companionship and more free time for pleasure, he has a wonderful time with his music, always the complete center of his life, and he no longer feels that he is missing out on anything. Although described as self-absorbed, Cherkassky is said to be a gracious, shy man with a good-natured, delightful personality.

Order and routine direct his life. He insists on having a piano available at all times, even during intermission at concerts. Although never nervous about his playing, he frets about whether the car will pick him up on time for the concert, whether his dressing room is arranged exactly as he ordered, and other such practical matters. Even his seemingly effortless virtuosity results from hard work and very regular, very careful preparation. Cherkassky practices faithfully four hours a day, and if he misses any of that time he makes it up at the next session.

Like everything else, Cherkassky's diverse, lively programs are most carefully planned. He even carries a small black book listing all the works he can play and all those that he has already played in public, each complete with the time it takes to play, some having the dates that he has performed them. For a typical season he prepares two recital programs and six or seven concertos. His immense repertoire, possibly the largest of any pianist living today, is due to his phenomenal memory. Although unquestionably a Romantic pianist, Cherkassky's large repertoire extends from Bach through the great masterpieces of the 19th century to the music of the 20th century (Berg, Boulez, Messiaen, Stockhausen, Stravinsky), and comes up to the present with works like Leonard Bernstein's Touches and Morton Gould's Boogie-Woogie Etude. He is at his shining best in the music of the 19th-century composers, especially Liszt, Chopin and the Russians (Tchaikovsky, Rachmaninoff, Prokofiev). He does not play much French music, sometimes a little Debussy or Ravel. He tries to learn a new work each year, often a contemporary piece. Perhaps his greatest delight is playing such confections as Godowsky's *Alt Wien*, the Albéniz-Godowsky Tango, the Rachmaninoff Polka and Eugene Pabst's Paraphrase on the Waltz from Tchaikovsky's *Eugene Onegin*.

Cherkassky does not take students, and says he has never taught because he is at a loss to explain what he does. His technique comes so naturally that he is unable to describe how he uses his fingers or what he does with the pedal or how he achieves muscle control. "I can do things quite intuitively myself. But I just couldn't possibly teach. One must be born with that gift." (Horowitz)

Josef Hofmann formed Cherkassky's playing style and his whole approach to pianism. Hofmann, says Cherkassky, was not exactly a teacher but more like a magnet. His personality dominated everything. "I believed in him like a god," said Cherkassky. "He had this craze for what he called his 'inner voices' and for the left hand." (Blyth) Pressed for specifics, Cherkassky is not too explicit. "I can't quite say what Hofmann taught me. Pedaling, dynamics, general vibrations. I learned an awful lot." (Rothstein) Music experts have been more specific about what Cherkassky got from Hofmann. "Mr. Cherkassky is one of the great technicians. That he had from the beginning. What he got from Hofmann was the ability to project a singing tone, never producing an ugly sound; the ability, common to Romantic pianists but now almost a lost art, to move the basses and to search out meaningful inner voices; and the trick of constant fluctuation of tempo without ever losing the basic meter." (Schonberg)

With Horowitz (d. 1989), Bolet (d. 1990) and Horszowski (d. 1993) gone, the style that Cherkassky inherited from Hofmann makes him one of the very last of the post-Romantic pianists, a descendant, if you will, of the so-called Golden Age, that era when musicians, most noticeably pianists, involved themselves wholeheartedly in the music, each one presenting a different, highly personal interpretation of the composers' intentions, each taking great license with the music in order to make it come alive, make it exciting. Except for the performances of Shura Cherkassky and Earl Wild, that bravura playing style is now almost extinct.

Unlike the modern pianist, Cherkassky looks upon playing the piano as a celebration of the art of music and the art of seeing what the piano can do. "He is not embarrassed that his playing dazzles, intoxicates, thrills. It is intelligent, artful playing, always." (*CE*, 28 Oct 1980) He is not a Romantic in the sense that he willfully distorts the score but plays, he says, spontaneously and with an element of improvisation. He plays exactly as he feels like playing at any given moment, and freely admits that five minutes before going onstage he does not know exactly how he is going to play. Gerard Schwartz, director of the Seattle Symphony and the New York Chamber orchestras, tells of conducting Cherkassky in seven performances of the Chopin F-minor Concerto. Each night Cherkassky made the work completely different, ranging from "emotionally reserved to sheer flamboyance. . . . With Shura all you can be sure of is that you can't be sure." (Wigler, "The Last Romantic")

Playing spontaneously or, as he says, "by intuition," he may take all sorts of liberties the first time, ignoring indicated dynamics or phrasing, then play the repeat impeccably, perhaps just to prove that he can. Critics deplore such spur-of-the-moment decisions, but Cherkassky revels in surprises. Like the late Jorge Bolet, he regrets that so many of today's pianists, especially the younger graduates of the competition circuit, are so calculating that they all play more or less alike, very accurately, always, but as he has said, "when you leave, you find you have forgotten that you ever heard them." Not so with Cherkassky's playing. His imaginative, unpredictable style reaches into the heart of his audience.

But Cherkassky is more than an exciting entertainer. He gives the same serious attention to everything he plays, whether a profound classical work or a rousing, lighthearted encore. And of course Cherkassky is a master pianist, with "a transcendental technique rarely encountered now. And by technique I do not mean the mechanical expertise of many contemporary young clinicians of the keyboard but a capacity to turn a black and white score into myriad lights and colors and above all to make a seemingly percussive and recalcitrant piano into a singing instrument." (Hough)

Over the decades reviewers have consistently marveled at Cherkassky's massive, all-around technical prowess: his fleet, rippling scalework; the way he spins out long melody lines; his shimmering pedal effects; his beautiful sound; his incredible "gift for holding a piece together even while constantly seeming to pull it apart rhythmically." (*NYT*, 20 Nov 1985) Even critics on the fence as to how they feel about Cherkassky—his unorthodox approach, his idiosyncratic *rubato* effects and voicings, the barely discernible breaks he allows between works on his programs—find it difficult to not enjoy a Cherkassky performance.

Purists of course will almost always be put off by his highly personal pianism. But even when his interpretations are questionable, Cherkassky's playing is so warm, colorful and in its own way authentic that invariably he com-

municates directly with his audience. About a decade ago Cherkassky began tap-
ing his practice sessions and that, he feels, has changed his playing, because
where he used to play inner voices a lot, he does not do that so much anymore.
However, Shura Cherkassky still "with innocent immediacy travels along with
the music, basking in the sound . . . exploring little-known paths with a heated
elegance. . . . 'Some people like my playing, and some people perhaps don't like
my playing,' he said, 'but I don't think anybody can call me boring'." (Rothstein)

Cherkassky has been a consistent Romantic. Critiques from 50 years
back, though written in the florid style of that day, could easily apply to his
playing today. At a Shanghai, China, recital played 60 years ago, Cherkassky
played "with his hands running across the keyboard like lightning and with his
heart in his fingertips." (*The Shanghai Times*, 22 Oct 1935)

A review of a 1939 recital in Oslo, Norway, is as fitting today as it was
then. Freely translated, it says, "When an artist like Shura Cherkassky sits at
the piano, *all one's old conceptions of piano playing are turned upside down*.
Without doubt he stands today in an exceptional position among the great pianists, both when technical mastery of the instrument and the spiritual grasp of
the music he interprets are considered. There is a sincerity in his playing which
breaks all conventional barriers and ties. He lives his music so intensely, sets it
forth so richly that it is no longer piano technique in the usual sense we are faced
with but prophesy, poetry, instantaneous improvisations of all human feeling
and passion. As marvelously subjective as Cherkassky is, he never encroaches
on the honor of the composer; he is respectful to and presents cleanly the music
he interprets, but with his flaming temperament and enormous knowledge of the
possibilities of the pianoforte he makes the works greater and deeper and more
glorious than we have known them to be before. With Cherkassky virtuosity is
driven up to its highest border; no difficulties exist for him." (*Morgenbladet-
Stener Kolstad*, 8 Nov 1939)

And more than 50 years later, Cherkassky, at age 81, remained, "purely
from a mechanical point of view, a staggering pianist. Any pianist—never mind
one who is an octogenarian—who plays Schumann's Symphonic Etudes with
such accuracy and power and the outer sections of Chopin's E Major Scherzo
with such delicacy and legerdemain commands attention. But that is where
Cherkassky's unique art begins." (*BaS*, 18 Nov 1991)

Cherkassky's grand performance (6 Sept 1986) of Schumann's *Kreisleriana* was "in every way what great Romantic piano playing is about: mercurial,
provocative, passionate, adventurous, shot through with vivid colour, irresistible
in its dramatic movement." (*FT*, 9 Sept 1986) Nearly two decades before that
recital, Cherkassky's "wildly eccentric, touchingly beautiful account of Schumann's eight *Kreisleriana* fantasies was perhaps the most successful of an
evening full of new insights and subtle turns." (*MT*, May 1968)

In a very early Liszt performance (31 Jan 1929), Cherkassky's "double-
octave playing . . . took the breath away not only as a feat of physical prowess,
but for its clean musical beauty." Yet even at this young age Cherkassky was
more than just a bravura pianist of the fast and loud type, "for although he
played Liszt [a transcription of Bach's G Minor organ Fantasia and Fugue; the B

Minor Sonata], he played it with his own very musical interpretation." (*MT*, 1 March 1929) And in a recital 55 years later he gave "a magical, satanic, absolutely marvelous account of Liszt's *Funérailles* . . . with some half-pedal witcheries on the final chords that no other pianist but Cherkassky would even dare to imagine successfully." (*FT*, 22 May 1984)

Notable in Cherkassky's unusual readings of Chopin are "a luscious tone, attention to the polyphonic side of the music, marvelously detailed phrasing, and a grasp of the overall shape of a work." (Met/Cho, see Bibliog.) Many critics call his Chopin playing magical. "Nobody plays Chopin the way Cherkassky does. Not that he's better than anybody else. He's just electrifyingly different." (*NYDN*, 15 March 1976)

In sum, Cherkassky is an extraordinarily talented pianist whose interpretations must be understood and accepted in the spirit in which they are offered. And, after seven decades of concertizing, he still plays the piano with the same joy and vitality of his youth. "In an age when even top-flight virtuosos seem interchangeably excellent, Mr. Cherkassky stands apart as a treasured iconoclast." (Horowitz)

For years Cherkassky disliked recording because he felt he could not be spontaneous in the cold atmosphere of the studio. But recording in the relaxed surroundings of the Nimbus studio in a castle in Wales changed his attitude. He has recorded at least eight compact discs for Nimbus, each containing one or more major works.

Cherkassky's first recording was a 78 rpm disc of Liszt's Concerto No. 1 for HMV. His many HMV records include the first ever recording of Prokofiev's Concerto No. 2 and a fine (presently out-of-print) set of the Chopin Etudes. His superlative reading of the Tchaikovsky Concerto No. 1, made for *Deutsche Grammophon*, is also unavailable at this writing.

A reissue of the Chopin Concerto No. 2 in F Minor, op. 21, is a welcome addition to the CD catalogue (see Discog.). "Cherkassky has seldom been recorded in such tip-top form. His sensitivity in unfolding Chopin's intimate musical language silences criticism. His tone has absolute purity . . . his is a masterful reading resplendent with the values of an older school of pianism." (*Gram*, Jan 1989) Other Chopin recordings, especially the Polonaises (see Discog.) and the Sonata No. 3 in B Minor (Nimbus 7701) are particularly delightful.

A recital blending traditional works with definitely unusual works includes the Franck *Prélude, Choral et Fugue*; the Grieg Sonata, op. 7; the fine Rachmaninoff Variations on a Theme by Corelli, op. 42; and the Messiaen *Etudes de Rhythme*, nos. 1 and 2 (see Discog.). This is Cherkassky at his recorded best. "His playing is bold, grand, fluid, beautifully shaped and technically superb. . . . The Franck unfolds magisterially, with exquisite phrasing details. . . . In the Messiaen, Cherkassky plays with incisive rhythm and wonderful splashes of brilliant sound. The Rachmaninoff is equally impressive." (*Fan*, March/April 1988)

Nimbus 5045 contains the Liszt Sonata in B Minor and Hungarian Rhapsody No. 2 along with Stravinsky's *Trois Mouvements de Petroushka*.

"Mr. Cherkassky's performance of the Liszt Sonata is especially memorable. This is grand playing of the old school—a big, noble conception, logically flowing, every note controlled, and above all full of variety of color." (Schonberg) Nimbus 5020 features the Schumann Symphonic Etudes and the Brahms Variations on a Theme of Paganini, each a formidable work in its own special way. Cherkassky chooses moderate tempos for both these masterworks, concentrating instead on the musical elements. This is especially noticeable in the Brahms.

SELECTED REFERENCES

Blyth, Alan. "Cheeky traditionalist." (interview) *Music and Musicians*, April 1969, p. 30.
Cantrell, Scott. "Hopeless romantic has a passion for piano." *Kansas City Star*, 14 April 1991, sec. A, p. 20.
"Free Spirit." *Time*, 9 Dec 1991, p. 19.
Horowitz, Joseph. "Shura Cherkassky—A Pianist Who Follows His Intuition." *New York Times*, 2 April 1978, pp. 17, 25.
Hough, Stephen, and Bryce Morrison. "Pianist to Pianist." *Gramophone*, Oct 1991, pp. 64–65, 146.
Kozinn, Allan. "The Last Romantic Demurs, But on the Other Hand. . ." *New York Times*, 10 Dec 1989, sec. 3, pp. 29, 32.
Montparker, Carol. "Shura Cherkassky, Sprightly Sage of the Piano." *Clavier*, Nov 1990, pp. 10–14.
Osborne, Richard. "Cherkassky in concert." *Records and Recording*, May 1969, pp. 22–23.
Pettitt, Stephen. "Perfect Pitch for the Ages of Man." *The Times* (London), 7 Oct 1991, p. 13 (Arts).
Rothstein, Edward. "Shura Cherkassky Makes Fervent Personality His Style." *New York Times*, 29 March 1981, sec. 2, p. 17.
Said, Edward W. "Uncertainties of Style." *The Nation*, 9 March 1992, pp. 312–315.
Schonberg, Harold. "The Poetry and Grandeur of Shura Cherkassky." *New York Times*, 1 March 1987, pp. 26, 28.
Wigler, Stephen. "At 80, pianist virtuoso Shura Cherkassky takes his time and enjoys his work." *Baltimore Sun*, 3 Jan 1993. An in-depth review of London 433654-2 CD.
———. "The Last Romantic." *Baltimore Sun*, 17 Nov 1991, sec. D, pp. 1, 3.
York, Nicholas. "Shura Cherkassky at 75." *Music and Musicians*, Oct 1986, p. 11.
See also Bibliography: Cur/Bio (Oct 1990); Ewe/Li; Kai/Gre; New/Gro; Ran/Kon; Sal/Fam; Sch/Gre.

SELECTED REVIEWS

AJ: 2 Nov 1990. *APP*: 20 April 1993. *BaS*: 3 Jan 1993. *CE*: 28 Oct 1980. *CST*: 4 March 1991. *CT*: 22 April 1985; 3 Dec 1986; 4 March 1991.

DFP: 28 Nov 1985. *DMN*: 9 Nov 1989. *FT*: 2 Jan 1974; 22 May 1984; 9 Sept 1986. *GM*: 2 Jan 1974; 9 Oct 1991. *LAT*: 6 Nov 1961; 17 Oct 1977; 1 May 1981; 20 Nov 1987. *LIN*: 18 Nov 1987. *MA*: 25 Dec 1926. *MM*: May 1965; May 1983; April 1985; Dec 1985; Jan 1987; May 1987; April 1988. *MT*: 1 March 1929; Sept 1956; May 1957; Sept 1957; May 1968; Jan 1969; April 1982. *NYHT*: 29 Nov 1931; 17 Oct 1940. *NYP*: 15 March 1976. *NYT*: 13 Nov 1924; 29 Nov 1931; 2 Feb 1936; 21 Jan 1941; 24 Oct 1944; 19 Nov 1960; 25 Nov 1961; 31 Jan 1977; 20 Nov 1985; 15 Dec 1986; 18 Nov 1987; 16 Nov 1989; 20 July 1990; 25 April 1994. *PI*: 19 April 1993. *SFC*: 18 April 1978; 30 April 1991. *STL*: 20 Oct 1991. TL: 2 Feb 1929; 1 Dec 1952; 9 Nov 1953; 22 April 1955; 4 March 1957; 2 Jan 1974; 3 Oct 1975; 21 May 1984; 16 Oct 1991; 24 Nov 1992. *WP*: 14 Feb 1986; 14 July 1987.

SELECTED DISCOGRAPHY

Cherkassky in Concert 1984, Vol. 1. Schumann: Symphonic Etudes, op. 13. Brahms: Variations on a Theme by Paganini op. 35. Hofmann: Kaleidoscope. Chasins: Rush Hour in Hong Kong. Nimbus NI 5020 (CD).
Cherkassky in Concert 1984, Vol. 2. Bach-Busoni: Chaconne. Berg: Sonata op. 1. Liszt: *Funérailles*. Beethoven: Sonata in E-flat Major, op. 27, no. 1. Nimbus NI 5021 (CD).
Chopin: *Andante spianato* and *Grande Polonaise*, op. 22; Sonata No. 3 in B Minor, op. 58. Liszt: Hungarian Rhapsody No. 2; Sonata in B Minor. Nimbus NI 7701 (CD).
Chopin: Concerto No. 2 in F Minor, op. 21; Fantasy in F Minor, op. 49. Menuet 160013-2. Kempe/RPO.
Chopin: Polonaises. DG (Resonance) 429516-2.
Chopin: Scherzo in B minor, op. 20. Schubert: Impromptus D. 899, nos. 2 and 3. Schumann: *Kreisleriana*, op. 16. Strauss-Godowsky: Paraphrase on "Wine, Women and Song." Nimbus NI 5043 (CD).
Eightieth Birthday Recital. Bach-Busoni: Chaconne in D Minor. Chopin: Nocturne in F Minor, op. 55, no. 1; *Tarantelle* in A Flat, op. 43. Gould: Boogie Woogie Etude. Hofmann: Kaleidoscope. Ives: Three-Page Sonata. Pabst: Concert Paraphrase from Tchaikovsky's *Eugene Onegin*, op. 81. Schumann: Symphonic Etudes, op. 13. London 433 654-2. Recorded at a Carnegie Hall recital on 2 December 1991. Winner of the 1993 Gramophone Award in the instrumental category.
Grieg: Sonata op. 7. Franck: *Prélude, Chorale et Fugue.* Messiaen: *Études de Rhythme*, nos. 1 and 2. Rachmaninoff: Variations on a Theme by Corelli, op. 42. Nimbus NI 5090 (CD).
Liszt: Concerto No. 1 in E-flat Major; *Liebestraum* No. 3; Hungarian Rhapsody No. 13; Faust Waltz; Don Juan Fantasy. Saint-Saëns-Godowsky: The Swan. Liadov: Musical Snuffbox. Testament 1033 (CD). Fistoulari/PO.
Liszt: Hungarian Fantasia; Hungarian Rhapsodies Nos. 2 and 5. Brahms: Hungarian Dances Nos. 17-20. DG (Resonance) 429 156-2.

Liszt: Hungarian Rhapsody No. 2; Sonata in B Minor. Stravinsky: *Trois Mouvements de Petroushka.* Nimbus NI 5045.

Schubert: Sonata in A Major, D. 664. Chopin: Variations on Mozart's "Là, ci darem la mano," op. 2. Bernstein: Touches. Pabst: Concert Paraphrase on Tchaikovsky's *Eugene Onegin,* op. 81. Nimbus NI 5091 (CD).

Shura Cherkassky Encores (Vol. 3). Albéniz/Godowsky: Tango. Balakirev: *Islamey.* Cherkassky: *Prélude pathétique.* Chopin: Waltz in E Minor. Debussy: Arabesque No. 1. Moszkowski: *Liebeswalzer.* Mozart: *Rondo alla turca.* Paderewski: *Menuet célèbre.* Rachmaninoff: *Elégie,* op. 3, no. 1; *Polka de W. R.* Rebikov: Christmas Tree. Shostakovich: Polka. Sibelius: Romance. Sinding: Rustle of Spring. Tchaikovsky: None but the lonely heart. London 433 651-2.

Shura Cherkassky Live. Albéniz-Godowsky: Tango. Chopin: Ballade in A-flat Major, op. 47; Etudes in C-sharp Minor, op. 10, no. 4, C-sharp Minor, op. 25, no. 7, B Minor, op. 25, no. 10; Preludes, op. 28, nos. 4, 6, 7, 10, 13, 17, 20, 23; Nocturne in F Minor, op. 55, no. 1. Rachmaninoff: *Polka de W. R.* Rubinstein: Melody in F, op. 3, no. 1. Schubert: Sonata in A Major, D. 664; *Moment musical* in F Minor, D. 780, no. 3 (arr. Godowsky). Scriabin: Prelude in D Major, op. 11, no. 5. London 433 653-2 (recorded London, 24 March, 4 May 1975).

Shura Cherkassky Piano Recital. Berg: Sonata, op. 1. Debussy: *L'Isle joyeuse.* Mendelssohn: *Rondo capriccioso,* op. 14. Poulenc: Toccata. Schumann: Sonata in F-sharp Minor, op. 11. Stravinsky: *Trois mouvements de Petrouchka.* Ermitage ERM 133 (CD).

⚜ ⚜ ⚜

CICCOLINI, ALDO: b. Naples, Italy, 15 August 1925.

> Ciccolini remains the most elegant, yet approachable, of pianistic practitioners.
>
> Daniel Cariaga (*Los Angeles Times,* 24 March 1986)

Even though almost every generation of Ciccolinis has produced musicians, Aldo Ciccolini was not, he says, purposefully directed to a career in music. He did not so much learn music as a youngster but more or less absorbed it while observing an older sister practice the piano. Whatever the learning process, by age nine Ciccolini showed sufficient promise that the Italian composer Francesco Cilèa arranged his admittance at the Naples Conservatory despite his being four years younger than the prescribed age. The years (1934–43) of study at the Conservatory, primarily piano and composition with Paolo Denza, a Busoni pupil, constitute all the musical training Ciccolini ever had. "I had only one teacher in my career," he once explained, "and after that I asked many great pianists to do me the honor of listening to my playing." (Chism)

Ciccolini gave his first recital at age 13 at the San Carlo Theater in Naples, and at age 15 completed his piano studies. He finished his composition courses in 1943; and that same year made his formal debut, playing the Chopin Concerto No. 2 in F Minor, again at the San Carlo Theater. Unfortunately, his debut came right in the middle of World War II, thus for the next few years surviving the war precluded all possibilities for a professional career.

After the war he restarted his musical life, and since then his no-nonsense career has been a straightforward march to success. In 1947 the Naples Conservatory appointed Ciccolini professor of piano, making him, at age 22, the youngest person up to that time to attain that rank. In 1948 he was awarded the St. Cecilia Prize in Rome. In 1949 he won the Grand Prize (shared with Ventsislav Yankoff of Bulgaria) at the prestigious Marguerite Long Competition in Paris, which most likely altered the course of his career. Like so many artists and musicians, Ciccolini decided to remain in Paris, and eventually became a French citizen. In the early 1970s he was appointed professor of piano at the Paris Conservatory, a post he still holds.

Taking the Grand Prize at the Long Competition no doubt ignited Ciccolini's long, eminently successful career. Shortly thereafter he gave his first recital (8 July 1949) in Paris, an event sponsored by the Italian ambassador to France, and before long he was making both concert tours (Europe, North Africa, South America) and recordings. He made his American orchestral debut on 2 November 1950 in New York, playing the Tchaikovsky Concerto No. 1 in B-flat Minor with the New York Philharmonic-Symphony Orchestra, conducted by Dimitri Mitropoulos; and the next month played his first New York recital (10 Dec 1950) at Town Hall. Ciccolini returned to America in 1951 to play the Schumann Concerto with Mitropoulos and the NYPSO, then, except for a brief return in 1957 to substitute for an ailing pianist as soloist with the New York Philharmonic Orchestra, he stayed away from the United States for a quarter of a century. Performing in America, it seems, had intimidated the 25-year-old pianist. In 1978, back in America for a third consecutive season, the 52-year-old Ciccolini explained the long hiatus: "A tour of your country can be very dangerous for a career. It is, for one thing, a physical drain. For another, your country is acquainted with the greatest musicians. New York audiences have heard much more of great music-making than any other place." (*NYT*, 13 Jan 1978)

Ciccolini played his first London recital on 23 January 1954 and, as in America, has returned there only intermittently. However, he has long held a reputation as one of the great pianists on the Continent; and his many performances in North America since reappearing in 1975 have fully confirmed that reputation. All told, there have been few setbacks in his career. His worldwide touring schedule—sometimes as many as 100 appearances a season—includes repeat engagements in Amsterdam, London, Los Angeles, San Francisco, New York, Milan, Paris, Sydney and Tokyo. He also teaches a few hours a week at the Paris Conservatory and gives master classes elsewhere. He manages this intensive performing and teaching schedule with the aid of meditation and yoga, disciplines he considers indispensable to a well-ordered existence. Ciccolini discloses little of his private life.

Reputedly an excellent teacher, Ciccolini can conduct classes in either Italian, French, English or Spanish. Students say his remarks, though sometimes very brief, are to the point and clearly formulated, and he often illustrates at the piano. He puts special emphasis on what he calls "mental practice" because, he says, technical problems are not the only difficulties for the pianist. The greatest problem is to project music, naturally, simply and with complete sincerity.

He learns a new work away from the piano in order to think about the music and how he is going to interpret it. Memorizing it completely before ever trying it on the keyboard, he thus becomes familiar with the structure of the piece and with its problems (of phrasing, tone, technique), "which cannot always be solved when one plays from notes. When at last I begin to work at the piano, I try to reproduce the tones and motions I have already determined. . . . Practice is facilitated when one learns to listen to one's own playing. It is not enough to reproduce each note: quality of tone, nature of attack, style of phrasing, are all part of study." (*Etude*, Sept 1953)

Ciccolini finds it heartening that so many contemporary performers carefully heed the composer's intentions. "Not only do we have to find out about the notes," he says, "but also about what is behind and in between them." The performer must really look at a score, not just look at the notes, but pay attention to those small signs which can be on certain notes, such as where they start, where they finish, or the way a *crescendo* is built or the value of a *sforzando*.

Italian by birth and French only by adoption, Aldo Ciccolini is completely at home in the French keyboard repertoire. Listening to his sympathetic playing of this music makes one feel that only a true Frenchman, with the possible exceptions of Walter Gieseking and Grant Johannesen, could sound so authentic and artistically satisfying. Some credit must be due Paolo Denza, Ciccolini's only teacher, who believed that knowing French music would develop a pianist's sense of color. Denza introduced Ciccolini to the repertoire now largely responsible for his fame.

His repertoire consists mostly of works by Debussy, Liszt, Ravel, Satie and Saint-Saëns, and includes some Beethoven, Chabrier, Chopin, Clementi, Falla, Franck, Mozart, Mussorgsky, Rachmaninoff, Scarlatti, Schubert and Schumann. Ciccolini has performed all five Saint-Saëns concertos, the Beethoven Concertos Nos. 3 and 4, the Tchaikovsky Concerto No. 1, the Schumann Concerto and the Shostakovich Concerto. He likes to present "collection" programs; for example, both books of the Debussy Preludes, the Liszt *Harmonies poétiques et religieuses*, and his striking all-Satie recitals. Contemporary music is not to his liking. "I must say that I've tried to become interested in contemporary music. I've been through an awful lot of it. But after years and years, I finally discovered I wasn't interested at all. I am even thinking to myself that I must be wrong, but I take full responsibility for what I am saying." (Malitz)

Ciccolini's New York debut (2 Nov 1950), a performance of Tchaikovsky's B-flat Minor Concerto with the New York Philharmonic-Symphony Orchestra under Dimitri Mitropoulos, received mixed reviews. After duly noting that the 25-year-old pianist had "very powerful muscles and virtuoso temperament," one critic concluded that he was obviously a gifted player. "He has brilliancy and also beauty of tone and he can generate excitement. But he did not prove a distinguished interpreter of the concerto, which, in his hands, lacked the grandeur and splendor so inherent in its measures." (*NYT*, 3 Nov 1950) On the other hand, another reviewer described Ciccolini as a "virtuoso of the first rank." (*NYHT*, 3 Nov 1950)

A review of Ciccolini's London debut recital (23 Jan 1954) also begins by admiring his brilliant technique, but adds that in Mozart's A Major Sonata, K. 331, this very fluency tempted him to speed too lightly over the surface of the music. However, "it was sensitive and delicate speeding, nonetheless, and in Franck's Prelude, Choral and Fugue such an emotionally light-weight approach was as refreshing as a breath of fresh air in a hothouse of geraniums." (*TL*, 25 Jan 1954) Later that year another London recital (16 Oct 1954) proved without doubt that Ciccolini was "master of his instrument and his repertory. His manner of playing is everything that the French admire in a pianist: clean of texture, keen of sensibility, aristocratic in approach." (*TL*, 18 Oct 1954)

Ciccolini's first New York recital after almost 25 years' absence—a classic Ciccolini program (Ravel, Satie, Mussorgsky) played at Carnegie Hall on 9 February 1975—received a rousing ovation. "It didn't take more than 10 bars of Ravel's *Pavane pour une infante défunte* . . . to make it very clear that the recital would be exceptional and Aldo Ciccolini never wavered from the high standard he set; an expressive, color-drenched performance. . . . In all, Ciccolini showed taste, refinement, power when needed and a sense of painting with music that went far beyond the norm." (*NYP*, 10 Feb 1975)

Ciccolini has a flair for programming provocatively contrasting works. One such event, a recital (5 March 1978) at Xavier University in Cincinnati, began with French music: two engaging Satie works (*Sports et Divertissements*, *Sonatine bureaucratique*); the monumental Prelude, Choral and Fugue of César Franck, and Ravel's *Sonatine*. It concluded with Rachmaninoff's passionate B-flat Minor Sonata. The encore was a powerful, pulsating performance of Falla's Ritual Fire Dance. "Where the Ravel offered shimmering and delicate effects, the Rachmaninoff is music full of passion and excitement. Here Ciccolini's fingers turned to pile-driving machines without ever losing their inherent link with the music itself." (*DDN*, 6 March 1978)

Ciccolini is justly famous for his Satie interpretations. At one offbeat performance (30 May 1979) described by Ciccolini as a "Caffé-Concert"—two shows before standing-room audiences at The Bottom Line, a Greenwich Village cabaret—he offered an entire program of "the whimsical works of the iconoclastic" Satie. "He played the familiar Gymnopédies and the less familiar Dissected Embryos with diffident mastery and passionate disdain." (*NYDN*, 1 June 1979)

Ciccolini, who has recorded all five Saint-Saëns concertos, proved conclusively in a live performance (2 April 1981) of the Saint-Saëns Concerto No. 4 with the Denver Symphony Orchestra under Sixten Ehrling that he is a formidable pianist of awesome ability who concentrates all his attention "to the task at hand, with none of the barnstorming flamboyance of an acknowledged virtuoso but the certitude of complete mastery. . . . What set Ciccolini apart in his performance was fabulous projection at all points of the work, and clarity of playing." (*DP*, 3 April 1981)

On 21 March 1986 Ciccolini played the complete set of Liszt's *Harmonies poétiques et religieuses* at the University of California, Los Angeles, proving beyond question that as a Lisztian "his credentials are impeccable." Ciccolini's performance reminded this critic of Fuller-Maitland's remembrance of Liszt's own playing: "'The peculiar quiet brilliance of his rapid passages, the noble proportion kept between the parts and the meaning and effect which he put into the music were the most striking points'—exactly describes Ciccolini's performance." (*LAT*, 24 March 1986)

Aldo Ciccolini's playing is at once both immensely satisfying and inspiring for an audience. As one critic described it, "Ciccolini avoids standard cliches, and his is one of the finest lyric talents of the piano today. . . . He makes the piano breathe like a human voice—like a variety of human voices." (*WP*, 21 July 1983) Another writer attributes Ciccolini's effect on an audience to the fact that he "belongs to the rare band of pianists who can create and sustain aural music. There is no trickery involved. His range of tonal color is prismatic. . . . It is always a type of color wholly indigenous to the piano, and it is never applied for its own sake; it rises from the dictates of the music, guided by an incessantly active imagination." (*LAT*, 17 Feb 1975)

Ciccolini has made superior recordings of much of the French keyboard repertoire; in fact his three *Grand Prix du Disque* awards are all for recordings of French music: the Satie collection, the Saint-Saëns concertos and the Ravel concertos. His interpretation of the five Saint-Saëns concertos (Grammy, 1973, see Discog.) stands as a model wherein exactly the right admixture of classic and romantic approach produces what must be near perfect results. His original LP recordings of Erik Satie's complete piano works won plaudits from even the severest critics (Grammy, Vol. 5, 1971). Now his recently recorded complete Satie on CD (see Discog.) clearly shows why the Italian-French pianist is so successful in this music: each of the short compositions is given its own careful, idiomatic reading, with tone color, timing, pedaling and phrasing all playing important roles. "In playing Satie's music, the most important thing to keep in mind is *simplicity*. This music is natural; all the atmosphere it generates comes from the fact that it is so straightforward." (Ciccolini, "Erik Satie's . . .")

The Ciccolini recordings of Debussy's complete solo piano music (see Discog.) rate equally with the few other sets—Fergus-Thompson, Jones, Trimo—available. His set not only has the advantage of being complete but, since it was recorded in 1991, the further advantage of being produced by the most modern technology. (Each of the five CDs in the set is available separately.) There are bound to be comparisons. For example, it would be difficult to better Gieseking's performance of the Preludes, but the sound is in no way comparable to that on the Ciccolini CDs. Those not familiar with Ciccolini's straightforward, sometimes classical approach, may feel that some selections are "too brightly lit, and stated rather than suggested." (*Gram*, June 1992) But Ciccolini's admirers and those who appreciate a variety of approaches to the music of Debussy and Ravel will find his set of Debussy's complete piano music most satisfying.

In 1989 Ciccolini signed a contract with Nuova Era, a new Italian company. Surprisingly, his initial project was to record all 32 Beethoven sonatas. The first issue—the last five sonatas—promised wondrous things to come. Even before its release, Nuova Era's marketing manager confidently announced that, "Ciccolini plays wonderfully. Trust me. His rendition of the last five sonatas is really superb. He has the maturity, the insight, the right pace." (*Fan*, Sept/Oct 1989) The marketing manager was absolutely right. These five recordings (see Discog.) prove that the "French music specialist" can hold his own with the best in Beethoven sonata interpretations. Even seasoned critics who have reviewed literally dozens of recordings of the late Beethoven sonatas agree that Ciccolini's version merits special attention. For example, "Ciccolini's 'Hammerklavier' is replete with instances of exceptionally finished pianism and subtle musicality. His chord voicing in the first movement is that of a consummate master. . . . The scherzo has a serene feeling and is playful. . . . But the highlight of this 'Hammerklavier' is the adagio sostenuto, one of the finest recordings of this long and difficult movement that I've heard." (*Fan*, March/April 1990)

Ciccolini's affinity with the music of Liszt shines through in his masterful projections of the variegated tone pictures comprising the *Années de pèlerinage* (see Discog.). Equally striking is his 1990 recording of the formidable *Harmonies poétiques et religieuses*. "In every one of the ten movements his rounded, cohesive conceptions are communicated with aplomb, polish and expressivity." (*ARG*, March/April 1992) "Ciccolini," writes another reviewer, "relishes the sense of meditation which goes hand in hand with Liszt's desire to wear his heart on his sleeve. Vastness, intimacy, other-worldliness, extroversion, spareness and richness, but above all spiritual sincerity, characterize this music. Ciccolini understands well these paradoxes, the marks of a true adventurer." (*TL*, 8 April 1991)

Included in the two Liszt CDs are seven operatic paraphrases—imaginative, technically challenging explorations of favorite tunes by Wagner, Gounod, Donizetti and Verdi. Originally recorded in 1982, just before the era of the CD, these are invariably sturdy, vivid performances.

SELECTED REFERENCES

Alan, Edward. ". . . .like apples from the apple tree." *Records and Recording*, June 1971, pp. 58–59. An extended review of Ciccolini's recordings of the Saint-Saëns concertos.

Beigel, Greta. "Opening the Door to Satie." *Los Angeles Times*, 9 Feb 1980, sec. 2, p. 10.

Chism, Olin. "Crossing the Boundaries for Art." *Dallas Times Herald*, 17 Sept 1985, pp. 1–2.

Ciccolini, Aldo. "Erik Satie's Piano Music." *Keyboard Classics*, May/June 1987, pp. 38–39.

―――. "Mental Practice." (interview with Stephen West) *Etude*, Sept 1953, pp. 16, 47.

Dumm, Robert. "Aldo Ciccolini: a return to Elegance." *Clavier*, Feb 1982, pp. 16–19.

Ericson, Raymond. "Neapolitan Pianist Plays With a French Accent." *New York Times*, 13 Jan 1978, sec. 3, p. 8.

Glass, Herbert. "Debussy Meets His Match in Aldo Ciccolini Showcase." *Los Angeles Times*, 20 Sept 1992, CAL, p. 51.

Hucher, Yves. *"Rencontre avec Aldo Ciccolini."* *Guide du Concert*, 21 June 1957, p. 1225.

Kentridge, Catherine. "The Refined Art of Aldo Ciccolini." *Music Magazine*, Jan/Feb 1984, pp. 23–24.

Malitz, Nancy. "Ciccolini's Piano Joins Satie's Wit For Irreverent Spectacle." *Cincinnati Enquirer*, 5 March 1978, sec. F, p. 4.

Perlmutter, Donna. "Aldo Ciccolini: The Pianist As Philosopher." *Los Angeles Times*, 21 March 1986, sec. 6, p. 8.

Soria, Dorle J. "Aldo Ciccolini and Erik Satie." *Musical America*, Oct 1979, pp. 6–9, 14.

See also Bibliography: Ewe/Li2; New/Gro; Ran/Kon; Rat/Cle.

SELECTED REVIEWS

CST: 18 Feb 1980. *DDN*: 6 March 1978. *DP*: 3 April 1981. *DTH*: 14 Sept 1985. *LAT*: 17 Feb 1975; 19 Oct 1976; 4 May 1979; 2 May 1983; 24 March 1986; 17 Feb 1987; 8 Nov 1989. *MH*: 18 Oct 1983; 25 Feb 1986. *MM*: April 1985. *NYDN*: 19 Feb 1975; 1 June 1979. *NYHT*: 3 Nov 1950; 26 Oct 1951. *NYP*: 10 Feb 1975; 27 Feb 1980. *NYT*: 3 Nov 1950; 26 Oct 1951; 10 Feb 1975; 6 Feb 1987; 28 June 1992. *NYTr*: 6 Feb 1987. *SFC*: 11 April 1983; 24 Sept 1985. *TB*: 10 July 1984. *TL*: 25 Jan 1954; 18 Oct 1954; 3 July 1961; 29 Nov 1965. *WP*: 21 July 1983. *WS*: 25 Feb 1980. *WT:* 22 July 1983.

SELECTED DISCOGRAPHY

Albéniz: Piano Concerto; *Iberia*; *Navarra*; *Catalonia*. IMG/Pickwick 1607 (CD). Bátiz/LSO.

Beethoven: Sonata in B-flat Major, op. 22; Sonata in F Minor, op. 57; Sonata in E-flat Major, op. 81a. *Nuova Era* CD 6886.

Beethoven: The Late Piano Sonatas: ops. 101, 106, 109, 110, 111. *Nuova Era* CD 6797/98 (2 discs).

Debussy: Complete Works for Solo Piano. EMI Angel CDC7 54447/51-2 (5 CDs).

Falla: *Danza ritual del fuego*. Liszt: *Chapelle de Guillaume Tell*; Consolations Nos. 5-10; *Funérailles*; Rigoletto Paraphrase. Mozart: Fantasy in C Minor, K. 475; Sonata in C Minor, K. 457. Ermitage ERM 405 (CD).

Falla: *Noches en los jardines de España*. Rodrigo: *Concierto de Aranjuéz*. Turina: *Danzas fantásticas*. Angel 63886 (CD). Bátiz/Royal PO.
Franck: *Les Djinns*; Symphonic Variations. Ricercar RIS 009058/059 (2 CDs). Strauss/Liège PO. Also contains four Franck orchestral works.
Liszt: *Les Années de pèlerinage* (complete). Angel CDMB-62640 (2 CDs).
Liszt: *Harmonies poétiques et religieuses*; opera paraphrases (7). EMI 54142 (2 CDs).
Mozart: Sonata in C Major, K. 309; Sonata in C Major, K. 330; Sonata in C Major, K. 545. Discover International DICD 920145.
Ravel: Concerto in G; Concerto for Left Hand. Angel CDM-69568. Martinon/*Orch. de Paris*.
Saint-Saëns: Concertos (complete). Angel CDMB-69443 (2 CDs). Baudo/*Orch. de Paris*.
Satie: Piano Music (complete). Angel CDC-49702, 49703, 49713, 49714, 49760.

CLIBURN, VAN (Harvey Lavan Cliburn, Jr.): b. Shreveport, Louisiana, 12 July 1934.

> He is a superbly equipped instrumentalist who makes musicianly sense and holds poetic ideals. Without effort or egotism he owns the unanswerable power of communication, the magic to which the spontaneous heart of the public is as responsive as is that of the most penetrating expert.
>
> Abram Chasins (*The Van Cliburn Legend*)

Here in the closing decade of the 20th century, far removed from the Cold War, how difficult it must be for anyone not personally familiar with that tense era even to imagine what Van Cliburn's "unanswerable power of communication" accomplished in the Russian spring of 1958. Americans, their pride badly bruised by the Soviet Union's successful launching of two Sputnik rockets in 1957, and Russians, isolated and distrustful behind the Iron Curtain, were worlds apart. Then Van Cliburn, a 23-year-old pianist from Texas, won the Gold Medal in the first International Tchaikovsky Competition in Moscow. In an as yet unmatched musical coup, Cliburn dazzled the Russians—plain citizens, political elite and musical intelligentsia alike—"with a display of technical skill that Russians have long considered their special forte." (*NYT*, 12 April 1958) And back home in the United States, Cliburn's totally unexpected victory rekindled American spirits.

From the very first auditions, the charismatic, outgiving Cliburn struck a responsive chord with Russian audiences—an emotional chord powerful enough to make them forget that Cliburn represented the United States of America, their feared enemy. If they were expecting an arrogant, warmongering American, the friendly, affectionate Cliburn must have been an enormous surprise. To discover that the playing of an American-born, American-trained pianist was, as one juror put it, "more Russian than the Russians," must have been a shock. On 14 April 1958 the jury officially announced that Van Cliburn had won. Melodramatic as it sounds, on that day his life changed; and today, nearly 40 years later, it is evident that what happened in Moscow decided the course of Cliburn's career.

The Russian people went absolutely wild over him. Many waited in lines all night to get tickets to his performances, and so many thousands were turned away that he opened his rehearsals to the public. They carpeted the stage with flowers and threw some of their dearest treasures over the footlights. They followed Cliburn in the streets and stormed his hotel, once again leaving their offerings. Cliburn, who had gone to Russia with three suitcases, needed 17 to carry home all those astonishing gifts.

His American homecoming reception is something else now difficult to believe. At the time, however, his out-of-the-blue musical conquest in the Soviet Union soothed America's hurt pride and, at least symbolically, erased some of the stigma of the Sputnik successes. Not to be outdone by the Kremlin, Robert F. Wagner, mayor of New York City, proclaimed 20 May 1958 as "American Music Day." Even more unbelievable, on that day New York honored Cliburn, a *concert pianist*, with a ticker-tape parade on Broadway, and an estimated 100,000 cheering spectators lined the parade route.

For the record, Cliburn went to that competition exceptionally well prepared, with years of excellent training and public performances behind him and a reputation as one of the best among his generation of American pianists. He had taken first place in America's most important piano contests, and he had already performed with important orchestras: Cleveland, Pittsburgh, Denver, Buffalo, Cincinnati, Dallas, Detroit, Houston, Indianapolis. Cliburn deserved his Moscow victory.

From birth, Van Cliburn had the caring support of generous parents— Harvey Lavan Cliburn, a purchasing agent for Magnolia Oil Company, and Rildia Bee (O'Bryan) Cliburn, a pianist who had studied at the Cincinnati Conservatory of Music and in New York with Arthur Friedheim, a Liszt pupil. She became a well-known piano teacher, and Cliburn grew up hearing her making music with her students throughout the day and her personal practicing at night. Listening and apparently absorbing, at age three Cliburn surprised his mother by playing by ear a piece one of her pupils had just played. She started teaching him when he was age four and was his only teacher until he went to Juilliard at age 17. By the time he was five, he could read at sight any pieces possible for his finger technique. By the fifth grade he was usually practicing three hours daily, one before school, one after school and one in the evening.

Cliburn made his first public appearance at age four on a program for the faculty and students of Dodd College in Shreveport, Louisiana. In 1940 the Magnolia Oil Company transferred Harvey Cliburn to Kilgore, Texas, thus Cliburn had all of his schooling in Kilgore, the town he still thinks of as "home." He was only 12 years old when he placed first in a statewide competition for young pianists, the prize being a guest performance with the Houston Symphony Orchestra, conducted by Ernest Hoffman. At that "prize" appearance (the concert was broadcast on the Texas Radio Network) Cliburn played the first movement of the Tchaikovsky Concerto No. 1 in B-flat Minor.

In the summers of 1947 and 1948, Cliburn took classes in harmony, theory, sight-reading, musical dictation and ensemble at the Juilliard School in New York. On 12 March 1948 Cliburn (at age 13 the Texas winner of the National Music Festival's nationwide competition to discover youthful talent) took part in a Carnegie Hall concert. That fall he enrolled at the Kilgore High School and, by taking extra courses in the summer, graduated in three years. By age 14 he was six-feet-four with hands capable of spanning a twelfth.

Cliburn studied piano with Rosina Lhévinne at Juilliard for three years. Thanks to his mother's rigorous training, he was already a very good pianist when he started at Juilliard. He had a natural way of playing, an awesome technique and a beautiful tone. Mme. Lhévinne, one of the great piano pedagogues of her time, shaped and refined his playing, and he emerged from Juilliard a more controlled and accomplished pianist. A formidable teacher in every way, Mme. Lhévinne required her students to have a minimum of 20 minutes of music memorized each week. She sought a limpid, not a percussive sound, and flexibility, not tightness in the playing.

Cliburn, obviously an outstanding student in a stellar Juilliard class (it included John Browning and Gary Graffman), collected a series of impressive awards. In 1952 he received the G. B. Dealey Memorial Award in Dallas, and also the Kosciuszko Foundation's Chopin Scholarship Award. In June 1953 at the Michael Memorial Music Competition in Chicago, cellist Paul Olefsky won first place, Cliburn the second. (He never placed second to any pianist.) In 1953 he also was awarded the Olga Samaroff Grant at Juilliard and won the school's annual concerto competition. He graduated in May 1954 (diploma course, not the degree course) with two honors—the Carl M. Roeder Memorial Award and the Frank Damrosch Scholarship for graduate studies.

Cliburn never had time for graduate work. Columbia Artists Management had already signed him to a contract, and he was well known in the musical community. He had spent two summers at Chautauqua performing with the Chautauqua Symphony Orchestra, conducted by Walter Hendl; and he had played professional recitals in Texas and Louisiana. Just before graduation he applied for the 15th Leventritt International Competition. Competing against top-level pianists, including John Browning and other Juilliard classmates, Cliburn emerged the winner in September 1954.

The Leventritt prize plunged Cliburn into a whirl of performing, including appearances with the New York Philharmonic Society and the Buffalo, Cleveland, Denver and Pittsburgh orchestras. At his first "prize" engagement, at Carnegie Hall on 14 November 1954, he played the Tchaikovsky B-flat Minor Concerto with Dimitri Mitropoulos conducting the New York Philharmonic Orchestra. An audience that "went bonkers," as one friend expressed it, brought Cliburn out for seven curtain calls. His career quickly gathered momentum. Within four months he played the rest of his Leventritt "prize" engagements, each enormously successful.

Cliburn played about 18 concerts in 1954–55, the first season after winning the Leventritt Competition. In 1955–56 he made about 30 appearances.

The next season (1956–57) he was booked for 23 engagements—a few orchestral performances, the others mostly community concert recitals in small towns. His schedule for the 1957–58 season showed only a few small town appearances, a dismal three-month gap, then a few more minor engagements.

Cliburn's seemingly guaranteed concert career had lost momentum. Why this happened is still not perfectly clear. Some were convinced that Cliburn's promising career stalled because here in America we promoted foreign talent and ignored native talent. But Howard Reich, in his excellent, comprehensive biography *Van Cliburn*, explains that a series of unforeseen incidents interrupted Cliburn's budding career. For one thing, he expected to be drafted into the army in 1957, so had not planned bookings ahead; however, he was disqualified because of chronic nasal hemorrhages. That left him free to give concerts, but he had very few engagements lined up. And there were family problems. A bad fall disabled Mrs. Cliburn to the point that she could not teach, and Cliburn returned to Texas to take over her students. Just as his mother improved, his father was hurt in an auto-bus accident, and Cliburn stayed on to help. He finally returned to New York in November, dejected at being away from performing for such a long time and not very hopeful about his future.

Having decided to enter the first Tchaikovsky Competition in Moscow, he practiced intensively, had a long lesson every Sunday with Mme. Lhévinne and consulted with Mitropoulous on the repertoire he would play in Moscow. On 22 March 1958 he played some of his Tchaikovsky Competition pieces for a few close friends. The next day he left for Moscow and the fateful competition that changed his life. The rest, as we hear so often, is history.

It is clear now, decades later, that the very day (14 April 1958) Cliburn won the Gold Medal in Moscow he stepped onto a merry-go-round that refused to let him off. He was, overnight, the center of international attention, the darling of the media, a political-cultural symbol, an idol of adoring fans. Without a break, he began a month of performances in Russia—Moscow, Leningrad, Riga, Kiev, Minsk—then returned home, where he met with more receptions, the thrilling ticker-tape parade and more and more performances. Meanwhile in early May he had signed a recording contract with RCA Victor.

On 19 May 1958 Cliburn faced the challenge of his first post-competition American concert. Playing the Tchaikovsky Concerto No. 1 and the Rachmaninoff Concerto No. 3 with the Symphony of the Air, conducted by Kiril Kondrashin (at Cliburn's request, allowed to leave Russia), Cliburn passed the acid test with flying colors. A repeat (26 May) of this program, broadcast live in full (two and a half hours) on radio station WQXR was, said the *New York Times*, "the week's event, television or no television."

The Cliburn carousel sped faster and faster. On 23 May 1958 he and his parents were at the White House for personal congratulations from President Eisenhower. He appeared on the "Steve Allen Show" on 25 May and on Edward R. Murrow's "Person-to-Person" program on 30 May. And of course he was always performing. ("Cliburn's pre-Moscow fee, about $800 a performance, jumped to about $2,000.) Concerts in Philadelphia, Washington, D.C., and New York preceded his departure (9 June 1958) for Europe to make his debuts in London, Paris, Amsterdam and in Brussels at the World's Fair. Cliburn again played the Tchaikovsky First and the Rachmaninoff Third concertos at his London debut (15 June) at the Royal Albert Hall, with Kiril Kondrashin conducting the London Philharmonic Orchestra. Both the United States and the Soviet ambassadors to Great Britain attended this performance—living evidence of Cliburn's new role as goodwill ambassador. And he was exceptionally good at it. "Van Cliburn behaved like a born statesman. He always said the right thing. He always made the right gesture." (Davidson)

In July Cliburn played a hectic round of concerts (before record-breaking crowds) in the United States and in August returned to Brussels for a second performance at the World's Fair. A so-called vacation beginning on 21 August 1958 included hours of practicing (often between midnight and six A.M. in the basement of Steinway Hall) to prepare for more 1958 concerts.

Cliburn's frantic performance pace continued. On 17 February 1959 he played three concertos (Mozart in C Major, K. 505, the Schumann, Prokofiev No. 3) with the New York Philharmonic Orchestra, conducted by Leonard Bernstein. Late in May of that year he began a monthlong tour of Europe (London, Paris, Milan, Lisbon). In 1960 Cliburn left Columbia Artists Management to sign with Sol Hurok, who employed Mrs. Cliburn as Cliburn's touring manager. It takes only a quick scanning of the stacks of Cliburn reviews to see how much he performed. For more than a decade he toured intensely—in the United States, in Europe, in Mexico (1962), in Israel (1962) and in Russia (1960, 1962, 1965, 1972). Eventually, critics began to complain, not only about the narrowness of his repertoire but sometimes also about his playing.

As early as 1959 a prophetic writer noted that if Cliburn, fortunate possessor of "what someone once called the incommunicable technique of magnificence . . . is forced by the curious truculence of popular demand to display it endlessly in playing Tchaikovsky, Rachmaninoff and Liszt, that will be a pity." (Poore) But a pianist needs time to practice, and Cliburn especially needed time to enlarge his repertoire. His managers, tempted by a flood of offers for their star pianist, particularly requests to hear him play the concertos that had made him famous, allowed him little time to work on his repertoire. It is easy to see how Cliburn himself, still only in his thirties and a natural showman overflowing with talent and enthusiasm, got trapped by his own extraordinary fame.

Some critics began to complain that Cliburn's playing sometimes seemed detached, aloof, leaden, mechanical or overly percussive. His limited repertoire, all too often mentioned, most likely accounts for the natural drop in Cliburn's engagements after 1970. Cliburn had simply overdone. In the early 1970s, recalls a colleague at RCA, "I began to feel he wasn't as enthusiastic about everything as he had been. . . . The old bite wasn't there. It was missing, and I thought he was tired." (Reich, *Van Cliburn*)

Cliburn himself, depressed at the deaths in 1974 of both his father and Sol Hurok, began to talk about taking an "intermission." Tired of the concert life, he now wanted a home with all his beloved treasures around him; and he wanted time to attend concerts, operas and the theater. About that time he stopped booking ahead. After honoring previously planned engagements, without any announcement, Cliburn ended his 20-year concert career with a final appearance in Toledo, Ohio, on 26 September 1978, playing the MacDowell

Concerto No. 2 with the Toledo Symphony Orchestra. He continued to live in New York until 1985, then moved to Fort Worth, Texas, where he is involved with the Van Cliburn Foundation, established in 1958 by Irl Allison. Since 1962 the Foundation has sponsored the Van Cliburn International Piano Competition, held every four years at Fort Worth, Texas, and now ranked among the most prestigious of its kind.

The years passed and Cliburn's "intermission" extended into a decade. He apparently practiced but would not perform publicly. Yet he was not forgotten. Honors bestowed during this sabbatical, as he began to call it, include an honorary degree from Texas Christian University in 1982; the Albert Schweitzer Award in 1983; the National Federation of Music Clubs' Presidential Citation in 1983; an honorary master of fine arts degree from Moscow Conservatory in 1990.

Cliburn emerged from his decade of self-imposed retirement for a private performance at a state dinner for Premier Mikhail S. Gorbachev, given by President Ronald Reagan at the White House on 8 December 1987. On 1 January 1988 he played at the dedication of the Bob Hope Cultural Center in Palm Desert, California, and gave a "beautifully shaped performance of Schumann's miniature 'Widmung' (Dedication). Beyond Cliburn's obvious ease and assurance on stage . . . he plays with control, elegance and his trademark delicacy of tone." (*CT*, 3 March 1988) His first public performance in 11 years was a benefit (19 June 1989) for the Mann Music Center in Philadelphia, playing the Tchaikovsky Concerto No. 1 and the Liszt Concerto No. 1 with Stanislaw Skrowaczewski conducting the Philadelphia Orchestra.

A few weeks later Cliburn made a triumphant return to Moscow, his first in 17 years, to play (2 July 1989) the same concertos (Tchaikovsky No. 1, Liszt No. 1) with the Moscow State Philharmonic Orchestra, conducted by Dmitri Kitayenko. Once again he played to wildly enthusiastic crowds in Moscow and Leningrad. And he played (8 Sept 1989) at the opening of the Morton H. Meyerson Symphony Center in Dallas, with the Dallas Symphony Orchestra, Eduardo Mata conducting. On 21 September 1990 he played the Tchaikovsky Concerto No. 1 with the Lincoln Symphony Orchestra, Robert Emilie conducting. He gave a solo recital (his first in a decade) in Kilgore, Texas, in early October and played (27 Oct) the Tchaikovsky Concerto No. 1 again at the Tilles Center (at the C. W. Post Campus of Long Island University in Greenvale, L.I.) with Mariss Jansons conducting the Leningrad Philharmonic Orchestra. On New Year's Eve of 1990 Cliburn played three concertos (Tchaikovsky No. 1, Liszt No. 1, Beethoven No. 5) in Fort Worth, Texas. On 1 May 1991 he played with Zubin Mehta and the New York Philharmonic Orchestra as part of Carnegie Hall's Centennial Festival. He seems not to have enlarged his repertoire, yet he had good reviews on the whole.

On 1 July 1994 Cliburn embarked on his first American tour in 16 years. Together with the Moscow Philharmonic Orchestra, Vassily Sinaisky conducting, he was scheduled to perform two of his old standbys—the Tchaikovsky Concerto No. 1 and the Rachmaninoff Concerto No. 3 in various cities. However, the Rachmaninoff was dropped before the initial performance (Hollywood Bowl), permanently replaced by some solo pieces. The tour was to include major American cities and end on 21 August. There were complications. The orchestra and soloist seemed ill-rehearsed—at least during the first several concerts. Cliburn's mother died on 3 August and there were some cancellations and some rescheduling of concert dates.

Van Cliburn's unique experience sets his concert career apart from those of the rest of his generation. Among them, only Cliburn knows what it means to be catapulted at a young age into instant, relentless celebrity with its contingent adulation, pressure, everlasting scrutiny and envy. He responded too generously to requests for performances, interviews, receptions, to just about everything. Whether he chooses retirement or a return to performing, he will always occupy a very special niche in musical history.

A good many pages have been devoted to Van Cliburn's repertoire, or, more precisely, his lack of repertoire. As early as the 1950s some critics scolded Cliburn for playing too many Romantic works and not enough of the Austro-German repertoire. After Moscow there was a specific caution: "What this gifted young man needs now is a more catholic study of music—not pianism, of which he needs little—and that with modern teachers. . . . What he is now being asked to do is a sure way to permanent intellectual disability." (*NYHT*, 20 May 1958)

Because there has been so much discussion about Cliburn's limited repertoire, it seems worthwhile to sum it up. The list compiled from Cliburn's recordings, from the discography published in the Reich biography and from dozens of critical reviews (dating from 1954 through 1991), indicates that he has mostly played these concertos: Beethoven Nos. 3, 4, 5; Brahms Nos. 1, 2; Chopin No. 1; the Grieg Concerto; Liszt Nos. 1 and 2; MacDowell No. 2; Mozart in C Major, K. 505; Prokofiev No. 3; Rachmaninoff Nos. 2, 3 and the Paganini Rhapsody; the Schumann Concerto; Tchaikovsky No. 1. These same sources show that Cliburn's solo repertoire contains little from the Baroque period apart from Bach's Toccata in C Minor. There are several Mozart sonatas and about five by Beethoven. The bulk of the repertoire comes from the Romantic period with Chopin's works dominating (Sonatas Nos. 2 and 3, about a dozen shorter works). The Liszt Sonata, Hungarian Rhapsody No. 12 and Mephisto Waltz are present, but one finds only a small group of short pieces by Schumann. From the later 19th century there are the Brahms-Handel Variations, op. 24, and a substantial group of shorter compositions; France is represented by about a dozen Debussy pieces and a few by Ravel; the Russian school is expectedly much in evidence—works by Prokofiev (Sonata No. 6), Rachmaninoff (Sonata No. 2, various preludes) and Scriabin. The outstanding contemporary work is the Barber Sonata.

Most certainly it was not problems with technique that limited Cliburn's repertoire. Fellow students at Juilliard recall how he dazzled them with his warm-up technique of playing swift scales in octaves and tenths with his hands crossed, a trick, said Cliburn, that does wonders in developing the left hand. It was not technique, but a matter of time. Fame plunged him into an exciting life, but it proved too demanding. Cliburn simply never found the time necessary to enlarge his repertoire. And possibly he resisted practicing. Cliburn has told interviewers that he enjoyed practicing until he reached his teens, but thereafter needed inspiration to make himself practice.

Cliburn's great flair for living and his warm, romantic nature permeate his playing. Believing that there is more to playing the piano than just hitting the right notes, he interprets a score with freedom and spontaneity. As a result, critics describe his playing as "poetic, beautiful and free with an exceptionally beautiful touch and a wonderful technique." (Cahn) At the same time, a natural elegance, dignity and taste pervade his sweeping style. His artistry is "the kind that begins where technique leaves off. His expressiveness ranges from ghostly sonorities and harplike trills to ringing double octaves that cleave the orchestra like a sword. He can shape passages with tensions and excitement, turn the weariest warhorse into a spirited charger." (*Time*, 19 May 1958)

Cliburn had achieved recognition even before Moscow. His performance (14 Nov 1954) of the Tchaikovsky Concerto in B-flat Minor, with Dimitri Mitropoulos conducting the New York Philharmonic Orchestra, prompted one reviewer to name him "the most talented newcomer of the season . . . he literally commands the piano as he plays and in many ways the music too. He is far from a finished performer as yet . . . but he has, in abundance, the qualities of fervor, audience appeal and musicianship which make for distinction." (*SR*, 27 Nov 1954)

Consider his concert reviews through the years. Just a few months after his phenomenal win in Moscow, Cliburn played (15 June 1958) two concertos for his London debut at Albert Hall. The *Musical Times* critic devoted a long column to the performance: "In Tchaikovsky's B flat minor Concerto and Rachmaninoff's Third in D minor every note fell into place with glorious punctuality; the playing was wonderfully alive and had delicacy as well as fire; the phrases were shaped and dynamically graded with loving care; the rhythm was irrestible as the wind." (*MT*, Aug 1958)

In those early years critics everywhere lavished compliments on Cliburn's playing. For example, a critique of his Boston debut (14 Oct 1960) at Symphony Hall—he played three of the most difficult sonatas in the repertoire: Liszt Sonata in B Minor, Rachmaninoff Sonata in B-flat Minor and the Barber Sonata—reads: "Mr. Cliburn is truly a little lower than the angels as an interpreter; he has the communicative gift that few artists of his age possess, Glenn Gould excepted; he digs deep into the substance of the music and it comes forth almost pure gold." (*CSM*, 15 Oct 1960)

A Hunter College recital (24 March 1962) presented two large-scale sonatas—Beethoven "*Appassionata*," op. 57, and the Liszt Sonata in B Minor— and also a group of Chopin pieces. "In Mr. Cliburn's recital there was virtually no excitement. . . . He impressed more as an extremely gifted pianist playing more or less by rote than as the artist he should be." (*NYT*, 26 March 1962) The following year Cliburn played (4 Oct 1963) a Carnegie Hall recital of Brahms, Beethoven, Barber and Chopin. The same critic sensed a definite improvement, noting that, "Mr. Cliburn's style is maturing and broadening. . . . He is fortunate in his tone and technique, and he still draws a warm sonority that is unique among pianists of his generation." But one caveat still persisted: "He will never take a chance, and he shies away from the improvisatory quality that the romantic pianists of the older generation possessed." (*NYT*, 5 Oct 1963)

Cliburn's performances became increasingly inconsistent. At a Hunter College recital (16 April 1966) he played so well that, wrote one reviewer, "It is heartening to see Mr. Cliburn at 31 years of age take his place among the music world's great." (*NYT*, 18 April 1966) But a Kennedy Center (Washington, D.C.) recital on 10 March 1973 was "strangely unsettled, marked with playing of a caliber that would be unacceptable from a top conservatory student." In Beethoven's "*Appassionata*" Sonata "he read the introduction as if it were a Bach adagio. . . . This same kind of disturbance made the slow movement one of the most perverse in history. It came out sounding more like an essay for the left hand than the great passage it truly is." (*WP*, 11 March 1973)

A review of a Los Angeles performance (11 March 1977) is typical of many criticisms appearing around that time. "The program traversed much the same repertory Cliburn has been performing season after season. . . . The pianist's technical equipment, temperamental flair and (for the most part) suavity of tone remain incontestable. So do the disconcerting signs of staleness and musical carelessness which cropped up throughout this recital." (*LAT*, 15 March 1977)

The announcement of Cliburn's return to the concert stage sent waves of excitement throughout the world of music. After being more than a decade "on sabbatical," he gave his first public performance (19 June 1989) at Philadelphia's Mann Music Center, playing two concertos which figured prominently in his early career: Tchaikovsky No. 1 in B-flat Minor and the Liszt No. 1 in E-flat Major. How did he fare? According to at least two major newspapers, Van Cliburn did very well indeed, thus effectively squelching the doomsayers. "As always, the big hands ate up the flashing octaves easily. The preternaturally long fingers managed staccato runs precisely and found an even touch for the pearly scales. The lyrical instinct and flair that from the beginning endeared the tall Texan to audiences surfaced winningly in the slow movements." (*NYT*, 21 June 1989) And this: "First, it became apparent that Cliburn had not forgotten how to play a concerto; then it began to seem possible that he had something new to say. . . . It would be hard to find a pianist anywhere who can communicate with an audience as powerfully, who can generate the kind of excitement that was witnessed here." (*WP*, 21 June 1989)

The next month Cliburn returned to Moscow. Thirty-one years after his glorious victory at the first Tchaikovsky International Piano Competition, he played (2 July 1989) the Liszt and the Tchaikovsky concertos, and drew bravos, screams and a standing ovation for his performances. Wrote an American critic who was present: "Every page of the two concertos was streaked with the sort of freedom of phrase, freshness and vivid imagination that comes only from a major musician at the zenith of his powers." (*DMN*, quoted in *JS*, 1 April 1990)

But a review of yet another performance (Los Angeles, 27 Oct 1990) of the Tchaikovsky Concerto No. 1, with the Leningrad Symphony Orchestra, reads, "Cliburn no longer sounds like a pianist with a technique in perfect working order. . . . Pages of fireworks were presented almost tenuously, without the bold, affirmative thrust that was once his to command." At the same time, Cliburn's "ability to conjure up an astonishing array of colors and tones from crystalline-yet-sure pianissimos to thundering fortissimos, all without apparent physical effort or strain, remains very much intact." (*LAT*, 29 Oct 1990)

Cliburn's performances on his 1994 tour were variable but his charisma remained unimpaired. As one critic noted after the pianist's Hollywood Bowl appearance, "The nuggets in the Tchaikovsky may have been few, but they were choice, and who among his contemporaries can match him in majesty, despite his limited range? Cliburn will never be the pianist we all thought he should be. But that is our problem, not his." (*Time*, 25 July 1994) The Metropolitan Opera concert (2 Aug 1994), with top prices at $150, was, at least from an audience standpoint, a smashing success—after the Tchaikovsky Concerto he received two standing ovations. But we have these comments from one reviewer: "Upon his 1989 return, critics wondered whether he would merely retrace his steps or begin where he left off. Since then, he has played virtually nothing but the Tchaikovsky First, and has shown little inclination to recapture his old repertory, let alone extend it. The pity is that there is a spark in Mr. Cliburn's playing that begs to be fanned into flame; but if he does nothing but trot out a single warhorse year after year, that spark will soon be smothered." (Kozinn)

Considering the relatively brief number of years before his "intermission," Cliburn's discography is substantial. The Tchaikovsky Concerto No. 1, recorded in Carnegie Hall on 30 May 1958 with Kiril Kondrashin and the RCA Symphony Orchestra, was enormously successful. "Others have played the famous Tchaikovsky Piano Concerto louder and faster, but none have played it with more authority, care and affection than Van Cliburn." (*OV*, Sept 1989) At the end of 1961 this recording had sold over a million copies, the first classical recording to do so.

In his recording of Rachmaninoff's Concerto No. 3 in D Minor, op. 30, with Kondrashin conducting the Symphony of the Air, "Cliburn plays each note—and there are quite a few—as if it were gold. . . . For devotees of Rachmaninoff's music, Cliburn is just the man for the job. . . . Things could be done differently but not better. Thus, his Rachmaninoff Three can stand next to Rachmaninoff's own recording, even if it is nothing like it." (*OV*, Sept 1989)

Cliburn recorded both Brahms concertos, No. 1 with Erich Leinsdorf and the Boston Symphony Orchestra, No. 2 with Fritz Reiner and the Chicago Symphony Orchestra (see Discog.). Each in its own way is stylish and satisfying. Some Brahms devotees prefer an emphasis on the "classic" elements in his music, others would opt for Brahms, the romantic. One reviewer felt that Cliburn covered both bases: "For my taste this is almost an ideal Brahms 1. . . . Cliburn is as masculine as he needs to be, but wonderfully lyrical where Brahms allows it." (*ARG*, July/Aug 1990)

Cliburn's recording of MacDowell's Concerto No. 2 with the Chicago Symphony Orchestra, Walter Hendl conducting, is the epitome of romantic playing, a glittering performance by a first-rate pianist. This very beautiful concerto with its overtones of Liszt could find no one better qualified than Van Cliburn,

whose "robust, unpressured, wonderfully spirited advocacy makes it bloom."
(*MA*, Sept/Oct 1991)

There are two Cliburn CDs of solo works by Chopin. Another album
couples the Chopin Concerto No. 1 in E Minor, op. 10, with Rachmaninoff's
"Paganini" Rhapsody, Eugene Ormandy conducting the Philadelphia Orchestra
(see Discog.). Wrote one reviewer: "I hear his mastery in the very first phrases
of the Chopin concerto, which is made exciting by the brio and accuracy of his
playing, but also by the sense we always get with Cliburn that he is in control
of the whole piece. . . . On the Rachmaninoff, which gives Cliburn an opportunity to demonstrate the further ranges of his technique and to exercise his taste
on a piece that is often overly romanticized, he is equally exciting." (*Fanfare*,
Sept/Oct 1989. Reprinted by permission.)

The Cliburn CD combining works by Barber, Debussy and Mozart (see
Discog.) is in itself unusual, and it contains some of his most musicianly playing, particularly in the Debussy and Mozart. Cliburn's Mozart is "beautifully
shaded, scrupulously stylish and sensitive to harmonic pulls towards the dark
side." (*Gram*, May 1991) As for the Debussy, supple and suavely textured, "the
slower, more evocative movements seem especially suited to Cliburn's poetic
way." (*ARG*, July/Aug 1991) Competing against other superb recordings of
the Barber Sonata, notably those by Horowitz and Browning, Cliburn "manages
to suggest an epic dimension, with song, dance, struggle and celebration held in
admirable balance." (*Gram*, May 1991)

Van Cliburn had a great impact on the musical world during those
comparatively few years from the late 1950s through the mid-1970s. Why? A
critic reviewing five of Cliburn's concerto recordings asks, "So what kind of
pianist was he? How does his artistry compare with that of the younger pianists
of today? . . . At his best Van Cliburn's direct and clean way with the music is
refreshing—so too is his ability to sustain the line of the music in solo passages. At his worst, his playing lacks personality; often there is little tension in
the interpretations." (*Gram*, Aug 1989)

Yet another critic, reviewing two of the same concertos, is of the opinion that no one has recorded the Beethoven No. 5 and Chopin No. 1 more sub-
limely than Van Cliburn: "His mastery of shape, of pulse and rhythm, his robust vigor and the sensitivity he displays in the modulations of each phrase,
make his grandly expressive playing gleam." (*Fan*, Sept/Oct 1989)

SELECTED REFERENCES

"The All-American Virtuoso." *Time*, 19 May 1958, pp. 58–60, 63–66.

Barthel, Joan. "Eight Years Later: Has Success Spoiled Van Cliburn?" *New
York Times*, 9 Oct 1966, sec. 2, p. 21.

Bernheimer, Martin. "Van Cliburn Disconcerted." *Los Angeles Times*, 13 July
1994, sec. F, pp. 1, 6.

Bracker, Milton. "Jubilant Cliburn Arrives Here After Piano Triumph in
Soviet." *New York Times*, 17 May 1958, p. 21.

Cahn, William. *Van Cliburn: The Amazing Story of a New American Hero*.
New York: Ridge Press, ca. 1959.

Chasins, Abram. "An Interview with Van Cliburn." *The Long Player*, Aug/Sept 1958, pp. 6, 188, 193, 211, 217, 222.

―――. *The Van Cliburn Legend*. New York: Doubleday and Co., 1959.

Davidson, John. "Every Good Boy Does Fine." *Texas Monthly*, May 1987, pp. 118–123, 171–172, 179–181.

Fleming, Michael. "Van Cliburn Reflects on the Past and a Possible Future." *New York Times*, 9 June 1985, sec. 2, p. 24.

Frankel, Max. "Russians Cheer U. S. Pianist, 23." *New York Times*, 12 April 1958, pp. 1, 12.

―――. "U. S. Pianist, 23, Wins Soviet Contest." *New York Times*, 14 April 1958, pp. 1, 18.

Henahan, Donal. "What Makes a Gifted Artist Drop Out in Mid-Career?" *New York Times*, 17 Aug 1986, sec. 2, p. 21.

Isacoff, Stuart. "An Exclusive Interview With Van Cliburn." *Keyboard Classics*, May/June 1985, p. 7.

―――. "The Rise and Fall and Rise of Van Cliburn." *Ovation*, Sept 1989, pp. 16–20, 71.

Isenberg, Barbara. "Intermission Over for Cliburn." *Los Angeles Times*, 15 April 1988, pp. 1, 17.

Kozinn, Allan. "Cliburn Saddles Up the Tchaikovsky Again." *New York Times*, 4 Aug 1994, sec. 3, p. 11.

Poore, Charles. "Books of The Times." *New York Times*, 14 April 1959, p. 33. A review of *The Van Cliburn Legend* by Abram Chasins.

Raabe, Nancy. "'American Sputnik' returns to orbit." *Milwaukee Sentinel*, 5 Aug 1994.

Reich, Howard. "The Cliburn Catalogue." *Chicago Tribune*, 22 Dec 1988, sec. 5, p. 7.

―――. "Hope tribute sparkles with Van Cliburn." *Chicago Tribune*, 3 March 1988, sec. 5, p. 15.

―――. "Power Playing." *Chicago Tribune*, 6 March 1988, sec. 13, p. 4.

―――. *Van Cliburn*. Nashville: Thomas Nelson, 1993. Contains a complete discography.

Sabin, Robert. "Two Conquests: Cliburn in Russia, Soviets Here." *Musical America*, May 1958, pp. 3, 5.

Schodolski, Vincent. "Van Cliburn, Soviets Renew Their Love Affair." *Chicago Tribune*, 4 July 1989, sec. 1, p. 12.

Taubman, Howard. "A Winner On His Merits." *New York Times*, 26 April 1958, sec. 2, p. 9.

Walsh, Michael. "The Reluctant Virtuoso." *Time*, 25 July 1994, p. 71.

Webster, Daniel. "Cliburn plans first concert in 10 years." *Boston Globe*, 25 Jan 1989, p. 45.

―――. "Cliburn's Sentimental Journey." *Philadelphia Inquirer*, 18 June 1989, sec. E, pp. 1, 13.

See also Bibliography: Cur/Bio (1958); Ewe/Mu; IWWM; Kai/Gre; Kol/Que; Moh/My; New/GrA; Ran/Kon; Rub/MyM; Sch/Gre; WWAM.

SELECTED REVIEWS

AJ: 22 Aug 1994. *ARG*: Nov/Dec 1994. *CED*: 24 April 1975. *CSM*: 15 Oct
1960; 28 Oct 1963; 21 Sept 1973. *CT*: 3 March 1988. *LAT*: 15 March
1977; 29 Oct 1990. *MA*: Nov 1963. *MH*: 17 Nov 1975. *MiT*: 8 March
1976. *MT*: Aug 1958. *NYHT*: 20 May 1958. *NYP*: 21 June 1989. *NYT*:
15 Nov 1954; 12 April 1958; 20 May 1958; 5 Aug 1958; 18 Oct 1958; 18
Feb 1959; 15 Feb 1960; 2 Aug 1961; 27 Nov 1961; 10 March 1962; 26
March 1962; 17 Jan 1963; 5 Oct 1963; 2 April 1964; 30 Oct 1965; 12 Jan
1966; 18 April 1966; 29 April 1968; 30 Oct 1968; 21 June 1989; 2 July
1989; 3 July 1989; 29 Oct 1990; 4 May 1991; 4 Aug 1994. *PEB*: 25 July
1978. *PI*: 20 June 1989. *SFC*: 8 Sept 1994. *SFE*: 8 Sept 1994. *SLT*: 7
Nov 1977. *TL*: 10 June 1958; 16 June 1958; 8 June 1959. *WP*: 11 March
1972; 22 March 1975; 20 June 1989; 22 Aug 1994.

SELECTED DISCOGRAPHY

Barber: Sonata, op. 26. Debussy: *La soirée dans Grenade; Etude pour les oc-
taves; La terrace des audiences du claire de lune; Jardins sous la pluie;
Reflets dans l'eau; Feux d'artifice.* Mozart: Sonata in C Major, K. 330.
RCA 60415-2.
Beethoven: Sonata in C Minor, op. 13; Sonata in C-sharp Minor, op. 27, no. 2;
Sonata in F Minor, op. 57; Sonata in E-flat Major, op. 81a. RCA 60356-
2.
Brahms: Concerto No. 1 in D Minor, op. 15; Variations and Fugue on a Theme
by Handel, op. 24. RCA 60357-2. Leinsdorf/Boston SO, 1974.
Brahms: Concerto No. 2 in B-flat Major, op. 83; Intermezzi, op. 117, nos. 1 and
2, op. 119, nos. 1-3. RCA 7942-2. Reiner/Chicago SO, 1961.
Brahms: Concerto No. 2 in B-flat Major, op. 83; Rachmaninoff: Rhapsody on a
Theme of Paganini, op. 43. RCA 09026-62695-2. Kondrashin/Moscow
PO. Live performances from 1972.
Chopin: Concerto No. 1 in E Minor, op. 11. Rachmaninoff: Rhapsody on a
Theme of Paganini, op. 43. RCA 7945-2. Ormandy/PO, 1969-70.
Chopin: Sonata No. 2 in B-flat Minor, op. 35; Sonata No. 3 in B Minor, op.
58. Liszt: Mephisto Waltz; *Sonetto del Petrarca* No. 123; *Un Sospiro.*
RCA 09026-60417-2.
Grieg: Concerto in A Minor, op. 16. Liszt: Concerto No. 1 in E-flat Major;
Concerto No. 2 in A Major. RCA 7834-2. Ormandy/PO, 1968, 1970.
MacDowell: Concerto No. 2 in D Minor, op. 23. Schumann: Concerto in A
Minor, op. 54. RCA 60420-2. Hendl, Reiner/Chicago SO, 1972.
My Favorite Chopin. Ballade in A-flat Major, op. 47; Barcarolle, op. 60;
Etudes op. 10, no. 3 and op. 25, no. 11; Fantasy in F Minor, op. 49;
Nocturne in B Major, op. 62, no. 1; Polonaise in A-flat Major, op. 53;
Scherzo No. 3, op. 39; Waltzes op. 64, nos. 1 and 2. RCA 60358-2.
My Favorite Encores. Chopin: Etude in C Minor, op. 10, no. 2; Nocturne in E
Major, op. 62, no. 2; Scherzo No. 2 in B-flat minor, op. 31. Debussy:
Clair de lune; l'Isle joyeuse; La plus que lente; Reflets dans l'eau; La Fille

aux cheveux de lin. Rachmaninoff: *Etude-tableau* in E-flat minor, op. 39, no. 5. Schumann-Liszt: *Widmung.* Scriabin: Etude in D-sharp Minor, op. 8, no. 12. Szymanowski: Etude in B-flat Minor, op. 4, no. 3. RCA 60726-2.

Prokofiev: Concerto No. 3 in C Major, op. 26 (Hendl/Chicago SO, 1960). Rachmaninoff: Concerto No. 3 in D Minor, op. 30 (Kondrashin/Symphony of the Air, 1958). RCA 6209-2.

Prokofiev: Sonata No. 6 in A Major, op. 82. Rachmaninoff: *Etude-tableau,* op. 39, no. 5; Prelude in D Major, op. 23, no. 4; Sonata No. 2 in B-flat Minor, op. 36. RCA 7941-2.

Rachmaninoff: Concerto No. 2 in C Minor, op. 18 (Reiner/Chicago SO, 1962). Tchaikovsky: Concerto No. 1 in B-flat Minor, op. 23 (Kondrashin, RCA SO, 1958). RCA 5912-2. Also Musical Heritage Society MHS 512488K (CD).

A Romantic Collection. Brahms: Rhapsody in E-flat Major, op. 119, no. 4. Granados: The Maid and the Nightingale. Liszt: Consolation No. 3; Sonata in B Minor. Rachmaninoff: Prelude in G-sharp Minor, op. 32, no. 12. Ravel: *Pavane pour une infante défunte*; Toccata (*Le Tombeau de Couperin*). Schumann: Romance, op. 28, no. 2. Tchaikovsky: Song of the Lark. RCA 60414-2.

The World's Favorite Piano Music. Beethoven: *Für Elise.* Brahms: Intermezzos, op. 117, no. 3 and op. 118, no. 6; Waltz in A-flat Major. Chopin: Fantasy-Impromptu. Debussy: *Reverie.* Liszt: *Liebestraum*; Consolation No. 5. Mozart: Turkish March. Rachmaninoff: Prelude in C-sharp Minor, op. 3, no. 2; Preludes, op. 23, nos. 5-7 and op. 32, no. 5. Schubert: *Moment Musical* No. 3; Schumann: *Traümerei.* Tchaikovsky: Barcarolle from The Seasons. RCA 60973 (CD).

⚜ ⚜ ⚜

CORTOT, ALFRED DENIS: b. Nyon, Switzerland, 26 September 1877; d. Lausanne, Switzerland, 15 June 1962.

The accomplishment of Cortot is a permanent possession of anyone who knows his work. Whenever such a person hears individuality of expression, personal inflection, beauty of tone, coexistent repose and élan, imaginative identification with the sonic world of a composer, true culture in piano playing, his memory whispers the name of Cortot.
Richard Dyer (*Boston Sunday Globe*, 2 October 1977)

Born in Switzerland of a Swiss mother and a French father, Alfred Cortot lived most of his life in Paris; and more often than not writers refer to Cortot as "a famous French pianist." He had already started music lessons with two older sisters before his family moved to Paris, where at age nine he was accepted at the Paris Conservatory preparatory class taught by Emile Decombes, a disciple of

Chopin. At age 15 Cortot was admitted to the advanced piano class of Louis Diémer, "the most remarkable pianist of his generation," said Cortot. "Diémer taught me piano. Music was revealed to me by Edouard Risler." Cortot graduated (1896) from the Conservatory with a first prize in piano; made a brilliant professional debut in Paris, playing Beethoven's Concerto No. 3 at one of the *Concerts Colonne*; and with Risler gave a series of two-piano recitals of arrangements of works from Wagner's operas.

Fascinated by Richard Wagner's music, Cortot in 1898 went to Bayreuth to learn more about Wagner's repertoire and style from Julius Kniese, chorus master at the *Festspielhaus*. He worked as a choral coach under Kniese and later became assistant conductor under Felix Mottl and Hans Richter. Fired with a zeal for Wagner's music, Cortot returned to Paris in 1901 and immediately plunged into a whirl of activity—as a conductor, not as pianist—designed to bring Wagner to French audiences. In 1902 he founded the *Société des Festivals Lyriques*, and on 17 May presented—and conducted—the first Paris performance of *Die Götterdämmerung*. In 1903 Cortot organized the *Association de Concerts Alfred Cortot*, which he directed for about two years, offering such important works as *Parsifal*, Beethoven's *Missa Solemnis*, Liszt's *St. Elisabeth* and the Brahms Requiem. In 1904 Cortot became orchestral conductor of the *Société Nationale* in Paris, which initiated concerts of contemporary music by young or unknown French composers. By the time he was 30, his many conducting activities had made Cortot a leading figure in French musical life.

He had not, however, abandoned the piano. In 1905 Cortot, violinist Jacques Thibaud and cellist Pablo Casals organized the Trio Cortot-Thibaud-Casals, a great chamber-music ensemble enchanting audiences for nearly three decades. And Cortot restarted his career as a solo pianist with three Romantic recitals (works by Chopin, Schumann and Liszt) at the *Salle Pleyel*. Subsequent tours of Europe (France, Germany, Austria, the Netherlands, Spain, Switzerland, Russia, Italy) and Great Britain quickly spread his fame as a virtuoso. Meanwhile, in 1907 Gabriel Fauré, director of the Paris Conservatory, appointed Cortot professor of the *classe supérieure de piano*, a post he held until 1919, the year he founded the *Ecole Normale de Musique*.

Cortot first came to the United States in 1918 on tour with the Paris Conservatory Orchestra, conducted by André Messager. On 20 October he played Saint-Saëns's Concerto No. 4 at the Metropolitan Opera House, and on 11 November 1918 he made his New York recital debut at Aeolian Hall. His second American tour (1919–1920)—he made six in all—was perhaps the most memorable. Within three months Cortot made 49 appearances at which he played four different recital programs and eight concertos; the five Beethoven concertos, Rachmaninoff No. 3, Saint-Saëns No. 4, and the Schumann Concerto. Cortot last toured the United States in 1929, performing a series of sonata recitals with Jacques Thibaud.

Cortot reached the height of his career between the two world wars. "During those 20 years he made more than 150 recordings, gave 183 public master classes at the *Ecole Normale,* gave 282 concerts in the United States, 292 in England and 1,425 in Europe, Russia and South America—not to mention more than 60 concerts with two orchestras that he founded during this period, the

Orchestre Symphonique de Paris and the *Orchestre de l'Ecole Normale.*" (Timbrell, "Alfred Cortot")

During World War II Cortot worked to aid fellow musicians, but unfortunately he also worked for the Nazi-controlled Vichy government. Like many other famous musicians, Cortot in 1933 had refused to play in Germany because of the rise of anti-Semitism. However, when the Germans occupied France, he served as Commissioner for Fine Arts under the Pétain government. He also conducted the orchestra of Radio Paris, controlled by the Nazis, and, worse in the public eye, in 1942 he played concerts in Germany. After the war Cortot was arrested, tried by a French purge committee and forbidden to engage in any professional activities for one year (April 1945–April 1946). The truth of Cortot's wartime status may never be known. One of his staunch supporters, insisting that Cortot was not a collaborator, claimed that each time he played a recital in Germany he did so in exchange for the release of French citizens deported to Germany as slave laborers. (Dumesnil)

Some historians contend that when Cortot returned to concertizing in 1946 he encountered such a storm of protest that he retired (1948) to Switzerland and concentrated on teaching. On the other hand, one of his pupils reports that when Cortot reappeared at the *Salle Pleyel*, 3,000 people crowded the hall with 300 more on the stage, and they gave Cortot a ten-minute ovation when he entered. Again, the exact truth is difficult to ascertain. He lived the rest of his life in Lausanne, commuting regularly to Paris to give his famous classes at the *Ecole Normale.* During the late 1940s and early 1950s he played more than 100 concerts a season. Cortot's final recital in Paris—an all-Chopin program at the *Salle Pleyel* on 17 October 1949, the exact 100th anniversary of Chopin's death—was enormously successful. In 1952 a final concert tour took him to Japan and South America, but not to North America. Even though memory and technique sometimes failed him, the elegance and sensibility of his playing were still unforgettable. Cortot made his very last appearance at the Prades Festival on 10 July 1958, performing an all-Beethoven program with Pablo Casals.

Cortot was an avid, discriminating collector of music manuscripts, books about music and musicians, paintings (usually portraits of composers) and autograph letters. After his death his vast library was dispersed, various portions being acquired by libraries in London, Chicago, Berkeley (California) and Lexington (Kentucky). A large quantity of his rare musical manuscripts now resides in the Pierpont Morgan Library in New York City.

Cortot's honors include the prestigious Gold Medal of London's Royal Philharmonic Society, a knighthood in the Spanish Order of *Isabel la Católica*, and the rank of *Chevalier de la Légion d'honneur* in France.

Alfred Cortot passionately loved his art and passionately pursued it—as solo pianist, ensemble pianist, conductor, collector, writer and teacher. He was an articulate author. His *Principes Rationnels de la Technique Pianistique*, a valuable sourcebook for advanced students, reiterates Cortot's advice that at least 15 minutes a day must be devoted to "Daily Keyboard Gymnastics," a kind of warm-up procedure. Cortot's *Studies in Musical Interpretation*, compiled and translated by Jeanne Thieffry, contains materials from his master classes. The three-volume set of Cortot essays collectively titled *La Musique française de Piano* (*French Piano Music*) reveal his encyclopedic knowledge of French repertoire. His lifelong devotion to Chopin inspired *Aspects de Chopin* (*In Search of Chopin*). Cortot was also a fine editor. His ideas about technique and interpretation can be found in his numerous study editions of the major works of Chopin, Liszt, Mendelssohn, Schubert, Schumann and Weber. (Each piece is prefaced with a French text by Cortot, giving the history, the aesthetic and pianistic interest, and the difficulties of the piece. On each page, the musical text in its strictly authentic version has comments by Cortot.)

His teaching involved two basic maxims: "Let the music speak for itself, and it will always be fresh;" and "perfecting musical expression is far more important than perfecting technique."

Cortot's teaching contained little of technique per se. It was assumed that students accepted for his master classes and private lessons had already acquired technical competence. He taught his students that to produce a beautiful tone required a great deal of arm control and much legato, that suppleness and mobility must be concentrated in the wrists and arms.

Based on his own experience, Cortot concluded that every difficult passage can be reduced to one or two basic problems. He instructed the student to work not only on the difficult passage but on the problems themselves, on restoring the fundamental character of the passage. Even in the fastest and most difficult passages, the sense of the music was always Cortot's first concern. Sometimes he demonstrated at the keyboard, often illustrating a point by imitating the pupil's manner of playing. He repeatedly reminded the student to be self-critical and to be always searching for new ways of coming closer to the composer.

His students seem to agree on his general teaching goals: strive for a singing tone, a smooth legato and accurate pedaling; avoid pounding, wild speed and any theatrical display; and have a quiet platform manner. The extensive list of eminent Cortot students testifies to his talents as a pedagogue. During his active teaching period of around 55 years, pianists like Dinu Lipatti, Gina Bachauer, Clara Haskil, Vlado Perlemuter and many others received his counsel, advice and suggestions. Almost without exception they regarded him as an important, valuable stimulus to their respective careers.

By no means a child prodigy, Alfred Cortot worked hard all his life to perfect his pianism. As an adult he practiced faithfully four hours a day and developed a superb though not flawless technique. But technique was never Cortot's strong point. He always had a reputation for missed notes and, especially in his later years, memory lapses. Nevertheless, Cortot's reputation as a truly great pianist endures. He endowed every composition, even overplayed works, with a wonderful youthfulness and vitality. His French romanticism rejected sentimentality and exaggeration.

Cortot instinctively grasped the architecture of a work. Even when he missed notes, Cortot kept going. He could have covered his mistakes with a convenient *rubato*, but he refused to break the emotional line or disturb the relationship of the larger parts to the whole. It was Cortot's keen understanding of the structure of the music—rhythmic, harmonic and formal—that maintained a proper balance in his fervent, poetic and always spontaneous-sounding interpretations.

He was intelligent, well-educated and well-read, but his approach to music was far from cerebral. He sincerely believed that emotion was both the source of music and the purpose of music, thus finding the means to penetrate the mind and emotions of the composer always came first. Virtuosity in itself meant nothing to Cortot. For him, playing the piano well meant the ability to express the spirit of the music. Some writers infer that this kind of psychological investigation may have been suggested to Cortot when at age 15 he was the pupil chosen by Diémer to play for Anton Rubinstein. Listening as Cortot played Beethoven's "*Appassionata*," Rubinstein then remarked, "One does not *play* Beethoven; one should re-create him." Whatever the source, Cortot learned the lesson well. His ability to capture the spirit behind the notes may have been his greatest gift. As many critics have pointed out, one always listened *through* Alfred Cortot to the music (Schumann, Chopin, Franck, Liszt, Debussy) that he played so incomparably. Above all, the most remarkable element of his playing—and one of the hallmarks of Cortot's style—was its *sound*, the sheer, wondrous beauty of his tone.

Alfred Cortot remains one of this century's greatest interpreters of the music of Chopin and Schumann. Their works appeared on almost every Cortot recital program and comprised the major portion of his repertoire. He also played a lot of Beethoven, Debussy, Liszt; works by other French composers (Fauré, Franck, Ravel, Saint-Saëns); works by a few Russian composers and other Romantic composers. His concerto repertoire included Beethoven's concertos; Chopin's Concerto No. 2 in F Minor, op. 21; Ravel's Concerto for the Left Hand; Saint-Saëns' Concerto No. 4 in C Minor, op. 44; and Franck's Symphonic Variations.

There are dozens and dozens of Cortot reviews, some of live performances, some of recordings, and it is interesting that almost all of them reflect his *personal* approach to, and understanding of, music. For example, "There was in his playing a combination of intellectual authority, aristocracy, masculinity and poetry. . . . He never made an impression merely as a technician, and he left flamboyance to the big virtuosos. Cortot was much more the re-creative musician, with severe elegance and logic to his playing." (Sch/Gre, see Bibliog.)

Cortot made his American debut on 20 October 1918 at the Metropolitan Opera House, playing the Saint-Saëns Concerto No. 4 with the Paris Conservatory Orchestra, conducted by André Messager. "Mr. Cortot . . . proved to be an artist of sincere and ardent temperament, backed by sound technique. He exhibited the 'new' Gallic traits, strong and stimulating, that seem to be more appreciated since the war." (*NYT*, 21 Oct 1918)

For his New York recital debut (11 Nov 1918), Cortot played a long program including works by Albéniz, Chabrier, Chopin, Debussy, Liszt and Saint-Saëns. Some critics seemed uncertain about his playing. "He is virile. He is brilliant. And he is too often as hard as nails. . . . The playing of the preludes of Chopin . . . was a hazardous undertaking for an artist whose method is

so Gallic, so academic. Of the Polish composer's spirit there was little trace."
(*NYT*, 12 Nov 1918) But American composer Deems Taylor, writing for
Musical America (16 Nov 1918), was more optimistic, noting in particular the
performance of the Chopin Preludes, and describing Cortot as "a master craftsman in the expressional and impressional possibilities of his instrument. . . .
On such an artist one may rely even if one disagrees with him. Clearly the effects he produces are intended, carefully thought out and as carefully wrought."

When Cortot performed the Franck Symphonic Variations and Vincent
d'Indy's Symphony on a French Mountain Air with the Boston Symphony
Orchestra under the baton of Henri Rabaud, one critic praised him for choosing
musicianly works and for bringing to them "musical taste and intelligence of the
highest order. . . . The performance of the Symphony, as well as the Variations,
was considered unsurpassed in the history of these concerts." (*MA*, 8 Feb 1919)

One of the artistic high points of Cortot's next American tour was his
performance (1 Jan 1920) of Rachmaninoff's Concerto No. 3 with the
Philadelphia Orchestra, conducted by Leopold Stokowski. Rachmaninoff, present in the audience, received enthusiastic applause for his "impressive score."
And evidently Cortot's playing of the Concerto was a great success: "Alfred
Cortot explores the spiritual depths of music. In the most genuine and unaffected way he is among the most poetic of pianists. Refinement is also one of
his characteristic artistic traits." (*MA*, 10 Jan 1920)

Less than three weeks later the pianist played a New York recital (20
Jan 1920) of works by four significant composers: Franck (Prelude, Choral and
Fugue); Chopin (12 Etudes selected from ops. 10 and 25); Debussy (Preludes,
Book I); Schumann (Symphonic Etudes). "Cortot," wrote one critic, "combines
the most distinguished and patrician qualities of French artistry with a bigness of
style and a breadth of perception not customarily deemed Gallic traits. . . . His
command of tonal and technical effect, of *nuance*, of rhythm, of glib and flawlessly clean articulation, is consummate." He gave the music of César Franck
"a character of mystical introspectiveness hitherto undiscovered by the numberless interpreters of this work. . . . Mr. Cortot's Chopin was exquisite, brilliant,
marvelously dextrous and often genuinely emotional." (*MA*, 31 Jan 1920)

That same season Cortot played all five Beethoven concertos with
Walter Damrosch and the orchestra of the New York Symphony Society. His
performance (17 Feb 1920) of the first three concertos "displayed a new warmth
of style, inspired by his evidently sincere affection for the music of Beethoven's
earlier period." (*NYT*, 18 Feb 1920) Two days later he played Concertos Nos. 4
and 5, and "gave a spirited, vital and engrossing performance, one of sensitive
values and brilliant moments in the familiar music." (*NYT*, 20 Feb 1920) But
Cortot was at his finest playing the French repertoire. When he played (12 Nov
1922) the Saint-Saëns Concerto No. 4 in C Minor, op. 44, with the New York
Symphony Orchestra, conducted by Walter Damrosch, "his performance was, not
to put too fine a point upon it, a prodigious achievement, an extraordinary tour
de force not merely of technique, but of insight into the music itself. . . . There
were an intensity, a finesse, a sweep of power in this interpretation that were of
a memorable musical value." (*NYT*, 13 Nov 1922)

Cortot had equal, if not even greater, success on the other side of the Atlantic. On 1 November 1920 he played Rachmaninoff's extraordinarily difficult Concerto No. 4 with the London Symphony Orchestra, Albert Coates conducting. "Mr. Cortot's playing was one of his finest achievements both in respect of technical perfection, variety of colour, and magnetic vitality. As an encore he played a Bourrée of Saint-Saëns for the left hand alone, and here his technique was if anything more remarkable still." (*MT*, 1 Dec 1920)

Of course there were always a few critics who found some of Cortot's unfortunate drawbacks irritating. A recital (30 Sept 1923) at London's Queen's Hall included music by Beethoven, Chopin, Liszt, Schumann. "In the more vigorous passages [Beethoven and Chopin] he allowed his left hand to overpower the right, and sometimes the music seemed to get out of his control. . . . But against these faults and a good number of wrong notes we must set the almost perfect performance of the 'Kinderscenen' and of the Mephisto Waltz, in which M. Cortot's wide range of tone-colour and his remarkable *leggierissimo* playing were heard to great advantage." (*TL*, 1 Oct 1923)

Alfred Cortot's reputation as a great pianist has not only endured but, since his death, it has had periodic bolstering accolades from other notable pianists. For example, this from Gina Bachauer: "Alfred Cortot was a great musician, but first and foremost he was a poet. . . . I think his Schumann was the most beautiful I have ever heard in my life." (*HF*, Nov 1963) And this from Mitsuko Uchida: "Alfred Cortot played all the wrong notes—but his is still the most inspired Schumann I've heard in my life." (*TL*, 3 Oct 1985)

Cortot's discography is more extensive than that of any other pianist except, perhaps, Artur Rubinstein. For an initial appraisal of Cortot on disc, the best source is Fred Gaisberg, producer for the Gramophone Company, which wanted to acquire a record library of Chopin's piano music. Gaisberg chose Cortot "because of his profound study and poetic performance of Chopin's works and also because he happened to have been trained by that great composer's last pupil and disciple, Decombes." (Gai/Mus, see Bibliog.)

Chopin's works form the core of the Cortot discography. He recorded the Etudes, Preludes, Waltzes, Impromptus, Ballades, Mazurkas (recorded shortly before his death), many Nocturnes and miscellaneous works. He disliked Concerto No. 1 and only recorded No. 2 in F Minor, op. 21. Most of the published discs date from shortly before World War I to around 1954. The discography is confusing because Cortot re-recorded many of Chopin's works. He recorded the Ballades, *Berceuse*, Etudes, B Minor Sonata and the Waltzes twice and recorded the Preludes and B-flat Minor Sonata three times. Since he never played anything the same way twice, there is much to be gained from most of these discs. In general, Cortot was at his technical and artistic zenith between the two world wars. The later recordings simply do not do him justice.

Chopin scholar James Methuen-Campbell describes Cortot as "a pianist who, despite memory lapses and unfortunate slips of the finger, possessed extreme virtuosity and one of the greatest musical intellects of all time, who managed to combine the two into a perfect blend, and who had a greater affinity with Chopin's music than any other pianist of our age." Methuen-Campbell singles out Cortot's recordings of the B Minor Sonata, the Waltzes and the Preludes, all dating from the 1930s, as possibly the most representative of Cortot at his best. (Met/Cho, see Bibliog.)

As with most of his recordings, Cortot's readings of Schumann contain much that is inspired and delightful, but also much that perplexes and disappoints. The finest examples are perhaps found in Volumes 2 and 3 of the Biddulph CDs (see Discog.). In the *Carnaval* his pacing is, according to one listener, "masterful, but his handfuls of wrong notes are not. . . . [Yet] in the Symphonic Etudes, from the opening theme to the final crashing chords Cortot is inspired and in fine technical form." The same reviewer would equate Cortot's *Kreisleriana* with those memorable performances by Argerich, Gieseking and Horowitz; and as for the *Kinderscenen*, "words cannot describe the beauty, imagination, voicing, and color." (Elder)

Debussy was another composer for whom Cortot had great affinity. He recorded the first book of Preludes, Children's Corner suite, and the Sonata for violin and piano (with Jacques Thibaud). These are available on CD together with Ravel's *Jeux d'eau* and the *Sonatine* (see Discog.). Cortot had at his disposal a great range of tone color, advantageous in this repertoire. "His Debussy playing shows a richly sensuous, virile approach to the music. Cortot's musical gestures, like his sound, are always highly personalized. . . . Emotional projection is everywhere, for Cortot never believed in simply letting the music 'speak for itself'." (Banowetz)

SELECTED REFERENCES

Banowetz, Joseph. "Reflections on Playing Debussy." *Piano Quarterly*, Fall 1982, pp. 42–46.

Clough, F. F., and G. J. Cuming. "An Alfred Cortot Discography." *Gramophone Record Review*, Dec 1957, pp. 135–136.

Cortot, Alfred. *In Search of Chopin.* (translated from the French *Aspects de Chopin* by Cyril and Rena Clarke). New York: Abelard Press, 1952, reprint by Greenwood Press, 1975.

———. *La Musique française de Piano.* 3 vols. Paris: Presses universitaires de France, 1944. Vols. 1 and 2 translated by Hilda Andrews as *French Piano Music*. New York: Da Capo Press, 1977.

———. "Pedagogic Principles of Piano Playing." *Etude*, Dec 1929, pp. 882, 937.

———. "Practical Aspects of Modern Pianoforte Study." (interview with Harriette Brower). *Etude*, Aug 1920, pp. 515–516.

———. *Rational Principles of Pianoforte Technique.* (translated by Le Roy-Metaxas). Paris: Salabert, 1972.

Dumesnil, Maurice. "Alfred Cortot." *The Piano Teacher*, Sept–Oct 1964, pp. 10–13.

Dyer, Richard. "Alfred Cortot: The music still lives." *Boston Sunday Globe*, 2 Oct 1977, sec. E, p. 20.

Elder, Dean. "The Art of Alfred Cortot." *Clavier*, Oct 1992, pp. 32–35. A discerning review of recent recordings.

Fermoy, Ruth. "Cortot." *Recorded Sound*, Oct 1964, pp. 266–269.

Gavoty, Bernard. *Alfred Cortot*. Paris: Éditions Buchet/Chastel, 1977.

Henderson, A. M. "Personal memories of Cortot as artist and teacher." *Etude*, April 1956, pp. 12, 59, 65.

Manshardt, Thomas. *Aspects of Cortot*. Northumberland: Appian Publications & Recordings, 1994.

———. "Studying with Alfred Cortot." *Clavier*, Jan 1994, pp. 20–21.

Nichols, Roger. "Alfred Cortot, 1877–1962." *Musical Times*, Nov 1982, pp. 762–763.

Obituary. *Musical America*, Aug 1962, p. 45. *Musical Times*, Aug 1962, p. 561. *New York Times*, 16 June 1962, p. 19.

Rothstein, Edward. "How to Play Chopin? Cortot Had Answers." *New York Times*, 8 Dec 1993, sec. 2, p. 33.

Thieffry, Jeanne. "Alfred Cortot's Studies in Musical Interpretation." (translated by Robert Jaques, foreword by Alfred Cortot). London: George G. Harrap & Co., 1937.

Timbrell, Charles. "Alfred Cortot: His Life and Legacy." *Piano Quarterly*, Fall 1984, pp. 19–28.

———. "A Cortot Discography." *Piano Quarterly*, Fall 1984, pp. 29–31. Additions and corrections to the Clough and Cuming discography (see above).

See also Bibliography: Ald/Con; Bla/Gra; Bro/Mod; Cal/MG; Cal/Mus; Car/Tal; Dan/Con; Eld/Pia; Ewe/Mu; Gav/Vin; Gol/Jou; Ham/Gre; Kir/Pab; Kol/Que; Lan/Mus; MGG; New/Gro; Nie/Mei; Ran/Kon; Rat/Cle; Rub/MyM; Sch/Gre; Woo/My.

SELECTED REVIEWS

MA: 16 Nov 1918; 8 Feb 1919; 10 Jan 1920; 31 Jan 1920. *MT*: 1 Dec 1920; 1 Dec 1921; 1 Jan 1926. *NYT*: 21 Oct 1918; 12 Nov 1918; 16 Nov 1918; 27 Dec 1918; 7 Jan 1920; 21 Jan 1920; 18 Feb 1920; 20 Feb 1920; 25 Jan 1921; 18 Feb 1921; 13 Nov 1922; 3 Dec 1922; 23 Feb 1923; 27 Nov 1929. *SFC*: 7 Nov 1929. *TL*: 23 Nov 1908; 17 Feb 1910; 30 June 1910; 1 April 1911; 24 Nov 1919; 15 Nov 1920; 28 Nov 1921; 1 Oct 1923; 16 Nov 1925.

SELECTED DISCOGRAPHY

Alfred Cortot plays Chopin. Ballades (rec. 1929); *Berceuse*, op. 57 (rec. 1926); 24 Preludes, op. 28 (rec. 1926). Music and Arts CD-317.

Alfred Cortot plays Chopin: The Celebrated 1926/33 Recordings. Ballade No. 1 in G Minor, op. 23; Barcarolle in F-sharp Major, op. 60; Fantasy in F Minor, op. 49; Polonaise in A Flat Major, op. 53; Sonata No. 2 in B-flat Minor, op. 35; Sonata No. 3 in B Minor, op. 58. Music and Arts CD-717.

Alfred Cortot plays French Concertos. Chopin: Concerto No. 2 in F Minor, op. 21 (Barbirolli, rec. 1935). Ravel: Concerto for the Left Hand (Munch/*Orch. du Con.*, rec. 1939). Saint-Saëns: Concerto No. 4 in C Minor, op. 44

(Munch/*Orch. du Con.*, rec. 1935); *Etude en forme de Valse.* GEMM CD 9491.

Alfred Cortot plays Liszt. Au bord d'une source (rec. 1924); Hungarian Rhapsody No. 2 (rec. 1926); Hungarian Rhapsody No. 11 (rec. 1925); Legend: St. Francis of Paola Walking on the Waves (rec. 1937); *La Leggierezza* (rec. 1931); *Rigoletto* Concert Paraphrase (rec. 1926); The Ring (Chopin-Liszt); Sonata in B Minor (rec. 1929); Spring (Chopin-Liszt). GEMM CD 9396.

Alfred Cortot plays Schumann. Concerto in A Minor, op. 54; *Davidsbündler-tänze,* op. 6; *Papillons,* op. 2. Biddulph LHW 003. Ronald/LSO.

Alfred Cortot plays Three Romantic Piano Favorites. Chopin: Concerto No. 2 in F Minor, op. 21 (Barbirolli). Franck: Symphonic Variations (Ronald/ LSO). Schumann: Concerto in A Minor, op. 54 (Ronald/ LSO). Music and Arts CD-718.

Alfred Cortot plays Weber and Liszt. Chopin-Liszt: Spring; The Ring. Liszt: Hungarian Rhapsody No. 11; *La Leggierezza* (acoustic recording); *La Leggierezza* (electric recording); Sonata in B Minor. Weber: Sonata No. 2 in A Flat Major, op. 39. Music and Arts CD-662.

Alfred Cortot: Rare 78's and previously unissued test pressings. Albéniz: *Malagueña* (rec. 1919); *Seguidillas* (rec. 1919); Chopin: "My Joys" (arr. Liszt, rec. 1923); *Polonaise-fantaisie,* op. 61 (rec. 1947); Prelude in C-sharp Minor, op. 45 (rec. 1947); "*Trois nouvelles etudes.*" (rec. 1947). Liszt: *Au bord d'une source* (rec. 1923); Etude "*La Leggierezza*" (rec. 1919); Hungarian Rhapsody No. 2 (rec. 1926); Hungarian Rhapsody No. 11 (rec. 1926); Rigoletto Paraphrase (rec. 1926); St. Francis Legend—Walking on the Water (rec. 1935). Saint-Saëns: Valse-Etude (rec. 1919). Scriabin: Etude in D-sharp Minor, op. 8, no. 12 (rec. 1923). Music and Arts CD-615.

Alfred Cortot: Victor Recordings of 1919–1926. Brahms: *Wiegenlied,* op. 49, no. 4. Chopin: Ballade in G Minor, op. 23; *Berceuse,* op. 57; Etude in A-flat Major, op. 25, no. 1; Etude in A Minor, op. 25, no. 11; Impromptu in A-flat Major, op. 29; Impromptu in F-sharp Major, op. 36; *Grand Polonaise brillante,* op.22; "My Joys," op. 74, no. 12; Valse in C-sharp Minor, op. 64, no. 2. Debussy: *La Fille aux cheveux de lin; Minstrels.* Ravel: *Jeux d'eau.* Saint-Saëns: Bourrée for left hand, op. 135; *Etude en forme de Valse,* op. 52, no. 6 (rec. 1919). Schubert: Litany. Weber: Invitation to the Waltz. GEMM CD 9386.

Chopin: *Oeuvres pour Piano: Cortot.* EMI CZS 7 67359-2 (6 CDs). This collection does not contain everything that Cortot recorded but rather the best examples from his Chopin discography, in some cases two recordings of the same work.

Cortot plays Debussy. Debussy: Preludes Book I (rec. 1930-31); *Le vent dans la plaine, La Fille aux cheveux de lin, Minstrels* (rec. 1928-29); Children's Corner; Sonata No. 3 for Violin and Piano (with Jacques Thibaud). Ravel: *Jeux d'eau; Sonatine.* Biddulph LHW 006 (CD).

Cortot plays Schumann, Vol. 2. *Carnaval,* op. 9; Symphonic Etudes, op. 13; Trio, op. 63. Biddulph LHW 004 (CD).

Cortot plays Schumann, Vol. 3. *Fantasiestücke*, op. 12; *Kinderscenen*, op. 15; *Kreisleriana*, op. 16. *Dichterliebe* (Panzéra). Biddulph LHW 005 (CD).

CURZON, SIR CLIFFORD: b. London, England, 18 May 1907; d. London, England, 1 September 1982.

> It is a conception that Curzon offers, not a succession of details.
> Stephen Wigler (*Rochester Democrat and Chronicle*, 5 October 1980)

He was an international concert star for three decades, yet Sir Clifford Curzon remained a reluctant luminary, frequently deserting the concert platform, sometimes for as long as five months, to study and work on his repertoire. Admitting that he was basically a solitary person, Curzon dreaded the concert stage and was happiest playing alone in his studio.

His father Michael Curzon was a London antique dealer, his mother Constance (Young) Curzon was an amateur musician, and both loved music. There was also a "musical" uncle, the composer Albert W. Ketèlbey, famous then but remembered now mostly because he composed such melodious tonal portraits as "In a Persian Market" (1920) and "In a Monastery Garden" (1915). Curzon's first musical memory was hearing Uncle Albert trying out his latest compositions on the Curzon's piano. "My father adored them. And I can remember . . . listening to those immortal melodies wafting up from downstairs; and I can remember the inexpressible longing they filled me with." (Gil/Boo, see Bibliog.)

Curzon started violin lessons at age five and a year later began piano study with his mother's voice teacher. While there is no mention of his being a child prodigy, at age 12 he was accepted at the Royal Academy of Music, where he became a pupil of Charles Reddie, a student of Bernard Stavenhagen, one of Liszt's best pupils. Curzon made wonderful progress, winning two scholarships and just about every piano prize offered at the RAM, including the prestigious McFarren Gold Medal. He also studied with Katharine Goodson, but it was Reddie, he felt, who had the greatest influence on his budding talent. At age 16 Curzon made his first public appearance, playing in a Bach triple concerto conducted by Sir Henry Wood at a Promenade Concert at the Queen's Hall. Promoted and encouraged by Sir Henry, Curzon played often at the Proms and with the Promenade Orchestra on tour, and in 1924, also under Sir Henry's direction, he gave the first performance in Great Britain of Germaine Tailleferre's *Ballade* for piano and orchestra.

By this time Curzon was teaching as well as performing, having been appointed a subprofessor at the RAM when he was 18 and made a full professor at 19. At about that same time he heard an Artur Schnabel recital and was so overwhelmed by Schnabel's playing (the Schubert posthumous Sonata in A Major, D. 960, was "a revelation of what piano playing could be"), he resolved to study with Schnabel. In 1928 he took leave from the RAM and spent two years in Berlin working with Schnabel, who showed him a broader, more profound approach to music and piano playing. (Curzon's admiration for Schnabel never waned and, until Schnabel's death in 1951, he checked in with him almost yearly for guidance.) Still not completely satisfied with himself despite a successful concert in Berlin, Curzon spent two years in Paris studying harpsichord with Wanda Landowska (not just his teacher but, as he said, "one of the dearest guiding lights in my life") and studying "just music" with Nadia Boulanger. While in Paris he performed with both the Colonne Orchestra and the *Société Philharmonique.*

Not compatible with teaching ("If I ever fell on hard times, I'd rather trim a hedge than teach."), Curzon resigned from the RAM when he returned to England in 1932 and began his concert career, steadily adding to his reputation with appearances at Royal Philharmonic Society concerts, with the BBC Symphony Orchestra and at important British festivals. In 1936 the British Council chose Curzon and violist Lionel Tertis to give a series of sonata recitals in Europe. In 1937 he played in Constant Lambert's *Rio Grande* (chorus, piano and orchestra) with the BBC Symphony Orchestra in Paris. In 1938 the British Council sent him on a solo tour of Europe.

Reserved and independent, Curzon bypassed managers and arranged his own American debut, renting New York's Town Hall for a solo recital (26 Feb 1939) and Carnegie Hall for his orchestral debut (10 March 1939)—a program of three widely contrasting concertos (John Ireland's Concerto in E Flat, the Mozart Concerto in A Major, K. 488, and the Tchaikovsky Concerto in B-flat Minor) with members of the New York Philharmonic-Symphony, conducted by Alexander Smallens. A spate of rave notices from the American critics prompted concert manager Arthur Judson to sign Curzon for an American tour the following year, but World War II intervened, and it was eight years before he returned to America. During the war he played dozens of recitals for the troops and for war workers all over Britain. After the war he resumed his career with performances in London, including BBC broadcasts, and several European tours with the BBC Symphony Orchestra.

Late in 1947 Curzon returned to America. On 30 November he played the Tchaikovsky Concerto No. 1 on a CBS broadcast with the New York Philharmonic-Symphony under Dimitri Mitropoulos, and on 20 December gave a Town Hall recital. He made a stunning success. "Curzon," said the *New York Times*, "must be reckoned among the greatest keyboard artists of the time." The *Herald-Tribune* was even more effusive: "Only too rarely in a lifetime of concertgoing is one permitted to hear such wonderful music-making. . . . He must indubitably be considered one of the greatest pianists of the time."

Arthur Judson booked Curzon for a tour (Nov 1948–March 1949) of America and Canada, 45 appearances, orchestral and solo, including two Telephone Hour radio guest spots. A typical Curzon tour, it was immensely successful. When he returned home in March 1949, he concertized in England, France and Belgium, and the following November he began a coast-to-coast tour (1949–50) of the United States. Curzon had a long, illustrious career, but with the many self-imposed sabbaticals he was never as active as demand would have allowed. Despite his limited American appearances (a New York recital in 1972 was his first there in a decade) and, for that matter, not playing regularly in his native England, Curzon "had achieved near-legendary status." (*NYT*, 3 May 1978)

He worked diligently at his craft, practicing a minimum of four and often eight hours daily and always traveling with a silent keyboard. "I practice and practice and work and work. I dare not take anything for granted." (Cur/Bio 1950, see Bibliog.) To prepare a work, he first read it through away from the piano, then played it, being concerned only with getting a general feeling for the composition. Finally, he broke down the piece bit by bit, beginning with full phrases and ending with the relationship of note to note. Achieving the right sound was just as important as technique. "A pianist without a beautiful and appropriate sound is like a human being in cardboard clothes," he said. "You have to clothe your music in the right sound. Paderewski used to have this to perfection." (*MM*, Feb 1979)

Early in his career Curzon won recognition for his mastery of the great romantic virtuoso concertos, and at one time his enormous repertoire included more than 50 concertos. He was a superb Tchaikovsky and Brahms player, and he championed many contemporary works. In 1946 he premiered Lennox Berkeley's Sonata, dedicated to him, and in 1951 he gave the world premiere of Alan Rawsthorne's Piano Concerto No. 2 in London. Ultimately Curzon's repertoire focused on the classical composers, predominantly Mozart, Beethoven, Schubert. He liked to say that he became a Mozart specialist almost in spite of himself, because so many orchestras kept requesting him to play Mozart.

Curzon and Lucille Wallace, an American from Chicago also studying harpsichord with Wanda Landowska, married in Paris in July 1931. Besides their shared love of music, they both enjoyed the quiet life, gardening, walking, mountain climbing and art collecting. In 1954 they adopted the two orphaned sons of the singer Maria Cebotari and Gustav Diessl. Mrs. Curzon died in 1977. Following a long illness, Clifford Curzon died 1 September 1982.

He was an uncompromising perfectionist. The intense, scholarly scrupulousness with which he approached music made him a demanding colleague, but "Crusty Curzon" was that way only on the surface, according to Peter Runkel, a student who knew Curzon well. "Underneath, he was so gentle, so caring, so exactly the opposite of what he tried to make people believe about him when he sprayed them, head to foot, with all of that non-stop fire and brimstone." (*PQ*, Spring 1988)

Curzon was made a Fellow of the RAM in 1939, made a CBE in 1958 and knighted in 1977. His honorary degrees include a D. Mus. from Leeds University (1970) and a D. Litt. from Sussex University (1973). In 1980 he received the Gold Medal of the Royal Philharmonic Society.

Curzon's much-praised playing reflects the strong influences of his famous teachers: a fastidious brilliance without showy display and an attention to purely musical considerations, both from Schnabel; poetry and freedom of expression, from Landowska; a sense of purpose and a feeling for style, from Boulanger.

Curzon's debut recital (26 Feb 1939) at Town Hall drew extravagant notices. "Few pianists of the day have the perfect control of nuance in prismatic softer tints, the invariably singing tone, the velvety fortissimo with strength behind it that gave these familiar pieces [Schubert's Four Impromptus, D. 899] unusual appeal." (*NYT*, 27 Feb 1939) And this from the erudite Oscar Thompson: "Here was no mere virtuoso of highly trained fingers but a lyric artist whose conceptions are distinctive and whose feeling for color and nuance is exceptional." (*NYS*, 27 Feb 1939)

A review of a Town Hall recital (20 Dec 1947) began: "Clifford Curzon . . . must be reckoned among the greatest keyboard artists of the time. . . . [He] played with extraordinary ease and security in every composition, regardless of its exactions. With such consummate artistry at all times, Mr. Curzon invariably made his highly imaginative and poetic readings convincing to a degree that disarmed criticism." (*NYT*, 21 Dec 1947)

His program (15 Feb 1953) of Beethoven, Schubert and Schumann at Boston's Symphony Hall proved that Curzon was "something of a rarity—the kind of pianist who combines extreme tenderness with monumental strength, volatile emotion with cold intelligence." (*CSM*, 16 Feb 1953) And the eminent composer-critic Virgil Thomson considered Curzon to be far and away the most satisfactory interpreter of the Romantic repertoire: "Schubert and Schumann are composers whom almost nobody plays convincingly any more. Certainly no one brings them to life with quite the delicacy and the grandeur of Mr. Curzon." (*NYHT*, 8 Jan 1950)

But at the 1964 Salzburg Festival it was Curzon's playing of Mozart (Concerto in B-flat Major, K. 595, with Georges Szell and the Berlin Philharmonic Orchestra) that overwhelmed one reviewer. Curzon gave "one of the few performances which I shall never forget. . . . The music, divine enough in itself, was winged into life with the most lucid phrasing and the most beautifully finished tone imaginable." (*RR*, July 1969)

In one of his last American appearances (2 May 1978) Curzon received high praise for his remarkable performance of the Mozart Concerto, K. 491, with the Philadelphia Orchestra under Eugene Ormandy. His playing "had logic, strength and integrity. The strength was manifest not in outsized dynamics but in the way a phrase uncoiled, inevitably finding its way into the total structure of the piece. This kind of tensile strength, so necessary in Mozart, is the secret of only a few musicians." (*NYT*, 3 May 1978)

The talented, modest and very private Curzon was a very special pianist. He played Mozart with "a matchless poise and eloquence" and interpreted Schubert with a "lyrical freshness that sounded effortless. . . . Yet his sense of drama, his beautiful touch . . . and his feeling for large-scale structures also made him an outstanding exponent of Liszt's sonata." (*TL*, 3 Sept 1982)

Since Curzon hated to make recordings just as much as he dreaded live performances, his discography is comparatively small and, unfortunately, many of the recordings are difficult to obtain through ordinary channels. It is hoped that they will be reissued, for most of them are superb examples of his playing.

In 1970 Curzon recorded two Mozart concertos (K. 466, K. 595) with the English Chamber Orchestra, conducted by Benjamin Britten. A recent reissue of these two masterworks substantiates the pianist's great feeling for Classical style. "Sir Clifford Curzon's playing is extraordinarily alert and concentrated; shaping and shading of even the minutest details is superbly subtle, while each movement has a sense of grand inevitability. This ability to focus intently upon foreground detail without losing the sense of the overall shape is one of the hallmarks of Curzon's genius." (*Good CD Guide* [1994]. Reprinted by permission.)

In 1964 Peter Gammond wrote, "Curzon is not a virtuoso in the theatrical sense, but only in the best sense. . . . His style is recognizable not by any eccentricities or mannerisms, but by an intense, singing quality that one despairs of defining in mere words." (Gammond) This is clearly evident in Curzon's recording of the Brahms Concerto No. 1 with George Szell and the London Philharmonic Orchestra (see Discog.). Here is the required virtuosity, the necessary dramatic gesture, but here also one finds a warm lyricism, a variegated color palette and the inimitable singing quality that was so much a part of Curzon's style.

A recent record catalogue lists almost 50 available recordings of the Beethoven "Emperor" Concerto, and in this formidable competition Sir Clifford's version, recently reissued on a CD, ranks among the very best. It is "a refined, thoughtful reading . . . almost Mozartian in the delicacy of the finale but with keen intelligence and inner concentration working throughout." (Pen/Gui [1984], see Bibliog.) In that same Penguin Guide a reviewer of a Schubert recording declares that, "Curzon's is perhaps now the finest account of the B-flat Sonata in the catalog. Tempi are finely judged, and everything is in fastidious taste. Detail is finely drawn but never emphasized at the expense of the architecture as a whole."

SELECTED REFERENCES

"Alone With a Piano." *Newsweek*, 8 Nov 1948, pp. 84–85.
Blyth, Alan. "Artur Schnabel, Pianist and Teacher." (interview with Curzon). *The Listener*, 25 April 1974, pp. 544–546.
———. "Clifford Curzon." *Gramophone*, May 1971, p. 1764.
Clough, F. F., and G. J. Cuming. "A Curzon Discography." *Audio and Record Review*, July 1964, p. 14.
Curzon, Clifford. "Bring Music into your Practice." *Etude*, Oct 1951, pp. 13, 63.
———. "Epilogue." In *The Book of the Piano*, ed. Dominic Gill. Ithaca: Cornell University Press, 1981, pp. 259–266.
———. "Schnabel's Life and Music." (book review) *Musical Times*, April 1962, pp. 232–233.
Gammond, Peter. "A Homebred Genius." *Audio and Record Review*, July 1964, pp. 12–13.
Horowitz, Joseph. "Sir Clifford Curzon Followed the Narrow Path to Mozart." *New York Times*, 30 April 1978, sec. 2, pp. 19–20.

Lebrecht, Norman. "The last word, in Mozart." *The Times* (London), 12 Sept 1982, p. 4.

Levinger, Henry W. "Clifford Curzon: A Profile." *Musical Courier*, 1 Jan 1955, p. 9.

Morrison, Bryce. "Sir Clifford Curzon." *Music and Musicians*, Feb 1979, pp. 22-23.

Obituary. *New York Times*, 4 Sept 1982, p. 15. *The Times* (London), 3 Sept 1982, p. 12.

Runkel, Peter. "Clifford Curzon Remembered." *Piano Quarterly*, Spring 1988, pp. 42–45.

———. "Memories of Clifford Curzon," Part 2. *Piano Quarterly*, Summer 1990, pp. 39–45.

See also Bibliography: Bro/Mas; Cur/Bio (1950); Dan/Con; Ewe/Li; Ewe/Li2; Kai/Gre; Rat/Cle; Sch/Gre; Woo/My.

SELECTED REVIEWS

CSM: 16 Feb 1953. *LAT*: 21 March 1970. *NYHT*: 11 March 1939; 8 Jan 1950. *NYS*: 27 Feb 1939. *NYT*: 27 Feb 1939; 11 March 1939; 1 Dec 1947; 21 Dec 1947; 9 Jan 1949; 27 Jan 1952; 10 April 1970; 3 May 1978. *RDC*: 17 March 1978. *TL*: 19 Jan 1934; 24 July 1946; 20 June 1977; 28 Feb 1980; 2 March 1980.

SELECTED DISCOGRAPHY

Beethoven: Concerto No. 5 in E-flat Major, op. 73; "Eroica" Variations, op. 35. London Treasury (Weekend Classics) CD 421 616-2. Knappertsbusch/ Vienna PO.

Brahms: Concerto No. 1 in D Minor, op. 15; Intermezzi, op. 117, no. 1, op. 119, no. 3. London 417 641-2. Szell/London SO.

Brahms: Concerto No. 1 in D Minor, op. 15. Franck: Symphonic Variations; Litolff: Scherzo (*Concerto symphonique*). Decca 425 082-2 (The Classic Sound). Szell/ London SO.

Brahms: Sonata No. 3 in F Minor, op. 5; Intermezzi, op. 117, no. 1 and op. 119, no. 3. London STS 15272.

Franck: Symphonic Variations. Grieg: Concerto in A Minor, op. 16. London STS 15407. Boult/London SO.

Grieg: Concerto in A Minor, op. 16 (Fjeldstad/London SO). Tchaikovsky: Concerto No. 1 in B-flat Minor, op. 23 (Solti/Vienna PO). London Treasury (Weekend Classics) 417 676-2.

Liszt: Sonata in B Minor; *Liebestraum* no. 3; *Valse oubliée* no. 1; *Gnomen-reigen*; *Berceuse*. London Treasury STS 15552.

Mozart: Concerto in D Minor, K. 466; Concerto in B-flat Major, K. 595. London 417288-2. Britten/English CO.

Mozart: Concerto in A Major, K. 488; Concerto in C Minor, K. 491. London Treasury (Weekend Classics) 433 086-2. Kertész/London SO.

Schubert: Fantasie in C Major, op. 15 ("Wanderer"). London LPS 83 (LP).

Schubert: Sonata in D Major, D. 850; Impromptus, D. 899, nos. 3–4; *Moments musicaux*, D. 780. Decca 443 570-2 (The Classic Sound).
Schubert: Sonata in B-flat Major, D. 960; Impromptus. London 417642-2.

CZIFFRA, GEORGES (György): b. Budapest, Hungary, 5 November 1921; d. Senlis, France, 17 January 1994.

A trite question: Who are your favorite composers?
The great Hungarian musicians, naturally: Liszt, Bartók, Kodály. Chopin, that goes without saying. Beethoven, whose work makes me think of a cathedral. Your French clavecinists. Schumann, the most emotional of all composers. Schubert, the greatest inventor. César Franck, the 'mystical lamb' who erases the sins of so many others.
Georges Cziffra (Gavoty, *Vingt Grands Interprètes*)

By age 35 György Cziffra—Hungarian-born and, from 1968, French by adoption—ranked as one of Hungary's most famous pianists. He had a thriving concert career, and in 1955 he received the coveted Liszt Prize, a singular distinction since previously Hungary had bestowed that honor only on composers. However, this wonderful career existed only within the sphere of Communist-dominated Hungary, and Cziffra happened to be a known activist against political and cultural repression. Right then, in 1956, the brave Hungarian uprising (23 Oct–14 Nov) provided him with a sudden opportunity to escape into Austria. His sensational debuts—in Vienna and Paris that year and in London and Chicago the next—opened the door to the usual international career. But Cziffra made only occasional tours abroad (Canada, the United States, Japan, Israel, for example). Most of his concerts were in Europe.

Clearly a musical prodigy, Cziffra studied with his father and at age five demonstrated his amazing talent for improvisation at the *Grand Cirque du Budapest*. He must have created a sensation—a five-year-old improvising fantasies on popular tunes and operatic melodies requested by the audience! When he was about eight and still studying with his father, Cziffra played for Ernst von Dohnányi, one of Hungary's greatest musicians. In 1930 he began studies, supervised by Dohnányi, at the Franz Liszt Academy in Budapest. He gave his first professional recital in Budapest at age 12. Others followed, and he soon had an impressive reputation in the Budapest musical community.

At age 16 Cziffra made his first tours (Scandinavia, Holland) outside Hungary, which in ordinary times might have signified a good start for a career; but World War II intervened, and Cziffra was confined to Hungary. He continued with his studies, played whatever public concerts were allowed and, most important, enlarged his repertoire. Conscripted (1941) into the Hungarian army, about four years later Cziffra was taken prisoner and served a year in a prisoner-of-war camp. Released in 1947, he resumed his studies at the Franz Liszt Academy, now working with the renowned pedagogue Prof. György Ferenczi, and earned his living playing jazz piano in Budapest bars and nightclubs.

Unfortunately, Cziffra's ongoing political activities caused him to spend three years (1950–53) in a work camp, and only after his release was he finally able to make a concert career, playing in Budapest and other large Hungarian cities. In 1955, the same year he won the Franz Liszt Prize, he was allowed to give concerts in Switzerland and Czechoslovakia. Such success was not enough. He needed relief from Hungary's repressive living conditions and the senseless restrictions on his musical career. The Hungarian revolt of 1956 made that possible. Cziffra, his wife (in 1942 he married Soleyka Abdin) and 13-year-old son walked for 10 days and nights to reach the Austrian border.

Within weeks Cziffra, his fame already known in much of Europe, had conquered "Vienna and Paris like a musical bombshell." (*MM*, Sept 1957) At his Vienna debut (17 Nov 1956), sponsored by the Viennese *Gesellschaft der Musikfreunde*, he played Scarlatti, Mozart, Beethoven and Liszt. His encores—his own arrangements of *Carmen* and Tales of the Vienna Woods—"brought down the house." At his Paris debut (2 Dec 1956) he played the Liszt Hungarian Fantasy at the *Théâtre du Châtlet*, with Pierre Dervaux conducting the Colonne Orchestra. Cziffra made his London debut at Festival Hall on 21 September 1957, playing the Liszt E-flat Concerto and the Hungarian Fantasy with the Royal Philharmonic Orchestra under Alexander Gibson. On his first North American tour, he made his United States debut (18 July 1957) at the Ravinia Festival in Chicago and played (23 July 1957) at the Hollywood Bowl. He made his New York debut on 31 October 1958, playing Liszt's Concerto No. 1 and the Hungarian Fantasy with the New York Philharmonic Orchestra, conducted by Thomas Schippers.

Cziffra appears to have performed only infrequently in Great Britain and America. There are reviews of London performances in 1957, 1959 and 1963, and American performances in 1957, 1958, 1984 and 1986: after his 1958 concerts in Los Angeles, he did not appear there again until 1984! However, in the intervening years, Cziffra pursued many musical and cultural projects in his adopted France (he became Georges, instead of György), especially the restoration (begun in 1966 with his son György Cziffra, Jr.) of the great organ in the Abbey of *Chaise-Dieu* (*Haute Loire*). In 1976 they founded a music festival at the Abbey, and the restored organ was heard again. Meanwhile Cziffra had purchased (1973) the nearly ruined 12th-century *Chapelle Royale Saint Frambourg*, located in Senlis, the small city where he lived outside of Paris. To restore this chapel and to provide assistance for young artists in all cultural fields, he established the Cziffra Foundation, a cultural and artistic trust formalized (30 Dec 1975) by presidential decree. The Franz Liszt Auditorium, opened in the restored chapel in 1977, has become a medium for young artists to present their exhibits, concerts and lectures. In 1983 Cziffra inaugurated a series of cultural exchanges between France and Hungary.

France, out of gratitude to her adopted son, in 1968 created the Cziffra Piano Competition at Versailles and also accorded Cziffra some of her highest honors: *Chevalier de la Légion d'honneur* (1973), *Commandeur des Arts et des Lettres* (1975), the *Médaille d'or de l'Académie Française* (1981).

György Cziffra, Jr., died in an accident (1981) just as he was beginning to make a career of his own as a conductor. From that time Cziffra refused orchestral engagements, and during the last several years he was conspicuously absent from the concert scene. He died on 17 January 1994, but the *Fondation Cziffra* continues in his memory.

It appears that Cziffra did not play the music of his countrymen Bartók or Dohnányi. Works by Chopin, Liszt and Schumann dominated his programs, and his two favorite vehicles with orchestra were seemingly the Liszt Concerto No. 1 and the Hungarian Fantasy. Unlike most pianists who look to Bach and Scarlatti when programming Baroque music, Cziffra would choose some charming *clavecin* pieces by Couperin, Lully and Rameau.

Indisputedly a virtuoso of the highest order, Cziffra obviously considered technical wizardry nothing to be ashamed of. He played many of the old Liszt warhorses and invariably dazzled his audiences. At the same time, his command of tone quality and color, his articulation and dynamic control were equally discernible in the 18th-century miniatures that he often played and recorded. However, he was always an unpredictable performer; and although performing different interpretations of the same compositions can be exciting when achieved by, say, Shura Cherkassky, Cziffra's performances, based on his mood of the moment, sometimes resulted in less than memorable readings.

His concerts were always interesting, whether one did or did not agree with all of his interpretations, because of his phenomenal technique and his often breathtaking performances of Liszt. He played Liszt's Hungarian Fantasy at his Paris debut (2 Dec 1956): "His technique in octaves is flawless, his tempi and fingering are astonishing, and he uses little pedal—his performance being made up of great musicianly hands and great musical intelligence." (*NY*, 15 Dec 1956) Six months later at his Los Angeles debut (23 July 1957) he played the Tchaikovsky Concerto No. 1, with Milton Katims conducting the Los Angeles Philharmonic Orchestra, and was congratulated for his power and tonal coloration. There were some gentle caveats: "He has a degree of imagination, though one had the impression that it is more a pianistic type of imagination than a purely musical one. He inclines to linger over lyrical passages . . . and he likes sudden bursts of speed." (*LAT*, 24 July 1957)

Unpredictable changes in tempo also marred Cziffra's performance of the Hungarian Fantasy, played (1 Aug 1957) with Georg Solti conducting the Los Angeles Philharmonic Orchestra. "It was disjointed, with so many sudden and illogical changes of tempo that even so expert an accompanist as Mr. Solti could not always outguess what the pianist was up to." Typical of Cziffra, at that same concert he gave a thrilling performance of the Liszt Concerto No. 1. "It was in a broadly scaled virtuoso style and it had something of the grand romantic manner that is becoming increasingly rare in piano playing." (*LAT*, 2 Aug 1957)

Cziffra won all-around critical approval when he played those same two Liszt works at his London debut (21 Sept 1957) with Alexander Gibson conducting the Royal Philharmonic Orchestra. "There is apparently no technical feat that lies beyond Mr. Cziffra's truly remarkable hands—hands capable of achieving the most rich and mellow warmth of tone in the biggest fortissimos, and of discovering the finest gradations of tone from a fortissimo down to a whispered pianissimo." (*TL*, 23 Sept 1957)

Cziffra's changeable playing, technical brilliance and the amazing individuality of his conceptions stamped him as a superb, if at times wayward, musician. At his American debut (18 July 1957) at Chicago's Ravinia Festival, he "won an ovation with his performance of the Grieg Concerto. His powerful hands had enormous reach and his tone was impressively grand." (*NW*, 29 July 1957) At his first performance (31 Oct 1958) with the New York Philharmonic Orchestra, he again played his two favorite Liszt compositions, and "was at his best in the Hungarian Fantasy, which gave him ample opportunity to glitter in the trills, lightening scales and fioritura of Liszt. . . . The embellishments had exactly the dazzling effect Mr. Cziffra intended." (*NYT*, 1 Nov 1958)

Cziffra played several times in London during 1959. On 30 January he played the Franck Symphonic Variations and the Tchaikovsky Concerto No. 1 with the Philharmonia Orchestra under the baton of Norman del Mar, and "the delicacy, dreamlike fluency, mercurial yet rhythmic playing in Franck was the very enchantment of piano playing." (*TL*, 31 Jan 1959) Cziffra repeated the Tchaikovsky Concerto on 13 September 1959, this time with Alexander Gibson and the London Symphony Orchestra—a "dazzling, albeit wayward" performance in which he was "minded to swerve the course of the music from true in order to gratify his passion for rapid octave passages, which to be sure he plays with dumbfounding brilliance." (*TL*, 14 Sept 1959)

Meanwhile Cziffra had played a solo recital (13 Feb 1959) in London—music by Beethoven, Schumann, Balakirev *and* Liszt—that was only partially successful. However, in the all-Liszt last half of the program, Cziffra was in his element. "To hear the lilt of the Valse Impromptu, the ethereal glitter of 'Feux Follets,' and the massive control with which he ennobled the Spanish Rhapsody, was to forget what he is not, as a pianist, in the exhilaration of hearing and watching what a thundering fine pianist he undoubtedly is." (*TL*, 14 Feb 1959)

Many years later, Cziffra's recital (8 Sept 1984) of works by Chopin, Liszt, Schubert and Schumann won high praise for his unorthodox yet fascinating playing, his old-fashioned but quite glorious music making: "Cziffra displayed all sorts of extremes of control in color, volume and articulation. Rubatos, by normal modern standards, were extremely free. Yet they were always tasteful, and nearly always effective." (*SFC*, 10 Sept 1984)

In a Chicago recital (2 Nov 1986), again playing works by Chopin, Liszt, Schubert and Schumann, Cziffra demonstrated his fabulous technique in "music that was quiet and lyric rather than flamboyant. . . . In *Les Jeux d'eau à la Villa d'Este* he had fountains going all over the stage. The imagery was magnificent. . . . If Cziffra's playing of Schubert, Schumann and Chopin were to be described in one word, it would be aristocratic. Everything he touches takes on a refinement, elegance and dignity that is quite uncommon." (*CST*, 3 Nov 1986)

As with his live performances, Cziffra's recordings overflow with his striking individuality. "The only other artist still playing who resembles him (slightly) is Shura Cherkassky, and the only pianist of the past with whom he might be compared is Ignaz Friedman. . . . This is not to say that any seasoned collector will be satisfied with each performance, but every band contains the sort of lively provocation that renders even a short journey with Cziffra so memorable. Call him eccentric, call him headstrong, call him whatever, his playing is not to be forgotten once heard." (*HF*, Oct 1984)

Cziffra made many recordings. His eclectic repertoire and his wide-ranging stylistic gamut can be heard in two contrasting recordings. The *Recital á Saint Frambourg*, a program of 18th-century French keyboard music (see Discog.) is a delight. Harpsichord pieces by Couperin, Rameau, Daquin and Lully performed on the piano? Yes! And they are a joy to hear.

From Rococo to high Romanticism is quite a leap, but here Cziffra was equally at home. His 1985 Liszt Album (EMI 2704171), chosen as one of *Stereo Review's* outstanding releases (Jan 1987), is a splendid "sampler" from the composer's repertoire—*Chasse-Neige*; *Gaudeamus igitur*; *Les Jeux d'eau à la Villa d'Este*; Mephisto Waltz; *Ricordanza*; *Saint François de Paul marchant sur les flots*; *Soirées de Vienne*; Valse Impromptu. "In terms of repertoire, the program is an intriguing one, balancing the familiar and the unfamiliar, bravura pieces with poetic ones. In terms of performance, it is on that heady level where an artist defines his own standards and renders comparisons pointless." This album, dedicated to the memory of Cziffra's son, is "an eminently worthy tribute to the memory of Franz Liszt as well." (*StR*, Jan 1987)

Some of Cziffra's finest recorded performances (made during the brief period after his imprisonment and before his flight during the 1956 Hungarian uprising) appear on a CD reissue, *The Hungaroton Recordings 1954–56* (see Discog.). Liszt dominates, and there is the expected brilliant virtuosity, but there is also a lyricism that permeates throughout. Many of the old favorites are found here—*Gnomenreigen*, *Les Jeux d'eaux à la Villa d'Este*, *Valse oubliée*. The Valse Impromptu and the flamboyant *Grand Galop chromatique* are less familiar but equally enjoyable. This CD collection also includes the formidable *Islamey* of Balakirev.

During the late 1950s when he was at his unsurpassed brilliance, Cziffra recorded a series of Liszt's Hungarian Rhapsodies. Ten of these have been reissued on CD by EMI (see Discog.) and some are well-nigh unbelievable. "Here is all his death-defying bravura; the dizzying changes of pace and direction, the hair-raising crescendos within the bar, the steam-drill left-hand accentuation, and the sky-rocketing flights that leave a trail of sparks in their wake." (*Gram*, Nov 1994)

One of the most important additions to the Cziffra discography, a 6-CD set of recordings (*Les Introuvables*, see Discog.), contains performances from various periods in the pianist's career. This set is a must for Cziffra admirers.

SELECTED REFERENCES

Camacho-Castillo, Mildred. "A Selected Cziffra Discography." *High Fidelity*, Oct 1984, p. 82.

Cziffra, Georges. *Des Canons et des Fleurs*. (translated from the Hungarian by György Cziffra, Jr.). Paris: Editions Robert Laffont, 1977.

"Cziffra Speaks His Mind." *HiFi Review*, Aug 1959, pp. 32-34.
Dixon, Thomas L. "Odd Man Out—Or In?" *High Fidelity*, Oct 1984, pp. 80, 82.
Fondation Cziffra. Booklet issued for the inauguration of the *Salle Franz Liszt*, n. d. The Foundation is still active: 1, Place Saint-Pierre, 60300 Senlis, France.
Freed, Richard. "Cziffra's Incomparable Liszt." *Stereo Review*, Jan 1987, p. 105.
Gavoty, Bernard. "György Cziffra." In *Vingt Grands Interprètes* (see Bibliog.), pp. 71–77.
"Georg Cziffra." *Guide du Concert*, 14 Dec 1956, p. 370.
"György Cziffra." *Music and Musicians*, Sept 1957, p. 5.
"The Infant Prodigy Who Made Good." *Music and Musicians*, Feb 1959, p. 7.
"Liszt Alive." *Newsweek*, 29 July 1957, p. 77.
Obituary. *Gramophone*, March 1994, p. 13.
See also Bibliography: IWWM; New/Gro; Ran/Kon; Rat/Cle.

SELECTED REVIEWS

CST: 3 Nov 1986. *CT*: 3 Nov 1986. *LAT*: 24 July 1957; 2 Aug 1957; 14 Sept 1984. *MA*: Dec 1984. *MT*: Nov 1957. *NW*: 29 July 1957. *NY*: 15 Dec 1956. *NYT*: 1 Nov 1958. *SFC*: 10 Sept 1984. *SJM*: 10 Sept 1984. *TL*: 23 Sept 1957; 31 Jan 1959; 14 Feb 1959; 12 June 1959; 4 Sept 1959; 14 Sept 1959; 3 June 1963; 31 Aug 1963.

SELECTED DISCOGRAPHY

Georges Cziffra: *Récital à Saint Frambourg*. Works by Couperin, Rameau, Lully, d'Acquin. EMI cassette 2C 269-73080.
György Cziffra: The Hungaroton Recordings 1954–56. Balakirev: *Islamey*. Field: Rondo scherzando. Grieg: Concerto in A Minor, op. 16 (Rozsnyai/ Hungarian SO). Liszt: Piano Concerto No. 1 in E-flat Major (Lehel/Budapest SO); *Etudes d'exécution transcendante*: No. 3 (*Paysage*), No. 5 (*Feux-follets*), No. 6 (*Vision*), No. 7 (*Eroica*), No. 10 (*Appassionata*); *Gnomen-reigen*; *Grand Galop chromatique*; Hungarian Rhapsodies: No. 2, No. 6, No. 12, No. 15 (Rakóczy); *Les Jeux d'eaux à la Villa d'Este*; Valse Impromptu; *Valse oubliée No. 1*. Schubert-Liszt: *Soirée de Vienne No. 6*; Schumann: *Traumes Wirren*. CDAPR 7021(2 CDs).
György Cziffra: Piano Recital. Chopin: Fantasy in F Minor, op. 49; Impromptu in F-sharp Major, op. 36. Cziffra: Improvisations on Rossini's overture to *William Tell*; Paraphrase on Rossini's *"La Danza."* Liszt: *La Campanella*. Ravel: *Jeux d'eaux; Sonatine*. Hungaroton SLPX 11945.
György Cziffra Recital. Chopin: Ballade in F Minor, op. 52; Etudes in E Major, op. 10, no. 3; A-flat Major, op. 10, no. 10; C Minor, op. 10, no. 12; A-flat Major, op. 25, no. 1; *Fantaisie-impromptu*, op. 66; Waltzes in A-flat Major, op. 42; D-flat Major, op. 64, no. 1; C-sharp Minor, op. 64, no. 2. Liszt: *Les Funerailles*; *Gnomenreigen*; Hungarian Rhapsody No. 2.;

Liebestraum No. 3; Transcendental Étude No. 10 in F Minor. Ermitage CD ERM 103.

Les Introuvables de Cziffra. EMI Classics 8 CDS CZS 67366-2. A collection of 8 CDs taken from various periods of Cziffra's career. They are: (1) Liszt; (2) Liszt, Cziffra; (3) C. P. E. Bach, Balakirev, Beethoven, Couperin, Hummel, Krebs, Lully, Mendelssohn, Rameau, Scarlatti, Schumann; (4) Beethoven, Brahms, Chopin; (5) Beethoven; (6) Schumann; (7) Franck, Grieg, Liszt; (8) Tchaikovsky.

Liszt: Concerto No. 1 in E-flat Major; Concerto No. 2 in A Major; Hungarian Fantasy; *Totentanz.* EMI 7476402 (CD). Cziffra, Jr./*Orchestre de Paris.*

Liszt: *Études d'exécution transcendante* (complete). EMI CDM 69111-2.

Liszt: Hungarian Rhapsodies Nos. 2, 6, 8–11, 12–15; *Rhapsodie espagnole.* EMI *Rouge et Noir* CZS7 67888 -2 (2 CDs). Rec. 1957–59.

Liszt Recital. Chasse-Neige; *Gaudeamus igitur*; *Les jeux d'eau à la Villa d'Este*; Mephisto Waltz; *Ricordanza*; *Saint François de Paul marchant sur les flots*; *Soirées de Vienne*; Valse Impromptu. EMI 2704171.

La Rendez-vous de Senlis. Bach-Busoni: Prelude and Fugue in D Major. Brahms: 15 Hungarian Dances. Chopin: *Introduction et Variations brillantes*, op. 12; Nocturnes, op. 9, nos. 1 and 2; Etudes, op. 10, nos. 3-5, 10, 12; Scherzo No. 2 in B-flat Minor, op. 31. Liszt: Polonaise No. 2; Transcendental Etude No. 10. Saint-Saëns: *Etude en forme de Valse.* Schubert: Impromptus, D. 899, no. 4, D. 935, no. 4. EMI 2-CZS 62880-2.

DICHTER, MISHA: b. Shanghai, China, 27 September 1945.

> The consistent solidity and virtuosity of Dichter's work have made him
> an enduring presence on the international concert scene.
> Howard Reich (*Chicago Tribune*, 1 July 1993)

Misha Dichter happened to be born in China only because Leon and Lucy
(Lhevine) Dichter, his Polish parents, had fled Warsaw, Poland, just ahead of
World War II's Nazi troops. They lived for a time in Shanghai, and in 1947
(Misha, their only child, was two years old) moved to Los Angeles, California,
where Leon Dichter established what proved to be a successful lumber business.
Neither of the Dichters had any musical interests nor did they own a piano; how-
ever, when their son became intrigued with a neighbor's piano, they let him, at
age six, start piano lessons.

  Up until the age of 12 his musical training was, at best, haphazard.
The last of his several miscellaneous early teachers happened to be a "wonderful"
pianist his parents had heard playing Russian songs in a Russian émigré restaurant, and immediately engaged him to teach their son. "Those are my roots,"
says Dichter, "and they gave me a very free early musical existence." (Kreader)
No wonder that, as he has said, he played as wildly as a gypsy until he studied,
from age 12 to 18, with Aube Tzerko, once a pupil of Artur Schnabel, who
trained him thoroughly in the Schnabel tradition, beginning with the Brahms
Exercises and months and months of scales and etudes.

  In 1961 Dichter placed first in a competition sponsored by the Western
Division of the Music Educators National Conference, and consequently per-

formed the Rachmaninoff Concerto No. 2 at the Santa Monica Civic Auditorium. Graduated from Beverly Hills High School in 1963, he enrolled at the University of California, Los Angeles, as an English major but stayed only two semesters. Within that time, Dichter won the Atwater Kent Award, was soloist with various local orchestras and, during the 1963–64 concert season, performed with the Los Angeles Philharmonic Orchestra at a Youth Concert.

Attending a two-week (June 1964) piano master class at UCLA conducted by Rosina Lhévinne, the famous piano pedagogue, changed Dichter's life. As soon as Mme. Lhévinne, obviously impressed with Dichter, invited him to study with her at the Juilliard School in New York, he gave up being an English major to become a music student. At Juilliard, Dichter received the Josef Lhévinne scholarship and first prize in the Beethoven Concerto contest. Leaving Los Angeles had of course also meant giving up his lessons with Aube Tzerko, a teacher so outrageously different from Rosina Lhévinne that Dichter finds it impossible to talk about one without mentioning the other.

Like his teacher Schnabel, Tzerko carried musical analysis to such extremes that students playing for him could barely get past the first measures of the first movement of a piece. Thus while studying with Tzerko, Dichter had acquired a repertoire of "about half a piece." Dichter's meagre repertoire must have appalled Mme. Lhévinne, a living advocate of the sweeping 19th-century pianism taught at the Moscow Conservatory, who taught not only technique and musicianship but also the 19th-century tradition of performance practice, even including stage deportment. She made him memorize a new composition every week for the next four months.

Dichter made his debut in Los Angeles, at a Young Musicians Foundation concert (8 Feb 1963) performed in Schoenberg Hall on the University of California campus. In 1966 he placed second in the third International Tchaikovsky Piano Competition in Moscow. RCA Victor signed him to a contract, and agents clamored for booking, but, being only too well aware that he knew only enough pieces for half a recital program and had only two concertos to offer an orchestra, Dichter sensibly followed Lhévinne's advice that he should return to school so that they could learn repertoire together. No doubt recalling Van Cliburn's hectic pace after winning the Tchaikovsky Competition eight years earlier, Madame cautioned Dichter against overexposure. Thanks to her wise counsel, Dichter avoided the post-competition pressures to perform too much too soon and kept his name before the public with a few (usually less than 10) engagements a year.

Dichter made his American orchestral debut (14 Aug 1966) at the Berkshire Music Festival in Lenox, Massachusetts, playing the Tchaikovsky Concerto No. 1 with the Boston Symphony Orchestra, Erich Leinsdorf conducting, and played the same concerto at his London debut (8 June 1967) with the New Philharmonia Orchestra, conducted by Igor Markevitch. Audiences wanted to hear him play that same Tchaikovsky Concerto and the flashy Chopin etudes he had performed at the competition. Dichter wanted to show that he could be serious and sober. "I went overboard trying to be introspective. I didn't want to show my natural, gut way of playing, which is basically gypsy." (Kreader) But as he delved increasingly into the inner mathematics of music, he played, he recalls, "with no emotion."

Acknowledging his natural inclination for playing Liszt ultimately solved his problems. Finally admitting that his "natural, gut way of playing" is basically gypsy and that he loved the Liszt Rhapsodies, the late Liszt pieces and the Liszt Sonata, he set himself to learning those flamboyant works. "Practicing those pieces had an effect on everything I played. Technically it was a quantum leap from about 1975 to 1979." (Kreader)

Since that time Dichter has pursued the busy life of the international concert artist, playing about 100 concerts a season. He also plays two-piano recitals with Cipa (Glazman) Dichter, his wife. Born in Brazil—her parents had fled from Russia during World War II—Mrs. Dichter met her husband while both were students at Juilliard. They married in 1968 and have two sons.

Dichter rarely, if ever, teaches one-on-one, but loves teaching master classes. On 1 July 1993 he celebrated a quarter-century of teaching classes at the Ravinia Festival by playing three concertos—Liszt No. 1, Tchaikovsky No. 1, Mozart K. 365 (with Cipa Dichter)—with the Chicago Symphony Orchestra. For the last two decades he has also taught master classes at the Aspen Music Festival.

Dichter's interests, past and present, make for a most interesting man. A talented cartoonist, he has often filled the time spent on planes and waiting in airports and at rehearsals drawing delightful pen and black ink sketches, many of which have been exhibited in New York art galleries. He loves (and studies) architecture, a passion very likely rooted in his interest in mathematics. He is an active chamber player, an accomplished writer, and he loves classic cars.

Throughout his career, reviewers have come up with disparate assessments of Misha Dichter's playing. There are those who see him as a keyboard master in the great virtuoso tradition, with a rare ability to communicate and a distinctive style. Such critics describe Dichter's playing with these words: elegance, eloquence, poetry, poise, authority, dignity. Critics disagreeing with those appraisals find Dichter's playing too objective, too analytical, sometimes too cold, even monotonous. They point out his narrow tonal palette, shallow sonorities, limited expressive powers.

He feels that a great many musicians attack a composition without first considering its architecture ("abstract foundation," as he calls it). His own approach to a work (based on the premise that he will not play a note without understanding its place in the whole) begins with an analysis of its mathematical substructure. He looks at the work as a unit in itself, then breaks it down (by section, phrase, motive, chord, note), always searching for the "totality of the tiniest little structures in relation to the entire work." (O'Brien) Of course, this exacting analysis has no effect on the emotional content of a performance, but it gives Dichter a feeling for form and a sense of freedom when he sits down to play. And the process never ends. When he starts reworking a piece he has played before, he applies to the current score the discoveries he had made on earlier work-ups of that particular piece. Every time the pianist prepares a piece anew, says Dichter, even those he may have played over and over, he can still find countless details hitherto overlooked.

At the same time, Dichter is well aware that understanding the music, no matter how completely, is not enough, that the performer must also feel the music. "I will be as emotional as I can be," he tells interviewers, "but only when I first have a thorough understanding of the score." And he approaches the emotional aspects of music in a highly individual manner: Once he has a full understanding of a work, he places it in his subconscious, and lets "the feeling govern the performance."

As this approach to a score indicates, Dichter is a faithful interpreter, his heritage from both Tzerko and Schnabel, who had instilled in him that the printed score is sacrosanct, that the pianist's interpretative conclusions must always be based on the score. Dichter once explained that while he approaches, say, Beethoven's Opus 111 and Liszt's Hungarian Rhapsodies with equal strictness, that does not mean, he says, that in performance he will "adhere to every note in the score, because in the outpouring of total abandon that the score evokes I must follow along with the passion. But I will know every note that Liszt or Beethoven wrote, and I will rarely move from what is on the page." (Silverman) Above all, Dichter strives to get the *sound* exactly right for each composer.

His commanding, much-admired technique does not come naturally. It required hard work. Piano students will be interested to learn that Dichter as a student did not practice the usual formal exercises of Czerny or Clementi. He mostly developed his technique by devoting a whole year to "just practicing various standard exercises such as scales, arpeggios, trills, and so forth." And he finds it helpful "to remember that music does not come from the fingers. One plays with the ear, not with the fingers. It is the inner ear which directs the blending and the articulation of tones. What I also believe is important is that much learning takes place away from the keyboard." (Mach)

Dichter is now known for playing the virtuoso masterpieces of the 19th and early 20th centuries, but early in his career he found Liszt "unplayable," not because he lacked the technique for Liszt, but simply because the music never *sounded* the way he wanted it to sound. But Dichter changed his mind about playing Liszt. In 1985 he told interviewers that he had been working extensively on Liszt's music, and that "studying Liszt is like studying with a great teacher." (*PI*, 17 June 1985) Indeed, Dichter's performances and recordings of the Liszt concertos and the Hungarian Rhapsodies are models of musicianly virtuosity.

He has little interest in adding contemporary works to his repertoire. "I'm in the middle of my career," he said in 1975, "and I still want to play only the pieces I know and adore." There are exceptions, like Marc Neikrug's Fantasy-Sonata (1972), not only written for Dichter, but based on the letters of his first name.

A collection of reviews of his playing, dating from 1963 to 1993, show that Dichter mostly plays Mozart, Beethoven, Schumann, Liszt, Schubert, Brahms, Rachmaninoff and, less frequently, Haydn, Stravinsky, Mussorgsky,

Prokofiev, Scriabin, Debussy, Albéniz. The reviews also show that he has performed these orchestral works: Tchaikovsky Concerto No. 1, Mozart Concerto in C Major, K. 503, Brahms Concertos Nos. 1 and 2, Liszt Concertos Nos. 1 and 2, all five Beethoven Concertos, the Grieg Concerto, the Schumann Concerto.

Dichter's various debut appearances in the 1960s were eminently successful. At his London debut (8 June 1967, Festival Hall), performed with the New Philharmonia Orchestra, conducted by Igor Markevitch, Dichter played the Tchaikovsky Concerto No. 1 "with stupendous strength and brilliance. . . . As an interpreter [he] combined romantic fervour with princely self-discipline, and given the right kind of partnership, this would have proved a debut in a thousand." (*TL*, 9 June 1967) And when Dichter played the Tchaikovsky for his debut (13 Jan 1968) with the New York Philharmonic Orchestra, he received a bear hug from conductor Leonard Bernstein and an ovation from the capacity audience. "His conception of the work was basically sensitive and personal. His tone was liquid and lovely in the softer passages, firm, but never hard in the fortissimos." (*NYT*, 15 Jan 1968)

A San Francisco recital on 7 January 1973—music by Mozart, Neikrug, Rachmaninoff and Schumann—was "as close to perfection as pianists can hope to achieve . . . . The playing was so sensible, so suave in all its parts and so free of clutter that Dichter's technique emerged as total servant to the music. . . . What is unique to Dichter is his rhythmic stability. His rubato was applied with a fine restraint, one that helped crest important ideas, and always with impeccable taste." (*SFC*, 9 Jan 1973)

Dichter gave a "ravishing" performance (17 March 1978) of Schubert's great Sonata in B-flat Major, D. 960, at the Metropolitan Museum of Art. "He commands a melting legato and can exquisitely control the softest shadings. The manner in which he fluttered through the scherzo, and the downward scamper of his right hand during the coda to the last movement, were prodigious feats of unadvertised virtuosity." (*NYT*, 19 March 1978)

Dichter's Los Angeles performance (1 April 1979) of the Liszt Sonata in B Minor drew this comment: "If he did not cast any particularly new light on the lengthy argument, at least he kept it firmly in line with enough flexibility for diversion, he propounded the drama with the proper fury and he was dauntless in facing up to the bravura." (*LAT*, 3 April 1979) But his all-Liszt recital (17 Feb 1980) at Alice Tully Hall "deserved all the cheers it received. . . . Too often, performances of [the Liszt Sonata] are merely empty and loud. . . . Mr. Dichter traveled a great distance beyond that kind of Liszt, into the realm of Romantic incantation." (*NYT*, 19 Feb 1980)

An early New York performance (12 Jan 1972) of the Brahms Concerto No. 1 with the Boston Symphony Orchestra, Michael Tilson Thomas conducting, warranted a substantial article in *Time* (24 Jan 1972). Calling him "probably the best of a new breed of pianists," this writer reports that Dichter attacked the Concerto "with directness and clarity, free of the quixotic and the chichi. It's a fiendishly difficult work, all uphill, all steep and sudden curves and yawning abysses, and Dichter took it at full throttle, the piano barely large enough to contain his ferocity." (Saal) Another critic, however, missed "an element of poetry, of color, of imagination. . . . There was drive rather than poetry; percussion rather than nuance." (*NYT*, 14 Jan 1972)

Sometimes even the finest performances are beset with problems. This was true when Dichter gave a solo recital (27 July 1992) at Los Angeles's open-air Greek Theatre. The sound technicians were evidently unable to compensate for the acoustical problems endemic to a structure more suited to ballet ensembles and rock bands. Yet, in spite of the sonic drawbacks, Dichter's program of Beethoven, Brahms, Liszt and Bartók showed him triumphing even under adversity: "It was an awesome demonstration of grace under pressure, longer musical lines and thoughts given full and honest expression without strain. Dichter's tremendous authority at the keyboard is the result of a comprehensive technique combined with an astute musicality." (*LAT*, 29 July 1992)

Recording principally for Philips, Dichter's acclaimed discs include music by Beethoven, Brahms, Chopin, Gershwin, Liszt, Mussorgsky, Schumann and Stravinsky. The extant discography is not extensive but it is representative of the pianist at his best. In his recording of the two Liszt concertos, made with the Pittsburgh Symphony Orchestra, André Previn conducting, "Dichter sails confidently over Liszt's technical obstacles while leaving many of the musical problems untouched: In quieter moments, the solo playing is neat and graceful, while in the finale of the E Flat concerto, Mr. Dichter's kinetic energy—and the virtuosity with which he controls it—border on the astonishing." (*NYT*, 15 May 1983)

A 1983 disc of five short works for piano and orchestra offers a comprehensive view of Dichter's special talents. It contains two obviously "popular" works—Gershwin's Rhapsody in Blue and the Addinsell Warsaw Concerto—and three equally interesting dazzlers—the Litolff Scherzo, Chopin's Fantasy on Polish Airs and Liszt's transcription of Weber's *Polacca Brillante* (see Discog.). As one reviewer put it, "If you don't own this gem of a CD yet, don't walk, run to get it. What you'll receive is a genuinely gorgeous showcase of artistry and sound. . . . Misha Dichter's breathtaking and flawless piano solos combined with the shimmering, yet often full-bore orchestral wizardry of the Philharmonia Orchestra make this disc a perfect addition to a cherished collection." (*Digital Audio*, March 1985)

He has recorded all of Liszt's 19 Hungarian Rhapsodies (see Discog.). One reviewer writes that while Dichter's set of Rhapsodies "has missed their basically improvisatory and folk-music character . . . this is the most technically accomplished set of the complete Hungarian Rhapsodies that I have yet heard." (*Gram*, Nov 1987)

An interesting Mussorgsky CD couples the keyboard version of the Pictures at an Exhibition with the orchestral transcription so expertly achieved by Ravel (see Discog.). "Dichter's performance is very much in the grand manner and his 'Great Gate of Kiev' is extraordinarily powerful and compelling. The whole performance is full of imaginative touches, with the various 'Promenades' used perceptively to change the mood between each picture." (*Gram*, June 1988)

In 1993 Dichter signed a multi-record agreement with MusicMasters Classics. This gives him the opportunity to begin recording repertoire that is particularly meaningful to him or which he has not had the opportunity to record in recent years. The first scheduled disc (March 1994) features an all-Brahms program including the Variations and Fugue on a Theme by Handel, op. 24.

SELECTED REFERENCES

Adler, Dick. "Return of the King." *Los Angeles Magazine*, March 1987, pp. 58–60.

Cariaga, Daniel. "Dichter: A Career On Schedule." *Los Angeles Times*, 27 Aug 1985, sec. 6, p. 2.

"Dichter, Back at Juilliard, Remembers Piano Teacher." *New York Times*, 12 March 1986 (Day by Day), sec. 2, p. 2.

Finn, Robert. "Pianist Misha Dichter takes swing from Liszt to Mozart in his stride." *Plain Dealer* (Cleveland), 24 July 1986, sec. E, p. 11.

Kreader, Barbara. "Misha Dichter." *Clavier*, May/June 1984, pp. 12–15.

Mach, Elyse. "Misha Dichter." (interview) *Piano Quarterly*, Winter 1975/76, pp. 19–22.

Marsh, Robert C. "Growth is the key for Misha Dichter." *Chicago Sun Times*, 27 Aug 1989 (Show), p. 7.

O'Brien, Valerie. "The Musician as Artist: Misha Dichter." *Ovation*, March 1980, p. 42.

Oestreich, James R. "Then There Is the Other Side of Misha Dichter." *New York Times*, 8 April 1990, sec. 2, pp. 27, 40.

Raymond, John. "Misha Dichter Works at Playing The Unplayable." *Atlanta Journal*, 25 Jan 1980, sec. B, pp. 1, 9.

"RCA Victor's Roundup—Young Americans with Russian Medals." *High Fidelity Magazine*, Jan 1967, pp. 20, 24.

Reich, Howard. "Many happy returns." *Chicago Tribune*, 1 July 1993, sec. E, p. 9.

Rhein, John von. "Misha Dichter: The Moscow winner has come a long way." *Chicago Tribune*, 6 April 1981, p. 2.

Saal, Hubert. "Misha of the New Breed." *Time*, 24 Jan 1972, p. 73.

Silverman, Robert. "Misha Dichter: Unabashed Musical Conservative." *Piano Quarterly*, Winter 1989/90, pp. 20–24.

"Sketching The Career Of Pianist Dichter." *Pittsburgh Press*, 19 June 1983, sec. E, pp. 1, 4.

Sweeney, Louise. "Music With Muscle." *Christian Science Monitor*, 18 July 1990, p. 12.

Tucker, Marilyn. "The Man With a Liszt to Fulfill." *San Francisco Chronicle*, 5 Dec 1979, p. 65.

Webster, Daniel. "A pianist liberated by romantic works." *Philadelphia Inquirer*, 17 June 1985, sec. D, pp. 1, 8.

Willis, Thomas. "Misha Dichter: Watching a career grow." *Chicago Tribune*, 2 May 1977, sec. 3, p. 9.

See also Bibliography: Dub/Ref; Ewe/Mu; Mac/Gre; New/GrA; Noy/Pia; WWAM.

SELECTED REVIEWS

CDM: 26 April 1993. *CDN*: 16 Feb 1970. *CST*: 2 May 1977; 29 July 1991.
CT: 15 Feb 1970; 1 July 1993. *IS*: 7 Jan 1978. *LAHE*: 4 April 1979.
LAT: 10 Feb 1963; 8 April 1968; 2 Feb 1970; 16 March 1971; 8 Sept
1973; 11 Sept 1975; 3 April 1979; 12 May 1982; 29 Aug 1985; 29 July
1992. *MH*: 10 March 1976. *MJ*: 6 Dec 1975. *NYT*: 15 Jan 1968; 22 Jan
1968; 28 Oct 1968; 22 March 1969; 24 Jan 1971; 14 Jan 1972; 22 Jan
1973; 19 March 1978; 19 Feb 1980; 2 May 1984; 18 Feb 1990. *PI*: 17
Nov 1990. *PP*: 2 Oct 1981; 23 June 1983; 15 Dec 1984. *SFC*: 9 Jan
1973. *SFE*: 15 March 1979. *SLT*: 8 March 1981. *ST*: 29 Jan 1991. *TL*:
9 June 1967. *WP*: 2 July 1990.

SELECTED DISCOGRAPHY

Addinsell: Warsaw Concerto. Chopin: Grand Fantasy on Polish Airs, op. 13.
   Gershwin: Rhapsody in Blue. Litolff: Scherzo (*Concerto symphonique*).
   Weber-Liszt: *Polonaise Brillante*. Philips 411123-2. Marriner/Philhar-
   monia.
Beethoven: Sonata in C Minor, op. 13; Sonata in C-sharp Minor, op. 27, no. 2;
   Sonata in A Major, op. 101. Philips 422475-2.
Brahms: Piano Concerto No. 2 in B-flat Major, op. 83. Philips 9500 414.
   Mazur/*Gewandhaus*.
Brahms: Fantasias, op. 116; Variations and Fugue on a Theme by Handel, op.
   24; Waltzes, op. 39. MusicMasters 67126-2.
Liszt: Concerto No. 1 in E-flat Major; Concerto No. 2 in A Major. Philips
   420896-2. Previn/Pittsburgh SO.
Liszt: The 19 Hungarian Rhapsodies. Philips 426 463-2 (2 CDs).
Misha Dichter plays Liszt. Au bord d'une source; *Funérailles*; Mephisto Waltz
   No. 1; Hungarian Rhapsody No. 11 in A Minor; Hungarian Rhapsody No.
   14 in F Minor. Schubert-Liszt: *Liebesbotschaft*. Philips LP 9500401, cas-
   sette 7300 639.
Mussorgsky: Pictures at an Exhibition. Philips 420708-2 (Includes the orches-
   tral version with de Waart and the Rotterdam Philharmonic Orchestra.)
Schumann: Fantasia in C, op. 17; Symphonic Etudes, op. 13. Philips 9500
   318.
Tchaikovsky: Concerto No. 1 in B-flat Minor, op. 23. RCA 6526-2.
   Leinsdorf/Boston SO.

DOUGLAS, BARRY: b. Belfast, Northern Ireland, 23 April 1960.

> I don't think of myself as a pianist, but rather as a musician who hap-
> pens to play the piano.
>
> Barry Douglas (*Ovation*, February 1987)

Barry Douglas was born in Ulster at just the wrong time to ensure that he would live through his childhood and early teen years in a Belfast often under siege from the sporadic, violent eruptions between Northern Ireland and the Republic of Ireland. Understandably the Belfast of the early 1970s had little time or incli- nation for musical or any other kind of cultural activities; but growing up in that sometimes culturally barren city has made little difference in Douglas's career.

Neither of his parents—his father owned a small business, his mother was a nurse—had studied music, but they knew enough to recognize that the four-year-old Douglas, who could pick out tunes on the piano, had an unusual aptitude for music. They gave him piano lessons and sent him at age nine to the Belfast School of Music. He made good progress (Douglas has absolute pitch, a remarkable memory and an exceptional sight-reading facility), but as a youngster he was not single-mindedly set on the piano. He played cello in the school or- chestra, clarinet in the school band and actually made his first public appearance, at age 11, playing the organ. Sometimes he conducted youthful choruses and or- chestras.

At about age 16, Douglas began piano studies with Felicitas Lewinter, a pupil of Emil von Sauer, who had studied with Liszt. Lewinter, as Douglas puts it, not only "scared" him into practicing, but sparked his interest in the pi- ano. With Lewinter urging him on to finding "the best sound for the piano," he began to practice more, up to four or five hours a day, and on her advice, in 1978 he began studying with John Barstow at the Royal College of Music in London. Barstow was the right choice. "I liked his style very much," says Barry. "As a teacher he wasn't so keen on talking about technique; he was more concerned with the structure and expression of music." (Elliott)

A teenager fresh from beleaguered Belfast, Douglas was totally unpre- pared for the music, the drama, the wonderfully rich abundance of cultural activi- ties available in London. Attempting to catch up, he heard all the music he could manage. In his four years (1978–82) with Barstow, friend and mentor as well as teacher, Douglas was able to hear concerts, operas and recitals in London, Wagner operas at Bayreuth and a Richter recital at the Touraine Music Festival in France. Absorbing these varied musical experiences enriched and broadened Douglas's knowledge of, and outlook on, music. "I went to opera all the time," he says. "I had never known before that I loved opera. So my influences have been many pianists, teachers, performers and symphonic performances, but what has really inspired me is the voice." (Duchen)

Douglas made an informal London debut on "Young Musicians 1980," an event sponsored by the Greater London Arts Association. Although allotted only 30 minutes, his performance of Liszt's B Minor Ballade showed that "he had the stormy reserves of technique and energy needed," and, as far as he got, his performance of the Mephisto Waltz No. 1 revealed a "clean-cut, exciting bril-liance." (*TL*, 13 Feb 1980) That same year the 20-year-old Douglas also won (second place, no first awarded) the International Paloma O'Shea Competition in Santander, Spain.

The year 1982 proved exceptionally eventful. On 3 May 1982 Douglas won a Concert Artists Guild of New York award, which guaranteed a New York recital. He also graduated from the Royal College of Music with the Cyril Smith Recital Award, and his "prize" recital (7 Dec 1982) in the Purcell Room of the Royal Festival Hall earned a good review, with the prediction that he had "a momentous career ahead of him on this showing." After graduation, he began three years of private, very productive studies with Maria Curcio, a pupil of Artur Schnabel. For one thing, Douglas made "a good first step" in technique working with Curcio, a teacher with "some very clever ideas for how to get spe-cific sounds with various positions of the arm and hand." (Elliott) The year 1982 also brought a major disappointment. Douglas entered the seventh International Tchaikovsky Competition in Moscow and was quickly eliminated in the first round.

He placed fifth at the Artur Rubinstein International Piano Master Competition in Tel-Aviv, Israel, in 1983, and in 1985 won the Bronze Medal at the seventh Van Cliburn Competition in Fort Worth, Texas. And, although he had decided not to put himself through the ordeal again, Douglas made a second attempt at the Tchaikovsky Competition in 1986. Prodded by friends and his manager, he made up his mind to go only ten days before the contest began. Fortunately he knew most of the required repertoire, and it took him only a week to learn the required piece by a Russian composer. This time Douglas not only survived round one but was the audience favorite from the start. And this time, in a field of about 150 entrants, he won the Gold Medal, the first westerner in 28 years (since 1958, when Van Cliburn took first prize at the first Tchaikovsky Competition) to win the Gold Medal alone, not sharing it as, for instance, John Ogdon had shared first prize with Vladimir Ashkenazy in 1982.

Between leaving college and winning the Tchaikovsky Competition, Douglas had struggled with trying to start a career. Nevertheless, by the time he entered the Tchaikovsky he was performing about 50 concerts a year and, accord-ing to London reviews, had made a good professional beginning. A critic at the *Manchester Guardian* thought that he had "already matured into a front-rank pi-anist." The *Daily Telegram* praised him for "a characteristically well-planned, stimulating program (that) confirmed that he is one of the most exciting, most absorbing, most thrilling communicative pianists of his generation."

One may wonder whether Douglas would or would not have gone on to international success, but without a doubt Moscow's prestigious Gold Medal ("I don't like to speculate where I would be without it," says Douglas) opened the door to an international career. Winning over Russian pianists made Douglas the darling of the media, generated a flood of engagement offers from around the world and brought him a recording contract from RCA. At first he enjoyed the extensive touring (everyone wanted him, of course, to play the Tchaikovsky Concerto No. 1 that he had played at the competition), as well as all the atten-tion (interviews, television appearances, autograph parties) and the mad scramble of promoters (at one point five Japanese agents) competing to sign him to a management contract. (For a most illuminating exposition on the promotional packaging of a "hot" young competition winner, see Isenberg.)

And management kept him very busy. He played more than 60 concerts in the year after winning his gold medal and made his first recording for RCA—naturally Tchaikovsky's Piano Concerto No. 1 and Mussorgsky's Pictures at an Exhibition, both vital to his Moscow success. He played a pianist in the delightful *Madame Sousatzka*, a movie starring Shirley MacLaine. He made his formal New York recital debut at Carnegie Hall on 8 April 1988. Aware of the increasing pace, Douglas wisely cut back. It took him about a year, as he puts it, "to find my own rhythm of working again. It's a faster rhythm now, but at least I am back in the frame of mind I was in before the competition." (Morrison) The best part of winning, he says, was having the chance to play with conductors and orchestras that, before Moscow, he could only dream about.

From his homes in London and Paris, Douglas tours around the globe (Europe, United States, Canada, Asia, Israel, Australia, New Zealand), performing about 100 concerts a year and, unlike most concert performers, apparently enjoying every minute. "Every day is different. I hate to be locked into a routine and, as well as being very hard work, it's a very exciting life—the fact that I can be in a different place playing with different musicians, meeting up with friends and colleagues around the world." (Duchen) However, he is less enthused about competitions and their importance—a surprising attitude, given the number of prizes and awards tendered Douglas.

Although Douglas has never deliberately targeted any specific area of piano repertoire ("If it's a good piece and it appeals to me then it doesn't really matter who wrote it."), he came to fame playing the music of the late Romantics. Generally speaking, his repertoire—charted from reviews and discography dating from 1986, the year he stepped into the international musical limelight, and extending through the early 1990s—includes these concertos: Brahms Nos. 1 and 2, Tchaikovsky Nos. 1 and 2, Prokofiev No. 3, Liszt Nos. 1 and 2, Beethoven No. 2, Rachmaninoff Nos. 2 and 3, the Britten Concerto; and includes solo works by Tchaikovsky, Prokofiev, Mussorgsky, Shostakovich, Haydn, Mozart, Beethoven, Schumann, Brahms, Liszt, Chopin and the more contemporary Webern, Berg, Corigliano.

Preparation for playing this repertoire involves studying each score away from the piano so as to ascertain the composer's artistic intention and, of course, practicing. Douglas normally practices about three hours a day, every day if at all possible, believing that missing a day of practice can make a difference, "not so much that anyone else would notice, but enough to affect my own fulfillment." (Morrison)

His approach to the music is intensely personal in that he is "very skeptical of the idea of performance tradition. If there is a tradition, maybe it's time to change it." (Finn) He tries to give each piece a fresh look, so that the audience will feel that it is newly composed. "Sometimes one can get bound up in traditional approaches to an interpretation or bad habits. It's nice to pare it down and start again. I think clarity and freshness are the key for me—but these are only words. I have to convey this musically." (*Gram*, March 1992)

That Barry Douglas is eminently successful in his profession is unquestioned. He is booked years ahead and can pretty much play when and where he wishes. But what of his pianism? He is "neither the careful middle-of-the-roader . . . nor the wilfully eccentric headline-maker. . . . [He is] a performer who starts with the powerhouse technique you'd expect of a major competition winner. . . . Added to that technical level is a big sonority; Douglas makes a big sound roll out of the piano, and he seems to have a romanticist's temperament in making large, powerful works emerge with lyricism instead of bombast." (Bargreen)

How does Douglas himself explain his approach to his art? To him, tone production is extremely important. "You really miss out if you don't think of this, and I want to be able to create all sorts of sounds with the piano." Additionally he claims to aim for "complete control, lots of fire and life, and fidelity to the text. That's what's so fantastic about performing music. There are so many links in the chain." (Marum)

On 5 February 1987 Douglas played the Tchaikovsky Concerto No. 1 in B-flat Minor at Albert Hall with the BBC Symphony Orchestra, conducted by Gianluigi Gelmetti. "His massive technique and superb coloristic sense made the first movement a marvel, and the second—the beautifully lit andantino semplice—a minor miracle; and one was temporarily induced to feel that Tchaikovsky is the greatest of all composers." (*STL*, 8 Feb 1987) When Douglas performed that concerto that same year in the United States at one of the Caramoor Festival concerts, a reviewer marveled at the maturity of his approach, the avoidance of eccentricities and exaggerations: "What distinguished his playing was the controlled clarity of his sound. In rapid passages there was precision, warmed with liquid tone. Technical virtuosity became expressions of true musical drama, not empty exercises." (*MA*, Jan 1988)

Douglas has proven himself equally adept with the Brahms Concerto No. 1 in D Minor. A 1987 performance at London's Festival Hall was a resounding success. "The hallmarks of his own increasingly distinctive performing personality are there, to be sure: the vivid and securely ballasted octaves, the resonant, arm-powered chord sequences, the serious and lucid passage-work. But, from that point on, Douglas the soloist retreats and Douglas the musician takes over." (*TL*, 23 March 1987)

He does not limit himself exclusively to playing large-scale, highly charged concertos. On 27 September 1989 Douglas played Beethoven's Concerto No. 2 in B-flat Major, op. 19, almost Mozartean in style and content, with the Baltimore Symphony Orchestra, conducted by David Zinman. By one account, the soloist "showed he is a pianist at home with the finesse and musical control needed for a work so firmly rooted in Classicism. . . . On the other side of the equation, Douglas could summon rhapsodic moments when the sheer warmth and feeling of Beethoven's melodies bloomed full." (*ES*, 28 Sept 1989)

Douglas's recital on 19 March 1988 at Washington's Kennedy Center Terrace Theater showed a predilection for unusual programming: the Brahms Ballade No. 4, op. 10, and the complete set of seven *Phantasien*, op. 116, plus

Tchaikovsky's Grand Sonata in G Major. The Brahms received the bulk of critical attention: "It is almost impossible to believe that the Brahms ballade could have been played better. . . . His timing [in opus 116] was so sensitive that such a succession of slowly paced, somberly colored pieces never lost interest. In the slowest of them, he was able to decelerate to almost a full stop, maintain the line of the music and yield an effect that was heartbreaking in its pathos." (*BaS*, 21 March 1988)

At the 1990 Belfast Festival, Douglas played a program of four sonatas, a demanding evening for both listeners and performer: Alban Berg's Sonata; the Liszt Sonata in B Minor; and Prokofiev's Sonatas Nos. 2 and 7. In his powerful performance of the Liszt Sonata, Douglas's "ability to sustain intensity over wide stretches was remarkable. This was an intellectual, even magisterial performance, with dazzling brilliance in bravura, stunning double octaves and a sustained weight of tone." (*BT*, 20 Nov 1990)

More recently, Douglas's recital (19 July 1994) at the University of Maryland featured music by Debussy (*Pour le piano*), Rachmaninoff (*Moments musicaux*) and Mussorgsky (Pictures at an Exhibition). One enthusiastic reviewer noted: "Douglas's performance served as an eloquent reminder that at such rarefied levels it will always be the magicians who rule." (*WP*, 20 July 1994)

Douglas made two recordings of the Brahms Concerto No. 1 in D Minor. After he won the Tchaikovsky Competition in Moscow, *Melodiya* promptly engaged him to record this Brahms Concerto with the USSR Symphony Orchestra, Vasily Sinaisky conducting. Later the *Melodiya* LP was transferred to an Olympia/Conifer CD (see Discog.), and despite the drawbacks— only fair sound production, noticeable coughing, uninformative notes—the recording is illuminating, a performance that "never fails for an instant to produce glorious, exciting, haunting, and emotionally charged music." (*Fan*, July/Aug 1989) However, Douglas's second reading—this time with Stanislaw Skrowaczewski and the London Symphony Orchestra—is far superior. "There is never any doubt that Douglas is technically, and in large measure emotionally, in command of this daunting work, and there is far better rapport here between pianist, conductor and orchestra than there was on the Melodiya issue." (*Gram*, March 1989)

Shortly after the Moscow competition, Douglas signed with RCA and his first recording for that label had to be the Tchaikovsky Concerto No. 1, performed with Leonard Slatkin conducting the London Symphony Orchestra (see Discog.). The CD earned a "Recording of Distinction" award from *Ovation*: "Douglas has a searing technique; but, at the same time, he is as sensitive to the poetry as to the brilliance." (*OV*, Feb 1987) And from another reviewer: "His easy bravura is always at the service of the music and his playing is full of affectionate insights and imaginative touches." (*Gram*, Jan 1987) The basic complaint about the CD stems from its length—only 37 minutes of playing time!

Douglas has recorded Tchaikovsky's Grand Sonata in G Major, op. 37, together with some shorter Tchaikovsky compositions (see Discog.). "The sonata's fist-shaking, folk-like first theme as marshalled by Douglas will whirl in your head for days. In the *Romance* and selections from the *Seasons*, Douglas exhibits a wonderful sense of line and spontaneous lyric flow." (*CL*, Sept 1990)

Douglas's second disc for RCA was a solo recital highlighting the Mussorgsky Pictures at an Exhibition plus two Liszt works—the "Dante" Sonata and a transcription of the *Liebestod* from Wagner's *Tristan und Isolde* (see Discog.). The "Pictures" have long been a staple item in his repertoire. "Douglas treats this masterpiece as a musical work of art, not as a vehicle for dumbfounding display. It therefore becomes, in his hands, a superb musical experience, exciting certainly—at times heartwarmingly so—but at all times dedicated to the genius of Mussorgsky and his unforgettable masterpiece." (Matthew-Walker)

Douglas's outstanding technique and his ability to project drama and passion make him a natural Liszt interpreter. Three concerted works—the two Concertos and the Hungarian Fantasy—are combined into one exciting CD, recorded with the assistance of the London Symphony Orchestra, Jun'ichi Hirokami conducting (see Discog.). One reviewer points out the splendid collaboration between conductor and soloist, and gives Douglas high marks for his technique, power and splendid articulation in complex passages: "More impressive, however, is a feeling for tempo relationships, an ability to characterize, to organize, and to communicate. . . . This offering is at the top of my list, and is in fact one of the finest concerto recordings I've ever heard." (*ARG*, May/June 1991)

Another Douglas CD contains the Liszt Sonata in B Minor, some smaller, late Liszt works, the Berg Sonata and Webern's Variations (see Discog.). One critic noted Douglas's skill in the austere Variations and his eloquent presentation of "the ebbs and flows of the Berg sonata." But, he continued, although Douglas played the Liszt Sonata with feeling, "on the whole, his faults are more in evidence here than his virtues. His vaunted technique seems clumsy, his tone clangorous and percussive, and it lacks propulsion and coherence." (*ARG*, March/April 1993)

Beethoven's Sonata in B-flat Major, op. 106, the mighty "*Hammerklavier*," is one of his acknowledged masterpieces for solo piano, and it is also one of the most difficult to perform successfully. Technique, articulation, phrasing, pedaling, architectural concept, all these and more must be under total control for a convincing reading. Douglas became attached to this work as a teenager, and it was in his repertoire by 1984. He performed the sonata many times before playing it on his 1988 Carnegie Hall debut recital and his recording shows just how far he has come in artistic maturity. From one review: "This is a broadly conceived, firmly controlled *Hammerklavier* that I enjoyed first and foremost for its honest-to-goodness musical truth." (*Gram*, June 1988)

More recently, Douglas has recorded an all-Prokofiev program, including the Sonata No. 2 in D Minor, op. 14, and the Sonata No. 7 in B-flat Major, op. 83 (see Discog.)—a challenge to even the finest pianists. Douglas gives a "masterly account" of the Second Sonata. "One has the distinct feeling that he has fully assimilated this music before committing it to disc. . . . Even when Prokofiev is in his muscular, knockabout mood, as in the second movement scherzo, and the fleet-footed finale, Douglas is always careful to temper any abrasiveness with an acute awareness for melodic shape and lyrical parentheses." (*Gram*, March 1992)

SELECTED REFERENCES

Bargreen, Melinda. "Pianist has to fight 'pretty face' publicity." *Seattle Times*, 26 Feb 1989.

Duchen, Jessica. "Quality Not Quantity." *Gramophone*, March 1992, p. 22.

Elliott, Susan. "Trying to Avoid the One-Genre Trap." *New York Times*, 22 July 1990, sec. 2, pp. 21, 26.

Finn, Robert. "Irishman is own man at keyboard." *Cleveland Plain Dealer*, 5 July 1987, sec. H, p. 7.

Ford, Jessica. "Barry Douglas' RFH debut." *Music and Musicians*, Jan 1983, pp. 33–34.

Howell, Georgina. "Starting On a High Note." *Sunday Times* (London), 21 Sept 1986 (Magazine), p. 57.

Isenberg, Barbara. "Starplayer: The Marketing of Barry Douglas." *Los Angeles Times*, 8 May 1988, CAL, pp. 8–9, 25–27.

Johnson, Stephen. "From Belfast to Beethoven." *Gramophone*, June 1988, p. 17.

———. "Piano Pictures." *Gramophone*, May 1987, p. 1512.

Marum, Lisa. "Barry Douglas, Pianist." *Ovation*, Feb 1987, p. 50.

Matthew-Walker, Robert. "Barry Douglas." *Music and Musicians*, May 1987, pp. 9–11.

Morrison, Richard. "Find your own rhythm." *The Times* (London), 19 Jan 1988, p. 16.

Reich, Howard. "The competition has just begun for Barry Douglas." *Chicago Tribune*, 22 July 1987, sec. 5, p. 3.

Schonberg, Harold C. "Enter Barry Douglas, an Irish Pianist With the Touch of a Winner." *New York Times*, 8 April 1988, pp. 13, 19.

Shulgold, Marc. "Pianist Barry Douglas: Mr. Low Key." *Los Angeles Times*, 3 Dec 1986, sec. 6, p. 8.

Tompkins, Kate M. "Barry Douglas." *Musical America*, Sept 1988, pp. 6, 10.

See also Bibliography: IWWM.

SELECTED REVIEWS

AJ: 5 Dec 1987; 24 March 1988. *BaS*: 21 March 1988; 28 Sept 1989. *BT*: 20 Nov 1990. *CT*: 23 July 1987; 23 July 1990. *DMN*: 9 Nov 1991. *DO*: 12 March 1991. *DP*: 24 Oct 1991. *DT*: 4 July 1986; 1 May 1987. *ES*: 28 Sept 1989. *GM*: 4 July 1986. *IrT*: 21 Nov 1990. *LAT*: 5 Sept 1988; 10 March 1989; 28 July 1989; 5 Nov 1991; 5 Feb 1994. *MA*: Jan 1988. *MT*: Jan 1986. *NewY*: 25 April 1988. *NYT*: 4 July 1986; 10 April 1988; 12 March 1990; 26 July 1990. *PI*: 21 Oct 1989. *SLPD*: 14 Oct 1989. *STL*: 8 Feb 1987; 2 Aug 1987. *TC*: 25 March 1991. *TL*: 13 Feb 1980; 23 March 1987; 1 May 1987; 31 July 1987. *WP*: 21 March 1988; 20 July 1994.

SELECTED DISCOGRAPHY

Beethoven: Sonata in C Major, op. 53; Sonata in F Minor, op. 57; Sonata in E
   Minor, op. 90. RCA Victor 09026-61280-2.
Beethoven: Sonata in B-flat Major, op. 106 ("*Hammerklavier*"); Andante Favori.
   RCA 7720-2.
Berg: Sonata, op. 1. Liszt: *Elegie* 2; *Nuages gris*; *Richard Wagner-Venezia*;
   Schlaflos; *Frage und Antwort*; Sonata in B Minor. Webern: Variations, op.
   27. RCA 09026-61221-2.
Brahms: Concerto No. 1 in D Minor, op. 15. RCA 7780-2. Skrowaczewski/
   London SO.
Brahms: Concerto No. 1 in D Minor, op. 15. *Melodiya* Australia MA3012 and
   Olympia/Conifer OCD 137. Sinaisky/USSR SO.
Liszt: Concerto No. 1 in E-flat Major; Concerto No. 2 in A Major; Hungarian
   Fantasia. RCA 7916-2. Hirokami/London SO.
Liszt: "Dante" Sonata. Mussorgsky: Pictures at an Exhibition. Wagner-Liszt:
   Isolde's Liebestod. RCA 5931-2. Also Musical Heritage Society MHS
   512953H (CD).
Prokofiev: *Amoroso*, op. 102, no. 4; March, op. 33ter; Sonata No. 2 in D
   Minor, op. 14; Sonata No. 7 in B-flat Major, op. 83; Waltz, op. 97, no.
   10; Waltz (War and Peace). RCA 60779-2.
Rachmaninoff: Concerto No. 2 in C Minor, op. 18; Preludes, op. 3, no. 2, op.
   23, nos. 2–7. RCA 09026 61679-2. Thomas/London SO.
Tchaikovsky: Concerto No. 1 in B-flat Major, op. 23. RCA 5708-2.
   Slatkin/London SO.
Tchaikovsky: Grand Sonata in G, op. 37; Romance in F, op. 51, no. 5; The
   Seasons, op. 37b ("May," "June," "August," "September," "October").
   RCA 7887-2.

VIDEO

Rachmaninoff: Concerto No. 2 in C Minor, op. 18. With Michael Tilson
   Thomas and the London Symphony Orchestra. RCA (Red Seal) 09026
   61786-3. Volume 4 of *Dudley Moore introduces Concerto!*

E

ENTREMONT, PHILIPPE: b. Reims, France, 7 June 1934.

> I think that my conducting has helped my playing immensely in terms of discipline, testing myself and developing a concept of the sound. I understand the total picture immeasurably better. It has also made me a more secure person, perhaps because I am now a happier person.
>
> Philippe Entremont (*Music Magazine*, May/June 1984)

"In Tunis the concert piano was so dirty he had to ask them to clean it. They did, with a hose, leaving the piano unsoiled but drowned. In South America the French Embassy sent him on a concert tour so deep into the interior that there were no pianos to play. In a Johannesburg concert he played the Rachmaninoff Second Concerto until three of the piano's legs collapsed." (Elder, "Philippe Entremont on Tour")

Philippe Entremont's life as a traveling pianist certainly has had its frustrating moments; but all things considered, he appears to have been destined for the concert life and would have it no other way. He is the son of professional musicians, his father Jean Entremont being a conductor and his mother Renée (Monchamps) Entremont a pianist, music teacher and former *Grand Prix* winner. Entremont remembers music study with his mother before he had reached age six, much of it solfège training, and that after years of "reading notes and rhythms," he advanced rapidly.

At about age eight he began private lessons in Paris with the famous Marguerite Long, pianist and pedagogue at that time retired from the Paris Conservatory. Although Entremont already had nearly four years of piano study behind him, he was so frightened at the thought of playing for the great Madame Long that at the audition he played his prepared piece entirely in the wrong key. Sufficiently impressed with his talent to overlook his nervousness, Madame accepted him as a pupil, and he had three highly disciplined (he called them "oppressive") years with her. An inflexible, demanding teacher, Madame Long ordered him to play her way—the only way, she insisted. He rebelled at times and she, he later realized, must have "despaired sometimes, seeing the negativeness of my approach. But she was wonderful, had a good heart." (Elder, "Philippe Entremont . . .") Most important, Marguerite Long taught him a great deal about sound and technique.

Entremont was awarded the Harriet Cohen Medal when he was only age 12, the same year he enrolled at the Paris Conservatory, primarily to study piano with Jean Doyen. The first year he won a first prize in solfège; at age 14 he won first prize in chamber music; at age 15 he earned his *Premier Prix* in piano. Despite his differences with Mme. Long, Entremont studied with her for another three years after graduating from the Conservatory.

He made his professional debut in Barcelona, Spain, in 1951. A contestant in the 1952 Queen Elisabeth of Belgium Competition in Brussels, Entremont ranked a disappointing tenth place behind first-prize winner Leon Fleisher. However, one critic, voicing the opinion that Fleisher and Entremont showed fairly equal innate talent, specifically mentioned Entremont's "magnificent playing of the Rachmaninoff Second Concerto . . . against special odds of a conductor who did not share his eminently correct tempos." (*NYT*, 8 June 1952) Entremont placed first in the prestigious Marguerite Long Competition in Paris in 1953 and, as so often happens, winning a gold medal brought the recognition needed to start a concert career. Entremont was prepared, for though just age 19, he had already acquired a substantial repertoire.

That same year (1953) he was chosen to tour the United States on an exchange program between the *Jeunesses Musicales de France* (part of the international movement begun in Belgium in the 1940s to promote talented young artists) and the National Music Council in New York. He made his American recital debut (4 Jan 1953) at the National Gallery in Washington, D.C., and the following day made his orchestral debut at Carnegie Hall with the National Orchestral Association, Leon Barzin conducting. Entremont's second American tour, under the same auspices, included a solo recital (1 April 1955) at the Grace Rainey Rogers Auditorium in New York. In 1956 his debut with the Philadelphia Orchestra and Eugene Ormandy led to an especially close relationship with that orchestra. Entremont became such a favorite with Philadelphia audiences that he was the first nonresident to be named "Goodwill Ambassador." Since that beginning in the 1950s, Entremont's many tours have covered the world.

Like pianists Vladimir Ashkenazy and Daniel Barenboim, Philippe Entremont is now recognized as both pianist and conductor. Taking up the baton came naturally. As a boy he had often attended his father's orchestra rehearsals (at age 13 he spent a whole month just with *Falstaff*), and had become acquainted with the orchestral repertoire. Now, after more than 20 years on the podium, Entremont obviously is immensely happy in his dual role. He actually began conducting, he says, "almost against my will. . . . I was asked by Columbia Records to record two Mozart concerti. They asked if I would be willing to conduct from the keyboard. I'm sure they were trying to save money. It was like a snowball; I have never stopped since." (Fruchter)

In 1975 the Vienna Chamber Orchestra engaged Entremont for a tour, the following year appointed him as music director, and in 1981 appointed him "conductor for life." He has led this ensemble, his great pride and joy, on tours of Europe, Japan, South America and North America. He has also been conductor for the New Orleans Philharmonic Symphony (1980–86), the Denver Symphony Orchestra (1986–89) and the *Orchestre Colonne* of Paris, beginning with the 1988–89 season. Entremont was recently appointed principal conductor of the Netherlands Chamber Orchestra in Amsterdam.

Entremont's hectic schedule (solo recitals, concerto performances, conducting engagements, recording) allows little time for teaching, but he enjoys working with students whenever possible. Between 1973 and 1980 he gave summer master classes (and was also director) at the *Académie Internationale de Musique Maurice Ravel* at St. Jean-de-Luz, France, an institution providing master classes on the interpretation of French music for young musicians of professional quality.

In the early years of his career Entremont played so often he became known as a "workhorse pianist." Even now he can be active 10 months a year, usually playing well over 100 concerts (as either soloist or conductor) spread over all five continents. But the indefatigable Entremont keeps telling interviewers how much he enjoys what he is doing, that his salvation lies in staying busy. Somehow, "he manages to run two orchestras, practice a couple of hours a day, and keep up his golf game. He also loves movies, museums and a good laugh." (Gray)

In recognition of Entremont's talent and hardworking career, France has made him a *Chevalier de la Légion d'honneur* and an *Officier de l'ordre national du mérite*. More recently Austria awarded him the First Class Cross of Honor for the Arts and Sciences. Entremont and his wife (m. Andrée Ragot 21 Dec 1955) lived in Vienna for many years but in 1993 moved back to Paris.

Entremont gets bored practicing technical exercises simply for the sake of technique, thus his practice sessions, usually three or four hours a day, consist largely of learning new works. At one time his substantial repertoire ranged from Beethoven to Gershwin, with emphasis on the brilliant Romantic masterworks. His more recent repertoire consists largely of Mozart, Haydn, the French composers and some Romantic music. In 1984, when asked by an interviewer what repertoire he preferred, Entremont replied, "We have Mozart and then the others." (Adamick)

This well-trained and immensely gifted musician has honed his inborn talent to a fine point of musical craftsmanship, and whatever the period or style of music, his playing bristles with (say reviewers) "vitality," "gusto," "brio," "brilliance." Entremont is known for his elegant style, fluent technique and expressive tone. Perhaps most fittingly, he "is one of those pianists without overwhelmingly universal appeal who nevertheless, by their very versatility, seem to have appeal for *everyone*." (Jones)

On the negative side, Entremont has been faulted, especially early in his career, for a lack of tone, for playing everything with the same tonal characteristics. Some reviewers even mention an unattractive tone quality, particularly in high-intensity playing. Other criticisms include the use of a mannered *rubato* in Chopin, a sometimes cavalier approach to details, a disregard for dynamic markings and overuse of pedal. These are, of course, just some of the highly subjective reactions which every artist appearing before the public must expect.

For his first American appearance with orchestra, Entremont chose to play the Liszt Concerto No. 1 and to give the American premiere of André Jolivet's complex, rhythmically venturesome Piano Concerto, written in 1950. On 5 January 1953 he played the concertos at Carnegie Hall with the National Orchestral Association, Leon Barzin conducting. Entremont was in his element with the Jolivet: "It was a performance done with the spirit and fire of youth, plus a technical and musical mastery of an extremely talented musician. The performance . . . brought down the house." However, the same critic felt that Entremont "showed his superficial feeling for Liszt's concerto—though he played it brilliantly enough." (*NYT*, 6 Jan 1953)

Entremont played the Jolivet Concerto again at his Philadelphia debut (2 Nov 1956) with Eugene Ormandy and the Philadelphia Orchestra. He also played the Rachmaninoff "Paganini" Rhapsody, but the Jolivet was the intriguing item, as was the soloist. Entremont had "speed, big tone, a sense of soul, flair. . . . Entremont played with a momentum that swept all before him. Few in the audience liked the Jolivet concerto much at first, but when the final notes faded there was a roar of approval." (*Time*, 12 Nov 1956)

At his first appearance (4 Jan 1958) with Leonard Bernstein and the New York Philharmonic Orchestra, Entremont played the Prokofiev Concerto No. 3 in C Major, a vehicle to test any soloist's technique. Entremont showed "great technical dash and accuracy, a sure sense of what he wanted from the piano and an ability to communicate his excitement to the audience." (*NYT*, 6 Jan 1958)

He has been a frequent participant at Lincoln Center's Mostly Mozart summer festivals. On 12 August 1971 he played two Mozart sonatas (K. 331 and K. 576), the Fantasy, K. 297, *plus* the great Schubert posthumous Sonata in B-flat Major. A reviewer who felt that the Schubert, a difficult work to bring off convincingly, was overinterpreted, still liked the overall program: "Philippe Entremont plays the piano with an appealing mixture of insouciance and confident charm. When his technical equipment is under reasonable control, as it was in his recital . . . one is certain to hear a good deal of pleasant music-making." (*NYT*, 14 Aug 1971) At another Mostly Mozart concert (10 Aug 1973) Entremont, in his dual role of pianist-conductor, played three Mozart concertos—K. 453 in G Major; K. 467 in C Major; K. 488 in A Major—to mixed critical reaction. "Considering the technical problems involved, Mr. Entremont did his job with skill and flair, although the performances did not always jell satisfactorily." While the ensemble frequently lacked real precision and sometimes covered up the soloist, "otherwise these readings had plenty of dash with safe, sensible tempos." (*NYT*, 12 Aug 1973)

On 7 March 1975 Entremont, commemorating the centenary of Ravel's birth, played an all-Ravel recital at New York's Avery Fisher Hall. His Ravel was persuasive: "He negotiates complex figurations fluently, the piano tone is silvery and cool, the playing is expressive without becoming overwrought, and a keen Gallic intelligence is in control." (*NYT*, 9 March 1975) And Entremont's performance (5 March 1983) of the Ravel Concerto in G with the Memphis Symphony Orchestra, Akira Endo conducting, "gave the feeling of impetuosity at the keyboard, along with the suggestion of insouciance that this score demands. He was altogether impressive and made the concerto tingle as only a pianist of great polish can do." (*CA*, 6 March 1983)

A Mozart evening (10 Dec 1985) in London's Queen Elizabeth Hall with Entremont and the Vienna Chamber Orchestra disappointed one critic. In the Concerto in E-flat Major, K. 271, "the piano sounded strangely muffled, as if the soloist's left foot were permanently depressing the soft pedal. It was not, I hasten to add, but that did not prevent the performance from lumbering." (*TL*, 12 Dec 1985) But at a 1987 Kansas City recital Entremont gave a very special reading of the Mozart Sonata in A Major, K. 331, playing "with utmost simplicity . . . always stressing the purity and sweetness of the melodies and playing with a wondrously light, poetic touch." (*KCT*, 12 Jan 1987)

Extensive worldwide touring and many New York recitals have established Entremont as one of the finest pianists active today. Currently Entremont the conductor (or conductor-pianist) seems to perform more often than Entremont the recitalist, but one hopes that he will strive to maintain his standards of excellence as a pianist, the role that brought him international recognition.

"As a young pianist Philippe Entremont epitomized the snappy, splashy, tempestuous virtuoso, earning him the label '*Le Pianiste Atomique*' from *Paris France-Soir*. His recordings (which have helped immensely in building his career) have the same characteristics." (Elder, "Philippe Entremont . . .") Entremont's recordings—as of 1989 he had 124 to his credit—have frequently won awards: the Edison Prize (1968), a Grammy Award (1972), three times a *Grand Prix du Disque* (1965, 1968, 1975).

Considering the fact that during the 1960s Entremont recorded virtually all of Chopin's solo piano music, it is surprising that only a portion exists in CD format. The one Odyssey album, however, stands as a fine example of his Chopin playing (see Discog.). For example, Entremont plays the waltzes beautifully, if objectively. "Actually, they could stand a *bit* more sentiment; there are moments when they take on a certain glacial glibness that is not very appropriate. These performances have a rhythmic drive and a purely pianistic verve that is quite exciting nevertheless." (Jones) The other compositions—ballades, scherzos—no less than the waltzes, equally project Entremont's Chopin playing style: elegant, technically superb, rhythmically vital but with an occasional tendency to sound "uninvolved" and to use *rubato* in an academic or mannered way.

He originally recorded Bartók's Concertos Nos. 2 and 3 with Leonard Bernstein and the New York Philharmonic Orchestra for a Columbia stereo album. Now those concertos, together with some other Bartók compositions, have been released on a Sony CD (see Discog.). "Entremont gives a good account of himself here. Tonally, his work is moderately restricted, but it is neither bleakly percussive nor overromantically inflected. His freewheeling, declamative extroversion fits in well with Bernstein's similarly debonair point of view." (*RIR*, 1970)

In 1960 Entremont recorded the Rachmaninoff Concerto No. 2 in C Minor, also with Leonard Bernstein and the NYPO. Presently it appears on a CD together with the "Paganini" Rhapsody plus several Preludes (see Discog.). An early reviewer gave the concerto performance high marks: "They play the uncensored, frankly impassioned, insistent score of the Concerto in C minor with all the fervor and natural sympathy it arouses in them. The result is a performance of manly eloquence. Entremont, the pianist, has the strength of steel, but he is never brutal." (*NYT*, 21 Aug 1960)

Entremont also recorded two other Rachmaninoff concertos—Nos. 1 and 4—with his favorite conductor and orchestra, Ormandy and the Philadelphia Orchestra. These are fortunately in reissue (see Discog.) along with the "Paganini" Rhapsody, also with Ormandy. Reviewers have been enthusiastic: "Finally! These are certainly the best recordings of both concertos. . . . How 'authentic' can you get? Entremont simply had to take his place in Ormandy's interpretations of two beautiful concertos." (*ARG*, Jan/Feb 1992)

In the late 1970s Entremont recorded all five Saint-Saëns Concertos with the Toulouse Capitole Orchestra under the baton of Michel Plasson. There are currently three recordings of the complete set—by Rogé, Ciccolini and Entremont. One critic with a seemingly good understanding of this style evaluates and compares the last two. For him, Entremont "is a pianist of skill and aplomb, fully equal to their technical demands, and he shows some understanding of the style. Nevertheless his tone often tends to harshness, and he fails to reveal all the wit in the writing." (*Gram*, May 1990) This reviewer finds the Ciccolini set to be more idiomatic, with a better piano quality and a more natural balance between soloist and orchestra.

Entremont, the quintessential French musician, has made an international career as a superb concert pianist and skilled conductor. His talent, his boundless energy, his winning personality, have placed him among the most illustrious musicians of our day.

SELECTED REFERENCES

Adamick, Paula. "The Esprit and Style of Philippe Entremont." *Music Magazine*, May/June 1984, pp. 18–19.
Chism, Olin. "Playful pessimism about the piano." *Dallas Morning News*, 9 Sept 1993.
Elder, Dean. "Philippe Entremont: 'Le Pianiste Atomique'." *Clavier*, March 1980, pp. 18–20.
———. "Philippe Entremont On Tour." *Clavier*, Feb 1994, pp. 8–12, 44.
Entremont, Philippe. "A French Sampler." *High Fidelity Magazine*, Nov 1971, pp. 32, 40.
Fruchter, Rena. "Conducting That Began by Chance." *New York Times* (N.J. ed.), 21 April 1991, p. 14.

Gray, Channing. "Famed French pianist to play the 'dead hall'." *Providence Journal*, 30 March 1990.

Gruen, John. "The Frenchman in New Orleans." *New York Times*, 3 Jan 1982, sec. 2, pp. 15, 20.

Jones, Robert T. "The art of Philippe Entremont." *American Record Guide*, March 1969, pp. 538–540.

Methuen-Campbell, James. "Voyage of Discovery." *Records and Recording*, Aug 1979, pp. 38–39.

"Philippe Entremont." Philadelphia Academy of Music program, 21 April 1968.

Schwartz, Jerry. "Visiting maestro doubles as pianist." *Atlanta Journal*, 5 Jan 1984, sec. C, p. 1.

Tucker, Marilyn. "Philippe Entremont: A Collector of Careers." *San Francisco Chronicle*, 27 Sept 1980, p. 35.

Webster, Daniel. "Pianist-conductor has lots to keep him busy." *Philadelphia Inquirer*, 12 July 1981, sec. F, p. 5.

See also Bibliography: Cur/Bio (1977); Dub/Ref; Eld/Pia; Ewe/Mu; IWWM; New/Gro; WWF.

SELECTED REVIEWS

CA: 6 March 1983. *CG*: 31 March 1983. *CPD*: 4 Aug 1975. *DP*: 18 Jan 1985; 17 March 1986. *GM*: 17 June 1961. *KCT*: 12 Jan 1987. *LAT*: 10 Jan 1969; 6 April 1970; 12 April 1976; 21 March 1977; 24 Oct 1977. *MA*: 15 Jan 1958. *NYP*: 9 Aug 1977. *NYT*: 8 June 1952; 6 Jan 1953; 2 April 1955; 6 Jan 1958; 27 March 1965; 13 Jan 1967; 14 Aug 1971; 12 Aug 1973; 9 March 1975; 17 Aug 1975; 3 Aug 1982; 4 April 1983; 18 Nov 1988. *SLPD*: 17 May 1982. *SLT*: 28 Feb 1980. *SPPP*: 25 April 1986. *Time*: 12 Nov 1956. *TL*: 10 March 1958; 28 June 1977; 19 Dec 1977; 2 March 1981; 12 Dec 1985. *WP*: 24 March 1980. *WS*: 2 July 1977.

SELECTED DISCOGRAPHY

Bartók: Concerto No. 2; Concerto No. 3; Concerto for 2 Pianos, Percussion and Orchestra; Concerto No. 2 for Violin and Orchestra; Rhapsodies for Violin and Orchestra. Sony Classical SMK 47511. Bernstein/NYPO.

Chopin: Ballades (4); Scherzos (4); Waltzes (19). Odyssey MB2K 45670 (2 CDs).

Debussy: Children's Corner; *Clair de lune*; *Deux Arabesques*; *Feux d'artifice*: *Images*, Books 1 & 2; *Pour le piano*. Sony Classical SBK 48174 (CD).

Entremont Plays Piano Favorites. Columbia MG 35185. A 2-LP album containing 22 well-known keyboard "favorites."

Franck: Symphonic Variations; Symphony in D Minor. Odyssey MBK 46276 (CD). Dutoit/PO.

The Gershwin Album. Concerto in F; Rhapsody in Blue; An American in
  Paris; Porgy and Bess (A Symphonic Picture). Columbia MG 30073 (2
  LPs). Ormandy/PO.
Grieg: Concerto in A Minor, op. 16. Saint-Saëns: Concerto No. 2 in G Minor,
  op. 22. CBS MYK-37805 (CD). Ormandy/PO.
Haydn: Piano Concerti. Concerto in D Major, Hob. XVIII:11; Concerto in C
  Major, Hob. XIV:12; Concerto in G Major, Hob. XVIII:4. Musical
  Heritage Society MHS 9027F(cassette). Entremont/Vienna CO.
Haydn: Piano Concerti, Vol. 2. Concerto in G Major, Hob. XIV:13; Concerto
  in F Major, Hob. XVIII:2; Concerto in F Major, Hob. XVIII:3; Concerto in
  C Major, Hob. XVIII:5. MHS 9176T (cassette) Entremont/Vienna CO.
Haydn: Piano Concerti, Vol. 3. Concerto in C Major, Hob. XIV:4; Concerto in
  F Major, Hob. XVIII: 7; Concerto in G Major, Hob. XVIII:9; Concerto in
  C Major, Hob. XVIII:10. MHS 9329W (cassette). Entremont/Vienna CO.
Liszt: Concerto No. 1 in E-flat Major; Concerto No. 2 in A Major
  (Ormandy/PO); Hungarian Fantasia (Ozawa/New PO); Sony Classical SBK
  48167 (CD). .
Mozart: Concerto in A Major, K. 414; Concerto in E-flat Major, K. 449. Koch
  Schwann 311157 (CD). Entremont/Vienna CO.
Mozart: Sonatas (complete). Pro Arte CDD-498, 499, 3410, 3411 (4 CDs).
Rachmaninoff: Concerto No. 1 in F-sharp Minor, op. 1; Concerto No. 4 in G
  Minor, op. 40; Rhapsody on a Theme of Paganini, op. 43. Sony Classical
  SBK 46541 (CD). Ormandy/PO.
Rachmaninoff: Concerto No. 2 in C Minor, op. 18; Preludes in C-sharp Minor,
  op. 3, no. 2; D Minor, op. 23, no. 3; E-flat Major, op. 23, no. 6; Rhap-
  sody on a Theme of Paganini, op. 43. Odyssey MBK 46271 (CD).
  Bernstein/NYPO.
Ravel: Concerto in G; Concerto in D (Left Hand); Gershwin: Concerto in F.
  Sony Classical SBK 46338 (CD). Boulez/Cleveland Orchestra.
Ravel: The Piano Works. Odyssey MB2K 45611 (2 CDs).
Saint-Saëns: Piano Concertos (5). CBS Odyssey MB2K 45624 (2 CDs).
  Plasson/*Orchestre du Capitole de Toulouse.*

$$\mathcal{F}$$

FELTSMAN, VLADIMIR: b. Moscow, USSR, 8 January 1952.

> I came here with very strict goals, very certain ideas. My idea was to
> be active and to play the piano. I think I've succeeded. I'm playing
> with major orchestras, and not only in America. I'm making records.
> So I'm having a perfectly normal, healthy musical life.
>   Vladimir Feltsman (*Louisville Courier-Journal*, 5 March 1989)

The unprecedented musico-political tale of Vladimir Feltsman effectively contra-
dicts the generally accepted truism that politics and the arts do not make for the
most compatible bedfellows. Indeed, it was political intervention that brought
Feltsman out of musical limbo in the USSR and, with much fanfare, launched
his musical career in the West.

Feltsman himself has never been political. He is the only child of
well-to-do parents. Both had studied at the Moscow Conservatory, and his father
Oskar Feltsman became a prominent composer of popular music. By Communist standards, Feltsman grew up in luxury; by any standards, he lived in a rich
cultural environment. Every season he went "hundreds of times" to hear concerts
at Bolshoi Hall or in the Small Hall of the Moscow Conservatory. Music and
musicians, not politics and politicians, dominated his life.

Not a startling child prodigy, Feltsman was more than six years old
when he began piano lessons with his mother Eugenia. A year later, enrolled at
Moscow's Central Music School, he became a pupil of Yevgeny Timakhin, who
had studied with the famous Russian pedagogue Konstantin Igumnov. As
Feltsman remembers it, he was about ten years old before he became serious
about music, meaning that he began serious practicing. For about five months

he practiced two or three hours a day, improving his technique with Hanon, Czerny, Cramer and Clementi studies. And he must have worked very hard. He was only 11 years old when he played the Beethoven Concerto No. 1 with the Moscow Philharmonic Orchestra.

At age 13 Feltsman played Kabalevsky's Concerto No. 3 with the orchestra of the Bolshoi Theater, and at age 15 he won first prize at the Concertina International Competition in Prague, Czechoslovakia. He was then accepted at the Moscow Conservatory and assigned to Professor Yakov Flier. Professor and pupil disagreed on the matter of repertoire. Flier wanted Feltsman to play more Russian works; Feltsman loved the Austro/German repertoire, and insisted on more Mozart, Beethoven and Schubert, as well as more contemporary works. By age 16 he was permitted to play some public performances, but when he began to program music by Olivier Messiaen, he had to fight with the authorities to be allowed to put the titles of the sacred pieces on the concert posters.

In 1971 the 19-year-old Feltsman won first prize at the prestigious Marguerite Long Competition in Paris, an accomplishment that brought him to the attention of *Gosconcert*, the all-powerful government booking agency (actually agent, manager and promoter all rolled into one). *Gosconcert* arranged more performances for him, and *Melodiya*, the official recording company (then the only one in the USSR), asked him to make some records. Feltsman first recorded the Schumann Sonata in F-sharp Minor and the Brahms *Phantasien*, op. 116; later made a Schubert disc ("Wanderer" Fantasy, Four Impromptus, D. 899); recorded both Chopin concertos and also recorded Kabalevsky's Concertos Nos. 2 and 3.

Feltsman taught at the Moscow Conservatory for two years after his own graduation, and meanwhile *Gosconcert* arranged performances for him. He was even sent outside Russia—twice to Belgium, once to Italy—as an outstanding example of the great musicians trained in the USSR. However, without explanation *Gosconcert* canceled a Feltsman 1972–73 tour of West Germany and Holland. Although he was one of *Gosconcert's* most promising young performers, for some reason Feltsman had been designated "not for export." For five years he was permitted to play only within the Soviet Union and in Prague and Sofia, both cities in Communist countries. But in 1977, after his marriage, Feltsman was sent on a two-month tour of Japan, and in 1978 he was sent on a tour of France. Why he was again "for export" has never been explained, but it seems clear that once Feltsman had married (his wife Anna, a biologist, was never allowed to travel with him), the authorities knew he would return.

At age 26 Feltsman, recognized as one of the USSR's most successful pianists, seemed to have the perfect career. He was giving recitals, playing with the best orchestras, making records and, by Soviet standards, living very well. What he did not have, to any degree, was artistic freedom. In May 1979 Feltsman applied for permission to emigrate to Israel with his family, not for political reasons, only to acquire the freedom to perform—and record—whatever and wherever he liked. However, merely applying for that visa cast Feltsman into musical limbo. Within two hours his tapes were ordered removed from the Moscow Radio library, and radio and television stations were forbidden to broadcast any of his performances. Within a day his records had been removed from all record stores, and two weeks later his engagement with the Moscow Philharmonic Orchestra was canceled just hours before he was to play. As a performing pianist, Feltsman no longer existed.

Shunned for two and a half years—he had not given a single public performance—Feltsman managed to tell his story to the *New York Times*, and the *Voice of America* broadcast the interview. That may be why the Ministry of Culture ordered *Gosconcert* "to give Feltsman a job" to keep him from airing his plight. Hoping to pacify him, *Gosconcert* booked him for about 32 concerts a year, but he had few good engagements and most of the time found himself playing in factories, nursery schools and the like in small provincial towns. He was forced to sell many of his books and scores to support his family, now living in a tiny Moscow studio.

Feltsman may have despaired, but he never gave up. He practiced four or five hours a day, enlarged his repertoire, studied new music, read a great deal, worked on his English and frequently played recitals for friends in his crowded one-room apartment. He fought his deplorable situation by seizing every opportunity to plead his case with Western journalists, visitors and diplomats. The sympathetic American community took up his cause, and on several occasions U.S. Ambassador Arthur A. Hartman invited Feltsman to play at Spaso House, the ambassador's official residence. It was at a Spaso House recital in 1984 that CBS Masterworks clandestinely recorded (with equipment smuggled into Moscow) Feltsman playing the Chopin Preludes, op. 28. The completed tape was smuggled out of the USSR, delivered to CBS in Paris for processing and later released by CBS Masterworks in the United States.

As growing concern over the plight of Jewish *refuseniks* (Soviet Jews not allowed to emigrate) aroused the international community, protests (from colleagues, diplomats and friends) against Feltsman's musical isolation increased accordingly. Concert promoter Norman Gladney had twice applied to *Gosconcert* for permission to have Feltsman perform—in New York (1982) and in Washington, D.C. (1984)—and had twice been refused. In June 1982 the National and Greater New York Conferences on Soviet Jewry had staged a dramatic "in absentia" American debut for Feltsman at New York's Avery Fisher Hall. Feltsman was heard playing (a tape of some of his Moscow performances), but no one was at the piano. Despite pressure from Jewish émigré groups, diplomats and a host of celebrities, nothing really happened until 1987, when Soviet-American cultural relations began to thaw.

After nearly eight years of musical isolation and the consequential notoriety, Feltsman had become a politico-cultural symbol of the world's growing concern about *refuseniks*. With the onset of *glasnost*, President Ronald Reagan, U.S. Secretary of State George Shultz and Ambassador Hartman brought the Feltsman case to Mikhail Gorbachev's attention, and, on 10 April 1987, *Gosconcert* informed Feltsman that he would play a recital on 21 April at the Great Hall of the Moscow Conservatory. According to reports, other *refuseniks*, friends and people from the various diplomatic missions filled the hall to hear Feltsman play his first recital (an all-Schumann program) there in nearly nine years.

Earlier efforts on his behalf now came to fruition. Leslie Gerber, a dealer in rare classical records and classical music programmer for radio station WDST-FM in Woodstock, New York, asked the radio station manager to broadcast a program of Feltsman's recordings. Going further, the manager, aided by the U.S. State Department, arranged a telephone interview with Feltsman. Mr. Gerber also explained Feltsman's situation to Dr. Alice Chandler, President of the State University of New York at New Paltz, and, on a visit to Moscow in January 1987, Dr. Chandler met with Feltsman. In June the Feltsman family received permission to emigrate, and Dr. Chandler sent him a formal proposal offering him a SUNY chair, a distinguished fellowship.

When the 35-year-old Feltsman arrived in America in August 1987, he was still something of a mystery to the musical public, even to record collectors. Only one of his recordings, the smuggled collection of Chopin Preludes, op. 28, made at the American ambassador's residence in Moscow, had come to America. Yet because of the vociferous, high-level pressure put on Feltsman's *refusenik* case, he was an acknowledged success before he arrived, even before he had played a note. As one writer succinctly put it, Feltsman's "starter kit included concerts at the White House and Carnegie Hall, a CBS Masterworks contract and a management deal with Columbia Artists. . . . Mr. Feltsman was also given a teaching post at the State University of New York at New Paltz, at a salary of $80,000 a year." (*NYT*, 14 April 1991) The overpublicized, glossy political wrappings enveloping that "starter kit" achieved instant stardom for Feltsman the political emblem and media darling. It also obscured Feltsman the pianist.

He played a private recital at the White House on 27 September 1987; made his professional American debut at Carnegie Hall on 11 November 1987; and made his orchestral debut (15 Feb 1988) with the New York Philharmonic Orchestra, playing the Brahms Concerto No. 2 in B-flat Major, with Zubin Mehta conducting.

Columbia Artists kept Feltsman extremely busy. During his first three seasons in America he played about 21 concerts in New York alone. He has played with virtually all of the major American orchestras and also played abroad. During his first years in the West he played more than 70 concerts a season, but now prefers to play between 50 and 60. And within his comparatively brief time in America he has been seen on CBS ("60 Minutes"), NBC ("Good Morning America" and "20/20") and PBS ("Live from Lincoln Center"). And of course he holds a secure position at SUNY, New Paltz, where normally he teaches a course in piano literature, takes a limited number of piano majors and also conducts master classes throughout the SUNY system. (For an interesting description of a Feltsman master class, see Gerber, *MA*, Jan 1989.)

Because of all the ballyhoo surrounding his arrival in the United States, Feltsman started at the top of the musical circuit, and there have been problems. It is very possible that all the attention, especially the media promotion, accounts for his acquired reputation for being arrogant, petulant and aloof (onstage and at rehearsals) and for being unfriendly to the public after concerts. It should be pointed out, however, that Feltsman was totally unfamiliar with the American after-concert protocol involving parties and receptions.

As for his playing, often the reviews have been only lukewarm; besides that, in 1989 Sony Classical (formerly CBS Masterworks) announced that his recording contract would not be renewed. They disagreed, says Feltsman, over repertoire. Sony wanted him to record Russian music, Feltsman wanted to record the German repertoire.

Seemingly aware of his image, Feltsman has made a genuine attempt to remedy the personality problems. He has a new recording contract with Music-Masters. Hopefully all will turn out well, for he is a highly talented, serious-minded pianist.

"I don't belong," says Vladimir Feltsman, "to the typical [Russian] school of stormy, athletic playing. . . . I've always been more European-oriented in my musical tastes. I guess about nine-tenths of my repertory is from Central European composers." (*RMN*, 1 Dec 1989) It is true that Feltsman's repertoire encompasses works by Bach, Mozart, Beethoven, Schubert, Schumann, Chopin, Liszt and Brahms; yet, the Feltsman discography and a portfolio of reviews encompassing, but not definitively, his years in the United States show that he does program some works by Russian composers. Mussorgsky's Pictures at an Exhibition appears often on his programs, and, less frequently, so do works by Rachmaninoff (Concerto No. 3, "Paganini" Rhapsody, Prelude in G-sharp Minor, Vocalise), Scriabin (Sonata No. 4), Prokofiev (Sonata No. 8 in B-flat Major) and Tchaikovsky (Concerto No. 1). He often programs excerpts from Olivier Messaien's *Vingt regards sur l'Enfant Jésus*. His concerto performances here in the United States include the Mozart in B-flat Major, K. 595, Beethoven No. 4, Brahms No. 2, Tchaikovsky No. 1, Rachmaninoff No. 3.

Although Feltsman is known for having a very large repertoire, built up during his years of isolation, he claims to be a lazy worker who practices only about three hours a day. Unlike most concert pianists, he loves to play exercises: "I do childish ones like Hanon for a few minutes because I love the feeling of checking my fingers, physically—the sense of well-being. Scales I do sometimes, but never fast and noisy, just in a middle tempo, gently, to be comfortable. . . . Mostly I practice with the ears, not the fingers." (Montparker)

Out of more than 35 Feltsman critiques only six or seven add up to all-out complimentary reviews, yet there is only one wholly negative commentary. Descriptive phrases recurring throughout these reviews overall portray him as an expert craftsman with taste, intelligence, flair, confidence and temperament. His playing is distinctive for a lucid, moderate-sized tone that never turns ugly in loud passages, a solid but not flashy technique, a clean, polished phrasing and moments of individuality. Negative comments dwell on a lack of structural integrity, a habit of overpedaling, a lack of tonal imagination. Critics seem to agree that an intellectual coldness in Feltsman's approach accounts for the excessive refinement in his playing. His performances are "well-crafted but lack warmth," they are "workmanlike rather than compelling."

In his first year or so in the United States, Feltsman's nonmusical fame definitely impinged on assessments of his playing. "Although American critics failed to agree on the exact measure of his musical excellence, they unanimously admired his independence, perseverance and courageous dedication to the integrity of classical music." (Cur/Bio 1988, see Bibliog.) Feltsman reviews covering the last six years provide a more judicious appraisal. On the whole, the exaggerated prediction (Feltsman would prove to be "the greatest Russian pianist of them all") created by the saga of Vladimir Feltsman, not by any piano performances of Vladimir Feltsman, has not come to pass.

His Carnegie Hall debut (11 Nov 1987)—a program including the Schubert Sonata in A Major, D. 664, three selections from Messiaen's *Vingt regards sur l'Enfant Jésus*, Schumann's Symphonic Etudes, op. 13—showed an unquestionably talented, deeply musical performer. "Feltsman owns a big technique, has taste and awareness of different styles, knows how to float and color a phrase and has staying power. The temperament, though somewhat cool in the modern style, breaks out into warmer regions at appropriate times." (*NYT*, 12 Nov 1987)

A Chicago reviewer hearing a repeat (8 Dec 1987) of that Carnegie Hall program admired Feltsman for "dexterity and finger speed as astonishing as those of any virtuoso on the current scene. . . . What he does superbly—one is even tempted to say matchlessly—is to exploit the sound world of music for its own sake, looking to its potential for ecstasy as well as its ability to beguile the ear." (*MA*, May 1988)

At his first appearance (15 Feb 1988) with the New York Philharmonic Orchestra, Zubin Mehta conducting, Feltsman played the Brahms Concerto No. 2—"a solid, musicianly performance [with] enough flashes of individuality to encourage one to want to hear him again. . . . Still, the results were often passionate in the manner of Tchaikovsky rather than persuasively Brahmsian." (*NYT*, 17 Feb 1988)

At his first Minneapolis recital (10 Oct 1988) Feltsman gave a spirited but uneven reading of Mussorgsky's Pictures at an Exhibition. Although each of the movements was more sharply defined in dynamics and tempo than many Western pianists would dare, there were problems. "Feltsman's fingers, though quick, strayed too often from the right notes, especially in thick chordal passages. And his range of pianistic color was very narrow indeed." Specifically, Feltsman's reading of Mozart's C-Minor Fantasy, K. 475, and Schumann's *Kreisleriana* had an unmistakable "Russian" accent; his "lugubrious" Mozart "too often sounded gluey because he refused to lift his fingers and let some air in. . . . He did bring out the wildness of Schumann's vision [*Kreisleriana*], but at the expense of tone quality, phrasing and simple accuracy." (*SPPP*, 12 Oct 1988)

Feltsman's playing at his Philadelphia recital debut (26 March 1991) induced one critic to compare his playing with that of other Russian pianists (Gilels, Richter, Ashkenazy, Gavrilov) known to Western audiences. His conclusion was that Feltsman is not of the same caliber as most of these: "The Schumann received a technically impressive, though stern reading. . . . Expressiveness in the Bach *Partita* was achieved through the slight misalignment of the right hand with the left. The left hand kept the tempo at metronomic regularity, while the right strayed with varying amounts of rubato. The result was a carefully controlled window of tension." (*PI*, 28 March 1991)

Feltsman's "lean, ringing tone and steel-clad technique" earned highest marks at a New York recital (21 Feb 1993) that included Schumann's *Kreisleriana*, the Bach-Busoni Chaconne, Beethoven's Sonata in A-flat Major, op. 110, and the Scriabin Sonata No. 4. Feltsman proved himself to be "a splendid pianist and a serious musician, but sometimes his gifts seem like a suit of armor, one that protects his music from harm but also separates it from the living, feeling and ultimately vulnerable side of human experience." (*NYT*, 23 Feb 1993)

Considering the comparatively few years that Feltsman has been in the West, he has to his credit a respectable discography. In his recording (1984) of the Chopin Preludes (see Discog.), available even before he arrived in the United States, "one hears a pianist of prodigious technique, a big temperament and no little tonal and expressive sensitivity. . . . You get the right sense of variety-within-unity in his readings, plus a searching emotionalism that is very Russian. It is an impressive document, and it makes one want to experience more of Feltsman's art. He is an individual pianist in the grand Romantic manner, that much is certain." (Rhein)

Reviews of Feltsman's Carnegie Hall debut recital (11 Nov 1987), recorded live and issued in a 2-CD format (see Discog.), have been largely favorable. For example, "Messiaen . . . suits Feltsman down to the ground. His greatest strength, to judge from the recital as a whole, is as a colourist. . . . The *Symphonic Studies* are the major work in the recital and the one by which Feltsman's pretensions to star status will be most severely judged. Many of the ingredients of that status are there for all to hear—again, the control of keyboard colour . . . the ability to orchestrate the texture . . . the instinct for creating and sustaining atmosphere." (*Gram*, May 1988) From another critic: "He has a formidable technique, but he uses it judiciously. . . . Above and beyond that, he has intelligence, imagination, rhythmic vitality, lyricism, tenderness, and poetry, particularly in such music as these Schumann études. . . . He captures the mystical, ecstatic atmosphere of the Messiaen [*Vingt regards*] expertly, and with an unusually multifarious tonal palette." (*MA*, July 1988)

In a Liszt recital, recorded in 1988 (see Discog.), Feltsman's reading of the B Minor Sonata is "a bold performance whose boldness convinces. It has an understated expressive force rarely encountered in the world of bland or overemphasized commercial recordings." (*Fan*, March/April 1990) In Feltsman's recording of the Tchaikovsky Concertos Nos. 1 and 3, with Mstislav Rostropovich and the Washington National Symphony Orchestra, his "is a relatively laid back view of the First Concerto. . . . The big first movement cadenza is wonderfully fluid and continuous, and the transition into the following coda is a dream. There is much sensitive dialogue between piano and orchestra, well captured by the recording." (*Gram*, Jan 1991)

Although Feltsman's recordings of the Prokofiev Concertos Nos. 1 and 2 are fine, one reviewer finds both performances too serious, lacking in wit. On the other hand, "it's hard not to admire the sheer technical control. . . . And both concertos are full of impressive interpretive touches: the dramatic tempo-bending in the cadenza-like passage in the First, the almost terrifying, zombie-like conclusion to the third movement of the Second, the exceptional voicing in the quieter music of the finale, the fine interplay between piano and orchestra throughout." (*Fan*, Sept/Oct 1989)

Feltsman's 1978 Paris recording of the Schubert "Wanderer" Fantasy is available, coupled with the *Moments musicaux*, D. 780 (see Discog.). The Fantasy is a superior reading from a superior interpreter: "When Feltsman chooses, he has a tremendous sound, which never degenerates into banging. . . . Where the composer provides no metronome marking, Feltsman interprets tempo indications with a latitude that sometimes startles, but in a revelatory way." The pianist also earns good marks for the *Moments musicaux*: "The way he permits the last of the six . . . just to fade away into nothingness speaks for his commendable humility before his musical material." (*MA*, July 1988)

Feltsman loves Bach, includes Bach in many recitals and has recorded a representative amount of the Bach repertoire. His performance of Bach's Goldberg Variations, recorded live on 26 October 1991 at the Moscow Conservatory, has drawn conflicting reviews. For one critic, the pianist's version "considerably distorts the emotional and structural integrity of what Bach wrote, but he does produce some quite beautiful music." (*ARG*, Jan/Feb 1993) For another critic, Feltsman has recorded "A Golden Goldberg . . . an electrifying performance—technically dazzling yet infused with romantic sensibility—that breathes fresh life into these intricate keyboard exercises." (*Time*, 18 Jan 1993)

Feltsman continued his perusal of Bach in 1992 with an album devoted to Book I of the Well-Tempered Clavier. And the following year he recorded three Bach keyboard concertos, conducting the Orchestra of St. Luke's (see Discog.). The readings in both albums are expectedly romantic *and* beautiful.

SELECTED REFERENCES

Ames, Katrine. "88 Keys to the City." *Newsweek*, 23 Nov 1987, pp. 78–79.
Ardoin, John. "A pianist's quest for the West." *Dallas Morning News*, 8 Sept 1990, sec. C, pp. 1, 3.
Bohlen, Celestine. "Moscow Lifts Ban on Pianist." *Washington Post*, 22 April 1987, sec. C, p. 3.
Cohen, Richard. "The Persistent Pianist." *Washington Post*, 27 Nov 1987, sec. A, p. 27.
Diehl, Jackson. "Soviet Pianist Allowed to Emigrate." *Washington Post*, 7 Aug 1987, sec. A, pp. 1, 26.
Dyer, Richard. "Vladimir Feltsman busy just being himself." *Boston Globe*, 10 July 1988, p. 84.
Ericson, Raymond. "An Isolated Soviet Pianist Plays Chopin's Preludes." *New York Times*, 1 June 1986, sec. 2, p. 26.
Feron, James. "For Pianist, A New Life In the U. S." *New York Times*, 19 Oct 1987, sec. 2, pp. 1–2.
Forsht, James L. "The Secret Concert Of Vladimir Feltsman." *Keyboard Classics*, May/June 1986, pp. 10–11.
Gerber, Leslie. "An Interview with Vladimir Feltsman." *Fanfare*, Jan/Feb 1988, pp. 365–374.

————. "Vladimir Feltsman, Teacher." *Musical America*, Jan 1989, pp. 17–18.

Goodman, Peter. "For Feltsman, A New Life In His Own Key." *Newsday*, 8 Nov 1987, pp. 13, 23.

Holland, Bernard. "For a Cause Célèbre, The Art of Building a Career." *New York Times*, 5 March 1989, sec. 2, pp. 27–28.

Isacoff, Stuart. "Vladimir Feltsman: On The Road Again." *Keyboard Classics*, March/April 1988, pp. 6, 8.

Kozinn, Allan. "Auspicious Debut for a Celebrated Russian Emigré." *Keyboard*, March 1988, pp. 54–56, 60, 62, 65.

McLellan, Joseph. "Feltsman's Rousing Return." *Washington Post*, 23 Nov 1987, sec. B, p. 1.

————. "A Soviet's Star-Spangled Debut." *Washington Post*, 28 Sept 1987, sec. B, pp. 1, 6.

Montparker, Carol. "Vladimir Feltsman: The End of an Eight-Year Odyssey." *Clavier*, Jan 1988, pp. 10–15.

Passy, Charles. "Vladimir Feltsman: Beyond the Hype." *Ovation*, Jan 1989, pp. 21–23.

Rhein, John von. "Secret recording gives public hearing to pianist's struggle to leave USSR." *Chicago Tribune*, 16 March 1986, sec. 13, p. 2.

Schmemann, Serge. "Soviet Pianist Performs, but Not in New York." *New York Times*, 20 June 1982, p. 6.

Schonberg, Harold C. "Vladimir Feltsman Recalls His Years as a Nonperson." *New York Times*, 30 Aug 1987, sec. 2, p. 19.

Stearns, David Patrick. "Born In The USSR." *Gramophone*, May 1988, p. 1556.

Swed, Mark. "Emigré Pianist Is on the Run—and Enjoying It." *Los Angeles Times*, 22 April 1988, sec. 6, pp. 1, 10.

See also Bibliography: Cur/Bio (1988).

SELECTED REVIEWS

BaS: 25 July 1991. *BG*: 20 Jan 1991. *BN*: 26 Oct 1989. *CaT*: 4 Feb 1991. *LAHE*: 18 Jan 1989. *LAT*: 27 April 1988; 18 Jan 1989; 13 July 1989; 18 May 1990. *LADN*: 27 July 1990. *MA*: May 1988. *MH*: 20 Oct 1987. *MJ*: 7 Nov 1989. *ND*: 13 Nov 1987. *NYP*: 13 Nov 1987. *NYT*: 28 Sept 1987; 12 Nov 1987; 17 Feb 1988; 31 Jan 1989; 11 Nov 1992; 19 Dec 1992; 23 Feb 1993; 21 Dec 1993. *PI*: 1 May 1989; 28 March 1991. *SFC*: 24 June 1988. *SPPP*: 12 Oct 1988. *Time*: 23 Nov 1987. *TL*: 26 May 1993. *V-P*: 18 Oct 1988. *WP*: 9 July 1988; 20 Feb 1989; 4 June 1992; 26 Sept 1994. *WT*: 21 Feb 1989.

SELECTED DISCOGRAPHY

Bach, J. S.: Concerto in D Minor, BWV 1052; Concerto in E Major, BWV 1053; Concerto in D Major, BWV 1054. MusicMasters 01612 67132-2. Feltsman/Orch. of St. Luke's.

Bach, J. S.: Goldberg Variations. MusicMasters 01612-67093-2 or MHS
   513260T (CD). Recorded live in Moscow, 1991.
Bach, J. S.: Well-Tempered Clavier, Book I. MusicMasters 01612-67105 (2
   CDs). Also MHS 523458Y.
Beethoven: Sonata in E Major, op. 109; Sonata in A-flat Major, op. 110;
   Sonata in C Minor, op. 111. Music Masters 01612-67098-2. Also MHS
   513654W (CD).
Brahms: Piano Pieces, op. 116, nos. 3, 4.. Schubert: Wanderer Fantasy, D.
   760. Schumann: Sonata No. 1 in F-sharp Minor, op. 11. Russian Disc
   RD CD 11 001.
Chopin: Preludes, op. 28. CBS MK 39966 (CD).
Liszt: *St. François d'Assise: La Prédication aux Oiseaux*; Sonata in B Minor;
   Tre Sonetti del Petrarca. CBS MK 44925 (CD).
Prokofiev: Concerto No. 1 in D-flat Major, op. 10; Concerto No. 2 in G Minor,
   op. 18; "Romeo bids Juliet Farewell" (Romeo and Juliet). CBS MK 44818
   (CD). Thomas/London SO.
Rachmaninoff: Concerto No. 3 in D Minor, op. 30; Rhapsody on a Theme of
   Paganini, op. 43. CBS MK 44761 (CD). Mehta/Israel PO.
Schubert: *Moments musicaux,* D. 780; Wanderer Fantasy, D. 760. CBS MK
   42569 (CD).
Tchaikovsky: Concerto No. 1 in B-flat Minor, op. 23; Concerto No. 3 in E-flat
   Major, op. 75. Sony Classical SK 45756 (CD). Rostropovich/National
   SO.
Vladimir Feltsman: American "Live" Debut. Beethoven: 6 Variations on an
   Original Theme, op. 76. Messiaen: *Noël; Première Communion de la
   Vièrge; Regard des prophètes, des bergers et des Mages* (*Vingt Regards sur
   l'Enfant Jésus*). Rachmaninoff: Prelude, op. 32, no. 12. Schubert: Sonata
   in A Major, D. 664. Schumann: Symphonic Etudes. CBS MZK 44589 (2
   CDs).

FIRKUSNY, RUDOLF: b. Napajedla, Moravia (now Czechoslovakia), 11
   February 1912; d. Staatsburg, New York, 19 July 1994.

> Has anyone ever heard Rudolf Firkušný give a poor recital, or even a so-
> so one? Perhaps, but in this listener's experience, the Czech-born
> pianist is not only one of the finest now performing, but also a remark-
> ably consistent one.
>
>   Donal Henahan (*New York Times,* 7 October 1974)

Rudolf Firkušný's family had a piano, but no one played. In fact, neither his father Rudolf Firkušný, an attorney, nor his mother Karla (Sindelarova) Firkušný
was musical. Firkušný was about four years old when his newly widowed
mother, who had moved with her three children to Brno, realized that her

youngest child could easily pick out tunes on the piano. She arranged lessons with a local flutist, who taught piano to small children; and by the time Firkušný was five he could play tunes by ear and could improvise. His mother took him to the composer Leoš Janáček, at the time head of the Brno Organ School, for advice. At their meeting Firkušný played Dvořak's Eighth Slavonic Dance and his own version of a little chorus from Janáček's opera *Jenufa*. Sufficiently impressed with Firkušnýs playing to overcome his aversion to child prodigies, Janáček agreed to supervise Firkušnýs musical education and to find a good piano teacher for him. There were conditions. Janáček insisted that he must have complete freedom in guiding Firkušnýs musical progress; that the boy must have a good general education and plenty of time for studies; and that while Firkušný could sometimes perform publicly, he could not go on tour. Apparently satisfied, Janáček enrolled Firkušný at the Brno Conservatory to study piano with Růzena Kurzová.

When Firkušný was six, Janáček himself began teaching him elementary theory and composition, "his own kind of harmony," as Firkušný recalled, very special and revolutionary for the time. For each lesson (two a week, lasting from half an hour to two hours) Firkušný had to bring a short original composition for them to go over together. Otherwise the lessons were spontaneous. They might play four hands at the piano, or Firkušný might play Janáček's latest opera for him, or Janáček might demonstrate at the piano. As Firkušný progressed, the lessons (now once a week or whenever Janáček asked to see him) became sessions for playing and analyzing scores (Janáček's scores and some by Stravinsky and Debussy) at the piano. In his own unconventional way, Janáček taught Firkušný to read scores, transpose and, as the pianist explained, "just about everything."

Everything came easily and naturally to Firkušný. Music was not work but more a pleasant hobby, and he advanced rapidly. Janáček also took his small pupil to the theater and opera, especially to the premieres of his own works, and instilled in him a great curiosity about all music, not just piano literature. He treated the boy as an adult, despite his young age, and saw to it that he was not exploited as a child prodigy but allowed to develop as a musician. Janáček's unorthodox training proved to be the greatest influence in Firkušnýs life.

From 1918 until his death in 1928 Janáček was Firkušnýs guide and mentor, even securing financial aid for him and his family, notably from Tomas G. Masaryk, Czechoslovakia's first president. At age 14 Firkušný was sent to the Prague Conservatory to expand his musical horizons and, as Janáček put it, to learn harmony, theory and counterpoint the old-fashioned way. Enrolled as a composer, Firkušný studied composition with Josef Suk, theory with Rudolf Karel and piano with Vilem Kurz. At the same time he still consulted with Janáček about particular interpretations, music in general and new works for study.

Firkušný made his first public appearance (14 June 1922) at age 10 in Prague, playing the Mozart Concerto in D Major ("Coronation") with the Czech Philharmonic Orchestra. At age 14 he made a very successful debut in Vienna, so stunning in fact that agents Gurmann and Knepler offered him a performance contract, a proposal immediately rejected by both Janáček and Kurz. Instead,

Firkušný completed his courses at the Conservatory and at the Gymnasium. At his Conservatory graduation the 17-year-old Firkušný played a piano concerto that he had composed. Even so, he abandoned the idea of becoming a composer. He was playing the piano all the time anyway, he was an excellent sight reader and, besides, he needed to earn money.

He also wanted to get away from Kurz, an excellent but domineering teacher, and study with Alfred Cortot in Paris. Having heard Schnabel's recording of the Brahms Concerto No. 2 and become fascinated with Schnabel's approach, so different from what he had learned, Firkušný also hoped to study with Schnabel in Germany. President Masaryk provided the funds for his protégé to go to Paris, but Firkušný's desire to become a Cortot pupil never materialized. After listening to Firkušný play, Cortot suggested that he needed an audience, not a teacher, and refused to accept him as a student. But Cortot asked him to judge final examinations at the *Ecole Normale* and engaged him to play in a concert he was about to conduct. Firkušný spent about a year (1932–33) in Paris trying to absorb what he called "the French sound."

In the summer of 1933 he studied with Schnabel, who, having left Hitler's Germany, was then at Tremezzo on Lake Como, Italy. Since Vilem Kurz had trained Firkušný exceptionally well in technique and since he was already concertizing, his lessons with Schnabel became discussions about music, with Schnabel often illustrating at the piano. The highly intelligent Schnabel opened up wonderful new possibilities for Firkušný in respect to the music itself, and he taught Firkušný to listen to music in a different way. Schnabel was his last teacher, but Firkušný never stopped refining his interpretations.

He played often in Europe in the 1930s, building an especially fine reputation in his native Czechoslovakia. His first American tour—he made his New York debut on 13 January 1938—was not an overly successful venture. In Prague preparing a tour of France when Germany occupied Czechoslovakia in 1939, Firkušný managed to get to Paris via Switzerland, leaving behind his belongings and music, including an irreplaceable score of Dvořak's Piano Concerto in G Minor—an unpublished copy revised, with Dvořak's permission, by Vilem Kurz. A Belgian diplomat rescued the score and sent it to Firkušný for a performance in Ostend. When the Germans occupied France, he fled to Portugal. With the Dvořak score in hand, he was invited to play in Lisbon and Oporto, performances that helped raise enough money to get him to London (a member of the Czech army in exile, he played recitals for soldiers and Red Cross units), and eventually to America.

In the summer of 1941 Firkušný played the Dvořak Concerto at Ravinia Park, Chicago, under the baton of Sir Thomas Beecham—the first United States performance of that work in 65 years. His Town Hall recital (14 Dec 1941) was, said Firkušný, his real American debut. All seven New York newspapers gave him good reviews, and Columbia Artists offered him a contract. Although well-launched, his career moved slowly during the war years. The needed spark came with a 1943 tour of South America. Booked for about six concerts, Firkušný drew a tremendous response and was invited to extend his tour. Tours in Mexico, Cuba and Central America followed, and in 1946 Firkušný returned to Europe for an extensive tour. He made his first tour of Israel in 1948–49. By that time he had become a fixture on the American concert circuit, playing in 50 cities that season.

Slowly, without fanfare, Rudolf Firkušný built an international reputation. For more than four decades he played all over the world, with some of this century's legendary conductors, and became one of this century's most respected pianists. On 28 May 1990 he played Martinů's Piano Concerto No. 2 with the Czech Philharmonic Orchestra, conducted by Rafael Kubelík, at Prague's Smetana Hall, an event that ended Firkušný's 44 years of voluntary exile—his way of protesting the years of totalitarian subjugation of his homeland. President Vaclav Havel led an emotional standing ovation for Firkušný's performance, and Czechoslovakia showered its famous son with honors: a doctorate from Charles University, the oldest university in Central Europe; the Gold Medal of the Performing Arts Academy of Prague; honorary citizenships from the cities of Prague and Napajedla, his birthplace. He was also made an honorary director of the Prague Conservatory.

Firkušný taught at the Juilliard School of Music from 1965. Because of his busy performance schedule, he took only a small number of advanced students. An American citizen since 1948, he lived in New York with his wife and two children. In 1989 Firkušný received the "Ethnic New Yorker Award" for his contributions to the cultural and communal life of his adopted city. On 19 July 1994 Firkušný died of cancer at his summer home in Staatsburg, New York.

Firkušný was as much renowned for his masterful performances of the Classical and Romantic repertoire (Mozart, Beethoven, Schubert, Brahms, Chopin, Debussy) as he was for his performances of early 20th-century repertoire, not only his beloved Czech music (almost every Firkušný program had at least one work by a Czech composer—Martinů, Smetana, Dussek, Suk, Dvořak, Janáček), but also the music of other contemporary composers (Barber, Menotti, Ginastera, Hanson, Floyd). As recently as the 1990 Edinburgh Festival, Firkušný played a "glorious recital of Czech piano music."

He prepared with about four or five hours of daily practice. Working away from the piano, he tried to recall to mind the composition in question, giving special attention to technically demanding passages and pinpointing any problems. The next step was to play through the entire work very slowly, as if for the first time. The refreshing sincerity, dignity and authority of Firkušný's detailed, beautifully executed interpretations revealed the thoroughness of his preparation and his respect for himself and the music.

Rudolf Firkušný was never a titan of the keyboard. Although possessing the power to unleash a technique that would stun any audience, he early in his career decided against razzle-dazzle flamboyance. He was without question a genuine musician's musician, a pianist whom other pianists made a special effort to hear. Modest and self-effacing, Firkušný was a reliable, unegotistical performer, greatly respected by fellow musicians and by critics. Like the man (courtly, friendly, the quintessential gentleman), his music (subtle, refined, elegant, warm) radiated with an inner serenity and an outward joy. Good taste always prevailed, bravura was inevitably tempered with innate musicianship and a true artistic spirit. Technically he was known for his facile touch, nimble and elegant fingerwork, discreet pedaling and delicate tonal shading.

Firkušný's reviews were for the most part as consistent as his playing style. Four decades ago at his Carnegie Hall recital (14 March 1947), the grand piece of the evening—Schumann's Fantasia in C Major, op. 17—was communicated "with the true romantic feeling; this with all legitimate warmth, ardor, and impetuosity, yet without exaggeration." (*NYT*, 15 March 1947) In another performance (Los Angeles, 1 March 1949) of that great Fantasia, Firkušný, although possessing the means to overwhelm his audience, chose "to be modest, self-effacing and musicianly, rather than flamboyant and spectacular. The final movement, in particular, was as fine a bit of romantic mood painting as one hears in a whole season of recitals." (*LAT*, 2 March 1949)

A New York recital (17 Jan 1968) included Beethoven's Sonata in C Minor, op. 10, no. 1, and Chopin's Sonata in B Minor, op. 58. While one critic wished for a greater range of dynamics, otherwise, especially in the slow movements, "the beautifully turned phrases and the absolute poise of the lyricism were such that the listener could wish for nothing finer." (*NYT*, 18 Jan 1968) In his performance (2 Aug 1977) of Beethoven's Sonata in E Major, op. 109, Firkušný surprised and pleased one reviewer by "treating it not as a ponderous and difficult utterance but rather as a wonderfully intimate lyrical fantasy, subtle and erudite it is true, but glowingly impressive." (*WS*, 3 Aug 1977)

At age 79 Firkušný played (17 Feb 1991) the Brahms Piano Concerto No. 1 with the Seattle Symphony Orchestra, Gerard Schwartz conducting, and clearly demonstrated that he still retained his technique and the elegance, wisdom and beauty of his phrasing: "His Brahms is neither feverish nor bombastic; Firkušný makes his points with the musical equivalents of a paintbrush, not a hammer." (*ST*, 18 Feb 1991)

The same lovely, understated lyricism so often admired in the Firkušný reviews was, interestingly enough, also the cause of negative criticism. The reviewer of a very early Los Angeles recital (28 Feb 1950) concluded that perhaps Firkušný did not achieve the full range of color contrasts on the piano "because he goes a shade too far in his effort to produce tones from a percussion instrument that are invariably soothing and agreeable to the ear." (*LAT*, 1 March 1950) Nearly 30 years later, at a Carnegie Hall recital (5 Dec 1979) Firkušný's performance of Schubert's A Minor Sonata, D. 784, "was beautifully fingered and elegant in style. Yet it did seem to lack something: a forward thrust, a variety of dynamics, the inherent bigness of the work." (*NYT*, 6 Dec 1979)

Some critics even wished for a little harshness to contrast with "all this beautiful tone production." But if, as most of the reviews indicate, Rudolf Firkušný's understated—but heartfelt—lyricism and his love for beautiful sound made him an old-fashioned pianist, "his playing should be cherished for itself and for its rarity." (*LAT*, 25 April 1983)

Despite his long career as concert artist, Firkušný accumulated only a small—but excellent—discography. As of this writing some of the fine LPs (the Capitol album of Debussy pieces and also the pianist's program of Chopin pieces) have not yet been reissued on CD.

In 1983 in Tokyo Firkušný played and recorded some music by three Romantic composers (*Rudolf Firkušný Plays*, see Discog.). Schubert's three Impromptus, D. 946, composed the year of his death, are not heard as often as the more familiar sets, but, as played by Firkušný, they emanate great charm. He also gave fine readings of Brahms's four *Klavierstücke*, op. 119, but the jewel of this Sugano CD are the *Davidsbündlertänze*, op. 6, Schumann's lengthy (28 min.) collection of kaleidoscopic miniatures. All are played with Firkušný's usual consummate musicianship.

In the Classic repertoire, Firkušný's recordings of six Mozart concertos with conductor Ernest Bour and the South-West German Radio Symphony Orchestra project with authority the melding of drama and lyricism that are so inherent in these compositions.

The most valuable of Firkušný's recordings are, arguably, his performances of music by his Czech compatriots. He was raised with this repertoire and actively promoted it throughout his long career. His 1972 LP recording of a program of Janáček pieces for *Deutsche Grammophon* was later transferred to CD. In 1989 Firkušný recorded the same music (with one small change) for RCA (see Discog.). Both versions are excellent (Grammy awards, 1972, 1991), the newer one perhaps benefiting from the performer's ever expanding maturity. "There is a Schubertian element at work here, more in spirit than in any physical sense, which Firkušný locates more consistently than all other players. It may lie in the freedom with which the pianist tackles innate lyricism, the certain and immediate establishment of atmosphere which comes through on record in all of his Janáček performances." (*Fan*, March/April 1991)

Firkušný's recording of Martinů's solo piano music won acclaim for both the composer and the pianist (Grammy 1989). A critic, after a brief discussion of the composer and his style for listeners unaccustomed to this music, described Firkušný's performances as "revelatory, not only of the stature of this music and his love for it, but of a deeply musical pianism; the clarity of his left-hand technique, in particular, is a marvel." (*Gram*, Dec 1989)

In the summer of 1993 Firkušný returned to Czechoslovakia to perform and record Martinů's Concertos Nos. 2, 3, and 4 with the Czech Philharmonic Orchestra. RCA has recently released these superb recordings as a *Rudolf Firkušný Tribute*. From one critic: "These are the finest recordings of all three of these concertos. . . . The pianism is sure. It captures all of the composer's quirky eccentricities and makes them cohesive in a way rarely before heard." (*ARG*, March/April 1995)

SELECTED REFERENCES

"At Least One Czech." *Time*, 20 Feb 1950, pp. 44, 46.

Campbell, Karen. "The Timeless Mastery Of Rudolf Firkušný." *Keyboard Classics*, Nov/Dec 1987, pp. 4–5.

Firkušný, Rudolf. "Rudolf Firkušný: An Old-School Virtuoso Reflects Upon This Century's Piano Traditions." (interview by Kyle Kevorkian). *Keyboard*, June 1987, pp. 20, 23.

"Firkušný's Dvořak." *Newsweek*, 28 Jan 1952, p. 86.

Freed, Richard. "Firkušný's Czech Celebration." *Stereo Review*, Aug 1992, pp. 65–66.

Levinger, Dr. Henry W. "The 'Continental' Approach." *Musical Courier*, July 1956, p. 2.

Lyons, James. "Rudolf Firkušný, Ambassador Without Portfolio to the Musical World." *Musical America*, June 1956, pp. 10, 33.

McLellan, Joseph. "The Long-Playing Success of Rudolf Firkušný." *Washington Post*, 29 April 1990, sec. G, p. 6.

Montparker, Carol. "Rudolf Firkušný: An Aristocrat with a Folk Tradition." *Clavier*, Feb 1984, pp. 12–15.

Mráček, Jaroslav. "Rudolf Firkušný at 75." *Musical America*, March 1987, pp. 14–15.

Obituary. *American Record Guide*, Sept/Oct 1994, p. 30. *New York Times*, 20 July 1994, sec. 2, p. 20.

Pareles, Jon. "A Firkušný Tribute to His Czech Countrymen." *New York Times*, 28 Jan 1983, sec. 3, p. 12.

Pincus, Andrew L. "Rudolf Firkušný: An era in music passes." *Berkshire Eagle*, 7 Aug 1994.

Reich, Howard. "Pianist Firkušný dabs vivid tableau." *Chicago Tribune*, 16 Oct 1988, sec. 5, p. 3.

———. "Soul of a Czech." *Chicago Tribune*, 14 Oct 1988, sec. 5, p. 3.

Rubin, Stephen E. "The Making of a Non-Superstar." *New York Times*, 8 April 1973, sec. 2, p. 19.

Whitney, Craig R. "Rudolf Firkušný Once Again Plays In Czechoslovakia." *New York Times*, 29 May 1990, sec. 3, p. 11.

See also Bibliography: Cur/Bio (1979); Dub/Ref; Ewe/Li2; Ewe/Mu; IWWM; New/Gro; Noy/Pia.

SELECTED REVIEWS

BaS: 16 April 1989. *CE*: 22 Feb 1976. *CPD*: 24 Nov 1986. *CST*: 26 May 1980. *CT*: 26 May 1980; 21 May 1984; 16 Oct 1988. *LAT*: 2 March 1949; 1 March 1950; 27 Jan 1954; 25 April 1983; 1 Nov 1984; 21 Aug 1992; 15 July 1993. *MA*: 25 Dec 1941. *MT*: March 1969; Sept 1984. *NYP*: 23 Aug 1977; 26 Aug 1981. *NYT*: 14 Jan 1938; 15 Dec 1941; 3 Feb 1943; 19 Jan 1946; 15 March 1947; 6 March 1958; 9 Feb 1963; 4 Feb 1964; 18 Jan 1968; 22 Nov 1970; 16 Jan 1974; 6 Dec 1979; 12 Nov 1986; 5 Feb 1988; 29 May 1990. *PI*: 18 July 1986; 18 June 1991; 9 Dec 1992. *SFC*: 3 Nov 1981; 8 Aug 1983. *ST*: 18 Feb 1991. *TL*: 10 Feb 1934; 6 Sept 1957; 26 Sept 1960; 2 Sept 1990. *WP*: 23 July 1983; 16 July 1985; 5 May 1990. *WS*: 3 Aug 1977; 13 Aug 1978.

SELECTED DISCOGRAPHY

Benda: Sonata No. 9 in A Minor. Dussek: Sonata in F Minor, op. 77. Dvořak: Humoresques, op. 101; Mazurkas, op. 56; Poetic Pictures, op. 85; Theme with Variations, op. 36. Smetana: Ten Czech Dances. Tomášek: Eclogue

No. 22 in F Major, op. 35. Voříšek: Impromptu No. 4 in A Major, op. 7. VoxBox2 CDX 5058.

Dvořák: Piano Concerto in G Minor, op. 33; Symphony No. 8. Multisonic 31 0019 (CD). Kubelík/Czech PO.

Dvořák: Concerto in G Minor, op. 33. Janáček: Concertino for Piano and Chamber Ensemble; Capriccio for Piano Left-hand, Brass, and Flute. RCA (Red Seal) 09026-60781-2. Neumann/Czech PO.

Franck: Symphonic Variations; Symphony in D Minor. RCA 60146-2. Flor/Royal PO.

Janáček: In the Mist; On an Overgrown Path; Piano Sonata 1.10.1905 ("From the Street"); "Zdenka" Variations. DG 429 857 (CD) (recorded 1972).

Janáček: In the Mist; On an Overgrown Path; Piano Sonata 1.10.1905 ("From the Street"). RCA 60147 (CD).

Martinů: *Les Ritournelles*; *Fantaisie et Toccata*; Piano Sonata No. 1; Etudes and Polkas: Book I, nos. 2 and 5; Book II, nos. 1, 2, 4 and 5. RCA Victor 7987-2.

Mendelssohn: Concerto in G Minor, op. 25 . Mozart: Concerto in D Major, K. 451; Concerto in C Minor, K. 491. Melodram CDM 18032. Rossi, Pradella, Schippers/*Orch. A. Scarlatti di Napoli.*

Mozart: Concerto in E-flat Major, K. 271; Concerto in D Major, K. 451; Concerto in B-flat Major, K. 456; Concerto in D Minor, K. 466; Concerto in C Minor, K. 491; Concerto in C Major, K. 503. Intercord Classical Creations INT820 546/8 (3 CDs). Bour/ SW German RSO.

Récital au Festival de Montreux. Beethoven: 6 Bagatelles, op. 126. Dvořák: *Tema con variazioni*, op. 36. Schubert: 3 Impromptus, D. 946. Smetana: *Esquisse*; *Furiant*; *Souvenir de Bohême*, op. 12, nos. 1 and 2. *Disques Montaigne* WM 334 789050.

Rudolf Firkušný Plays. Brahms: *Klavierstücke*, op. 119. Schubert: Impromptus, D. 946. Schumann: *Davidsbündlertänze*, op. 6. Sugano CD SCD-83001.

Rudolf Firkušný Tribute. Martinů: Piano Concertos Nos. 2, 3 and 4. RCA Victor 09026 -61934-2. Pešek/Czech PO.

FISCHER, ANNIE: b. Budapest, Hungary, 5 July 1914; d. Budapest, Hungary, 10 April 1995.

> Annie Fischer played the Beethoven First Piano Concerto as if she owned it, which in a way she does. Lustrous and rich, this is the kind of piano sound that we don't hear much these days with the slap-and-tickle virtuosi.
>
> Ed Mattos (*Washington Post*, 14 March 1984)

During the course of the 20th century, Hungary has produced far more excellent composers and pianists than the law of averages or the size of the country would dictate. Pianist Annie Fischer, was one of these fine Hungarian musicians. Throughout her long, active career the publicity-shy Fischer fiercely guarded her privacy, thus little is known about her personal life. She shunned interviews and any public exposure apart from the concert stage. Even the biographical sheet issued by her agent reveals only the barest essentials of her background.

Annie Fischer was born in Budapest, trained in Budapest and, apart from spending several war years in Sweden, always lived in Budapest. She studied for nine years (1923–32) at the Royal Academy of Music (from 1925 the Franz Liszt Academy): three years in Arnold Székely's preparatory class; four years of academy classes, under Székely's guidance; and two years in Ernst von Dohnányi's famed master class. Considered the best pupil of her group, Fischer was twice awarded (1928–29, 1929–30) the Liszt Prize granted by the Hungarian government.

At age 10, Fischer took part in a student concert (28 Feb 1925), playing the second and third movements of Beethoven's Concerto No. 1 in C Major, accompanied only by a string orchestra. On 29 November 1928 she performed her first concert outside of Hungary, playing the Mozart A Major Concerto, K. 488, and the Schumann Concerto in A Minor, op. 54, with the *Tonhalle* Orchestra in Zurich, Switzerland. The youthful pianist's stylish, mature playing astonished even the most critical musicians, not only because of her technical command of the piano but because of the spiritual depth of her interpretation. Fischer also appeared at the Festival of Hungarian Music held (April 1930) at the *Salle Pleyel* in Paris, performing Leo Weiner's Concertino for Piano.

Although the youngest of the 100 participants at the first Franz Liszt International Piano Competition, held in Budapest in 1933, Fischer was awarded first prize (Louis Kentner placed third) by the judges, among them Emil von Sauer, one of Liszt's most eminent pupils. It was Fischer's sensational performance of Liszt's Sonata in B Minor that overcame the competition, and it was her remarkable success in taking first prize that launched her international career. Recitals and orchestral performances with Europe's major orchestras firmly established her reputation as one of her era's finest pianists. During 1941–46, when World War II disrupted most of Europe, Fischer and her husband Aladár von Tóth (married in 1937, Fischer was widowed in 1968) lived—and performed—in Sweden. They returned to Budapest in 1946, and Fischer resumed her international career.

Annie Fischer was greatly admired and much honored in her native country. In recognition of her artistic achievements, Hungary three times (1949, 1955, 1965) gave her its highest cultural award, the Kossuth Prize. In 1965 she was named Honorary Professor at the Franz Liszt Academy. Other honors include recognition as Decorated Eminent Artist and as recipient of the Red Banner Order of Labour (1974).

Fischer was far better known and appreciated in Europe than in North America, partly because she disliked making recordings, the prime channel of publicity for performing artists, and partly because she spent comparatively little time in America. She made her American orchestral debut on 5 February 1961 at Carnegie Hall, playing Mozart's Concerto in E-flat Major, K. 482, with George Szell and the Cleveland Orchestra. But Fischer's Boston debut came as late as 1982, in the 49th season of her career; previous to this she had not played in America for a decade. Although she performed in Canada, the United States, Australia, New Zealand, Japan and the USSR, Fischer toured mostly in Europe.

Like Alfred Cortot, Annie Fischer did not give technically impeccable performances. Invariably her listeners extolled her superb interpretations, ravishing sound and profound musicianship. With equal consistency, the reviews mention her sprinkles—often splashes—of wrong notes and her memory lapses. But the technical insecurities rarely mattered. Fischer's playing enthralled, in a far more important sense, because her deeply musical nature reached the essence, the very heart and soul, of the music. Few pianists achieved her kind of beguiling and satisfying pianism. "To begin with, Annie Fischer is a great instrumentalist . . . despite the fact that in the first half of her program [19 Nov 1982, Boston] she splattered more notes than you'd hear in a season of recitals by lesser performers. . . . Her superiority as a pianist manifests itself first in an extraordinary quality of tone. . . . Everything she does at the piano makes a direct connection between the fullest content of the music and the minds and hearts of the audience." (*BG*, 22 Nov 1982) In New York, Fischer's recital (27 Feb 1986) at the Metropolitan Museum of Art brought a similar reaction. Again, there were a lot of wrong notes, but "her ability to knit the notes together into something no mere score can convey sounded close to magisterial." (*NYT*, 2 March 1986)

In her seventies Fischer still impressed with her physical strength and virility, her precise articulation and the heart and intensity in her playing. She commanded a great range of keyboard color and her ever-present spiritual concentration created an unusually satisfying projection to almost everything she attempted. Fischer was mainly concerned with the music—"how best to do justice to the composer, and how to convey her personal attitudes. These attitudes are always ingratiating, they leave a feeling of having heard more in the music than you thought was there." (*LAT*, 1 March 1985)

Her large repertoire extended from Bach to Bartók, but she became most renowned for her especially fine readings of Mozart, Beethoven and Schubert. At a London recital (23 April 1987) Fischer's performance of the Schubert Sonata in B-flat Major, D. 960 (she recorded it and played it often) "had marvellous concentration and intensity—the andante especially delivered with a simple, unaffected eloquence. . . . Her scherzo had an easy, joyful swing. . . . The finale was full of streaming clouds and fierce winds." (*FT*, 24 April 1987)

Mme. Fischer's all-Beethoven recital (9 Oct 1984) in London included three early sonatas and the mighty "*Waldstein.*" A natural Beethoven player, Fischer was in her most glorious form: "The Waldstein crowned the occasion. . . . The vistas of the sonata were rendered newly wide and surprising as much in supporting detail as in the shaping of the main themes." (*FT*, 11 Oct 1984)

In another all-Beethoven London recital (8 Nov 1987), Fischer's performances of four Beethoven piano sonatas "were littered with wrong notes but . . . they mattered not one jot. . . . It is only her insistence on taking risks that produces those wrong notes, and there was no greater proof that those risks are justified than her tremendous account of the 'Appassionata' Sonata." (*TL*, 9 Nov 1987)

Fischer performed (26 May 1966) Bartók's Third Piano Concerto at London's Festival Hall with "great integrity." Supported by the New Philharmonia Orchestra under Rafael Frühbeck de Burgos, she played the Bartók "with just the right blend of rhythmic flexibility and dynamic precision. From the first fluent entry in the opening movement to the last gestures of virtuosity in the finale she displayed an idiomatic insight and a tonal control which made this one of the season's outstanding concerto interpretations." (*MM*, Aug 1966)

Annie Fischer held her own with the finer pianists of this century. She had a secure reputation acquired through a combination of innate talent and hard work. "It is no derogation to describe Fischer as a pianist of the old school; she is one of the most appealing survivors of an earlier era. . . . She is never explosive or volcanic in the contemporary manner. She has plenty of technique, but she never parades it, and an occasional clinker is not a tragedy. She commands power, but she never seeks to overwhelm. And no matter what the dynamics, she always makes the piano sing with the intimacy of a lied singer." (*LAT*, 1 March 1985)

Mme. Fischer made many records for EMI and other labels in the 1950s and early 1960s, then stopped because she did not like recording. The series of Mozart concertos, recorded variously (1958–59, 1966) with Wolfgang Sawallisch, Efrem Kurtz and Sir Adrian Boult, represent a milestone of Mozart performance practice. One looks in vain for a better stylistic comprehension and pure musical approach. "Annie Fischer's technical evenness, rhythmic solidity, limpid tone, and elegant phrasing produce a singing, subtle Mozart." (*CL*, Dec 1991)

A performance of Beethoven's Concerto No. 3 with Heribert Esser and the Budapest Symphony Orchestra (see Discog.) added yet another illustrious reading of this great work. For one reviewer, this is "a direct, straight-as-an-arrow interpretation, as authentically Beethovenian in character as one can hope to find." And, in the Schubert Impromptu, D. 935, no. 1, on the same disc, "the gentle flowing character of the music is projected with an effortlessness and sincerity that are unprecedented in my experience." (*ARG*, March/April 1992)

Another EMI compact disc contains the Liszt Sonata in B Minor from 1953 and the great Schubert Sonata in B-flat Major recorded in 1968. The Schubert in particular makes the album eminently worthwhile, because of Fischer's unique understanding of the sonata's lyricism and design. Another Fischer reissue on CD features a 1960 live performance of the Bartók Concerto No. 3 with Ferenc Fricsay conducting the Bavarian Radio Symphony (see Discog.). Most striking are Fischer's "bell-like clarity of tone, her directness of approach, her sensitive response to changes of musical character, her absolute refusal to play harshly. . . . The performance is completely authentic in style and accent." (*BG*, 15 March 1990)

SELECTED REFERENCES

"A Debut at 68." *New York Times*, 26 Aug 1982, sec. 3, p. 16.
Dyer, Richard. "Intimacy, mastery move audience in Annie Fischer recital."
    Boston Globe, 9 April 1990, pp. 30, 32.
Harrison/Parrott Ltd. Publicity information.
Jacques Leiser. Publicity information.
Kovács, János. "Fischer Annie és Szenkár Jená." *Muzsika*, Nov 1958, pp. 3–4.
Obituary. *New York Times*, 13 April 1995, sec. 2, p. 10. *The Times*
    (London), 12 April 1995, p. 19.
Vásáry, Tamás. "Annie Fischer." *Musical America*, Oct 1982, p. 1.
See also Bibliography: New/Gro; Ran/Kon.

SELECTED REVIEWS

BG: 22 Nov 1982; 6 March 1984; 19 March 1985; 9 April 1990. *BH*: 19
    March 1985; 10 April 1990. *FT*: 11 Oct 1984; 24 April 1987; 28 April
    1987. *LAT*: 21 Oct 1982; 1 March 1985; 4 March 1988. *MM*: Aug 1965;
    Aug 1966; Nov 1966; Jan 1978; July 1985; Jan 1988. *MT*: July 1957;
    July 1983. *NYDN*: 16 Nov 1982. *NYT*: 6 Feb 1961; 14 Feb 1968; 15
    Nov 1982; 5 March 1984; 2 March 1986; 15 April 1990. *PP*: 28 April
    1990. *SFC*: 1 Nov 1982. *TL*: 13 Feb 1956; 1 Feb 1960; 16 Nov 1960;
    30 Aug 1961; 23 May 1962; 20 Sept 1966; 7 May 1970; 16 Feb 1971; 9
    March 1973; 17 March 1975; 9 Oct 1978; 20 Oct 1981; 10 Oct 1983; 25
    April 1987; 9 Nov 1987. *WP*: 14 March 1984.

SELECTED DISCOGRAPHY

Bartók: Concerto No. 3. Tchaikovsky: Symphony No. 6. *Orfeo* CD-200891.
    Fricsay/ Bavarian RSO.
Beethoven: Concerto No. 3 in C Minor, op. 37. Mozart: Fantasy and Fugue in
    C Major, K. 394. Schubert: Impromptu in F Minor, D. 935, no. 1. *Hun-
    garoton* HCD 31493. Esser/Budapest SO.
Beethoven: Sonata in D Minor, op. 31, no. 2; Sonata in C Minor, op. 111.
    Odéon LP P33CS 1807.
Liszt: Concerto No. 1 in E-flat Major. Angel CDM 64144. Klem-
    perer/Philharmonia. Also contains orchestral works by Mendelssohn and J.
    Strauss.
Liszt: Sonata in B Minor. Schubert: Sonata in B-flat Major, D. 960. *Hungaro-
    ton* HCD 31494.
Mozart: Concerto in D Minor, K. 466; Concerto in C Major, K. 467; Rondo in
    D Major, K. 382. *Hungaroton* HCD 31492. Lukács/Budapest SO.
Mozart: Concerto in D Minor, K. 466; Concerto in A Major, K. 488. EMI
    (Angel) CDZ 67000-2. Boult/PO.
Mozart: Concerto in C Major, K. 467; Concerto in E-flat Major, K. 482. EMI
    (Angel) CDZ 67002-2. Sawallisch/PO.

Mozart: Concerto in C Minor, K. 491; Concerto in B-flat Major, K. 595. EMI
   (Angel) CDZ 67001-2. Kurtz/PO.
Schumann: Concerto in A Minor, op. 54; *Carnaval*, op. 9. Price-Less CD
   D16492. Klemperer/PO.
Schumann: Fantasia in C Major, op. 17; *Kreisleriana*, op. 16. Price-Less CD
   D18894.

FISCHER, EDWIN: b. Basel, Switzerland, 6 October 1886; d. Zurich,
   Switzerland, 24 January 1960.

> Fischer was a player of genius (an overworked word, but one I use
> rarely), not a composer's genius but a true performer's genius. His
> playing is at the same time both absolutely *right* and daring.
>
> Alfred Brendel (*Records and Recording*, March 1975)

Edwin Fischer, one of the rare magical pianists in musical history, has for years
occupied a unique niche in the pantheon of great piano masters. Yet Fischer's
very individuality calls up the mind-provoking thought that, given today's insistence on perfect precision at all cost, he might find it difficult to please a contemporary audience and even more difficult to get a good review from a late 20th-
century critic. No one ever claimed that Fischer had an impeccable technique;
his greatness lies in the profound humanity of his playing.

   Edwin Fischer apparently began life with music all around him, and we
know that music was all he ever wanted. Both sides of his family were musical.
His father, oboist in the Basel municipal orchestra and violist in a string quartet,
originally came from a family of musical instrument builders in Prague, Czechoslovakia. Fischer's mother, born Anna Friedli, also came from a musical family. A lifelong bachelor, Fischer lived simply and, in the eyes of his admiring
students, remained forever young, in love with life and with music.

   He began piano studies at age four, and at age 10 was enrolled at the
Basel Conservatory, chiefly to study (1896–1904) with the composer Hans
Huber. After his father died in 1904, Fischer's mother, at great hardship, took
him to Berlin to study at the Stern Conservatory with Martin Krause—a Liszt
pupil who later taught Claudio Arrau. (Fischer adored his mother and never
forgot the "sacrifices" she endured for the sake of his music. He lived with her
until her death.) Fischer himself taught at the Stern Conservatory from 1905
until 1914, later taught (1931–35) at the Berlin *Hochschule für Musik*.

   By 1916 he had acquired a reputation as a pianist. He gave recitals and
frequently appeared as guest artist with orchestras directed by imposing conductors like Arthur Nikisch, Felix Weingartner, Willem Mengelberg, Bruno Walter
and Wilhelm Furtwängler. But Fischer's career—never spectacular—progressed
at his chosen pace. He accepted only as many concert engagements as he knew

he could handle and, refusing to travel by air, he played only in Europe and Great Britain.

A lifelong devotee of chamber music, Fischer in 1930 formed his own chamber orchestra, with which he revived the 18th-century practice of leading the orchestra from the keyboard. He was conductor of the Lübeck *Musikverein* (1926–28) and the Munich *Bachverein* (1928–32), and also played in a trio with the Italian cellist Enrico Mainardi and the German violinist George Kulenkampff (later replaced by Viennese violinist Wolfgang Schneiderhan). Fischer believed that playing ensemble music and training and conducting his own chamber orchestra broadened his musical knowledge and indirectly improved his piano playing.

After nearly 40 years in Germany, Fischer in 1942 returned to his native Switzerland, living in Zurich and Hertenstein, a village on the shore of Lake Lucerne. He resumed his performing career after World War II, still restricting engagements to Europe and Great Britain. Some of today's major pianists (Alfred Brendel, Paul Badura-Skoda) attended Fischer's famous summer master classes at Lucerne.

In the last years of his life failing health badly affected Fischer's playing, yet he was driven to continue, not for income but because playing was his whole life. In 1954 paralysis affecting his hands (for months he could not even hold a pen, let alone play the piano) was the final blow. Apart from an attempt at a concert two years later at Eppstein, West Germany, Fischer never played again; and without his music, his life virtually ended. "It is very sad to think of Lipatti who died too soon, but it is even sadder to think that Edwin Fischer died too late." (Barzetti)

Fischer was an articulate author and a careful, musicianly editor. His book on the Beethoven Sonatas, originally a series of nine lectures, has a personal approach with emphasis on Fischer's experiences and his enjoyment of music rather than on dissection and analysis. Another lecture series, published as *Reflections on Music*, includes such diverse subjects as "Art and Life," "On Musical Interpretation," "Frederic Chopin" and "Beethoven's Piano Works." He also published a fine study of J. S. Bach. In addition, Fischer edited Bach's keyboard works (Copenhagen, 1954–56) and Mozart's piano sonatas (Milan, 1966). The University of Cologne awarded Fischer an honorary doctorate for his distinguished services to music.

Fischer had a solid German training, and he played the traditional classical repertoire—Bach, Beethoven, Brahms, Chopin, Handel, Mozart, Schubert, Schumann. He also had an unusual "philosophic turn of mind and a markedly individual approach to music making." (Matthews) What made him special was the deep humanity of his playing—an indefinable glow that critics and admirers have attempted to define, not always lucidly, with words like "honesty," "grandeur," "simplicity," "tenderness," "naïveté," "humility," even "love." Somehow Fischer transferred his own warm, honest and generous nature into his music and *that*, more than any distinct technical skills, made his playing great.

His technical arsenal included an instinctive feeling for determining the overall shape and structure of a work just by sight-reading it. And he could shape a phrase so eloquently that it would unfold, evolve and breathe so naturally as to leave no one in doubt of its meaning and purpose. However, Fischer told his students that it was equally important that a composition should not emerge as a series of details, no matter how perfectly accomplished, but as an overall harmonic structure in which all these details should fit.

He laid down cardinal rules about tempos for his students, but in his own playing he often took liberties according to his emotional mood at the moment he sat down to play. Fischer never established the correct tempo for a work at the beginning, but took his tempo from sections in which the rhythmic pattern was either noticeably expanded or speeded up in relation to the rest of the piece.

In his simple, direct approach to music Fischer sought just the right balance between the composer's intentions and his own personal emotions about the music. But his constant striving for this balance resulted, at least in the opinion of some critics, in his playing all composers' music very much alike. The main objection was that whoever the composer, whether Bach, Mozart, Beethoven or Brahms, there was very little difference in Fischer's playing.

If, as students have noted, Fischer never missed a day of practice, why have so many paragraphs been devoted to his wrong notes and occasional memory lapses? Why was such a strongly disciplined musician so often unpredictable? Fischer countered the criticism with his opinion that in modern times technique (meaning virtuosity) mattered little, that it was far more important for the performer to find the inner spirit of a work, then use his own personality to recapture that spirit. "Although he had no real virtuosity, and did not sound as if he had ever possessed it, he played each note in every passage as if it really mattered and not as a dazzling display of sheer bravura." (Barzetti)

His tone was neither strikingly beautiful nor powerful, but it charmed listeners because it was always deeply eloquent. Fischer's playing, says Alfred Brendel, had a "sonority and richness of expression which doesn't come at all easily to many of today's players." (*MM*, Dec 1976)

His playing, we know, was not perfect, but it was wonderfully unique in being intimately related to his own high-minded, sweet nature. If Fischer's exalted thoughts on music may now read like a text from another planet, they are still worth repeating for what they tell us about his playing: "All study, all talent, all application will not suffice if one's whole life is not directed towards being a mediator of great thoughts and feelings. . . . One must live a life of purity in every detail, even down to the morsel one is putting into one's mouth. Prepared in this way, that Something will appear which is unteachable, that grace of the quiet hour when the spirit of the composer speaks to us, that unconscious moment, when one is raised out of oneself, call it intuition, grace—then all ties are loosed, all hindrances swept away." (Fischer, *Reflections*)

The finest tributes to Fischer's playing come from some of today's finest pianists. Alfred Brendel, a student at Fischer's master classes in Lucerne in 1949, 1950 and 1956, wrote that Fischer's playing "has a particular freshness and intensity of communication which reaches you, more directly than from any other performer I know. There is no curtain between him and you. He produced a marvellously relaxed sound, pianissimos that really carried and ferocious fortissimos that were still relaxed and never strident." (*RR*, March 1975)

Daniel Barenboim, who as a boy sat in on some of Fischer's classes in Salzburg and later heard him play in concert, describes how Fischer "was able to play legato without the pedal, which meant that he could use it for additional expression. . . . There was also a natural luminosity of sound when he played chords, as, for instance, at the beginning of the slow movement in Schubert's *Wandererfantasie*. That was quite wonderful. To me, he played the Mozart concertos exactly as they should be played. He had a liveliness in the fast movements and a simplicity and richness of expression in the slow movements that I shall always remember. . . . He had a wonderful gift of making everything sound improvised; he often gave you the feeling that he was making things up as he played. Fischer may not have been a great virtuoso, nor even pretended to be one, but his playing was quite breathtaking." (Barenboim, *A Life in Music*, 1991, Scribner's, Weidenfeld and Nicolson. Reprinted by permission.)

Paul Badura-Skoda, a Fischer student and one of his greatest admirers, describes Fischer as "a creative pianist, in type very close to Artur Schnabel— i.e., he played the same repertoire based on Beethoven, Schubert and Brahms. But Fischer's approach was slightly different, less intellectual than Schnabel's. When Fischer sat down to play, it was as if the composer himself played and improvised a piece, a sonata, or a fantasy. As a person, Fischer was very kind, very interested in his students. And one of the great inspirations he gave to me was his credo that an artist must strive for perfection as a human being, combining talent with virtue." (Elder, *Pianists At Play*, © 1982 by The Instrumentalist Company. Used by permission.)

Fischer had a grand style—warm, eloquent, sincere, infinitely alive— but in the end it may simply be his great joy in playing that endeared him to audiences and made any problems (technique, interpretation, whatever) insignificant.

Considering the globe-spanning itineraries of the modern pianist, Edwin Fischer performed within a relatively small arena in Europe and in Great Britain. Fortunately there are, in English, critiques of Fischer's London concerts as well as comments on his playing expressed by colleagues or pupils who heard him in live performance. An inconsistent performer, his playing had all the temperament and imagination of virtuosity; yet he was not a virtuoso in the true sense. How surprising to read that at an early London recital (1 Dec 1924) it was Fischer's strong finger work that most impressed the reviewer: "His scale passages are extraordinarily clear-cut, and the decision in all he does is satisfying. . . . But in the use of these powers he is inclined to run to extremes of tone and of pace, which have a disintegrating effect on Mozart's Fantasia and Chopin's Ballade in G Minor." (*TL*, 2 Dec 1924)

Ten years later another London critic described Fischer's outstanding qualities as not pianistic, but intellectual, imaginative and curiously inconsistent: "A part of his inconsistency lies in a queer antagonism to the composer's dynamic marks; this was especially evident in the Hammerklavier Sonata, for instance in the broken chords before the return of the theme in the Scherzo.

Fischer played them *pianissimo*. This antagonism appears to be no part of a general conception of the work, but rather eccentricity. Two pieces by Brahms were wonderfully played, showing Fischer at his best, full of fire and imagination." (*MT*, Feb 1934)

A typical review states that Fischer's playing "has a fine vigour; it is fierce, earnest, tender and eccentric. It is reminiscent in some ways of Eugen d'Albert, though Fischer has neither the passion nor the virtuosity of d'Albert. Musically speaking, Fischer's weakness lies in a certain lack of concentration— scarcely any movement is ever consistently good. One passage will be professional, another filled with imagination and tenderness, a third eccentric to a degree, taking thought neither for the composer nor the pianoforte." (*MT*, June 1934)

However, a later London review contained nothing but praise. On 23 February 1947 Fischer, performing Beethoven's Concerto No. 4 with Basil Cameron and the London Philharmonic Orchestra, played "with that deeper insight that distinguishes the maturity of years from all other kinds of interpretation by younger artists, however gifted. It was at once rhapsodic and intellectual." (*TL*, 24 Feb 1947)

To commemorate the 200th anniversary of the death of J. S. Bach, Fischer played three concerts (23 Jan, 26 Jan, 2 Feb 1950) at the *Salle Gaveau* in Paris. He presented all the Bach concertos for from one to four keyboards and chamber orchestra. He conducted from one keyboard, and three of his "disciples" (Helena Costa, Reine Gianoli, Karl-August Schirmer) assisted at the other keyboards. Not performances for purists, they were meant for those who loved Bach and loved sincere and devoted music making. "No one is more qualified to give such homage to the old master," wrote one reviewer. "Fischer's authority, his prestigious touch, also the care with which he chose the soloists to assist him, have assured the high quality of these concerts." (*LM*, 2 Feb 1950)

Fischer continued his "Bach year" with two acclaimed concerto evenings in London. On 20 November 1950 he played the Concertos in D Minor and E Major plus the Brandenburg Concerto No. 5, conducting the Philharmonia Orchestra from the keyboard. "He obtained wonderful moulding of phrasing by fine gradation of tone. This, of course, is all wrong; the eighteenth century went in for contrasts, not nuances of tone. . . . But wrong or not, it was magnificent, and Bach's spirit came through more alive than in many a stylistically more correct interpretation." (*TL*, 21 Nov 1950)

In February 1953 Fischer, conducting the Philharmonia Orchestra from the piano, played all five Beethoven Concertos and the "Triple" Concerto in two London concerts (Concertos Nos. 1 and 4 and the "Triple" Concerto on 5 February and Concertos Nos. 2, 3 and 5 on 12 February). One critic, noting momentary lapses of memory and fistfuls of wrong notes, also wrote: "What will stay in the mind is the authority, power and insight of Fischer's understanding of Beethoven. The old man raved sometimes but it was the raving of a Lear, shot with flashes of poetry." (*MT*, April 1953)

According to his pupils, Fischer did not like to make recordings. No doubt his live performances were better, but "Fischer's unique variety of tonal production—and his attention to rhythm, phrasing, punctuation, sustained line, and the drama or mood inherent in the music he was playing—many times prevailed over a certain inhibition he seemed to feel when faced with the coldness of the studio microphone." (*Fan*, July/Aug 1990) There are a number of Fischer's performances available on CD; some come from early commercial recordings, others were taken from radio concerts.

Fischer was the first to record (1933–36) Bach's Well-Tempered Clavier in its entirety (see Discog.). Some critics find that overall his recording comes close to that made by Wanda Landowska, but a disappointed reviewer found the transfers to CD to be poor and Fischer's performances to be "somewhat lackluster." (*Fan*, July/Aug 1990) Alfred Brendel considers Fischer's Bach performances as classic examples of an artist who used the piano to its fullest possible effect: "Listen to the best of the *Wohltemperierte* recordings, for instance, most of the slower pieces, and there you have piano playing that is completely 'timeless' in its mood. . . . Perhaps, at times, Fischer would sacrifice detail to the beauty and style of a piece—he had the most relaxed technique I have ever seen—but he was, within himself, an enormously vital musician." (*RR*, June 1971)

Fischer often performed the Bach concertos for from one to four claviers and chamber orchestra, usually touring with three of his students assisting. His performance of three of the best-known concertos is available on CD (see Discog.). Again, these are not for the purist. Fischer frequently doubled the melodic lines in octaves, thickened Bach's original chords, indulged in romantic alternations of hushed *pianissimos* and fierce *forte* outbursts. Also noticeable is that rhythmic unsteadiness present in more than one recording. However, for the Bach lover searching for sheer beauty, for eloquently expressive and finely nuanced cantabile lines, these interpretations will bring eminent satisfaction.

Considering his great affinity for Mozart, Fischer made few Mozart recordings: discs containing four concertos and also two versions of K. 466, one on 78 rpm and one in LP format. All the concertos, save the 1954 LP performance of K. 466, are available in one collection (see Discog.). Of course, they vary in quality. "His good qualities are evident on these discs: graceful phrasing, great beauty of tone and sensitive nuances, liquid passage work, plus delicacy and purity. Against these have to be set missed or split notes, muffed ornaments and, worst of all, a seemingly fundamental instability of pace." (*Gram*, Feb 1991) Another reviewer writes, "they have great historical significance, not only for interpretive merit but, in many cases, for being phonographic premieres as well. . . . All are remarkable for their prevailing stylishness, tension, clarity of voicing, and commitment." (*Fan*, May/June 1991)

Fischer recorded the Beethoven Concertos No. 3, No. 4 and No. 5. Concertos Nos. 3 and 4, with the pianist conducting the Philharmonia Orchestra, date from 1954. There are two versions of Concerto No. 5; the first, a 1939 78 rpm, was performed with Karl Böhm and the Dresden State Orchestra; the second, a 1951 LP, was made with Wilhelm Furtwängler and the Philharmonia Orchestra. The latter performance is the superior one, particularly in its CD transfer (see Discog.). For one critic, this is one of the most rewarding performances of the concerto ever recorded: "Fischer was not a commanding virtuoso, but his masterly response to the concerto's extraordinary energy and vision grips the attention, as does his constant illumination of detail and phrase." (*Gram*, March 1988)

A recent CD brings back three of Fischer's earliest Beethoven sonata performances, all recorded in London: the Sonata in F Minor, op. 57 ("*Appassionata*") in 1935; the Sonata in C Minor, op. 13 ("*Pathétique*"), and the Sonata in A-flat Major, op. 110, both in 1938 (see Discog.). These inspired interpretations from the 1930s have long been praised for their insight and their spirituality. Fischer's only Handel recordings, the 1931 Chaconne in G Major and the Suite No. 3 in D Minor (Präludium, Air, Presto), recorded in 1934, add a further dimension of pleasure to this welcome CD.

Although Fischer's name in recorded history is irrevocably linked to Bach, Mozart and Beethoven, his readings of Romantic composers are none the less compelling. One CD offers the Schumann Fantasia in C Major, op. 17, and the great Brahms Sonata in F Minor, op. 5 (originally recorded in 1949). From one review: "What I like about Fischer's performances is their sense of direction: here, plainly, is a musician who knows the essentials of both the Brahms and the Schumann. . . . While a listener may sometimes be surprised by the degree of Fischer's personal elaborations and his shaping of phrases, there is something eminently unfussy about both interpretations." (*MA*, July 1988)

Fischer's recordings are fraught with inconsistencies. Reading various critiques and reviews, one could understandably be bewildered by the sometimes contradictory comments concerning his recordings. His pupil Badura-Skoda admitted that Fischer "certainly gave his greatest performances when he wasn't recording, and this is part of the mystery of creation. In his own words he said, 'You cannot create if you are under observation. Everything that creates in nature or in art does so in hiding.' . . . So the very best recordings are those which were taken when he did not know that he was being recorded. Despite that, many excellent recordings of his playing do exist." (Reed)

Other thoughts on this particular quandry appear in a letter written by Fischer pupil Alfred Brendel. Brendel had previously expressed his admiration for Fischer as man and musician in a chapter of his book *Musical Thoughts & Afterthoughts*. This letter only emphasizes his feelings and gives a straightforward appraisal of his teacher. Writing of the Mozart concertos, Brendel admits that Fischer's performances have been variable: "His cadenzas are deplorable . . . and a steady maintenance of tempo was not one of his major concerns." But for Brendel, Fischer's well-known nervousness in performance could turn into an asset: "Fischer's nervous excitability could generate some of the most immediately moving and exhilarating playing one could ever hope to hear. . . . His spontaneity and freedom could, at times, be matched by superlative control, pianistic, musical and emotional. . . . While Fischer's performances may not be for purists, there is, in his best playing, a musical and emotional purity that, to me, makes considerations of 'historical' fidelity irrelevant." (*Gram*, May 1991)

SELECTED REFERENCES

Barenboim, Daniel. *A Life In Music*. London: Weidenfeld and Nicolson, 1991.

Barzetti, Marcella. "Edwin Fischer." *Recorded Sound*, Winter 1961–62, pp. 152–157.

Bouboulidi, Rita, with Carol Montparker. "Remembering Edwin Fischer." *Clavier*, Oct 1987, pp. 22–25.

Elder, Dean. *Pianists at Play*. Evanston: The Instrumentalist Company, 1982, p. 113.

Fischer, Edwin. *Beethoven's Pianoforte Sonatas*. (translated by Stanley Godman). London: Faber and Faber, 1959.

————. *J. S. Bach: eine Studie*. Potsdam: Eduard Stichnote, 1945.

————. *Reflections on Music*. London: Williams and Norgate Ltd., 1951.

Gavoty, Bernard. *Edwin Fischer*. Geneva: Editions René Kister, 1954. (*Series Les Grands Interprêtes*)

Haid, Hugo, ed. *Dank an Edwin Fischer*. Wiesbaden: F. A. Brockhaus, 1962.

Hughes, Eric. "Edwin Fischer Discography." *Recorded Sound*, Winter 1961–62, pp. 158–163.

Matthews, Denis. "Edwin Fischer." *Recorded Sound*, July 1970, pp. 649–654.

Mozart: Sonate per Pianoforte, Revisione di Edwin Fischer. 2 vols. Milano: Edizioni Curci, 1955.

Obituary. *The Times* (London), 26 Jan 1960, p. 15. *Musical Times*, March 1960, p. 175.

Olsen, Henning Smidth. *Edwin Fischer: A Discography. Danmarks Biblioteksskole* 1974.

Reed, Christopher. "Paul Badura-Skoda." *Clavier*, Nov 1986, pp. 5–11.

Smithson, Roger. *The Recordings of Edwin Fischer*. Second Edition. Watford: Hill and Garwood, 1990.

See also Bibliography: Ald/Con; Bro/Mod; Coo/Gre; Dan/Con; Doe/Tra; Kol/Que; MGG; New/Gro; Rat/Cle; Rub/MyM; Rub/MyY; Sch/Gre.

SELECTED REVIEWS

Figaro: 25 Jan 1949. *LM*: 2 Feb 1950. *MT*: Feb 1934; June 1934; April 1953. *TL*: 24 June 1913; 2 Dec 1924; 5 Dec 1924; 24 Feb 1947; 21 Nov 1950; 6 Feb 1953.

SELECTED DISCOGRAPHY

Bach: Brandenburg Concerto No. 2 in F Major, BWV 1047; Chromatic Fantasy and Fugue, BWV 903; Concerto in E Major, BWV 1053; Concerto for 3 Claviers, BWV 1064; Fantasy and Fugue in A Minor, BWV 904; Fantasy in C Minor, BWV 906. EMI *Références* CDH 7 64928-2. Fischer/CO.

Bach: Concerto No. 1 in D Minor, BWV 1052; Concerto No. 4 in A Major, BWV 1055; Concerto No. 5 in F Minor, BWV 1056; Brandenburg Concerto No. 5, BWV 1050. EMI *Références* CDH7 63039-2. Fischer/CO.

Bach: Well-Tempered Clavier, Books 1 and 2. Angel CDH-63188 (3 CDs).

Bach-Busoni: Prelude and Fugue in E-flat Major. Bach-Fischer: Ricercar from "The Musical Offering." Beethoven: Sonata in A-flat Major, op. 110. Handel: Chaconne in G Major. Marcello-Bach: Adagio from Concerto in D Minor. Mozart: Sonata in A Major, K. 331. Schubert: Impromptu in B-flat Major, D. 935, no. 3. Pearl GEMM CD-9481.

Beethoven: Concerto No. 5 in E-flat Major, op. 73; Sonata in A-flat Major, op. 110. Dante HPC 007 (CD). Böhm/*Sächsische Staatskapelle Dresden*, rec. 1938-39.

Beethoven: Concerto No. 5 in E-flat Major, op. 73; Sonata in D Major, op. 10, no. 3. Angel (EMI) CDH-61005. Furtwängler/Philharmonia, rec. 1951.

Beethoven: *Sonate per pianoforte*, Vol. 1. Sonata in C Minor, op. 13; Sonata in C Major, op. 53; Sonata in E Major, op. 109. Hunt CD-513.

Beethoven: Sonate per pianoforte, Vol. 2. Sonata in D Major, op. 10, no. 3; Sonata in D Major, op. 28; Sonata in C Minor, op. 111. Hunt CD-514.

Brahms: Concerto No. 2 in B-flat Major, op. 83. DG 427778-2. Furtwängler/ Berlin PO.

Brahms: Sonata in F Minor, op. 5. Schumann: Fantasy in C Major, op. 17. EMI/Pathé Marconi 2905751.

Edwin Fischer: The First Beethoven Sonata Recordings. Beethoven: Sonata in C Minor, op. 13; Sonata in F Minor, op. 57; Sonata in A-flat Major, op. 110. Handel: Chaconne in G Major; Suite No. 3 in D Minor (Präludium, Air, Presto). CDAPR 5502.

Mozart: Concerto in E-flat Major, K. 482; Concerto in C Minor, K. 491; Rondo in D Major, K. 382. Arkadia CDMP-409.1. Fischer/Danish CO.

Mozart: Piano Concertos and Solo Works. Concerto in G Major, K. 453; Concerto in D Major, K. 466 (London PO); Concerto in E-flat Major, K. 482 (Barbirolli/CO); Concerto in C Minor, K. 491 (Collingwood/London PO); Concerto in C Major, K. 503 (Krips/Philharmonia); Rondo in D Major, K. 382; Sonata in C Major, K. 330; Sonata in A Major, K. 331; Fantasia in C Minor, K. 396; Fantasia in C Minor, K. 475; Ronanze in A-flat Major, K. Anh 205; Minuet in G Major, K. 1. EMI *Références* CHS7 63719-2 (3 CDs).

Schubert: Impromptus, D. 899, D. 935. Dante HPC 006 (CD).

FLEISHER, LEON: b. San Francisco, California, 23 July 1928.

> The great challenge for the pianist is to make a line, an inexorable line, from note to note, just by depressing a series of keys. It isn't easy.
>
> Leon Fleisher (*Piano Quarterly*, Spring 1990)

For pianist Leon Fleisher achieving that "inexorable line, from note to note," has been not just a great but a doubly difficult challenge. A genuine piano prodigy and a student of the incomparable Artur Schnabel, Fleisher made his professional debut with the San Francisco Symphony Orchestra at age 14 and a smashing New York debut with the New York Philharmonic-Symphony at age 16. By the time he was 18 he had played two Carnegie Hall recitals and more than 20 engagements with major symphony orchestras. At age 23 he won the prestigious Queen Elisabeth of Belgium Competition, and he was barely out of his twenties when the Ford Foundation named him one of the 10 best concert artists in America.

Designated as the heir apparent to his teacher Artur Schnabel, Fleisher surely was destined for a predictably great future. But his flourishing professional career lasted only a dozen years. At age 37, because of the inexplicable failure of his right hand, he faced a wholly new challenge: How could he keep on making music? A quarter of a century later Fleisher, now in his mid-sixties and still not able to play the piano with two hands, is indeed making music. He has a new career as a conductor and, meeting his greatest challenge, he is still a performing pianist, producing that "inexorable line," as he puts it, with the repertoire of music written for piano, left hand alone.

Music has been his life's passion. At age five he began piano studies with Lev Shorr (who later taught Stephen Kovacevich), and his rapid advancement conjured up visions of fame and fortune in the minds of his parents, both immigrants (Isidor Fleisher came from Russia, Bertha [Mittelman] Fleisher from Poland) who had settled in San Francisco. Fleisher remembers his childhood as one completely geared to shaping him into a famous pianist. Instead of formal schooling, he had mostly private tutors and apparently few childhood diversions.

He was only seven years old when he gave his first public recital in San Francisco, and only nine the year he played a concerto with the San Francisco WPA orchestra, conducted by Alfred Herz, and the year he met Artur Schnabel. Confident of young Fleisher's talent, Herz devised a scheme to make Schnabel, who detested prodigies, listen to the boy play. Herz simply invited Schnabel, a good friend and bridge crony, to dinner, and as they left the dining room Fleisher, surreptitiously brought into the house by Mrs. Herz, began to play. He must have played very well, for Schnabel, who normally refused any student under age 16, invited Fleisher to come to his home in Tremezzo, Italy, for training.

Fleisher studied with Schnabel for 10 years, starting at age 10 with six months' work in Tremezzo. After the Schnabels left Europe in 1939 because of World War II, the lessons continued intermittently in New York City at the Schnabel apartment on Central Park West. As a teenager, Fleisher went into the city by subway for his lessons (by 1944 his family had moved from San Francisco to Washington Heights, New York), and what with lessons, practicing and commuting, music consumed most of his time. Instead of attending school, he had a tutor for academic studies, concentrating on English literature and history.

Schnabel's method of teaching—students attended each other's lessons—made it possible for each student to learn and absorb while not always having to be the one in the spotlight. The pupil having the lesson would play his piece on a Steinway grand piano, then Schnabel, playing on a small upright piano, would demonstrate changes and improvements; and, as Fleisher remembers it, invariably Schnabel sounded better on the upright than any student on the grand.

Schnabel was far more concerned about having students learn how to communicate the musical idea than in their acquiring technical perfection. Listening to Schnabel's knowledgeable, intimate discourses on each piece, Fleisher would cover his scores with playing reminders—"like a string of pearls" or "like liquid gold." "It was wonderful," says Fleisher, "he was giving us 60 years of knowledge about a piece. There was so much to learn, so much to remember. We used to reel out of lessons." (Briggs) Fleisher has never forgotten. Artur Schnabel, he says, "gave me my musical identity, my musical life."

Fleisher made his professional debut (16 April 1943) performing the Liszt Concerto No. 2 in A Major with the San Francisco Symphony Orchestra, conducted by Pierre Monteux. He was only age 14 but even then showed himself to be "a grand musician and a colossal pianist, one who has every device of keyboard craftsmanship literally at his fingertips, whose playing is rich and warm-hearted and intense both with intellect and with feeling." (*SFC*, 17 April 1943) A year later he played (4 Nov 1944) the Brahms Concerto No. 1 in D Minor with the New York Philharmonic-Symphony Orchestra, again with Pierre Monteux conducting. Fleisher gave his first New York recital on 28 January 1946, the second on 27 January 1947, and by then had also already played 26 engagements with major symphony orchestras.

After 10 years with Schnabel, Fleisher developed what he describes as a passive attitude, and Schnabel, aware that Fleisher was "waiting for his pronouncements," stunned him by suggesting that they stop the lessons. This abrupt change in his life, "plus the usual teen-age problems, threw me into a slump and I found myself unable to practice for about four years. My concerts began dropping off, understandably—I was playing badly." (Susa) Critical reviews of the time confirm his problems. His playing at the second Carnegie Hall recital raised questions. Some passages were touching, others were mechanical. Fleisher played some sections in a slow, searching manner, but rushed others. "And though his tone was generally soft and melting, it was also sometimes hard and metallic." (*NYT*, 28 Jan 1947)

Adrift without Schnabel ("I was lost—I could always go to Schnabel and get the answers."), Fleisher stopped playing and spent about three years in Paris in a kind of voluntary seclusion. In hopes of revitalizing his stalled career, he decided to enter the 1952 Queen Elisabeth of Belgium Competition in Brussels. To prepare, he practiced fiendishly for six months, surprising himself by remembering many of the things Schnabel had said about various works. Inspired and renewed, Fleisher competed at Brussels, and from a field of more than 70 contestants the jury (13 members, among them critic Olin Downes and pianists Marguerite Long, Artur Rubinstein, Robert Casadesus and Rudolf Firkušný) awarded the coveted first prize to Fleisher. He was the first American ever to win a major European music competition. It fulfilled all his hopes. Deluged with bookings, he immediately set off on a series of recitals and orchestral appearances in Europe, and for the next decade he pursued a heavy schedule of performing, mostly in Europe, the United States, Canada and South America.

Fleisher was appointed in 1959 to the Andrew W. Mellon Chair at the Peabody Conservatory of Music in Baltimore, and he is still on that faculty. That same year (1959) the Ford Foundation awarded Fleisher—selected as one of the 10 best concert artists in America—a grant to commission a work from a composer of his choice. Accordingly, in the fall of 1963 Fleisher gave the first performance of Leon Kirchner's Second Piano Concerto, with the composer conducting the Seattle Symphony Orchestra.

Fleisher's brilliant career (his reputation as one of his generation's finest pianists is well-documented) lasted only a brief 12 years. About 1962 he began to notice a weakness in his right index finger as he played trills. There was no pain, but sometimes while practicing—often seven or eight hours a day—he would feel a tingling or numbness in his right forearm. Soon his fingers began to curl inward as he played, and sometimes go limp. If he practiced harder, the condition worsened. Doctors were unable to pinpoint the cause, and ultimately the problem affected his playing. (Naomi Graffman's article is the best source for information on the history of Fleisher's disability.)

On 28 October 1964, Fleisher's performance of two Mozart Concertos (K. 451, K. 488) with the Festival Orchestra of New York, Thomas Dunn conducting, disappointed just about everyone. "Mr. Fleisher either was having a bad evening or he is not the pianist I had been led to believe him to be. . . . At times, his right hand did not seem to know what his left was doing." (*NY*, 7 Nov 1964) And this: "In neither work was he a really convincing exponent. . . . Fleisher's finger work in these two concertos was curiously uneven." (*NYT*, 29 Oct 1964) After struggling to get through "by dint of great effort" a Cleveland concert in April 1965, Fleisher and George Szell, his longtime mentor and colleague, mutually agreed that Fleisher had to bow out of their forthcoming State Department tour (western Europe and Russia) and cancel all future engagements. Only a pianist can even begin to imagine what this horrific blow meant to Fleisher.

He believes that he caused his injury by overdoing—too many performances, too much practicing. As a student with Schnabel, a pianist more concerned with communicating the musical idea of a work than the mechanics of piano playing, Fleisher had practiced about four or five hours a day. When, during his post-Schnabel days in New York, he encountered young technical wizards like Gary Graffman, he decided his own playing was inadequate and began to practice up to seven or eight hours a day. On top of that, he accepted too many engagements—22 performances in New York alone in one season, according to reports. Whatever the cause, Fleisher had to come to terms with just about the worst catastrophe for a pianist. Nothing had changed in that he still needed to make music, always his life's passion. He began to learn works written for orchestra and piano, left hand alone (the Ravel Concerto for the Left Hand, the Prokofiev Concerto No. 4 in B Flat, Britten's Diversions for Piano Left Hand and Orchestra), and he turned to conducting.

Although he had no training at all as a conductor, as a young pianist he had played many times with orchestra, especially with Pierre Monteux and George Szell. Besides, as a youth he had spent several summers at Monteux's conducting school in Hancock, Maine, although not as a conducting student. When the school first opened, there were not enough students to make an orchestra. Fleisher and a few other young pianists would play arrangements of symphonies (four hands, one piano) and the would-be conductors would conduct.

Fleisher also had the advantage of knowing a good many orchestral parts, because Schnabel had always insisted that pupils learning a concerto must also have intimate knowledge of the orchestra score. These experiences stood Fleisher in good stead when he took up the baton. In 1967 he cofounded (with Dina Koston) the Theater Chamber Players of Washington, D.C. Basically, Fleisher learned conducting by conducting. He conducted the Annapolis Symphony Orchestra between 1970 and 1982. He was associate conductor of the Baltimore Symphony Orchestra from 1973 to 1978. On 24 August 1970 he made his New York conducting debut at the Mostly Mozart Festival, and he has been guest conductor with a wide variety of orchestras (Boston, Chicago, Cleveland, Montreal, San Francisco, Seattle, Detroit, Dallas, Vancouver, Brussels and more).

Meanwhile for 17 years Fleisher fought his disability (ultimately diagnosed as *focal distonia*, a nerve disorder causing a spasmodic dysfunction of the hand or fingers, even at rest) with a diversified array of treatments and therapies. The muscles in his right hand seemed so much improved after an operation (Jan 1981) for carpal tunnel syndrome that he attempted a comeback at playing with two hands—a performance (16 Sept 1982) of César Franck's Symphonic Variations with the Baltimore Symphony Orchestra, Sergiu Comissiona conducting, at the opening of the orchestra's new Joseph Meyerhoff Symphony Hall. Responding to the audience uproar, the "reborn lion" also gave a "splendidly introspective reading of Chopin's Nocturne in D Flat, op. 17, no. 2." (*NYT*, 18 Sept 1982) Audience and critics were pleased, but Fleisher himself was painfully aware that he could sustain playing with two hands for only short periods of time. He canceled the "handful" of orchestra engagements scheduled, with high hopes, by his agents at Columbia Artists Management, and forged ahead. "Looking back," he told a 1982 interviewer, "I'd say what seemed at the time to be an irretrievable tragedy, turned out really to be the 'expander' of my life—a life now filled with satisfaction." (Beigel)

Today Fleisher, in his mid-sixties and still ranked among America's best pianists, plays only the repertoire composed for the left hand alone. Admitting (in the 1982 Margles interview) that he had been somewhat slow in fully exploring that repertoire, "probably because I have felt in the back of my mind that I was going to come back to playing with two hands," Fleisher has since then added considerably to his left-hand repertoire—solo works as well as works written for orchestra and piano, left hand. His first major solo recital in 25 years—played (3 Nov 1990) at Washington's Kennedy Center of the Performing Arts—consisted solely of works for piano, left hand alone. On 23 July 1994 Fleisher premiered a new Piano Concerto for the Left Hand, written for him by Lukas Foss and performed with Seiji Ozawa and the Tanglewood Music Center Orchestra.

Married three times, Fleisher is the father of five grown children. He has for many years lived in Baltimore, where he still teaches. Privately educated in his youth and self-educated as an adult, he is extremely well-read and conversant on a broad range of topics. His press material adds that he is also "a redoubtable bridge and ping-pong player (he once achieved the finals in a New

York citywide ping-pong tournament), holds a certificate as a lifeguard, collects toy and ornamental lions and gives a hilarious imitation of the Marx Brothers."

Obviously a performer who enjoys teaching, Fleisher, just as obviously, is very good at it. In May 1990 he received the Johns Hopkins University President's Medal in recognition of his 30 years of distinguished teaching—he is the Mellon Professor of Music—at the Peabody Conservatory, where his students have included André Watts and Louis Lortie. "What Leon did for me," says Watts, "went way beyond teaching me what he knew about music." (Levine)

Students flock to Fleisher's master classes, whether at Peabody, the Salzburg *Mozarteum*, the Paris Conservatory, Chicago's Ravinia Festival, Toronto's Royal Conservatory of Music, or elsewhere. In 1985 he was appointed artistic director of the Tanglewood Music Center. "The greatest teacher for me since Schnabel," says Fleisher, "was teaching itself. Tracking down the errors in a pupil's playing became a fascinating project, and I enjoyed searching for ways to correct them." (Susa) Like Schnabel before him, he gives his students everything he knows about a piece, not just what they are ready to absorb. The teacher, he says, must both inform the student and show him how to learn on his own. "Music is a language," he says. "It has certain principles. Although the maxims are not so inviolable that they cannot be broken, knowing them allows you to break them from time to time. I have always said my students learn the most from me after they have left me." (Montparker)

Because of his own experience, Fleisher advises his students to allow ample time between practice sessions for muscles to heal. And even though winning the prestigious Brussels piano competition revitalized his own career, he generally warns students against competitions, because today there are too many and they have lost their value. He encourages his students to believe in themselves and to commit their lives to making music. Being practical, he also advises that they find a way to keep a roof over their heads.

Fleisher's early programs of two-hand performances show works by (among others) Bach, Beethoven, Brahms, Mozart, Schubert, Liszt, Chopin, Weber, Franck, Debussy, Ravel. Reviews from that early period show that he achieved his greatest fame playing works by Beethoven and Brahms.

After acknowledging in 1990 that he did not expect to play again with two hands, Fleisher has more than ever explored and performed the repertoire for piano, left hand alone. Surprisingly, there are a great many of these pieces. (Research done by Norman Malone of De Paul University has uncovered about 450 such works.) Ravel and Prokofiev composed works for orchestra and piano, left hand, for Paul Wittgenstein, the pianist who lost his right arm during World War I. Scriabin composed a Nocturne and Prelude for left hand after he hurt his right hand competing with classmate Josef Lhévinne at the Moscow Conservatory. Felix Blumenfeld composed a difficult Etude to help strengthen the left hand. Leopold Godowsky, who never had problems playing with two hands, wrote the fiendishly difficult ("he must have been a sadist," quips Fleisher)

Symphonic Metamorphosis on the Schatz-Walzer Themes from Johann Strauss's The Gypsy Baron for piano, left hand. Fleisher plays all of these works.

His solo repertoire also includes Brahms's arrangement of the Chaconne from Bach's Partita No. 2 for solo violin; Saint-Saëns's Six Etudes for the Left Hand, op. 135; a Suite by Max Reger; a four-movement Sonata by Carl Reinecke; and Dinu Lipatti's Sonatine for Left Hand. Jeno Takács' Toccata and Fugue, op. 56, and Jean Hasse's Silk Water were both written expressly for Fleisher.

With orchestra, Fleisher has played (many times) the Ravel Concerto for the Left Hand; the Prokofiev Concerto No. 4; Britten's Diversions for Piano, Left Hand, and Orchestra; Franz Schmidt's Quintet in G for Strings and Piano, Left Hand, and also his Piano Concerto No. 2 for Left Hand; Erich Wolfgang Korngold's Suite for Piano, Left Hand, and Strings; Gunther Schuller's Concerto for Piano, Three Hands (two pianos), and Orchestra.

Fleisher has become the foremost living exponent of the repertoire for piano, left hand alone. Polishing and perfecting his left-hand technique, he has reached new heights of virtuosity; and once again Fleisher's reviews unanimously confirm his standing as one of his generation's finest pianists. His approach to music has indeed remained constant. Like his teacher Schnabel, his playing shows a strict respect for the musical text. Again like Schnabel, Fleisher does not just play a melodic line; he makes it sing on the keyboard. Just as Fleisher's playing has maintained its consistently high level, whether playing with two hands or the left hand alone, reviews of his performances are consistently similar. These reviews, early and late, describe Fleisher's playing style as "compelling," "patrician," "musically penetrating," "intellectually penetrating" and particularly notable for its "warmth of feeling and sensuous beauty." He has a firm, often prodigious technique, a secure sense of rhythm, an innate grasp of formal structure, a command of dynamics both sensitive and capable of myriad variation.

Beyond that, Fleisher plays the piano as though he enjoys every note, every phrase. Radiating energy, he creates a "rare spark" that seems to pass between him and his audience. "Not the kind of spark that stemmed from mere dramatics or showmanship. What he had was the kind of flame that was ignited by rubbing the smallest phrase just so, and then building from there." (*Time*, 7 Sept 1970) That description of Fleisher playing with two hands still holds today. He has lost the use of his right hand, but not that spark or his exceptional gifts for playing the piano. In 1993 the release of his first compact disc in the Sony Classical project to record the left-hand repertoire verifies that Fleisher is still "that rarest of pianists: totally in command of a thrilling virtuoso technique coupled with a profound musicianship and a warm, obviously compassionate nature." (Belt)

Only 16 years old, Fleisher garnered an auspicious array of reviews for his New York debut (4 Nov 1944), playing the formidable Brahms Concerto No. 1 in D Minor with the New York Philharmonic-Symphony, Pierre Monteux conducting. "He showed a broad command of the piano, based on sound, sensitive musicianship. His technique was remarkable; his interpretation, surprisingly mature." (*NW*, 20 Nov 1944) And this: "He at once established himself as one of the most remarkably gifted of the younger generation of American keyboard artists. . . . Virtuosity such as Mr. Fleisher made known at this debut still remains a rarity." (*NYT*, 5 Nov 1944)

During his early career Fleisher, who seems to have an instinctive feeling for the clarity and rhythmic stability demanded by Classic style, played a lot of Beethoven and Mozart concertos. On 1 March 1962, when he played the Mozart Concerto in A Major, K. 414, at Town Hall with the Esterhazy Orchestra, conducted by Daniel Blum, his "poised and beautiful playing . . . was remarkable on many counts. One was its purity of style, for he approached Mozart with an air of easy assurance. . . . And there was much subtlety of nuance, even though every note sounded spontaneous." (*NYT*, 2 March 1962)

Although Fleisher performed innumerable times with orchestra, at no time did he neglect his recital repertoire. At his first Carnegie Hall recital (28 Jan 1946)—a program of difficult, eclectic music by Bach, Mozart, Beethoven, Liszt, Chopin and Sessions—he played "with abundant virtuosity, at times with an excess of it. It was clear that his talent for the piano is not only natural but well-cultivated. These were the dash, brilliance and exuberance of a young man who knew he could make the piano do anything he wanted." (*NYT*, 29 Jan 1946)

A decade later a Los Angeles program (10 Jan 1956) received high praise: "He is one of the best equipped and most sensitive of the younger pianists and the more difficult the task with which he confronted himself the better he played. . . . It is rare for so young a musician to realize the lyrical qualities of this music [the Schubert Fantasy, the high point of the evening] so well." (*LAT*, 11 Jan 1956)

By 1964 Fleisher's right-hand difficulties had become noticeable to his audiences, although few could have known of the specific problem. He kept performing, but less and less. After 17 years of silence, broken only by his 1982 "comeback" performance of the Franck Symphonic Variations, Fleisher reclaimed his long-interrupted career with a repertoire of works—both solo and concerto—for left hand alone. At a Los Angeles performance (12 Jan 1984) with Michael Tilson Thomas conducting the Los Angeles Philharmonic Orchestra, Fleisher played the Ravel Concerto for the Left Hand with "unflagging energy and grace, with crackling rhythmic bite where appropriate, with stunning bravura flash and an invariably impeccable sense of proportion." (*LAT*, 14 Jan 1984) Performing the Ravel with Zubin Mehta and the New York Philharmonic Orchestra, Fleisher "turned in a wonderful reading. The soloist enters with a bravura cadenza, introduced by full orchestra, the kind of entrance a virtuoso relishes, and Fleisher played it with commanding strength. He maintained this impressive level throughout the section, modifying his touch to one of evocative poetry in the blues-like middle portion of the piece. . . . The jaunty ending was brilliant and witty, and had the audience on its feet with 'bravos' instantly." (*NYTr*, 14 Dec 1988)

Fleisher, who also frequently plays the Prokofiev Concerto No. 4 (a work composed for left hand and orchestra, but not as important or appealing as the Ravel Concerto), gave an especially pleasing performance (24 Jan 1987) of the Prokofiev with the Baltimore Symphony Orchestra, Grzegorz Nowak conducting. In the second movement, "Fleisher made the music sing rapturously over the rich fabric of the accompaniment." In the third movement, "his hand supplied both hammer strength and feathery grace." And in the final movement, "Fleisher made the last notes run off the top of the instrument in an exquisite shimmer of near silence." (*BaS*, 26 Jan 1987)

In recent years Fleisher has begun to give recitals for solo piano, frequently in combination with at least one chamber work. His solo recital (his first in 25 years) at Kennedy Center's Terrace Theater on 3 November 1990 was a joyous occasion for the Washington, D.C., audience, "the return of a master musician, whose commanding tone, powerful technique and intelligent musicality place him in the first rank of pianists." (*WP*, 5 Nov 1990) The program included arrangements and transcriptions (Bach-Brahms Chaconne, Strauss-Godowsky "Metamorphoses"); works originally conceived for one hand (Scriabin Prelude and Nocturne, Blumenfeld Etude); and a work especially commissioned by Fleisher (Chacony by Robert Saxon). Together with two violinists and a cellist, he also played Erich Wolfgang Korngold's Suite for Piano, Left Hand, and Strings.

On 23 July 1994, Fleisher gave the world premier performance of Lukas Foss's Piano Concerto for the Left Hand, with Seiji Ozawa conducting the Tanglewood Music Center Orchestra, and "endowed the work with his personal dignity and substance and with a masterly control of tonal shading." (*BG*, 25 July 1994)

Fleisher recorded all five Beethoven concertos with George Szell and the Cleveland Orchestra in 1959 and 1961. Highly regarded at the time (Grammy, Concerto No. 5, 1961), with the passing years these recordings have become a landmark of Beethoven pianism. Now in CD reissue, they still maintain their original reputation: "These performances share the same exalted status enjoyed by the sets compiled by Emil Gilels, Wilhelm Kempff, Solomon and, of course, Fleisher's teacher, Artur Schnabel. Fleisher's are large-scale readings that wring every ounce of drama from the concertos, without neglecting their classical proportion or—in the case of the Fourth and Fifth Concertos—their nascent romanticism." (*BaS*, 16 Aug 1987) "From the day it first appeared," wrote another reviewer, "I knew that this was the Beethoven concerto set I had been waiting for: With a wonderful consistency, all five compositions emerged with splendid virility, a firm sense of contour and direction, and impressive tonal solidity." (*OP*, Dec 1987)

Another notable collaboration with Fleisher, Szell and the Cleveland Orchestra was recorded over 35 years ago: the Franck Symphonic Variations and the perennial Rachmaninoff "Paganini" Rhapsody. These two works (now reissued along with an exciting reading of Ravel's *Alborada del gracioso*) were one of the first stereo recordings made by the Cleveland Orchestra. Fleisher's performances, which must compete with versions by many, many other fine pianists, are excellent. The rapport between pianist and conductor produces poetic, polished interpretations of two of the most popular concerted compositions in the repertoire.

At age 21 Fleisher performed the Mozart Concerto in A Major, K. 488, with Bruno Walter and the Los Angeles Philharmonic Orchestra at a concert (12 June 1949) recorded live. The CD reissue (see Discog.) shows an unusually mature and sensitive pianist at work. Fleisher's is a Mozart energized "by all sorts of rhythmic and dynamic nuances, by phrasings that lend suppleness and profile to motifs and scales, and by an awareness of how to project the music's emotional variety without violating its Classical frame." (*Fan*, Jan/Feb 1990) Fleisher's recording of the Mozart Concerto in C Major, K. 503, made in 1959, now appears on CD with the complete Beethoven concertos (see Discog.). Because of the CD format, "the reduction in tape-hiss exposes a number of subtle nuances in the pianist's tonal and dynamic shadings that make me admire more than ever his chiseled, unaffected, buoyant reading." (*Fan*, Sept/Oct 1987)

Recently Fleisher has embarked on a long-term project with Sony Classical, the objective being to record the left-hand repertoire. The first CD released has Fleisher, Seiji Ozawa and the Boston Symphony Orchestra performing three of the works originally commissioned by left-hand pianist Paul Wittgenstein: the Britten Diversions, Prokofiev's Concerto No. 4 and the Ravel Concerto in D. This highly recommended album is a delight. "Fleisher plays all three works with tremendous authority and conviction, yet with a keen appreciation of their stylistic differences. The Ravel . . . is full of imposing tonal weight and drama. . . . By way of contrast, Fleisher's Prokofieff has an unusual degree of neoclassical clarity and energy, while the Britten variations have all the necessary characterization of mood and atmosphere." (Donald Manildi, *American Record Guide* [May/June 1993]. Reprinted by permission) Further commentaries only strengthen the importance of this CD. "While never underpowered, Fleisher stresses the Ravel's beauty and elegance rather than the overtly dramatic qualities; the lesser-known Prokofiev and Britten works bounce along with neoclassical wit." (*Gram*, May 1993)

The second CD to date in the Sony project contains music written for solo piano, left hand—Bach-Brahms: Chaconne; Blumenfeld: Etude, op. 36; Godowsky: Symphonic Metamorphoses; Saint-Saëns: Etudes, op. 135; Saxton: Chacony; Takács: Toccata and Fugue, op. 56. "Here is an enjoyable programme which provides an interesting and valuable sample of this specialized repertoire." (*Gram*, Oct 1993)

SELECTED REFERENCES

Ardoin, John. "Pianist Fleisher's song of courage." *Dallas Morning News*, 8 Feb 1992, sec. C, p. 1.

Beigel, Greta. "The Aches and Pains of a Decade's Promising Pianists." *Los Angeles Times*, 30 Sept 1984, CAL, pp. 50–51.

Belt, Byron. "Pianist Fleisher carves niche as left-hand virtuoso." *Sunday Republican* (San Francisco), 28 March 1993, sec. F, p. 6.

Braggiotti, Mary. "Prodigy a Cynic on Marriage." *New York Post*, 16 Jan 1946, Magazine, p. 1.

Briggs, John. "Two Leons Collaborate On Concerto." *New York Times*, 29 Nov 1964, sec. 2, p. 14.

Delacoma, Wynne. "Pain Taught Fleisher a Music Lesson." *Chicago Sun-Times*, 12 July 1994.

Downes, Olin. "Competition At Brussels." *New York Times*, 8 June 1952, sec. 2, p. 7.

Dubal, David. "An Interview with Leon Fleisher." *Piano Quarterly*, Spring 1990, pp. 17–19.

"Fleisher's Beethoven." *Music Magazine*, Nov 1961, pp. 18–19.

Freed, Richard. "Leon Fleisher's Triumphant Return." *Stereo Review*, June 1993, pp. 76, 78.

Graffman, Naomi. "Leon Fleisher's Long Journey Back To The Keyboard." *New York Times*, 12 Sept 1982, sec. 6, pp. 55, 58, 87–93.

"Hand of Fate." *Newsweek*, 31 Aug 1970, pp. 64–65.

Horowitz, Joseph. "Pianist Approaches Quintet in G Single-Handed." *New York Times*, 21 Oct 1977, sec. 3, p. 20.

"Kindling a New Flame." *Time,* 7 Sept 1970, p. 47.

Kupferberg, Herbert. "To The Left." (interview) *Gramophone*, April 1993, p. 11.

Lembo, Elaine, and Joseph McLellan. "A First for Fleisher." *Washington Post*, 8 March 1984, sec. B, p. 4.

"Leon Fleisher—Prodigy, American Style." *Musical America*, 10 Dec 1944, p. 11.

Levine, Joe. "Eavesdropping on angel babble." *Johns Hopkins Magazine*, June 1985, pp. 10–15.

Libbey, Theodore W., Jr. "The Return of Leon Fleisher." *New York Times*, 2 May 1982, sec. 2, p. 23.

Margles, Pamela. "Leon Fleisher Returns." *Music Magazine*, Nov/Dec 1982, pp. 10–15.

McLellan, Joseph. "Sonata for a Southpaw." *Washington Post*, 3 Nov 1990, sec. D, pp. 1, 6.

Montparker, Carol. "The Indomitable Leon Fleisher." *Clavier*, Oct 1986, pp. 6–11.

Nachman, Gerald. "Stadium Star." *New York Post*, 4 Aug 1964, Magazine, p. 3.

Rockwell, John. "Leon Fleisher's Other Careers." *New York Times*, 22 July 1979, sec. 2, p. 19.

Susa, Conrad S. "Leon Fleisher." *Musical America*, Dec 1964, p. 105.

Tommasini, Anthony. "Fleisher revives works for left hand." *Boston Globe*, 25 Sept 1988, p. 91.

Walsh, Michael. "The Sound of One Hand." *Time*, 29 March 1993, p. 62.

See also Bibliography: Cur/Bio (1971); Dub/Ref; Ewe/Li2; Ewe/Mu; Hag/Thi; Mac/Gr2; New/GrA; Noy/Pia; Ran/Kon; Sal/Fam; WWAM.

SELECTED REVIEWS

BaS: 26 Jan 1987. *BG*: 25 July 1994. *BH*: 12 Oct 1991. *BJ*: 27 June 1984. *DMN*:1 Sept 1984; 10 Feb 1992. *LAT*: 11 Jan 1956; 20 Aug 1959; 16 Aug 1962; 18 Aug 1962; 14 Jan 1984; 25 May 1990. *NY*: 7 Nov 1964.

NYHT: 6 Nov 1944. *NYS*: 6 Nov 1944. *NYT*: 5 Nov 1944; 29 Jan 1946; 28 Jan 1947; 1 Jan 1954; 2 March 1962; 18 Nov 1963; 29 Oct 1964; 4 Dec 1964; 22 Sept 1972; 18 Nov 1975; 2 Sept 1982; 18 Sept 1982; 18 May 1984; 4 Dec 1988; 28 Jan 1990. *NYTr*: 6 Nov 1944; 14 Dec 1988. *PP*: 2 March 1984. *SFC*: 17 April 1943; 18 Sept 1982; 22 March 1993. *SFE*: 20 March 1993. *WP*: 19 Feb 1986; 5 Nov 1990.

SELECTED DISCOGRAPHY

Beethoven: The 5 Piano Concertos. Mozart: Concerto in C Major, K. 503. CBS M3K 42445 (3 CDs). Szell/Cleveland Orchestra.

Brahms: Concerto No. 1 in D Minor, op. 15. Odyssey cassette YT-31273. Szell/Cleveland Orchestra.

Brahms: Concerto No. 2 in B-flat Major, op. 83. Odyssey cassette YT-32222. Szell/Cleveland Orchestra.

Britten: Diversions, op. 21. Prokofiev: Concerto No. 4 in B-flat Major, op. 53. Ravel: Concerto for the Left Hand. Sony Classical SK 47188 (CD). Ozawa/Boston SO.

Franck: Symphonic Variations. Rachmaninoff: Rhapsody on a Theme of Paganini, op. 43. Ravel: *Alborada del gracioso*. CBS MYK-37812 (CD). Szell/Cleveland Orchestra.

Grieg: Concerto in A Minor, op. 16. Schumann: Concerto in A Minor, op. 54. Odyssey cassette YT-30668. Szell/Cleveland Orchestra.

Leon Fleisher Recital. Bach (arr. Brahms): Chaconne in D Minor. Blumenfeld: Etude in A-flat Major, op. 36. Godowsky: Symphonic Metamorphoses of the Schatz-Waltzer. Saint-Saëns: Six Etudes, op. 135. Saxton: Chacony. Scriabin: Two Pieces, op. 9. Takács: Toccata and Fugue, op. 56. Sony Classical SK 48081 (CD).

Mozart: Concerto in A Major, K. 488. AS Disc AS 412. Walter/Los Angeles PO. Also Paulina Carter with Weber *Konzertstück*, op. 79.

Schubert: Fantasy in C Major, D. 760 ("Wanderer"); Sonata in A Major, D. 664. Sony Classical SBK 47 667 (CD).

FRAGER, MALCOLM: b. St. Louis, Missouri, 15 January 1935; d. Pittsfield, Massachusetts, 20 June 1991.

> He has the unusual ability to dazzle the ear—as all good concerto pianists should do—but his playing is not for the ear alone. It also fulfills the basic function of music as an emotional language that speaks to the heart.
>
> Harold Rogers (*Christian Science Monitor*, 12 August 1963)

From time to time there appears a pianist with qualities surpassing musicianship, qualities capable of turning music into "an emotional language that speaks to the heart." Malcolm Frager was that kind of pianist, one of the few for whom making music required much more than a great technique. Frequently likened to Myra Hess, Frager "fused all his forces—technical, intellectual, emotional—into a single aim. And this goal, as Dame Myra once explained, is 'the music, and the meaning of the music'." (*CSM*, 11 Dec 1965)

Malcolm Frager was the son of Alfred Monroe Frager, a hosiery manufacturer, and Florence (Friedman) Frager, ethnic Jews who had converted to the Christian Science faith. Frager began piano lessons at age four with his grandmother, later studied with an aunt named Evelyn Rubinstein and at age six played his first recital, at Baldwin Hall in St. Louis. At age seven he began studies with Carl Madlinger, a former pupil of Isidor Philipp in Paris. Madlinger was responsible for laying the foundation of the technical expertise that would later characterize much of Frager's pianism. With Madlinger, half of every lesson (Frager studied with him for seven years [1942–49]) consisted of technical exercises to develop young fingers and to strengthen individual muscles as they grew. At age 10 Frager made his debut (1945) playing the Mozart Concerto in G Major, K. 453, with the St. Louis Symphony Orchestra, conducted by Vladimir Golschmann.

A musical prodigy but never treated as such, Frager enjoyed a normal childhood at home with his parents until he reached age 14 and they sent him to New York for advanced piano studies with the famed pianist and pedagogue Carl Friedberg, once a pupil of Clara Schumann. In his six years (1949–55) with Friedberg they rarely discussed technique, only matters relating to music interpretation. Instead of attending regular high school, Frager worked (1949–51) with tutors for about three hours a day at the Tutoring School of New York. Not typical and certainly not easy for a teenager, his routine consumed every moment of his life. Seeking a change, he spent the summer of 1952 in France studying with Robert Casadesus and Nadia Boulanger at the American Conservatory in Fontainebleau, where he was awarded the *Prix d'excellence*.

When he returned to New York he gave his debut recital at Town Hall on 28 December 1952, and no doubt intended to pursue a musical career. But since his father, fearing it was impossible to make a living playing the piano, made it clear that he would not support such a career unless his son went to college, Frager entered (1953) Columbia University as a Russian language major.

He graduated magna cum laude in 1957—fluent in Russian, French, Spanish and German, and familiar with Polish and Italian.

Music was never out of his life. While at college he kept up his practicing and also the lessons with Friedberg until 1955, the year Friedberg died. At the same time, receiving awards and entering competitions put his name before the public. In 1955 he placed second at the Geneva International Piano Competition; in 1956 he received the Michaels Memorial Music Award in Chicago; in 1958 he received the Career Award of the National Society of Arts and Letters. A runner-up for three consecutive years (1955, 1956, 1957) in the prestigious Leventritt International Competition, Frager tried again in 1959 and on 30 September 1959 was declared first-prize winner for his playing of Prokofiev's Concerto No. 2 in G Minor. Frager's own explanation for his success is interesting, considering that he was only 24 years old when he won the Leventritt. "I believe the reason I was selected as the winner was because of a change in my own attitude about myself and my reason for competing. I decided not to show off with a huge repertoire. I listed only the pieces that I felt most close to and I included only three concerti. I worked to prove that my motivation was to play well without wanting something from the audience—or in this case, the judges." (Novik)

Frager played concerts in Canada and the United States after his Leventritt success, and made his debut (1 May 1960) with the New York Philharmonic Orchestra, conducted by Leonard Bernstein. That same month of May (and less than a year after winning the Leventritt) Frager, without telling anyone but his parents, entered the Queen Elisabeth of Belgium Competition in Brussels. His performance of the Prokofiev Concerto No. 2 and the Haydn Sonata in E-flat Major, Hob. XVI:52, earned him the victory (28 May 1960), his prize being a cash award, a recording contract with RCA Victor and a number of European engagements. On his return to America, Frager and his fellow prizewinners (Americans captured 6 of the 12 awards) received bronze medallions from New York City's mayor Robert F. Wagner for having brought distinction to themselves and to their country.

Winning two important competitions launched a career that often kept Frager on tour as long as nine months a year. He first performed in London on 10 November 1961, playing the Beethoven Concerto No. 4 with Otto Klemperer conducting the Philharmonia Orchestra. In 1963 he made a six-week tour (25 recitals) in Russia, Estonia, Latvia and Lithuania. Accompanied on this trip by his wife (married Morag Macpherson of Glasgow, Scotland, in October 1962), Frager had an enormous success, not only as a pianist but as an ambassador of goodwill. The Russian people showered him with gifts and adulation; Russian officials, indulging in the suspicion typical of the times, were less than enthusiastic about an American who spoke their language.

At the end of the tour Frager and Vladimir Ashkenazy, after a five-year correspondence, finally got together again in Moscow. The two young pianists had become acquainted in New York in 1958, the year Ashkenazy made his first American tour. To the lonely Ashkenazy, who could not speak English and had been mostly kept isolated by the Russian "companion" sent with him by State officials, the Russian-speaking Frager must have seemed like a gift from the

gods. Now in Moscow, they decided to give the two-piano recital so often discussed in their letters. Setting a date, they practiced only about ten days and performed on 14 June 1963, a concert so successful that they gave three more
within the next five days.

Once begun, Frager's career never slowed down. He typically played
well over 100 concerts a season, most of them in North America and Europe.
His debut appearance (1963) at the Berkshire Music Festival at Tanglewood (he
played the Prokofiev Concerto No. 2 with the Boston Symphony Orchestra,
conducted by Erich Leinsdorf) was the first of many collaborations with that conductor and orchestra. Frager and his family became so attached to the Berkshires
that in the early 1970s they moved from New York to a 70-acre farm near
Tanglewood. He had a separate barn studio for practicing, and from that home
base he made his tours throughout the world.

He enjoyed teaching but had to limit himself to master classes. From
1983 he gave two weeks of master classes each year in Lucerne, in conjunction
with the International Music Festival. He also gave master classes at the St.
Louis Conservatory of Music, which honored him with a doctorate.

A versatile musician with multiple interests, Frager in 1966 discovered
an early version (1875) of Tchaikovsky's Piano Concerto No. 1. In 1967 he un-
earthed the manuscript of the original orchestration of Schumann's Piano
Concerto, having traced it to a West German village. (When conductors permitted, he played this somewhat more exuberant version in concert.) In 1978 he
was the first person to gain access to a monumental cache of musical
manuscripts missing from the Prussian State Library in Berlin since World War
II. This collection (it included the Beethoven Symphonies Nos. 7, 8 and 9;
Beethoven's Piano Concertos Nos. 3 and 5; and more than 100 Mozart compositions) had been removed from the Berlin library in 1941, stored first at a castle,
then a Benedictine monastery and finally ended up at the Jagiellonian Library in
Kraków, Poland. For his part in locating the collection and helping to make it
available, Frager received (1987) the Golden Mozart Medal from the
International Mozart Foundation in Salzburg, Austria. (Pincus, "The Lenox musician . . .")

Frager apparently was ill for about a year prior to his death, but there
was no publicity. He made his last appearances in July 1990 as guest artist at
the annual Summerfest of the Baltimore Symphony Orchestra. Performing the
Mozart Concerto in A Major, K. 488, at the opening concert on 10 July 1990,
Frager slipped a strain of "Happy Birthday" into the first-movement cadenza as a
birthday surprise for conductor David Zinman. The last work he performed (28
July) was the one with which he began his career, the Mozart Concerto in G
Major, K. 453.

After Baltimore, Frager canceled all the rest of his engagements. His
death at the age of 56 ended a career in full bloom with even greater potential.
His wife and daughter survive him.

When Malcolm Frager told interviewers that "building a repertoire includes familiarity with the entire Well-Tempered Clavier of Bach, all the sonatas
of both Mozart and Beethoven, the complete piano works of Schubert,

Schumann, Chopin and Brahms," he was essentially describing the foundation of his own large repertoire—so large that in one season alone he played 18 concertos and several recital programs during 5 tours (60 concerts) of Europe. Orchestras obviously liked him; once invited to perform with, for example, the orchestras of Boston, Cleveland, New York, Chicago, Philadelphia, St. Louis, Frager was asked back again and again.

He enriched his traditional repertoire with 20th-century works by Prokofiev and Bartók. His entry in the *New Grove Dictionary of Music and Musicians* states that he played "Mozart, Beethoven, Schubert and Schumann with warmth and a sense of intimacy"; and played Bartók and Prokofiev "with a special insight" and "unusual flexibility." The *London Times* obituary puts it this way: "Frager was particularly fond of interpreting Beethoven, Schubert, Schumann and Brahms, but was just as comfortable in the more flamboyant repertory of the 20th century." (*TL*, 1 July 1991)

Hours of practice maintained Frager's large repertoire. Even as a child he was forever practicing, trying to sight-read and to improvise. As an adult he practiced at least eight hours a day—and loved it. He often said that he could play the piano all day and most likely into the night. Not, however, on the day of a performance, the danger being that (as he put it) "the performance is over by the time you get on stage."

He also liked to practice away from the piano, reading a score and listening to the melodies mentally. That was one bit of advice he offered young pianists: "Once a piece has been memorized don't go on playing it over and over again. Practice it mentally. In this way the piece will not become fixed at any level of performance. It will continue to grow, to unfold." (*CSM*, 12 Aug 1963) He had other suggestions for aspiring concert pianists: acquire repertoire when young; know the chamber music literature thoroughly; study conducting and learn score reading; know as much as possible of other music literature; and go to a variety of concerts.

It hardly matters whether Frager's fluent, note-perfect technique was an inexplicable gift or the reward of constant practicing. That technique seemingly never failed him. Almost every review, early and late, in its own way emphasizes that he had remarkable technical command ("flawless technique," "clean-cut precision," "impeccable control," "steely fingers"). But for Frager technique was the means, not the end. In his view the best way to learn a new work was first of all to examine the qualities inherent in the piece.

Intelligent, well-educated and highly literate, Malcolm Frager also seems to have been a modest man living harmoniously within his personal sphere of fame, family and friends. He loved to read, especially on tour, and was known to read through one author's (Melville, Austen, Hawthorne, for instance) entire body of work in a season. Never the prima donna, he was friendly with his audiences and with people in general, easy to interview, and generally uncomplaining. There are concert pianists who are obsessed with having the perfect piano. Frager just accepted the piano offered and played it to the best of his—and its—ability. Once a pedal fell off the piano in the middle of a South American concert, and the unruffled Frager simply sat on the stage chatting with the audience in Spanish while a technician repaired the wayward pedal. This depiction of Frager, culled from interviews, suggests that his mind and his quiet, unassuming nature clearly influenced his approach to the piano.

Reviewers' comments on Frager himself ("calm," "poised," "immensely self-possessed," "utterly composed") and on his playing ("reticent mastery," "relaxed, natural pianism," "unsophisticated simplicity," "direct, uncomplicated, uncluttered playing") prove beyond question that Frager achieved his goal of wanting to be the same offstage and onstage, so that (as he must have told a dozen interviewers) "there would be no dichotomy between who I am and what I am."

An individualist but never to the extent of distorting the original text, his playing had style, taste and refinement; scrupulous honesty and seriousness; energy and insight. Some critics complained that sometimes his playing had too much drive, was too consistent, too inflexible; that there were times when his precise playing failed to generate the dramatic tension some works demand; that sometimes his playing was too cool, too straightforward.

Frager played his recital debut at Carnegie Hall on 31 October 1960, and the enthusiastic audience loved him and his playing. Critics also were impressed. His reading of the B-minor Scherzo "was Chopin playing of taste and skill . . . elegant, secure and pianistically impeccable." And his playing of the Prokofiev Sonata No. 6 "was staggering. . . . His performance had the kind of sweep, authority and pianistic finish that one would ordinarily expect only from a pianist many years senior to Mr. Frager." (*NYT*, 1 Nov 1960) In March of 1962 his recital at Washington's Constitution Hall again pleased the critics. "His control makes even the most difficult passages fall into position as musical ideas that are related to the composition, rather than as scintillating ends in themselves for the glory of the performer." (*CSM*, 26 March 1962)

At their first Moscow recital duo-pianists Frager and Ashkenazy played compositions taken from the classic repertoire for two pianos: Mozart Sonata in D Major, K. 448; Schumann's Andante and Variations; the Chopin Rondo; and finally the exciting Bartók Sonata for Two Pianos and Percussion. "Ashkenazy played with great excitement and vigor, and Frager—who also charmed the audience with his perfect Russian—was every bit his match. But the thing that made the evening electrifying was the evidence of such joy in music making, the proof of such harmony in friendship." (*Time*, 21 June 1963)

Frager's London program (Brahms Sonata, op. 1, and three Haydn sonatas) on 31 January 1965 revealed his "splendid technique and an unsophisticated simplicity which somehow enables him to unlock musical secrets without fussy detail or applied espressivo." (*MM*, April 1965) And this: "As a pianist pure and simple he had an admirably incisive yet mellow touch; his fingers never fumbled or miscalculated their speed of descent in obtaining the precise dynamic shading required." (*TL*, 1 Feb 1965)

Frager developed a warm rapport with the Boston Symphony Orchestra. After one of their many Tanglewood performances (the Mozart Concerto in B-flat Major, K. 450, with Erich Leinsdorf conducting), the orchestra's concertmaster, Joseph Silverstein, told a critic that when an artist played often with them, orchestra members usually found "the chinks in his armor. His flaws show up. But not with Frager. He just keeps getting better and better." Apparently the critic agreed: "Mr. Frager has achieved the art that conceals art. He makes you think and feel the music. . . . Scales come forth skimmingly. Phrases are elegantly shaped. His unpercussive tone does not assail the ear. . . . But when he is playing Mozart, you do not really think of all these things. You feel the wonder that is Mozart." (*CSM*, 16 July 1966)

As an 11th-hour substitute at Oberlin College for a suddenly ill Horacio Gutiérrez, Frager gave an "Olympian performance" (4 April 1978) of works by Haydn, Schumann and Chopin. "A musician of logic and taste, he discreetly defined polyphonic voices, weighed accents and delayed cadential resolutions. Playing with intense concentration and marvelous freedom from personal mannerisms, he allowed each work to speak with clarity, unfold naturally and soar to the heights on its own inner momentum." (*CPD*, 6 April 1978)

The high point of Frager's University of Maryland recital on 18 July 1988 was the Weber Sonata No. 1 in C Major, op. 24, "a composition with its sprawling affective gestures rooted in operatic idioms. . . . He did not dwell on its affectations but neither did he disregard them, and they made their point more strongly for this restraint. Tempos were exquisitely chosen and Frager found an ideal balance of weight for his textures." (*WP*, 20 July 1988)

About a year later, a Chicago recital gave pause to reflect on Frager's mature pianism. At age 25 he was "a spectacular technician who excelled in works that did not call for the high romantic style. Nearly 30 years later, the technique still is spectacular, but the maturity of outlook, the warmth of humanity, the pure delight in beauty essential to the romantic style, now are central to his point of view." (*CST*, 15 May 1989)

Frager made very few recordings. As one of the benefits of winning the Queen Elisabeth Competition in 1960, he made his first major recording in Paris, an RCA stereo disc containing the two selections that he played at the Competition: Prokofiev's Concerto No. 2 in G Minor, with the Paris Conservatory Orchestra conducted by René Leibowitz (Grammy, 1960), and the Haydn Sonata in E-flat Major (LSC-2465). "The Haydn is suavely done, the phrasing turned in high classical style. . . . Tonal brilliance is found in abundance in the Prokofiev. It is an exciting recording of a stunning, incisive performance. Mr. Frager has the technique that dazzles the ear and the subjectivity that moves the heart—a rare combination to be found in a 25-year-old." (*CSM*, 1 Nov 1960)

Frager frequently turned down invitations to record, feeling they would not be helpful to his artistic development. And, of course, he played only the music that he felt comfortable with, an ideal not always coinciding with record producers' desires or demands. His recordings of the Beethoven Concertos Nos. 3 and 5 and the Schumann Andante and Variations (with Ashkenazy) are out of print. Recordings available at this writing include a fine album of American Piano Music, the Strauss *Burleske*, a Chopin album, some Haydn and Mozart concertos and the Schumann Concerto in A Minor.

Frager's disc of four Haydn concertos is perhaps misnamed. Called concertos, these works are more like divertimentos, written in *style galant* with little counterpoint or thematic development. However, as miniatures they are charming. As one reviewer noted, "Frager and the tiny orchestra give the music what it needs: clarity, buoyant rhythms, elegant sonority. They are obviously not bored by its innocent simplicity, and their playing conveys pure pleasure." (*Fan*, March/April 1989)

Recorded on a Bösendorfer Imperial grand piano with a beautiful tone quality, Frager's Chopin album (see Discog.) is a grand example of his artistry. There are four Mazurkas, the op. 43 *Tarantelle*, a Polonaise, the Sonata No. 3 in B Minor, op. 58, and the popular *Andante spianato* and *Grande Polonaise*, op. 22. "Frager's way of shaping individual phrases, his connecting of a series of phrases into a continuous section, his breathtaking technique, his superb tonal command, his overall handling of the instrument proclaim him a master artist. . . . The disc concludes with a magnificent performance of the magnificent op. 58, with an irresistible combination of power, poetry and elegance." (*Fan*, July/Aug 1991)

SELECTED REFERENCES

Eckert, Thor, Jr. "Pianist Frager is artist, teacher, thinker." *Christian Science Monitor*, 25 June 1986, pp. 1, 6.
Frager, Malcolm. "The Manuscript of the Schumann Piano Concerto." *Current Musicology*, 15 (1973), pp. 83–87.
Gray, Channing. "Pianist with a taste for the rare in repertoire." *Journal* (Providence, Rhode Island), 13 Feb 1987, sec. D, p. 5.
Murphy, George. "Pianist Frager works to stay on top." *Rochester Democrat and Chronicle*, 17 Jan 1980, sec. C, pp. 1–2.
Novik, Ylda. "Malcolm Frager." *Piano Quarterly*, Spring 1977, pp. 17–18, 20.
Obituary. *Clavier*, Sept 1991, p. 45. *New York Times*, 21 June 1991, sec. 2, p. 7. *The Guardian* (Manchester), 25 June 1991, p. 39. *The Times* (London), 1 July 1991, p. 16.
"Oh, Vladimir! Oh, Malcolm!" *Time*, 21 June 1963, p. 46.
Peters, Frank. "Everyone Needs To Be The Soloist Once In A While." *St. Louis Post-Dispatch*, 5 Oct 1980, sec. B, p. 5.
Pincus, Andrew L. "Concert pianist Malcolm Frager dies at 56." *Berkshire Eagle* (Pittsfield, MA), 21 June 1991, sec. B, p. 1.
———. "The Lenox musician and the missing Mozart script." *Berkshire Eagle*, 17 March 1991, sec. G, p. 5.
Rogers, Harold. "Speaking Through the Affections." *Christian Science Monitor*, 12 Aug 1963, sec. 2, p. 1.
Sabin, Robert. "Frager Wins Leventritt Piano Award." *Musical America*, Oct 1959, pp. 3, 28.
Tucker, Diane. "American Pianist Wins Two Major Awards." *Christian Science Monitor*, 15 Oct 1960, Youth Section, p. 1.
Wigler, Stephen. "Malcolm Frager's Subdued Success." *Baltimore Sun*, 8 July 1990, sec. F, pp. 1, 6.

See also Bibliography: Cur/Bio (1967, 1991); Mac/Gr2; New/GrA; WWAM.

SELECTED REVIEWS

AJ: 11 April 1980. *BaS*: 22 Feb 1982; 11 July 1990. *CO*: 1 April 1982. *CPD*: 6 April 1978. *CSM*: 26 March 1962; 19 Jan 1963; 15 July 1964; 11 Dec 1965; 16 July 1966; 29 May 1985. *CST*: 6 Jan 1975; 15 May 1989. *FT*: 28 Nov 1985. *KCS*: 5 May 1983. *LAT*: 15 Dec 1965; 16 Nov 1968. *MiT*: 12 Aug 1977. *MM*: April 1965. *NYP*: 13 Feb 1976. *NYT*: 29 Dec 1952; 2 May 1960; 1 Nov 1960; 26 July 1963; 3 Aug 1963; 8 May 1965; 3 July 1965; 15 Jan 1966; 2 Nov 1966; 8 May 1970; 1 March 1990. *SLPD*: 21 Sept 1979; 30 Oct 1985. *TL*: 11 Nov 1961; 18 Feb 1963; 1 Feb 1965; 31 Jan 1972. *WP*: 5 March 1962; 8 May 1987; 20 July 1988.

SELECTED DISCOGRAPHY

Haydn: Concertos in C Major, Hob. XIV:12; C Major, Hob. XVIII:5; F Major, Hob. XVIII:7. Koch-Schwann *Musica Mundi* CD 316 013F1. Frager/ RIAS Sinfonietta.

Malcolm Frager plays. Foerster: On the Sea. Gilbert: Mazurka. Huss: Prelude op. 17, no. 2. Nevin: Étude in Form of a Scherzo, op. 18, no. 2. MacDowell: Twelve Virtuoso Studies op. 46. Paine: Romance op. 12. Parker: Valse gracile op. 49, no. 3. New World LP NW 206.

Malcolm Frager plays Chopin. Polonaise in A-Flat Major, op. 53; *Andante spianato* and *Grande Polonaise*, op. 22; *Variations Brillantes* on a Theme from *Ludovic* by Halévy op. 12; Mazurkas op. 6; *Contredanse* in G-flat Major; *Tarantelle* in A-Flat Major, op. 43; Sonata No. 3 in B Minor, op. 58. TELARC CD-80280.

Mozart: Concerto in C Major, K. 415; Concerto in G Major, K. 453. Vivace E-515 (CD). Chakarov/Festival Sinfonietta. Also Fidelio 1819.

Mozart: Concerto in A Major, K. 488. Vivace G-217 (CD). Chakarov/Festival Sinfonietta.

Prokofiev: Concerto No. 2 in G Minor, op. 16. Haydn: Sonata in E-flat Major, Hob. XVI:52. RCA Victor LSC-2465. Leibowitz/*Orch. du Conservatoire de Paris.*

Schumann: Concerto in A Minor, op. 54. Beethoven: Violin Concerto in D Major. Chesky CD52. Horenstein/Royal PO.

Strauss: *Burleske* in D Minor. EMI Classics CDZC-64342. Part of a 3-CD collection of the composer's orchestral works. Kempe/Dresden SO.

VIDEO

Mozart on Tour. Concerto in D Major, K. 175. Philips 070 239-3. Vol. 2. Previn/ *Orchestra della Radiotelevisione della Svizzera Italiana.*

FREIRE (Pinot Freire), **NELSON** (José): b. Boa Esperanza, Brazil, 18 October 1944.

> Although [Freire] has never become as celebrated as his playing deserves, he is surely among the handful of greatest players before the public.
>
> Stephen Wigler (*Baltimore Sun*, 18 July 1988)

True, Nelson Freire has never become a "famous celebrity," and, moreover, it seems very unlikely that he ever will fit into that category. An anomaly among today's high-visibility virtuosos, Freire maintains a low profile because he believes that pianists should not perform too often. Where some pianists still play more than 100 concerts a season, Freire schedules only from 50 to 60 appearances. Nevertheless, those live concerts and his recordings have been enough to certify his standing as one of today's finest pianists. He has been compared to such legendary giants as Josef Hofmann, Alfred Cortot and Sergei Rachmaninoff, and more than once recognized as the undisputed heir to the late Artur Rubinstein. Pianists, piano aficionados and record collectors certainly know Freire's worth, but among the general public he is not nearly as prominent as his much-praised playing warrants.

Even as a toddler of three, Freire would drop everything to join his older sister whenever she played the family's upright Zimmerman piano. Before long Freire could play by ear almost any piece he heard her play, and it took him only a matter of hours to learn to read music. Such remarkable talent definitely needed guidance, but Boa Esperanza was too small a town to have a qualified piano teacher. Freire's parents—his father was a pharmacist, his mother a schoolteacher—located a Uruguayan teacher named Fernandez in Varginha, the closest city, yet still a four-hour bus trip. After about a dozen lessons, Fernandez recommended that Freire's parents move to Rio de Janeiro, where they would find exactly the right teacher. Moving to the capital meant leaving family, friends and work, but the Freires made the change for the sake of their son's musical career.

Finding the right teacher in Rio de Janeiro proved both difficult and frustrating, largely because at age five Freire had already developed his own way of playing and balked at the normal routine of lessons and practice, especially tedious scales and exercises. He was age seven—and a few prospective teachers had come and gone—when his desperate parents learned of Lucia Branco, a pianist who had studied with a pupil of Liszt. Talking with Freire and listening to him play, Branco concluded that, as she frankly told his parents, the child was a phenomenon but also, in her words, completely "nuts." Branco recommended that he study with Nise Obino, one of her former pupils who, in her view, was likewise "nuts." Three months of almost daily lessons with Obino prepared Freire to start lessons with Branco, and he continued to work with both teachers until he left for Europe at age 14.

The recitals he gave under their tutelage made him a famous child prodigy, and his picture often appeared on the front page of Rio de Janeiro's important newspapers. He was only 10 when Boa Esperanza named a street after him, and only 12 when he was invited to participate in Rio de Janeiro's first International Piano Competition (1956). Lucia Branco agreed that the competition would be a good experience for Freire, but at the same time warned him that he would have little chance competing against so many older, more seasoned pianists. Freire actually prepared just enough music (Chopin's Nocturne in C-sharp Minor, op. 27, no. 1; the Etude in F Major, op. 10, no. 8; and the Polonaise in A Flat) for the first round. However, he made it to the semifinals, where he played a Chopin mazurka, another etude and the Ballade No. 4, and became one of 12 finalists. In the final round the 12-year-old's performance of the Beethoven "Emperor" Concerto persuaded the jury, which included Lili Kraus, Marguerite Long and Guiomar Novaes, to award him first prize.

Juscelino Kubitschek, president of Brazil, rewarded Freire's amazing success with a government-funded scholarship for study abroad. Freire decided on Vienna, went there alone at age 14 and for two years studied with Bruno Seidlhofer. On impulse, Freire entered the 1964 Vianna da Motta Competition, arriving in Lisbon just two days before it began and without even knowing the title of the required work. Undaunted by drawing first place in the lots, Freire learned the piece—a composition by Carlos de Seixas—in two days, and went on to win the competition. That same year Freire was awarded the Dinu Lipatti Medal in London. This recognition together with first place in the da Motta Competition generated playing engagements.

Concertizing mostly in South America and Europe, Freire came to prominence in 1966 with, according to *Time* magazine, "a galvanically Promethean" performance of Tchaikovsky's Piano Concerto No. 2 in West Germany. His very successful London debut (17 Feb 1968) at Wigmore Hall so impressed Ernest Fleischmann, manager of the Los Angeles Philharmonic Orchestra and also recording supervisor for CBS, that he signed Freire to record four popular piano and orchestra works—Tchaikovsky Concerto No. 1, Liszt's *Totentanz*, the Grieg and Schumann concertos—with the Munich Philharmonic Orchestra, conducted by Rudolf Kemp. Freire, at the time relatively unknown in the United States, stunned the critics with this CBS album (see Discog.). After hearing it, James Goodfriend of *Stereo Review* called Freire a "cockeyed sensation" and Irving Kolodin of *Saturday Review* described him as a "hurricane of pianistic power."

Freire made his first American appearance (23 Jan 1969) in Los Angeles playing the Bartók Concerto No. 1 with the Los Angeles Philharmonic Orchestra, conducted by Pierre Boulez. On 21 August 1969 he appeared at the Hollywood Bowl, playing the Schumann Concerto in A Minor, op. 34, with the LAPO under André Previn. Freire first played in New York on 31 December 1969, performing the Rachmaninoff Concerto No. 4 with the New York Philharmonic Orchestra, conducted by Rafael Frühbeck de Burgos. Scheduled to play the Rachmaninoff twice, Freire actually performed it five times in six days because an attack of flu caused Jeanne-Marie Darré to cancel her engagement. The final performance of the Rachmaninoff began at 7:30 P.M. on 5 January 1970. The moment Freire finished he was rushed by limousine to the Garden City High School in Long Island, 25 miles distant, where he warmed his hands under hot water, stepped onstage at 8:40 P.M. and performed his first American recital—a "knuckle-crunching" program including Beethoven's "*Waldstein*" Sonata, the Chopin B-minor Sonata, and works by Bach, Liszt and Villa-Lobos. A year later Freire played his first New York recital (9 Jan 1971) at Hunter College. By that time, critics were ranking him as one of the most exciting new pianists of this or any other age.

Living in Paris since 1990, Freire tours mostly in South America, Europe, the United States, Canada, Israel and Japan. He plays regularly but not all that often. A New York recital in February 1975 was his first appearance there in four years; and a London appearance in 1977 was the first time in ten years. However, he has often performed at the University of Maryland International William Kapell Piano Competition and Festival.

A 1970 *Time* article reported that Freire preferred the dreamy picturesque worlds of Schumann, Chopin, Liszt, Tchaikovsky, even Rachmaninoff. Freire's programs show that he also plays Bach, Mozart, Schubert, Brahms, Villa-Lobos, Strauss-Godowsky, Franck and Ravel. Martha Argerich, Freire's close friend who sometimes plays two-piano music with him, says that Freire is always looking for new works to play or new books to read.

Given his "grand manner" style, it is understandable that among the older generation of pianists Freire most admires Sergei Rachmaninoff, Josef Hofmann, Walter Gieseking and Novaes. Novaes, whom he had known and loved from childhood, attended his concerts whenever possible and often helped him, giving her views on how to play certain works. She inspired him, says Freire, not by what she said but by the way she said it.

Nelson Freire is a great natural musician. Shy and reserved, his personality never intrudes on the music. Although his playing is, to be sure, spontaneous and individual, he always shows a musicianly respect for score indications and for the piano itself. The late Albert Goldberg once said that Freire could let the music ripple and sing with the utmost grace and ease, and the next moment, and just as effortlessly, he could deliver up a volley of octaves like a burst of artillery fire. Other critics agree: "When it comes to technique, Freire can do anything that any other famous pianist can do, except so much better. His command of color is literally incomparable. . . . The iridescent clarity of his playing frequently defies belief. Like the late Glenn Gould, Freire seems to have a tiny brain in each finger." (*S-L*, 14 July 1990)

A review of a program (Mozart, Brahms, Chopin, Villa-Lobos, Albéniz) on 19 July 1985 at the University of Maryland International Piano Festival concisely sums up Nelson Freire's remarkable talent. "Of the numerous elements that constitute Freire's mastery of his instrument and his repertoire, three were dominant: a broad range of sonority that Freire controlled at will, an uncanny sense of timing in the buildup and release of rhythmic tension, and an unfailing ability to make the piano sing." (*WP*, 22 July 1985)

When one finds a negative Freire review, the only complaint seems to be that his playing at times is too personal. For example, when he made his New York debut (31 Dec 1969), he played very beautifully, "but he gave the concerto [Rachmaninoff No. 4] the kind of polite, well-integrated performance that did little to help the cause of the music." (*NYT*, 1 Jan 1970) And a critic at his first Los Angeles recital (10 March 1972) wrote: "Freire has a remarkable control of tonal nuance and variety of color and his tone is invariably mellow and edgeless. But many of his effects were simply too intimate and subdued for effective projection in a large hall." (*LAT*, 13 March 1972)

Only 23 years old when he made his London debut (17 Feb 1968) at Wigmore Hall, Freire's interpretative skills had not totally matured according to one critic, but he played an exacting program "with fluency, brilliancy, strength and authority. . . . Except for some questionably fast tempi he showed as musicianly a respect for each score's written symbols as he did for the piano itself." (*TL*, 19 Feb 1968)

Only a little more than a year later his Los Angeles performance (21 Aug 1969) of the Schumann Piano Concerto "left no doubt that he belongs to the contemporary elite. His Schumann was grandiose in score, crisp in rhetoric, logical in structure. . . . Not the mellowest or most indulgent of interpretations . . . but it was fresh, manly and tasteful." (*LAT*, 23 Aug 1969) A New York reviewer attending this same performance agreed: "Freire does perform the notes swiftly, surely and confidently, but he also performs them subtly, sensitively and responsively. Unlike some of his chronological equivalents, whose playing has more than a suggestion of the computerized, Freire's impulses, as experienced live, are no less spontaneous, impulsive, and stimulating than they were in his recording." (*SR*, 6 Sept 1969)

Freire gets high marks for his Chopin performances. In a New York recital (13 Feb 1975) at Hunter College he played Chopin's F-minor Fantasy and the Scherzo in B Minor "with a self-involvement, as opposed to self-intrusion, in the music. He brought the pieces to appropriate climaxes without becoming percussive tonally, and there were personal accents to provide a true Romantic spirit." (*NYT*, 15 Feb 1975) At his recital (13 Dec 1984) in Miami, Florida, "His way with the B-flat Minor Scherzo was typical of his utterly natural gift for phrasing, his instinct for the re-creation of music. . . . But the real jewel of Freire's Chopin group was the fourth Mazurka of Op. 24, which few pianists in my experience have played with nobler or deeper expression." (*MH*, 15 Dec 1984)

Freire's performance (27 July 1991) of the Beethoven Concerto No. 5 ("Emperor") with the Baltimore Symphony Orchestra, David Zinman conducting, prompted one reviewer to name him as the undisputed heir to the late Artur Rubinstein: "There is the same physical beauty of the playing—gorgeous tone from top to bottom at all dynamic levels—and a kind of technique that makes playing the piano seem as natural and as easy as breathing." (*BaS*, 29 July 1991)

Given Freire's distinctive talents and his fine concert reviews, it is surprising that he has made so few recordings. But, expectedly, each of the available discs is truly worth having. *Nelson Freire in Recital* was recorded live on 13 December 1984 in Miami, Florida. Although there is some disturbing audience noise, the excitement and enthusiasm more than compensate. One reviewer had "only praise for Freire's playing: the glitter and brilliance of *Poissons d'Or* and *O Polichinelo*, the sensuous rhythmic undulations of Albéniz and Villa-

Lobos, and the direct and unaffected musicianship of the Chopin group." (*Fan*, March/April 1988) Another critic, equally enthusiastic about this album, rates Freire as "perhaps the greatest living pianist in mid-career who has yet to be recognized for the great artist that he is. . . . Nelson Freire truly is the pianist's pianist of our time." (*MA*, Sept 1988)

Heitor Villa-Lobos is represented on a fine CD containing a good sampling of his characteristic keyboard compositions. "Freire's major work here, played with spectacular virtuosity, is *Rudepoema*, a violent and noisy musical portrait, so it is claimed, of Artur Rubinstein, who did so much to champion Villa-Lobos's cause." (*Gram*, Dec 1987)

Freire's recordings (now on CD) of both the Grieg and the Schumann concertos, with Rudolf Kempe conducting the Munich Philharmonic Orchestra, have been enormously successful. His Grieg, said one reviewer, is "wild and wonderful—the best I've ever heard." (*ARG*, July/Aug 1990) Freire plays both concertos with "plenty of flair and excitement. This recording has everything. . . . There is no better pairing of these two concertos if you like dark, rich sound." (*ARG*, Nov/Dec 1990)

SELECTED REFERENCES

Elder, Dean. "Nelson Freire: 'the boy from Brazil'." *Clavier*, Jan 1977, pp. 14–17.
"Joyful Discovery." *Time*, 19 Jan 1970, p. 64.
Press Material, Columbia Artists, 1994–95.
Wigler, Stephen. "Publicity-shy pianist Freire arrives for concerts with BSO." *Baltimore Sun*, 13 Dec 1990, sec. E, pp. 1, 4.
See also Bibliography: New/Gro.

SELECTED REVIEWS

BaS: 18 July 1988; 14 Dec 1990; 29 July 1991; 13 July 1992; 27 Dec 1992. *CiP*: 23 July 1990. *DP*: 3 April 1982. *LAT*: 25 Jan 1969; 23 Aug 1969; 30 July 1970; 15 Feb 1971; 13 March 1972. *MH*: 15 Dec 1984. *NYT*: 1 Jan 1970; 11 Jan 1971; 15 Feb 1975; 28 Feb 1977; 6 April 1984. *S-L*: 14 July 1990. *SMH*: 29 April 1994. *SR*: 6 Sept 1969. *TL*: 19 Feb 1968; 16 May 1977; 12 March 1979; 12 Dec 1980. *WP*: 24 July 1982; 22 July 1985; 19 July 1988. *WS*: 14 Feb 1977. *WS-N*: 7 Aug 1975.

SELECTED DISCOGRAPHY

Chopin: Ballade No. 3 in A-flat Major, op. 47; *Berceuse*, op. 57; 3 *Ecossaises*, op. 72; Polonaise in A-flat Major, op. 53; Prelude in C-sharp Minor, op. 45, Scherzos (4). Teldec 8.44075 (CD).
Chopin: Nocturne in B-flat Minor, op. 9, no. 1; Nocturne in E-flat Major, op. 9, no. 2; Nocturne in F Major, op. 15, no. 1; Nocturne in F-sharp Major, op. 15, no. 2; Nocturne in G Minor, op. 15, no. 3; Nocturne in C-sharp Minor, op. 27, no. 1; Nocturne in D-flat Major, op. 27, no. 2; Nocturne in

E Minor, op. 72, no. 1; Nocturne in C-sharp Minor, op. 72, no. 2; Fantasy in F Minor, op. 49. Teldec 8.44076 (CD).
Chopin: Sonata No. 3 in B Minor, op. 58. Liszt: Sonata in B Minor. Columbia M 31128 (LP).
Grieg: Concerto in A Minor, op. 16. Schumann: Concerto in A Minor, op. 54. Liszt: *Totentanz*. Tchaikovsky: Concerto No. 1 in B-flat Minor, op. 23. Columbia M2X 798 (2 LPs). Kemp/Munich PO.
Grieg: Concerto in A Minor, op. 16. Schumann: Concerto in A Minor, op. 54. Odyssey MBK 46269 (CD). Kemp/Munich PO.
Nelson Freire in Recital. Albéniz: *Evocacion*; *Navarra*. Albéniz-Godowsky: Tango. Chopin: Impromptu in F Sharp, op. 36; Mazurka in B-flat Minor, op. 24, no. 4; Mazurka in C-sharp Minor, op. 41, no. 1; Scherzo in B-flat Minor, op. 31. Debussy: *Poissons d'or*. Mozart: Sonata in A Major, K. 331. Rachmaninoff: Prelude in G-sharp Minor, op. 32, no. 12. Villa-Lobos: The Baby's Family (3); *A Lenda do caboclo*. Audiofon CD 72023.
Schubert: Impromptus, D. 899. Sony Classical SBK 47667 (CD).
Tchaikovsky: Concerto No. 1 in B-flat Minor, op. 23. Odyssey MBK 46268 (CD). Kemp/Munich PO.
Villa-Lobos: *As três Marias*; *Preludio* (*Bachianas brasileiras* No. 4); *Próle do Bébé*; *Rudepoêma*. Teldec 8.43686 (CD).

VIDEO

Ravel: *La Valse* (with Martha Argerich). In *Scarlatti Debussy Ravel*. Sony Video LP.

FRIEDMAN, IGNAZ: b. Podgórze, near Kraków, Poland, 14 February 1882; d. Sydney, Australia, 26 January 1948.

> Friedman was something of a genius not only because he ranked with the great pianists of his day, but—more important—because in him was a living and relishing sense of life, and a capacity to feel the whole of the experience that came his way; and to convey it to others simply by living it in his mind all over again.
>
> Neville Cardus (*The Listener*, 19 August 1954)

Friedman spent his earliest years mostly on the move with his father, a clarinet-tist and violinist in a small orchestra traveling throughout Poland, the Balkans, the Austro-Hungarian empire and possibly in Greece and Turkey. Ultimately— Friedman was about 10 years old—his father joined a theater orchestra in Kraków (Josef Hofmann's father was also a member), and the family settled down.

Said to be able at age eight to transpose Bach fugues into any key, Friedman must have had his first music lessons from his father during the itinerant years. In Kraków he studied with Flora Grzywinska for about 10 years until he went to Leipzig. Grzywinska, as the mature Friedman often acknowledged, developed his technique and introduced him to music literature, not only piano literature but also that for chamber music, opera and lieder. He was 18 years old when he moved to Leipzig to study composition with Hugo Riemann at the University of Leipzig. He also attended seminars on aesthetics and Baroque music and heard as many concerts as he possibly could manage.

The following year (1901) Friedman played in Vienna for the famous pedagogue Theodor Leschetizky, who abruptly dismissed him with the advice that he not even attempt a career as a pianist. (This was a favorite Leschetizky tactic for deflating youthful egos; Paderewski and Moiseiwitsch got the same treatment.) Leschetizky did eventually accept him as a pupil, and Friedman's technical expertise (by age 15 he knew all the Czerny exercises) so delighted Leschetizky that in class he often, without warning, would throw up his arms and shout out in fun, "Friedman! Come play for us the Czerny Etude, No. 33." After four years with Leschetizky, Friedman became one of his assistants. One of the first pupils Leschetizky sent to him for preparatory study was Maria Schidlosky, a Russian pianist who had studied in Rome with Sgambati. She and Friedman married in 1909 and made their home in Berlin.

Meanwhile Friedman made a brilliant Vienna debut (22 Nov 1904), playing three concertos (Brahms No. 1 in D Minor, Liszt No. 1 in E-flat Major, Tchaikovsky No. 1 in B-flat Minor) with a local Viennese orchestra; and his exciting playing set in motion a 40-year, globe-encircling concert career. Starting in 1905, he made dozens and dozens of exhaustive tours, playing an estimated 2,800 concerts—he sometimes performed on seven successive days—in Europe, the Americas, Asia, Australia, New Zealand, Iceland, Turkey, Egypt, South Africa and Palestine. He appeared with virtually all the famous conductors of his day, and he played a great deal of chamber music with artists like Casals, Feuermann, Elman and Auer.

The Friedmans lived in Berlin from 1909 until World War I forced them, in 1914, to move to Copenhagen. The war also forced Friedman to cancel his first tour of the United States, due to start in 1915, and six years would pass before he made his American debut on 7 January 1921. He toured North America frequently during the 1920s, was absent during 1930–34 and returned for tours in 1935 and 1937. In 1938 he sought Josef Hofmann's aid in finding a teaching position in the United States, but Hofmann, no longer director of the Curtis Institute, could offer little help, and other inquiries also disappointed.

Fortunately for Friedman, the piano duo of Vronsky and Babin canceled their 1940 tour of Australia, and the Australian Broadcasting Commission invited Friedman as replacement. On tour in Spain when they received the news, the Friedmans managed to get to Marseilles and sail on one of the last ships out of France before the German invasion. They settled in Vauclause, a town overlooking the Heads, the entrance to the Sydney harbor, and Friedman resumed his schedule of teaching, composing and touring (Australia, New Zealand, Indonesia).

On 24 July 1943 Friedman was performing an all-Chopin program in Sydney, and as he played the Preludes, his left hand lost some control. It improved enough so that after the intermission his performance of the Sonatas went well; however, the next morning his left hand was completely numb. Initially diagnosed as neuritis, his condition was later thought caused from diabetes. He never recovered sufficiently to perform again in public, but he continued to teach in Sydney. Friedman died on 26 January 1948 from complications following abdominal surgery.

Neville Cardus, who often visited Friedman at Vauclause, described his good friend as "a man of wit and great charm; he was indeed one of the wittiest men I have ever known. . . . He was a widely read man, with a rare knowledge of English literature, and he was much more informed of English music than is common amongst Continental musicians." (Cardus)

Friedman composed more than 90 works, including a piano concerto, a quintet for piano and strings, three string quartets, some songs and a large number of compositions for piano solo. He often included his own works on recital programs, and they were appreciated by his contemporaries; today they are largely forgotten. A serious, conscientious editor, Friedman produced a new edition of Chopin's piano compositions for Breitkopf and Härtel and edited the piano music of Liszt and Schumann for Universal Edition.

Reputedly an excellent teacher (following the precepts of his own teacher Leschetizky), Friedman taught whenever his busy concert schedule permitted. Students, said Friedman, should always be able to do with the left hand what they can do with the right: "They need not purchase special arrangements of their studies to do this . . . simply do it." At the same time Friedman warned against thoughtless repetition in practice: "Think while practicing. There must not be one measure that is not played musically. . . . Students should use their brains and be more analytical and less emotional." In one of his published articles Friedman discussed what he considered the most important elements of pianistic training: "What is the most difficult thing in pianoforte playing? . . . I must say that in teaching the most difficult thing is to teach rhythm and color. Technic, that is, the mechanical side of technic, the rapid scales, arpeggios, octaves, etc., are mere trifles beside rhythm and color. Of the two, probably rhythm is more difficult to achieve than color. . . . Rhythm is the life of music, color is its flesh and blood. Without either all interpretative art is dead." (Friedman, "What is the Most Difficult Thing . . .")

Ignaz Friedman's repertoire was enormous and diverse. Just the 95 programs (out of Friedman's estimated 2,800 concerts) printed in George Kehler's *The Piano in Concert* (Keh/Pia, see Bibliog.) list works by nearly 50 composers of various nationalities. Starting in the 18th century with Bach, Scarlatti, Handel and Rameau, this long list also includes Gluck, Haydn, Mozart, Beethoven, Weber, Schubert, Mendelssohn, Schumann, Chopin, Liszt, Brahms, Saint-Saëns, Debussy, Ravel, Albéniz, Dohnányi, Bartók, Kodály, Tchaikovsky, Glazunov, Scriabin and a host of lesser composers popular then but not often heard today. In his concerts Friedman played Bach only in transcription—Bach-Busoni, Bach-Tausig, Bach-Liszt—and only half a dozen Beethoven sonatas. But when he performed the Romantic repertoire, especially Chopin, Schumann, Brahms—he breathed life into every work he played.

Friedman had all the technique required to perform this vast repertoire. That technique, extraordinarily brilliant, clean and precise, had been developed from technical exercises, not from practicing excerpts from standard compositions. "Have technique first," he said, "then take up the study of the standard compositions. Have all the possibilities of technique 'in the pockets' and thus preserve the freshness of the composition, otherwise it will be played without 'fantasy'." (Kinscella) Serene at the piano, Friedman played without unnecessary gestures, "no flinging of the hand in the air, no sudden removal of the fingers from the keyboard, as though it were sending out an electrical shock." (Cardus)

As an interpreter, Friedman held to the theory that it is the duty of the pianist to make the composition *live*; that the finest music comes from the best of the composer *and* the best of the artist. Granting that the composer should come first, Friedman still insisted that the pianist had the right to put himself into a composition if he could do so "without offense to the composer, and with good taste." As reviews corroborate, Friedman at times carried his highly individual interpretative ideas to excess.

Performance reviews from Holland and Spain provided attractive publicity for Friedman's first tour of the United States and Canada (Jan–March 1921). From Amsterdam: "The public was carried away by the wonderful playing of this rare virtuoso." (*De Tijd*, 14 March 1920) And from Madrid: "Ignaz Friedman is undoubtedly one of the greatest living artists." (*La Tribuna*, 7 April 1920) And, "The colossal pianist completely conquered his audience." (*El Mundo*, 10 April 1920)

Friedman's New York debut on 7 January 1921 was, seemingly, an unqualified success. "Mr. Friedman disclosed at once and all through the afternoon technical powers of the most unusual sort, an extraordinary brilliancy and speed, a command of the mechanism of piano playing that accomplished the most exacting technical tasks without apparent effort, and without attempt at turning this mastery into a means of personal display." (*NYT*, 8 Jan 1921)

As he passed through America on his various tours, Friedman was lionized as few pianists had ever been. After a Kansas City recital (14 Feb 1922), one critic declared that, "not in many years, certainly not in the memory of the younger generation, has there been such piano playing or such a response to piano playing as there were yesterday afternoon when Ignaz Friedman appeared on the stage of the Schubert Theater. At the end there were cheers; not one, but many." (*KCT*, 15 Feb 1922)

However, not all critics agreed. In 1923 the tireless Friedman played three recitals at New York's Aeolian Hall, programs that, unlike those of, say, Schnabel, were designed to please and excite his audiences. At the first program (13 Jan 1923) he played a substantial group of Chopin works, the Bach-Busoni Chaconne and the extraordinarily difficult Strauss-Godowsky *Fledermaus* paraphrase; and his Chopin playing was "sensational in the highest sense of polished cameo-phrase and bell-toned inner harmonies." (*NYT*, 14 Jan 1923) A review of the second recital (3 Feb 1923)—Friedman played his usual Chopin pieces, *plus* Schumann's Fantasia, op. 17, and the Brahms-Paganini Variations—was cautious: "Mr. Friedman is fond of the extremes of power, loud and soft; and sometimes overdoes their contrast. There were many beautiful passages in his performance of Schumann's 'Fantasy,' great vigor and spirit, sometimes to the point of superfluity. There was also an excess of hesitant *rubato*." (*NYT*, 4 Feb 1923) One review for the third program (22 March 1923)—the usual Chopin group, Beethoven's Sonata in E Minor, op. 90, and the Mendelssohn Serious Variations—mentioned only the music, the small audience and the long, insistent applause.

Another formidable program (Bach-Tausig Toccata and Fugue, Beethoven Sonata in E Minor, op. 90, Schumann *Carnaval*, Strauss-Godowsky Artist's Life, a Chopin group and several other compositions), played in New York on 1 March 1924, drew similar half-and-half criticism: "There are certain performances in which everything [is] fully thought out in advance, and carried through with complete effectiveness. Yet these performances leave something to be desired. It is felt that . . . the performer had to be as economical as possible of feeling and enthusiasm." (*NYT*, 2 March 1924)

Friedman's London recital (23 Feb 1925), a program including the Beethoven Sonata in C Minor, op. 111, a Chopin group, Schumann's Symphonic Etudes and the Liszt Mephisto Waltz, drew unanimous praise: "It is no exaggeration to say he created a sensation by his technique alone. It looked so simple, this man seated bolt upright at the piano with never a disfiguring gesture, reeling off shimmering trills and cascades of chords, and yet behind his amazing technique, hidden somewhere in the impassive figure, there was a soul." (*YO*, 24 Feb 1925)

But not all critics were unconditionally won over with Friedman's pianism. After a five-year absence his New York recital of 6 March 1935—a long, difficult program including the Bach-Busoni Chaconne, Schumann *Kreisleriana*, a group of nine Chopin compositions, and works by Mozart, Ravel, Debussy and Strauss—inspired one critic to praise "the piano wizardry that abides in the fingers of Ignaz Friedman. [It] provided a stimulating and at times exciting demonstration of what a remarkable technique can mean. . . . In many of its details Mr. Friedman's playing was supreme playing of its kind, but in its larger aspects it was not the supreme kind of playing." (*NYT*, 7 March 1935) A few weeks later Friedman again played (30 March 1935) in New York, and his all-Chopin program drew this critique: "There could be different opinions of Mr. Friedman as a Chopin interpreter. He has a superb technic, which combines power and tonal charm, though an occasional tendency to force tone. He has the big manner. Sometimes this manner degenerates into the merely formidable." (*NYT*, 31 March 1935)

Regardless of Friedman's tendencies to let technique carry the day, to ignore or distort dynamics or other expression marks of the composer, he remained in good repute with his audiences and with most critics. He held to his highly individualistic concept of performance practice to the end of his career. And critics held to their views, though always tempered with undisguised admiration: "If extreme virtuosity and marvelous control of tone were ends in themselves, [Friedman's recital] could have been whole-heartedly endorsed. But again, as on many a previous occasion here, the Polish pianist employed his phenomenal keyboard gifts primarily with an eye to effect in interpretations which were eccentric to an unusual degree and displayed little reverence for the composers' ideas." (*NYT*, 28 Feb 1937)

Friedman's many piano rolls were mostly recorded for Duo-Art (see Discog.). In the 1920s and 1930s he recorded a large number of discs for Columbia, and his unpredictability in his concert performances shows clearly in his recordings. The two-CD album *Romantic Rarities*, volume 2 (see Discog.) provides a good sampling of his pianism, although limited to one composer, Chopin. As stated in the liner notes, the proportion of Friedman's rejected takes to those published was exceptionally high, so these recordings should represent some of the pianist's best performances on disc. A basically unimpressed reviewer describes Friedman as "an impulsive, unpredictable player of such waywardness that Leschetizsky at first refused to teach him." (*Gram*, Jan 1993) Then there is Chopin specialist James Methuen-Campbell, who has stated: "The place of Ignaz Friedman in the history of Chopin playing is unique and unassailable." Methuen-Campbell signals the Mazurkas, some of the Etudes, the F-Minor Ballade as among Friedman's finest performances, and commends Friedman for his discipline and musical consistency, tonal shading and great rhythmic subtlety. (Met/Cho, see Bibliog.)

For an appraisal of Friedman's pianism, the definitive source is the four-CD album containing his solo recordings from 1923 to 1936 (see Discog.). Here are the Chopin Mazurkas for which he was famous (as a youngster he reportedly danced mazurkas in the street); the Nocturnes, including the gorgeous E-flat Major, op. 55, no. 2; the Etudes, of which op. 10, no. 7 in C Major is extraordinary, as is op. 25, no. 6, the Etude in Thirds. This collection also includes works by Beethoven, Liszt and Mendelssohn, and there are also two talks—on Paderewski and on Chopin—taken from New Zealand radio broadcasts. The only dour note to this collection is the Grieg Concerto, Friedman's only concerto recording. Unfortunately the unidentified orchestra is under-rehearsed and the conductor ill-prepared.

Friedman's recordings stand as a testimonial to his controversial pianism. "Their greatness is that they bring the music to life and represent a challenge to the purists and digital-sound lovers who contemplate music as an abstraction or sonic bath rather than as a living entity." (Evans)

SELECTED REFERENCES

Cardus, Neville. "Pianist in Exile." *The Listener*, 19 Aug 1954, pp. 286–287.
Evans, Allan. "Ignaz Friedman." Liner notes, Pearl CD IF 2000 (see Discog.).
Friedman, Ignaz. "Americans Appearing in Europe Need Artistic Development." (interview) *Musical America*, 16 Jan 1926, p. 8.
———. "Quo Vadis Piano?" *Etude*, Nov 1926, pp. 807, 859.
———. "Self-Development A Necessity for the Pianist." In Brower, *Modern Masters*, see Bibliog.
———. "What is the Most Difficult Thing in Piano Playing?" *Etude*, May 1921, pp. 297–298. Also in Coo/Gre, see Bibliog.
Howard, Geoffrey. "Ignaz Friedman." Liner notes, Pearl Opal album 802/3.

Kinscella, Hazel Gertrude. "What Enters Into the True Piano Technique?" *Musical America*, 24 March 1923, pp. 11, 36.

Kramer, A. Walter. "A Modern Poet in Tonal Art." *Musical America*, 4 July 1914, p. 32.

Obituary. *New York Times*, 27 Jan 1948, p. 25.

"World Awaits Musical Messiah, Says Friedman." *Musical America*, 15 Jan 1921, p. 29.

See also Bibliography: Ald/Con; Bro/Mod; Coo/Gre; Dan/Con; Ewe/Li; New/Gro; Rat/Cle; Rub/MyM; Rub/MyY; Sal/Fam; Sch/Gre.

SELECTED REVIEWS

BN: 8 March 1924. *DT*: 24 Feb 1925. *KCS*: 2 March 1926. *KCT*: 15 Feb 1922. *LDN*: 24 Feb 1925. *LMP*: 24 Feb 1925. *MA*: 31 March 1923; 25 March 1935; 10 April 1935; 10 March 1937. *NYHT*: 7 March 1935. *NYT*: 8 Jan 1921; 4 Dec 1921; 14 Jan 1923; 4 Feb 1923; 23 March 1923; 6 Jan 1924; 10 Jan 1924; 2 March 1924; 10 Jan 1926; 31 Jan 1926; 31 Oct 1926; 12 Dec 1926; 15 Jan 1928; 27 Oct 1929; 7 March 1935; 31 March 1935; 28 Feb 1937. *TP*: 21 March 1924. *YO*: 24 Feb 1925.

SELECTED DISCOGRAPHY

Aliabiev-Liszt: The Nightingale. Chopin: Nocturne in G Minor, op. 37, no. 1; Nocturne in B Minor, op. 62, no. 1; Polonaise in B-flat Major, op. 71, no. 2. Liszt: *Reminiscences de Don Juan*. Liszt-Friedman: Hungarian Rhapsody No. 14. Moszkowski: Serenade, op. 15, no. 1. Paganini-Liszt-Busoni-Friedman: *La Campanella*. Schubert-Liszt: *Der Erlkönig*. Strauss: On the Beautiful Blue Danube, op. 314. Foné 90 F 10 CD. From Duo-Art piano rolls.

Ignaz Friedman Piano Recital. Pearl Opal 802/3. All of the material on this LP album appears on the later Pearl CD collection IF 2000.

Ignaz Friedman: The Complete Solo Recordings 1923–1936. Anon-Friedman: Judgement of Paris. Beethoven: Sonata in C-sharp Minor, op. 27, no. 2. Chopin: *Berceuse*, op. 57; Ballade in A-flat Major, op. 47; Impromptu, op. 36; Etudes, op. 10, nos. 5, 7, 12; op. 25, nos. 6, 9; Mazurkas, op. 7, nos. 1–3; op. 24, no. 4; op. 33, nos. 2, 4; op. 41, no. 1; op. 50, no. 2; op. 63, no. 3; op. 67, nos. 3–4; op. 68, no. 2; Nocturne in E-flat Major, op. 55, no. 2; Polonaise in A-flat Major, op. 53; Polonaise in B-flat Major, op. 71, no. 2; Prelude in D-flat Major, op. 28, no. 17; Sonata in B-flat Minor, op. 35 (2 movts.); Valses, op. 34, no. 2; op. 64, no. 1; Friedman speaks on Chopin. Dvořák: Humoresque. Friedman: *Elle Danse*, op. 10, no. 5; *Marquis et Marquise*, op. 22, no. 4; Music Box, op. 33, no. 3. Gärtner-Friedman: Viennese Dances Nos. 1, 2, 6. Gluck-Brahms: Gavotte. Hummel: *Rondo Favori* in E-flat Major. Grieg: Concerto in A Minor (Gaubert/SO). Liszt: Hungarian Rhapsody No. 2. Mendelssohn: Scherzo (Capriccio) in E Minor; Songs Without Words, op. 19, nos. 3, 6; op. 30, no. 6; op. 38, nos. 2, 6; op. 53, nos. 2, 4; op. 67, no. 2; op. 102, no. 5.

Mittler: Little Nana's Music Box. Moszkowski: *Serenata*, op. 15, no. 1.
Mozart: *Rondo alla Turca* (Sonata, K. 331). Paderewski: Minuet in G
Major; Friedman speaks on Paderewski. Paganini-Liszt-Busoni-Friedman:
La Campanella. Rubinstein: Romance; Valse Caprice. Schubert-Friedman:
Alt Wien. Schubert-Liszt: Hark, Hark the Lark! Schubert-Tausig: *Marche
Militaire* in D-flat Major. Suk: Minuetto. Pearl IF 2000 (4 CDs).
Pupils of Leschetizky. Chopin: Nocturne in E Flat, op. 55, no. 2. Pearl OPAL
CD 9839.
Romantic Rarities. The Celebrated Chopin Recordings (1924–36). *Berceuse*,
op. 57; Etudes, op. 10, nos. 5, 7, 12; op. 25, nos. 6, 9; Impromptu, op.
36; Mazurkas, op. 7, no. 1; op. 33, nos. 2, 4; Nocturne in E-flat Major, op.
55, no. 2; Polonaise in B-flat Major, op. 71, no. 2; Prelude in E-flat Major,
op. 28, no. 19; Waltz in A Minor, op. 34, no. 2. CDAPR 7014 (2 CDs).

GABRILOWITSCH, OSSIP SALOMONOVITCH: b. St. Petersburg, Russia, 7 February 1878; d. Detroit, Michigan, 14 September 1936.

> He played like no one else, and no one could play like him. Others played differently—were more thunderous, or cultivated a cyclonic virtuosity, or became miniaturists. . . . Gabrilowitsch remained, as man and artist, simply incorruptible, nobly himself. It would be entirely impossible to replace him.
>
> Olin Downes (*New York Times*, 20 September 1936)

Olin Downes—and, it seems, every other writer and critic who knew Gabrilowitsch personally—seldom discussed Gabrilowitsch's piano playing without adding a word about his caring nature. Becoming one of the most admired, most sought-after pianists of his day could easily have changed him; but to the end of his life Gabrilowitsch retained the modesty and thoughtfulness that so impressed his contemporaries. Pianist, conductor and chamber musician, he was one of the busiest musicians of his time, but personal commitments never kept him from lending a helping hand to unemployed or aspiring fellow artists—musicians, painters, writers, even scholars.

Ossip Gabrilowitsch was a complex personality—"always like a violin strung up to pitch," said his wife. Personally retiring and not one to boast of his own success, he vociferously defended his convictions and could, when called for, be straightforward to the point of bluntness. He was fun-loving, teasing and joyous; he could also be pessimistic, sometimes sorely depressed by the sorry state of the world. It would be hard to find a better description of Gabrilowitsch than that written by Bruno Walter in a letter (11 Nov 1936) to composer Daniel Gregory Mason: "Ossip was unique. His humanity was as strong in him as talent and spirit. Most astonishing was . . . that he, pessimist, skeptic, illusionless about man and fate, was at the same time serene, even gay, open-hearted to everybody, generous in thoughts and deeds." (Mason)

Gabrilowitsch always lived comfortably. He was the third son and youngest child of Solomon Gabrilowitsch, a Russian attorney, and Rose (Segal) Gabrilowitsch, of German-Russian ancestry, both vitally interested in music and art. By age three Gabrilowitsch could sing songs in perfect pitch, and at about four showed such an interest in the piano that his brother George, 11 years older, began giving him lessons. Before too long he was placed in the hands of an experienced pedagogue, a Madame Olga Theodorovitsch.

Gabrilowitsch studied at the St. Petersburg Conservatory for six years (1888–94): piano with Victor Tolstov; composition, theory and orchestration with Anatole Liadov and Alexander Glazunov; and various courses in general subjects. At the same time he was tutored at home in history, mathematics and languages. At age 11 Gabrilowitsch was selected to perform at the Conservatory concerts; by the time he was 13 years old, he was playing recitals at private salons and at social gatherings. He graduated (1894) with highest honors and the coveted Rubinstein Prize in piano playing.

Pressed by several important musicians to begin concertizing, he intuitively chose, with his father's full approval, to seek further training. Anton Rubinstein and Anna Essipoff, a faculty member at the Conservatory, urged him to study with Theodor Leschetizky in Vienna, and Essipoff, the former wife and assistant of Leschetizky, coached him for weeks to prepare him for his examination. Leschetizky accepted him in 1894, and two years later he gave such a successful debut concert (17 Oct 1896) in Berlin that he was immediately invited to give a second. His playing so impressed Hermann Wolff, the well-known concert manager, that he arranged for Gabrilowitsch to play a Beethoven concerto with the Leipzig *Gewandhaus* Orchestra, conducted by Arthur Nikisch. Before that season ended, Wolff arranged for a fourth performance.

Gabrilowitsch's fast-growing reputation in Europe induced the Everett Piano Company to bring him to America for a series of concerts, thus on 12 November 1900 he made his American debut at Carnegie Hall, playing the Tchaikovsky Concerto No. 1 with Emil Pauer (and "an orchestra of some sixty-five men") and also solo works by Beethoven, Chopin, Rubinstein and Liszt. On that same first tour (1900–01) Gabrilowitsch made two orchestral appearances and played three solo recitals in Boston. Other American tours followed in 1902–03, 1906–07, 1908–09; 1914–15; 1915–16. By then Gabrilowitsch had become one of the great pianists of his day.

In 1898 Leschetizky had introduced Gabrilowitsch, who was in Vienna on a visit, to Samuel Clemens (Mark Twain) and his daughter Clara, at the time a Leschetizky pupil. Three years later Gabrilowitsch and Clara became engaged; however, with Gabrilowitsch constantly touring and Clara, having given up her piano studies, now studying voice in London and elsewhere, they postponed marriage until 1909. During their long engagement, they corresponded frequently and

GABRILOWITSCH, OSSIP   287

visited together as much as possible. Clara developed into a pleasant mezzo-soprano, and after their marriage the Gabrilowitsches often gave recitals together.

Before his marriage Gabrilowitsch had taken time to spend several months (1905–06) in Leipzig studying conducting with the renowned Arthur Nikisch and in 1906 had made his conducting debut in Paris. Conducting became a second—and important—career, but he never gave up the piano and often would appear as pianist and conductor on the same program. Not too long after his marriage, Gabrilowitsch was appointed conductor of the *Konzertverein* Orchestra in Munich. He and his wife lived there for four years (1910–14), and Nina, their only child, was born in Munich in 1910.

The Munich years ended abruptly in September 1914 after the German military arrested Gabrilowitsch, a Russian citizen, as an enemy alien. Upon his release, he and his family escaped to Zurich, leaving almost everything behind. Although later able to send for clothes and a few personal belongings, they could not claim their books, music and manuscripts—all items subject to seizure by the Germans. Gabrilowitsch established residence in the United States and later (1921) became an American citizen.

In 1915, the season following his arrival in America, he undertook a mammoth historical piano series—six recitals tracing the development of pianism from Bach to the early 20th century. In 1916 he also made his American debut as a conductor with an all-Tchaikovsky program (30 Dec 1916) in New York, and he also played the Tchaikovsky Concerto No. 1. In 1918 he was appointed principal conductor of the Detroit Symphony Orchestra, a post he held for 17 years. And his "happy combination of musical genius with natural leadership and a tireless capacity for administrative detail gradually raised the Detroit Orchestra from mediocrity to eminence, establishing a solid music tradition in that midwestern industrial city." (Lichtenwanger) For a time (1928-31) Gabrilowitsch also shared the directorship of the Philadelphia Orchestra with Leopold Stokowski. His performances of Bach's St. Matthew Passion (in Detroit on 30 March 1926 and in New York on 7 April 1928) were high points in his conducting career. Gabrilowitsch not only led his orchestra and chorus entirely from memory, but also played the keyboard accompaniments to the soloists' recitatives.

Despite his conducting duties, he still managed to give many solo piano recitals, play concertos with orchestras, give joint recitals with his wife, play ensemble music, especially with the Flonzaley Quartet, and perform enormously popular two-piano recitals with Harold Bauer. The joyous Bauer-Gabrilowitsch duo recitals drew packed houses. During the 1925–26 season the indefatigable Gabrilowitsch played ten recitals in ten different cities with Bauer; gave six lecture-recitals (18 Oct 1925 to 21 Feb 1926)—a repeat of his earlier historical series, this time with lectures; and celebrated the 25th anniversary of his New York debut with a Carnegie Hall recital (21 Nov 1925, a Chopin-Schumann program) and a nostalgic performance (17 Nov) of the Tchaikovsky Concerto No. 1 (as at his debut), with Leopold Stokowski conducting the Philadelphia Orchestra. In twenty-five years of orchestral concerts, wrote one critic, he had not heard the Tchaikovsky presented "with the breadth, the fire and the nobility of conception that characterized it last night. . . . Mr. Gabrilowitsch gave of it a fabulous interpretation. We say 'fabulous' because this was the kind of playing, in its great lines, its unlimited power and rich musical feeling, that is said to have been frequent in a former day—which it certainly is not in this one." (*NYT*, 18 Nov 1925)

Gabrilowitsch's performance (14 March 1935) of the Chopin E Minor Concerto at the closing concert (he played and conducted) of the Detroit season turned out to be the last time he ever conducted the Detroit Symphony Orchestra or played in Orchestra Hall. Plagued with intestinal hemorrhaging for some months, in May 1935 he was told he had cancer. In the meantime he had one final concert to play under his agreement with Leon Barzin and the National Orchestral Association—a herculean undertaking of five concerts at which Gabrilowitsch played 16 concertos (or other concerted works) illustrating the history of the concerto from Bach to the 20th century.

Although gravely ill on the day before the final concert of the series, Gabrilowitsch insisted on playing and the next day had to be hospitalized. Two operations proved unsuccessful, and he died on 14 September 1936. At the public funeral services held in Orchestra Hall, the Detroit Symphony Orchestra played Schubert's Unfinished Symphony and the *Liebestod* from Wagner's *Tristan und Isolde*.

Mrs. Gabrilowitsch reported that her husband had neither the time nor the inclination to teach; that he really did not enjoy "imparting musical knowledge," either in classes or private lessons; and that he did not like to be asked questions. (Clemens) However, while they were living in Munich, a small group of piano students boarding together in a Berlin pension coaxed Gabrilowitsch into giving them lessons. An assistant first prepared the students, and once a month Gabrilowitsch came from Munich, stayed at the pension and for two or three days conducted long class sessions. A fine teacher, "he tried to retain whatever was good," said one of these students, "so that we might preserve our individuality, even though our ideas were quite different from his." (Brower)

Gabrilowitsch taught by example, that is, by having the pupil *hear* the right sound needed for interpretation. At lessons he sat at a second piano and frequently illustrated the desired tonal effect. Passing on what he had learned from Leschetizky, he (1) insisted that students listen, listen, listen and never be satisfied with a tone quality unless it was exactly what they wanted; (2) instructed them to use the Leschetizky method of high-arched hand position, loose wrist and firm fingers, "which buried themselves deeply into the keys"; and (3) reminded them that there is no such thing as an unimportant detail, that a sixteenth note is just as significant as a whole note. (Gabrilowitsch's articles in *Etude* explain his teaching in detail.)

Perhaps most helpful for these students was hearing Gabrilowitsch himself practicing during his stays at the pension. As a schoolboy and at the St. Petersburg Conservatory he had done the usual grinding practice, but with Leschetizsky he had learned that too much practice can be more harmful than too little, that quality ("concentration means everything"), not quantity, is the secret of good practice. For the rest of his life he practiced about two hours, three at the most, constantly listening to what he was playing, concentrating on every phrase and criticizing every note.

Like Leschetizky, Gabrilowitsch believed that playing a difficult passage over and over destroyed spontaneity and "robbed musical feeling of its bloom." Thus, as his wife describes it, at practice sessions she would hear him very carefully and thoughtfully play a short passage, or a page, then leave the piano to "look out of the window, as if to erase mistakes from his memory, at the same time losing himself in the deepest concept of the composer. I never heard him repeat a phrase over and over, and doubtless for this reason there was an improvisatory quality in his performance that was rare." (Clemens) Being musical director of the Detroit Symphony Orchestra inevitably reduced his practice time, but with his fine memory and limber fingers, Gabrilowitsch still, as reviews prove, gave wonderful piano performances.

Leschetizky's ideas about technique ("merely a means to an end," "music begins where technique leaves off") greatly influenced Gabrilowitsch's playing, thus tone production and tone coloring always took precedence over technique. The secret, for Gabrilowitsch, lay in complete relaxation, in acquiring the right touch—the player's means of creating dynamic shading and thus the distinguishing characteristic that differentiates one pianist's sound from that of another. As he poetically expressed it, "A fine technique without the requisite touch to liberate the performer's artistic intelligence and 'soul' is like a gorgeous chandelier without the lights." (Gabrilowitsch, "Touch")

His approach to a composition involved first understanding the entire piece—its musical construction and its poetic message—and then attempting to capture the beauty of tone to express that message. Reviews of the mature Gabrilowitsch's playing prove beyond any doubt that he had the necessary poetic gifts. Remarkable for their similarity, these reviews reveal that taste, not personality, dominated his playing; that the romantic aura and feeling of spontaneous improvisation enthralled listeners, even most critics. His playing, said reviewers, revealed complete ease, immaculate articulation, singing touch, temperament, intelligence, great polish, romantic outlook, sentiment (but never sentimentality), restraint (yet depth of expression) and a beautiful, translucent tone.

There are dozens of glowing appraisals of Gabrilowitsch's playing. Daniel Gregory Mason placed him among the few rare pianists (Paderewski, Rachmaninoff) who were what he called "transformers," meaning an artist "who intuitively catches the composer's vision of beauty, and by his skill, his feelings, his loyal self-subordination, realizes for us not its letter but its spirit, catches for us its inner meaning, gives to us the utterance that is above the notes, in all its magic." (Mason)

There was an unmistakable romantic aura about Gabrilowitsch, even in his appearance, and his interpretations were often extremely romantic. Critic Olin Downes agreed that those interpretations might upset the classicist, but in his view Gabrilowitsch's rich musical nature, profound understanding and sincerity justified his approach. For him, Gabrilowitsch was the kind of master interpreter whose "interpretations had this quality of true greatness; they gave you the feeling of harmoniousness and inevitability. . . . Always the listener was fascinated, absorbed. Always he was responding, as he listened, to beauty, feeling and the divine union of imagination and form." (*NYT*, 20 Sept 1936)

After hearing Gabrilowitsch's first American recital (26 Nov 1900), a critic wrote, "The most winning feature of his playing is the tone, which is simply luscious. It is not altogether complete in variety, but owing to a caressing touch it is always lovely." (*NYT*, 27 Nov 1900) A second recital on 30 November 1900 may have lacked authority, but the reviewer indulged in some eulogistic descriptions that would be echoed over and over throughout Gabrilowitsch's career: "Especially was it plain that his melting tone color in such music as that of the introspective and self-weary Chopin . . . wove its subtle spell about the feminine heart. This is a pianist who has moments of perfect loveliness. These come when the music and his far-away mood, his utter abstraction of manner, with its self-critical insistence on the letter of every nuance, are in complete harmony." (*NYT*, 1 Dec 1900)

Critic Henry T. Finck had to be won over: "When Gabrilowitsch made his début in New York he played, I thought, somewhat crudely and with rather excessive 'storm and stress.' Huneker raved over him from the start and soon I found that he had stolen a march on me; the more I heard Ossip the more I admired him, and ultimately I ranked him with the super-pianists." (Fin/My, see Bibliog.) As the years progressed Gabrilowitsch's playing appeared to take on the elements of fire and virtuosity deemed necessary in that era. He also began programming unusual items, something that not many of his contemporaries would care to emulate. He played the Glazunov Sonata No. 1 during his 1906–07 tour. On his 1908–09 tour he offered Daniel Gregory Mason's Elegy in Variation Form, which was received with much less enthusiasm.

Regardless of his programs, the reviews were now glowing. For example, "There are few players that make the piano so attractive an instrument to hear as does Mr. Gabrilowitsch. There was not a moment during the recital yesterday when the tone was not beautiful. . . . His tempos, also, are subject for unqualified admiration." (*MA*, 17 Nov 1906)

Audiences often went wild with enthusiasm (frequently Gabrilowitsch's encores absorbed as much time as the recital itself) and would not leave until someone came from backstage and closed the piano. His six historical recitals (1915–16) in New York were sensational. (The series was repeated in Boston and Chicago.) From first to last, audiences were held spellbound by Gabrilowitsch's ability to project so many styles so convincingly. "In carrying to so triumphant a conclusion this arduous series of historical recitals, Mr. Gabrilowitsch has performed a feat that will not quickly be forgotten and one that should be accorded a high place by the annalist of New York's present concert season." (*MA*, 18 March 1916)

Gabrilowitsch celebrated the 25th anniversary of his New York debut with an extremely busy, fulfilling year. His 21 November 1925 Carnegie Hall celebratory recital received lengthy, enthusiastic plaudits from all of New York's leading papers. "In twenty-five years Mr. Gabrilowitsch has gained his sway over the American public by the most legitimate and artistic means. These were days of sensationalism, but he has maintained inviolate his selfless devotion to his art, his sanity, his rare perceptions of beauty." (*NYT*, 22 Nov 1925) And also: "Mr. Gabrilowitsch's fine art has been repeatedly dissected and commented upon. He rose nobly to the expectations of an unusual anniversary Saturday. The Schumann of the great fantasia was portrayed with the musical emphasis upon his contemplative moods. The Schumann of the G minor sonata attained heights of noble eloquence, and Mr. Gabrilowitsch's readings of Chopin were masterly, forceful and full of fire." (*NYS*, 22 Nov 1925)

During the 1934–35 season Gabrilowitsch presented another series of "surveys," but on an entirely different level—16 works for piano and orchestra in five concerts with the National Orchestral Association under the baton of Leon Barzin. This glorious survey of concerto literature included masterful examples by J. S. Bach, Beethoven, Brahms, Chopin, Mozart, Rachmaninoff, Schumann and Tchaikovsky; and it proved to be a fitting climax to Gabrilowitsch's career.

At the first concert (27 Oct 1934) one critic found the Larghetto of the Bach (Concerto in A Major) "one of the most moving episodes in the literature. Similarly the Mozart [Concerto in D Minor, K. 466], which we think Mr. Gabrilowitsch plays better than any pianist before the public today, was a thing of beauty. . . . Beethoven's loveliest concerto [No. 3 in C Minor] had a reading so compelling as to arouse tumultuous acclaim." (*MA*, 10 Nov 1934) And the Beethoven Concertos Nos. 4 and 5 and Choral Fantasy on the second program (29 Dec 1934), "were performed with a devotion and a degree of technical excellence that made every moment significant." (*NYT*, 30 Dec 1934) Each concerted piece on the third concert (16 Feb 1935) was a genuine experience: "Mr. Gabrilowitsch played [the Chopin Concerto in E Minor] with the most sensitive poetry and a style becoming its period." In the performance of the Schumann Concerto the pianist, "completely changing his style, revealed the full measure of its loveliness and intimacy of appeal. In the virtuoso sense, at least, Liszt's concerto [No. 2 in A Major] climaxed the concert; and in other senses too." (*NYT*, 17 Feb 1935)

Gabrilowitsch played both Brahms Concertos at the fourth concert (9 March 1935). His "complete command of keyboard technique enabled him to surmount the thorniest of the many problems these compositions impose; but there was no virtuosity for its own sake. Passage work and figurations were so presented as to assert for them their measure of organic strength, with nothing of extraneous brilliance. The soloist was incorporated in the orchestra." (*NYT*, 10 March 1935) Although gravely ill as he reached his fifth and last concert (23 March 1935), Gabrilowitsch, performing the Franck Symphonic Variations, the Tchaikovsky Concerto No. 1, the Strauss *Burleske* and the Rachmaninoff Concerto No. 2, concluded his herculean project "after having lavished on each of his numbers all that head, heart and fingers could bring to them." (*NYT*, 24 March 1935)

Gabrilowitsch made very few recordings. He made numerous piano rolls for reproducing pianos; but comparing any one of these to his recording of the same composition, one is struck with a considerable divergence in performance, for the roll shows little of the pianist's famous touch and the tempo is frequently inaccurate. The most ambitious of Gabrilowitsch's disc recordings is the Schumann Piano Quintet, op. 44, made with the Flonzaley Quartet in 1924

(see Discog.). He also recorded the Arensky Waltz for two pianos with Harold
Bauer, and one must agree with Harold Schonberg that "a lovelier piano disc has
never been made." (Sch/Gre, see Bibliog.)

The 1992 VAIA CD (see Discog.) contains at least one version of every
work Gabrilowitsch ever recorded, including previously unissued recordings. He
programmed many short, miniature compositions on his recitals, and these he
recorded exclusively; there are no sonatas or suites. "Gabrilowitsch considered
clear, distinct phrasing an indispensable principle of piano playing, and his
recordings are all eloquent testimony to this. . . . All are enriched by
Gabrilowitsch's uncomplicated, poetic approach." (MacAlear) Two of his own
pieces which he recorded offer proof of his considerable compositional talents.

"As old as they are Gabrilowitsch's records still demonstrate what most
present-day pianists can't do. Many a budding virtuoso can play faster than
Gabrilowitsch did, most can play louder, but very few if any can play rapidly and
still maintain his kind of finger articulation, and fewer still can coax such a tone
from the piano. You don't get Gabrilowitsch's kind of piano playing any more
and it's our loss." (Lewis)

SELECTED REFERENCES

Brower, Harriette. "Gabrilowitsch As He Appeared to One of the 'Gabbites'."
    Musical America, 1 Nov 1913.
Clemens, Clara. *My Husband Gabrilowitsch*. New York: Harper & Brothers,
    1938.
Downes, Olin. "Ossip Gabrilowitsch." *New York Times*, 20 Sept 1936, sec.
    9, p. 7.
Gabrilowitsch, Ossip. "Memorizing Music Successfully." (interview with
    Edwin Hughes). *Etude*, May 1914, pp. 327–328.
———. "Progress in Piano Playing and Conducting." (conference with R. H.
    Wollstein). *Etude*, Dec 1934, pp. 701–702.
———. "Theodor Leschetizky: A Great Master of the Piano." *The Piano
    Teacher*, March/April 1963, pp. 8–10.
———. "Touch—the Great Essential of Fine Pianoforte Playing." *Etude*,
    March 1909, pp. 153–154.
Horvath, Cecile de. "Lessons with Ossip Gabrilowitsch, Piano Virtuoso and
    Conductor." Part I. *Etude*, Dec 1938, pp. 781–782.
———. "Lessons with Ossip Gabrilowitsch." Part II. *Etude*, Jan 1939, pp. 14,
    64.
———. "Lessons with Ossip Gabrilowitsch." Part III. *Etude*, Feb 1939, pp.
    89, 123.
———. "Lessons with Ossip Gabrilowitsch." Part IV. *Etude*, March 1939, p.
    155.
———. "Safonoff and Gabrilowitsch." *Piano Teacher*, Jan/Feb 1962, pp. 16–
    19.
Lewis, John Sam. "Ossip Gabrilowitsch." *Record Research*, Jan 1978, p. 13.
Lichtenwanger, William. "Ossip Gabrilowitsch." In *Dictionary of American
    Biography*, (Dic/Am, see Bibliog).

MacAlear, Robert. "Ossip Gabrilowitsch: His Issued and Unissued Recordings."
Liner notes for VAIA/IPA 1018.

Mason, Daniel Gregory. "Gabrilowitsch in Detroit." In *Music In My Time*.
New York: Macmillan Company, 1938, pp. 310–330.

Obituary. *Musical Times*, Oct 1936, p. 945. *New York Times*, 15 Sept 1936,
p. 29. *The Times* (London), 15 Sept 1936, p. 12.

"Piano Players and their Achievements." *New York Times*, 18 Nov 1900, p.
22.

See also Bibliography: Ald/Con; Bro/Pia; Cha/Spe; Coo/Gre; Dow/Oli; Ewe/
Mu; Fin/My; Kau/Art; Kol/Que; Lah/Fam; MGG; New/Gro; Nie/Mei;
Rat/Cle; Rub/MyM; Rub/MyY; Sal/Fam; Sch/Gre.

SELECTED REVIEWS

LAT: 28 Jan 1916. *MA*: 17 Nov 1906; 22 Dec 1906; 12 Jan 1907; 20 April
1907; 13 Feb 1909; 10 Feb 1912; 20 Nov 1915; 18 Dec 1915; 18 March
1916; 10 June 1916; 25 Feb 1929; 10 Nov 1934. *NYS*: 22 Nov 1925.
NYT: 13 Nov 1900; 27 Nov 1900; 1 Dec 1900; 3 Nov 1902; 11 Jan 1909;
7 Feb 1909; 28 March 1915; 14 Nov 1915; 25 Feb 1916; 16 April 1916;
28 Nov 1916; 1 Jan 1917; 3 March 1917; 25 Jan 1919; 27 Nov 1921; 18
Feb 1923; 28 Oct 1923; 26 Oct 1924; 14 Nov 1925; 18 Nov 1925; 22 Nov
1925; 21 Dec 1925; 10 Jan 1927; 29 Oct 1930; 28 Oct 1931; 22 Feb 1932;
15 Nov 1932; 25 April 1933; 6 Nov 1933; 4 Nov 1934; 30 Dec 1934; 17
Feb 1935; 10 March 1935; 24 March 1935. *NYTr*: 22 Nov 1925. *SFC*: 4
Aug 1926. *TL*: 3 June 1897; 18 June 1897.

SELECTED DISCOGRAPHY

Ossip Gabrilowitsch Concert. Chopin: *Fantaisie Impromptu*, op. 66; Etudes,
op. 10, no. 8, op. 25, no. 2; Waltz in E Minor. Fauré: Romance No. 3.
Gabrilowitsch: Melodie in E Minor, op. 8, no. 1. Leschetizky: Intermezzo
in Octaves, op. 44, no. 4. Mendelssohn: Spinning Song, op. 67, no. 4.
Rachmaninoff: Prelude in C-sharp Minor. Sapellinikoff: Elf's Dance, op. 3.
Schubert: *Moment musical*, op. 94, no. 3. Schumann: *Novelette*, op. 99,
no. 9. Everest. Archive of Piano Music. X-924. From Duo-Art piano
rolls.

Ossip Gabrilowitsch (His Issued and Unissued Recordings). Arensky: *Près de la
Mer*, op. 54, no. 4; Waltz (from Suite for two Pianos, op. 15: with Harold
Bauer). Bach–Saint-Saëns: Bourrée (Violin Partita in B Minor). Delibes:
Passepied from *Le Roi s'amuse*. Gabrilowitsch: Caprice, op. 3; Melody in
E Minor, op. 8. Glazunov: Govotte, op. 39, no. 3. Gluck-Brahms:
Gavotte. Grainger: Shepherd's Hey. Moszkowski: *En Automne*, op. 36,
no. 4.. Schütt: Rococo-Minuet (with Harold Bauer). Schumann: *Novelette*,
op. 99, no. 9; Quintet for Piano and Strings, op. 44 (with the Flonzaley
Quartet); *Warum* (*Fantasiestücke*, op. 12). VAIA/IPA 1018 (CD).

GAVRILOV, ANDREI: b , Moscow, USSR, 21 September 1955.

> Combative, compulsive and intense, Andrei Gavrilov is a unique star in the pianistic firmament, one who leaves an indelible mark on everything he plays.
>
> Bryce Morrison (*Gramophone*, June 1992)

"Combative," "compulsive," "intense"—all fittingly apply to Andrei Gavrilov. Since he is also, as he freely admits, highly emotional and impulsive, it is not surprising to learn that the young Gavrilov growing up in the former USSR was a rebellious nonconformist—more aesthetically than politically. In that respect he was like his father Vladimir Gavrilov, a well-known painter who, says his son, died at age 47, worn down by pressure to conform and lack of artistic freedom. Unlike the father, the pianist son weathered the ups and downs of living in what he calls the "cultural chaos" of the former Soviet Union. He is now a German citizen, reveling in the free yet organized cultural atmosphere of his new homeland.

At age three Gavrilov began piano lessons with his mother Assanetta Yegiserian, a graduate of the Moscow Conservatory, and she watched over his development all through his school years. Starting at age six, he studied at the Central Music School under the guidance of Tatiana Kestner, a "very German" pedagogue. As a student of Alexander Goldenweiser, Kestner had what Gavrilov recalls as a rational approach to music, at least when compared to that of his mother, a strong advocate of "emotional richness" in music. But these two formidable teachers formed a kind of collaboration in regard to his training, and, he now says, "it did me a lot of good."

Gavrilov was about 16 years old the day he was called off the football field (he was team captain) and instructed (he had no say in the matter) to enter the 1974 Tchaikovsky Competition. About a year and a half earlier he had become a pupil of Lev Naumov, under whose tutelage he would later study at the Moscow Conservatory, and it was Naumov who prepared him for the contest. Naumov, with his marvelous sense of musical fantasy and imagination, led Gavrilov to "a new understanding of the essence of music, a new attitude to the form, to the psychology of performance. . . . One can work with him at a piece forever and discover something new." Before Naumov, says Gavrilov, "there was my ungovernable temperament—I was simply raging at the instrument and was already playing super-difficult compositions, but on the other hand there was no profound understanding of music yet." (Zil/Rus, see Bibliog.) Clearly, Naumov has been the strongest musical influence in his life.

Gavrilov took first place at that fifth Tchaikovsky Competition, very likely because the "jury and audience alike were bowled over by his flame-throwing technique, by the unique drive and physicality of his playing." (Morrison, "Settling In") And winning that 1974 Tchaikovsky Competition brought Gavrilov's name to the attention of the international musical world. Later that year his career took another big step forward when a telegram from the Salzburg Festival invited him to substitute for an indisposed Sviatoslav Richter. It was a wonderful opportunity, but he had to cope with an audience expecting the great Richter. As he later told the story, "The audience booed; they hated me. . . . I felt so excited—so angry—that I played the programme of Scarlatti, Haydn, Mozart, and then just went on and played more and more and more— Rachmaninov, Prokofiev, the lot. It was childish and I wouldn't do it now, but it worked. At the end they went crazy and the police had to help me escape, like a pop star." (Finch, "Full-frontal assault")

Gavrilov's career quickly moved ahead and beyond the USSR. In 1976 Richter invited him to perform at the Touraine Festival in France; and that autumn Gavrilov "stole" the Helsinki Festival by giving a performance of the Rachmaninoff Concerto No. 3 (with Paavo Berglund and the Bournemouth Symphony Orchestra) "that brought down the house." (*TL*, 8 Sept 1976) He also made his first London appearance that year, performing (22 Nov 1976) the Prokofiev Concerto No. 1 and the Ravel Concerto for Left Hand, also with the BSO. London loved Gavrilov. On 5 July 1977 he received more rave reviews for his performance of the Tchaikovsky Concerto No. 1, performed with the London Symphony Orchestra under David Atherton. In September 1978 he made his debut in Germany as soloist with the Berlin Philharmonic Orchestra and followed it with a 30-performance tour of West Germany. In 1979 he gave 12 concerts in Japan.

He was not doing so well at home. Soviet authorities worried about his having so many performances outside of the USSR, away from their control. Not only that, the curious, rebellious Gavrilov had openly criticized the Minister of Culture, read all of the banned works of Solzhenitsyn and found out for himself the true facts, not the doctored official version, of Russia's history. Such behavior had to cause problems. The KGB watched him at all times, at home and abroad, and once, after he had refused to perform at the Kremlin for Brezhnev, the KGB threatened to send him to one of their notorious "psychiatric" clinics.

In 1979 the USSR's invasion of Afghanistan ended all cultural exchanges between East and West, giving those shadowing Gavrilov the perfect opportunity to rein him in. For three years he was not allowed to give concerts (except for workers at factories), had to sell some of his possessions to survive and, in effect, became a nonperson, so much so that former friends avoided him completely for fear of becoming contaminated by his political troubles. Tensions between East and West eventually eased, as they always do, and Gavrilov's situation likewise improved. In 1984 he was again performing abroad. "Andrei Gavrilov," wrote a London critic, "has scorched his way into London after five long years' absence. Last night he performed a recital of Scriabin and Rachmaninov which will surely be remembered as one of the great musical events of the year." (*TL*, 20 Aug 1984)

Wanting to make up those lost five years, Gavrilov announced that he hoped to perform at least 70 percent of the time in the West, and he and his wife therefore requested permission to stay in Great Britain. Gavrilov later became a German citizen and makes his home in Germany, where the people, he says, live with music all the time. In the last decade he has performed extensively, especially in Great Britain, Europe (Germany, Italy, Switzerland, Austria), Japan, Canada and the United States.

Gavrilov does not teach. About 10 years ago he stated that he was firmly convinced that it is impossible for an active concertizing pianist to be both performer and pedagogue, and there is no evidence that he has since changed his mind.

Although he loves to play the piano, he hates the traveling part of the concert life, much preferring to be at home practicing his repertoire or doing manual work, especially welding. In 1990 Gavrilov proudly announced that he had done all the manual work for his home in Wiesbaden, had even put much of the furniture together. He enjoys all the arts—theater, movies, painting, literature.

Apart from the Tchaikovsky award, he was the winner in the 1975 International UNESCO Competition in Bratislava; in 1989 he was the recipient of the *Premio Internationale Academia Musicale Chigiana.*

Gavrilov's rip-roaring technique was not a gift, but the result of hard work, continuing hard work. Years of daily practice at the Central Music School—an hour and a half of scales, Czerny and Hanon—laid the foundation; and since then he has maintained and improved his technique with a regular practice routine. Like Shura Cherkassky, Gavrilov thinks regular practice is so important that when forced to miss a day, he considers the lost hours as a debt that he must make up. He normally spends about three-fourths of practice time on the music for his programs, the rest on new pieces, music he does not know. Hating any kind of edited compositions, Gavrilov tries always to work with the Urtext. He will of course investigate the comments of various authorities on a particular piece, but says that "when an editor's hand pushes through the staff, it drives me crazy."

Basically his repertoire extends from Scarlatti to Stockhausen and concentrates on the major works of Scriabin, Rachmaninoff, Liszt and Chopin. Gavrilov himself says that he loves to play difficult works and different styles, and that specializing in one single field is the worst thing possible.

Onstage playing the piano Gavrilov appears intense, overpoweringly energetic and dramatic. As for his way of playing the piano, London music critic Joan Chissell seems to have set the formula of appreciation for Gavrilov's blistering piano style way back in 1976, the year he made his first sensational appearances in the West—at the Tours and Helsinki festivals. Chissell became an instant, ardent admirer of "this young Russian wizard," and in her first reviews described his playing with these words and phrases: transcendental virtuosity, crystalline delicacy, fiery strength, the magical delicacy of his bravura, the refinement of his touch. We presently have an accumulation of nearly 20 years of reviews representing many different critics' opinions about Gavrilov's playing. Their particular words and phrases clearly reiterate the Chissell formula: demon of the keyboard, lion of the keyboard, a pianist of torrential power, spectacular virtuosity, fearless bravura, dynamic yet subtle cantabile playing, crystalline delicacy, lyrical delicacy, musical sensitivity and so on.

At the 1976 Touraine Festival: "There was a wild abandonment in his playing of Ravel's 'Scarbo' and Balakirev's 'Islamey' that one would have called reckless if it had not had a precision and control seemingly and miraculously beyond the possibility of error. . . . It was the poetry of his performance that stirred one most. Liszt's 'La Campanella' had a poise, a delicate and luminous clarity, that you would have thought quite impossible at such a rapid tempo." (*STL*, 11 July 1976)

At his London debut (22 Nov 1976) Gavrilov played two concertos: the Prokofiev Concerto No. 1 in D-flat Major, op. 10, and Ravel's Concerto for the Left Hand, with Paavo Berglund conducting the Bournemouth Symphony Orchestra. "Prokofiev's first concerto left no doubt of Mr. Gavrilov's masterly technique, physical strength, and tireless musical commitment. . . . Ravel's concerto for left hand alone was hardly less a triumph of pianistic virtuosity, with unusual clarity and precision in dispatch of the most awkward passages." (*TL*, 23 Nov 1976)

Gavrilov performed often in London from 1976 through 1978, was restricted to the USSR for several years and did not play again in London until 19 August 1984—really the start of his international concert career. Substituting on short notice for an indisposed Boris Christoff, Gavrilov played (21 March 1985) the Rachmaninoff Concerto No. 2 with the London Philharmonic Orchestra under James Conlon. His was "a young man's Rachmaninov, full of bounding energy in the opening movement." And in the finale, "he released a torrent of feeling and virtuosity—sometimes leaving James Conlon and the LPO a little bemused by his unpredictable headstrong approach." (*DT*, 22 March 1985)

Gavrilov received "several standing ovations" at his first American performance (29 July 1976)—an all-Russian program at the Newport Music Festival. But a decade passed before he made his first American tour, where his scorching performances drew mixed reviews. At his first Los Angeles appearance (17 April 1985) he played an all-Chopin program—the four Ballades, six Etudes from Opus 10 and the Sonata in B-flat Minor—and "failed to establish himself as an important Chopin interpreter. Instead, he excited a large, and largely undiscerning, audience by fast, passionate and blurred playing of all the many climaxes in this program, and by generally neat hurdling of technical challenges." (*LAT*, 18 April 1985) However, another reviewer at that same event saw Gavrilov as "a phenomenal technician as well as an artist with original and telling ideas and an amazing command of the music he plays. His interpretations were mature beyond his years yet still full of youthful zest." (*LAHE*, 18 April 1985)

A review of Gavrilov's "sensational" performance at his Midwest debut (1 July 1985), at Ravinia's Murray Theater, provides a very perceptive analysis of his approach: "In some respects his pianism is a throwback to the Russian piano style of the late-19th century, particularly as represented by Rachmaninoff and Horowitz. With Gavrilov, there is much the same combination of prodigious power and crystalline lyricism that set these great pianists apart, along with a highly individual sense of Romantic phrasing." (*CT*, 2 July 1985)

Back in London later that year, Gavrilov received a devastating review for his performance (24 Sept 1985) of the Rachmaninoff Concerto No. 2 with Guido Ajmone-Marsan conducting the London Philharmonic Orchestra, specifically because of his rash virtuosity: "Such an absence of sensibility or the finer musical virtues is doubly distressing given Gavrilov's phenomenal gifts, and it is to be hoped that he will quickly re-find his truest musical as well as technical form." (*MM*, Nov 1985)

By 1986, a decade after his spectacular leap into the West, other reviews of Gavrilov's playing had become noticeably harsh. On 8 March 1986 he played the Rachmaninoff Concerto No. 3 with the Baltimore Symphony Orchestra, under David Zinman. Right at the start, "the piano part roared off on its own, creating utter chaos vis-a-vis his accompanists. Thereafter Mr. Gavrilov either shoved Mr. Zinman precipitously ahead or kept him waiting with exaggerated *Luftpausen*." (*NYT*, 10 March 1986)

But Gavrilov gave a knockout performance (13 Nov 1986) of Ravel's Concerto for the Left Hand with the Detroit Symphony Orchestra, Sixten Ehrling conducting. He "evoked strong, physical images of the sort that put him in a line with such as Hofmann, Lhévinne, Richter and Gilels. Each phrase bounded upward and outward toward its manifest destiny. Each technical barrier was demolished. And forget sentimentality." (*DeDN*, 15 Nov 1986)

Gavrilov remains a controversial pianist. He played (10 Feb 1990) the Ravel Concerto for Left Hand with the Scottish National Orchestra, Raymond Leppard conducting, with "power and thunder almost beyond description. . . . But Andrei, the axeman of the keyboard, is also a poet. And to the exotic, fragrant passages of this mesmerising piece he brought an exquisite delicacy and weightless clarity of sound that were breathtaking." (*GH*, 12 Feb 1990)

One of Gavrilov's recital programs for the 1993–94 concert season had music by Schubert (3 Impromptus), Ravel (*Gaspard de la nuit*) and Prokofiev (Sonata No. 8). Reviews of the Toronto performance (5 Feb 1994) and the New York performance (9 Feb 1994) differ. Performing the Schubert in Toronto, "Gavrilov established an intimate rapport with the audience while foregrounding a warm, full-textured sound that never obscured the delicate lines of the music." Playing the formidable Ravel triptych, "he seemed completely at ease with the difficult glissandi and sylph-like, sliding figures of the work's *Ondine* section, and his tone control in *Le Gibet* was a marvel." (*TS*, 7 Feb 1994) However, in the New York performance (9 Feb 1994), Gavrilov showed "a pianist's gargantuan technical appetite for devouring" both the Ravel *Gaspard* and Prokofiev's Eighth Sonata, but in the Schubert (3 Impromptus from D. 935) his "technical confusions were startling. . . . Yet more puzzling was Mr. Gavrilov's seeming oblivion to Schubert's ambiguous harmony and how it prods and tugs at melodic movement." (*NYT*, 12 Feb 1994)

Gavrilov has made numerous recordings from a varied repertoire ranging from Bach and Handel to Scriabin. In 1985 he recorded all seven Bach solo keyboard concertos with Jurij Nikolaewski and a Russian chamber orchestra, and during 1984–87 he recorded the complete set with the Academy of St. Martin in the Fields, conducted by Sir Neville Marriner (see Discog.). The 1985 discs appear to be no longer available, but Marriner's orchestra and Gavrilov get high marks for their version. In Gavrilov's readings, "every note has a pin-point clarity, often sharpened by a detached touch that gives extra buoyancy to his already exceptionally tautly-sprung rhythm." (*Gram*, April 1987) And his piano performance of the six Bach French Suites should dispel the prejudices of the most ardent purists. "The notes unfold naturally, without eccentricity, with beautiful tone and communication." (*CL*, May/June 1987)

Gavrilov's Scriabin album (see Discog.) contains some of the most beautifully played Scriabin works recorded to date. "Even in those rare pieces in this recital that call for power and obvious virtuosity it is the controlled restraint with which he deploys these qualities that is most impressive, and elsewhere his playing has a contained eloquence, a refined lyricism and an ability to convey almost secret, private emotions that is ideally suited to the music." (*Gram*, Aug 1986)

Gavrilov sparkles in his Russian repertoire in a CD containing a 1979 recording of the Tchaikovsky Concerto No. 1 (Muti/Philharmonia), a 1977 recording of the Prokofiev Concerto No. 1 (Rattle/London SO), the Tchaikovsky Theme and Variations, op. 19, no. 6, Prokofiev's fiery *Suggestion diabolique*, op. 4, no. 4, and Balakirev's transcendental *Islamey* (see Discog.). "The playing on this occasion is dazzling. The Prokofiev concerto is brilliant and brimming with excitement. . . . The Tchaikovsky is an imposing reading." (*ARG*, July/Aug 1993)

Although the Rachmaninoff Concerto No. 2 has been recorded dozens and dozens of times, there is arguably always room for a fresh approach, and Gavrilov (with Muti and the Philadelphia Orchestra) gives us that on a CD also including the Rhapsody on a Theme of Paganini, another time-worn favorite (see Discog.). "This is Rachmaninoff in a no-nonsense, high-octane virtuosic . . . Earl Wild sort of mold. The pianist's dexterity is stunning, not much *rubato* is applied, and more attention is paid to rhythmic propulsion and an impressive dynamic range than to phrasing or creating a rich sonority." (*ARG*, Jan/Feb 1992)

In 1990 Gavrilov signed an exclusive contract with *Deutsche Grammophon*, under which he has already recorded the Chopin Sonata No. 2 and the four Ballades, three Prokofiev sonatas, the Schubert Impromptus and a Grieg album and plans to record Bach (French Suites, English Suites, Goldberg Variations), Beethoven (Concertos, Diabelli Variations), Liszt (Transcendental Etudes) and others. The new DG Chopin CD (see Discog.) contains the Sonata No. 2 in B-flat Minor and the four Ballades. Critics differ on this CD. One reviewer hears "a composed and mature Gavrilov, someone able to storm high heaven, if necessary, without loss of refinement, someone in fact acutely aware that Polish passion in Chopin was counter-balanced by Gallic finesse." (*Gram*, June 1992) On the other hand, another critic sees Gavrilov's reading of the Sonata as "nearly a disaster. The first two movements are full of strange articulation and arbitrary emphases, mannerisms which call attention to themselves and away from the music. . . . The *Ballades* are not as grotesque as the sonata, but they also have arbitrary touches and never come across with as much rhetorical conviction as I would like to hear." (*Fan*, Sept/Oct 1993)

A reviewer of Gavrilov's CD collection of three Prokofiev sonatas (see Discog.) flatly states that, "Gavrilov's reading of the first movement of the Seventh Sonata is one of the finest I've heard. . . . The Eighth Sonata is perhaps, overall, the finest performance of the whole disc. . . . I liked his gentle, unimpeded sense of flow in the opening *Andante dolce*." (*Gram*, June 1992)

Another *Deutsche Grammophon* CD, the eight Schubert Impromptus, surprised some who view Gavrilov's flamboyant approach as basically inimical to Schubert's music: "Gavrilov is straightforward in his approach to the Impromptus, using *rubato* with tasteful restraint; it is sensitive, musicianly playing, often poetic, without dissolving into sentimental mush." (*Fan*, Nov/Dec 1993) An even more unusual—for Gavrilov, that is—offering appears in a collection of two dozen short compositions drawn from Grieg's corpus of Lyric Pieces (see Discog.). With a large group of such highly contrasted works, mixed reactions are inevitable. "It is when the music is slow that Gavrilov has a tendency to sound unconvincing." Yet, the "overtly dance-like *Lyric Pieces* are all splendidly done . . . [and] I have never heard the 'Nocturne' from Op. 54 played more beautifully." (*Gram*, Dec 1993)

Some of Gavrilov's recordings have been internationally recognized as eminently superior: best concerto (Ravel) in *Gramophone's* 1978 awards; 1981 *Deutscher Schallplattenpreis* (Prokofiev); *Grand Prix du Disque* for Scriabin (1985) and Rachmaninoff (1986) solo recordings; *High Fidelity International Record Critics Award* for the Scriabin album (1985).

SELECTED REFERENCES

Brissaud, Pascal. "*Aventures et nouvelles aventures d'Andrei Gavrilov.*" *Le Monde de la Musique*, July/Aug 1992.
Finch, Hilary. "Full-frontal assault." *The Times* (London), 24 Sept 1985, p. 9.
————— "Striking 20-finger exercise of rite." *The Times* (London), 26 Sept 1992 (Weekend Times), p. 3. A review of the Stravinsky CD (see Discog.) by Ashkenazy and Gavrilov.
"Gavrilov—The Richter Connection." *Gramophone*, Jan 1985, p. 846.
Houlahan, Mike. "The day the music died." *The Evening Post* (New Zealand), 5 March 1992.
Malitz, Nancy. "Slava at Sixty." *Ovation*, March 1987, pp. 12–17.
Morrison, Bryce. "A Rebel With Many Causes." *Gramophone*, Sept 1990, p. 468.
————— "Settling In." (interview) *Gramophone*, June 1992, p. 21.
Parry, Gareth. "Moscow allows Gavrilov to stay." *The Guardian* (Manchester), 21 March 1985, p. 3.
Passy, Charles. "Two From Feltsman's Schooldays." *Ovation*, Jan 1989, p. 22.
Shuik, Bella. "Andrei Gavrilov in the West." *The World & I*, May 1987, pp. 213–219.
"Soviet Pianist Asks to Stay in Britain." *New York Times*, 7 March 1985, sec. 3, p. 17.
Webster, Daniel. "Soviet pianist revels in playing West again." *Philadelphia Inquirer*, 16 July 1985, sec. D, pp. 1, 8.
See also Bibliography: IWWM; Zil/Rus.

SELECTED REVIEWS

BG: 14 Oct 1985. *CSM*: 1 May 1985. *CT*: 2 July 1985; 12 Nov 1986.
DeDN: 15 Nov 1986. *DT*: 22 March 1985; 7 Dec 1991. *FT*: 15 May
1990. *GH*: 12 Feb 1990. *GM*: 23 March 1985. *LAHE*: 18 April 1985.
LAT: 18 April 1985; 17 Oct 1985. *MA*: Sept 1985. *MM*: Nov 1985.
NDN: 30 July 1976; 13 July 1985. *NYP*: 19 Dec 1986. *NYT*: 29 April
1985; 15 Sept 1985; 24 Oct 1985; 10 March 1986; 12 Feb 1994. *SFC*: 3
May 1985. *SLPD*: 22 Sept 1991. *STL*: 11 July 1976. *TL*: 8 July 1976; 8
Sept 1976; 23 Nov 1976; 7 July 1977; 4 Sept 1978; 20 Aug 1984; 20 Nov
1985; 3 June 1988; 5 Dec 1991. *TS*: 7 Feb 1994.

SELECTED DISCOGRAPHY

Bach: Concerto No. 1 in D Minor, BWV 1052; Concerto No. 2 in E Major,
    BWV 1053; Concerto No. 4 in A Major, BWV 1055; Concerto No. 5 in F
    Minor, BWV 1056. EMI Classics CDD 7 64055-2. Marriner/ASMF.
Bach: Concerto No. 3 in D Major, BWV 1054; Concerto No. 6 in F Major,
    BWV 1057; Concerto No. 7 in G Minor, BWV 1058; French Suite No. 5
    in G Major, BWV 816. EMI Classics CDD 7 64293-2. Marriner/ASMF.
Bach: French Suites (6). Angel CDCB-49293 (2 CDs).
Balakirev: *Islamey*. Prokofiev: Concerto No. 1 in D-flat Major, op. 10
    (Rattle/London SO); *Suggestion diabolique*, op. 4, no. 4. Tchaikovsky:
    Concerto No. 1 in B-flat Minor, op. 23 (Muti/Philharmonia); Theme and
    Variations in F Major, op. 19, no. 6. EMI Classics CDM 7 64329-2.
Chopin: *Études,* op. 10; *Études*, op. 25. EMI CDC 7 47452-2.
Chopin: Sonata in B-flat Minor, op. 35; Ballades (4). DG 435622-2. (rec. 1991)
Grieg: Lyric Pieces. DG 437 522-2. Twenty-four selections from the com-
    poser's extensive sets of miniatures.
Prokofiev: Prelude, op. 12, no. 7; Romeo and Juliet, op. 75; *Suggestion dia-
    bolique*, op. 4, no. 4. Ravel: *Gaspard de la nuit*; *Pavane pour une infante
    défunte*. DG 437 532-2. These 1993 recordings (except the Prelude) are not
    reissues of previous works but new readings.
Prokofiev: Sonata No. 3 in A Minor, op. 28; Sonata No. 7 in B-flat Major, op.
    83; Sonata No. 8 in B-flat Major, op. 84. DG 435439-2.
Rachmaninoff: Concerto No. 2 in C Minor, op. 18; Rhapsody on a Theme of
    Paganini, op. 43. EMI Classics CDC 7 49966. Muti/Philharmonia.
Rachmaninoff: Five Preludes; Four *Moments musicaux*; Two *Études-tableaux*;
    Élégie, op. 3, no. 1. Angel CDC 47124.
Ravel: Concerto for the Left Hand; *Gaspard de la nuit*. Angel CDM 69026.
    Rattle/London SO.
Schubert: Impromptus D. 899 and D. 935. DG 435 788-2.
Schumann: *Carnaval*, op. 9; *Papillons*, op. 2; *Faschingsschwank aus Wien*, op.
    26. Angel CDC 49235.
Scriabin: Sonata No. 4 in F Major, op. 30; 24 Preludes, op. 11; Etude, op. 42,
    no. 5. Angel CDC-47346.

Stravinsky: Concerto for 2 pianos; *Le Sacre du printemps*; *Scherzo à la russe*; Sonata for 2 pianos. London 433 829-2. With Vladimir Ashkenazy.

VIDEO

Rachmaninoff: Concerto No. 2 in C Minor, op. 18. In *Vladimir Ashkenazy in Moscow*. EMI Classics 7 40305-3. Ashkenazy/Royal PO.

GIESEKING, WALTER WILHELM: b. Lyons, France, 5 November 1895; d. London, England, 26 October 1956.

> I think that Gieseking will long be remembered as the incarnation of supreme craftsmanship. Perhaps one could find a few pianists more inspired, more powerful in their conception, but none who could manage as well as Gieseking to turn absolute craftsmanship into art with a capital A.
>
> Marcella Barzetti (*Recorded Sound*, Spring 1962)

By all odds a superb pianist born to pureblood German parents (Wilhelm and Martha [Bethke] Gieseking) and bearing the Teutonic-sounding name of Walter Wilhelm Gieseking would have become a formidable specialist in the music of one of the mighty German masters—Beethoven, Brahms, even Schumann. But Gieseking, finding his métier at the far opposite end of the musical spectrum, became his era's most remarkable interpreter of early 20th-century French music. Even now Walter Gieseking's Debussy and Ravel recordings admirably hold their own with other more recent versions.

Who can say whether or not living his first 15 years mostly in the congenial climate of southern France and Italy made a difference? Gieseking happened to be born in France because his father (a physician and amateur entomologist), having left Germany in order to evade military service, chose to practice medicine along the French and Italian Rivieras, selecting locations where he could better pursue his passion for entomology. The youthful Gieseking felt entirely sympathetic with the warm Latin environment of the Mediterranean, and apparently knew very little about his German heritage.

He was educated irregularly by private tutors and started piano lessons at age four, but during those early years he had no consistent or serious musical training. "I've played the piano ever since I can remember," he once said, "but since there have never been any professional musicians in the family [his father learned piano and flute] and since my father preferred a normal child to an unhealthy *Wunderkind*, it never occurred to me that my talent would ever be anything more than a hobby." (*MA*, 23 Jan 1926) By age seven, however, playing the piano had become an important part of his life. The family returned to Germany in 1911, and Gieseking, then age 16, became a pupil of Karl Leimer at the Hanover Conservatory. Three years of study with Leimer, the only important teacher Walter Gieseking ever had, completed his musical training.

His official debut had to be postponed while he served two years (1916–18) in the German army, assigned as a musician. After the war he restarted his career, but with the French government having confiscated the family estate in France, thus vastly depleting their resources, he earned his living accompanying, giving piano lessons, playing chamber music and coaching opera singers. His official Berlin debut (1920), at which he played works by Debussy and Ravel, was a tremendous success. "The critics came and lavished such praise that Gieseking had to give seven Berlin recitals during his first season." (Gel/Mus, see Bibliog.) His reputation spread so quickly that he was well-known in Europe by the time he made his London debut on 15 October 1923. He made his American debut on 10 January 1926, and during the 1930s toured widely throughout Europe, the United States and South America.

Although Hitler's armies were already on the move in Europe when Gieseking completed his 13th American tour early in 1939, he elected to return to Germany instead of seeking refuge in America as so many other European musicians chose to do. During the war he performed willingly for Nazi organizations, and also played nearly 200 concerts outside of Germany, in either occupied or neutral countries. Although arranged through regular concert agents, these foreign bookings always had to be confirmed by Nazi authorities in Berlin. Whether out of conviction or fear, Gieseking closed his letters with "Heil Hitler," and even allowed the Nazis to influence his recital programs. "He dropped his best known interpretations, Debussy and Ravel, when the war started and resumed Franck after the Nazis decided Franck was German." (Clark)

The Third Reich fell in May 1945. Gieseking, blacklisted by the American military government for allowing himself to be used as a cultural agent of the Nazi party, defended himself on the grounds that he had never been a member of the Nazi party (a true statement) and that as an artist he was not concerned with politics. The German denazification court and the American military government cleared him of all charges in December 1946. (Further information on Gieseking's wartime activities can be found in the articles by Clark, Harrington and Snowden.) At his first postwar appearance (21 Dec 1947) in Paris, playing two concertos (Mozart, Liszt) with the Colonne Orchestra under Paul Paray, Gieseking so thrilled his audience that a few weeks later hundreds had to be turned away from his first postwar recital (17 Jan 1948), held at the *Palais de Chaillot*. On 9 October 1948 he made his first London appearance in 11 years, playing two concertos (Brahms No. 2, Schumann) with the Philharmonia Orchestra, conducted by Willem van Otterloo.

Resuming his career in the United States proved more difficult. Gieseking's 14th American tour, scheduled for 1949, had to be canceled because immigration officials, under pressure from the Department of Justice and anti-Nazi organizations (picket lines patrolled outside Carnegie Hall, where Gieseking was to appear), ordered him to be deported. But elsewhere this "indefatigable trouper," as one writer called him, toured extensively (in 1952 he flew 75,000 miles), playing to crowded halls in Europe, Australia, South America and Japan. American authorities finally permitted him to return; and his first American concert in 15 years, played on 22 April 1953 at Carnegie Hall, received a warm reception. Thereafter Gieseking played almost every season in America.

A devoted family man—Gieseking and Anna Maria Haake married in 1925—he often took his wife, or one of his two daughters, sometimes all three, along on concert tours. At home in Wiesbaden he filled his days playing the piano, gardening, working on his famous butterfly collection (a hobby inherited from his father) and pursuing his favorite sports of swimming and mountain climbing. Huge, powerful looking and a vegetarian who neither drank spirits nor smoked tobacco, Gieseking gave the impression of unbounded vitality and good health.

He taught for most of his life, chiefly private students. He often taught summer piano classes with Karl Leimer and, from 1947 until his death in 1956, held master classes at the State Conservatory at Saarbrücken, at that time under Allied occupation and controlled by France. Master of four languages, he could conduct classes in French, German, English or Spanish.

On 2 December 1955 a bus transferring passengers from fogbound Frankfurt to the Stuttgart airport struck a bridge pillar on the fog-enshrouded *Autobahn*. Mrs. Gieseking died in that accident, and the pianist suffered severe head injuries. By March 1956 he was sufficiently recovered to begin a ten-week American tour. The recital he gave in Munich on 11 October 1956 turned out to be his final appearance. In mid-October he launched an ambitious recording project (some Schubert, all the Beethoven sonatas) in London; completed six double-sided LP records within six-and-a-half days; and the next day underwent emergency surgery for pancreatitis. Gieseking died (26 Oct) shortly after the operation.

Because he possessed an uncanny keyboard facility, Walter Gieseking was always prepared to play the piano, yet he never (as Mrs. Gieseking emphatically affirmed) practiced regularly and rarely more than three hours at a session. Gieseking credited Karl Leimer with teaching him that the mind must control practicing, that mental concentration is far more important than special studies or finger exercises. (Gieseking later instructed his own students to concentrate on every note when practicing; to play not with the fingers but with the ears; to strive for a singing tone—"always the melody beautifully singing; all the other notes *pianissimo*"; and always to play exactly what the composer wrote.)

Mental concentration was also a main factor in learning a new work. Gieseking first studied the score in detail, without a piano, mentally solving all problems of technique and interpretation before ever trying to play the piece—a natural approach for a pianist with such extraordinary musical resources. "He possessed a photographic and aural memory that was perhaps unparalleled in our time; it is said that he played in public works that he had read through only once. Furthermore, he could play the left-hand part of any passage from memory. He was a fantastic sight-reader and could and did sight-read anything. . . . When a student performed a concerto, he played the orchestral parts, always without a score of course. What he played, just using those phenomenal ears of his, excelled all existing piano reductions." (Elder, "Study," part I)

Although always at his superior best interpreting the music of Debussy, Ravel and Mozart, whose works formed the nucleus of his repertoire, Gieseking was by no means a narrow specialist. The truth is that his immense facility and natural musical talents made it possible for him to play almost everything. He was "as catholic as Cook's . . . Bach today does not preclude Bartók tomorrow, nor does an evening with Haydn prevent acquaintance with Hindemith or Haba in the morning." ("Are You Planning")

His programs reveal that almost every Gieseking recital began with Bach; that he invariably included one or more of his favorites (Debussy, Ravel, Mozart); that he also frequently played works by Beethoven, Brahms, Schumann and Schubert; that he performed a surprising amount of contemporary music. Gieseking told one interviewer that he played all contemporary music "suitable for my instrument—all schools, all nationalities." (*MA*, 23 Jan 1926) One New York recital (26 Nov 1930) offered nothing but works by "modern living composers." And at one of his appearances (2 Feb 1933) with the New York Philharmonic-Symphony Orchestra, Bruno Walter conducting, Gieseking played Arthur Honegger's Concertino and Richard Strauss's *Burleske*.

Whatever the composition or composer, Gieseking played the piano with a magical mix of delicacy and strength that *induced* tone from the keyboard, never forced it. No musicologist or critic ever described him as a powerhouse virtuoso, but he was a virtuoso musician who used his exceptional technique with exquisite taste and sensitivity. From first to last, critics dwelt upon Gieseking's beautiful tone quality and color, raving over his "impalpable *pianissimi*," "gossamer magic," "silvery nuances," "unearthly beauty," his "musical sensitivity." That critical theme—tone quality and color—dominated reviews all through Gieseking's career.

"The young pianist Gieseking," wrote a *Züricher Post* critic in the early 1920s, "though a German, initiated us into the mysteries of modern French piano music as no one else did ever before. . . . No one else seems to have succeeded in reaching such surprising individuality and coloring of tone as Gieseking." In 1935 an editor of *Etude* wrote that "the sonorities and tone qualities which he draws from the piano have brought an altogether new expressiveness to the instrument." In 1948, after Gieseking's first postwar London appearance (10 Oct), *The Times* critic noted that "beauty of detail has always been the salient characteristic of Mr. Gieseking's playing, especially the finer shades of tone and a wonderful bell-like resonance from the top octaves of the instrument." (*TL*, 12 Oct 1948)

This gorgeous tone color that so impressed critics derived in large measure from Gieseking's wonderfully skillful pedaling. He used the pedal not to cover technical mistakes but to generate color. "His use of complicated pedaling, disciplined by an acute ear and precise technique, yielded remarkable results: the pedal was transformed from a mediocre retoucher into a skillful colorist." (Holcman) Gieseking never lost that unique skill. At his all-Debussy recital of 4 February 1955, the year before he died, "there was a chasteness and classical quality to his pedaling, which he used to bring out delicate tonal adjustments and subtle gradations of dynamics." (*NYT*, 5 Feb 1955)

The minimal amount of disapproving criticism scattered through Gieseking's reviews fault him for sometimes failing to create sufficient emotional tension to realize the full dramatic power of a work; for being too objective or too serious at times—in other words, not spontaneous and sometimes monotonous playing. He always played with great polish but, wrote one critic, "one feels that only too often he is merely playing notes—playing them beautifully, to be sure, but without much feeling of tension, drama or spontaneity." (*NYT*, 5 Dec 1954)

Gieseking's first London recital (15 Oct 1923) had only "small" movements, said one critic, not sufficient "of testing his interpretative power." But "his command over piano tones, and his pianissimo now and then becomes as nearly nothing as is possible to imagine." (*TL*, 19 Oct 1923) Three years later in a New York program (8 Feb 1926) Gieseking achieved "unusual richness and fineness of effect within a relatively small dynamic scale. His extensive technic need not be discussed. . . . The distinction of Mr. Gieseking's appearance are his poetic sentiment and imagination, the intimacy of his musical expression and his exquisite adjustment of tone values. . . . The performance was a model of finished pianism, of musicianship and sensitive feeling." (*NYT*, 9 Feb 1926)

One brilliant success succeeded another. The "dazzling artistry" and "glowing beauty" of Gieseking's playing at his New York recital of 23 January 1927 inspired only effusive praise. For example, "Mr. Gieseking played the recital like an archangel. The sheer wonder of it eludes recounting. In his performances were crystallized every element of beauty, every shaft of eloquence, every lineament and proportion of what is great and sentient and noble and subtle in the contemporary school of piano playing." (*NYWT*, 24 Jan 1927)

For the rest of his career Gieseking received consistently excellent reviews. A critic hating a new Castelnuovo-Tedesco Sonata played at a London recital (26 Oct 1929) still admired Gieseking as "one of the finest executants of the day. . . . He is not one of the intellectual pianists. . . . He is a true pianist, getting all his effects by technical means and not by force of personality or taking thought." (*MT*, 1 Dec 1929)

The eminent musicologist Henri Prunières, reporting (dateline 10 Dec 1931) on the concert season in Paris, wrote that Walter Gieseking had just played two magnificent concerts: "He is a magician of the piano, and there are few pianists capable of extracting from a piano such suave, delicate and finely colored sonorities as this virtuoso. I do not like his interpretation of Beethoven . . . but as soon as it is a question of bringing out the plastic and poetic merits of a sensual music such as that of Mozart or Debussy, what splendor!" (*NYT*, 27 Dec 1931)

Gieseking's performance (11 Nov 1937) of the Rachmaninoff Concerto No. 2 with the New York Philharmonic-Symphony revealed another facet of his artistry: "A performance that cannot be forgotten by those who heard it, playing of a kind that makes one think of the traditions of a Rubinstein. In fact, it is not easy to believe that we can hear a greater interpretation of this work from any pianist before the public today. Mr. Gieseking played with a power, beauty and fire which swept the orchestra and the audience with him." (*NYT*, 12 Nov 1937)

On 3 March 1955 Gieseking played the Mozart Concerto in C Major, K. 467, and Franck's Symphonic Variations with the New York Philharmonic-Symphony, Guido Cantelli conducting. "He can convey a wealth of hues within a narrow dynamic compass. Thus in the Mozart concerto he did not go above a mezzoforte more than a few times, and yet he managed to suggest variety and nuance. . . . In Franck's Symphonic Variations . . . there were places where his affinity for color and nuance were displayed with appealing effect. But there were also stride and sweep in his playing." (*NYT*, 4 March 1955)

To the very end of his life Gieseking charmed audiences and most critics. His all-Debussy program (4 Feb 1955) at Carnegie Hall "evoked excitement, transparency, and movement throughout. Occasionally he would choose to hold his audience hypnotically suspended through an ethereal pianissimo or a section of tremulous repose. With endless refinements of touch and pedaling, one phrase grew out of another. Climaxes developed with the inevitable force and upward sweep that stamp the musician and the architectural master. . . . Gieseking's pedaling was a miracle." (Cha/Spe, see Bibliog.)

On 11 October 1956 Gieseking played what would prove to be his last recital—a Munich program consisting of the Beethoven Sonata op. 31, no. 3, Schumann's Sonata in F-sharp Minor, the Debussy *Suite bergamasque* and Ravel's *Sonatine*. This recital, wrote one critic, "surpassed any previous performance." (Pinson)

Gieseking left an extensive recorded repertoire, produced principally with Angel (EMI) and Columbia. In 1953 he recorded all of Mozart's solo piano music (see Discog.) and all of Debussy's. (He recorded the complete piano works of Ravel in 1956.) The Mozart recording began in July 1953 at EMI's Abbey Road studio. Gieseking recorded through the summer and finished the following December. At the end of 1954 EMI released a sumptuous—and highly successful—limited edition. "The password at Angel Records this month is 'M' for marvelous. . . . Mozart's 63 works for piano solo played by Walter Gieseking was on the list of the year's best by nearly every reviewer who summed up 1955 on discs." (*Carnegie Hall*, Jan 1956)

The original LPs have been reissued on 8 CDs. Opinions vary. According to one reviewer, Gieseking's offerings stand up well: "No other great pianist brought as much variety of tone and style to each composer as did Gieseking. His Mozart has a miraculous speed and evenness; trills, turns, and passage-work ripple like hovering humming-birds. His *piano* dynamic is softer than that of some contemporary Mozarteans, but his singing tone and joy are unsurpassed." (*CL*, April 1992) However, another reviewer was "doubly astonished and reluctant to find that Gieseking lent his great gifts and prestige to further the fictional nineteenth-century tradition of Mozart as a miniaturist. . . . The playing here is as angular and static as it is wonderfully rounded and forward-moving in Gieseking's Debussy and Ravel." (Cha/Spe, see Bibliog.)

The release on CD of four Mozart concertos (see Discog.) adds a felicitous quartet of master performances to the available Gieseking discography.

"Gieseking is inspired and magically communicates the music's essence. He employs much nuance and color and knows how to use accents to achieve grandeur." (*CL*, Dec 1991)

Having the complete Debussy *Préludes* now available on CD (see Discog.) introduces Gieseking's magical playing to a new generation. Recorded in 1953, the *Préludes* are still vivid reminders of Gieseking's incredible affinity for French music. "Gieseking loved the music of Debussy and throughout his career played the solo works more and with greater success than any other pianist. . . . He interprets each prelude definitively and achieves a kaleidoscopic view that makes the music gripping. His technique, voicing, evenness of touch, and beauty of tone are so perfected that the listener experiences the music's essence, not just its notes." (*CL*, April 1990)

Gieseking had already recorded both Debussy and Ravel in the 1930s. Soundwise these early recordings (Debussy *Préludes* [Book I], *Estampes* and *L'Isle joyeuse*; the Ravel *Gaspard* and *Miroirs* excerpts [rec. 1936–38]), reproduced on Pearl CD 9449 (see Discog.), cannot compare with the later recordings of the 1950s. "This is regrettable in music that relies so heavily on subtleties of touch and color. Enough can be heard, however, to make evident the superlative level of pianistic imagination Gieseking lavished on the impressionistic literature." (*ARG*, July/Aug 1991)

Gieseking's recordings of Ravel's solo piano works were made in 1956 and presented by Angel as a deluxe 3-LP set (Angel 3541). When this album first appeared, one critic wrote: "Any lingering doubts that he is one of the greatest living interpreters of Ravel should be dispelled by this album. Most arresting of all is Gieseking's sharp sense of style. For he is a many-sided artist. But above all, the performances have a transcending bigness, a vaster vision, which governs the ebb and flow of tempo, dynamic shadings, phrasing, color. Perhaps it is this very breadth of approach which endows each little detail with its evocative power." (*NYT*, 8 July 1956)

Those who would hear Gieseking in an eclectic repertoire can do no better than listen to the two Pearl Retrospective CDs (see Discog.). "His memorable playing of the Bach, Beethoven, and Mendelssohn works [Vol. 1] is in some ways matchless. . . . The two Arabesques [Debussy] . . . are played with such freshness that they almost seem to breathe a fragrance." (*ARG*, Nov/Dec 1992) The second volume includes recordings made from 1924 to 1951, music by Bach, Beethoven, Chopin, Falla, Liszt and Scriabin. A review of this second volume offers a general appraisal of the pianist. "Walter Gieseking . . . perhaps the greatest tone colorist of his time . . . used his control of touch, pedalling, and tone to produce limpid phrases, ethereal sounds, and transparent textures that we can hardly believe come from a percussion instrument." (*ARG*, Jan/Feb 1994)

SELECTED REFERENCES

"Are You Planning a Pianistic Tour? Let Walter Gieseking be Your Baedeker." *Musical America*, 23 Jan 1926, p. 7.

Barzetti, Marcella. "Walter Gieseking." *Recorded Sound*, Spring 1962, pp. 168–173.

Clark, Delbert. "A Review of Gieseking's Record Since 1934." *New York Times*, 8 Feb 1948, sec. 2, p. 7.

Clough, F. F., and G. J. Cuming. "Walter Gieseking: A Microgroove Diskography." *Gramophone Record Review*, July 1957, pp. 703–707.

Corrigan, John. "Remembering Walter Gieseking." *Clavier*, Nov 1986, pp. 12–16.

Elder, Dean. "Masters of the Past." *Clavier*, April 1990, p. 36.

———. "Study with Gieseking." *Piano Teacher*, Jan–Feb 1964, pp. 2–6.

———. "Study with Gieseking," Part 2. *Piano Teacher*, March–April 1964, pp. 6–8.

Gieseking, Walter. "The Amazing Musical World of Today." (interview with Oliver Daniel). *Etude*, Jan 1939, pp. 7–8.

———. "Increasing the Resources of the Piano." (interview with David Ewen). *Etude*, July 1935, pp. 399, 434.

———. "On Playing Mozart." Liner notes, Seraphim album ID-6047.

———. "On Playing Ravel." Liner notes, Angel album 3541-35.

———. "Practical Considerations in Pianoforte Interpretation." (interview with Florence Leonard). *Etude*, Sept 1929, pp. 645–646.

Gieseking, Walter, and Karl Leimer. *Piano Technique*. New York: Dover Publications, Inc., 1972.

Harrington, Rev. Donald. "The Ministers' Corner." *Community News*, Community Church, Park Ave., N.Y., 13 Feb 1949, p. 22. A sympathetic look at the Gieseking "collaboration" episode.

Holcman, Jan. "Au Revoir to Walter Gieseking." *Saturday Review*, 29 Dec 1956, pp. 34–35.

Kammerer, Rafael. "Gieseking—His Death Closed A Chapter in Great Artistry." *Musical America*, 15 Nov 1956, pp. 9–10.

Obituary. *Le Guide du Concert*, Nov 1956, p. 183. *Musical Times*, Dec 1956, p. 659. *New York Times*, 26 Oct 1956, pp. 1, 14. *The Times* (London), 27 Oct 1956, p. 11.

Pinson, Hilda. "Gieseking: 1896–1956." *Saturday Review*, 24 Nov 1956, p. 69.

"Return Engagement." *Time*, 4 May 1953, p. 87.

Snowdon, Edward W. *Some Notes on "The Gieseking Case."* Pamphlet published by Gieseking's North American managers, Wagner and Snowdon, 25 Aug 1948, 11 p.

See also Bibliography: Bla/Gra; Bro/Mod; Cur/Bio (1956); Eld/Pia; Ewe/Li; Ewe/Mu; Gav/Vin; Gel/Mus; MGG; New/Gro; Nie/Mei; Rub/MyM; Sch/Gre.

SELECTED REVIEWS

BET: 15 Jan 1927. *BN*: 22 Jan 1926. *CEA*: 5 Feb 1927. *LAT*: 8 Feb 1954; 14 Feb 1955; 24 Aug 1955; 16 April 1956; 17 Aug 1956. *MA*: 24 March 1928; 2 Feb 1929. *MT*: 1 Dec 1923; 1 Nov 1926; 1 Dec 1929; Feb 1934.

NYT: 11 Jan 1926; 9 Feb 1926; 25 March 1926; 24 Jan 1927; 3 Feb 1928; 24 Jan 1929; 1 April 1929; 13 Oct 1930; 27 Dec 1931; 22 Feb 1932; 20 Feb 1933; 19 Feb 1934; 11 March 1934; 28 March 1935; 12 Nov 1937; 23 Jan 1939; 16 March 1939; 23 April 1953; 5 Feb 1955; 4 March 1955; 30 March 1955; 23 March 1956; 8 July 1956. *NYWT*: 24 Jan 1927. *Time*: 22 Feb 1926. *TL*: 19 Oct 1923; 12 Oct 1948; 13 Oct 1948; 15 Oct 1951; 7 Dec 1953; 14 Dec 1954.

SELECTED DISCOGRAPHY

Bach: English Suite No. 6 in D Minor. Schumann: *Davidsbündlertänze*, op. 6; *Kreisleriana*, op. 16. Urania ULS 5155-CD. *Forlane* UCD 16590.
Beethoven: Concerto No. 1 in D Major, op. 15 (Rosbaud/Berlin SO). Chopin: Barcarolle, op. 60. Franck: Symphonic Variations (Wood/London PO). Liszt: Concerto No. 1 in E-flat Major (Wood/London PO). The Classical Collector FDC 2008.
Beethoven: Concerto No. 4 in G Major, op. 58; Concerto No. 5 in E-flat Major, op. 73. Angel Laser Series CDZ 7 62607-2. Galliera/Philharmonia.
Beethoven: Concerto No. 5 in E-flat Major, op. 73 (Rother/Berlin RSO). Franck: Symphonic Variations (Cluytens/*Orch. Natl. de France*). Schumann: Concerto in A Minor, op. 54 (Wand/Cologne RSO). Arkadia CDHP 588. The Beethoven "Emperor" Concerto is the only surviving stereo recording of a complete work taped by German Radio (Fall 1944) during World War II.
Beethoven: Sonatas in C Minor, op. 13; E Major, op. 14, no. 1; G Major, op. 14, no. 2; E-flat Major, op. 27, no. 1; C-sharp Minor, op. 27, no. 2. Angel Laser Series CDZ 7 62857-2.
Debussy: *Préludes* Books 1 & 2 (Complete). Angel CDH 7-61004.
Gieseking: A Retrospective—Vol. I. Bach: Partita No. 1 in B-flat Major. Beethoven: Bagatelle in E-flat Major, op. 33, no. 1; Sonata in G Major, op. 49, no. 2; Sonata in E Major, op. 109. Brahms: Capriccio in F-sharp Minor, op. 76, no. 1; Intermezzo in B-flat Minor, op. 117, no. 2. Chopin: Barcarolle, op. 60. Debussy: Two *Arabesques*. Fauré: Nocturne in E-flat Major, op. 36. Mendelssohn: *Andante and Rondo capriccioso*. Poulenc: *Mouvements perpétuels*. Scriabin: Four Pieces, op. 51. Pearl GEMM CD 9930.
Gieseking: A Retrospective—Vol. 2. Bach: Italian Concerto. Beethoven: Sonata in D Minor, op. 31, no. 2. Chopin: *Berceuse*; Mazurka, op. 17, no. 4. Falla: Nights in the Gardens of Spain (Schröder/Hessian RSO). Liszt: Hungarian Rhapsody No. 13. Scriabin: Sonata No. 5 in F-sharp Major, op. 53. Pearl GEMM CD 9011.
Mozart: Complete solo works. EMI CHS 7 63688-2 (8 CDs).
Mozart: Concerto in D Minor, K. 466; Concerto in C Major, K. 503; Concerto in C Minor, K. 491; Concerto in A Major, K. 488. EMI *Références* CHS 763709-2. Karajan, Rosbaud/PO.

Rachmaninoff: Concerto No. 2 in C Minor, op. 18; Concerto No. 3 in D Minor, op. 30. Music and Arts CD-250. Mengelberg/*Concertgebouw*. Public performance recorded in 1940.

Ravel: Complete Works for Piano Solo. Angel 3541 (3 LPs). Theorema TH 121163/164 (2 CDs). Pirated from Angel?

Ravel: *Gaspard de la nuit*; *Alborada del Gracioso (Miroirs)*; *La Vallée des cloches (Miroirs)*. Debussy: *Préludes*, Book I; *Pagodes (Estampes)*; *Jardins sous la pluie (Estampes)*; *L'Isle joyeuse*. Pearl GEMM CD 9449.

Walter Gieseking: Broadcast Recitals, 1949–1951. Bach: English Suites, Nos. 2 in A Minor, 3 in G Minor, 4 in F Major, 6 in D Minor; French Suites Nos. 2 in C Minor, 5 in G Major; 15 Two-Part Inventions; Three-Part Inventions Nos. 1–5, 7–15. Beethoven: Sonatas ops. 31, no. 1, 78, 79, 90, 81a, 101, 106, 111. Schumann: Symphonic Etudes, op. 13; Three Romances, op. 28; *Waldscenen*, op. 82. Music and Arts CD-743 (4 CDs).

Walter Gieseking: His First Concerto Recordings. Beethoven: Concerto No. 1 in C Major, op. 15. Mozart: Concerto in E-flat Major, K. 271; Sonata in B-flat Major, K. 570. APR 5511 (CD). Rosbaud/Berlin SO. Rec. 1936–37.

Walter Gieseking: Historic broadcast performances 1944–1950. Bach: Chromatic Fantasy and Fugue, BWV 903. Beethoven: Sonata in A-flat Major, op. 110. Debussy: *Reflets dans l'eau*. Mozart: Sonata in A Major, K. 331; Sonata in D Major, K. 576. Ravel: *Ondine*. Scarlatti: Sonata in E Major, K. 380; Sonata in G Major, K. 427. Music and Arts CD-612.

❖ ❖ ❖

GILELS, EMIL GRIGORYEVICH: b. Odessa, USSR, 19 October 1916; d. Moscow, USSR, 14 October 1985.

> Mr. Gilels was a big, rich-toned pianist who could ride triumphantly over an orchestra in the mainstream Romantic piano concertos—those of Beethoven, Chopin, Liszt, Brahms and Tchaikovsky, all of which he recorded. He wasn't always note-perfect, but he commanded his repertory with an élan that made such flaws seem insignificant. And unlike some powerhouse virtuosos, he had a poetic gift that enlivened slow movements.
>
> John Rockwell (*New York Times*, 16 October 1985)

Emil Gilels was born in the Ukrainian city of Odessa, a provincial yet extraordinarily musical port on the Black Sea which has spawned far more than its fair share of internationally famous pianists. (Benno Moiseiwitsch, Simon Barere and Shura Cherkassky also were born in Odessa.) Located in the south where it had direct contact with Europe, particularly Italy, Odessa often engaged European musicians, notably Italian opera companies, to perform at the city's large opera house. "Young people there at that time," said Gilels, "could not help being caught up in music." (Blyth)

Although there were no professional musicians in the family, Gilels remembered that his father, an amateur musician, loved to sing religious songs while accompanying himself on the piano. Perhaps it was his father, then, who arranged for the six-year-old Emil to start lessons with Yakov Tkach, who had studied with Raoul Pugno in Paris. Tkach, chiefly concerned with developing technique, even wrote in all the fingering and pedaling on the scores. He usually assigned studies by Bertini and Herz, for despite having studied with Pugno and lived in France, Tkach was a proponent of the old German school with a repertoire, said Gilels, that "ended with Beethoven's *Sonata Pathétique* and the E-flat Concerto of Liszt." Tkach's small but strong-minded pupil was concerned only with making music, and he refused to play works that meant nothing to him. Nevertheless, Gilels later acknowledged that Tkach had given him a good start toward being both a pianist and a musician.

Gilels gave his first full public recital (11 June 1929) at age 12 in the hall of the All-Ukrainian Revolutionary Association. His playing "was very far from childlike, being accomplished and well-rounded. Neither in technique nor in rendition was there anything slipshod." (*Vecherniye izvestiya*, 18 June 1929) After hearing that recital, Bertha Reingbald, a teacher at the Odessa Institute of Music and Drama, decided to take Gilels as a pupil to prepare him for advanced training at the Moscow Conservatory. During his years (1930–34) with Reingbald, he practiced about four hours a day and developed a broader repertoire. Gilels always credited Reingbald with giving him a musical foundation, what he termed "a musical stability." She also prepared him to compete in the National Competition of the Ukraine, held in Kharkov. He won first prize, which may be why in 1931 the Ukrainian government granted him a scholarship.

The following year Gilels played for Artur Rubinstein, then on tour in Russia. Many years later Rubinstein recalled that Odessa meeting: "I was asked by a piano teacher at the local conservatory to hear her pupils. You know how boring such an ordeal usually is, but by God there was a boy—I remember as if it happened yesterday—short, with a mass of red hair and freckles, who played. . . . I can't describe it. . . . All I can say is—if he ever comes here I might as well pack up my bags and go." (Seroff, "Russia's Emil Gilels")

On 7 May 1933 Gilels won first prize at the first All-Union Competition of Performing Musicians, and although only age 16 he could have begun a career right then. He chose instead to complete his studies in Odessa, and after graduation (1935) he moved to Moscow to begin postgraduate studies with the eminent pedagogue Heinrich Neuhaus at the Advanced Technical School of the Moscow Conservatory. That same year Gilels gave his first performance of the Tchaikovsky B-flat Minor Concerto and made his first recording in Moscow. Working with Neuhaus for two years (1935–37), Gilels improved his technique and acquired the mental discipline necessary for a concert career. He also took classes in history, philosophy and aesthetics, and the "resulting broadening of his intellectual activities was reflected in his playing." ("Don't Clap for Me")

In 1936 Gilels won second prize at the third International Piano Competition in Vienna. In May 1938 he won the prestigious Queen Elisabeth

International Competition in Brussels. On 9 September 1938 he was appointed as assistant to Neuhaus at the Moscow Conservatory and, as his concert schedule permitted, he taught there (associate professor in 1947, full professor in 1952) for the rest of his life.

Only a year after his appointment he took leave in order to undertake (in Odessa) a concentrated study of the entire repertoire of two-piano music, which he performed (until 1953) with Yakov Flier. Gilels loved to play ensemble music and, again as concert schedules allowed, he played it throughout his life. His early chamber-music experience consisted of playing sonatas with his sister Elizabeth, a well-known violinist; in 1949 he formed a Trio with Mstislav Rostropovich and Leonid Kogan (Gilels's brother-in-law); he later performed with the Amadeus Quartet and played piano duets with his daughter Elena, also a concert pianist.

Gilels's American debut, scheduled at the 1939 World's Fair in New York, would most likely have been the start of an international career had not World War II intervened. Confined within the USSR by the war, he gave some concerts in the larger cities, but more often played for veterans in hospitals and soldiers at the front, and on one occasion (1943) even in occupied Leningrad. After the war he performed (1948) at the third International Spring Festival in Prague, Czechoslovakia—his first performances outside the USSR. He played a recital on 29 May; on 1 June he played the Tchaikovsky Concerto No. 1 with the Czech Philharmonic Orchestra, conducted by Konstantin Ivanov; and on 11 June he gave his first concert in Warsaw.

For the next seven years Gilels toured with immense success both in and out of the Soviet bloc countries. In June 1951 he was one of 11 Soviet artists allowed to participate at the May Music Festival in Florence, Italy. On 21 February 1952 he gave his first concert in Scandinavia; made his London recital debut at Royal Albert Hall on 9 December 1952; and his first tour of Belgium in 1953. In 1954 he played (5 Feb) at a conference of foreign ministers at the Soviet Embassy in Berlin and went on to Paris to play (14 Feb) three concertos (Beethoven No. 1, Tchaikovsky No. 1, Prokofiev No. 3) with the *Orchestre de la Société des Concerts du Conservatoire*, André Cluytens conducting, and play two Paris recitals (26 Feb, 6 March).

Meanwhile the Soviet Union had joined UNESCO, and in 1954 Columbia Artists Management initiated negotiations to bring Gilels and other Russian musicians to the United States. Thus Gilels made his long postponed American debut on 3 October 1955 in Philadelphia, playing the Tchaikovsky Concerto No. 1 with the Philadelphia Orchestra, Eugene Ormandy conducting—the opening event in a new era of Soviet-American cultural exchanges. (According to the *New York Times* [4 Nov 1970], Gilels was the first Soviet pianist to appear in America since 1928.) It also obviously signaled the start of a new international career. Gilels and the Philadelphia Orchestra repeated their performance in New York on 4 October. He gave a solo recital at Carnegie Hall on 11 October and appeared again at Carnegie Hall on 16 October to play with the Symphony of the Air. He completed that busy year in America with a performance (celebrating the 10th anniversary of the United Nations) of the Tchaikovsky Concerto No. 1 with Leonard Bernstein and the New York Philharmonic Society at the United Nations Assembly Hall on 24 October, then made a tour that included Washington, D.C., Chicago, Boston and Cleveland.

Gilels toured regularly and intensively for the rest of his life, giving hundreds of concerts in the Soviet Union, Europe, North America and Great Britain. By 1968 he was touring nine or ten months a year and spending his summers practicing (5 or 6 hours a day) new works. On 11 June 1979 he celebrated 50 years on the concert platform with a recital at the Odessa School of Music. Less than two years later Gilels had an early warning that those 50 years had taken a toll when he collapsed in his dressing room right after playing a recital (2 Feb 1981) at the Amsterdam *Concertgebouw*. But he kept performing until about a year before his death on 16 October 1985. He was survived by his wife, pianist-composer Farizet Khutzyostova (m. 1947), and his daughter Elena (b. 1950), also a concert pianist.

Honored in the international community and venerated in his homeland (he joined the Communist Party in 1941), Gilels was awarded the Stalin Prize in 1946 and declared a "People's Artist" in 1954. He received the Order of Lenin (then the USSR's highest honor) in 1961 for his performances during World War II and again in 1966 in recognition of his high status as an international piano virtuoso. France awarded him the Order of *Commandeur Mérite Culturel et Artistique de Paris* in 1967, and King Baudoin of Belgium awarded him the Order of Leopold in 1968.

Gilels had an immense repertoire (reportedly about 400 compositions) encompassing music of an extremely wide psychological range—from Scarlatti, Bach and Mozart to Stravinsky and Shostakovich. Apparently equally interested in Classical and Romantic music, he never specialized. "I like all music," Gilels told a 1972 interviewer, "and have tried many styles. . . . I don't make any firm distinction between Classical and Romantic music. I believe that fundamentally it's the same, it's music. . . . It's really a matter of quality, what one calls classical, what one calls music in the highest sense." (Lewinski)

Gilels was still in his twenties when he began systematically to add Russian music to his repertoire, and his programs over the years indicate that he ultimately accumulated an enormous body of works by Russian composers, including Kabalevsky, Scriabin, Stravinsky, Shostakovich, Prokofiev, Balakirev, Tchaikovsky, Rachmaninoff and Medtner. On the other hand, his programs also show that he often played all five Beethoven concertos and played all the Tchaikovsky and Brahms concertos. Gilels knew almost all the piano works of Beethoven and played all-Beethoven and all-Mozart recitals.

"If piano playing of utter magnificence means anything in your life, keep a sharp lookout for Emil Gilels," reported Herbert F. Peyser in 1936. Peyser, music critic abroad for the *New York World-Telegram*, had heard Gilels play just two pieces—a gigue arranged by Leopold Godowsky and Rachmaninoff's Prelude in G Minor—but that was enough "to establish Emil Gilels as a perfectly enormous pianistic talent. . . . There is something stupendously elemental, something that takes the listener's breath in the way he attacks even a gigue transcription." (Peyser)

Peyser may sound extravagant to modern ears, but he provides firsthand evidence that Gilels was always a remarkable pianist, even when isolated within the training and traditions of just one school, which happened to be the Romantic Russian school of Anton Rubinstein and the great pedagogue Theodor Leschetizky—traditionally a virtuoso style depending on intense, spontaneous emotion to create a new artistic concept every time a work is performed. But Peyser was right. "As time went by, he [Gilels] shed his early propensity towards virtuosity and searched deeper into his wide repertory which stretched from Bach through Mozart to Bartók and Prokofiev." (*TL*, 16 Oct 1985)

When in form, Gilels could match any pianist, living or dead, in virtuosity, yet he "always seemed more concerned with the human values of music—warmth, beautiful tone, communication of a work's essence and structure." (Potter) With Gilels, it was not technical perfection but an amazing intensity and zeal in his playing that captured the listener's attention. His unique virtuosity throbbed with a powerful, dynamic emotion—a sheer musical force ("a high-voltage current that does not cease for a single moment," "an uninterrupted stream of onrushing music," "a lion's grip") that awed critics and thrilled audiences. Most important, Gilels had the musical scholarship and innate classical simplicity needed to control his pulsating virtuosity.

He told interviewers that he envisioned musical form as a living, creative process more than an architectural pattern. His was a personal concept of musical form, but Gilels had both the ability to immediately grasp the structure, development and overall idea of a work and the capability to clearly convey the composer's intention. He was famous for his solid, awesome *fortissimo* and his tender, expressive *pianissimo*. Almost all, if not all, the Gilels reviews speak of his astonishingly beautiful piano tone. Some critics likened the way he laid on piano colors (multilayers of sound, rich in nuances) to the way an artist applies color to a painting. For instance, Gilels "consciously looks for, and usually finds, the tone appropriate to the music of this or that style. His instrument sounds differently, depending on whether he plays works by Scarlatti, Mozart, Beethoven, Schumann, Chopin, Brahms, Rachmaninoff, Scriabin, Debussy or Prokofiev." (Barenboim) This ability to find exactly the right sound for each work he played gave one reviewer the impression that, as played by Gilels, pieces by Bach, Schubert, Schumann, Prokofiev and Stravinsky were performed by the pianist *on five different instruments.*

We have a fitting, if flowery, description of Gilels's "almost unbelievable" performance of the Tchaikovsky Concerto No. 1 at his Philadelphia debut (3 Oct 1955): "Approaching the concerto in the spirit of a protagonist, Gilels unleashed torrents of energy on the soaring melodies and rippling counterpoints of the first movement, now blending with, now struggling against, the swelling orchestral resources. We beheld the master of a ferocious, wildly triumphant overpowering bravura style, the likes of which have rarely been seen since the passing of Franz Liszt. . . . Here was a magnificent technique wedded to great emotional power." (*Etude*, Dec 1955)

Making his fifth tour of the United States in 1964, Gilels was playing better than ever. "Once objective and calculating, he now plunges deeply into a work with daring abandon. . . . A fireplug of a man with square, stubby hands, Gilels foregoes note-picking accuracy for a more fluid style of fingering." (*Time*, 18 Dec 1964) The tour itself covered 20 cities in the United States and Canada. At one Carnegie Hall recital (6 Nov 1964) Gilels's playing "not only was exceptional purely on the pianistic level, but his ability to communicate directly to the listener the very core of the music he played was also on the highest artistic level." (*NYT*, 7 Nov 1964)

His twelfth American tour included performances of all five Beethoven concertos with the Cleveland Orchestra.   On 11 June 1979 he celebrated 50 years on the concert stage with a recital in Odessa.   The following November he was soloist with Zubin Mehta and the New York Philharmonic Orchestra.   The concerto, Tchaikovsky No. 1, was the same one he played at his New York debut in 1955. His playing in 1979 "was grander, more highly inflected, exhibitionistic and forceful.   Yet it had its moments of poetry too, and once in a while an endearing vulgarity in an old-fashioned manner. . . . His articulation in these rapid passages [*prestissimo* section, second movement] was something to marvel about." (*NYT*, 15 Nov 1979)

Gilels was active musically to the end of his life.   He gave a recital in London on 5 February 1984 and another that same year in October.   The major work of Gilels's February program was the "*Hammerklavier*" Sonata, "a reading very much his own, a reading majestically spacious and strong yet at the same time laying more emphasis on Beethoven as seer than stormer of high heaven." (*TL*, 6 Feb 1984) After the second recital, devoted mainly to a group of Scarlatti sonatas and Debussy's *Pour le piano*, a reviewer, astounded at the variety of tone colors bestowed on the Scarlatti, asked himself where Gilels found these sounds: "Hidden somewhere deep in the keyboard, for depth is one clue to the frightening penetration of his playing." (*TL*, 16 Oct 1984)

Gilels was indeed one of the most highly regarded pianists of his generation.   His splendid technique, physical strength, discipline and command of tonal nuance gave him an international reputation with both audience and critics. "In the 1960s a certain youthful impulsiveness and exuberance gave way, without any corresponding loss of energy or excitement in the playing, to a greater sense of stillness and inner concentration—qualities that have brought to his performances a new depth of intensity and coherence." (New/Gro, see Bibliog.)

Gilels's recordings were beginning to become generally available shortly before he came to the United States. Many of these recordings, now considered classics, have been reissued in CD format. For example, his sensational performance of the Liszt-Busoni Fantasy on Mozart's Marriage of Figaro (Gilels learned it in 40 days) that won first prize at the 1933 All Union Musicians' Contest. Gilels recorded it in 1935 (see Discog.).

A good way to hear Gilels as an all-around pianist is to listen to a CD of varied works and composers. One of the best (Multisonic 0091) takes the listener from Haydn through Beethoven and Chopin to Ravel. The Haydn Sonata in C Minor (Hob. XVI:20) is truly outstanding. "Tempos are broad, repeats are observed and the result is wonderful. Gilels uses the space he has created to bring color and life to every note and to phrase like a great singer." (*ARG*, Sept/Oct 1992)

Gilels's recordings of both Brahms Concertos with Eugen Jochum and the Berlin Philharmonic Orchestra won a Grammy award in 1973, and are now available as a 2-CD set (see Discog.). One critic praised Gilels's reading of Concerto No. 1 for its "majesty and breadth, poetry and fire" and the "rare depth and inwardness of feeling" in the slow movement. And as for Concerto No. 2, "Gilels and Jochum bring such warmth and humanity to the score as well as a magisterial authority that they carry all before them." (*Gram*, Sept 1986) Another critic, disappointed with Concerto No. 2, "found the pianist in what may charitably be called a ruminative mood. Tempos are slow and exasperating, and there's a lack of energy in his playing in even the most heroic passages." (*ARG*, May/June 1993) Earlier, in 1958, Gilels had recorded Concerto No. 2 with Fritz Reiner and the Chicago Symphony Orchestra (Grammy, 1958). This recording, remastered and issued on CD, reveals Gilels in all his youthful vigor. "The performance of the concerto remains one of the genuine gramophone classics of all time." (*ARG*, July/Aug 1991)

There are presently available two CDs of the Tchaikovsky Concerto No. 1 in B-flat Minor, op. 23. The best is a recording made from a live performance (19 Nov 1979) at New York's Lincoln Center, with Zubin Mehta conducting the New York Philharmonic Orchestra. Similarly there are two CDs of Concerto No. 2 in G Major, op. 44, both recorded live performances—one from 1959, with Kiril Kondrashin and the USSR Symphony Orchestra, the second, from 1972, Gilels playing with Evgeni Svetlanov and the USSR State Academy Symphony Orchestra. The 1972 version "is hugely exciting. . . . Gilels' playing is masterly." (Pen/Gui, see Bibliog.)

The ultimate discussion of Gilels's recordings must forcibly center around the Beethoven sonatas. His producer (Rinke) relates how reluctant Gilels initially was to undertake a project of putting the entire set to disc. But he eventually relented, taking his time, however, and unfortunately time ran out. They worked for seven years and were nearing the end of the project. The producer had already booked the final recording sessions for February and May of 1986 to coincide with the pianist's 70th birthday. However, Gilels died in 1985, leaving five sonatas unrecorded. Most critics agree that the uncompleted set stands as an eloquent testimonial to the great artistry of the Russian pianist. "Emotionally, he is wild horses, and technically, he shows a feline sureness and quickness. Poetically, powerfully he pours out his soul, shaping long singing lines that gain strength from his attention to detail." (*CL*, Jan 1988) And also: "He was in many ways an ideal Beethoven pianist. His rich sonority . . . never allowed even the most stark passages to sound threadbare. . . . Beethoven's dissonances come across with penetrating clarity in Gilels' hands, and he could also scale his sonority down to a whisper." (*OV*, Nov 1987)

As to the individual sonatas, choice is rather a matter of personal preference. Many will prefer DG 419 162-2, a disc containing the "*Waldstein*," op. 53; "*Appassionata*," op. 57; and "*Les Adieux*," op. 81a. For one reviewer, this "immediately establishes a claim to being one of the most desirable of all Beethoven piano sonata collections yet to be released on CD." (*Gram*, Aug

1986) There are also those who feel that Gilels gives his finest readings in the late Beethoven sonatas (Grammy, Op. 106, 1984). "Gilels' recordings of Opp. 109 and 110 are inspired, the most moving I have heard since Gieseking's." (*CL*, Jan 1988)

Gilels recorded the five Beethoven concertos with George Szell and the Cleveland Orchestra—"a Beethoven collection that for purity of musicianship, grasp of the early 19th century style, and illumination of detail is a match for any Beethoven concerto cycle ever recorded." (*NYT*, 20 Oct 1968) Unfortunately this collection has not been reissued on CD. There is, however, a set of concertos recorded live on successive evenings in Prague in November 1958, but they can in no way compare to those made by other notable pianists, for example Barenboim, Fleisher, or Rudolf Serkin.

A collection of Scriabin works (see Discog.) taken from various live performances in Russia are spectacular. Gilels' readings of the Third and Fourth Sonatas "bear not only his own unmistakable stamp of genius but seem vividly evocative. . . . And the Four Night Pieces [Schumann] . . . are played with something very close to perfection." (*ARG*, July/Aug 1990)

SELECTED REFERENCES

Allen, John. "Discs: Beethoven and Chopin—concertos by the mile." *Christian Science Monitor*, 31 Jan 1969, p. 4.

Barenboim, Lev. "Emil Gilels." *Music in the USSR*, Jan/March 1985, pp. 13–16. Includes a Selected Discography.

Blyth, Alan. "What Gilels likes." *London Times*, 22 Feb 1973, p. 14.

"Don't Clap For Me—Save It For My Friend." *Music and Musicians*, April 1957, p. 7.

"The Evolution of Emil." *Time*, 18 Dec 1964, p. 67.

Henahan, Donal. "Is There Anything New About Beethoven?" *New York Times*, 20 Oct 1968, sec. 2, p. 27.

———. "The Return of Emil Gilels." *New York Times*, 11 Feb 1977, sec. 3, p. 11.

———. "Who will replace the old guard of Soviet music?" *New York Times*, 27 Oct 1985, sec 8, p. 19.

"An Interview with Artist-Teacher Emil Gilels." *The Piano Teacher*, March/April 1962, pp. 4–5.

Lewinski, Wolf-Eberhard von. "Emil Gilels." *Records and Recording*, Dec 1972, pp. 21–22.

Obituary. *Clavier*, Dec 1985, p. 32. *London Times*, 16 Oct 1985, p. 18. *Los Angeles Times*, 16 Oct 1985, sec. 2, p. 6. *New York Times*, 16 Oct 1985, sec. 2, p. 6. *Washington Post*, 16 Oct 1985, sec. C, p. 6.

Peyser, Herbert F. "Piano Contest Prize Winner." *New York Times*, 12 July 1936, sec. 9, p. 5.

Potter, Tully. "Emil Gilels." *Hi-Fi News & Record Review*, Jan 1981, pp. 84–85. Includes a Selected Discography.

Richardson, Trevor. "Berlin Partnership." *Records and Recording*, Dec 1972, pp. 20–21.

Rinke, Hanno. "Recording With Gilels." *Gramophone*, Sept 1986. p. 346.
Schwarz, Falk. "Emil Gilels" (interview) *Recorded Sound*, July 1981, pp. 1–13. Includes a discography.
Seroff, Victor. "Musical Fireworks Behind the Iron Curtain." *Etude*, Jan 1949, pp. 5, 8.
————. "Russia's Emil Gilels." *Saturday Review*, 29 Oct 1955, pp. 41–42, 53.
"Soviet Russia's top pianist makes sensational debut in America." *Etude*, Dec 1955, pp. 12, 62-63.
"Soviet Virtuoso." *Time*, 17 Oct 1955, p. 83.
See also Bibliography: Cur/Bio (1956); Ewe/Li2; Ewe/Mu; Kai/Gre; Mac/Gr2; Moh/My; New/Gro; Rat/Cle; Rub/MyM; Zil/Rus.

SELECTED REVIEWS

CPD: 20 Jan 1977. *CSM*: 9 March 1977. *CST*: 26 Nov 1979. *CT*: 26 Nov 1979. *HP*: 5 Nov 1979. *KCS*: 25 Oct 1978. *LAHE*: 25 Oct 1979. *LAT*: 30 Jan 1958; 19 Feb 1960; 24 March 1962; 16 Dec 1964; 12 March 1969; 13 Jan 1977; 14 Nov 1978; 25 Oct 1979. *MM*: Jan 1978; July 1983. *MT*: June 1957; July 1957; Sept 1967; May 1982. *NY*: 15 Oct 1955. *NYP*: 12 Feb 1977. *NYT*: 5 Oct 1955; 12 Oct 1955; 13 Jan 1958; 27 Jan 1958; 4 Jan 1960; 19 Jan 1960; 23 Jan 1960; 1 Feb 1962; 7 Nov 1964; 24 Nov 1964; 25 Nov 1964; 18 Nov 1966; 10 Dec 1966; 3 Feb 1969; 31 March 1969; 6 Nov 1970; 17 Oct 1979; 15 Nov 1979; 18 April 1983. *PEB*: 28 Jan 1977. *SR*: 22 Oct 1955; 29 Oct 1955. *TL*: 10 Dec 1952; 27 Oct 1955; 24 April 1957; 26 April 1957; 6 May 1957; 23 Feb 1959; 26 Feb 1959; 6 Nov 1965; 8 Nov 1965; 11 July 1967; 14 July 1967; 18 March 1968; 17 Oct 1968; 14 June 1976; 21 Sept 1977; 4 March 1980; 6 May 1980; 20 Aug 1980; 19 Nov 1980.8 March 1982; 6 Feb 1984; 16 Oct 1984.

SELECTED DISCOGRAPHY

Beethoven: Concertos (5). Multisonic 31 0106-2 (3 CDs). Sandling/Czech PO.
Beethoven: Sonata in D Major, op. 10, no. 3; Sonata in E-flat Major, op. 31, no. 3; Variations, op. 35. DG 423136-2.
Beethoven: Sonata in C Minor, op. 13; Sonata in E-flat Major, op. 27, no. 1; Sonata in C-sharp Minor, op. 27, no. 2. DG 400036-2.
Beethoven: Sonata in C Major, op. 53; Sonata in F Minor, op. 57; Sonata in E-flat Major, op. 81a. DG 419162-2.
Beethoven: Sonata in B-flat Major, op. 106. DG 410527-2.
Beethoven: Sonata in E Major, op. 109; Sonata in A-flat Major, op. 110. DG 419174-2.
Brahms: Concerto No. 1 in D Minor, op. 15; Concerto No. 2 in B-flat Major, op. 83. Fantasias, op. 116. DG 419158-2 or MHS 523359K (2 CDs). Jochum/Berlin PO.

Brahms: Concerto No. 2 in B-flat Major, op. 83. Haydn Variations. RCA 60536 (CD). Reiner/Chicago SO.

Chopin: Concerto No. 1 in E Minor, op. 11; Concerto No. 2 in F Minor, op. 21. Sony Classical SBK 46336 (CD). Ormandy/PO.

Chopin: Polonaise in A Major, op. 40, no. 1; Polonaise in C Minor, op. 40, no. 2; Sonata in B Minor, op. 58. DG 431587-2.

Emil Gilels at Carnegie Hall. Bach: Prelude and Fugue in D Major, BWV 532. Beethoven: Sonata in C-sharp Minor, op. 27, no. 2; 32 Variations in C Minor. Chopin: Etude in F Minor, op. 25, no. 2; Etude in A-flat Major, op. posth. Medtner: *Sonata reminiscenza* in A Minor, op. 38. Prokofiev: Scherzo and March (*The Love for Three Oranges*). Ravel: *Pavane; Jeux d'eau.* Music and Arts CD-773. Recorded 7 February 1969.

Emil Gilels in Concert. Chopin: Ballade in G Minor, op. 23; Don Juan Variations; Nocturne in E-flat Major, op. 55, no. 2. Debussy: *Mouvement*; *Hommage à Rameau*; *Reflets dans l'eau.* Ravel: *Alborada del gracioso.* Schumann: *Arabeske*, op. 18; 4 Pieces, op. 32. Music and Arts CD-747.

Emil Gilels in Recital. Bach-Siloti: Prelude in B Minor. Beethoven: Sonata in A-flat Major, op. 26. Prokofiev: Prelude in C Major, op. 12; Sonata No. 3 in A Minor, op. 28 (*Allegro tempestoso*); *Visions fugitives*, op. 22 (selections). Rachmaninoff: Daisies, op. 38, no. 3; Preludes, op. 3, no. 2, op. 23, nos. 3, 6 and 10, op. 32, no. 11; Vocalise, op. 34. Scriabin: Etude in C-sharp Minor. Music and Arts CD-746.

Grieg: Lyric Pieces (20). DG 419749-2.

Haydn: Sonata in C Minor (Hob. XVI:20). Beethoven: Sonata in F Minor, op. 57. Chopin: Sonata No. 2 in B-flat Minor, op. 35. Ravel: *Valses nobles et sentimentales.* Multisonic 0091.

Liszt: Sonata in B Minor. Beethoven: Sonata in C Major, op. 53; Sonata in A Major, op. 101. Music and Arts CD-759. Rec. 1966.

Mozart: Sonata in B-flat Major, K. 281; Sonata in A Minor, K. 310; Fantasia in D Minor, K. 397; Variations in F Major, K. 398. DG 413997-2.

Musique du 18e Siècle. C. P. E. Bach: *Sonate en la majeur.* Bach-Busoni: *Prélude et fugue en ré majeur* BWV 532. Clementi: *Sonate en ut majeur.* Haydn: *Sonate en ut mineur.* Rameau: *La Villageoise; Tambourin.* Scarlatti: Sept sonates. *Le Chant du Monde* LDC 278981/82 (2 CDs).

Prokofiev: Sonata No. 8 in B-flat Major, op. 84; Eight *Visions fugitives*, from op. 12. *Melodiya* C10-06129-30.

Rachmaninoff: Concerto No. 3 in D Minor, op. 30. Saint-Saëns: Concerto No. 2 in G Minor, op. 22. Shostakovich: Prelude and Fugue in D, op. 87, no. 5. Testament SBT 1029 (CD). Cluytens/*Orch. du Con.*

Recordings 1930–84. Debussy: *Clair de lune.* Debussy-Boruika: Nocturne No. 2 (*Fêtes*). Liszt: Hungarian Rhapsody No. 6. Liszt-Busoni: Fantasia on two themes from Mozart's "The Marriage of Figaro." Ravel: Toccata (*Le Tombeau de Couperin*). Scriabin: Five Preludes, op. 74; Sonata No. 3 in F-sharp Minor, op. 23; Sonata No. 4 in F-sharp Major, op. 30. Olympia OCD 166.

Schubert: *Moments musicaux*, D. 780; Sonata in A Minor, D. 784. Liszt: Sonata in B Minor. Orfeo C332931B (CD). Rec. 1970.

Scriabin: Etude in C-sharp Minor; Preludes, op. 74; Sonata No. 3 in F-sharp
   Minor, op. 23; Sonata No. 4 in F-sharp Major, op. 30.   Schumann:
   Nachtstücke, op. 23. MCA 32107 (CD).
Tchaikovsky: Concerto No. 1 in B-flat Minor, op. 23; Violin Concerto. Sony
   Classical SBK 46339 (CD). Mehta/NYPO.
Tchaikovsky: Concerto No. 2 in G Major, op. 44. Mozart: Concerto in C
   Major, K. 467. *Mezhdunarodnaya Kniga* MK 417106 (CD). Kondrashin/
   USSR SO (1959).
Tchaikovsky: Concerto No. 2 in G Major, op. 44. Olympia/Conifer OCD229.
   Svetlanov/USSR State Academy Orch.

GODOWSKY, LEOPOLD: b. Soshly, near Vilnius, (Russian) Lithuania,
   13 February 1870; d. New York City, New York, 21 November 1938.

Godowsky is a pianist for pianists, as Shelley is a poet for poets.
                                                  James Huneker (*Variations*)

Attributed statements and entertaining anecdotes in Jeremy Nicholas's excellent
biography *Godowsky: The Pianists' Pianist* prove that Huneker's pithy assessment of Leopold Godowsky was right on the mark. Godowsky gave his most
remarkable performances offstage, playing for intimate gatherings of friends and
colleagues, especially other pianists. His laurels as one of this century's greatest
pianists were bestowed on him by other great pianists stunned by the incomparable virtuosity of his playing at these informal get-togethers. Godowsky the
public pianist was a precise scholar and technical wizard and usually nothing
more. Playing in private, a more relaxed Leopold Godowsky performed pianistic
marvels that left other master pianists breathless. As many often said, no public performance or Godowsky recording could match the freedom and beauty of
Godowsky's playing in an intimate atmosphere, in the presence of admiring
friends and colleagues.
      Perhaps most remarkable of all, Godowsky was a self-taught musician.
He was not sent early to music school; he never had advanced training, except for
three frustrating, unproductive months at the Berlin *Hochschule*; he never had
private instruction from Liszt or Leschetizky or any other master pedagogue of
his time, or even from any of the lesser pedagogues. Jeremy Nicholas,
Godowsky's biographer, considers that Godowsky's "aptitude for self-study has
rarely been equalled in musical history."
      Certainly Leopold Godowsky was not "born into music." Neither of
his parents, both of Polish-Jewish ancestry, was the least bit musical or, it
seems, even interested in music; and Godowsky himself repeatedly claimed that
in his whole life he had not had so much as three months of lessons. His father
Matthew Godowsky, a physician, undoubtedly intended that his only son would

enter the medical profession, but his father died of cholera when Godowsky was only 18 months old. That sad event changed the course of Godowsky's life.

Within a year or so his nearly destitute mother Anna (Lewin) Godowsky had moved into Vilnius under the protection of her friends Louis and Minna Passinock; and Louis Passinock, a good amateur violinist enraptured with music, soon recognized that Leopold Godowsky was an infant prodigy. Passinock dreamed of making him a violin prodigy, so Godowsky had violin lessons; but even as young as age three he was secretly playing the piano ("as natural and necessary as breathing," he would later say) at every possible moment. Minna Passinock knew enough about the piano to explain the basics, but on his own Godowsky instinctively knew how to pick out tunes he heard played. He was soon composing, and when he was five years old a minuet he had written convinced "Uncle Louis" Passinock that he was meant for the piano.

There is to date no record of Godowsky's schooling. He remembered his childhood as endless (and wonderful) hours at the piano, playing every kind of piece he could get hold of. When he encountered seemingly impossible passages, he "isolated" those parts and worked tirelessly on them until he could play them as easily as the simple passages. It sounds like a drudgingly difficult childhood, but remember that Godowsky was *voluntarily* teaching himself the piano. Those childhood hours alone at the piano obviously were delightful, but having to play chamber music almost every evening (into the early morning hours) with Uncle Louis's adult friends was physically and mentally exhausting for such a small child. On the other hand, the experience gained in those endless home recitals partly explains how "Godowsky acquired his fabulous manual dexterity and comprehensive technique at an age when most people are learning the notes of the scale." (Nicholas)

Godowsky's first public recital, played at age nine in Vilnius, led to others. His rare talent attracted the attention of one Monsignor Selinsky, a beneficial patron who gave young Godowsky music, books and toys, often invited him to dine and to hear music, and gave helpful advice during the long sessions when Godowsky played for him. "Uncle Louis" Passinock, more interested in making money with his young charge, arranged a concert tour for Godowsky (and himself) in some of the nearby towns; but after the first concert (a great financial and artistic success), a critic-lawyer named Knorosovsky accused Passinock of exploiting the child and ultimately stopped the tour.

It was also Knorosovsky who later arranged a full scholarship for Godowsky at the St. Petersburg Conservatory, a gift that Uncle Louis, determined to keep control of his possibly income-producing prodigy, refused to accept. Infuriated but persevering, Knorosovsky literally kidnapped the boy (with assistance from Anna Godowsky) and sent him to friends in Bialostok to prepare for an audition with Anton Rubinstein at the St. Petersburg Conservatory. Unfortunately for Godowsky, his mother, succumbing to Passinock's entreaties, brought the boy back to Vilnius, an action that deprived Godowsky of studying, free of charge, with the finest teachers in Russia.

With the child once more in his keeping, Uncle Louis organized a second tour of concerts (by "the 11-year-old sensational piano phenomenon, assisted by Louis Passinock, Violinist"), this time in towns of East Prussia, out of reach, he hoped, of the powerful pen of critic Knorosovsky. When that tour ended at Königsberg, a banker named Feinberg offered Passinock compensation if he would allow the boy to go to Berlin. Uncle Louis agreed, and Godowsky went to live with the Feinbergs. Well prepared with hours of daily practice in the Feinberg music room, Godowsky passed the entrance examination at the Berlin *Hochschule für Musik*. Feinberg found him lodging in Berlin and gave him money to live on, but within three months the precocious 13-year-old had become totally disenchanted with the *Hochschule*. When his mother and Uncle Louis suddenly appeared in Berlin, Godowsky gladly agreed to accompany them to America.

Within weeks of his arrival in New York on 29 November 1884, the 14-year-old Godowsky had begun an American career. He made his American debut (7 Dec 1884) with the Clara Louise Kellogg Company; performed (22 Dec 1884) with the soprano Emma Thursby at the Ross Street Presbyterian Church in Brooklyn; early in 1885 made several appearances at the New York Casino, alternating weekly with Teresa Carreño; and toured America and Canada with a troupe organized by Major Pond, a prominent impresario of the time. That same year (1885) he toured in the Northeast and in Canada with the Ovide Musin Concert Company, apparently on his own, for there is no mention of his mother or Passinock accompanying him. He made barely enough to exist during that first tour, and at the end of the second Musin tour, along the West Coast, Musin abandoned him. Penniless and only 15 years old, Godowsky managed to get back to New York, where he sought help from Leon Saxe, a tobacco baron and patron of the arts.

In July 1886 Saxe took Godowsky to Europe, intending to have him study with Liszt at Weimar, but hearing en route of Liszt's death, they moved on to Paris, where Godowsky hoped he might study with Camille Saint-Saëns. Although Saint-Saëns refused to teach him, the two formed a close friendship and soon were spending every Sunday together. Godowsky would play all morning, but it was never really a lesson. Saint-Saëns would offer bravos, encouragement, perhaps a suggestion here and there, but that was all. In the afternoon Saint-Saëns would play from his own scores, and, as Godowsky often recalled, "talk most delightfully about music." Undoubtedly those long musical Sundays in Saint-Saëns's Paris apartment broadened Godowsky's intellectual and musical horizons. Besides these musical encounters, Saint-Saëns offered practical advice and took Godowsky to a gym to get into condition for touring.

Living in Paris until he was almost 21 years old, Godowsky gave some concerts, played often in salons and established a fine reputation as a pianist. Aware now that he lacked schooling, during these four years he began teaching himself (as he had taught himself to play the piano) a variety of subjects—art, languages, philosophy, history, science. Saint-Saëns's friendship gave him entree into the most exclusive social and musical circles of Paris. And at Saint-Saëns's insistence, Godowsky joined *La Trompette*, a society sponsoring about 15 or 20 concerts a season, which gave him further exposure, both as a composer (his compositions were first published in Paris) and as a pianist.

On 12 June 1890 he played a solo recital in London which was reviewed by famed critic George Bernard Shaw. In Beethoven's 32 Variations,

Godowsky proved to be "a brilliant and all-too-rapid executant. . . . He next tried Schumann; and though the difficulties of the Etudes Symphoniques seemed to give him no trouble, a certain shyness, rather engaging than otherwise, prevented him from standing on his merits emphatically enough to get full credit for his performance. By this time, however, the audience had come decidedly to like him; and when he got on to Chopin, with whom his musical instinct and natural grace of expression had their way unembarrassed, his battle was won." (*The World*, 18 June 1890)

Godowsky returned to the United States in October 1890, and that year was appointed to the faculty of the New York College of Music. He gave his first Carnegie Hall recital on 24 April 1891. On 30 April 1891 he married Frieda Saxe, daughter of Leon Saxe, and the following day became an American citizen. In the early years of his marriage Godowsky taught regularly to support himself and his wife. Besides his appointment at the New York College of Music, he taught (1893–95) at the South Broad Street Conservatory in Philadelphia and from 1895 to 1900 was head of the piano department at the Chicago Conservatory of Music. By the turn of the century Godowsky had performed throughout the United States and in Canada and had become highly successful as a pianist and as a teacher. In 1897 the esteemed Theodore Thomas, founder of the Chicago Symphony Orchestra, signed Godowsky to play a concert with his string quartet (composed of CSO members), and was so impressed with Godowsky that he engaged him for the remaining five concerts in the series. Fearing that the young pianist might "vegetate" in Chicago, Thomas advised him to go back to Europe and make a name for himself. Godowsky apparently agreed. On 4 July 1900 he sailed for Europe with his wife and three children.

Jeremy Nicholas, Godowsky's biographer, marks the Berlin debut recital (6 Dec 1900) as the turning point in Godowsky's career. His monumental program and breathtaking technique caused a furor. Reports of the time indicate that the audience went wild, critics eulogized and the following morning "all Berlin was ringing Godowsky's name." Immediately engaged for five additional performances, Godowsky overnight became one of the highest paid instrumentalists in the profession. He returned to America to fulfill engagements with Theodore Thomas in Chicago and make a tour (15 March–3 April 1901) of the United States and Canada, then returned to Europe. He made his adult London debut with a solo recital in spring of 1901 and on 21 June 1901 played the Brahms Concerto in D Minor with the London Philharmonic Society.

The Godowskys lived in Berlin from 1901 to 1909. He taught privately and made a handsome income with annual tours of Europe and the Near East. Early in 1909 he was appointed director of the Piano Masters School at the Imperial Academy of Music in Vienna, with the title of Royal Professor, a singular honor for a Polish Jew. And five years (1909–14) of teaching master classes in Vienna further enhanced Godowsky's standing as a major pedagogue. Students from America and Europe flocked to his classes, but apparently teaching rarely interfered with Godowsky's composing or concertizing. He toured widely, especially in Europe, often performing more than 70 concerts a season. He even returned to America for tours in the 1912–13 and 1913–14 seasons. Theodore Thomas's advice proved exactly right for Godowsky. After a dozen or so years in Europe, he ranked as one of the most distinguished pianists in the world.

A compulsive worker, he must have had an inexhaustible store of energy to withstand for so many years the demands of life as pianist, teacher, composer and father of four. His life revolved around the piano—playing it and composing for it. He reveled in company, even when working at composing, and had a reputation as a most sociable, witty (sometimes cutting) and engaging host. He loved to play for friends, students and colleagues in his own secure surroundings, and it was at those intimate gatherings, as we read over and over again, that Godowsky's playing so astounded even other pianists. Who can say why? The philosophical theory is that the congenial Godowsky's other self harbored doubts and depressions that hampered (dampened might be a better word) his public performances. The musical theory is that Godowsky's obsessive attention to the text restricted his interpretative skills.

Ignoring signs that World War I was imminent, the Godowskys barely managed to get to England (from Belgium where he was performing) just ahead of the advancing German army; and they arrived in New York in November 1914. He played some concerts during the war and gave very profitable master classes in New York City, Los Angeles and Seattle. America was his home for the rest of his life, but he traveled extensively. After the war he resumed his intensive concert schedule, performing around the world. Tours of Europe, Java, India, Japan and Egypt kept him away from the United States for five years (1922–27).

More than 40 years of that hectic existence ultimately took its toll. On 17 June 1930, while recording the Chopin Nocturnes, Godowsky suffered a stroke so disabling that he never again played in public. One cruel event followed another: his son Gordon committed suicide in 1932 and his wife Frieda died in 1933. Desolate and deeply depressed, Godowsky drifted aimlessly from friend to friend, hotel to hotel, from America to Europe and back again. He managed to give a series of master classes in Los Angeles in August 1933 and another series in New York in June 1934. In May 1935 he visited Heinrich Neuhaus, a former pupil, in Russia. Confined to bed for much of 1937, Godowsky died 21 November 1938, following an operation for an intestinal obstruction. His daughters Dagmar and Vanita and his son Leopold, a musician-chemist who with another musician, Leopold Mannes, invented the Kodachrome film process, survived him.

The indefatigable Godowsky was a prolific composer and a fastidious editor. As editor-in-chief (1912–22) for the *Progressive Series of Piano Lessons*, published by the Art Publication Society of St. Louis, Godowsky personally selected and proofread everything involved in this project—compositions, text, exercises, studies. His own published music, listed in the catalogue compiled by Leon Saxe, contains many fascinating works for piano—elaborate paraphrases, transcriptions, studies in rhythm, concerto cadenzas, left-hand pieces, exotic tone poems. "One needs unbiased ears to listen to Godowsky's music. Much of it is unprecedented in its dense interplay, its elaborate detail and contrapuntal texture and represents the *ne plus ultra* of pianistic polythematic tonal writing."

(Nicholas) Its extreme difficulty may be why pianists have shown very little interest in Godowsky's piano music in the half-century since his death. However, a current record catalogue lists over 12 CDs containing performances of his compositions played by at least eight different pianists.

The most famous—perhaps infamous—of his keyboard works are the 53 published studies on Chopin Etudes, "paraphrases in which the originals are dressed richly but reverently in the harmonic and polyphonic garb of Godowsky's own imagination." (Lichtenwanger) These Chopin Studies are "probably the most impossibly difficult things ever written for the piano . . . fantastic exercises that push piano technique to heights undreamed of even by Liszt." (Sch/Gre, see Bibliog.)

Godowsky had a wonderful memory and a huge repertoire. The Nicholas biography lists 38 selected programs from the years 1892–1930, and another selected 50 programs from the years 1892–1930 have been printed in *The Piano in Concert* (Keh/Pia, see Bibliog.). Since there are only seven duplicates in these 88 programs, these two sources supply a good overview of Godowsky's broad repertoire. Of particular interest are the eight historical recitals—a survey of the entire 19th-century piano literature—that he played at the Chicago Conservatory of Music during the 1897–98 season.

Considering his own phenomenal technique, it is interesting, as reported by his pupils, that Godowsky rarely mentioned technique, that is, mechanical technique. The fact is that he held the view that "piano technique" was a term including every component of a piano performance—approach, preparation, interpretation, the whole. "Notes from a Godowsky Master Class" explicitly details this Godowsky theory. (Haven) Godowsky urged students to develop correct mental and muscular practice habits, specifically what he termed the "weight-release principle." He believed that relaxed arm weight and economy of motion are the "foundation stones" of technique. The finger, he said, should rest with easy arm weight on the key. For more power, use more weight; for less power, hold back some of the weight. "Together with Teresa Carreño, who developed similar theories on weight and relaxation from watching Anton Rubinstein practice, Godowsky was the first great concert pianist to consciously adopt and then teach the principle of weight release, rather than muscular impetus, as the most efficient method of playing." (Nicholas)

As in his own playing, he urged his students to pay close attention to the written text. Godowsky himself, obsessively faithful to the text, abhorred the kind of pianists who "seek liberty in lawlessness and originality in individualistic distortions." He was forever checking against the score (even with works that he might have played a hundred times in the course of his career) and comparing the various versions of the different editions published. Yet his pupil Neuhaus reported that Godowsky's own music scores were literally covered with his personal comments and notations, Godowsky's method, surmised Neuhaus, of thinking things out.

Godowsky of course had the technique to play his wide-ranging repertoire and his own fiendishly difficult works. Contemporary writers attempting to describe his technique employed words like "prodigious," "magical," "transcendent," "crystalline." Other great pianists of the day who heard Godowsky simply wondered "how he did it." All agreed that his playing was precise, clean-cut and well articulated; that he never used his technique for showy effect; that he played everything with deceptive ease and simplicity, even music that other pianists would find impossibly difficult.

A musician of the highest musical integrity, Godowsky's strict attention to the text accounts for the incredibly fine quality of his playing. It also explains the lack of emotion in his playing. The unfavorable comments in Godowsky's reviews generally complain that his tone was too often dry and pallid, without depth; that his interpretations, too, were often colorless, without emotional impact. Playing for the public, his musical fidelity resulted in an amazingly precise performance, but so depersonalized that it conveyed to the audience only the printed music, little more. Awestruck audiences applauded his breathtaking technique and the clarity and eloquence of his playing, but rarely were they inspired or emotionally involved. Audiences perhaps never heard his best playing, for it was only at those small private gatherings that Godowsky, free of nerves and inhibitions, unleashed his imagination along with his ferocious technique.

The unstinting admiration of some contemporary critics suggests that they, too, heard Godowsky play in an intimate setting: "In his playing he is transcendental. . . . It is the fine equilibrium of intellect and emotion that compels our admiration. . . . He is a powerful man with muscles that are both velvet and steel. . . . He is master of the art of playing the piano beautifully. His exquisitely plastic phrasing, artistic massing of colors, above all the nobility of his conception—little wonder I call him a Brahma of the keyboard." (Hun/Var, see Bibliog.)

"There was general agreement that his technique was prodigious, transcendent. . . . His outstanding contribution to piano playing lay in his extraordinary development of the ordinarily weaker and subordinate left hand. Through his playing and composing of pieces for the left hand alone he initiated a trend that influenced Scriabin and many later musicians." (Lichtenwanger)

The late Jorge Bolet, a Godowsky champion, defended him against those professional pianists condescendingly describing Godowsky as the musician who tampered with the Chopin Etudes. Bolet believed that Godowsky, like Liszt, advanced "the mechanics of piano playing, to a degree previously unimagined. . . . Godowsky symphonicized (if there is such a word) piano playing to a greater extent than any other composer who has ever lived. What Godowsky did with rhythms, polyrhythms and textures can only be termed ingenious." (Dub/Ref, see Bibliog.)

By the turn of the century Godowsky was recognized as the foremost Chopin interpreter of the day and one of the great pianists of all time. When he made his Berlin debut (6 Dec 1900), every seat in Beethoven Hall was taken and almost every professional pianist in Berlin attended. The sensational reviews of that debut marked a turning point in Godowsky's career. For example: "Leopold Godowsky is the best pianist now living and in many respects the greatest I ever heard. Most assuredly no artist now living possesses the same most marvellous technique, a technique which in point of finesse and subtlety does not yield an iota to that of de Pachmann, and which, as far as brilliancy as well as accuracy is concerned, can vie successfully with the one which made and still makes Rosenthal famous." (*MC*, 8 Dec 1900)

On 4 December 1912 Godowsky's solo recital at Carnegie Hall earned a glowing review: "Without any desire to disparage his other qualities it must be conceded that the most astonishing element in Mr. Godowsky's performances is sheer technical perfection. . . . Every known stumbling block, old or new, from the warehouse of technical difficulties, is surmounted by him completely, and with a magnificent absence of all apparent effort. . . . Viewed from the interpretative standpoint the artist's playing was characterized by breadth, massiveness and brilliancy of style and a mood of fiery impetuosity." (*MA*, 7 Dec 1912)

An enthusiastic audience—there were even chairs on the stage—loved every minute of Godowsky's Aeolian Hall recital of 17 October 1915, but critics' opinions were mixed. This from an admiring reviewer: "Godowsky represents the final word in artistic sincerity. He is straightforward, unpretentious, humble in his treatment of the master works. He does not obstruct with his own personality your view of the composer. If you do not hold with the degree of emotion of heart or soul with which he invests his readings, you must at the same time applaud him for his intelligence, his authority and polish." (*MA*, 23 Oct 1915) A less impressed critic wrote: "There must necessarily be a deep interest in the performance of one who has so consummately mastered certain things, though his mastery does not extend to all, not even to the most vital and fundamental things, in musical art. It cannot be said that Mr. Godowsky is invariably a great interpreter of the greatest music, or that he often touches deeply the heart or fires the imagination." (*NYT*, 18 Oct 1915)

But there were those who regarded Godowsky as the perfect pianist in all aspects of pianism. After a 13-year absence he played a London recital on 26 February 1927, and his playing of the Brahms Rhapsody in E-flat Major, op. 119, no. 4, and his own transcription of a movement from a Bach Violin Sonata tempted one critic to write a eulogy of his technique: "But technique is not the whole of Godowsky; he is also the poet, and this is revealed, not so much by the wordy descriptions which he has written for his 'Java' Suite, as by his Chopin playing. Here, the height of his attainment is most fully revealed. His idiom is a subtle compound of imagination and efficiency." (*MT*, 1 April 1927)

As with other early 20th-century piano giants, it is only by Godowsky's recordings that he may be judged today, and here we are extremely fortunate. He left a considerable recorded legacy, more than 200 piano rolls and discs embracing more than 150 compositions. A glance at his discography (see Nicholas, Appendix B) shows that he had at his command a good-sized portion of the entire piano repertoire.

Godowsky preferred the piano roll to the early primitive acoustic recording process. On more than one occasion he publicly stated (for publicity purposes) that the piano roll faithfully reproduced his playing, which was of course only partially true, depending on the company, the playback apparatus, the engineers, etc. In any case, he made his first piano roll in 1907 and continued making rolls until the mid-1920s. Those who would hear Godowsky playing his own music must listen to the rolls, for he made very few discs of his own works.

Most of the approximately 90 compositions he recorded on disc were made acoustically. Because of the early space limitation of the disc (4 minutes), most of these are short compositions. When a larger work was attempted, it was often horribly mutilated by cuts and omissions. However, during the later part of Godowsky's recording career, the more sophisticated electrical process made it possible to record more substantial compositions like the Beethoven Sonata in E-flat Major, op. 81a, and the Schumann *Carnaval*.

Regardless of the recording process, Godowsky never felt that his recordings did him justice. He was so uncomfortable in the studio, so concerned that his performances be "perfect," so meticulous in his preparations that the end product was frequently disappointing. The technique was there in abundance and the works were performed to perfection, but the results often gave the impression of a cool, almost machine-like performance. Of course there were many exceptions. Godowsky's 1929 performance of the Grieg Ballade in G Minor, op. 24, stands as one of the high points in recorded pianism.

In 1913 Godowsky recorded for the American Columbia Gramophone Company. Most of these early discs have noticeably poor sound, dim treble response and annoying surface noise. However, another Columbia session in 1916 produced a charming Chopin Waltz in A-flat Major, op. 42, illuminating Godowsky's technical prowess and musicality.

In 1920 he signed a contract with the American Brunswick Company and recorded for them until late 1926. These later acoustic recordings are far superior to the earlier Columbia discs. The Chopin Fantasy-Impromptu, op. 66, reveals the essence of Godowsky's artistry—eloquent technical facility, beautiful cantabile phrasing. The Polonaise in A Major, op. 40, no. 1, and the A-flat Impromptu, op. 29, also show exquisite phrasing and feeling for style. Unlike most pianists of his day (and ours!), he included American music in his repertoire. The Brunswick catalogue lists works by Camille Zeckwer, Eastwood Lane and Edward MacDowell.

By 1928 the electric process of recording solo piano music was a comparatively sophisticated mechanism. Godowsky signed with the English Columbia Company in June of that year and remained their featured recording artist until his untimely illness. In 1928 he recorded some Chopin Nocturnes and in 1929 three works of sizeable proportion: the Grieg Ballade in G Minor, op. 24, Beethoven's Sonata in E-flat Major, op. 81a, and the Schumann *Carnaval*, op. 9. Here the pianist is in his element, and he appears "almost relaxed" with these superb readings. The Grieg is unmatched even today. "Only marginally less inspired is Godowsky's radiant and serene reading of the *Les Adieux* Sonata, while in *Carnaval* he assiduously avoids any trace of sentimentality, opting instead for an elegant blend of understatement and vigour." (CDAPR 7010, liner notes)

Almost all of Godowsky's recordings have been reissued on CD by Appian Publications and Recordings (APR) in two sets, each containing 2 CDs (see Discog.). The first set (APR 7010) contains all of the pianist's recordings for English Columbia, made between 1928 and 1930, and his only recordings of extended length. Included are the fine Grieg Ballade, the beautifully phrased, rhythmic Chopin Sonata No. 2 in B-flat Minor and 12 eloquently played Nocturnes. The second set (APR 7011), an anthology of his American Columbia and Brunswick recordings made between 1913 and 1926, contains a dazzling Chopin Scherzo No. 4 (his last studio recording, made in 1930) and a private recording of The Gardens of Buitenzorg, the only known example of his playing after his stroke.

SELECTED REFERENCES

Adler, Clarence. "Leopold Godowsky." *The Piano Teacher*, July–Aug 1963, pp. 2–4. Reprinted in *The AMICA Bulletin*, May/June 1993, pp. 117–119.
Brower, Harriette. "Godowsky's Writings On Piano." *Musical America*, 19 April 1913, p. 21.
Cooke, James Francis. "The Genius of Leopold Godowsky." *Etude*, April 1953, pp. 26, 62.
———. "The Real Significance of Technic." In *Great Pianists on Piano Playing* (see Bibliog.), pp. 132–142.
Godowsky, Leopold. "Background in Music Study." *Etude*, June 1936, pp. 345–346.
———. "The Best Method is Eclectic." *Etude*, Oct 1933, pp. 645, 710.
———. "The Best Method is Eclectic." (Part 2) *Etude*, Nov 1933, pp. 737, 784.
———. "The Laws Governing Technic and Interpretation." In *Piano Mastery* (Brower, Second Series, see Bibliog.), pp. 61–79.
———. "A Master Pianist on Music Study." (Part 2). *Musical America*, 20 July 1918, p. 14.
———. "A Master Pianist on Music Study." (Part 3) *Musical America*, 10 Aug 1918, p. 19.
———. "Piano Music for the Left Hand." *Musical Quarterly*, July 1935, pp. 298–300.
———. "The Place of Technic in Pianoforte Playing." *Etude*, Jan 1913, pp. 13–14.
Haven, Dale. "Notes From a Godowsky Master Class." *Music Teacher*, July–Aug 1963, pp. 5–8.
Hodgson, Leslie. "Godowsky: Great Musical Mind and Personality." *Musical America*, 10 Dec 1938, p. 11.
Huneker, James. "A Brahma of the Keyboard." In *Variations* (see Bibliog.), pp. 225–232.
Kipnis, Igor. "New Light on Godowsky." *Clavier*, Oct 1990, pp. 19–21.
"Leopold Godowsky." In *Music and Musicians in Chicago*, ed. F. Ffrench (see Bibliog.), pp. 114–115.
Lichtenwanger, William. "Leopold Godowsky." In *Dictionary of American Biography*, vol. 22 (Supplement Two), pp. 243–244.
Miller, Douglas. "The Godowsky Centenary (born February 13, 1870)." *Musical Opinion*, March 1970, pp. 302–305.
Neuhaus, Heinrich. "My Recollections of Godowsky." (translated by Beatrice L. Frank). *Clavier*, Oct 1990, pp. 15–18.

Nicholas, Jeremy. *Godowsky: The Pianists' Pianist*. Northumberland: Appian
  Publications & Recordings, 1989. A full-length biography.
Obituary. *Los Angeles Times*, 22 Nov 1938, p. 1. *Musical America,* 25 Nov
  1938, p. 32. *New York Times*, 22 Nov 1938, p. 23.
Philipp, Isidor. "Recollections of Leopold Godowsky." In *A Birthday Offering
  to Carl Engel*. New York: G. Schirmer, Inc., 1943, pp. 179–180.
*Progressive Series of Music Lessons for the use of Conservatories, Teachers and
  Students*. L. Godowsky, Editor-in-Chief; Dr. W. S. Mathews, Editor;
  Emil Sauer, Co-Editor. St. Louis: Art Publication Society, 1913.
Saxe, Leonard S. "The Published Music of Leopold Godowsky." *Music Library
  Association Notes*, March 1957, pp. 165–183.
Schonberg, Harold C. "He Makes Every Other Pianist Sound Like A Peasant."
  New York Times, 8 Feb 1970, sec. 2, pp. 17, 28.
————. "A piano giant is rescued from ghostdom." *New York Times*, 11 June
  1989, sec. 2, pp. 29–30.
See also Bibliography: Ald/Con; Bro/PiS; Cal/MG; Cal/Mus; Cha/Spe;
  Coo/GrP; Dub/Ref; Ewe/Mu; Hun/Uni; Hun/Var; Kau/Art; Kol/Que;
  Lah/Fam; Met/Cho; MGG; New/Gro; Neu/Art; Nie/Mei; Rub/MyM;
  Rub/MyY; Sal/Fam; Sch/Gre; Sha/Mus.

SELECTED REVIEWS

CDJ: 18 Oct 1920. *CDN*: 18 Oct 1920. *CEP*: 18 Oct 1920. *LAT*: 23 May
  1919. *MA*: 30 Nov 1912; 7 Dec 1912; 28 Dec 1912; 23 Oct 1915; 20 Nov
  1915; 12 Feb 1916; 27 Oct 1917; 6 Nov 1920. *MT*: 1 July 1890; 1 April
  1927. *NYT*: 15 Jan 1892; 28 Nov 1912; 4 March 1914; 18 Oct 1915; 14
  Nov 1915; 13 Dec 1916; 21 Oct 1917; 30 Jan 1919. *TL*: 13 June 1901; 18
  Jan 1902; 25 Jan 1902; 16 May 1902; 18 March 1903; 30 Jan 1911; 22
  May 1911; 20 March 1912; 12 Oct 1920; 28 Feb 1927.

SELECTED DISCOGRAPHY

Godowsky The Pianists' Pianist. An anthology of his American recordings
  (1913–26) plus a private recording and his last commercial recording.
  Albéniz: Tango in D, op. 165, no. 2. Bishop-Godowsky: Home, sweet
  home. Chopin: Etudes, op. 25, nos. 1 and 3; Fantasy-Impromptu, op. 66;
  Scherzo in E Major, op. 54; Waltzes in A-flat Major, op. 34, no. 1, A-flat
  Major, op. 42, C-sharp Minor, op. 64, no. 2. Chopin-Liszt: *Chants polon-
  ais*, op. 74, nos. 1 and 5. Debussy: Golliwog's Cakewalk (Children's
  Corner); Minstrels (Preludes I). Dohnányi: Concert Study in F Minor, op.
  28, no. 6. Godowsky: The Gardens of Buitenzorg (Java Suite); Humoresque, The Hunter's Call & Military March (Miniatures). Henselt: *Wiegenlied* in G-flat Major, op. 45. Lane: The Crapshooters. Liszt: *Gnomenreigen*; *La leggierezza*; *Liebestraum* No. 3. MacDowell: Witches' Dance,
  op. 17, no. 2. Mendelssohn: *Andante & Rondo capriccioso*, op. 14. Songs
  without words, op. 62, no. 1, op. 64, no. 2. Rubinstein: Melody in F, op.
  3, no. 1; *Rêve angélique*; Romance in E-flat Major, op. 44, no. 1.

Schubert-Godowsky: *Morgengrüss*. Schubert-Tausig: *Marche militaire*.
Schütt: *A la bien-aimée*, op. 59, no. 2. *Etude mignonne*, op. 16, no. 1.
Sinding: Rustle of Spring, op. 32, no. 3. Verdi-Liszt: *Rigoletto* para-
phrase. Zeckwer: In a boat. CDAPR 7011 (2 CDs).
Godowsky The Pianists' Pianist. The complete UK Columbia recordings
(1928–30). Beethoven: Sonata in E-flat Major, op. 81a. Chopin: Twelve
Nocturnes (op. 9, nos. 1 and 2; op. 15, nos. 1 and 2; op. 27, nos. 1 and 2;
op. 32, no. 1; op. 37, nos. 1 and 2; op. 48, no. 2; op. 55, no. 1; op. 72);
Sonata No. 2 in B-flat Minor, op. 35. Grieg: Ballade in G Minor, op. 24.
Schumann: *Carnaval*, op. 9. CDAPR 7010 (2 CDs).

GODOWSKY PLAYED BY OTHERS

18 Studies on Chopin Etudes. Ian Hobson, piano. Arabesque Z-6537 (CD).
53 Studies after Chopin's Etudes. G. Douglas Madge, piano. Dante PSG
8903/4, 8905/6. (4 CDs).
Leon Fleisher Recital. Symphonic Metamorphoses of the Schatz-Waltzer (left
hand). Sony Classical SK 48081 (CD).
Piano Music. Godowsky: *Alt Wien*; Passacaglia. Godowsky-Schubert: Ballet
Music from Rosamunde; *Moment musical* No. 3; 3 Song Transcriptions
(*Gute Nacht, Das Wandern, Ungeduld*); Godowsky-Strauss: *Künstlerleben*.
Godowsky-Weber: Invitation to the Dance. R. de Waal, piano. Hyperion
CDA 66496.
Triakontameron. G. Douglas Madge, piano. Dante PSG 9009 (CD).
Waltzermasken. G. Douglas Madge, piano. Dante PSG 8908 (CD).

GOULD, GLENN HERBERT: b. Toronto, Canada, 25 September 1932; d.
Toronto, 4 October 1982.

> Every great artist makes us see or hear the world otherwise. Glenn
> Gould, for whom clarity was never the enemy of mystery, showed us
> all that it is possible to go through life without having to keep a foot
> on the loud pedal most of the time.
>
> Geoffrey Payzant (*Glenn Gould: Music & Mind*)

Unorthodox and inimitable, Glenn Gould has inspired an outpouring of print
(books, articles, analyses, interviews, conversations, critiques, commentaries,
memories), some of it written by Gould himself, most of it written in the decade
following his death. The pro and con discussions set forth in these writings essentially dwell on the same Gould themes: his life and concert career; the influences on his development; his eccentricities; his musical goals, style and repertoire; the recording-television-radio years; critical reviews and final assessments.

The cut-and-dried biographical data suggest that Gould almost always lived a strange, isolated life. An only child—son of Russell Herbert Gould, a prosperous Toronto furrier and amateur violinist, and Florence (Greig) Gould, a part-time voice teacher—Glenn Gould was only age three when his mother, holding him on her lap at the piano, realized that he had absolute pitch. By age five he could play the simple tunes she taught him. Even as a child, he lived only for music. His parents desperately wanted him to have what they considered a normal childhood, but Glenn refused to take part in any of the usual boyhood activities, shunned sports and was always keenly aware of his hands. Robert Fulford, Gould's best friend through childhood and adolescence, cannot remember a moment when Gould was not an outsider.

Gould studied music with his mother until he was ten, then enrolled (1943) at the Toronto Conservatory (later the Royal Conservatory of Music), where he studied piano with Alberto Guerrero, a Chilean pedagogue; organ with Frederick C. Silvester; and theory with Leo Smith. Robert Fulford recalls that in high school (Malvern Collegiate Institute) Gould was more often absent than present and sometimes was tutored in private by one of the teachers. At Malvern from 1945 to 1951, Gould completed his courses but not the requirements necessary for matriculation. However, he was only 12 years old when he passed (1945) the Royal Conservatory's associate examination for solo piano and only age 13 when he passed (1946) the music theory examinations and was awarded the Associate Diploma of the Conservatory with highest honors.

Gould came to local public attention in Toronto when at age 11 he won (15 Feb 1944) the "piano trophy competition" at the annual Kiwanis Music Festival, taking first place ahead of older, supposedly more advanced students. In 1946 he took first place in the open Bach Prelude-and-Fugue category at that same festival. He gave his first important public performance as organist, not as pianist, in a Casavant Society concert (12 Dec 1945) held at Toronto's Eaton Auditorium. The 13-year-old was "never at fault," wrote one reviewer. "He played Mendelssohn's chorale and lovely variations [from the sixth organ sonata] as only a great artist could. . . . The Bach G Minor Fugue was pedalled as clearly as a song." (*TT*, 13 Dec 1945) A few months later Gould, still only age 13, played (8 May 1946) the first movement of Beethoven's Concerto No. 4 with the orchestra of the Royal Conservatory. "The boy's playing showed how beautiful piano music can be . . . and how awesome are the ways of genius in a child. For Glenn Gould is a genius." (*TT*, 9 May 1946)

On 20 October 1947 Gould gave his first professional solo recital, a Toronto event arranged by impresario Walter Homburger, Gould's manager from 1947 to 1967. Even then Gould's preoccupation with the essence of each work was in evidence: "Here was a player who conceived movements, entire compositions as wholes, and whose every detail was calculated to reveal total structures." (*GloM*, 21 Oct 1947) Gould played his first network radio recital on 24 December 1950. By age 20 he had appeared on about eight other Canadian Broadcasting Company programs, made about 10 appearances with various Canadian orchestras, and made a solo recital tour through Canada's western provinces.

By the time he made his American recital debut (2 Jan 1955) in Washington, D.C., Gould had become, as *Music in Canada* (1955) describes him, one of the most outstanding musicians the country had produced. For that American recital debut, Gould, true to form, chose a program that few pianists at the time would have thought of performing, or dared to perform: Bach's Partita No. 5 in G Major and five Three-Part Inventions; the Beethoven Sonata in E Major, op. 109; Webern's Variations, op. 27; the Alban Berg Sonata; pieces by Gibbons and Sweelinck. One review included: "Few pianists play the instrument so beautifully, so lovingly, so musicianly in manner, and with such regard for its real nature and its enormous literature. . . . Glenn Gould is a pianist with rare gifts for the world." (*WP*, 3 Jan 1955) When David Oppenheim, director of Columbia's Masterworks Division, heard Gould play this same program in New York, he immediately offered Gould a recording contract. Gould's first recording for CBS—the Bach Goldberg Variations, released in January 1956—became a best seller and cemented Gould's reputation as one of the leading pianists of his age.

Gould continued to reap accolades on his first concert tour (1956–57) through the United States and Canada. He made his American orchestral debut on 13 March 1956, playing the Beethoven Concerto No. 4 with the Detroit Symphony Orchestra, conducted by Paul Paray; and his New York orchestral debut (26 Jan 1957), playing the Beethoven Concerto No. 2 with the New York Philharmonic-Symphony, Leonard Bernstein conducting. His first European tour began in early May 1957 with four concerts in Moscow and four in Leningrad. Gould made his Berlin debut (May 1957) on that same tour, playing the Beethoven Concerto No. 3 with the Berlin Philharmonic Orchestra, Herbert von Karajan conducting. In May 1958 he made his debut with the Philadelphia Orchestra, playing the Beethoven Concerto No. 4 with Eugene Ormandy conducting. During the 1958–59 season Gould had three months of nonstop activity on a second European tour (Austria, Belgium, Germany, Italy, Sweden), including a Salzburg performance (Aug 1958) of the Bach Concerto in D Minor, with Dimitri Mitropoulos conducting. That December Gould was in Israel, where he played 11 concerts in 18 days. In May and June of 1959 he was scheduled to play all five Beethoven Concertos with the London Symphony Orchestra, Josef Krips conducting, but at least one of these performances was canceled by Gould. By now the media had begun to make much of his frequent concert cancellations due, he always said, to illness.

During 1963 and 1964 he lectured at the Gardner Museum in Boston, the University of Cincinnati, the University of Toronto, Hunter College and Wellesley College. When in June 1964 he received an honorary doctorate from the University of Toronto, the unpredictable Gould chose to deliver the convocation address rather than play a brief piano recital, customary at such a ceremony.

At that moment Glenn Gould was at the peak of success, a superstar on the lucrative concert circuit, with more proffered engagements than he could possibly accommodate; but, unannounced, he had already made his final concert appearance, a recital in Chicago's Orchestra Hall on 28 May 1964. For nearly a decade, Gould had not only been playing concerts but also making radio broadcasts, appearing on television, recording, writing, composing and lecturing. Although brief, his concert career had been intense, and he was tired of the whole "hideous, traumatic experience," the "onerous burden" of public performances. He had frequently mentioned leaving the concert stage, but no one had taken him seriously. At this point, frustrated with what he called the "non-take-twoness" of the concert experience—the finality of a concert performance, the inability of the artist to correct finger slips and any other mistakes—Gould simply stopped. (*Glenn Gould: Concert Dropout*, see Discog.)

Since he apparently had unbounded energy for projects that interested him, the remaining 18 years of his life were immensely productive. He made more than 80 recordings, produced (and performed in) many radio programs, and appeared on television. He also wrote prolifically—essays, interviews, program notes for some of his own recordings and more than 40 articles with such provocative titles as "Glenn Gould Interviews himself about Beethoven," "Memories of Maude Harbour or Variations on a Theme of Arthur Rubinstein," "The Search for Petula Clark." Gould's recording of Hindemith's Three Piano Sonatas won a Grammy award, but his liner notes are "in some ways, better than the record itself." (Page, *Glenn Gould Reader*)

Withdrawing from public performance when only in his early thirties was, Gould always claimed, according to plan. Further, before his untimely death, he had let it be known that when his long-running contract with CBS Masterworks came to an end, which would be shortly after Gould's 50th birthday, he planned "a major change of gears." He gave no details, only hinted that he might try conducting. However, about three years earlier he had confided to Andrew Kazdin, his CBS producer for more than 15 years, that at age 50, in accordance with the "master timetable" for his career, he would publicly announce that he was about to stop making recordings. But Gould also confided that he had a devious hidden agenda: He would continue recording secretly in Toronto (where he already owned all necessary recording equipment); process the tapes into finished masters; hold them in reserve while his already issued records rose in value (Gould was sure they would become collectors' items); at the propitious time reveal all or part of his secret stockpile, and hopefully make a fortune.

Whether Gould would have fulfilled his grand recording scheme or whether he had indeed used his rare gifts to attain his full potential as an artist will never be known. Disabled by a massive stroke just two days after his 50th birthday, Glenn Gould died in Toronto on 4 October 1982.

Opinions differ on the subject of who or what influenced Gould's musical style. During a 1959 interview on Radio Canada, Gould himself stated that his organ studies—pursued intermittently for about six years—had provided the groundwork for his keyboard technique and for his great love of Bach. He also frequently mentioned that as a teenager he had admired Schnabel's recordings; Rosalyn Tureck's recordings of Bach, which confirmed his own ideas as to how Bach should be played; and the recordings of Leopold Stokowski, a musician who, like Gould himself, did not feel bound to follow every detail of the composer's score.

But apparently Gould rarely talked about what he had learned from Alberto Guerrero, his teacher for nine years; and the omission suggests that Gould disapproved of what he called Guerrero's "excessive *rubato*" style. Some writers believe that Gould did not really begin to learn about music until he finished his studies with Guerrero and, in 1952, at age 20, withdrew to his parents' cottage at Uptergrove, about 90 miles north of Toronto, to devote himself to rethinking the way the piano ought to be played. However, John Beckwith, another Guerrero pupil in Gould's time, feels that Guerrero definitely influenced Gould's playing style, especially Gould's low posture at the keyboard and his use of pure finger technique as opposed to weight techniques. Beckwith says that Gould's "basic attitude to music stemmed from Guerrero's example initially, divergent though they were in outlook and taste later on." (Beckwith's informative "Shattering a Few Myths," in John McGreevy's *Glenn Gould by Himself and His Friends*, is important to any study of Gould.)

Writers may appear to give inordinate attention to Gould's eccentricities, but since they influenced both his personal life and his professional career, they cannot be ignored. From the time he left the concert platform until his death, Gould determinedly kept out of the public eye, preserving his privacy with a passion bordering on paranoia. Very, very few individuals ever got close to him. His extremely selective choice of friends—usually one friend at a time, later put aside to make room for another "close" friend—protected the isolation he craved. Only a handful of people, if that many, ever knew where he lived. (For example, Andrew Kazdin, Gould's producer at Columbia, never saw the inside of Gould's apartment.) Gould refused to shake hands, ostensibly fearing injury, but obviously he hated to be touched at all.

Working mostly at night, often from midnight to dawn (very difficult for his crew), Gould often retired at five or six in the morning and started another day about three in the afternoon. He made almost all contacts, business and personal, by telephone, sometimes hours-long phone calls. Co-workers recall how Gould would phone and, without ever asking whether his calling was convenient, plunge into an hour, even a two-hour phone conversation.

Glenn Gould was also a hypochondriac, to the extent that he carried with him his own box of pills, other medicines and towels, and he regularly used tranquilizers such as Valium and Nembutal. He had a deadly fear of getting sick, especially of catching a cold. All year round he wore a coat, beret or cap, gloves and scarf. Fearing drafts, Gould never permitted air conditioning to be turned on in the studio, despite the intensely hot lights and the enclosed environment. He carried bottled water with him, sometimes had a glass by the piano when he performed.

Before practicing, before a concert and intermittently during recording sessions, Gould soaked his arms and hands in water heated to the boiling point and took a calming tranquilizer. Other eccentricities appeared at the piano. Every Gould performance included extraneous noises (humming, singing, crooning) and various motions (weaving low over the keyboard, or playing with his head flung back and eyes closed) that distracted audiences and frustrated sound technicians. If playing with only one hand, Gould often waved the other hand around, conducting himself. Even worse, when waiting for his cue in a concerto, he frequently conducted the orchestra from the piano bench, irritating conductors to the extreme. He had an absolute fixation about having just the right piano and piano bench. Gould's bench was actually a chair, specially adapted (many times!) to suit his low posture at the keyboard. Only 14 inches tall, with sawed-off legs, this chair folded into a case, and, until it literally disintegrated, Gould carried it to every performance.

His piano, raised on wooden blocks, had to have the exact hair-trigger specifications Gould required for his kind of playing, which meant that a piano tuner had to stand by at every performance and throughout every recording session. The pre-World War II Steinway CD 318 that he used for years, up to the time when further readjustment became impossible, and the second-hand Yamaha that replaced it were both modified along the lines of an 1895 Chickering (stored in his apartment) that had exactly the tactile grab and immediacy Gould demanded. He wanted a piano that would minimize pianistic sounds—washes of harmonies, impressionist colors, the sustaining pedal.

Glenn Gould stressed that his musical goal was to rethink the repertory in a radically different fashion. His musical knowledge and instincts awed colleagues, but at no time in his life, not even during his brief concert career, did Gould look upon music as a means of communicating with an audience; on the contrary, he never felt any kind of rapport with his audiences. Nor was his aim merely to reproduce the expressed intentions of the composer or to achieve a beautiful piano tone. For Glenn Gould, making music meant probing the heart of a score, and to that end no amount of takes and retakes, splicing and editing, was ever too much. It follows, then, that in youth and in maturity, he was always far more interested in the structure of music than in its emotional aspect.

Structure—or as Gould sometimes called it "the backbone"—was the essence in all his music making. Increasingly he emphasized structure "at the expense of conventionally understood 'expression.' Vocal-style inflection, even the large-scale dynamic gradings which had helped him achieve such sweeping grandeur and momentum in his earlier years, fell more and more by the wayside. . . . In his quest for the dehumanized beauty of pure structure, Gould lost a legion of former admirers. . . . As time progressed, Gould relied less and less on dynamic gradations, preferring to sculpt phrases and elucidate the music's contrapuntal weave by means of articulation, rhythm and embellishment." (Siepman)

Just as Gould's articulation—dry, detached, overemphasized—will perhaps always arouse debate, his peerless precision and breathtaking finger technique will always remain a matter of wonder. "With a technique that knew of no difficulties, Mr. Gould could dissect a work, cleanse it of its standard interpretative manners and restore to it an almost ecstatic excitement." (*NYT*, 5 Oct 1982)

Rhythmically he favored "a motoric rat-a-tat martellato with an almost callous contempt for the kind of *rubato* which he ascribed to Edwin Fischer (while confessing never to have heard him). But within this framework of temporal rigidity, the slightest agogic deviation became an eloquent and often exhilarating structural tool." (*PQ*, Winter 1990-91)

Gould's intensely personal ornamentation frequently dismayed colleagues and irked musicologists. Embellishing not merely to decorate but to emphasize points of structure, he never worried about removing or adding ornaments according to his feelings about the performance of the moment. Believing that a score should be treated as though it were a film script requiring molding and editing by the artist, Gould would add or subtract octaves, change tempos, omit repeats, roll chords, and indulge in other personal exaggerations, distortions and outrageous departures from tradition.

Gould's whole approach to music may rest on the fact that he thought music was more mental than physical. As he told one interviewer, "One does not play the piano with one's fingers, one plays the piano with one's mind. . . . If you have a clear image of what you want to do, there's no reason it should ever need reinforcement. If you don't, all the fine Czerny studies and Hanon exercises in the world aren't going to help you." (Dubal) Of course, only a Glenn Gould, endowed with a "terrifyingly secure" technique and innate cognition, could use this approach. Gould in his youth practiced about four hours daily; during his recording years he rarely practiced regularly, and when he did it would be for only an hour, or less, at a time.

He told more than one interviewer that polyphonic music was the only music that really interested him, and he seemed to have a compulsion for stressing the polyphonic aspect of everything he played. Gould was known to be able to read a book and simultaneously carry on a telephone conversation. Another "contrapuntal" story relates how Gould in 1954 treated some friends to an informal run-through of both the accompaniment and vocal part, all memorized, to Schoenberg's The Book of the Hanging Gardens. "I can remember," recalled one friend, "following the score and noting not only how accurately he sang those difficult pitches simultaneous with playing the piano part, but also with what ferocious intensity he carried off the performance." (Canin)

Robert Fulford, Gould's best boyhood friend, remembers that Gould's musical tastes were fastidious from the beginning: "By his late teens he had staked out what was to be the ground of his taste during the first flowering of his career. He liked the eighteenth century and the twentieth but had little time for the nineteenth and no patience at all for anything that carried the name 'romantic'." (Fulford) Gould basically never changed; to the end of his life he detested romanticism of any kind. Interviewed just a year before his death, he reiterated his theme that the major portion of the piano recital repertoire is a "colossal" waste of time, that the music of the entire first half of the 19th century, except for some Beethoven, is "full of empty theatrical gestures, full of exhibitionism." To the astonishment of colleagues, Gould rejected the music of Chopin, Debussy, Liszt, Schumann, Schubert and even many early works of Beethoven.

He loved Bach and the early and middle works of Mozart. His repertoire also included works by composers as disparate as Sweelinck, Gibbons, Bizet and Sibelius. The only 20th-century composers he thought worth playing were those having a strong inclination to counterpoint—Berg, Hindemith, Krenek, Schoenberg and Webern.

Just as he lived his life exactly the way he pleased, Gould played only music that he really liked. Sometimes, for the sake of controversy or whatever unknown reason, he would outdazzle the dazzlers, as on a 1975 CBC television program when he played Ravel's *La Valse* "as though bent on surpassing those virtuosi who dust off the more spectacular transcriptions of Liszt . . . to dazzle us with the sheer physical improbability of their display." (Payzant)

A review of Gould's American orchestral debut (13 March 1956) with the Detroit Symphony Orchestra is singularly untechnical but not incongruous. A forerunner of most of Gould's reviews, it describes exactly the way Gould played—and behaved—all through his brief career and how most audiences usually responded: "Gould saunters to the piano. . . . Seating himself on his special chair, his contortions begin. . . . He convulses on an orchestral *sfz* while waiting for his own re-entrance. He sings and from my third-row seat I heard a frequent buzzing. I could find no other than the pianist to whom I might attribute this. The completely full house snickered a bit at first, but I don't think they could have been more attentive. . . . Gould won his audience and he held them as few have done." (Viets)

Gould made his New York orchestral debut (26 Jan 1957) with the New York Philharmonic-Symphony, Leonard Bernstein conducting. Although one reviewer could not refrain from noting Gould's eccentric performance mannerisms, he found nothing at all eccentric about his reading. "Aside from a few punched and percussive tones—Mr. Gould's tone does get less pleasant as it increases in amplitude—he knew what he was doing and did it with complete efficiency." (*NYT*, 28 Jan 1957)

Gould's Carnegie Hall recital (7 Dec 1957) included Mozart's Sonata in C Major, K. 330, Schoenberg's Suite, op. 25, a Sweelinck organ fantasy and Bach's Goldberg Variations. Apart from Gould's mannered, precious performance of the Mozart sonata, it was an evening of exciting piano playing. "Everything Mr. Gould did was unconventional, and (the Mozart always excepted) everything he did made sense. . . . [In the Goldberg Variations] he sometimes punched his tone a bit, and once in a while his dynamics seemed outsized; but always there was variety, a fine musical intelligence, an extraordinary ability to separate voices and a pair of hands that were unerring." (*NYT*, 9 Dec 1957)

Gould's performance (25 May 1959) of Beethoven's Concerto No. 5 with the London Symphony Orchestra, conducted by Josef Krips, elicited the by now usual kind of enthusiastic but disturbed reactions. The critic remarked on Gould's exceptionally low chair, the piano raised on wooden blocks; he described how he almost lay back, crossing his left leg over his right; and noted that now and again he sipped a glass of water and beat time with his foot. Despite all this, the reviewer praised Gould's performance for its clarity, "not only what one might call technical clarity, but extreme clarity of the mind. . . . To an unusual degree, he was evidently thinking of the solo part as belonging to the whole texture; he listened keenly to the orchestra. . . . Gould's performance was finely conceived and finely carried out." (*MT*, July 1959)

In one of his most publicized erratic performances, Gould played (6 April 1962) the Brahms Concerto No. 1 in D Minor with the NYPO, conducted by Leonard Bernstein, who before the performance announced that while he could not agree with Gould's remarkably broad tempos and frequent departures from Brahms's dynamic indications, he would nevertheless conduct because he found

Gould's ideas so fascinating and believed the concept deserved a hearing. (The performance was recorded, *Historic Brahms*, see Discog.)

Augmenting the relatively few reviews of live concerts are the excellent appraisals of Gould's playing found in the mass of written material. For example: "Glenn's performances were both unique and inimitable. His total command of staccato, voicing and articulation was exceptionally well-suited to Baroque music. . . . To play with such individuality and yet such complete artistic persuasiveness is perhaps the rarest of all performing gifts, and Glenn was one of the handful of each era who possessed this magic." (Canin)

The recording studio atmosphere, sterile and uninspiring for many musicians, was home to Glenn Gould. He was one of the first classical musicians to treat recording as a distinct art form, similar to movie making. Usually he prepared six or seven equally valid interpretations for each work he recorded. The final product consisted of tapes and "takes" (Gould's memory for details of every take was legendary among co-workers) from one or several of these interpretations, and Gould strongly believed that his spliced constructions had all the spontaneity and energy expected in a live performance. In his view, recorded music should create a one-to-one relationship between performer and listener and should have a calming (he used the word "tranquilizing") effect, not arouse the kind of excitement usually expected at a live concert.

Glenn Gould was good at this recording process because somehow he was able "to bring together and unify into one logical musical entity a sum total of individual parts which for most other pianists would make little or no sense. This unique ability was one of the most amazing aspects of his work, and perhaps the most irreplaceably precious." (*PQ*, Winter 1982-83) Andrew Kazdin's *Glenn Gould at Work* provides an insightful account of Gould at work during the recording years.

The Gould recordings—the complete Mozart sonatas, nearly all of Bach's solo keyboard works and works by such varied composers as Beethoven, Berg, Bizet, Gibbons, Haydn, Krenek, Schoenberg and Richard Strauss—comprise one of the largest, arguably most popular discographies consistently appearing in record catalogues. Gould recorded music not just to preserve it—or preserve a performance of it—but to explore the "limitless possibilities" (his phrase) available in the recording medium. He was 25 years with Columbia Masterworks and absolutely controlled his recording studio. His concert career may have been marked—and sometimes marred—by the demands and idiosyncracies of Gould's brilliant, idealistic concept of pianism, but his recording career was consistent and mostly reflective of his genius. It was his first CBS recording—the Goldberg Variations, released in 1956—that quickened his career.

Despite his avoidance of the romantic repertoire, Gould was at heart a passionate player. Many of his recordings show a grace and good humor that make them seem like captured improvisations—personal, inspired, free. He refused to play the romantic repertoire in public, but played it in the studio. Gould recorded Bizet's *Variations chromatiques* —"one of the very few masterpieces for solo piano to emerge from the third quarter of the 19th century," according to Gould. He also recorded some Grieg; some Sibelius; his own and

Liszt's transcriptions of Beethoven symphonies and Wagner orchestral works (see Discog.); and some keyboard works of Richard Strauss.

Through the years 17 Gould albums received Grammy awards—for Bach (1910, 1962–65, 1970–71, 1973–74, 1977, 1979–80, 1982), Beethoven (1983), Hindemith (1973), Strauss (1984) and an early recital of 20th-century piano music (1959).

The CBS (now Sony Classical) reissues collectively titled *The Glenn Gould Legacy* are valuable reminders of his often brilliant, often quixotic genius. Volume 2 (3 CDs) lavishly exhibits Gould's uncompromising way with Beethoven, Mozart and Haydn (see Discog.). The Beethoven Concerto No. 1, recorded with Vladimir Golschmann and the Columbia Symphony Orchestra, contains Gould's own bizarre cadenzas. The slow movement lacks the inner give-and-take so necessary between orchestra and soloist. The finale, however, highlights the exquisite articulation that was so much a part of Gould's pianism. The orchestra for the Beethoven Concerto No. 2, recorded in Moscow in 1957 and originally released on a *Melodiya* disc, is definitely second-rate, but "it is Gould's spontaneity in colouring the writing in different registers, in treating fast passages with an unmannered expressivity—in a word, his 'musicality'—that make this a memorable reading." (*Gram*, Sept 1986) Volume 2 also contains the last three "late" Beethoven sonatas which originally appeared on Gould's second recording for CBS. These very personal interpretations from the young Glenn Gould show examples of his great gifts (left-hand clarity, contrapuntal expertise) and of some self-indulgent eccentricities (inappropriate *rubatos*, disquieting tempos).

His Bach recordings show Gould playing—and playing magnificently—the music he seemingly most enjoyed. Both versions of his Goldberg Variations (1956, 1981) are available on CD. Possibly the second version is better because of Gould's superior technique and the fine sound quality. However, the early version, with its bracing tempos, youthful élan and typical Gould clarity of textures, "is still a performance full of the joy of music." (*Fan*, Jan/Feb 1988)

Not all of Gould's recorded performances come from the recording studio. Music and Arts label has issued a series of live performances and radio broadcasts that provide even more examples of Gould's incredible skills (see Discog.). Especially notable are his broadcast performances of Beethoven's Concerto No. 2, with Ernest MacMillan conducting the Toronto Symphony Orchestra; and Beethoven's famed 32 Variations in C Minor—all devoid of Gould's sometimes disturbing interpretative ideas. Another CD contains two live performances with the Baltimore Symphony Orchestra, Peter Adler conducting. The Brahms Concerto No. 1 is particularly fine: "Gould's ringing tone, clarity in the measured trills, sensitivity to contrapuntal details, and masterful accentuation highlight this moving performance." (*CL*, May/June 1990)

Paradoxically, Glenn Gould's final recording had nothing to do with the keyboard. In the summer of 1982 he conducted—and recorded—a performance of Wagner's Siegfried Idyll with a pickup chamber orchestra he assembled in Toronto. "Gould had long loved the piece; he had transcribed it for solo piano and recorded it in the early '70s. Gould's orchestral recording of Siegfried Idyll, which was in final mixes at the time of his death, must be the slowest in history and is of melting and surpassing tenderness [see Discog.]. Once heard, it renders most traditional interpretations cursory, and its release is a major addition to the Gould canon." (Page, "Glenn Gould's Last Stand")

Beginning in 1992, Sony Classical issued the first of a series of 16 video cassettes taken from Gould's various CBS television appearances. Perhaps the most intriguing of these—at least from a performer's point of view—is SHV 48424, the Bach Goldberg Variations, filmed in New York City in April and May 1981.

The argument about whether Glenn Gould did or did not use his phenomenal gifts to full potential will no doubt linger for decades. He was, to be sure, a puzzling musician, an enigmatic genius and one of the finest musical minds of his time.

SELECTED REFERENCES

Aikin, Jim. "Glenn Gould." *Contemporary Keyboard*, Aug 1980, pp. 24–28, 30–32, 36.

Asbell, Bernard. "An Interview with Glenn Gould." *Horizon*, Jan 1962, pp. 88–93.

Bazzana, Kevin. "Glenn Aplenty: Sony Classical's New Glenn Gould Edition and Glenn Gould Collection." *Fanfare*, Jan/Feb 1993, pp. 28–35.

Beckwith, John. "Shattering a Few Myths." In McGreevy, *Glenn Gould By Himself and His Friends*, pp. 65–74.

Bernheimer, Martin. "A Keyboard Symphony From a Concert Dropout." *Los Angeles Times*, 26 May 1968, CAL, p. 37.

Canin, Martin. "Looking Back." *Piano Quarterly*, Winter 1982–83, pp. 7–10.

Canning, Nancy. *A Glenn Gould Catalog*. Westport, Conn.: Greenwood Press, 1992.

Colgrass, Ulla. "Glenn Gould." (interview) *Music Magazine*, Jan/Feb 1981, pp. 6–11.

Cott, Jonathan. *Conversations with Glenn Gould*. Boston: Little, Brown and Company, 1984. Contains a discography and a listing of Gould's radio and television programs.

Distler, Jed. "Gould's Bach or is it Bach's Gould?" *Classical Pulse*, Feb 1995, p. 32. An evaluation of *The Glenn Gould Collection* on video.

Dubal, David. "Glenn Gould: A Last Interview." *Piano Quarterly*, Fall 1984, pp. 55–57.

Friedrich, Otto. *Glenn Gould: A Life and Variations*. New York: Random House, 1989.

Fulford, Robert. "Growing Up Gould." In McGreevy, *Glenn Gould By Himself and His Friends*, pp. 57–63.

"Glenn Gould: Concert Dropout." Col. BS 15. A recorded conversation with John McClure.

"Glenn Gould interviews himself about Beethoven." *Piano Quarterly*, Fall 1972, pp. 2–5.

Goldsmith, Harris. "Glenn Gould: An Appraisal." *High Fidelity*, Feb 1983, pp. 54–55.

Gould, Glenn. *Arnold Schoenberg: A Perspective.* University of Cincinnati, 1964.

———. "Memories of Maude Harbour or Variations on a Theme of Arthur Rubinstein." *Piano Quarterly,* Summer 1980, pp. 27–30.

Hurwitz, Robert. "Encounters with Glenn Gould." *Ovation,* Oct 1983, pp. 18–22.

Kazdin, Andrew. *Glenn Gould at Work: Creative Lying.* New York: E. P. Dutton, 1989. A history of Gould's recording career, complete with discography.

McGreevy, John, editor. *Glen Gould, By Himself and His Friends.* Toronto: Doubleday, 1983. Contains a bibliography of Gould's various writings for periodicals.

McLellan, Joseph. "Glenn Gould, First & Last." *Washington Post,* 10 Oct 1982, sec. F, p. 6.

———. "Pure Gould." *Washington Post,* 5 Oct 1982, sec. B, p. 1.

Obituary. *Los Angeles Herald Examiner,* 5 Oct 1982, sec. C, pp. 1, 5. *Los Angeles Times,* 5 Oct 1982, sec. I, pp. 1, 18. *New York Times,* 5 Oct 1982, pp. 1, 25. *San Francisco Chronicle,* 5 Oct 1982, p. 28. *The Times* (London), 6 Oct 1982, p. 14.

Page, Tim. "Glenn Gould." (interview) *Piano Quarterly,* Fall 1981, pp. 14–24.

———. *The Glenn Gould Reader.* New York: Alfred A. Knopf, 1984.

———. "Glenn Gould's Last Stand." *Classical,* Jan 1991, pp. 34–40.

Payzant, Geoffrey. *Glenn Gould: Music and Mind.* New York: Van Nostrand Reinhold, 1978, revised 1984.

Roberts, John P. L., and Ghyslaine Guertain, eds. *Glenn Gould: Selected Letters.* Toronto: Oxford University Press, 1992.

Rothstein, Edward. "Confessions of a Gould Devotee." *New York Times,* 4 October 1992, sec. 2, p. 27.

Sachs, Harvey. "Glenn Gould." In *Virtuoso* (see Bibliog.), pp. 176–196.

Shames, Laurence. "Glenn Gould: 1932–1982." *Keyboard Classics,* Jan/Feb 1983, pp. 12–13.

Siepman, Jeremy. "Glenn Gould and the Interpreter's Prerogative." *Piano Quarterly,* Winter 1990/91, pp. 29–37.

Silverman. Robert J. "Glenn Gould: Commentary." *Piano Quarterly,* Fall 1981, p. 13.

———. "Memories of Glenn Gould." *Music Magazine,* Nov/Dec 1983, pp. 15–17.

Stanton, David. "A Cry for the Individual." *Piano Quarterly,* Fall 1984, pp. 50–53.

Stearns, David Patrick. "Gould Remembered." *Gramophone,* Aug 1987, p. 264.

Viets, Edward. "Glenn Gould. . .a début and a personality." *Etude,* Oct 1956, pp. 15, 42.

See also Bibliography: Cur/Bio (1960); Doe/Tra; Dub/Ref; Ewe/Li; Ewe/Mu; Kol/Que; Mac/Gre; New/Gro; Ran/Kon; Rat/Cle; Sac/Vir; Sch/Gre.

SELECTED REVIEWS

GloM: 21 Oct 1947. *LAT*: 11 March 1957; 11 Jan 1959; 27 April 1961. *MC*:
1 Feb 1955. *NYT*: 12 Jan 1955; 28 Jan 1957; 9 Dec 1957; 14 March
1958; 14 Feb 1959; 8 April 1959; 18 March 1961; 7 April 1962. *SFC*: 16
Jan 1959; 17 Feb 1962. *TL*: 21 May 1959; 1 June 1959; 15 Aug 1960.
TT: 13 Dec 1945; 9 May 1946; 15 Jan 1947. *WP*: 3 Jan 1955.

SELECTED DISCOGRAPHY

The Art of the Young Glenn Gould (broadcast recordings). Beethoven: Concerto
No. 2 in B-flat Major, op. 19 (1951, MacMillan/Toronto SO); Concerto
No. 3 in C Minor, op. 37 (1955, Ungar/CBC SO); 32 Variations in C
Minor, WoO 80. Music and Arts CD-284.
Bach: Concerto in D Minor, BWV 1052. Beethoven: Concerto No. 2 in B-flat
Major, op. 19. Sony Classical (Glenn Gould Edition) SMK 52686 (CD).
Slovák/Leningrad Conservatory Orch., rec. 1957.
Bach: Concertos 1-5 and 7 (BWV 1052-56 and 1058). Sony Classical SM2K
52591 (2 CDs). Bernstein, Golschmann/Columbia SO.
Bach: English Suites (complete); Partita in B Minor (BWV 831). CBS M2K-
42268 (2 CDs).
Bach: French Suites (complete). CBS MK-42267 (2 CDs).
Bach: Goldberg Variations (rec. 1955); 2 Fugues (WTC II). Sony Classical
SMK 52594 (CD).
Bach: Goldberg Variations; Three-Part Inventions. Sony Classical (Glenn Gould
Edition) SMK 52685. Recorded live 25 August 1957.
Bach: Goldberg Variations (rec. 1981). CBS MK-37779 (CD).
Bach: Toccatas (6). Sony Classical SM2K52612 (2 CDs).
Bach: Two-Part Inventions; Three-Part Sinfonias. Sony Classical 52596 (CD).
Beethoven: Concerto No. 5 in E-flat Major, op. 73 (Ancerl/SO); Variations, op.
34; Trio in D Major, op. 70, no. 1 (w/Schneider, Nelsova). Music and Arts
CD-639.
Beethoven: Sonata in B-flat Major, op. 106. Mozart: Fantasy in C Minor, K.
396. Music and Arts CD-617. Rec. 1967.
Bizet: *Premier Nocturne*; *Variations Chromatiques*. Grieg: Sonata in E Minor,
op. 7. Sibelius: Sonatinas; Three Lyric Pieces. Sony Classical SM2K
52654 (2 CDs)
Brahms: Concerto No. 1 in D Minor, op. 15. Strauss: *Burleske*. Music and
Arts CD-197. Adler/Baltimore SO. Rec. 1962.
Byrd: Hugh Ashton's Ground; First Pavan and Galliard; Sixth Pavan and
Galliard; Sellinger's Round; Voluntary for My Ladye Nevell. O. Gibbons:
Fantasia in C Major; Italian Ground; "Lord of Salisbury" Pavan and
Galliard. Sweelinck: Fantasia in D. Sony Classical SMK 52589 (CD).
Glenn Gould: 1956 & 1967 Broadcast Recitals. Bach: Art of the Fugue, nos.
11, 13, 9; English Suite No. 1 in A Major; Partita No. 6 in E Minor;
Toccata in D Minor. Gibbons: Pavanne and Galliard. Music and Arts CD-
272.

Glenn Gould: Concert Dropout. Columbia BS 15. A recorded (LP) conversation with John McClure.

The Glenn Gould Edition. A project by Sony Classical to present the most comprehensive collection of Gould's performances, including the CBS catalogue, unreleased studio recordings plus the radio and television material recorded for the CBC. (See Sony Classical catalogue for listing.)

Glenn Gould in Salzburg. Bach: Goldberg Variations. Mozart: Sonata, K. 330. Schoenberg: Suite, op. 25. Sweelinck: Fantasia. Memoria 991-007 (CD). Rec. 1959.

The Glenn Gould Legacy, Vol. 2. Beethoven: Concerto No. 1 in C Major, op. 15; Concerto No. 2 in B-flat Major, op. 19. Sonata in E Major, op. 109; Sonata in A-flat Major, op. 110; Sonata in C Minor, op. 111. Haydn: Sonata in E-flat Major, Hob. XVI:49. Mozart: Sonata in C Major, K. 330; Fantasia and Fugue in C Major, K. 394. CBS M3K-39036 (3 CDs). Goldschmann/Columbia SO.

The Glenn Gould Legacy, Vol. 3. Brahms: Intermezzos, op. 76, nos. 6 and 7; op. 116, op. 4; op. 117, nos. 1-3; op. 118, nos. 1, 2, 6; op. 119, no. 1; Rhapsody in B Minor, op. 79, no. 1. Grieg: Sonata in E Minor, op. 7. Sibelius: Three Sonatinas, op. 67. R. Strauss: Sonata in B Minor, op. 5. Wagner (tran. Gould): Dawn Music, Siegfried's Rhine Journey (*Götterdämmerung*); Prelude (Act 1, *Meistersinger*). CBS M3 42107 (CD).

The Glenn Gould Legacy, Vol. 4. Berg: Sonata, op. 1. Hindemith: Sonata No. 3. Krenek: Sonata No. 3, op. 92, no. 4. Prokofiev: Sonata No. 7 in B-flat, op. 83. Schoenberg: Three Pieces, op. 11. Scriabin: Sonata No. 3 in F-sharp Minor, op. 23; Sonata No. 5 in F-sharp Major, op. 53; Two Pieces, op. 57. CBS M3K-42150 (3 CDs).

Hindemith: Sonatas for Piano (3). Sony Classical SM2K 52670 (CD).

Historic Brahms by the New York Philharmonic. Concerto No. 1 in D Minor, op. 15; Academic Festival Overture; Alto Rhapsody (Marian Anderson); Variations on a Theme by Haydn. New York Philharmonic/WQXR 1987 Radiothon Special Edition Historic Recordings Vol.VII Monaural 871/2. Preceding the Concerto No. 1 is the famous "disclaimer" spoken by conductor Leonard Bernstein. Available ($23) on cassette or LP from Radiothon, New York Philharmonic, Avery Fisher Hall, 10 Lincoln Center Plaza, New York, NY 10023-6973.

The Young Glenn Gould—1947 to 1953. Bach: Italian Concerto. Berg: Sonata, op. 1. Mozart: Music for Piano, Four Hands: Sonata, K. 497 (*Allegro di molto*); *Andante* in G Major, K. 501; Sonata, K. 521 (*Allegro*); Fantasy in F Minor, K. 594. With Alberto Guerrero. Mastersound DFCDI-024.

Wagner (trans. Gould): Dawn Music (*Götterdämmerung*); Prelude (Act 1, *Die Meistersinger*); Siegfried Idyll; Siegfried's Rhine Journey (*Götterdämmerung*). In addition, this CD contains the orchestral Siegfried Idyll, Gould's only recording as conductor and his final recorded performance. Sony Classical SK 46279 (CD).

VIDEO

Glenn Gould: A Portrait. Kultur 1188.
The Glenn Gould Collection. A collection of 16 video cassettes (available separately) presenting various television appearances made throughout the years. Sony Classical.
Highlights from The Glenn Gould Collection. Sony Classical SHV 48433.

GRAFFMAN, GARY: b. New York, New York, 14 October 1928.

> In a way he is the great architectural draftsman among his contemporaries. He applies himself to the notes in a scrupulous manner, making everything clear, and the music comes out in an architectural manner. But what authority!
>
> Harold C. Schonberg (*New York Times*, 21 March 1967)

In November 1979 at age 51 Gary Graffman closed the door on his very successful 30-year career as a performing pianist. Like his good friend and fellow pianist Leon Fleisher, Graffman had developed right-hand problems. They are not yet solved, but after a year of silence, the determined Graffman was back on the concert platform, performing the Ravel Concerto in D, for left hand alone. He has also, like Fleisher, developed new careers. Graffman is director at the Curtis Institute of Music, where he also teaches; he has published a delightful book of memoirs; and he continues to perform, now playing exclusively the repertoire composed for the left hand alone.

The thoroughly American Graffman (born, raised, trained and based in New York City) derives from a rich Russian heritage. His father Vladimir Graffman studied violin with Leopold Auer at the St. Petersburg Conservatory and, after emigrating to America, became Auer's assistant at the Mannes School of Music in New York. Graffman's mother Nadia (Margolin) Graffman belonged to a wealthy landowning family from Kiev. Forced out of Russia by the 1917 revolution, the Graffmans eventually settled in New York, the birthplace of their only child.

Graffman had violin lessons (on a special small instrument) with his father at a very early age, but even at age three the piano fascinated him. Piano lessons with Cosby Dansby Morris prepared him for the entrance examination at the Curtis Institute of Music in Philadelphia, and at age seven, on scholarship, Graffman began 10 years (1936–46) of studies at Curtis, primarily with Isabella Vengerova, who taught him the Romantic piano tradition and the Russian way of slow practice and beauty of sound.

Graffman's parents and the Curtis faculty all frowned on prodigy exploitation, but he was permitted to give a few public performances. In 1936 he was soloist with the Philadelphia Symphonette, directed by Fabien Sevitzky, and in 1939 he played the Haydn D Major Concerto with the Indianapolis Symphony Orchestra, again with Sevitzky conducting. The reviews were remarkable, not the usual condescending comments: "It was the playing of a prodigy, whose technical equipment is astonishing. . . . It was a bit terrifying to hear a young-ster . . . play with all the assurance, ease and poise of a pianist three times his age, and, as a matter of fact, play with more maturity and artistry than many a pianist of thirty." (*IN*, 27 March 1939) At his first New York recital, played at Carnegie Chamber Music Hall on 28 April 1940, the 11-year-old Graffman "played with a searching sense of style and an almost uncanny amount of musi-cal understanding and poetry for a child of his years." (*NYT*, 29 April 1940)

Being a childhood prodigy meant a somewhat restricted life, no doubt, but Graffman was neither exploited nor overly protected. His parents were re-laxed enough about his talent to permit him to play baseball, and he remembers childhood as happy and enjoyably busy. Graduated at age 18 from both the Curtis Institute and the Columbia Grammar School in New York, Graffman spent the next year (1947–48) at Columbia University. Meanwhile in 1947 his winning a special award as runner-up in the piano competition sponsored by the Rachmaninoff Fund made possible his debut with the Philadelphia Orchestra: on 28 March 1947 he played the Rachmaninoff Concerto No. 2 with Eugene Ormandy conducting the orchestra.

In 1949 Graffman won the coveted Edgar M. Leventritt Award and that brought him engagements with three orchestras: New York Philharmonic-Symphony, Cleveland and Buffalo. On 25 February 1950 he played the Brahms Concerto No. 1 with the New York Philharmonic-Symphony under Leonard Bernstein. After a year in Europe studying on a Fulbright grant, Graffman re-turned home in the fall of 1951 and began touring for the Columbia Community Concert series.

Graffman and Naomi Helfman, also a musician, married in December 1952, and thereafter she usually accompanied him on his tours. In the spring of 1953 he performed five different concertos while touring the United States with the Little Orchestra Society, conducted by Thomas Scherman. By the following year he was playing regularly with major orchestras throughout the country. Simultaneously, in the early 1950s, Graffman received coaching from Vladimir Horowitz in New York and from Rudolf Serkin at the Marlboro School and Festival in Vermont.

In 1955 Graffman made his recording debut on the RCA Victor label and undertook his first foreign tour, throughout South America. His first European tour, begun in the fall of 1956, launched an international career em-bracing all five continents. Usually spending 10 months a year on the road, within six years Graffman made seven tours of Europe, a second South America tour and a whirlwind around-the-world tour. Until his right hand failed in 1979, Graffman remained one of the busiest of pianists, traveling almost constantly.

His Carnegie Hall concert of 4 April 1973 celebrated the 25th anniver-sary of his professional debut there, and "by then he had become the only pianist ever to record with all six principal symphony orchestras of America; the only American pianist to have recorded all three of Tchaikovsky's piano concertos; one of the few pianists to have played with twenty-two major American orches-

tras and to have made thirty-eight appearances with orchestras in a single season." (Ewe/Mu, see Bibliog.)

But in 1979 Graffman's high-riding career came to a full stop. The
fourth and fifth fingers of his right hand had begun to curl inward involuntarily
as he played. As his wife recalled, he had to work twice as hard to accomplish
less, and practicing more only made things worse. The exceptionally dependable
Graffman (he had missed only a handful of concerts during his career) was forced
to cancel all future engagements. Unlike Leon Fleisher, Graffman's problem
was not caused by excessive practicing but, he believes, from mistreating an old
injury to the fourth and fifth fingers of his right hand, which he strained trying
to bring sound out of an unresponsive piano at a 1967 Berlin performance. If he
had allowed that injury to heal properly, he might have been fine. But Graffman, determined to fulfill his many concert contracts, changed his fingering in
order to speed up the recovery process, that is, he began playing octaves with his
thumb and third finger instead of thumb and fifth finger. Compensating in that
fashion (using muscles not intended for those functions) caused an imbalance
that, after so many performances, ruined his right hand.

Graffman, like Fleisher, has endured years of treatments and therapies.
However, after a year of canceling engagements, he was back playing for the
public, not with two hands but with the left hand alone. He began this second
career with performances of the Ravel Concerto in D, written for left hand alone,
and later added Prokofiev's Concerto No. 4, Britten's Diversions on a Theme for
piano left hand and orchestra, Rorem's Concerto No. 4, Korngold's Concerto in
C-sharp Minor, op. 7, and Korngold's Suite for Piano, left hand, two Violins
and Cello. Graffman may now be playing a restricted repertoire, yet judging by
the reviews, he is still one of America's finest pianists.

He began teaching at the Curtis Institute in 1980 and in 1986 became
director. As a teacher he advocates that the Chopin Etudes (all of them) should
be learned and used as technical studies as quickly as possible. And he consistently discusses pedaling, an art that he feels is not taken seriously, even is often
neglected, by pianists. Incorrect pedaling, he says, can as easily destroy a performance as artistic pedaling can enhance it.

Graffman's autobiography *I Should Have Been Practicing* is well-writ-
ten, informative, often witty and consistently interesting. Reviews have been
unanimously favorable. As for Gary Graffman himself, a review of his book
supplies the perfect assessment: "Graffman's self-portrait is the most attractive
(if unwittingly so) in his album. He is urbanity itself: cultured, gracious, moderate, literate." (*NW*, 11 May 1981)

On 7 May 1991 the Commonwealth of Pennsylvania honored Graffman
with the Governor's Arts Award, the citation reading that "his leadership of
Curtis has been credited with restoring the institution to pre-eminence among the
world's great conservatories of music." (*PI*, 7 May 1991)

Graffman has said that his repertoire for two hands was limited because
instead of adding new works, he spent time polishing works he already knew in
order to keep his interpretations from becoming stale. That may be, but some
50 reviews covering three decades of Graffman performances show a fairly large

repertoire encompassing Classic and Romantic works from the 19th and early 20th centuries. Works by Beethoven, Brahms, Chopin, Haydn, Liszt, Mendelssohn, Prokofiev, Rachmaninoff, Schubert and Schumann dominate the programs. Also included, though less frequently, in this particular set of reviews, are works by Balakirev, Bartók, Debussy, Handel, Mozart and Mussorgsky.

The impressive consistency of reviews throughout Graffman's career provides a definitive appraisal of his attitude, approach and playing. Intelligent and scholarly, Graffman is (in words lifted from reviews) a sincere, dedicated and confident musician with a big virtuoso style and a broad approach. He has a flawless technique, seemingly effortless in its power and control, and he plays with clarity, elegance and logic. But his musical integrity, profound musicianship and refined taste may be his greatest assets. Nearly every critic seems compelled to also mention that Graffman's playing was (in their words) often too severe, too austere, too cold, or too impersonal; that it lacked charm, imaginative flair or a sense of joy; that its relentless rhythmic drive sometimes made for a brittle tone and too little color. Taken together, these faults add up to really one comment: Graffman, a magnificent architectural draftsman, gives a firmly structured performance rather than a passionate, grandiloquent performance.

Reviews from one stage of Graffman's career closely resemble reviews from any other stage. To begin at the beginning, here is a review from 40 years ago of Graffman's performance (11 Nov 1954) of the Prokofiev Concerto No. 3 with the Los Angeles Philharmonic Orchestra, conducted by Alfred Wallenstein: "His fingers are fast and unfailingly accurate. . . . He has surprising power for chords and octaves and there is a rhythmical drive to his playing. . . . But he also has something more than superficial virtuosity, for his tone in even the most strenuous passages was round and solid in quality and there was a constant play of imagination and musical sensitiveness." (*LAT*, 12 Nov 1954)

A Graffman London recital (12 Nov 1956) ended with Liszt's arrangements of three Caprices by Paganini: "His prestidigitation here was almost beyond belief." Throughout the recital, however, "he made it clear that he was not only a virtuoso of the first order but also an extremely sincere and sensitive musician—of the aristocratically impersonal school of thought though, rather than one of those who identify themselves with every note." (*TL*, 19 Nov 1956)

Identical critical themes prevailed in the 1960s. Graffman played (30 April 1964) Rachmaninoff's Rhapsody on a Theme of Paganini with the New York Philharmonic Orchestra, conducted by Leonard Bernstein: "What we get from Mr. Graffman is the plan of the music rather than its poetry (though poetry is not missing), its architecture rather than its song. . . . Mr. Graffman succeeds completely on his own terms. . . . He has a flawless technique. . . . His tone is big, clear and penetrating. . . . His musical ideas have strength and integrity." (*NYT*, 1 May 1964)

The 1970 reviews follow the same critical pattern. Graffman's challenging program in Los Angeles on 28 October 1972 included Beethoven's C Minor Sonata, op. 13, Brahms's Variations and Fugue on a Theme of Handel, Ravel's *Gaspard de la nuit* and Balakirev's *Islamey*. One review began, "Gary Graffman is a wonderful pianist. But sober. . . . Brahms's huge canvas . . . disappointed the most. Its reading was utterly straightforward. . . . His Beethoven, on the other hand, benefited from such soberness. . . . This reading made wonderful sense." (*LAT*, 30 Oct 1972)

Three years later another *Los Angeles Times* critic reviewed a Graffman recital (6 Dec 1975) with Liszt's B Minor Sonata on the program. "He has never before played so impressively. . . . He laid out the massive structure with an unerring sense of proportion. . . . He had immense reserves of power, producing massive sonorities without ever belaboring the instrument or verging on harshness. . . . This was an orchestral conception." (*LAT*, 8 Dec 1975)

Graffman's meticulous pianism, keyboard brilliance and poetic insights illuminated his performance (16 Jan 1976) of the Chopin Concerto No. 1 in E Minor with the Cincinnati Symphony Orchestra, Uri Segal conducting. Graffman was at his very best in the concerto's slow movement. "While the two outer sections provided ample chance to dazzle and the coda with its bravura display was set forth with a great sense of joie de vivre, it was the lingering romanza that proved the real delight. Graffman made it sing." (*DDN*, 18 Jan 1976)

For more than a decade now Graffman has been playing only the repertoire written for the left hand alone, and the reviews have been excellent. At one of his first left-hand-alone performances in New York he played the Ravel Concerto in D with the American Philharmonic Orchestra, Rohan Joseph conducting. Maintaining the tension and the magisterial sweep, Graffman's Ravel was "richer, darker in tone, a bit slower in pace, more cumulative in impact, than is customary. . . . He remains one of America's finest pianists." (*CSM*, 3 Feb 1982)

On 16 April 1989 Graffman, conductor Sidney Rothstein and the Reading Symphony Orchestra delivered an exciting performance of Benjamin Britten's Diversions on a Theme for Left Hand and Orchestra, op. 21, a work bristling with difficulties and one not many pianists undertake to study. "It was astonishing to watch Graffman's hand bounce high over the keys in a kind of demon dance, or his thumb etch feathery melodies as the rest of his fingers fashioned intricate accompaniments. . . . Graffman is still one of the finest musicians on the concert stage." (*RE*, 17 April 1989)

Graffman's performance (31 Jan 1991) of the Prokofiev Concerto No. 4, for the left hand, with the Atlanta Symphony Orchestra, Yoel Levi conducting, proved once again that he "remains as fine a musician as he ever was, in complete command of every note. With a lean and focused tone that can easily thunder and just as easily whisper, Mr. Graffman combined precision and power with stylistic acumen." (*AJ*, 1 Feb 1991)

Graffman opened the 1991 Muhlenberg College Piano Series with an "electrifying" program of music for the left hand: Carl Reinecke's Sonata, op. 179, Max Reger's Four Special Studies, Brahms's arrangement of the Bach Chaconne in D Minor for solo violin and Erich Korngold's Suite, op. 23 (performed with four young musicians from the Curtis Institute). "Anyone listening with closed eyes would have been certain he was using all ten fingers. Arpeggios were even as were the scales. The firm tone was well-balanced, the technique pyrotechnical." (*MoC*, 19 Oct 1991)

The following year Graffman's performance (15 July 1992) of this same program at the University of Maryland's International Piano Festival "stood out for its breadth of expression." This critic singled out the Brahms transcription as the most impressive part of the recital: "Bach's original effort to create polyphony from a non-chordal instrument translates well for left-hand perform- ance, as evidenced by Graffman's careful blending of the lines. He turned Brahms's adaptation into a noble creation." (*WP*, 20 July 1992)

Ned Rorem's demanding Piano Concerto No. 4, for left hand, was writ- ten for Graffman, who played it at Carnegie Hall on 5 February 1993, with André Previn conducting the orchestra of the Curtis Institute. It was, reported the *New York Times* critic, "an electrifying performance." Another reviewer, likening Graffman to Paul Wittgenstein, the pianist who lost his right arm in World War I yet reportedly could do more with one hand than many pianists can accomplish with two hands, wrote: "The same might be said of Graffman. Rorem's keyboard writing gives no quarter." (*NYP*, 8 Feb 1993)

Graffman made many LPs before his right hand failed. His recordings of concertos by Tchaikovsky, Rachmaninoff, Prokofiev, Brahms, Chopin and Beethoven (performed with the orchestras of New York, Philadelphia, Cleveland, Chicago and Boston) are models of excellence in concerted musicianly playing. His recording of Gershwin's Rhapsody in Blue with Zubin Mehta and the Los Angeles Philharmonic Orchestra was one of the all-time best sellers for this perennial favorite.

Although most of the LP recordings are out of print, several of the most significant have been reissued on CD (see Discog.). One of the finest, the Tchaikovsky Concerto No. 1 in B-flat Minor, with the Cleveland Orchestra, conducted by George Szell, was a huge success when it appeared, and this daz- zling performance remains a strong contender among the many versions available today. Graffman's 1969 performance of the concerto is, wrote one reviewer, "among the best I know: vivid, full of color and fire, technically impeccable, tonally glistening, and wonderfully integrated with the razor-sharp orchestral ac- companiment." (*Fan*, Sept/Oct 1988) Another fine Tchaikovsky album, the Concertos Nos. 2 and 3, performed with Eugene Ormandy and the Philadelphia Orchestra, received a Grammy award in 1965.

Graffman's commanding performance of the Prokofiev Concertos Nos. 1 and 3 (reissued with the Sonata No. 3, see Discog.) has set a standard for 20th- century Russian performance practice. Their availability on CD is a tribute to the pianist's total concept of this idiom. According to one critic, "There is ex- citement aplenty, for Szell's well-known propensity for razor-sharp playing suits Prokofiev to a T. . . . It is a worthy souvenir of Gary Graffman's playing as a soloist with orchestra before he lost the use of his right hand." (*Fan*, Jan/Feb 1989)

In 1965 Graffman recorded Rachmaninoff's Concerto No. 2 and the "Paganini" Rhapsody with Leonard Bernstein and the New York Philharmonic Orchestra. Today a current record catalogue lists over 40 available recordings of that Concerto and around 30 versions of the Rhapsody.   The reissue of Graffman's 1965 performances may have been intended only as a souvenir of the pianist at the height of his career, but the recording still rates high. Graffman's "performances really take wing—his delivery of the treacherous first theme in the concerto finale is one of the classiest on record, and much of the Rhapsody is extremely fine." (*Gram*, March 1991)

Composed in 1991 and recorded in 1993, Ned Rorem's Piano Concerto for Left Hand and Orchestra is the first recording by Graffman since being restricted to left-hand repertoire, and he plays the eight-movement work with all the requisite panache and vivacity.

SELECTED REFERENCES

Cariaga, Daniel. "Graffman: Imperturbable, As Always." *Los Angeles Times*, 2 Aug 1981, CAL, pp. 57-58.
———. "Graffman Looks Back, Ahead." *Los Angeles Times*, 24 Oct 1978, sec. 4, p. 18.
Dunning, Jennifer. "When a Pianist's Fingers Fail to Obey." *New York Times*, 14 June, 1981, sec. 2, p. 1.
Graffman, Gary. "Artist's Life." *Keynote*, Oct 1988, pp. 20, 24.
———. *I Really Should Be Practicing*. Garden City, N.Y.: Doubleday & Company, Inc., 1981.
———. "Korngold Was More Than a Movie Composer." *New York Times*, 15 Sept 1985, sec. 2, p. 17.
Graffman, Naomi. "The Care and Feeding of Pianists." *Clavier*, July/Aug 1986, pp. 8–11.
Henry, Derrick. "Concert pianist plays in key of left." *Atlanta Journal*, 31 Jan 1991, sec. F, pp. 1, 4.
Kimmelman, Michael. "A pianist teaches others the music he can no longer perform." *Philadelphia Inquirer*, 22 Feb 1985, sec. C, pp. 1, 3.
Montparker, Carol.   "Gary Graffman, Reassessing Priorities." *Clavier*, July/Aug 1982, pp. 10–12.
Peña, Susan. "Graffman's brilliant career." *The Eagle* (Reading, PA), 9 April 1989, sec. B, pp. 22, 27.
Perlmutter, Donna. "A Mysterious Musical Malady Lingers On." *Los Angeles Times*, 3 July 1988, CAL, pp. 56–57.
"Post-Prodigies." *Time*, 2 Dec 1957, p. 72.
Roos, James. "Two pianists thrive on sound of one hand playing." *Miami Herald*, 21 Oct 1990, sec. I, p. 3. (Fleisher and Graffman.)
Schonberg, Harold C. "Graffman Marks Debut 25 Years Ago." *New York Times*, 6 April 1973, p. 30.
———. "Mr. Graffman." *Newsweek*, 17 Feb 1969, pp. 114–115.
See also Bibliography: Cur/Bio (1970); Dub/Ref; Ewe/Li2; Ewe/Mu; IWWM; Jac/Rev; New/GrA; Ran/Kon; WWAM.

SELECTED REVIEWS

AJ: 24 Sept 1990; 1 Feb 1991. *CPD*: 12 Jan 1978. *CSM*: 3 Feb 1982. *CT*: 1 May 1978. *DDN*: 18 Jan 1976. *DFP*: 10 Jan 1978. *IN*: 27 March 1939. *IT*: 27 March 1939. *LAT*: 12 Nov 1954; 3 March 1960; 10 Jan 1970; 9 March 1971; 30 Oct 1972; 13 Sept 1973; 14 Jan 1975; 8 Dec 1975; 28 Aug 1982.

MA: 1 Jan 1949. *MiT*: 16 March 1992. *MoC*: 19 Oct 1991. *MT*: March 1958. *NYP*: 8 Feb 1993. *NYT*: 29 April 1940; 28 Dec 1948; 27 Feb 1950; 1 Nov 1952; 31 July 1963; 4 April 1964; 1 May 1964; 29 Oct 1965; 20 Oct 1966; 18 Dec 1967; 1 Nov 1971; 6 April 1973; 1 May 1974; 21 Dec 1976; 8 Feb 1979; 25 Dec 1984; 9 Feb 1993. *PI*: 1 Oct 1988; 25 Feb 1989; 14 Dec 1994. *RT*: 17 April 1989. *TL*: 19 Nov 1956. *WP*: 20 July 1992. *WS*: 10 Dec 1975.

SELECTED DISCOGRAPHY

Brahms: Concerto No. 1 in D Minor, op. 15. RCA Victrola LP VICS-1109. Munch/Boston SO.

Brahms: Variations and Fugue on a Theme by Handel, op. 24; Variations on a Theme by Paganini, op. 35. Columbia MS 7276 (LP).

Chopin: Ballades (4); *Andante spianato* and *Grande Polonaise*, op. 22. RCA Victrola LP VICS-1077.

Chopin: Concerto No. 1 in E Minor, op. 11. Mendelssohn: *Capriccio brilliant* op. 22. Victrola cassette ALK1-5396. Munch/Boston SO.

Prokofiev: Concerto No. 1 in D-flat Major, op. 10; Concerto No. 3 in C Major, op. 26; Sonata No. 3 in A Minor, op. 28. CBS Great Performances MYK 37806-2. Szell/Cleveland SO.

Rachmaninoff: Concerto No. 2 in C Minor, op. 18; Rhapsody on a Theme of Paganini, op. 43. CBS Masterworks MYK 36722 (CD). Bernstein/NYPO.

Rorem: Piano Concerto for Left Hand and Orchestra. New World 80445-2. Previn/Curtis SO.

Schubert: Sonata in C Minor, D. 958; Wanderer Fantasy, D. 760. CSP LP AMS-6735.

Tchaikovsky: Concerto No. 1 in B-flat Minor, op. 23. Rachmaninoff: Preludes in G Minor, op. 23, no. 5; G-sharp Minor, op. 32, no. 12; A Minor, op. 32, no. 8. CBS Great Performances MYK 37263-2. Szell/Cleveland SO.

Tchaikovsky: Concerto No. 2 in G Major, op. 44; Concerto No. 3 in E-flat Major, op. 75. Columbia MS 6755. Ormandy/PO.

GRAINGER, PERCY ALDRIDGE: b. Brighton, near Melbourne, Australia, 8 July 1882; d. White Plains, New York, 20 February 1961.

> All his life, Grainger had a talent for making pig-headed decisions and a positive genius for hitching his wagons to the wrong stars. It is difficult to name anyone in the twentieth century who made such a splendid mess of a career which had such portentous beginnings. It is surprising that he was able to salvage so much.
>
> John Bird (*Percy Grainger*)

John Bird's readable, inclusive biography does full justice to Grainger, a bewilderingly complex, eccentric individual, and to Grainger, the equally complex, eccentric artist (pianist, composer, folk-song collector, author, editor, teacher).

As Harold Schonberg once described him, Grainger was "a whale of a pianist," but contrarily this alluring (a favorite word in Grainger reviews) pianist hated the piano (a nasty percussion instrument, as he called it), and all his life planned for the day when he could quit the concert platform and devote all his time to composing. That was never to be. From the time he first began to make money, the amazingly generous Grainger gave it away. At one count, he was wholly supporting nine relatives and helping 14 others, this in addition to the subsidies he handed out so freely to budding composers and the small royalty checks he sent to the folk singers who had helped him collect songs. There simply never was a time when he could afford to stop concertizing.

Grainger's English father John Henry Grainger, a hard-drinking yet talented architect, migrated to Australia in 1877; his Australian mother Rosa Annie (Aldridge) Grainger, was a strong, handsome woman who loved music. Just about everything written about Percy Grainger describes Rose (as she was always called) Grainger as an obsessively possessive mother who absolutely dominated the life of her only child. Thus any discussion of Percy Grainger must be prefaced with a word about his mother. They often read to each other, especially heroic, bloodthirsty Nordic sagas, which seem to have influenced Grainger's entire life. Before he reached his teens he had read Freeman's *History of the Norman Conquest*, portions of the *Anglo-Saxon Chronicles* and George Webbe Dasent's English translation of the Icelandic *Saga of Grettir the Strong*—a story, said Grainger, that "remained the strongest single artistic influence in my life, providing me (so it seemed to me) with an ideal example of what Nordic art should be—shapely yet 'formless,' many-sided yet monotonous, rambling, multitudinous, drastic, tragic, stoical, ruthlessly truth-proclaiming." (Taylor, "III")

With this turbulent literature Rose Grainger, a total believer in the superiority of the fair-haired, blue-eyed "Nordic" race, instilled in her small son her own bigotry and narrow-mindedness. She even bleached his hair to preserve the fair-haired look she worshipped, a pretense that Grainger would continue for many years. A nonconformist beneath her proper outer trappings, Rose Grainger, said her son, "was scornful of prosperity, law, Christianity and general rightness." She was also a dreadful mother. The abnormal relationship she locked herself into with her son; her jealousy, so intense that Grainger married (at age 46!) only after her death; her compulsive need to control every aspect of his life and career; all of these must be held responsible for creating the warped, yet somehow endearing, eccentric portrayed in Bird's fine biography.

Rose Grainger kept a whip in the front hall, her weapon for handling her inebriated husband and for punishing George Percy (about 1912 Grainger changed his name to Percy Aldridge Grainger) when he displeased her. In her own way she adored the boy, but she gave him a bizarre upbringing. She isolated him from other children and even, apart from three months in 1894, kept him away from school. She taught him English, music and a little history; he studied French and a smattering of art and elocution with private tutors. It was always Grainger and his mother, just the two of them against the world. She lived with him, ran his life and usually tagged along on his tours until her final illness; and in all those years they were separated only about five or six times. Her possessiveness destroyed many of Grainger's adult friendships and molded him into the neurotic, insecure man he grew up to be.

As her husband's drinking increasingly affected his earning ability, Rose Grainger, an adequate pianist, took in private pupils and later taught piano at a nearby school. She began teaching Grainger when he was five years old (a natural talent, even at that young age Grainger could improvise at length on themes by Mozart and Haydn), and at about age 10 he began lessons with Louis Pabst, an esteemed German pedagogue. A year or so later he made his debut (9 July 1894) in Melbourne. By the time he had played three more public performances (30 Oct 1894; 13 Feb 1895; 14 May 1895), Grainger had become Melbourne's prodigy, a "flaxen-haired phenomenon," said the critic of *The Age*, "who plays like a master on the piano." Meanwhile, Pabst having returned (1894) to Europe, Grainger began music lessons with Adelaide Burkitt, a Pabst pupil.

Since Grainger's parents had separated when he was about eight years old, he really never knew his father, although they kept in touch. It was his mother who now decided, after his successful prodigy concerts, that Australia was not the place for advanced musical training. With funds from a benefit concert arranged by Melbourne supporters, in May 1895 mother and son left for Frankfurt, Germany. Grainger enrolled at the Hoch Conservatory to study piano with James Kwast, a Dutch pianist, and composition with Iwan Knorr, a German composer. To pay for it all, his mother taught English classes in the evening. As young as he was, only 13, Grainger soon let it be known that he was dissatisfied with both Kwast and Knorr. He stayed with Kwast, but left Knorr to study composition with Karl Klimsch, a Frankfurt graphic artist and amateur musician, an association, says Grainger's biographer, that "was to become one of the most important in Grainger's early life." It was Klimsch, an ardent Anglophile, who first introduced Percy Grainger to "the beauties of English and Scottish folk song some ten years before he was to meet Grieg and involve himself in the activities of the first English folk-song revival." (Bird, *Percy Grainger*)

With Rose Grainger facing health problems, Grainger assumed the supporting role, earning income by giving recitals, accompanying singers and teaching piano classes for children. During these Frankfurt years he made friends with a group of young English students, among them Cyril Scott, Balfour Gardner and Roger Quilter, then beginning to advance their modern ideas about form, harmony and rhythm. Their influence changed Grainger's ideas on traditional musical concepts and inspired him to explore modern music being written by English and Australian composers.

Grainger and his mother settled in London in 1901 and that year attending a London "society recital" (3 July) by Australian contralto Maggie Stirling greatly changed his life. The accompanist failed to appear, and Grainger was called out of the audience to assist. He made such a marvelous impression, not only accompanying the singer but playing a solo performance of Schumann's *Faschingsschwank aus Wien*, all without advance notice, that invitations for "at-home" performances soon began to overwhelm him.

He lived in London for 13 years, extremely busy, productive years, said by some to be the happiest in his life. In 1902 he toured Great Britain with a musical group put together by the aging Adelina Patti. Early in 1903 he met the 37-year-old Ferruccio Busoni, then touring in England, and Busoni offered to give him lessons in Berlin, free of charge. As things turned out, the lessons lasted only for a few weeks in July of that year, largely because two such colorful temperaments could not get along. Grainger disliked Busoni's authoritative attitude with his students, and Busoni ridiculed Grainger for not practicing enough. The major problem was that Grainger, as always, really only wanted to compose. Still admiring Busoni as a pianist, he gave up and returned to London on 23 July 1903.

Then began a decade of steady performing, sometimes as many as 100 appearances a season, a number all the more incredible in view of the fact that Grainger almost always walked from one concert town to the next, carrying provisions and bare necessities in a backpack. (His evening suit, purchased in 1909 and still in use in the 1940s, was sent ahead by train.) When walking was impossible, he traveled by train, coach class. From September 1903 to May 1904, Grainger toured through Australia, New Zealand and South Africa. He toured in Denmark in 1905; through Great Britain in 1906; made an extended tour through Great Britain and Northern Ireland in 1906–07; was again in Australia and New Zealand in 1907–08; and toured through Scandinavia, Holland and Germany in 1908–09. In between tours Grainger often played in London. Being London's favorite society pianist gave him income and exposure. He also gave private piano lessons when time permitted.

In 1905 Grainger joined the English Folk Song Society and in 1906 began to use the Edison Bell phonograph to record British folk songs on wax cylinders. Over the next four years he collected more than 500 of these songs, many of which he later reworked into more elaborate folk-song settings, published as "British Folk-Music Settings." (Grainger, "Collecting. . .")

Grainger met Edvard Grieg in 1906 and Frederick Delius in 1907, two friendships that greatly influenced his life and philosophy. He had learned Grieg's A Minor Concerto with Kwast in Frankfurt and had orchestrated (July 1898), as an exercise, three of Grieg's Lyric Pieces. Grainger played the Grieg Concerto at Leeds in 1907 (Grieg, engaged to conduct, had meanwhile died), and ultimately became famous for his performances of this concerto.

Grainger and his mother moved to the United States in September 1914. With his eclectic tastes in music and his contempt for the classical tradition upheld by most pianists of his time, Grainger found America like a breath of fresh musical air. Besides that, after his New York debut (11 Feb 1915) and a series of performances during the 1915–16 season, he had captured the affections of American concert goers. America was "home" for the rest of his life. He took American citizenship in 1918 and in 1921 settled with his mother in White Plains, New York.

Grainger enlisted in the United States Army in June 1917 and served two years. A musician third class, he first played saxophone and oboe in the 15th Coast Artillery Corps Band at Fort Totten. As soon as the band leader realized who Grainger was, he promptly promoted him to rehearsal conductor. At the band's bond-selling concerts, audiences quickly recognized Grainger and insisted on his playing piano solos. Trying to think of piano pieces suitable for every kind of audience, he began improvising on the old English Morris dance Country Gardens. As the tours continued, his improvisations gradually crystallized into definite form, and one day in the barracks he wrote down a final version. Those improvisations, Grainger's most popular composition, sold at a rate of about 35,000 copies a year for 20 years.

Discharged from the army in February 1919, Grainger began an endless round of tours, and every summer from 1919 to 1931 he taught a five-week session at Chicago Musical College. He toured in Oregon, British Columbia, New Mexico, California, Colorado and Ohio in 1919–20, and returned to the Pacific Coast and Canada in 1922. As he was performing in Los Angeles on 30 April 1922, his mother, long in poor health, committed suicide by throwing herself from the 18th floor of the Aeolian Building in New York. To offset his deep depression at her loss, Grainger toured frantically in both Europe (Scandinavia and Holland in late 1922) and in Australia (1924, 1926).

During the 1924 tour he started giving a new kind of "lecture–recital" concert, talking as much as he played, usually music determined by his own cultural tastes. Grainger was little concerned that these programs might go against the mainstream of audience taste, and the results were often controversial.

Never fond of the piano, he now began to hate it and even tried, says his biographer, "to drop the label of star virtuoso," preferring to bypass major musical centers and instead play for music clubs, schools, colleges and country music festivals. It took time. By the mid-1940s his performances (about three a week) were mostly away from the mainstream concert circuit. The rest (about 15 or 20 a season) were usually orchestral performances in large cities (Washington, D.C., Philadelphia, Minneapolis, San Francisco, Detroit, Chicago).

Typical of the flamboyant Grainger, his marriage (9 Aug 1928) to Ella Strom, a Swedish poet and painter, took place at the Hollywood Bowl before an audience estimated at 22,000 people. The Swedish Lutheran ceremony, embellished with a 126-member orchestra and an a capella choir, was held after a concert in which Grainger both played and conducted. He also composed the orchestral wedding music (To a Nordic Princess). Ella Strom had to be a strong woman to endure life with the erotic, erratic Grainger. Married to a man who found the greatest pleasure in flagellation, "only she knew the full measure of his joys and frustrations, his saintliness and cruelty and his genius and aberrations." (Bird, *Percy Grainger*)

Percy and Ella Grainger made their home in New York. He taught at New York University for just one year (1932–33), then he and his wife spent many months (1933–35) cruising the South Seas and in Australia, where he toured for the Australian Broadcasting Commission, gave radio talks and planned for the construction of a Grainger Museum to be built on the campus of the University of Melbourne. Officially dedicated in 1938, this museum was not meant to eulogize Grainger. He envisioned it as an ethnological research center, a "repository for the nucleus of an historic Australian music collection." (Radic) Back in America by the end of 1935, he toured tirelessly to raise money for the museum, a burden to the end of his life. In 1940, worried about World War II and the dangers of living in the big city of New York, the Graingers moved to Springfield, Missouri.

An operation for cancer slowed him down only a little in 1953. In 1955 he made a final visit to Australia, in 1957 a last visit to Denmark. Even after a second operation in 1957, Grainger set out to play 12 concerts spaced from North Carolina to California. At his last public appearance, on 29 April 1960 at Dartmouth College, he gave a lecture and conducted a performance of his last major work The Power of Rome and the Christian Heart. (Bird) Grainger died on 20 February 1961. Although he had requested no public or religious ceremony of any kind, his body was flown to Australia for a Christian burial service and interment in the Aldridge family vault in Adelaide.

All things considered, what was Percy Grainger really like? A complex man constantly pursuing some new (often unattainable or illogical) goal, Grainger's life, habits, music, just about everything about him, was contradictory. The mass of published information depicts two very opposite Graingers. The public Grainger was a warm, friendly child of nature with a remarkable zest for life and everything (except the piano!) in it. Fanatically dedicated to nature, he let weeds engulf his house because the lawn mower was a "menace to nature"; used an ice box, not an electric refrigerator; refused to have screens (an "undemocratic barrier" between him and the insect world); and abstemiously avoided meat, coffee, tea, tobacco and alcohol.

Beneath this gentle, happy facade lived the unbelievably opposite Grainger, a man fascinated with blood and violence, tormented by doubts and inner conflicts ("possessed by angels of darkness as well as of light"), a man blatantly reveling in "sadistic fantasy and practice toward others and, more often, toward himself." (Doerschuk) These two conflicting portraits—a radiant outer Grainger, a darkly twisted inner Grainger—made for a most perplexing personality.

Ultimately the ongoing battle between the demands of his concert life and his passionate need to compose affected his playing and his reputation. He disappointed audiences expecting pyrotechnical performances like those they were hearing from Hofmann, Rachmaninoff and Horowitz. Even worse, Grainger for his part seemed not to care; however, to the end of his life he had a small special following.

Largely ignored in his final years and nearly forgotten for some years after his death, Grainger is apparently making a comeback. Initially inspired by Benjamin Britten's evening of Grainger music at the 1966 Aldeburgh Festival, it has progressed slowly. A few years later Britten recorded (with Peter Pears and others) some of Grainger's music. And in 1970 Britten helped to organize a Grainger Festival in London. In 1987 Salem College in Winston-Salem, North Carolina, held a two-day Percy Grainger Festival. Melbourne-born pianist Leslie Howard, a Grainger specialist who has collected all of Grainger's keyboard music, frequently gives lecture-recitals at which he plays Grainger's music and talks about Grainger's life and work. And John Bird's biography seems to have prompted an ever increasing collection of articles on Percy Grainger.

Grainger enjoyed teaching, in fact he often said that he liked everything about music education. Reportedly an inspiring—and assuredly always lively—teacher, he usually had a waiting list of students angling to get into his summer master classes (1919–31) at the Chicago Musical College. His lectures (1932–33) at New York University promulgated his theory that music is a worldwide art, equally as important in its more primitive phases as in its most artful phases. Using recorded illustrations and live music (when he could round up the instruments), he introduced these students to a sampling of the native musics of Africa, Asia and the South Sea Islands. In these same lectures he also began to discuss his long-held theory of Free Music, implying that his own earlier "pioneering experiments in irregular rhythms and complex harmony . . . had led, via Cyril Scott's piano sonata, to the creations of Schoenberg, Hindemith and Stravinsky." Grainger's statement on Free Music, written 6 December 1938, is reprinted in the Bird biography.

Basically Grainger taught that practicing scales is a waste of time, that the music itself is the best source for exercise and practice. (He personally hated practicing and usually waited until he had a performance due, then put in hours at a time to prepare.) If a student had a well-developed technique, he let it alone. To make a student aware of a certain technical problem, he prescribed an appropriate work that would highlight the special difficulty. Further, Grainger would go into great detail about pedal effects (half-pedaling, pedal-fluttering), especially the sostenuto pedal, because "the most wonderful tonal colors can be produced by artistic use of the pedals."

With all his students Grainger advocated his personal (and ridiculous) theory that the very best music was written by composers with fair hair and blue eyes. What a pity that this highly intelligent and genuinely creative man was denied the proper education that would have enabled him to analyze (and discard) the many outrageous views deeply instilled in him by his mother. Some of his statements, written and spoken, "contained the germ of genius (see, for example, his essays on Elastic Scoring and Free Music), yet a few would be so crass and mulishly stupid as to make his friends and colleagues want to run and hide with embarrassment." (Bird, *Percy Grainger*)

A largely self-taught composer, Grainger was unwilling to write in a "form in which one performer is exalted at the expense of a hundred others." He wrote no symphony, concerto, opera or oratorio, and restricted himself mostly to the smaller forms—choral pieces, piano solos, chamber music.

Grainger's well-balanced and consistently interesting recitals were unconventional then, and they are unthinkable today. Decidedly different, almost every single one included arrangements (Grainger's or another composer's) of folk songs or dances as well as works by contemporary composers. He was a faithful, vociferous champion of modern composers, but he was also famous for his performances of Grieg.

Reviews reaching across three decades outline a typical Grainger program. He began almost every recital with Bach (usually in transcription by Busoni, Liszt or Tausig), the influence no doubt of his early studies with Louis Pabst and his brief time with Busoni. Every recital also included works by Romantic composers, predominantly Chopin and Brahms, to a lesser extent Schumann, Liszt and Grieg. Usually there would be works by French composers (Debussy, Ravel, Franck, Fauré) and/or Spanish composers (Albéniz, Granados), and of course the folk-music arrangements and modern works. (For more information, see "Percy Grainger's Concert Repertoire," two articles published [Dec 1978, July 1979] in the *Grainger Society Journal.*)

Grainger told one interviewer that he "had to practice more than most pianists because I have almost no technique." Yet invariably reviewers commented on his effortless, natural technique, praising him for the cleanness and clearness of his touch, his ability to bring out the parts, his strong sense of rhythm. He had a "free, easy swing at the piano, a superb tone, an effortless and completely natural technique. . . . He was one of the keyboard originals—a pianist who forged his own style and expressed it with amazing skill, personality and vigor, a healthy, forthright musical mind whose interpretations never sounded forced." (Sch/Gre, see Bibliog.)

Occasionally reviewers acknowledged his faults—a sometimes abrupt breaking up and distorting of the musical phrase, unnecessarily noisy *fortissimos*, wayward rhythms, overly boisterous playing, an outrageous disregard for traditional playing standards. Yet Grainger's playing could disarm any criticism and "annihilate academic standards and critical hair-splittings by the indomitable strength and the kind of extemporaneous quality that is back of it." (Buchanan, "Percy Grainger. . .")

Grainger may have hated the piano, belittled his own playing, feared an audience almost more than anything in the world and worried constantly about memory failure, yet reviews of his playing, spanning the years 1909 through 1940, prove incontestably that he was a great pianist in an original mold. His American debut performance (11 Feb 1915) absolutely captivated New York audiences and critics, who put him in the rank of exciting performers like Paderewski and Kreisler. What stands out in all these rave reviews of this debut recital is how much the reviewers admired (and enjoyed!) Grainger's refreshing individuality.

Once he began to play, Grainger's anxieties and dislikes evaporated. Appearing at ease and happy to be there, he immediately established a warm bond with his audience, and he played with absolute conviction. The distinctly personal qualities of his playing—individuality, vitality, joyfulness—pleased critics as much as audiences: "As a pianist, Mr. Grainger is absolutely *sui generis*. In no respect does he suggest any other player now before the public. To set forth precisely the elements whereby he is unique is a baffling test. But subtly intangible as they are their effect is irresistible. Grainger's performances are surcharged with electricity, with veritable musical ozone. . . . In these days of mediocrities and anemic conservatory playing such manifestations of genius freshen the heavy air of the concert hall like clear, cold mountain blasts." (*MA*, 20 Feb 1915)

Modern pianists might envy the extravagant critical praise heaped on Grainger in his lifetime. On 12 March 1915 he played the Grieg Concerto in A Minor with the New York Philharmonic Society, Josef Stransky conducting, and "played that concerto as no other pianist has ever played it here, with a poetic insight, a variety of tonal effects and shadings, a tenderness and delicacy in the soft passages, and a dash and brilliancy in the final movement that were altogether enchanting." (*NYEP*, 13 March 1915) Again, when he played (31 Oct 1915) the Tchaikovsky Concerto No. 1 in B-flat Minor with Walter Damrosch conducting the New York Symphony Orchestra, Grainger "played this Russian music as no Russian has played it. The power, the virility, the dash, the brilliancy of it were astounding." (*NYEP*, 1 Nov 1915)

Grainger's playing was not all virility, dash and brilliance. On one occasion he played Beethoven's 32 Variations in London "with magnificent power and intellectual grasp. He gave them the unity which is unnoticed by average players, so that their cumulative power was very remarkable." (*TL*, 31 May 1911) Another time, playing Brahms's Variations on a Theme of Handel, Grainger gave a "masterly performance full of character and variety." (*TL*, 1 Dec 1909)

A review of a Toronto recital (10 Feb 1928) sums up Grainger's style: "He is a brilliant technician, and his temper is high-strung with an uncanny instinct for the delicacy of discord, its rightful proportion in the beautiful. He glories in color—bright, vivid, rich, changeful color—and the swing of his rhythms catches you up . . . before you know it. His tone rings sweetly as a silver bell, and always beautifully and clearly—and his touch has a hundred gradations and the clinging sympathy of a master who sings to himself as he plays." (*TET*, 11 Feb 1928)

On 8 January 1930 Grainger played one of his few totally different programs, different because there was no folk arrangement and no modern music. The first half of this Boston recital consisted of Preludes and Fugues from Bach's Well-Tempered Clavier; the rest of the program consisted of Chopin's Barcarolle and Sonata No. 3 in B Minor, Ravel's *Ondine* and the Debussy *Homage à Rameau*. And he still pleased the critics: "In his playing of these compositions Mr. Grainger displayed the highest, the most indispensable qualities of a pianist who has technical proficiency, sensitiveness and imagination. Few piano recitals in past years have been so musical." (*BH*, 9 Jan 1930)

Percy Grainger's comeback still moves slowly, but the reviews of his performances prove him to be one of the 20th century's great pianists.

Grainger recorded over a long period, from 1908 to 1957. Among the first artists to cut piano rolls for Duo-Art, he began around 1915 and continued making piano rolls until 1930, long after the emergence of acoustic and electrical recordings. Some of these are still of interest, for he frequently recorded the same compositions on piano roll and disc. To make his 1921 piano rolls of the Grieg Concerto in A Minor, the clever Grainger first recorded the solo part, then recorded the orchestral reduction and superimposed one on the other to make the completed rolls. His disc recording of the Grieg Concerto was taken from a public performance in Denmark on 25 February 1957, with Per Drier conducting the Aarhus Municipal Orchestra. Comparing the two (see Discog.) is revealing, for despite the harsh tone quality in the disc and the fact that Grainger was already suffering from cancer, his interpretative and technical powers were still intact. (Incidentally, his published edition of the Grieg Concerto for Schirmer has remained the definitive one.) Grainger also recorded the Schumann Symphonic Etudes twice—on piano roll (see Discog.) in 1925 and on disc in 1928.

Grainger began recording discs for the Gramophone Company in 1908, was under contract with the Columbia Graphophone (later Phonograph) Company from 1917 to 1931 and later made recordings with the Decca Company. After his death there apparently was no attempt to reissue his recordings, even from a historical standpoint. Now Pearl and Biddulph records have already remastered a number of Grainger's significant recorded performances and many others may be heard on the Gustafson Piano Library cassettes (see Discog.).

Two Pearl CDs containing some of Grainger's best playing give cause for a re-evaluation of his role in 20th-century pianism. In the first volume, "Grainger piles into the Bach organ transcriptions with a big, incisive sonority and tremendous rhythmic vitality." Another outstanding item is the performance of Debussy's *Pagodes*, taken from a recorded 1948 recital at the University of Texas. "Grainger speaks about the Debussy before playing it (as an encore) with the most incredible array of provocative tonal balances and rhythmic emphases." (*ARG*, Nov/Dec 1992) In addition, there is also a spontaneous, impassioned reading of the Schumann Sonata in G Minor, op. 22.

The second Pearl CD contains three excellent works by which to judge Grainger's performing abilities—Schumann's Symphonic Etudes, op. 13, and the two great Chopin Sonatas, Nos. 2 and 3. "The Sonatas have tremendous vitality, bold tone colours and a rhythmic athleticism which distinguishes them from any other pianist. The phrasing is so convincing that Grainger makes one wonder how the works could be performed in any other way." (Met/Cho, see Bibliog.) The Sonata in B Minor, op. 58, appeared in 1925 as Columbia's first complete instrumental sonata of the electrical recording era. "This performance has stood the test of time and is the recording to which connoisseurs always turn when Grainger's greatness as a pianist is being discussed. . . . It stands as one of the high points of recorded piano playing." (Bird, *Percy Grainger*)

The Biddulph collection has the Schumann Symphonic Etudes and Chopin's Sonata in B Minor, and in addition the magnificent Brahms Sonata in F Minor, op. 5, one of the truly formidable large-scale works for piano solo. According to one critic, Grainger's is "a truly heroic reading of Brahms's youthful F minor Sonata—one of the few that actually succeeds in making the work sound like a young man's music. . . . This is the playing of a man who lived his music, and whose hands served to liberate spontaneous interpretative ideas." (*Gram*, April 1993)

It is hoped that more of Grainger's recorded repertoire, including the Grieg Concerto, will be reissued on CD for, as Harold Schonberg so aptly puts it, he was indeed a "whale of a pianist." Our century has produced few musicians so interesting.

SELECTED REFERENCES

Bacon, Ruth Orcutt. "Percy Grainger, A Remembrance." *Grainger Society Journal*, Fall 1986, pp. 3–5.

Bird, John. "More Than A Pianist." *Keyboard Classics*, Jan/Feb 1989, pp. 7, 52–53.

————. *Percy Grainger*. London: Faber and Faber, 1982.

Buchanan, Charles L. "Analyzing The Greater Grainger." *Musical America*, 25 Aug 1917, p. 6.

————. "Percy Grainger: Pianist And Composer." *Musical America*, 29 July 1916, pp. 9–11.

Dilsner, Laurence. "Percy Grainger: some personal reflections." *Clavier*, Nov 1982, pp. 13–15.

Doerschuk, Bob. "Percy Grainger: Remembering a Pioneering Composer & Pianist On His Hundredth Birthday." *Keyboard*, Aug 1982, pp. 23–32.

Dorum, Eileen. *Percy Grainger: The Man Behind The Music*. White Plains, N.Y.: Pro/Am Music Resources, Inc., 1989.

"George Percy Grainger (1882–1961)." In *Australian Dictionary of Biography*. Melbourne: Melbourne University Press, 1983, pp. 69-72.

Grainger, Percy. "Collecting with the Phonograph." *Journal of the Folk-Song Society*, III/12 (1908/09), pp. 147–242.

————. "Edvard Grieg: A Tribute." *Grainger Society Journal*, Autumn 1987, pp. 8–10.

————. "Is Music Universal?" (Part 1) *New York Times*, 2 July 1933, sec. 9, p. 4.

————. "Is Music A Universal Language?" (Part 2) *New York Times*, 9 July 1933, sec. 10, p. 4.

————. "Modernism in Pianoforte Study." *Etude*, Sept 1915, pp. 631–632.

————. "New Ideas on Study and Practice." (Part I) *Etude*, Dec 1925, pp. 845–846.

————. "New Ideas on Study and Practice." (Part II) *Etude*, Jan 1926, pp. 23–24.

————. "Reaching Your Goal at the Keyboard." (interview with Myles Fellowes). *Etude*, Feb 1941, pp. 79–80, 134.

————. "The Specialist and the All-Round Man." In *A Birthday Offering to Carl Engel*. New York: G. Schirmer, Inc., 1943, pp. 115–119.

The Grainger Society Journal. Published twice a year by The International Percy Grainger Society, the Journal contains pertinent articles and resource materials.

Howes, Frank. "Percy Grainger." *Recorded Sound*, Summer 1961, pp. 96–98.
Josephson, David. "Conversation with Ella Grainger." *Grainger Society Journal*, July 1993, pp. 3–91.
———. "Percy Grainger." Lecture, Brown University, April 1976.
Lawrence, A. F. R. "Records of Percy Grainger as an interpreter." *Recorded Sound*, Summer 1962, pp. 43–48.
Loriaux, Maurice. "Reminiscences of Percy Grainger." *Grainger Society Journal*, Summer 1989, pp. 29–31.
Mellers, Wilfrid. *Percy Grainger*. Oxford: Oxford University Press, 1992.
Mossman, Joseph. "Remembrance of Grainger." *Grainger Society Journal*, Fall 1986, pp. 23–25. Reprint from *Des Moines Register*, 1979.
Obituary. *Musical America*, April 1961, pp. 69–70. *Musical Times*, April 1961, p. 245. *New York Times*, 21 Feb 1961, p. 35. *The Times* (London), 21 Feb 1961, p. 13.
Orga, Ates. "Percy Grainger 1882–1961." *Music and Musicians*, March 1970, pp. 28–36, 70.
Pears, Peter. "Percy Grainger." *Recorded Sound*, Jan 1972, pp. 11–15.
Radic, Therese. "A Pilgrim Looks at Grainger." *The Age*, 5 Aug 1978, p. 25.
Schonberg, Harold C. "No One's Laughing At Percy Grainger Anymore." *New York Times*, 25 April 1976, sec. 2, p. 19.
Scott, Cyril. "Percy Grainger: The Man and the Musician." *Musical Times*, July 1957, pp. 368–369.
———. "Percy Grainger: The Music and the Man." *Musical Quarterly*, July 1916, pp. 425–433.
Slattery, Thomas C. *Percy Grainger*. Evanston: The Instrumentalist Co., 1974.
Taylor, Robert Lewis. "I–A Matter Of Kicking Out At Space." *New Yorker*, 31 Jan 1948, pp. 29–35.
———. "II–The Running Pianist." *New Yorker*, 7 Feb 1948, pp. 32–39.
———. "III–Top Notes Glassy." *New Yorker*, 14 Feb 1948, pp. 32-40.
See also Bibliography: Bro/PiS; Coo/Gre; Ewe/Li; Fin/My; Kau/Art; MGG; New/Gro; Nie/Mei; Sch/Gre; Woo/My.

SELECTED REVIEWS

BET: 12 Jan 1925; 7 Feb 1927; 9 Jan 1930. *BH*: 11 Jan 1925; 9 Jan 1930. *BP*: 11 Jan 1925. *CSM*: 12 Jan 1925. *MA*: 20 Feb 1915; 20 March 1915; 18 Dec 1915; 29 Jan 1916; 18 Feb 1928. *MS*: 4 Jan 1928. *NYEP*: 13 March 1915; 1 Nov 1915; 8 Dec 1920. *NYS*: 12 Feb 1915; 1 Nov 1915; 8 Dec 1920. *NYT*: 12 Feb 1915; 9 Dec 1915; 9 Nov 1916; 8 Dec 1920; 6 Jan 1925; 9 Feb 1928; 9 Nov 1929; 17 Jan 1932; 17 Feb 1936; 10 April 1940. *NYTr*: 1 Nov 1915. *TET*: 11 Feb 1928. *TL*: 17 June 1908; 1 Dec 1909; 22 June 1910; 31 May 1911; 30 April 1913; 1 July 1914.

SELECTED DISCOGRAPHY

A. Played by Grainger

Bach-Grainger: Toccata and Fugue in D Minor. Bach-Liszt: Fantasy and Fugue in G Minor; Prelude and Fugue in A Minor. Chopin: Etude in B Minor, op. 25, no. 10; Sonata No. 2 in B-flat Minor, op. 35; Sonata No. 3 in B Minor, op. 58. Biddulph LHW 010 (CD).

Brahms: Sonata No. 3 in F Minor, op. 5; Waltz in A-flat Major, op. 39, no. 15. Schumann: Romance in F-sharp Major, op. 28, no. 2; Sonata No. 2 in G Minor, op. 22; Symphonic Etudes, op. 13; *Warum?* Biddulph LHW 008 (CD).

Chopin: Sonata in B-flat Minor, op. 35; Sonata in B Minor, op. 58; Waltz in A-flat Major, op. 42. Grainger: Brahms Cradle Song; Country Gardens; Danish Folksongs (2); Gum-Suckers March; Gum-Suckers March with orchestra; Irish Tune from County Derry; Jutish Medley; Mock Morris Dances; Molly on the Shore, One Day More, My John; Paraphrase on Tchaikovsky's Waltz of the Flowers; Shepherd's Hey; Shepherd's Hey with Orchestra; Spoon River Folksong. Gustafson Piano Library Cassette GPL 103.

Grainger: Suite on Danish Folksongs; Water-Music 'Hornpipe' by Handel. Grieg: Norwegian Bridal Procession, op. 19, no. 2; To Spring, op. 43, no. 6; Wedding Day at Troldhaugen, op. 65, no. 6. Guion: Sheep and Goat Walkin' to the Pasture; Turkey in the Straw. Liszt: Hungarian Fantasy; Hungarian Rhapsody No. 2; Hungarian Rhapsody No. 12; Liebestraum No. 3; Polonaise in E Major. MacDowell: To a Water-Lily (Woodland Sketches). Scharwenka: Polish Dance, op. 3, no. 1. Scott: *Danse negre*; Cherry Ripe; Lento. Sinding: Voices of Spring, op. 32, no. 3. Gustafson Piano Library Cassette GPL 104.

Grieg: Concerto in A Minor, op. 16. Schumann: *Etudes symphoniques*, op. 13; Romance, op. 28, no. 2; Sonata in G Minor, op. 22; *Warum? (Phantasiestücke*, op. 12). Strauss: 'Ramble on Love' from *Rosenkavalier* (arr. Grainger). Gustafson Piano Library Cassette GPL 105.

Percy Grainger plays. Bach-Busoni: "Ich ruf zu Dir." Bach-Grainger: Toccata and Fugue in D Minor. Bach-Liszt: Fantasia and Fugue in G Minor; Prelude and Fugue in A Minor. Chopin: Etude in B Minor, op. 25, no. 10; Etude in C Minor, op. 25, no. 12. Debussy: Golliwog's Cakewalk; *Pagodes (Estampes)*; Toccata (*Pour le piano*). Grainger: Molly on the Shore. Grieg: Wedding Day at Troldhaugen. Schumann: Sonata No. 2 in G Minor, op. 22. Pearl GEMM CD 9957.

Percy Grainger plays-Volume II. Byrd-Grainger: Carman's Whistle. Chopin: Sonata No. 2 in B-flat Minor, op. 35; Sonata No. 3 in B Minor, op. 58. Schumann: *Etudes symphoniques*, op. 13; Romance in F-sharp Major, op. 28, no. 2. Stanford-Grainger: Irish Dance No. 1. Pearl GEMM CD 9013.

Percy Grainger plays Grieg. Ballade, op. 24; Concerto in A Minor, op. 16; *Erotikon*; To Spring, op. 43, no. 6; Wedding Day at Troldhaugen, op. 65, no. 6. From Duo-Art piano rolls. Klavier KS-101.

Percy Grainger plays Schumann and Liszt. Liszt: Hungarian Rhapsody No. 12;
   Polonaise No. 2. Schumann: *Etudes symphoniques*, op. 13; Romance, op.
   28, no. 2. From Duo-Art piano rolls. Klavier KS-109.

B. Grainger's Music Played by Others
Percy Grainger: Piano Music, Leslie Howard, piano. Vol. 1: Musical Heritage
   Society MHS 522701 (2 CDs); Vol. 2: MHS 512773.
Percy Grainger: Complete Piano Music, Martin Jones, piano. Nimbus NI
   5220, 5232, 5244, 5255, 5286.

GUTIÉRREZ, HORACIO: b. Havana, Cuba, 28 August 1948.

> I work every day of my life to improve my sound. It has to do with
> listening to oneself. Some people have a basically better sound than
> others to begin with.
>
>   Horacio Gutiérrez (*Clavier*, September 1982)

Josephine (Fernández) Gutiérrez, Horacio's mother, was a serious musician
(unfortunately, in prerevolutionary Havana it was unseemly for a Spanish lady to
become a concert pianist), and when she realized that her two-year-old son could
not say the words of a little Spanish song but easily picked out the melody on
the piano, she immediately started him with piano lessons.
      At age five Gutiérrez became a pupil of César Perez Sentenat, a former
pupil of Joaquin Nin in Paris, and he studied with Sentenat for about seven
years. In 1959 (the year Fidel Castro assumed control in Cuba), the 11-year-
old Gutiérrez made his orchestral debut with the Havana Symphony Orchestra,
Gonzales Mantici conducting. A year later Sentenat recommended further training in Prague, but Gutiérrez's parents hesitated, fearing that in communist
Czechoslovakia they would have little to say about their son's musical training.
Even in Cuba, saya Gutiérrez, everyone's life was already "completely controlled
by the communists. At any given moment, the government could order us to
drop everything and go and cut sugarcane. No one, including musicians, was ex-
empt." (*LAT*, 1 Feb 1980)
      Rather than go to Prague, in 1961 Tomás Gutiérrez arranged his fami-
ly's escape, first to Colombia, then to the United States. They spent about a
year in Miami, where Horacio had free lessons and a Baptist Church let him
practice on its piano. In 1962 they moved to Los Angeles, and there Gutiérrez
began lessons with Sergei Tarnowsky, who had taught Vladimir Horowitz at the
Kiev Conservatory. Tarnowsky, once a pupil of the famed Anna Essipoff at St.
Petersburg, schooled Gutiérrez in the so-called Russian method, a technique using the arm rather than finger weight to develop ease and facility at the keyboard
and to achieve rich, wonderful sounds. During these student years, Gutiérrez appeared twice in the youth concerts of the Los Angeles Philharmonic Orchestra.

He was also soloist in a New York Philharmonic Young People's Concert (1966) under Leonard Bernstein, and in 1967 (Gutiérrez became an American citizen that year) he won first prize in the San Francisco Symphony Orchestra auditions. His first concert with the SFO was so impressive that he was invited to return in 1969.

Sponsored by Enid Daily, patron of the arts and also a Tarnowsky student in Los Angeles, Gutiérrez studied (1967–70) with Adele Marcus at Juilliard in New York. The year he graduated he was invited to play the Prokofiev Sonata No. 7 at the formal opening (30 Nov 1970) of Juilliard's Paul Recital Hall. That same year Enid Daily also provided funds for Gutiérrez to enter the fourth International Tchaikovsky Competition. He later admitted that he had hated every minute of Moscow, especially the long waits in restaurants when he wanted to be practicing. But Moscow liked Gutiérrez. He won the silver medal, and he was the only contestant invited to give recitals in Moscow and Leningrad and to return to Russia later for an extended tour (Feb 1971).

Gutiérrez made his professional orchestral debut (22 Aug 1970) with Zubin Mehta and the Los Angeles Philharmonic Orchestra, and his New York recital debut (12 May 1972) at Hunter College. (Gutiérrez and Patricia A. Asher, a fellow student at Juilliard, married in July 1972.) Since then he has performed regularly, especially in North America, South America, Israel and the Soviet Union. In 1982 he was awarded the Avery Fisher Prize, a noncompetitive award given to young artists for outstanding achievement in music: ten thousand dollars in cash, engagements with the New York Philharmonic Orchestra and the Lincoln Center Chamber Music Society, a solo recital on the Great Performers at Lincoln Center series and recording opportunities. Gutiérrez, a favorite of New York concert audiences, frequently appears at the Mostly Mozart Festival and on the Great Performers series. He has often appeared on television in the United States, Great Britain and France, and in 1988 received an Emmy Award for his fourth appearance with the Chamber Music Society of Lincoln Center.

Gutiérrez's active repertoire appears somewhat limited against those of some of his contemporaries. He first established his reputation performing the big Romantic concertos—Brahms No. 1 in D Minor, Tchaikovsky No. 1 in B-flat Minor, Rachmaninoff No. 3 in D Minor, Prokofiev No. 2 in G Minor and No. 3 in C Major. In the 1980s he added the Brahms No. 2 in B-flat Major, Chopin No. 2 in F Minor and the Mozart Concertos K. 459 and K. 491. He has played this concerto repertoire countless times with many of the world's major orchestras. Gutiérrez shuns what he calls the "encyclopedic" approach to music. He will not, for example, play all of the works of Chopin or all of Scriabin just to be able to say that he plays it. While he admits that the more works a pianist knows, the more he grows as an artist, he is also convinced that the performer needs time to live with the music, to digest it.

With his phenomenal digital skills, technique is never a problem. Gutiérrez considers himself basically a purist, as often as possible playing the music as written, that is, neither overly emotional nor coolly objective. Inspiration, being inspired to respond to the music, to be completely abandoned at any given time, does concern him: "Sometimes you're in a small town with no pressures and you can give some of the best concerts of your life with very little work because you're inspired and the music comes fresh." Despite his extraordinary talent, Gutiérrez suffers from nerves, and not only before a concert. "I'm nervous every day. I walk around with some stress all the time like permanent baggage." (*CL*, Sept 1982)

He frequently teaches master classes, and at one point felt that the ideal schedule for him would be to concertize for about six months and give intermittent master classes the rest of the year. He stresses the importance of tone, highly important to him, with his students. Admitting that tone is difficult to teach, Gutiérrez believes that the teacher can at least increase awareness of an ideal sound, and in striving for that sound the student will ultimately achieve his best tone, one distinctly his own.

Gutiérrez had acquired a youthful reputation before he went to Juilliard. After graduation in 1970, also the year he became a popular favorite at the Tchaikovsky Competition in Moscow, his career gathered momentum. Even at this early stage he was known for his technical prowess and, more important, for the fact that he used it for musical means. His performance (27 March 1972) of Rachmaninoff's Concerto No. 3 with the Houston Symphony Orchestra, Lawrence Foster conducting, was not only technically outstanding but musically thrilling, sensitive and highly communicative. "Though Gutiérrez could—and did—command a large and resounding tone when the occasion demanded, he also demonstrated an uncommon plasticity, lyricism and sweet gentleness in his playing. He . . . brought a great deal of poetic imagination to his interpretation of the concerto. . . . He proved that he is clearly much more than a mere keyboard virtuoso; he is a real musician." (*HP*, 28 March 1972)

This fiendishly difficult Rachmaninoff concerto has stayed in Gutiérrez's repertoire. Fourteen years later he played it at the Great Woods Center for the Performing Arts (Mansfield, Mass.) with the Pittsburgh Symphony Orchestra under Michael Tilson Thomas, and he tamed its pianistic gymnastics "with less apparent effort than any other pianist before the public today. His octave and chord technique is probably the best in the business. . . . His superhuman digital technique is always at the service of an unindulgent, lyrical expressivity and live-wire energy." (*BG*, 4 Aug 1986)

Gutiérrez's astonishing command of the keyboard makes him a natural Liszt pianist. At a Carnegie Hall recital (9 Jan 1974), his octaves near the end of the Liszt B Minor Sonata reminded one critic of a rocket taking off: "Musically it would have been better had he taken the passage a trifle slower; but in the face of such awesome energy and accuracy, who was going to complain? . . . There was a beautifully modulated tone, and no breakup in climaxes, and over-all rhythm and vitality. Seldom has a young pianist displayed this kind of sheer authority in so demanding a piece." (*NYT*, 11 Jan 1974)

A recital at Lebanon, Pennsylvania, included one of Gutiérrez's many thrilling performances of Liszt's Mephisto Waltz. "Regardless of the ferocious speed, Gutiérrez' trills and tremolos never lost their uniformity, runs and octave work were carried out as flawlessly as they were featherly light and, throughout it all, the man controlled the piano." (*DNL*, 14 Sept 1984)

When Gutiérrez played (25 July 1985) Chopin's F-minor Concerto at the Hollywood Bowl with the Los Angeles Philharmonic Orchestra, Michael Tilson Thomas conducting, his performance, in its naturalness, fluency, abundant detail and romantic ambiance "had a quality of singing and communication" that reminded one critic of other pianists'—Novaes, Rubinstein—performances of that same work: "In all cases, the Chopin style was unmistakable, and complete." (*LAT*, 27 July 1985)

On 4 November 1992 Gutierrez opened his Carnegie Hall recital with the grand Haydn Sonata in C Major, Hob. XVI:50. "Fineness of articulation and shining tone were the raw materials here. . . . Where symmetry was needed, it was provided; Haydn's surprises were carefully prepared." The Liszt Sonata served most nobly as the recital's finale, for the pianist "negotiated its well-worn paths with admirable skill and a sober sense of design." (*NYT*, 10 Nov 1992)

Like every other pianist, Gutiérrez has faults, mostly stemming from a surfeit of natural gifts. Reviewers have complained that his blazing technique sometimes overshadows the music, that he does not always penetrate the meaning of the music. Other complaints: that his minute attention to details results in a lack of focus; that his dizzying speed is at times both dazzling and destructive; that he lacks the singing touch; that he does not always bring off the long lines.

When Gutiérrez plays, however, the faults rarely matter. He is a very popular, sought after pianist, and has most likely collected hundreds of reviews. Ruffle through a stack—any stack—of these critiques, and certain words and phrases repeatedly catch the eye. In the sum, Gutiérrez emerges as a phenomenally strong, speedy and fluent pianist. He is a powerhouse, whose playing glitters, sparkles, even explodes with brilliance. There are times when his sensational performances can sway critics to superlatives and impel audiences to their feet. In other words, Horacio Gutiérrez is a virtuoso, Romantic pianist, renowned for his digitally phenomenal pianism (a level of articulation few pianists of any generation reach) and his remarkable power. With his clean and persuasive touch, his stylishly unsentimental presentations and, in later years, more subtle tone colors, Gutiérrez stands out as a big—but never overblown—pianist.

Gutiérrez has made surprisingly few recordings, which is regrettable considering his wonderfully successful live performances and his ever growing reputation as a top-rank pianist. The recordings he has made compete favorably with some of the outstanding discs now available.

His debut disc, the Liszt and Tchaikovsky concertos (see Discog.), received highly enthusiastic reviews, the Tchaikovsky in particular for the freshness of approach and vibrant, sensitive interpretation. Gutiérrez's gift for revitalizing frequently played concertos—the old warhorses—can also be detected in his recording of the Grieg and Schumann concertos (see Discog.). In the third movement of the Schumann Concerto the delightful rhythmic peroration is achieved with masterful articulation and phrasing.

His recording of the Brahms Concerto No. 2 must compete with the more than 40 other versions listed in the 1995 Schwann record catalogue, but for one reviewer Gutiérrez has created one of the most euphonious readings ever heard, whether on disc or on the concert stage, a recording that in terms of sheer opulence will not be matched for some time to come. Interestingly enough, this same reviewer finds Gutiérrez's playing expert but undercharacterized: "It lacks the spiky forthrightness, brashness, and lyric grace of Leon Fleisher, or the rhetorical grandeur and coloristic variety of Claudio Arrau." (*Fan*, July/Aug 1989)

Gutiérrez's recording of the Prokofiev Concertos Nos. 2 and 3 (see Discog.), works that seem to be naturally suited to his temperament and talent, have received all-around superb critiques. In "the massive Second Concerto . . . he comes through heroically, producing mammoth tone and neatly shifting into spiky brilliance for the sardonic scherzo." (*MA*, July 1991) "The Third Concerto is also excellent, ranking right along with Ashkenazy, Cliburn, and Graffman or the older recordings of Gilels, Kapell, and the composer himself." (*ARG*, July/Aug 1991) And from England: "Horacio Gutiérrez is as real a virtuoso as they come, and he goes through the thickets of notes in Prokofiev's Second Concerto like the proverbial knife through butter. . . . The Third Concerto confirms that the more notes there are flying around the happier Gutiérrez is." (*Gram*, May 1991)

SELECTED REFERENCES

Barron, James. "A Pianist Who Won't Rush into Things." *New York Times*, 4 April 1982, sec. 2, pp. 19, 25.

Beigel, Greta. "Pianists: Problems, Politics." *Los Angeles Times*, 1 Feb 1980, sec. 5, pp. 1, 15.

Bunke, Joan. "Pianist Gutierrez loves Chopin 'with a passion'." *Des Moines Register*, 30 Oct 1985, Datebook, p. 15 .

Freedman, Guy. "New Star in the Firmament." *Music Journal*, Dec 1975, pp. 8–9.

"Gutiérrez Seeks Balance in Pianistic Repertory." *New York Times*, 1 May 1987, sec. 3, p. 32.

Johnson, Lawrence. "If you love a romantic, Gutierrez is your pianist." *Detroit News*, 5 Feb 1993, sec. D, p. 1.

Martinez, Al. *Rising Voices: Profiles of Hispano-American Lives*. New York: New American Library Signet Book, 1974, pp. 80–83.

Montparker, Carol. "Horacio Gutiérrez: On An Express Train Called Success." *Clavier*, Sept 1982, pp. 20–22.

Shulgold, Marc. "Gutiérrez—A Rare Summer Appearance." *Los Angeles Times*, 21 July 1985, CAL, p. 55.

Valdes, Lesley. "Piano Roles: Method Acting At The Keyboard." *Keyboard Classics*, July/Aug 1983, pp. 4–6.

See also Bibliography: IWWM; WWAM.

SELECTED REVIEWS

AJ: 20 Sept 1979. *BG*: 4 Aug 1986. *BH*: 3 Aug 1986. *CST*: 11 Oct 1975; 8 May 1978. *CT*: 30 May 1986; 18 July 1993. *DeDN*: 14 Feb 1992. *DNL*:

14 Sept 1984. *HP*: 28 March 1972; 1 Sept 1986; 11 Feb 1991. *IS*: 9 Nov 1990. *LAT*: 24 Aug 1970; 19 April 1975; 27 July 1985; 13 Jan 1988; 16 May 1989. *MH*: 15 Dec 1976. *MM*: Nov 1983. *NYP*: 14 Aug 1986. *NYT*: 2 Dec 1970; 7 May 1972; 14 May 1972; 11 Jan 1974; 10 May 1976; 29 May 1980; 8 April 1982; 26 March 1988; 10 Nov 1992. *OrS*: 16 April 1988. *PEB*: 9 Jan 1981. *PI*: 21 Nov 1986. *PL*: 5 Aug 1986. *PP*: 5 Oct 1984; 14 Oct 1985. *TL*: 25 Nov 1974. *V-P*: 13 Nov 1978. *WP*: 11 Oct 1985.

SELECTED DISCOGRAPHY

Brahms: Concerto No. 2 in B-flat Major, op. 83.   Telarc   CD-80197. Previn/Royal PO.
Grieg: Concerto in A Minor, op. 16. Schumann: Concerto in A Minor, op. 54. Angel S-37510. Tennstedt/London PO.
Liszt: Concerto No. 1 in E-flat Major. Tchaikovsky: Concerto No. 1 in B-flat Minor. Angel S-37177, cassette 4AE-34421. Previn/London SO.
Liszt: Sonata in B Minor; Mephisto Waltz. Angel RL-32087.
Prokofiev: Concerto No. 2 in G Minor, op. 16; Concerto No. 3 in C Major, op. 26. Chandos CD CHAN 8889. Järvi/*Concertgebouw*.
Rachmaninoff: Concerto No. 2 in C Minor, op. 18; Concerto No. 3 in D Minor, op. 30. Telarc 80259 (CD). Maazel/Pittsburgh SO.
Tchaikovsky: Concerto No. 1 in B-flat Minor, op. 23.   Rachmaninoff: Rhapsody on a Theme of Paganini, op. 43. Telarc CD-80193. Zinman/ Baltimore SO.
Tchaikovsky: Concerto No. 1 in B-flat Minor, op. 23. Encore CDE 5 68123-2. Previn/LSO.

$\mathcal{H}$

HASKIL, CLARA: b. 7 January 1895, Bucharest, Romania; d. 7 December 1960, Brussels, Belgium.

> One of the most characteristic aspects of her playing was that nothing seemed to commence or end. The music simply materialized.
>
> Peter Feuchtwanger (*Recorded Sound*, July 1976)

That was the secret of Clara Haskil's rare talent: "the music simply materialized" in a deceptively easy flow of silvery sound, breathing life and light into everything she played. Sadly, Clara Haskil's own life had little of the joy and loveliness she poured into her music. A genuine child prodigy, she paid a terrible price for her gift. It took away her childhood and youth, alone an enormous loss to bear, but for Haskil there would be more. In her late teens she developed scoliosis, a lateral curvature of the spine, and that was but the first of a succession of ailments. She lived most of her life with pain, at times nearly unbearable pain, and how, one wonders, did she manage such serenely beautiful piano playing?

Isaac and Berthe (Moscuna) Haskil, her parents, were cultivated Sephardic Jews. Her mother and her mother's sister (Clara Moscuna, for whom Clara Haskil had been named) had both studied piano, and the sister at age 18 had obtained a first prize in piano at the Bucharest Conservatory. How far she might have gone will never be known; Clara Moscuna died of tuberculosis at age 20. Isaac Haskil, a merchant and obviously a music lover, provided music lessons for all his daughters. Lili, the firstborn, became a highly respected piano pedagogue in Bucharest; Jeanne, the youngest, played violin in orchestras; and Clara became a master pianist.

Her talent for the piano appeared at age three when her mother discovered that, without any instruction, Clara could play the pieces she heard her sister Lili practicing. Mme. Haskil quickly started teaching Clara, and after her husband died in 1899 she supported her family, with help from her brother Isaac Moscuna, by teaching piano and giving language lessons.

At the end of that same year (1899) Clara's innate skills astounded Georges Stefanesco, a professor of voice at the Bucharest Conservatory. As a test, he played a Mozart piece she had never heard. She not only immediately played it back to him, but repeated it, transposed to another key. That feat may have decided her future. After another year of study with her mother, in 1901 she entered the class of a Mme. Zenide at the Bucharest Conservatory. Her amazing performances soon attracted the attention of the Queen of Romania, who provided a scholarship for advanced studies.

Had her father lived, Clara Haskil's own life might have been entirely different—and happier. She might have remained with her family, instead of being taken over, at age 7, by her uncle Avram Moscuna, an austere, dominating bachelor. In April 1902 he took her to Vienna to explore possibilities for her further education. He first had her play for Anton Door, the celebrated Austrian pianist, and she so impressed Door that he published an article about her in the Vienna *Neue Freie Presse*. "This child is a miracle," he wrote. "She has never had any music lessons. She was only shown the value and names of the notes. More did not seem necessary, for every piece of music that is played to her she repeats by ear without mistake, providing she can manage it with her small hand. . . . Indeed, even more, she plays a work in any key which is suggested to her. When I put an easy sonata by Beethoven before her she sight-read it on the spot."

Her teacher in Vienna was Richard Robert, the remarkable pedagogue who numbered Rudolf Serkin and George Szell among his students. Robert and his wife were extremely kind to her. Having no children of their own, they became a second family, and she spent a great deal of time with them. At her first public appearances in November 1903, the eight-year-old Clara played the Mozart Concerto in A Major, K. 488, with Hilda Stern accompanying on a second piano, and also the Haydn Trio in G Major, with Arthur Mikolasch and Rudolf Schmidt Altherr. On 16 November 1903 she gave a recital in Vienna, playing a Schubert Sonatina (with Franz Mittler playing violin), a Handel Fughetta, a Grieg *Albumblatt* and some Variations by Beethoven. The next year she performed at a Liszt festival held in Vienna's famed Bösendorfer Hall.

She was getting exceptional reviews and lots of attention in Vienna, but her Uncle Avram decided she must go to the Paris Conservatory, at that time considered the finest in the world. Although hating to lose her, Robert agreed and prepared Clara for a final recital, a long, eclectic program (15 April 1905) including a Prelude and Fugue of Bach, a Rondo by C. P. E. Bach, Variations in B-flat Major by Handel, Weber's *Rondo brillante* in E-flat Major, Schumann's Prophet Bird and a Chopin Polonaise. Only 10 years old, Clara Haskil played like one twice her age. As wonderful as that was, she must have dreaded leaving the kindly Roberts, who during her three years in Vienna had helped so much in filling the terrible emptiness she felt without her mother and sisters. Apart from her beloved music, she had a largely dreary, lonely childhood, and she grew up to be a shy, self-effacing, reserved woman.

Clara and the uncompromising Avram presented themselves at the Paris Conservatory in the autumn of 1905, with a letter of introduction from Richard Robert. Gabriel Fauré, director of the Conservatory, decided that Clara would be eligible for the class reserved for foreign students, and he asked Joseph Morpain, one of his own former students, to prepare her for the Conservatory's entrance examination. (Like Robert, Morpain took an instant liking to Clara and remained a close friend until his death.) For some reason, perhaps because of her young age, Clara was not immediately enrolled in the Conservatory, but spent two uninspiring years in the elementary class of Mme. Allen-Chené. In 1907 she began studying with Alfred Cortot, but to the end of her life Haskil would declare that she obtained very little from him. She may have seen little of him. Cortot, only 30 years old at the time and very busy with his own career, often turned over his class to Lazare Lévy or Mme. Giraud-Letarse.

In 1910, at age 15, Clara Haskil obtained a *premier prix* at the Paris Conservatory from a jury that included Fauré, Moriz Moszkowski, Raoul Pugno and Ricardo Viñes. At graduation she received her degree, a grand piano from the house of Pleyel and 400 francs from an anonymous donor—one of the first of a succession of patrons and friends who provided Haskil comfort and support. About this time her uncle was taken ill while in Bucharest, and Clara's mother and Jeanne came to be with her in Paris. But they were barely settled when Avram returned and moved in with Clara, forcing Mme. Haskil and Jeanne to find other lodging.

After graduation Haskil decided to start giving concerts rather than working with another teacher. In 1911 she played in Vienna, Paris, Bucharest, St. Gall (Switzerland), Milan and Zurich. She received warm reviews for a Zurich recital (17 July 1911): "This truly extraordinary talent already possesses a maturity in the taste, style, plastic form, rhythm and personality which, with much older great artists, comes from a life of experience, disillusion and struggle." (Spycket, *Clara Haskil*) Ferruccio Busoni heard this recital (her program included the Bach-Busoni Chaconne) and invited her to study with him in Berlin. She never did (her mother and uncle vetoed the proposal), and regretted it all her life.

Haskil gave several concerts in 1913 (Monte Carlo, Paris, Lausanne) before the progressing scoliosis forced her to give up playing. Hospitalized for four years in a clinic at Berck-sur-Mer, France, she was initially confined in a plaster body cast, later a modified cast that at least allowed her once in a while to play the piano. It was a miserable period of her life. A patron sent her to Switzerland to recuperate fully, and in December of 1918 Haskil finally returned to Paris, determined to resume her career, but not at all sure how to go about it. Incredibly, despite those four years away from the piano, her unique gifts, as she soon proved, remained intact. She was scheduled to play Mozart's Concerto in B-flat Major, K. 595, with Hermann Scherchen and the orchestra of the *Société des Concerts du Conservatoire*, but at the only rehearsal, the evening before the concert, it was discovered that the publisher had sent the wrong orchestral parts—those for the Mozart Concerto in D Minor, K. 466, a work Haskil had not played in two years. Nevertheless, she played the concerto flawlessly, and at the end of the rehearsal the orchestra rose spontaneously and gave her a rousing cheer.

Clara Haskil's career progressed at a snail's pace, and in retrospect we can only speculate as to the reasons why. Incapable of any kind of display, Haskil never projected herself (she crept onto the stage, as one writer put it); besides, she was struggling in an era favoring flamboyance, and her quietly eloquent playing might easily have been overlooked. More than anything else, Haskil's lack of self-confidence must have affected her career. She seldom thought that she had played well, and sometimes feared she had played so badly that she would come off the stage near tears and utterly inconsolable.

At first, between 1920 and 1924, she played only within her own familiar geographical circle—Switzerland, France, Romania, Belgium, Austria, Italy. She made her American debut at Aeolian Hall in New York on 3 November 1924, and then gave several performances in Boston. She first played in England on 14 January 1926, in Manchester, where she played the Bach Concerto in D Minor and Chopin's Concerto No. 2 with the Hallé Orchestra, conducted by Sir Hamilton Harty. During December 1926 she gave five performances of the Schumann Concerto, op. 54, with Leopold Stokowski and the Philadelphia Orchestra.

In 1927 Haskil and Avram took a flat in Paris, and she lived there until 1940. She continued to tour, slightly enlarging her European touring circle with performances in Holland, Germany and Spain. After her uncle died in 1934, she was, for the first time in her 39 years, free to make her own way. It was the beginning of a new era for Clara Haskil. In 1937 D. E. Inghelbrecht founded the *Orchestre National de la Radiodiffusion Française* (Jeanne Haskil was a member), and often invited Clara to perform with his young, enthusiastic musicians. On 10 April 1937 she played the Brahms Concerto No. 2 with them, a great success even though she had learned the score in just eight days. That year she filled about 20 performing engagements, a very modest showing compared with the careers of fellow virtuosos; nevertheless, her career was moving ahead steadily, if very slowly.

She first met Dinu Lipatti (introduced by Nadia Boulanger) at the home of the Princesse de Polignac, a faithful Haskil supporter. He was 19 years old, she was middle-aged, but they formed a devoted, lasting friendship. When in the same city, they either met or talked on the phone daily. Even though apart most of the time, Lipatti and "Dear Clarinette," as he called her, maintained a steady correspondence. In one of his *Libertates* articles about musical life in Paris, Lipatti described a Haskil performance: "The Piano Concerto in E Flat by Mozart, which I heard recently in a magical interpretation given by the well-known artist, Clara Haskil, convinced me once again of the grandeur and extraordinary organic structure of this masterpiece. Clara Haskil's interpretation was truly astonishing, and she surpassed herself in this performance." (Tanasescu)

A foreigner living in France and, even worse, also a Jew, Haskil had no choice but to get out of Paris before the Germans arrived to take over the city.

In the spring of 1941 her sister Jeanne and a few musicians from the *Orchestre National* took Haskil along on a precarious nighttime escape to the unoccupied zone. They stopped at Rennes, then went on to Marseilles, where French Radio had relocated. Always frail, it was a hard trip for Haskil, and she gratefully accepted an invitation to stay with the Countess Pastré, a generous patron of the arts who had opened her chateau at Montredon, on the sea near Marseilles, to refugee artists.

Haskil's troubles had not ended. While at Montredon she began experiencing migraine headaches and eyesight problems, and in May 1942 underwent surgery for the removal of a tumor on her optic nerve. Finally, in November 1942, just a few days before Hitler's troops occupied Marseilles, Haskil obtained a Swiss visa and escaped to Switzerland, where Jeanne was now working as a violinist. Haskil became a Swiss citizen in 1949 and lived in Vevey for the rest of her life.

With the end of the war, the fragile but indomitable Haskil tried to pick up the threads of her concert career. In October of 1946, after a five-year absence, she played in Paris; shortly thereafter she performed a series of radio broadcasts for the BBC; and on 22 December 1946 she played a recital at Wigmore Hall. She also made her first professional recording, for the Decca label, performing Beethoven's Concerto No. 4 with the London Philharmonic Orchestra, conducted by Carlo Zecchi.

The year 1949 stands out as a turning point in Clara Haskil's career. A Dutch impresario named Konig organized a series of Dutch concerts and radio broadcasts for her, and while not financially profitable, they were warmly received by critics. As her reputation spread, Haskil began to earn enough to support herself independently of her benefactors. In 1952 she played about 70 concerts, in 1954 about 80 concerts and in 1955 about 85 concerts. She played with the finest orchestras and conductors and, an ideal chamber musician, with great string players—Casals, Ysaÿe, Enescu, Szigeti, Stern. In 1957 France rewarded her artistry with an appointment as *Chevalier de la Légion d'honneur.*

In 1949 Clara Haskil was already 54 years old and had been concertizing for more than a quarter-century. Fame had come to her very late, and she enjoyed it for just one brief decade. Her delicate health kept failing, but she kept performing. In 1956 she gave four performances of the Beethoven Concerto No. 3 with Charles Münch conducting the Boston Symphony Orchestra and two performances of the Mozart Concerto in D Minor, K. 466, with Paul Paray and the New York Philharmonic-Symphony. She also made recordings, particularly two memorable performances with her friend Geza Anda (see Discog.). But a severe bout with pneumonia in November 1957 ended her 1957–58 season, and although she recovered, thereafter a severe heart problem complicated her life. After three months away from the piano, without even practicing, Haskil, with Geza Anda, gave a performance in Lucerne (16 April 1958) of Mozart's Concerto in E-flat Major for two pianos, with Joseph Keilberth conducting the *Schweizerisches Festspielorchester.*

For the final seven years of her life Haskil had a happy, rewarding partnership with violinist Arthur Grumiaux. Like all their concerts, one in Paris on 1 December 1960 was eminently successful. A few days later she traveled to

Brussels to play a recital of sonatas with Grumiaux, but shortly after arriving at the Midi railroad station, she stumbled, fell down a flight of steps and was taken to the clinic at Longchamps in Brussels. An operation proved unsuccessful, and Clara Haskil died early in the morning on 7 December 1960.

Clara Haskil never taught, even in those lean times when she had to turn to generous patrons for support, and it is easy to see why she avoided teaching. To begin with, the reserved, insecure Haskil was, as she expressed it, incapable of giving the least advice. Besides, one must remember her precarious health, the almost daily pain. Although she never taught, she would listen to young pianists and comment on their playing, often with pertinent remarks more meaningful than any lessons could be. After one young pianist finished playing the first movement of Schubert's Sonata in B-flat Major for Haskil, she said, "'You didn't hold this chord long enough.' When asked: 'But does it matter, it is only a quaver longer?' Haskil replied: 'Yes, but a quaver in eternity.' She observed the smallest detail without drawing attention to it, so that each musical event sounded inevitable but never predictable." (Feuchtwanger)

Haskil had an abundance of natural gifts—large, elastic hands, a remarkable memory and unerring musical instincts. Her memory dumbfounded her colleagues, and there are numerous anecdotes. Alfred Cortot, for instance, told of preparing an immense schedule of works for Haskil to go through with him in the upcoming year, and how within three months she had mastered every work on the list. Haskil also had an unbelievable sight-reading gift. At first sight of a score, she could not only play all the notes but grasp the whole musical essence of the work. With such gifts, it is no wonder that she had an incredible ease at the piano, that the music seemed to flow out naturally and spontaneously.

If we sift through the reviews and articles, Haskil emerges as a pianist of "delicious" sensitivity, one who observed the smallest detail in the music without drawing attention to it. And for that reason, one had to listen attentively to her playing or else miss the essence of her art. She had a simple approach, a profound sense of style and she played quietly, lightly, gracefully, but always with absolute authority. Writers use the term "luminous" to describe her brand of brilliance, a virtuosity due to subtle shadings rather than pyrotechnics. She had an astonishing tonal range, and one felt that she was incapable of making any sound that would have offended the composer. A faithful interpreter, Haskil made the listener feel as though the music flowed directly, without intrusion, from the composer to the listener.

Haskil owed her fame to her interpretations of Mozart, Schubert and Schumann, and in her later years was considered to be the foremost Mozart player of her time. But she played many other composers (Scarlatti, Beethoven, Chopin, Brahms, Falla, Ravel). She often played from contemporary repertoire (Bartók, Hindemith, Badings) and would play unusual (at that time) items, such as the Schubert Sonata in B-flat Major and the Schumann *Waldscenen* and *Bunte Blätter* in their entirety.

Although announced as Haskil's first recital in New York, her Town Hall program on 25 January 1927—music by Bach-d'Albert, Bach-Busoni, Schumann, Chopin, Brahms, Liszt, Debussy, Ravel and Liapounoff—took place some two years after she initially played in that city. Reaction was guardedly favorable. "She showed unmistakable talent in the form of a musical tone, fleet fingers, warmth in the playing of melodic passages and considerable virtuoso instinct. . . . A certain lack of musical experience was probably responsible for too great a care for notes and a too meticulous regard for technical details in the impressionistic pieces [Debussy, Ravel]." (*NYT*, 26 Jan 1927) Paradoxically, this "care for notes" and this "regard for details" were to be part and parcel of Haskil's style.

Actually, Haskil had first appeared in New York on 3 November 1924. At that recital, "Her Chopin group was really captivating, but for some reason Schumann [Symphonic Etudes] escaped her." (*NYT*, 4 Nov 1924) However, the reviewer neglected to clarify his misgivings.

Haskil, nearly 56 years old when she made her London debut (22 Dec 1946) at Wigmore Hall, impressed critics with her mature, authoritative interpretations and her extremely delicate tone control. In three Scarlatti sonatas written for the harpsichord, she "exploited the dynamic possibilities of the piano without sacrificing the crispness and sparkle." In Beethoven's Op. 111, "every variation of the Arietta was satisfying to the ear as a musical moment in itself yet fitted into a perfectly judged scheme embracing the magnitude of the sonata as a whole." (*TL*, 23 Dec 1946)

On 2 November 1956, her first U.S. appearance in 30 years, Haskil played the Beethoven Concerto No. 3 with Charles Münch and the Boston Symphony Orchestra. She played the concerto "with a rare kind of fire, poetry and sadness." Boston critics were ecstatic. "The Herald's Rudolph Elie called it 'one of those magical revelations that occurs in music once in a generation . . . the most beautiful performance of Beethoven's *Third Concerto* I ever heard or expect to hear again'." (*Time*, 12 Nov 1956)

Wrote one critic of her London recital of 16 June 1957: "She avoids all flamboyance at the keyboard and concentrates her fastidious technique into the spirit of the music itself." (*MT*, Aug 1957) An acknowledged master of the Romantic repertoire, Haskil was also a supreme interpreter of Mozart concertos. She played them more than those of any other composer, not all of them, as do some of our contemporary virtuosos, but what she played she played exquisitely.

Take, for example, the D Minor, K. 466, known for its romantic *Sturm und Drang*. On 15 November 1956, when Haskil played it at Carnegie Hall with the New York Philharmonic-Symphony, Paul Paray conducting, it became a "glowing experience. . . . Her playing had firmness of design and profundity of perception. Here was an artist of power as well as sensitivity." (*NYT*, 16 Nov 1956) And from another reviewer: "I was entirely unprepared for her powerful phrasing and projection of the piano's opening statement, and the similar force of her playing throughout the work. It was the performance of a first-rate musician and pianist." (*Nat*, 8 Dec 1956) Haskil's performance (6 April 1959) of the same concerto with Colin Davis and the Philharmonia Orchestra at Festival Hall illuminated Haskil's salient Mozart style: "One of the marvels of her intensely concentrated performance was the tension she could sustain throughout. . . . Her feeling was of the truest kind, deep down below the surface, while her piano playing was a marvel of limpid clarity." (*TL*, 7 April 1959)

On 3 April 1959 Haskil played Mozart's Concerto in B-flat Major, K. 595, with the Philharmonia Orchestra, conducted by André Vandernoot, at London's Festival Hall. "This was exquisite in performance and wholly admirable in interpretation. Her playing had about it the intimacy of chamber music though it was not lacking in the more imposing qualities of noble pianistic display." (*TL*, 4 April 1959) And on 9 April Haskil played the Mozart Concerto in A Major, K. 488, again with Vandernoot and the PO. In addition to the usual praises, one critic found exactly the right summation, writing that the pianist "simply expunged from the concerto what was temporal and found instead what is eternal." (*TL*, 10 April 1959)

Haskil felt uncomfortable in the silence of the recording studio. Even though plagued by stage fright, she always needed an audience in order to give her very best. This is what makes some of her recorded concerts so exceptional (*Clara Haskil en Concert.*, see Discog.). Haskil recorded consistently only after World War II. In the late 1940s she recorded (78 rpm) the Beethoven Concerto No. 4, accompanied by the London Philharmonic Orchestra, Carlo Zecchi conducting. In 1950 she recorded the Bach Concerto in F Minor with Pablo Casals conducting the Prades Festival Orchestra. Her association with Philips began in 1951, with the Schumann Piano Concerto.

Haskil was at the height of her powers when she recorded the Schumann Concerto with Willem van Otterloo and the Hague Philharmonic Orchestra (see Discog.), and her unaffected simplicity and engaging eloquence were noticeably in evidence: "Every detail is most sensitively cherished yet never does she allow pursuit of expression to undermine structure. Her *ritenutos* and tempo changes are exactly as Schumann requests them, no more, no less." (*Gram*, June 1988)

Given Haskil's consistently fine performances, it is difficult to choose among the many recordings that she made. Her reading of Chopin's Concerto No. 2, made the year of her death, is extraordinary. Interestingly, she used her teacher Cortot's arrangement, where the long initial *tutti* is shortened and woodwinds are added from time to time. Accompanied by Igor Markevich and the Lamoureux Orchestra, Haskil shows that her talents were admirably suited to Romantic repertoire: "More beautiful playing of the *Larghetto* could scarcely be imagined: in her hands this rapturous movement is quite magical. While producing brilliance when it is called for, there is always refinement." (*Gram*, Aug 1986)

A number of Haskil's Mozart concerto recordings have been reissued on CD. Only a month before her death she recorded two of these—K. 466 in D Minor and K. 491 in C Minor—with Igor Markavitch and the Lamoureux Orchestra. One reviewer applauded the "neatness, poise and shapeliness of her playing . . . and her feeling for Mozartian style." (*Gram*, Nov 1984)

Other memorable recorded performances include Falla's Nights in the Gardens of Spain, again with Markevitch and the Lamoureux, where Haskil "brings to it all the refinement and sensitivity that made her one of the world's leading Mozart players. By concentrating on the melodic rather than the sensuous aspect of it she gives the piece a certain steely quality that is entirely suited to its Spanish atmosphere." (*TL*, 15 July 1961) And her reading of Schumann's Abegg Variations, op. 1, impressively illustrates her incredible technique and range of tone color.

In February 1995 (*Gramophone*) it was announced that Philips will bring out *Clara Haskil: The Legacy,* a 12-CD set which includes all the recordings Haskil made for that label between 1951 and 1960. This includes the solo repertoire (3 CDs), the concertos (4 CDs) and the chamber music (5 CDs).

SELECTED REFERENCES

Amyot, Etienne. "Clara Haskil: a memoir." *Recorded Sound*, July–Oct 1976, pp. 557–558.

"Clara Haskil concert programmes." *Recorded Sound*, July–Oct 1976, pp. 559–576.

Feuchtwanger, Peter. "Clara Haskil." *Recorded Sound*, July–Oct 1976, pp. 550–556.

Gavoty, Bernard. *Clara Haskil*. Geneva: René Kister, 1963. (Series Great Concert Artists).

Gelatt, Roland. "Music Makers." *High Fidelity*, Feb 1961, p. 57.

"Grande Ambiance." *Time*, 12 Nov 1956, pp. 116–117.

Obituary. *Hi Fidelity*, Feb 1961, p. 57. *Musical Times*, Jan 1961, p. 39. *New York Times*, 8 Dec 1961, p. 35.

"Piano Concertos from Mozart to Prokofiev." *The Times* (London), 15 July 1961, p. 11.

Russell, Sheridan. "Some recollections of Clara Haskil." *Recorded Sound*, July–Oct 1976, p. 558.

Spycket, Jerome. *Clara Haskil*. Lausanne: Van De Velde/Payot, 1975.

————. "Clara Haskil." Liner notes for *Clara Haskil en Concert* (see Discog.).

Tanasescu, Dragos, and Grigore Bargauanu. *Lipatti*. White Plains, N.Y.: Pro/Am Music Resources Inc., 1971.

Wolfensberger, Rita. *Clara Haskil*. Bern und Stuttgart: Scherz Verlag, 1961.

See also Bibliography: New/Gro; Ran/Kon; Rat/Cle; Sch/Gre.

SELECTED REVIEWS

GM: 15 Jan 1926; 30 April 1956. *MA*: 1 Dec 1956. *MT*: Aug 1957. *Nat*: 8 Dec 1956. *NYT*: 4 Nov 1924; 12 Nov 1925; 26 Jan 1927; 16 Nov 1956. *TL*: 23 Dec 1946; 17 June 1957; 4 April 1959; 7 April 1959; 10 April 1959; 8 June 1959.

SELECTED DISCOGRAPHY

Bach: Concerto for 2 pianos and orchestra in C Major, BWV 1061 (with Geza Anda). Mozart: Concerto for 2 pianos and orchestra in E-flat Major, K. 365

(with Geza Anda). EMI *Références* CDH 7 63492-2. Galliera/Philharmonia, rec. 1956.

Bach: Toccata in E Minor, BWV 914. Beethoven: Sonata in C Minor, op. 111. Debussy: Two Etudes. Ravel: *Sonatine*. Scarlatti: Sonata in B Minor, K. 87; Sonata in C Major, K. 132; Sonata in E-flat Major, K. 193. Schumann: Variations on ABEGG, op. 1. (recorded live 11 April 1953, Ludwigsburg). Stradivarius STR 13602 (CD) or AS Disc 124.

Beethoven: Concerto No. 3 in C Minor, op. 37. Sonata in E-flat Major, op. 31, no. 3. Philips 434 168-2. Markevitch/Lamoureux SO.

Beethoven: Sonata in D Minor, op. 31, no. 2; Sonata in E-flat Major, op. 31, no. 3. Philips 420088-2.

Beethoven: Sonata in E-flat Major, op. 31, no. 3. Mozart: Variations on a Minuet of Duport, K. 573. Schubert: Sonata in A Minor, D. 845. Schumann: *Kinderscenen*, op. 15 (recorded live 7 Sept 1956, Besançon Festival). Music and Arts CD-542.

Chopin: Concerto No. 2 in F Minor, op. 21 (Markevitch/Lamoureux). Mozart: Concerto in E-flat Major, K. 271 (Sacher/Vienna SO); Concerto in D Minor, K. 466 (Markevitch/Lamoureux); Concerto in A Major, K. 488 (Sacher/Vienna SO); Rondo in A Major, K. 386 (Paumgartner/Vienna SO). Falla: Nights in the Gardens of Spain (Markevitch/Lamoureux). Schumann: Variations on ABEGG, op. 1; *Waldscenen*, op. 82; *Kinderscenen*, op. 15. Philips 426964-2 (4 CDs).

Clara Haskil at the Ludwigsburg Festival, 11 April 1953. Bach: Toccata in E Minor, BWV 914. Beethoven: Sonata in C Minor, op. 111. Debussy: Etudes, Nos. 7, 10. Scarlatti: Three Sonatas. Schumann: *"Abegg"* Variations, op. 1. Ravel: *Sonatine*. Music and Arts CD-859.

Clara Haskil en Concert. Beethoven: Concerto No. 4 in G Major, op. 58 (Cluytens/*Orch. Nat.*). Chopin: Concerto No. 2 in F Minor, op. 21 (Kubelík/*Orch. du Cons.*). Mozart: Concerto in F Major, K. 459 (Silvestri/ON); Concerto in C Minor, K. 491(Cluytens/ON). *Disques Montaignes* TCE 8780 (2 CDs). Series *Les grands concerts inédits du théâtre des Champs-Elysées*.

Clara Haskil Plays Mozart Concertos. Concerto in E-flat Major, K. 271 (Ackermann/Northwest German RO, 1954); Concerto In D Minor, K. 466 (Munch/Boston SO, 1956). Music and Arts CD-715.

Clara Haskil Plays Mozart and Beethoven. Mozart: Concerto in B-flat Major, K. 595 (Klemperer/Kölner Gürzenich SO, 1956). Beethoven: Concerto No. 3 in C Minor, op. 37 (Munch/Boston SO, 1956). Music and Arts CD-716.

Mozart: Concerto in E-flat Major, K. 271; Concerto in F Major, K. 459. *Preludio* PHC-2140 (CD). Schuricht/Stuttgart RSO.

Mozart: Mozart: Concerto in E-flat Major, K. 271; Concerto in A Major, K. 488; Rondo in A Major, K. 386. Philips 420782-2. Sacher/Vienna SO.

Mozart: Concerto in D Minor, K. 466 (Klemperer/Lucerne FO); Concerto in B-flat Major, K. 595 (Klemperer/Kölner Gürzenich SO). AS Disc AS 612 (CD).

Mozart: Concerto in F Major, K. 459 (Fricsay/Berlin PO); Concerto in B-flat Major, K. 595 (Fricsay/Bavarian SO). DG 431872-2.

Schumann: Concerto in A Minor, op. 54. *Kinderscenen*, op. 15; *Waldscenen*, op. 82; Variations on ABEGG, op. 1. Philips 420851-2. Otterloo/The Hague PO.

HESS, MYRA: b. London (Hampstead), England, 25 February 1890; d. London, 25 November 1965.

> The chances are that never in her life was she guilty of an ugly sound. And her interpretations were marked by sanity, lucidity, proportion, grace and style. Dame Myra was one of the most civilized of pianists.
>
> Harold C. Schonberg (*New York Times*, 27 November 1965)

In her richly productive lifetime Myra Hess attracted loyal, loving friends, and their reminiscences (*Myra Hess, By Her Friends*) tell a great deal about both the musician and the woman. Their Myra was a warm and charming companion with a quick wit, delicious humor and a brilliant gift for mimicry. "She made a lifelike Queen Victoria under a lace doily, and her rolled-orange performance of the black-note Study of Chopin was a triumph of skill and ingenuity. . . . My favourite was her imitation of a mechanical piano, correct and deadly." (Lassimonne) Hardly the Victorian that her somber appearance might suggest, Hess was a lifelong smoker, enjoyed a cocktail, loved cards and games and told a very good story. However, she could be fussy about small matters and very critical of professional incompetence, yet friends and critics alike respected and admired her unwavering idealism and honesty.

Julia Myra Hess—to her regret the "Julia" disappeared when she was about three—was the youngest of four children born to Frederick Solomon Hess and Lizzie (Jacobs) Hess, both of German-Jewish ancestry. Her intelligence and strong will came from her stern father, her looks and temperament—small, dark and fun-loving—from her mother. At age five Hess began piano lessons with Mrs. Florence Reason, a neighborhood teacher. By the time she was eight years old Hess had passed the Trinity College aptitude test, becoming the youngest pupil ever to receive a Trinity College Certificate. The next year she made her first public appearance when, as she recalled some 50 years later, her father made her take part in a charity concert.

Thanks to her mother, Hess had a normal childhood despite music's demands and her father's insistence that she perform publicly for money. She attended Oak Hill Park and St. Leonard's schools for girls and continued her musical studies at the Guildhall School of Music with Julian Pascal and Orlando Morgan. While at Guildhall, Hess was awarded the Steinway Medal and, in 1902, the Ada Lewis Scholarship. In the autumn of 1903, at age 13, she entered the Royal Academy of Music, where the Lewis Scholarship provided her with free tuition for the regular three-year course, including two lessons each week with Tobias Matthay, who was to be her only piano teacher and an enormously strong influence throughout her life.

Matthay taught Hess about musical integrity and how to focus her inherent but undisciplined musical instincts. For a final practice before a performance, he taught her to go through the program silently, with the music before her, to keep the ear fresh and the mind alert. That may be why the works Myra Hess played countless times during her long career always retained their freshness. Matthay's final word to all pupils before stepping onstage would be, "Enjoy the music!" Whenever horrible stage nerves struck, always a problem for Hess, remembering Matthay's "enjoy the music" helped to calm her down. In time she passed along that comforting phrase to her own students.

While studying with Matthay, Hess played in concerts all over London as well as at the RAM student concerts, and at graduation in 1906 she took all honors in her class, including the Walter MacFarren Gold Medal for pianoforte. That completed her formal studies. Myra Hess never approached any famous teachers or entered international piano competitions. In her own words, "Matthay left me my individuality and taught me everything else." (McKenna) Hess adored Matthay and his wife and she spent a great deal of time at their home. Every year, even after she had acquired a worldwide reputation, she would preview her season's programs for him, and always turned to him for advice. (After his death in 1945, she paid him the crowning tribute: "He is always beside me when I play.") In 1906 she became his first assistant at the Tobias Matthay Pianoforte School in London, founded in 1905 while he was still teaching at the RAM.

On 14 November 1907 Hess made her London debut, a concert she organized herself, although it is not known who paid the expenses. (Her father would not have helped under any circumstances. His business was close to bankruptcy, and in any case he considered her concert a foolish waste.) Hess hired the Queen's Hall, engaged the New Symphony Orchestra and its young conductor Thomas Beecham, and for her part of the program played the Beethoven Concerto No. 4, Saint-Saëns's Concerto No. 4, Chopin's F-sharp Minor Nocturne and the Etude, op. 25, no. 11. She made a successful debut, but no professional engagements came of it. Knowing that in order to build a reputation she had to keep herself before the public, Hess quickly arranged two recitals (25 Jan and 22 Feb 1908) at Aeolian Hall, charging popular prices to help cover expenses. Later that year she played (2 Sept 1908) Liszt's E-flat Concerto at one of Sir Henry Wood's Promenade Concerts, the first of her more than 90 collaborations with Sir Henry.

In the lean years following her debut Hess taught long hours and seized every opportunity to play, whether in public or at private affairs. She toured Great Britain with the London String Quartet and as a two-piano team with friend Irene Scharrer. She also appeared with singers, among them Nellie Melba and Lotte Lehman, and with violinists, including Fritz Kreisler and Joseph Szigeti. The fees were absurdly low, but these performances kept her name before the public. Years later Hess told a BBC interviewer, "My reputation in England was built by giving a recital every season, and it took every penny I could save to pay for it." (McKenna) No wonder success came slowly. The musical world was not ready for Myra Hess. When she made her debut, the most popular, most successful pianists (Hofmann, Paderewski, Godowsky, for example) were speed and thunder virtuosos, each with a highly personal, freewheeling playing style. Her style—intimate, tasteful, impeccable—was very different. Hess played the notes as written. A purist, she never tampered with the music or the musical pulse, never rearranged the music for spectacular effect.

Myra Hess's first real success came in Holland, where she first toured in 1910 with the violinist Aldo Antonietti. By 1912 she was often performing with chamber groups in Amsterdam. She made her Amsterdam orchestral debut (10 Feb 1912) with an exquisite performance of the Schumann Concerto in A Minor with the *Concertgebouw* Orchestra, Willem Mengelberg conducting. Stunning reviews propelled her into immediate stardom in Holland. She grew to love the Dutch people, and they in turn remained one of her most faithful audiences. On that first Holland tour Hess and Antonietti had fallen in love, but he wanted marriage and children while Hess's intense devotion to the piano and her ambition for a concert career far outweighed her desire for marriage. Later admirers Mischa Elman and Benno Moiseiwitsch proposed marriage with no restrictions on her career, but Hess was completely absorbed in and dedicated to music. Later on she would say of her decision not to marry, "One sacrifices a great deal, but there are compensations."

Living at home with her parents had become increasingly unpleasant. Having declared bankruptcy, her father insisted that she stop losing money paying for her own recitals and play the piano in music halls to help support the family. In the early summer of 1914 Hess moved into her own lodgings, teaching long hours to support herself, then practicing far into the night. World War I presented performing opportunities that otherwise may not have materialized. Between 1918 and 1920 she made more than 50 appearances with orchestras in London and throughout the provinces. Myra Hess had finally arrived in Great Britain, and by 1920 she was playing nearly 100 concerts a year.

The critic César Saerchinger, who had heard Hess play many times in London, convinced the New York agent Annie Friedberg to book Hess for an extensive American tour. She began with an intimate New York recital (12 Jan 1922) at Steinway Hall and made her formal debut (17 Jan 1922) at Aeolian Hall. Less than a hundred people were scattered about the 1,200-seat auditorium; however, Henry Krehbiel and Richard Aldrich, two leading New York critics, attended and wrote exceptionally favorable reviews. Requests for bookings flooded Annie Friedberg's office, and she began organizing next season's Hess tours. Meanwhile, Hess completed that first long tour across America and into Canada. She traveled alone, got homesick and exhausted, but she made lasting friends in America, especially Frederick and Julia Steinway. In future years Hess always toured with a secretary-companion.

America seems to have been a catalyst for bringing out Myra Hess's mature creative powers. Her regular and highly successful North American tours earned her a reputation not only as a great woman pianist but as one of the world's greatest musicians. American audiences loved her even though, as Annie Friedberg fretted, she never packaged herself. Friedberg worried about Hess's sober, unpretentious onstage appearance and the fact that Hess played what was then considered serious, even austere, programs. Hess hated publicity, shunned grand social events, continued to wear mostly black onstage and never included popular numbers on her programs.

Her youthful repertoire had been large and included contemporary music and virtuoso pieces, but by the end of the 1920s Hess had honed her repertoire to what she liked to call "the roast beef of music," meaning Bach, Beethoven, Brahms, Mozart, Scarlatti, Schubert and Schumann, with occasional portions of "the shrimp cocktails of music," meaning Debussy and Ravel. She played all the Mozart concertos, Beethoven Concertos Nos. 5 and 6, the Brahms concertos; also the Schumann and Grieg concertos, and the Franck Symphonic Variations. And she played often. A typical itinerary included four months in North America, the rest of the season divided between Holland and Great Britain. She played in a few other European countries, but Holland remained her favorite. After 1956 she regularly participated in the Edinburgh Festival. Hess, who had a very special relationship with Pablo Casals, appeared at the Casals Festival at Perpignan (1951) and at Prades (1952), where she played sonatas, trios and piano quartets with artists like Isaac Stern, Joseph Szigeti and the "beloved Pau" himself.

In 1936 King George V acknowledged Hess's success with a C. B. E. (Commander of the Order of the British Empire) award. But by 1939 the years of following a relentlessly heavy schedule made her hate traveling. She also detested having to arrange playing dates two or three years in advance. Nervous, irritable and subject to periods of depression, Hess was dreading an upcoming seven-month tour of America and Australia when Britain's entry into World War II (3 Sept 1939) completely changed her life. She canceled the tour and offered her services in the evacuation of London children to the country.

London's wartime blackout created a dismal cultural blackout as well. Theaters, movies and concert halls were closed, museums and art galleries were stripped of their art works. The British people had only the BBC radio, and that offered mostly news and endless emergency instructions. To relieve the strain and soothe war-torn nerves, Hess conceived the idea of giving lunchtime cham-ber-music concerts somewhere in central London, charging low prices so that all classes of people could attend. When she mentioned her idea to friends in late September 1939, Denise Lassimonne suggested giving the concerts in the National Gallery, almost empty because its art treasures were stored in deep caves in Wales. Within an incredibly short time, friends with connections helped to turn Hess's idea into a reality, and she herself played the first concert (10 Oct 1939), just in case only a handful of people attended. Far from a failure, nearly a thousand people crammed into the National Gallery dome to hear the music, while others had to be turned away.

The National Gallery Concerts—they quickly expanded to include solo recitals, chamber music, orchestral and choral music performances—continued without interruption five days a week for six and one-half years despite the blitz, bombs and rockets. If not touring Britain, making speeches or broadcasting to North America for war aid, Myra Hess was at the Gallery. She took a large part in planning the programs and played 146 concerts herself. For her wartime ser-vices, King George V in June 1941 made her a D. B. E. (Dame Commander of the British Empire). On 17 January 1942 she became the 48th recipient of the Royal Philharmonic Society's Gold Medal, being only the second woman to receive that honor. Over the years Hess received honorary doctorates from seven British universities.

Myra Hess wanted desperately to continue the National Gallery Concerts after the war, not only to offer music for all audiences but to give young, unknown musicians a chance to play in public. The Gallery trustees, however, decided that the National Gallery was meant only for paintings, and the final concert—the 1,698th performance—was played (10 April 1946) by the Griller Quartet. The £15,000 raised over the years by the one-shilling admission price went to the Musicians' Benevolent Fund. The war years took a tremendous toll on Hess's stamina and health, but what the Gallery concerts did for the morale of war-weary Londoners can never be truly measured.

Her first postwar tour of America—beginning with a Town Hall recital (12 Oct 1946)—was triumphant and exhausting. She was 56 years old and drained by the war years, but for Myra Hess a life without her music was inconceivable. She simply could not stop. In 1949 she began to use her music onstage at times. Some New York critics disapproved, but Hess never lost her loyal audiences in the United States, Canada and Holland. In the 1950s she usually restricted herself to two tours a year: an American tour in late winter to early spring and a Dutch tour in mid-autumn. During these "vintage years," as Marian McKenna would call them, she gave 14 sold-out recitals (Dec 1946–Feb 1959) at Carnegie Hall, a remarkable achievement matched only by great pianists like Rubinstein, Horowitz and Paderewski. (Myra Hess idolized Paderewski and always kept his picture on her piano to remind her, as she put it, "of what beautiful piano playing is." It is interesting that she, a "purist" pianist, considered Paderewski, a pianist who so often played wholeheartedly with his personality, the greatest of all pianists.)

After a heart attack in September 1960, Dame Myra was rarely free from some kind of circulatory problem. Her 1960 concerts were canceled, but she returned to America to play at Yale on 24 January 1961 and at Hunter College on 28 January 1961. Within a week she suffered a cerebral thrombosis that paralyzed her left side. Although by April she was able to return home to London, she never fully recovered but steadily deteriorated, mentally and physically. She should have retired then, but having dedicated herself so exclusively to music, she could not give up. On 8 September 1961 she played the Beethoven Concerto No. 4 at Albert Hall with Sir Adrian Boult; on 27 September played two Mozart concertos (K. 414, K. 457) with Harry Blech and a chamber orchestra at Royal Festival Hall; and she made her final public appearance (31 Oct 1961), playing the Mozart Concerto, K. 488, with Boult and the London Philharmonic Orchestra. Fittingly enough, this was a gala concert marking the 21st anniversary of the Battle of Britain. Almost exactly 21 years earlier Dame Myra had played that same concerto at one of the National Gallery Concerts.

She recorded two programs for the BBC in December and January but, finally facing her condition, she asked that one not be broadcast. A press release on 2 April 1962 announced that Dame Myra had canceled all engagements because of rheumatism in her hands and that her pupil Stephen Bishop-Kovacevich would substitute for her at the Proms in August. Of course, it was more than rheumatism. Seriously ill and knowing she could never play again, she retreated into a deep depression. Since she lived beyond her powers to perform and performing had been her whole life, Myra Hess's last three years were full of sadness.

Dame Myra preferred playing to teaching. She taught out of necessity at the beginning of her career (about 1910 to 1920) when she was struggling to get public notice and paying for her own recitals. She taught again at the end of her career. Every lesson with Hess began with a pair of Preludes and Fugues from the Well-Tempered Clavier, just as all her life she herself had begun every practice session with some of those works. Eventually she began many of her recital programs with three Bach Preludes and Fugues.

Hess will be remembered also for her hauntingly beautiful piano arrangement of Bach's chorale "Jesu, Joy of Man's Desiring" (Cantata No. 147). She made it in 1920, began to play it for friends and occasionally performed it as an encore. In 1926 Oxford University Press published the first of many printings. She later made a two-piano arrangement and one for four hands, but it is with the solo work that her name has become lastingly associated. Hess once admitted having made more money on that single arrangement than from all her performances of "unadulterated Bach."

Making music meant everything to Myra Hess. She had no other life and allowed nothing—not love or family or duty—to interfere with her art. Howard Ferguson, a longtime friend and colleague who knew Hess very well, felt that after World War II her playing showed a new dimension, that though it always had been intensely musical and aglow with warmth and humor, after the war "there was an added serenity and depth that enabled her to communicate the subtlest essence of composers such as Mozart and Schubert, and of works like the last three Beethoven sonatas." (*MT*, Jan 1966) In his memoirs Sir Henry Wood, another close colleague and friend, recalled Dame Myra's first London Promenade Concert (1908), when she played the Liszt Concerto No. 1: "Myra Hess has never lost the fascination she exerted over her audience then. She is perhaps best known for her rich, romantic interpretation of the Schumann concerto but she displays no less musical style—which is often intense—when she plays the Brahms concerto in B flat." (Woo/My, see Bibliog.)

Like Sir Henry Wood, the finest critics were consistently fascinated by Myra Hess's playing. Her Town Hall recital of 8 November 1930 earned this accolade: "The playing of Miss Hess grows each season in resource and charm, but, happily, it does not change in essentials. Her style is the product of artistic traits deep within her. Its development is steady, consistent, inevitable, and it seems to grow richer every year." (*NYT*, 9 Nov 1930)

Hess's orchestral appearances received the same laudatory reviews, particularly her performances of Beethoven, Mozart and Schumann. When she played (10 Jan 1931) the Beethoven Concerto No. 4 with Serge Koussevitzky and the Boston Symphony Orchestra at Carnegie Hall, New York's leading critics outdid each other in praise. "The program would have been memorable if only for the spell of Miss Hess's performance. . . . Miss Hess was destined by nature for the interpretation of this work." (*NYT*, 11 Jan 1931)

Her Town Hall program on 20 January 1934 was hardly tailored for the general public: the Bach Italian Concerto and French Suite No. 5 and Brahms's colossal Sonata, op. 5. Yet one reviewer mentions the overflowing audience, remarking that Miss Hess could fill Town Hall any time and as many times as she wished. "She was always a poet, sensitive and exquisite, finely touched and richly gifted, and an interpreter of the sacerdotal kind—dedicated and absorbed and self-effacing. But she has ripened from a lyric poet into an epical and dramatic one." (*NYHT*, 21 Jan 1934)

A review of Dame Myra's Los Angeles recital—Bach, Beethoven, Schumann—of 25 March 1957 accurately describes the essential characteristics of her playing: "One forgot all about technique and tone and all the other argot of musical description and simply reveled in the music itself, revealed with such clairvoyance that one constantly had the feeling of overhearing the ideal image that must have been in the minds of Bach, Beethoven and Schumann." (*LAT*, 26 March 1957)

Many Hess recordings are again available. She began her recording career in the United States in 1928 with Columbia Records, recording around 20 compositions during that one year. Despite the primitive recording techniques, several of these records, made at the height of her youthful mastery, are a joy to hear. The Schubert Sonata in A Major, D. 664 (see Discog.), for example, has the special freshness, lyricism and gorgeous tone quality that were inimitably Dame Myra's own. At this stage of her career she had an eclectic repertoire, performing and recording Bach, Griffes, Falla, Debussy, Mendelssohn, as well as Beethoven, Brahms and Schumann, the composers she concentrated on later in life.

Dame Myra recorded some works for British Columbia from 1931 through 1937 and several for the Gramophone Company. With the development of the long-play record, she made some notable pressings, particularly the Schumann Concerto and Symphonic Etudes, several Beethoven sonatas and some chamber music. Her Schumann recordings remain among the great performances of all times.

Franck's Symphonic Variations (with Basil Cameron and the City of Birmingham Orchestra), the Schumann Concerto in A Minor (with conductor Walter Goehr and an unidentified orchestra) and Schumann's *Carnaval* appear on a recent Hess reissue (see Discog.). "The first movement of the Schumann Concerto is gripping principally because every utterance from the piano has an unshakeable dignity. . . . The metrical aspect of Schumann's *Carnaval* . . . is judged to perfection. Rubatos sound entirely natural." The performance of the Franck Symphonic Variations "is, above all, deeply expressive, with a wonderful feeling of release and exhilaration at the end for the last variation." (*Gram*, Feb 1994)

"The living being is gone. What remain after Myra Hess are her achievements: the introduction of a purer, cleaner style of interpretation of the classics to those who had been unaware that such possibilities existed; the unforgettable National Gallery Wartime concerts, enshrined in the memory of the many thousands who were there; the universal popularity of *Jesu Joy* . . . and, of course, the recordings." (Pearl GEMM 288, liner notes)

SELECTED REFERENCES

Amis, John. "Dame Myra Hess remembered." *Musical Times,* Feb 1990, p. 85.

Bishop, Stephen. "Studying with Myra." In *Myra Hess: By Her Friends*, pp. 75–77.

Chissell, Joan. "Pen Portrait: Dame Myra Hess." *Musical Times*, Feb 1957, pp. 71–72.

Clough, F. F., and G. J. Cuming. "Myra Hess Discography." *Recorded Sound*, Oct 1966, pp. 104–106.

Ferguson, Howard. "Myra Hess." *Recorded Sound*, Oct 1966, pp. 102–103.

Goldberg, Albert. "Dame Myra Hess." (interview) *Los Angeles Times*, 3 April 1955, sec. 4, p. 5.

Hess, Myra. "How to Play Beethoven." In *Myra Hess: A Portrait*, pp. 277–278, see McKenna.

Lassimonne, Denise, compiler. *Myra Hess: By Her Friends*. New York: The Vanguard Press, Inc., 1966. Edited and with Introduction by Howard Ferguson.

McKenna, Marian C. *Myra Hess: A Portrait*. London: Hamish Hamilton, 1976.

Obituary. *Musical Times*, Jan 1966, p. 59. *New York Times*, 27 Nov 1965, pp. 1, 28. *The Times* (London), 27 Nov 1965, p. 8.

Sabin, Robert. "Dame Myra Hess—Shy and Scholarly Yet a Woman of the World." *Musical America*, 1 Feb 1956, pp. 10, 23.

Saerchinger, César. "A Lady in Her Own Right." *Saturday Review*, 28 Feb 1953, pp. 56–57.

Schonberg, Harold C. "Grand Lady of Keyboard." *New York Times*, 27 Nov 1965, p. 28.

———. "Great Pianists From the Past Re-emerge" *New York Times*, 17 June 1990, sec. 2, pp. 23, 26. CD reviews of Hess and Moiseiwitsch.

———. "Taste, Style, Charm." *New York Times*, 5 Dec 1965, sec. 2, p. 15.

"Tributes to Dame Myra Hess (1890–1965)." Seraphim album M 60009, liner notes.

See also Bibliography: Ald/Con; Bro/Mas; Bro/Mod; Cal/MG; Cal/Mus; Cur/Bio (1943); Dow/Oli; Ewe/Li; Ewe/Li2; Kau/Art; Rat/Cle; Sch/Gre; Tho/Mus.

SELECTED REVIEWS

LAT: 25 April 1949; 25 March 1955; 30 March 1955; 26 March 1957. *MA*: 28 Jan 1922; 10 Dec 1927. *MT*: 1 April 1927. *NYEP*: 12 Jan 1931. *NYHT*: 9 Nov 1930; 11 Jan 1931; 21 Jan 1934; 23 Nov 1947. *NYT*: 18 Jan 1922; 7 Feb 1922; 6 Jan 1923; 11 March 1923; 19 Feb 1926; 9 Nov 1930; 11 Jan

1931; 20 Feb 1933; 20 Jan 1935; 13 Oct 1946; 2 Nov 1947; 23 Nov 1947; 14 Jan 1951; 27 Jan 1957; 25 Feb 1959. *TL*: 15 Nov 1907; 27 Jan 1908; 19 Nov 1908; 11 April 1913; 28 April 1914; 19 May 1915; 3 Nov 1916; 27 Sept 1920; 19 Dec 1921; 18 Jan 1922; 7 Feb 1922; 14 Oct 1930; 24 Feb 1947; 10 Dec 1952; 6 Feb 1953; 28 Sept 1961.

SELECTED DISCOGRAPHY

Bach: Adagio from Toccata, Adagio and Fugue (arr. Hess); "Jesu, Joy of Man's Desiring" (arr. Hess); Prelude in D Major. Beethoven: Bagatelle in E-flat Major, op. 126, no. 3; *Für Elise*; Sonata In E Major, op. 109; Sonata in A-flat Major, op. 110. Brahms: Intermezzo in C Major, op. 119, no. 3; Waltz in A-flat Major, op. 39, no. 15. Granados: *La Maja y el ruiseñor.* Mendelssohn: Song without Words, op. 102, no. 5. Scarlatti: Sonatas in C Minor (K. 11), G Major (K. 14). EMI (Great Recordings of the Century) CDH 7 63787 2.

Brahms: Concerto No. 2 in B-flat Major, op. 83; *Schicksalslied.* AS 415 (CD). (Bruno Walter Rarities) Walter/NYPO.

Franck: Symphonic Variations (Cameron/Birmingham SO). Schumann: Concerto in A Minor, op. 54 (Goehr/SO); *Carnaval.* op. 9. Bach-Hess: "Jesu, Joy of Man's Desiring." Dutton Laboratories CDLX 7005.

Mozart: Concerto in E-flat Major, K. 271 (Casals/Perpignan FO). Schumann: Concerto in A Minor, op. 54 (Mitropoulos/NYPO). Melodram 18024 (CD).

Mozart: Concerto in E-flat Major, K. 449 (1954); Concerto in D Minor, K. 466 (1956). Music and Arts Programs, CD-275. From radio broadcasts. Walter/Philharmonic SO.

Dame Myra Hess. Vol. I. Bach: Gigue (French Suite No. 5); Bach-Hess: "Jesu, Joy of Man's Desiring." Beethoven: Cello Sonata in A Major, op. 69 (w/Emanuel Feuermann). Brahms: Capriccio in B Minor, op. 76, no. 2. Chopin: Nocturne in F-sharp Minor, op. 15, no. 2. Debussy: *Poissons d'or*; Préludes, Book I (a) *La Fille aux cheveux de lin*, (b) Minstrels. Dvořak: Slavonic Dance in C Major, op. 46, no. 1. Mendelssohn: Song without Words in A-flat Major, op. 38, no. 6. Schubert: Ballet Music (Rosamunde), arr. Ganz; Sonata in A Major, D. 664. Pearl GEMM CD 9462.

Dame Myra Hess. Vol. II. Griffes: The White Peacock (Roman Sketches op. 7, no. 1). MacDowell: AD 1620 (Sea Pieces op. 55, no. 3). Schumann: *Carnaval*, op. 9; Concerto in A Minor, op. 54 (Goehr/SO). Pearl GEMM CD 9463.

Dame Myra Hess: Legendary Public Performances, 1949–1960. Beethoven: Concerto No. 4 in G Major, op. 58 (Boult/BBC SO, 1952); Concerto No. 5 in E-flat Major, op. 73 (Kurtz/Phil-SO, 1953). Mozart: Concerto in A Major, K. 414 (Scholz/Am. CO, 1956); Concerto in C Major, K. 467 (Stokowski/Phil-SO, 1949); Concerto in B-flat Major, K. 595 (Scholz/Am. CO, 1956). Brahms: Concerto No. 2 in B-flat Major, op. 83 (Walter/Phil-

SO, 1951). Music and Arts CD 779 (4 CDs). Also contains a recital with Isaac Stern, rec. Edinburgh Festival, 1960.

Myra Hess: The complete solo American Columbia recordings. Bach: Allegro in G; Gigue in G (French Suite No. 5); Jesu, Joy of Man's Desiring; Prelude and Fugue in C-sharp Major (WTC I). Beethoven: Bagatelle in B-flat Major, op. 119, no. 11. Brahms: Capriccio in B Minor, op. 76, no. 2; Intermezzo in C Major, op. 119, no. 11. Debussy: *La Fille aux cheveux de lin*; Minstrels; *Poissons d'or.* Falla: Ritual Fire Dance. Griffes: The White Peacock. Mendelssohn: Duetto, op. 36, no. 6; Spinning Song, op. 67, no. 4. Palmgren: Cradle Song. Ravel: *Pavane pour une Infante défunte.* Scarlatti: Sonata in C Minor, K. 11; Sonata in C Major, K. 159. Schubert: Ballet Music from *Rosamunde*; Sonata in A, D. 664. Schumann: *Vogel als Prophet.* Biddulph LHW 024.

Myra Hess: A Vignette. Brahms: Piano Trio in C Major, op. 87 (w/d'Aranyi, Cassadó). Haydn: Sonata in D Major, Hob. XVI:37 (I). Mozart: Concerto in C Major, K. 467 (Heward/Hallé Orch.). Schubert: Sonata in A Major, D. 664; Piano Trio in B flat Major, D. 898 (w/d'Aranyi, Salmond). CDAPR 7012 (2 CDs).

Schumann: Concerto in A Minor, op. 54; Symphonic Etudes, op. 13. Seraphim M 60009. Goehr/SO.

HOFMANN, JOSEF CASIMIR: b. Podgorze, near Kraków, Poland, 20 January 1876; d. Los Angeles, California, 16 February 1957.

> Hofmann was a monarch among pianists—one of the few phenomenally gifted virtuosos of his generation. All the qualities that make for superlative artistry were inherent in him.
>
> *Los Angeles Times*, 17 February 1957

Josef Hofmann's awesome "inherent qualities" made him one of the greatest pianists of all time. A prodigious worker who lived for music and constantly thought about music, the gifted Hofmann, unlike most pianists, required only a moderate amount of practicing to maintain his almost perfect technique. And even as a small child an innate sense of beauty and a natural emotional intensity distinguished his playing.

His inborn gifts may have come from his parents, both professional musicians: Casimir Hofmann, professor of piano, harmony and composition at the Warsaw Conservatory and also conductor at the Warsaw Municipal Opera; and Matylda Hofmann, a singer at the Kraków Municipal Theater. It seems that even as an infant their son showed an unusual interest in music. He was about three years old when the family relocated in Warsaw and about four when he started piano lessons, initially with his sister Wanda and then for about a year with his father's sister, a professional piano teacher. At that point his father, impressed by his son's rapid development, took over his instruction, and before long Hofmann was performing in public.

In his unpublished "Autobiography" (a 1956 manuscript now at the International Piano Archives at the University of Maryland, College Park), Hofmann recalls making his public debut at age five at the Warsaw Opera House. He was too short to reach the pedals, so his father, sitting on his left side, pedaled for him. About this same time Hofmann appeared at a charity concert held at a spa near Warsaw, and the small boy's public performances caused such a sensation that his father was besieged with requests for more. Resisting these early offers, Casimir Hofmann allowed his son to appear only occasionally at charity events.

Hofmann was about seven years old when the great pianist and pedagogue Anton Rubinstein heard him play in Warsaw and advised Hermann Wolff, the German impresario, to "snap up" this musical phenomenon. "I do not believe in *Wunderkinder*," said Rubinstein, "but I believe in this one." (Bowen) The equally impressed Wolff wanted to send the boy touring immediately, but Casimir Hofmann waited until his son was nine years old before allowing Wolff to arrange an extended tour through Europe (Germany, France, Netherlands, Norway, Denmark, Sweden) and Great Britain. Wherever the boy played, he caused a furor. In Berlin Hofmann played the Beethoven Concerto No. 1 with the Berlin Philharmonic Orchestra, conducted by Hans von Bülow. His first London appearance (9 June 1886) led to more recitals and a performance (25 June 1886) of the Beethoven Concerto No. 1 with the Philharmonic Society.

The next year Abbey & Grau, American concert managers, arranged Hofmann's first American tour, a staggering schedule requiring the 11-year-old pianist to play about 80 concerts, at the rate of four a week, and paying him $10,000. For his American debut, performed on 29 November 1887 at the Metropolitan Opera House in New York City, Hofmann played the Beethoven Concerto No. 1 and the Weber-Liszt Polacca for Piano and Orchestra, with Adolph Neuendorff conducting the orchestra, and some solo pieces. At these early concerts he also improvised on themes submitted by anyone from the audience, sometimes famous musicians of the day; for instance, Teresa Carreño gave him a theme at one concert, Walter Damrosch submitted one at another; and at a Washington, D.C., performance, John Philip Sousa sent up a theme. Hofmann's playing, and particularly his improvising, caused such excitement at his debut concert that at intermission half the audience rushed to the box office to purchase tickets for upcoming concerts, and the next morning some 600 people were lined up at the box office.

Within three months of his debut Hofmann had played more than 50 concerts, including at least another 17 at the Metropolitan Opera House. Then the Society for the Prevention of Cruelty to Children intervened, on the grounds that Hofmann was being exploited by his father, and the remaining concerts of the tour had to be canceled. An anonymous benefactor, later known to be financier Alfred Corning Clark, offered Casimir Hofmann $50,000 to support the family while Hofmann took further training, on the condition that the boy would not appear on the concert stage until he was 18 years old. His father accepted the offer, and the Hofmanns immediately returned to Germany.

Considering young Hofmann's intensive schedule and the fact that at age 11 he was supporting his entire family, the group of influential businessmen who urged the SPCC to stop the concerts did Hofmann a great favor. However, years later Hofmann claimed that continuing with the performances would have been better for him. When he returned to America and Britain a decade later, critics were extra harsh on a former prodigy, and it took him years to recapture the sense of ease he felt as a child on the concert stage. It was the approval of Russian audiences, who had not heard him as a prodigy and so had nothing to compare, that restored his shattered self-confidence.

After that abrupt departure from America in 1888, Hofmann's family settled in Berlin. He studied theory and composition with Heinrich Urban and developed his piano technique with Moriz Moszkowski, who ultimately admitted that the teen-age Hofmann knew so much more and played so much better than he did that he had nothing more to teach him. At age 16 Hofmann became a private pupil of Anton Rubinstein—the greatest influence in his life. Hofmann went to Dresden from Berlin (once a week in winter, twice weekly in summer), and over a two-year period (1892–94) had about 40 lessons, some of them lasting two hours. Years later Hofmann told his wife that Rubinstein never played for him during these lessons, but explained, analyzed, elucidated everything he wanted Hofmann to know, then, to preserve his individuality, left him to his own judgment.

Hofmann made his adult debut at age 18 at a Hamburg concert (14 March 1894) performing Rubinstein's Concerto in D Minor, with Rubinstein himself conducting. Although he had not played in public for nearly seven years and Rubinstein had allowed him less than three days to prepare the concerto, at the only rehearsal Hofmann played so beautifully that the usually formal Rubinstein rushed to embrace him before the whole orchestra. After that concert, Rubinstein dismissed him as a pupil: "I have told you all I know about legitimate piano-playing and music-making. . . . And if you don't know it *yet*, why, go to the devil!" (Hofmann, *Piano Playing*) Hofmann never saw Rubinstein again. The master soon returned to Russia, where he died on 19 November 1894.

Meanwhile that same autumn (1894) Hofmann had set off on his first tour since his enforced retirement. He began in England, meeting there for the first time Alfred Corning Clark, who had traveled from America to hear him. The first of his annual tours of the United States began in 1898 with two Carnegie Hall recitals (3 March, 11 March). For the next 40 years Hofmann toured the concert circuit—Russia, Europe, North and South America, Mexico—returning again and again, especially to Russia and America. He usually summered in Switzerland and tried to take every third year off to rest. In 1914 he left war-threatened Europe, settled in the United States and in 1936 became an American citizen. In 1924 he was appointed head of the piano department (Shura Cherkassky is his most famous pupil) at the newly organized Curtis Institute of Music in Philadelphia and was director from 1927 to 1938. In 1933 he received an honorary doctorate from the University of Pennsylvania. Hofmann celebrated (28 Nov 1937) the 50th anniversary of his American debut with a concert at the Metropolitan Opera House, a golden jubilee gala that probably stands as one of the most exciting events in the annals of American music. The lavish souvenir program lists an impressive honorary committee which included the President of the United States and Mrs. Roosevelt; and also an organizing committee, a musician's committee and a citizen's committee, three entities including just about every prominent business and social name in New York and every well-known musician of the era.

By all accounts, Hofmann had a stormy personal life. In 1905 he married Marie Eustis, a divorcee 11 years his senior, divorced her in 1924 and that same year married Betty Short, a pupil 30 years his junior. (This marriage was kept secret until 1927.) He had one daughter by his first marriage, three sons by the second. After he moved to Los Angeles in 1939, he began restricting his tours and made his final New York appearance on 19 January 1946. What with family problems and sometimes poor performances, Hofmann's final years were sad.

Those who knew him remember Josef Hofmann as a very private person with a highly disciplined mind and immense powers of concentration. "Scientific precision characterized both the man and the artist," said Abram Chasins, who knew him well. Hofmann spoke Polish, English, German and French, and for diversion (to escape from music, which was always on his mind), he played tennis, poker and chess.

Hofmann began composing as a small child, was already publishing by age 11 and in his lifetime produced more than 100 works, many under the pseudonym Michel Dvorsky. They range from scintillating salon waltzes to technically demanding pieces, including five piano concertos, and are uniformly romantic, appealing and eminently pianistic.

Somehow he also found time to write prolifically. As music editor of *The Ladies Home Journal* from 1907 to 1917, Hofmann published more than 60 columns on pedagogy, pianism and related subjects. His question-and-answer column in that magazine gave students and teachers the rare opportunity of having their questions answered, free of charge, by one of the greatest pianists of all time. In 1908 Hofmann published excerpts from some of these columns under the title *Piano Playing: A Little Book of Simple Suggestions*. In 1909 he published *Piano Questions Answered*. In 1915 he combined the two books under the title *Piano Playing, with Piano Questions Answered*. These publications and Hofmann's numerous articles on piano playing published in *Etude* magazine are just as valuable today in addition to being entertaining (see Miller).

Hofmann was a dedicated teacher and greatly respected, but some students found him too remote personally and his musical and analytical ideas too abstract to be inspiring or practical. He advised students to play the Chopin Etudes ("nothing better for all needs") to improve technique and never to overdo expression.

Brilliant and versatile, Hofmann—pianist, composer, author and teacher—was also an inveterate inventor and experimenter. By the end of his life he owned more than 70 patents and had invented such diverse items as shock absorbers, pneumatic springs, hydraulic snubbers, oil burner gadgets, piano sound amplification devices, even a steam automobile—a "splendid, self-constructed automobile," according to Constantin von Sternberg, who rode in it with Hofmann from Berlin to the shores of the Baltic Sea.

Hofmann's concert programs (1887 to 1946) show an enormous repertoire in the early part of his career and an inexplicably small repertoire at the end of his career. In November 1916 in Leningrad he gave a remarkable historical series—21 recitals at which he played 255 different compositions, all from memory. (Duncan Stearns's article in *Clavier* of April 1992 lists all of these works and the circumstances leading to this incredible feat.) Hofmann obviously expanded his repertoire with Rubinstein, who required him to prepare 10 Bach Preludes and Fugues and two Beethoven sonatas for each lesson. (Husarik) And his repertoire kept growing: at least 300 different works appear on the recital programs recorded in Husarik, Kehler (Keh/Pia, see Bibliog.) and the Eustis diaries of Hofmann's foreign tours (Graydon).

A specialist in Romantic music, Hofmann played a great amount of Beethoven, Chopin, Liszt and Schumann, and some Schubert and Brahms. All his life he played Rubinstein's works. He played almost no Bach in public except in transcription by Liszt, d'Albert or Tausig, only one piece by Handel, no Haydn or Mozart sonatas. He apparently had very little interest in French music and, except for some short pieces by Rachmaninoff and Prokofiev, played little music written by major 20th-century composers. He liked American music and even gave recitals of music written exclusively by American composers. But as he grew older Hofmann reduced his repertoire and concentrated on the major works of Schumann, Chopin and Beethoven.

Writers still rave over Hofmann's technique—greater than that of even today's technical wizards, "but more significant was his application of that technique to serve musical ends." (Moreno) Hofmann was, "without question one of the greatest pianists of all time and arguably the possessor of the most perfect playing mechanism of any pianist of the modern era." (Methuen-Campbell) Because of his unbelievable technique, Hofmann's ascetic playing not only survived but triumphed in an era when "titanic" pianists were all the rage. His playing, matchless in its emotional intensity and tone coloring, was "always guided by a profound perception of beauty." (*LAT*, 17 Feb 1957)

To begin with, Hofmann had been endowed with an extraordinary memory. His personal method for memorizing music employed, as he put it, four distinct memories—"the visional, the auricular, the muscular and the formal." In his view, what the pianist's mind and imagination will contribute to a performance is far more important than any mechanical perfection. Indeed his practicing was always more mental than physical. Abram Chasins, who worked on and off with Hofmann over a long period (1926–42), told the story that once while traveling on a train with Hofmann, he started to speak, but Hofmann held up a hand and shook his head. "Excuse me," he said, with eyes closed, "I'm practicing." (Cha/Spe, see Bibliog.)

Before even touching the keys Hofmann first determined the tempo, the manner of touch and, above all, the attack of the first note. He next determined the character of the piece—whether dramatic, tragic, lyric, romantic, humorous, heroic, sublime, mystic, or whatever. Thus Hofmann approached a work by first mentally analyzing the form, line, emotional significance, dynamic intensities and contrasts; he then turned to the details of phrasing, nuance and color. With this mental process complete, he would settle down to the keyboard to work on actual sound. He found so much to do in the piece he was preparing that he did little technical work outside the composition itself.

A scientist, Hofmann understood the piano as few people can. "He had an enormous musical palette, and his interpretations ranged from the diabolic to the ethereal." (Moreno) A master at using the full dynamic range of the instrument and exploiting every possible resource to the maximum, Hofmann used his pianism to "interpret" the music, an approach he had learned from Rubinstein. Thus, though he rarely strayed from the written notes, he had no compulsions about changing phrasing, highlighting notes and motives not indicated by the composer, even filling out chords. But most critics accepted this as part of his mystique. Hofmann seldom played a repeated passage the same way twice, a practice he admitted originating with Rubinstein. "He never played for me. He only talked and I, understanding him, translated his meaning into music and musical utterances. Sometimes, for instance, when I played the same phrase twice in succession, and played it both times alike, he would say: 'In fine weather you may play it as you did, but when it rains play it differently'." (Hofmann, *Piano Playing*)

Like Rubinstein, a stickler who used to follow every note on the page as Hofmann played, Hofmann taught his students that fidelity to the letter and spirit of a score is all-important. In his own playing service to the music always came first, even though he often altered details so as to make a work more effective. He described himself as belonging "to the small class of pianists who yield to the inspiration of the moment and improvise the composition at the piano."

A brilliant technician and elegant interpreter, Hofmann was lionized all over the world and ranks among the great pianists of his or any age. Unfortunately, as with so many early pianists, we are forced to rely on often primitive recordings to judge his playing; and even at their best such recordings do not reveal an artist at *his* best. But "those who heard his piano playing can never forget the man's aristocracy, flowing line, sensuous sound, brilliant technique and, above all, feeling of spontaneity. Hofmann, somehow, made every other pianist sound thick. His colleagues knew it. Among professional pianists he was acknowledged a miracle." (Sch/Fac, see Bibliog.)

The general appraisals of Hofmann's playing border on the ecstatic. An example: "A consummate poet, a spiritual aristocrat of the keyboard. . . . Hofmann is unique because he is not only Hofmann, he is a dozen other pianists as well. . . . [With Hofmann] music comes to us re-created, not through the exercise of a great temperament or a great imagination, but through the exercise of an impeccable gift for the making of beautiful sound, sound more superbly disciplined and woven together than we hear it from the fingers of any other contemporary pianist." (Buchanan)

Hofmann's American debut (29 Nov 1887) at the Metropolitan Opera House was a resounding triumph. The 11-year-old prodigy played the first movement of Beethoven's Concerto No. 1 "with a complete mastery of the technical difficulties, with rich and varied tone. . . . In the second movement, the tenderness of sentiment, the poetic insight into the meaning, the symmetrical conception of the movement as a whole, and the ability to make the music not only arouse the intelligence but move the heart of the hearer, displayed by this child, were simply wonderful. . . . The feeling, the intelligence shown by young Hofmann in this movement, were far and away beyond his years. They showed that he was a born musician." (*NYT*, 30 Nov 1887)

Fifty years later Hofmann's golden jubilee concert (28 Nov 1937), also held at the Metropolitan Opera House, heartily reaffirmed that early appraisal: "All the qualities of the greatest playing are his: the power and the delicacy; the lightening virtuosity and the capacity to make the keyboard sing; the richness of tone-coloring . . . the incorruptible taste and sense of form . . . the emotional intensity which is the more thrilling for its superb direction and control." (*NYT*, 29 Nov 1937)

During the 50-year span between these two appearances, Hofmann enjoyed a concert career scarcely paralleled by any other pianist, past or present. Overflowing audiences invariably demanded—and received—numerous encores. Throughout his Carnegie Hall recital of 26 October 1907, "he showed a degree of musicianship which stamped him as one of the greatest of living pianists. Fine sentiment, exquisite tonal coloring, a wonderful—at times astounding—facility of expression, are all among the characteristics of his art, which at once lends itself to a striking virility and poetic delicacy of utterance." (*MA*, 2 Nov 1907)

Audiences and critics applauded even his most adventuresome programs, for example, his recital (25 Jan 1919) of music exclusively by American composers. "Hofmann made of the veriest trifles sonorous shapes of beauty. His tone-color was ravishing. It would be dangerous to criticize his selection, for, as Henry James has pointed out, it is always a risk to ask an artist why he selects any particular theme for treatment. That should be the poet's secret. This holds good in the Hofmann case. He played what he liked because he liked it." (*NYT*, 26 Jan 1919)

A 1934 Queen's Hall recital included three very substantial works—the Brahms-Handel Variations, Chopin Sonata in B-flat Minor and Beethoven's Sonata, op. 111. Hofmann's playing "should be, in one respect, the ideal for every pianist; he is indeed the pianist's pianist; and properly to appreciate Hofmann's art is to feel physically what Hofmann is feeling. Hofmann's touch—in the real sense of physical sensation—is, in its intimacy and variety, astonishing. His wonderful legato robs the instrument of its percussive quality; the pianoforte 'sings,' compelled by a perfect physical continuity of touch." (*MT*, Feb 1934)

A Carnegie Hall recital on 8 March 1941 revealed that Hofmann had not lost one iota of his magnetism. But his playing had changed: "There is a quality in Mr. Hofmann's piano playing which one can describe only by the adjective transcendental. Master of a technical equipment of fabulous proportions and range, he has none of the hardness and glitter of the tribe of virtuosi. He remains the dreamer and the poet, the musician who says in tones things which cannot be expressed in words." (*MA*, 25 March 1941)

Hofmann's last appearance with orchestra (25 June 1945) was at Lewisohn Stadium, where he played the Schumann Concerto in A Minor with the New York Philharmonic-Symphony under the direction of Alexander Smallens. His final New York appearance, a Carnegie Hall recital (19 Jan 1946) proved a fitting climax to his illustrious career. Hofmann "accomplished some of his most distinguished playing of recent years. On the eve of his seventieth birthday . . . the eminent pianist made it evident that he still remained unrivaled in his command of singing tone and as a master of color on the keyboard." (*NYT*, 20 Jan 1946)

Considering his long, active career, Hofmann made a surprisingly small number of commercial recordings. His first discs (1903–04) were made for the Gramophone and Typewriter Company (later HMV) in Berlin. Between 1911 and 1919 he made a number of Columbia recordings, and these and the ones he made for Brunswick in 1923–25 are the only commercial recordings that he allowed to be released. Later on he did allow privately made discs of his Golden Jubilee concert at the Metropolitan Opera House to be made available. After his death, the International Piano Archives and RCA released some 1935 test pressings Hofmann had made for HMV in England and RCA in the United States. A number of his live concert recordings (1935–47) and some previously unissued discs have been made available on LP and on CD.

Hofmann's involvement with recording is a fascinating story in itself. He made piano rolls for the Hupfeld, Ampico, Welte and Duo-Art companies from 1913 to 1927. Over 60 rolls were made (Sit/Cla, see Bibliog.) and many of these have been made available on LP format. Hofmann was well recompensed for his efforts: his contract with Duo-Art granted him the sum of $1,000 for each completed roll.

The Columbia collection (see Discog.) reveals Hofmann's catholic tastes, including as it does not only a quantity of Chopin, Liszt and Mendelssohn but works by American composers Fanny Dillon, Constantin von Sternberg and Horatio Parker. Due to 78 rpm limitations of space, some compositions—like the brilliant Liszt Tarantella for instance—were forcibly abbreviated, but the Tarantella still remains one of Hofmann's most dazzling virtuoso performances. Another fine example is Rubinstein's *Valse Caprice*.

VAIA is to be commended for initiating a series with the general title *The Complete Josef Hofmann*. The first volume contains both Chopin Concertos as performed in the mid-1930s with the New York Philharmonic Orchestra, conducted by Sir John Barbirolli. One must of course listen beyond the sound quality of the old 78s, but the rewards are great. These are magnificent performances by a consummate artist, whose rhythmic drive, delicate filigree work and refined tonal control breathe an air of authenticity into Chopin's masterpieces.

The second volume of the complete recordings includes the famous Golden Jubilee concert of 1937 and fragments from Hofmann's penultimate appearance. The highlights of this CD are the Rubinstein Concerto No. 4 in D Minor, op. 95, and Hofmann's own *Chromaticon*, performed with the Curtis Institute Orchestra (augmented with members of the Philadelphia Orchestra) and conducted by Fritz Reiner. In addition to the musical value and interest, the CD memorializes an historical event. The CD even includes the encores—by Beethoven, Mendelssohn, Moszkowski and Rachmaninoff—and also four Chopin compositions taken from a Carnegie Hall concert of 24 March 1945. The Nocturne in C Minor, op. 48, no. 1, and the Mazurka in C Major, op. 33, are outstanding examples of Hofmann's finest Chopin playing. Volume three contains the recordings Hofmann made for Columbia from 1912 to 1918 and his Gramophone and Typewriter recordings of 1903; the acoustic Brunswick recordings of 1922–23 are in volume four.

SELECTED REFERENCES

Bowen, Catherine Drinker. *"Free Artist": The Story of Anton and Nicholas Rubinstein.* New York: Random House, 1939.

Buchanan, Charles L. "A Consummate Poet, a Spiritual Aristocrat of the Keyboard." *Musical America*, 9 Feb 1918, p. 9.

Cassini, Leonard. "Josef Hofmann." *Recorded Sound*, Oct 1968, pp. 331–334.

Chasins, Abram. "Josef Hofmann: Hail and Farewell." *Saturday Review of Literature*, 30 March 1957, pp. 47, 49, 60.

———— "My Lessons with Josef Hofmann." *Keyboard Classics*, Sept/Oct 1983, pp. 4–7.

Downes, Olin. "Still a Prodigy after Fifty Years." *New York Times Magazine*, 21 Nov 1937, sec. 8, pp. 12, 26.

Eaton, Quaintance. "Dr. Josef Hofmann Marks Debut Anniversary." *Musical America*, 25 Jan 1935, pp. 6-7.

————. "Hofmann's Golden Jubilee." *Musical America*, 25 Nov 1937, pp. 6–7, 9.

————. "Hofmann Jubilee Witnessed by Brilliant Throng." *Musical America*, 10 Dec 1937, pp. 7, 36.

Goldberg, Albert. "Hofmann At Fourscore." *New York Times*, 15 Jan 1956, sec. 2, p. 9.

Grant, F. R. "Michel Dvorsky: An Obituary." *Musical America*, 31 Jan 1920, p. 4.

Grau, Robert. "How Henry E. Abbey Lost Fortune Over Hofmann." *Musical America*, 20 April 1912, p. 26.

Graydon, Nell S., and Margaret D. Sizemore. *The Amazing Marriage of Marie Eustis & Josef Hofmann.* Columbia: University of South Carolina Press, 1965.

Hofmann, Josef. "How Piano Playing Has Progressed." (Part 1) *Etude*, Dec 1911, p. 812.

————. "How Piano Playing Has Progressed." (Part 2) *Etude*, Jan 1912, p. 14.

————. "The Indispensables in Pianistic Success." (Part 1) *Etude*, Jan 1920, pp. 7–8.

————. "The Indispensables in Pianistic Success." (Part 2) *Etude*, Feb 1920, pp. 81–82.

————. "A Musical Educational Renaissance." *Etude*, Oct 1936, pp. 611–612.

————. *Piano Playing* (A Little Book of Simple Suggestions). New York: The McClure Company, 1908.

————. *Piano Playing with Piano Questions Answered.* Reprint with new introduction by Gregor Benko. New York: Dover, 1976.

————. "Practical Ideas on Artistic Pedaling." *Etude*, Sept 1921, pp. 563–564.

————. "What Is the Purpose of Music Study?" *Etude*, Nov 1944, pp. 617, 663, 667.

Husarik, Stephen. *Josef Hofmann (1876–1957), The Composer And Pianist, With An Analysis Of Available Reproductions Of His Performances.* Ph.D. Dissertation, University of Iowa, 1983. Available through University Microfilms.

Josef Hofmann Golden Jubilee. Souvenir booklet for Jubilee concert. Metropolitan Opera House, 28 Nov 1937.

"Josef Hofmann's Jubilee." *New York Times*, 28 Nov 1937, sec. 4, p. 8.

"Jubilee." *Time*, 6 Dec 1937, pp. 38–39.

Kammerer, Rafael. "Death of Hofmann Stirs Memories of Unique Artistry." *Musical America*, March 1957, pp. 7–8.

Kipnis, Igor. "Three Great Pianists on Victrola." *Stereo Review*, March 1971, p. 102.

Methuen-Campbell, James. "An Appreciation of Josef Hofmann." *Clavier*, April 1986, pp. 11–13.

Miller, Bonny H. "The Josef Hofmann Years at the Ladies' Home Journal." *Piano Quarterly*, Spring 1990, pp. 25–35.

Moreno, Joseph. "Berkowitz on Hofmann." *Clavier*, April 1992, pp. 20–22.

"Mr. Abbey's Coming Stars." *New York Times*, 29 Oct 1887, p. 5.

Obituary. *Musical Times*, April 1957, p. 219. *New York Times*, 18 Feb 1957, pp. 1, 27. *The Times* (London), 19 Feb 1957, p. 13.

"The Piano Prodigy." *New York Times*, 4 Dec 1887, p. 16.

Pleasants, Henry. "The Incomparable Pianism of Josef Hofmann." *Stereo Review*, Dec 1975, p. 130.

Stearns, Duncan. "Hofmann's 1916 Recitals." *Clavier*, April 1992, p. 23.

Wile, Raymond R. "Genius to Genius." *American Record Guide*, Sept 1977, pp. 6–8, 56–58. Some unpublished correspondence between the Edison Laboratories and the young Josef Hofmann.

See also Bibliography: Bro/PiS; Cha/Spe; Coo/GrP; Dow/Oli; Ewe/Li; Ewe/Li; Ewe/Mu MGG; New/GrA; Nie/Mei; Rat/Cle; Rub/MyM; Rub/MyY; Sch/Fac; Sch/Gre.

SELECTED REVIEWS

MA: 2 Nov 1907; 7 Dec 1907; 15 Nov 1910; 17 Dec 1910; 16 Jan 1915; 5 Feb 1916; 9 Feb 1918; 1 Feb 1919; 25 April 1938; 25 March 1941. *MT*: 1 Dec 1920; 1 April 1924; 1 Aug 1926; 1 Nov 1926; Feb 1934. *NYA*: 9 Feb 1936. *NYHT*: 9 Feb 1936. *NYP*: 10 Feb 1936. *NYS*: 24 Nov 1918. *NYT*: 30 Nov 1887; 7 Feb 1888; 20 Nov 1901; 30 Oct 1910; 4 Dec 1910; 14 Jan 1912; 28 Jan 1912; 28 Nov 1912; 29 Oct 1913; 10 Dec 1913; 31 Jan 1915; 28 Jan 1917; 24 Nov 1918; 26 Jan 1919; 14 Jan 1923; 3 Jan

1924; 13 Jan 1930; 9 Nov 1930; 20 Jan 1935; 9 Feb 1936; 29 Nov 1937;
14 March 1938; 7 Nov 1940; 9 March 1941; 30 June 1942; 21 March
1943; 29 July 1944; 25 March 1945; 26 June 1945; 20 Jan 1946. *TL*: 17
Oct 1887; 8 Nov 1887; 21 Nov 1894; 27 May 1902; 22 Oct 1920; 29 Oct
1920;4 Oct 1926; 30 Nov 1937.

SELECTED DISCOGRAPHY

The Complete Josef Hofmann, Vol. 1. Chopin: Concerto No. 1 in E Minor,
op. 11; Concerto No. 2 in F Minor, op. 21. Includes a short interview
with Hofmann. VAIA/IPA 1002 (CD). Barbirolli/NYPO.
The Complete Josef Hofmann, Vol 2. Beethoven-Rubinstein: Turkish March.
Chopin: *Andante spianato et Grande Polonaise,* op. 22; Ballade No. 1 in G
Minor, op. 23; *Berceuse*, op. 57; Etude in G-flat Major, op. 25, no. 9; Nocturnes, op. 9, no. 2, op. 15, no. 2, op. 48, no. 1; Mazurka, op. 33, no. 3;
Waltzes, op. 34, no. 1, op. 42, op. 64, no. 1. Hofmann: Chromaticon, for
Piano and Orchestra. Mendelssohn: Spinning Song, op. 67, no. 4. Mosz-
kowski: *Caprice espagnole*, op. 37. Rachmaninoff: Prelude in G Minor,
op. 23, no. 5. Rubinstein: Concerto No. 4 in D Minor. VAIA/IPA 1020
(2 CDs). A fascinating reissue of Hofmann's Golden Jubilee Concert at the
Metropolitan Opera House. Hilsberg, Reiner/Curtis Institute Orchestra.
The Complete Josef Hofmann, Vol. 3. *The Columbia Recordings (1912–1918)*:
Beethoven: Sonata in C-sharp Minor, op. 27, no. 2 (1st movt.). Chopin:
Berceuse, op. 57; Fantasy-Impromptu, op. 66; Impromptu, op. 29;
Polonaise in A Major, op. 40, no. 1; Waltz in A-flat Major, op. 34, no. 1;
Waltz in C-sharp Minor, op. 64, no. 2; Waltz in E Minor, op. posth.
Chopin-Liszt: "The Maiden's Wish." Dillon: Birds at Dawn. Gluck-
Brahms: Gavotte. Grieg: *Papillon*, op. 43, no. 1. Hofmann: The
Sanctuary. Liszt: *Liebestraum* No. 3; Tarantella; *Waldesrauschen*.
Mendelssohn: Hunting Song, op. 19, no. 3; *Rondo capriccioso*, op. 14;
Spinning Song, op. 67, no. 4; Spring Song, op. 62, no. 6. Moszkowski:
Caprice espagnole, op. 37; *La Jongleuse*. Paderewski: Minuet in G Major.
Parker: *Valse gracile*. Rachmaninoff: Prelude in C-sharp Minor, op. 3, no.
2; Prelude in G Minor, op. 23, no. 5. Rubinstein: "*El Dachtarawan*";
Valse-caprice. Schubert-Liszt: *Der Erlkönig*. Schubert-Tausig: *Marche mil-
itaire*. Sternberg: Etude in C Minor. *The Gramophone and Typewriter
Recordings (1903)*: Chopin: Polonaise in A Major, op. 40, no. 1.
Mendelssohn: Hunting Song, op. 19, no. 3; Spring Song, op. 62, no. 6.
Schubert-Liszt: *Der Erlkönig*. Schubert-Tausig: *Marche militaire*.
Columbia Recordings Appendix: Chopin: Nocturne in E-flat Major, op. 9,
no. 1; Waltz in E Minor, op. posth. Grieg: *Papillon*, op. 43, no. 1.
Mendelssohn: Spinning Song, op. 67, no. 4. Rachmaninoff: Prelude in C-
sharp Minor, op. 3, no. 2. VAIA/IPA 1036-2 (2 CDs).
The Complete Josef Hofmann, Vol. 4. The Acoustic Brunswick recordings of
1922 and 1923. Scarlatti-Tausig: Pastorale and Capriccio. Gluck-Brahms:
Gavotte. Beethoven-Rubinstein: Turkish March. Rubinstein: Melody in F,
op. 3, no. 1. Hofmann: Nocturne (from "Mignonettes"). Rachmaninoff:

Preludes op. 3, no. 2, op. 23, no. 5. Wagner-Brassin: Magic Fire Music. Chopin: Scherzo No. 1, op. 20 (abbr.); Nocturne op. 15, no. 2; Waltz op. 64. no. 2; Polonaise op. 40, no. 1. Chopin-Liszt: My Joys. Liszt: Concert Study No. 1; Hungarian Rhapsody No. 2. VAIA/IPA 1047-2.

Josef Hofmann plays Chopin. Nocturnes op. 27, no. 2, op. 55, no. 1; Polonaises op. 40, no. 1, op. 53; Waltzes op. 34, no. 1, op. 42, op. 64, no. 1. Klavier Records (LP) KS 118. Recorded from Duo-Art piano rolls.

Legendary Pianists of the Romantic Era. Concert 1. Gluck: *Melodie.* Gottschalk: The Banjo. Rubinstein: Romance op. 44, no. 1. Schytte: Forest Elves op. 70, no. 5. Scriabin: Poem op. 32, no. 1. Weber: Rondo: Perpetual Motion op. 24. Woods: *Valse phantastique.* Klavier Records (LP) KS 114. Recorded from Duo-Art piano rolls.

Legendary Pianists of the Romantic Era. Concert 2.. Moszkowski: *Guitarre* op. 45, no. 2. Rachmaninoff: Prelude op. 23, no. 5. Rubinstein: Barcarolle No. 2; Valse Caprice in E-flat Major. Schumann-Tausig: *El Contrabandista.* Schütt: *Valse Bluette,* op. 25. Sternberg: Third Concert Etude op. 103. Klavier Records (LP) KL 121. Recorded from Duo-Art piano rolls.

Romantic Rarities, Vol. 1. *The Unpublished HMV Recordings.* Beethoven: Sonata in E-flat Major, op. 31, no. 3 (Scherzo). Chopin: Nocturne in F-sharp Major, op. 15, no. 2. Chopin-Liszt: *Chant polonaise* No. 1. Chopin: Waltz in A-flat Major, op. 42. CDAPR 7013.

HOROWITZ, VLADIMIR: b. Kiev, Russia, 1 October 1903; d. New York, New York, 5 November 1989.

> People normally went to Schnabel recitals in order to hear intelligent performances of Mozart or Beethoven or Schubert. They go to Horowitz recitals in order to hear Horowitz. This does not mean that Horowitz's performances are necessarily unintelligent; but initially, at least, one listens to Horowitz in the same way that one looks up at a shooting star: it is obviously dazzling; and it is difficult not to be awed by that aspect of it."
>
> Harvey Sachs (*Virtuoso*, 1982)

What to say about Horowitz? So much is already in print about this one-of-a-kind genius—articles, interviews, reviews, critiques and at least four full-scale books. Glenn Plaskin's mammoth (607 pages) *Horowitz: A Biography* was published in 1983. After Horowitz's death in 1989, three additional full-length books appeared in rapid succession. In 1991 David Dubal's *Evenings With Horowitz: A Personal Portrait* (321 pages). In 1992 Harold C. Schonberg's *Horowitz: His Life and Music* (427 pages). In 1993 Dubal's *Remembering Horowitz: 125 Pianists Recall a Legend* (383 pages). Each is important in its own special way, and together they provide a rich, well-rounded portrait of this spellbinding pianist. Given the wealth of information so readily available, it would indeed be presumptuous to attempt here more than an overall survey of Horowitz's life, performance style and some of his outstanding recordings.

Records that might confirm where and when Vladimir Gorovitz (Horowitz) was born no longer exist. He grew up in Kiev, but may have been born in Berdichev, a settlement of the Jewish pale southwest of Kiev. Regarding the year of his birth, Horowitz himself said that he was born in 1903, not 1904 as stated in most reference books.

His family was prosperous, cultured and very musical. Simeon Gorovitz, his father, was the Kiev representative of both Westinghouse and the German *Allgemeine Elektrische Gesellschaft*. Sophie (Bodick) Gorovitz, his mother, was a competent pianist who had studied at the Kiev Conservatory. Horowitz had his first piano lessons with his mother, starting at about age five, and in 1912, just a month before his ninth birthday, entered the Kiev Conservatory. A child who devoured all the music he could find, young Horowitz had already explored a wide variety of repertoire, including fourhand reductions (played with his mother) of symphonies, operas and chamber works. He had also become a remarkably good sight reader. Despite these impressive achievements, Horowitz always insisted that he had not been a child prodigy. True, he had never been pushed into performing for the public as a child, but his childhood accomplishments do seem extraordinary.

His first teacher at the Conservatory was Vladimir Puchalsky, his mother's former teacher, and it was not a good beginning. The talented but totally undisciplined Horowitz had already acquired his own way of playing the piano; Puchalsky, an unyielding traditionalist, naturally attempted (unsuccessfully) to mold him into a more conventional pianist. At age 12 Horowitz began lessons with Sergei Tarnowsky, who also had difficulty controlling Horowitz's free approach to the piano, but the two got along a little better. Although Horowitz never acknowledged it, in his four years with Tarnowski he developed into a stunning pianist.

He was an all-around poor student in regular school and barely got by in his other classes, but his sensational piano performances at the Conservatory made him a teen-age superstar. Life revolved around him, especially at home, where he got his own way or threw violent tantrums. A cousin remembered Horowitz as a conceited, self-centered and arrogant young man, a social misfit without friends. Sadly, so was Horowitz the man, only more so. But how he played the piano!

In 1919 Horowitz began studying with Felix Blumenfeld, his third and final teacher, and this proved to be a happy arrangement, largely because Blumenfeld had studied with Anton Rubinstein, Horowitz's great idol. "Blumenfeld," said Horowitz, "was exactly the teacher I needed because he was creative. It was with Blumenfeld that I started to develop my flat-finger technique. I started to practice in a sort of portamento which made my fingers like steel." (Dubal, *Evenings with Horowitz*)

Horowitz graduated from the Conservatory in 1920, and out of necessity (his family lost everything when the Communists took over Kiev) he began giving concerts to help. Not many attended his debut performance in Kiev on 30 May 1920. But word spread fast about the thrilling playing of the 17-year-old pianist, and he played to full houses at his next two Kiev recitals. The same thing happened in Kharkov. Unknown when he gave his first recital there in the fall of 1921, at his third Kharkov concert, the hall was sold out. In the next two seasons he played all over Russia, often with the violinist Nathan Milstein. (Money being short everywhere, many of their fees were paid with food, clothing, even supplies.) In 1923 the Milstein-Horowitz performances in St. Petersburg attracted packed houses, and the following season (15 Oct 1924–18 Jan 1925) Horowitz as soloist conquered that city (then renamed Leningrad) with 20 concerts encompassing 10 programs including, according to Horowitz, 44 large-scale works and 66 smaller pieces.

His unbelievable technique and supercharged style made him Russia's most famous pianist. Yet Horowitz had for a long time been thinking of leaving Russia, and now that he was eligible for the military draft, the prospect of a more successful, more profitable career in the West looked all the more tempting. Granted a visa on the grounds that he would be going to Germany to study with Artur Schnabel, Horowitz left Russia in September, 1925, not knowing that 61 years would pass before he returned home. Once in Berlin, he set to work practicing for his Berlin debut, learning German and attending concerts and the opera. Both his Berlin debut recital (2 Jan 1926) and his orchestral debut (8 Jan 1926)—a performance of the Tchaikovsky Concerto No. 1 in B-flat Minor with the Berlin Symphony Orchestra, conducted by Oskar Fried—stunned audiences. His recital on 14 January sold out, and the laudatory reviews produced many offers to play and an invitation from the Welte-Mignon piano roll company.

Horowitz's "big break," as he always called it, came in Hamburg. He played a recital there on 19 January 1926, and the next day was called upon, with just two hours' notice (the scheduled soloist fainted at the dress rehearsal and had to cancel), to play the Tchaikovsky Concerto No. 1 with the Hamburg Symphony Orchestra, Eugen Pabst conducting. That chance performance—as it turned out, a wildly bravura performance—created pandemonium in the concert hall. Horowitz's next Hamburg recital caused yet another furor, and he left for Paris with a contract for ten concerts in Germany the next season (1926–27).

After his Paris debut recital (12 Feb 1926) at the Paris Conservatory, and five additional performances, he had become the darling of the city. Meanwhile he was already booked for the upcoming 1926–27 season: more than 60 concerts spread over nine countries (Germany, France, Italy, Belgium, Holland, Hungary, Austria, Spain and England). Except for England, where he made little impact, Horowitz stirred up an ardent public following, although as always, "critics gave him mixed reviews, praising his unsurpassed virtuosity but often condemning his undeveloped musicianship." (Dubal, *Evenings with Horowitz*)

Horowitz's American debut (12 Jan 1928), playing the Tchaikovsky Concerto No. 1 with the New York Philharmonic Society Orchestra, Sir Thomas Beecham conducting, ended up a wild contest between soloist and conductor. Horowitz won, overriding Beecham's too slow tempos with a volcanic display of virtuosity that literally stampeded the audience. Criticism was mixed.

While every reviewer was obviously bowled over by the unbelievable Horowitz technique, "not one of them appeared convinced that he was a complete musician. . . . In addition to inappropriate tempi and imperfect balances, Horowitz was also roundly taken to task for an unnecessarily strident and pompous tone." (Plaskin, *Horowitz*)

Horowitz played his American recital debut (20 Feb 1928) in Carnegie Hall, and again the critics divided. But it really mattered little what reviewers wrote. By the end of his first American tour (3 months, more than 30 concerts), the American public had taken to Horowitz, and he returned to Paris (he kept an apartment there until World War I) with a guarantee of 45 American engagements the next season. That tour began with a Carnegie Hall recital (2 Nov 1928), at which the "thunderous applause . . . whenever Mr. Horowitz pounded his loudest," could not hide the uneven quality of his playing. "His appearances here," continued this reviewer, "have given rise to some misgivings regarding the true significance of his deeper musical gifts, and last night the doubters had further justification for their fears." (*NYWT*, 3 Nov 1928) As always, such reviews made little impression on audiences. They flocked to Horowitz's concerts, followed his every move and made him one of the greatest of international celebrities.

For several years he toured exhaustively in both Europe and the United States. In 1933 he played Beethoven's "Emperor" Concerto with the mighty Toscanini and his orchestra, and later that year Horowitz surprised the musical world by marrying (21 Dec, in Milan) Wanda Toscanini, the conductor's daughter. A great deal has been written about the Horowitzes' strange life together and the heartbreaking story of their only child (Sonia, born in Milan in 1934, died under mysterious circumstances in Geneva in 1975). Why did they marry at all? The best guess is that Wanda saw herself becoming vastly important as the wife of this internationally famous pianist, and that Horowitz saw untold benefits in being the son-in-law of the great Toscanini. Strong-willed and overprotective, Wanda Horowitz was not only wife but mother, companion, critic and above all business manager. Living with the eccentric, selfish Horowitz was a thorny cross to bear, but she stayed with him (they were separated but always in touch between 1949 and 1953) until his death 56 years later.

Coping with family life distracted Horowitz; coping with the raging Toscaninis (who could not talk without screaming) depressed him. Even worse, the classicist Toscanini constantly badgered Horowitz about his overly brilliant virtuosity. It all took a toll on his playing. With every concert (about 75 in the 1934–35 season) he seemed more exhausted, more tense. Some critics noted that his tone had become even harsher and metallic, that his frenzied energy obliterated any chance of true emotion in his playing. Yet a few critics detected a new maturity in Horowitz's playing, more insight into the music and less personal exhibition. On 14 March 1935 Horowitz gave an absolutely superb performance of the Brahms Concerto No. 1 in D Minor with Toscanini conducting the New York Philharmonic-Symphony Orchestra, and the reviews praised his musicianship: "His playing has seldom had the splendor of tone, the firmness of grasp and outline, the awareness of the composer's requirements." (*NYT*, 15 March 1935)

Horowitz would be just 32 years old that year, but in the eight years since his American debut he had kept to a grueling concert schedule, and he was clearly burned out. Bursting with tension and often bothered with a nervous stomach (or colitis), in November he began canceling engagements. His London concerts in March and April of 1936 received harsh notices, and that painful season finally ended with a Trieste performance on 2 May 1936. Horowitz disappeared from the concert platform for two years.

He had his appendix removed in September 1936, developed phlebitis after the operation and had to spend three months immobilized with his foot propped on a pillow. Theories abound concerning this two-year hiatus. One says continuing poor health kept him away; another says that Horowitz needed time to think because he had come to realize how much his fame depended on pure technique. "The mechanical precision of his playing had become so stupefying that no listener could any longer pay attention to the truly musical aspects of the work." (Bla/Gra, see Bibliog.)

Horowitz spent most of those two years in Switzerland trying to recover his mental and physical health. In later years he often said that only the understanding counsel and support of his friend Rachmaninoff (Horowitz idolized him) got him through this "nervous breakdown." He tested himself with a charity performance in Zurich on 26 September 1938 (Rachmaninoff was in the audience), then scheduled a 1938–39 concert season, with the condition that he must have more time to rest between engagements.

That season he played in Europe, though not in Germany and Italy because of Hitler and Mussolini, and he felt that his musical outlook, his musicianship, had changed. For the public, his return was a triumph. Horowitz played the Brahms B-flat Concerto with Toscanini at the Lucerne Festival on 29 August 1939. Three days later Germany invaded Poland, and shortly after that the Toscanini family, including the great Horowitz, sailed for the United States.

He performed all over America during World War II. An unparalleled success, in the 1940s Horowitz became the highest paid performing artist in America. His fiendishly difficult transcriptions, usually the rousing finale of a program, stirred audiences to fever pitch, most especially his spine-tingling paraphrase of Sousa's "Stars and Stripes Forever." The fact that his colleagues and most critics disdained his choice of repertoire had no impact on Horowitz's phenomenal drawing power. But by the late 1940s he was again, for one reason or another (cold, flu, abdominal problems, bronchitis), canceling concerts. Exhausted, overwrought and unable to come to terms with long-simmering problems at home, Horowitz separated from his wife in 1949. Although he lived in a hotel until they reunited in 1953, the Horowitzes kept in constant touch, and Mrs. Horowitz, as always, kept a firm hand on his business affairs.

He began his 1951–52 European tour in London on 8 October 1951, playing the Rachmaninoff Concerto No. 3 with the Royal Philharmonic Orchestra, Walter Susskind conducting. It was his first London appearance in nearly 13 years, but the Londoners had not forgotten him. Even the critics were pleased. On the other hand, his Festival Hall recital (8 Nov 1951), another tour de force as far as his audience was concerned, disappointed the critics. "A brittleness in Horowitz's playing became apparent. Underneath a brilliant shell of pianism there seemed to lurk something detached and calculating, something too far removed from the Byronic grandeurs, the luxuriating self-abandonments of Liszt's B Minor Sonata." (*MT*, Dec 1951)

Horowitz fulfilled two engagements in Paris in November, canceled the rest of that season's tour and returned home to America. (Horowitz had become a U.S. citizen in 1944.) On 12 January 1953 he celebrated the 25th anniversary of his American debut with a thrilling performance of the Tchaikovsky Concerto No. 1, George Szell conducting, at the New York Philharmonic's Pension Fund benefit concert at Carnegie Hall. But the next month he gave a New York recital (25 Feb 1953), and the critics savaged that performance, especially Horowitz's playing of Schubert's posthumous Sonata in B-flat Major.

That may have triggered Horowitz's next disappearance, although he was truly tired of touring (he hated the train travel, hotel living, restaurant food). Exhausted, ill and depressed, he canceled, at the last minute, a Minneapolis concert scheduled for 11 March 1953. This time he was off the concert stage for 12 years. The reasons for Horowitz's physical collapse and mental depression are still not fully known. He rarely left the house for about two years. He made a few recordings during this long intermission, practiced about an hour and a half a day, read a lot and watched movies.

Before he performed for the public again in 1965, he had a few secret tryout concerts at Carnegie Hall for small, select audiences. As always, his public remained faithful. They lined up, some all night, at Carnegie Hall to purchase tickets for his "comeback" recital announced for 9 May 1965. And they gave him a standing, rousing ovation. Next day most critics added their plaudits. Not only was Horowitz's transcendental virtuosity, unbelievable fingerwork and subtle pedaling all still in place, but most critics noted a new maturity, a more reflective approach, less of a nervous-sounding attack, an even richer quality of sound. Wrote one reviewer: "Aside from an inconsequential inaccuracy here and there, the line of thought, top and bottom, was implemented by a sense of internal structure and tonal design that spoke its own testimony to the fulfillment he has achieved in these recent years. . . . Old Horowitz or new, this was the order of artistry for which pianos are made to be played." (*SR*, 22 May 1965)

A year passed before Horowitz's next two New York concerts, both at Carnegie Hall. He would now play only on Sunday afternoon, never evening concerts. Three years later, tense and agitated, he stopped performing, this time for five years. Possibly a cold contracted in Boston had led to further complications. Or it may have been another nervous breakdown. Or he stopped because he was furious over a Boston review that said his technique was wonderful, but his music making abominable. He put himself in the hands of a psychiatrist, and by 1971 was almost back to his old self. He made recordings in 1971, 1972 and 1973, but he did not concertize, not until 1974, when he gave a recital at Cleveland's Severance Hall on 12 May. "Mr. Horowitz, making another of the returns to the recital stage for which he has become renowned, put on a typically flabbergasting Horowitzian show, in which there were many moments that perhaps no living pianist could equal." (*NYT*, 13 May 1974) Horowitz went on to play about 20 concerts in Canada and the United States in the 1974–75 season. Having overcome his fear of flying made touring somewhat easier; besides, he traveled like a potentate, with an entourage that catered to his every whim.

On 8 January 1978 Horowitz celebrated the 50th anniversary of his American debut at Carnegie Hall, playing the Rachmaninoff Concerto No. 3 with Eugene Ormandy conducting the New York Philharmonic Orchestra. It was his first appearance with an orchestra in 25 years, and his frantic pace of recent years showed in his playing. He had not lost that remarkable electricity, but his playing seemed exaggerated, calculated, artificial.

Horowitz had pushed himself too far. But he kept going, playing golden jubilee concerts around the country. In December 1978 he underwent prostate surgery, but once recuperated he went back to performing, with a concert in Atlanta on 18 March 1979. By the end of the following year his playing on one occasion had become "so subtle and subdued that, in soft passages, some listeners were straining to hear the famous Horowitz tone that in previous years would have effortlessly soared over them. Horowitz seemed to be weakening physically, his strength sapped by the hectic pace he had been keeping for five seasons." (McAlear)

On 22 May 1982 he gave his first London concert in three decades (the last one had been on 19 Oct 1951), and, even if the audience apparently did not notice, Horowitz seemed exhausted and completely out of touch with reality. For some reason he insisted on performing that season (1982–83), and his two recitals in Tokyo proved disastrous. The Tokyo press raged that his horrible performances had cheated the Japanese public, and RCA not only had to abandon its plans for a "Horowitz in Tokyo" album, but was unable to salvage enough material to make even one compact disc. After Tokyo, the Horowitzes went into seclusion. A new doctor and different therapy put him on the long road to recovery, and in the spring of 1985 he played once again for his devoted following— via a video titled "Horowitz: The Last Romantic," a recital recorded and filmed in Horowitz's own living room. This time the resilient Horowitz returned to his public less nervous, obviously relaxed, and the mannerisms and affectations had gone from his playing.

Two Paris recitals (26 Oct, 2 Nov 1985)—he had not played there for 34 years—absolutely overwhelmed the critics. Two concerts at *La Scala* in Milan, on 17 and 24 November, his first appearances there in half a century, equally confounded Italian critics. He was, they said, even greater than his legend. Horowitz was back touring, and better than ever.

In April 1986 he made a dramatic, highly orchestrated and highly publicized return to Russia, his first look at his homeland in 61 years. The Russian public went mad over him, and television crews dogged his every step. His Moscow recital (20 April 1986) was televised to the United States and to most of western Europe, and the film of that performance, titled "Horowitz in Moscow," won a Grammy award in 1988. After Moscow, Horowitz played in Leningrad, Hamburg, West Berlin, London and Tokyo, and his three Tokyo recitals more than made up for his earlier fiasco in 1983.

The amazingly rejuvenated Horowitz began his next season (1986–87) with a White House recital, on which occasion President Reagan presented Horowitz with the Medal of Freedom. On 15 December 1986 he played in the gala opening performance at the newly refurbished Carnegie Hall, and that, as it turned out, was the last time he appeared on an American stage. Early in 1987 he was back in Europe (Amsterdam, Berlin, Hamburg, Vienna). And in these, his final years, the magnificent Horowitz often received glowing, sometimes even ecstatic reviews. His concert in Hamburg on 21 June 1987 was his final appearance. Active to the last with recordings and videos, Horowitz died unexpectedly of a heart attack at home on 5 November 1989. He is buried in the Toscanini family vault at the *Cimitèrio Monumentale* in Milan, Italy.

Horowitz received the *Grand Prix du Disque* in 1970 and 1971; the *Prix Disque Montreuil* in 1971; the Royal Philharmonic Society Gold Medal in 1972; the United States Medal of Freedom in 1986; the Wolf Foundation Prize in 1983. In 1986 France made him a Commander of the *Légion d'honneur* and Germany bestowed on him the Federal Service Cross.

It really makes little difference that most writers portray Horowitz as a complex, neurotic, self-centered man, just as it makes little difference what one concludes from the reviews of his playing. No one can ever doubt that Vladimir Horowitz was a pianistic genius.

As a teacher Horowitz was arguably more a destructive than constructive force, and some of his pupils have never recovered. "In the context of teaching, Horowitz, fundamentally self-immersed, seemed blind to the devastating effects of his volatile temperament. His kindness could just as easily evaporate and be replaced by capricious, insensitive behavior. He postponed lessons and dropped some students without explanation, undercut self-confidence by withholding enthusiasm for the concerts and recordings of his protégés, and even denied that some had ever taken lessons with him." (Plaskin, "The Secret Career. . .")

In 1944 Horowitz accepted Byron Janis, then age 16, as his first student and worked with him for four years. His other students were Gary Graffman (1953–55); Coleman Blumfield (1956–58); Ronald Turini (1957–63); Alexander Fiorillo (1960–62); and Ivan Davis (1961–62). Graffman and Janis attained fame as concert pianists. The other Horowitz students were for the most part disappointed and disillusioned. Both Fiorillo and Blumfield, forbidden to perform while with Horowitz, were abruptly terminated and not permitted to call themselves Horowitz students. Ronald Turini and Ivan Davis fared better. Graffman reports, "He gave me a hell of a lot of his time very graciously." Janis, Horowitz's first student, was also the favorite student. He literally became a part of the Horowitz family. Horowitz used what Janis recalled as a trial-and-error approach. "There was a lot of experimenting going on—Horowitz deciding what to do and what not to do. Many of his ideas were sound, some not. After a long struggle, I later discarded things that weren't me." (Plaskin, "The Secret Career. . .") Janis also admitted that he had many psychological problems related to those years with Horowitz. "The weight of his personality was too much for me and I had a breakdown." (Plaskin, "A Lesson. . .") In 1976 Horowitz began teaching one or two advanced pupils at the Mannes College of Music, but he resigned in 1978.

Horowitz knew that much of his fame rested on his reputation as a technical wizard, and he made no attempt to apologize for it. His concept of technique went far beyond dexterity, speed, facility. In one interview he said, "But what is technique? It is having a good voice and knowing how to sing well. The piano's voice is the tone, the balancing of the notes, the coloring. . . . It takes the coordination of mind, heart, and finger. If by technique is meant the total of phrasing, shading, pedaling, then I am happy to be called the greatest technician." (Klein)

He normally practiced one and a half or two hours, never more than three or four hours, because, as he said many times, too much practicing makes playing mechanical. In 1960 Horowitz told an interviewer that it was "not necessary to repeat the work all the way through. A piece can be practiced 100 times and when it is taken to the stage it can sound simply like practicing the 101st time—it is not fresh. In my work I play a new large-form composition all the way through to obtain an overall viewpoint of its meaning and structure. Then I do not play it all through again until it is ready for public performance." (Holcman)

Horowitz had learned the invaluable art of listening from Felix Blumenfeld, his teacher in Kiev, who would tell him, "*Listen* to yourself, Volodya." And, as Horowitz often said, "This is what I tell young pianists who come here. 'Listen and sing.' We listen to old *bel canto* singers, to Battistini, Anselmi and Sobinov. Such line they had. Playing the piano should be like that." (Klein)

Horowitz was usually more impressive in short pieces or in works depending on spectacular playing for their effect than in pieces that required a sustained artistic vision and a sense of larger forms. He was at his best in the Russian repertoire—Prokofiev, Rachmaninoff, Scriabin—particularly in works demanding extraordinary technique. "His Beethoven was mostly forgettable, particularly the slow movements that are often the heart of the music. His Mozart and Scarlatti were much prized by some connoisseurs, but mainly for technical finesse—marvels of legato phrasing and the production of remarkable pianissimo tone—rather than for any musical sensitivity. . . . His performance of Chopin and Schumann miniatures often achieved magic through utter simplicity of phrasing and pure, limpid tone." (McLellan, "Horowitz . . . ")

When asked in 1975 about his repertoire, Horowitz replied, "Well, it's very large. I play just about everything—privately. And not only the piano literature. . . . I continue to love Scriabin passionately. . . . I consider Clementi the start of really large-scale pianism. . . . I particularly enjoy the French repertoire." (Morrison). Fellow pianist Murray Perahia confirms that Horowitz "knew all the repertory and could play pieces he hadn't done in 20 years— Beethoven, Scriabin, Chopin. He always counseled me to be freer, but he was upset when people tried to imitate his style. He didn't like the terms Classical or Romantic. He simply said to play from the heart." (*NYT*, 6 Nov 1989)

Horowitz had very few concertos in his active repertoire: Tchaikovsky No. 1; Rachmaninoff No. 3; Brahms Nos. 1 and 2; the Beethoven No. 5 and several Mozart concertos.

Horowitz was absolutely fearless at the piano. He took risks. And he had that ravishing sound and those unbelievable hands. No wonder he drew audiences like a magnet. A half-century ago they made Horowitz a superstar, and they never failed him. Critics are another story. Always divided over Horowitz's free playing, since his death the ongoing battle between the ardent supporters and disdainful detractors has mushroomed into full verbal combat (see Taruskin and letters in reply, *NYT*, 19 Dec 1993).

Both the Horowitz devotees and their opposites (those who never succumbed to his bewitching playing) have ardently defended their views. In the words of one supporter, "Horowitz, like all great pianists in the Romantic mainstream, can spin a long singing melodic line, as well as underpin it with a near kaleidoscopic highlighting of bass and inner voice lines. His ability to delineate these lines, and to shade and color subtleties of harmonic tension are second to none in either originality of conception or technical realization. It is at times tempting to term him the greatest contrapuntal player alive!" (Banowetz)

And this from a British devotee: "His technique is effortless, comprehensive, with strength and delicacy finely proportioned. So brilliant is his execution that many music-lovers call him superficial, or wanting in depth. . . . It is not easy to praise Horowitz too much, if only we approach his playing from the right point of view. . . . Horowitz has no 'message' for us straight from the high gods of music—only musical pleasure, born of the piano, lovely colours, patterns and scents, and pulsations of the aesthetic senses." (Cardus)

Those not in sympathy with the Horowitz pianism express their views in equally strong terms: "His technique is brilliant, his musicianship questionable, his performances always exciting but often maddening. . . . I believe that it is dangerous to regard Horowitz's or anyone else's technique as an art in itself; and I also believe that most musicians find Horowitz's way with the standard repertoire cloying, although they may be amazed by his playing in general and enlightened by certain of its details. His eccentricities may fascinate, but in the end, they remain eccentricities." (Sachs)

And this: "It is nearly impossible for him to play simply, and where simplicity is wanted, he is apt to offer a teasing, *affettuoso* manner, or to steamroll the line into perfect flatness. . . . Horowitz illustrates that an astounding instrumental gift carries no guarantee about musical understanding." (New/Gro, see Bibliog.)

The final word belongs to Horowitz's very large, very faithful audiences. They are the ones keeping alive the legend of their magnificent pianist.

In June of 1928 the Victor Talking Machine Company released Horowitz's first records for the phonograph as distinct from the some 20 compositions he performed on Welte (1926) and Duo-Art (1928) piano rolls. The first Victor recordings included the glittering *Carmen* variations and the Chopin Mazurka in C-sharp Minor, op. 30, no. 4. Beginning in 1930 with his recording of the Rachmaninoff Concerto No. 3, Horowitz recorded exclusively for RCA Victor and the British parent affiliation, The Gramophone Company, until 1962, when a purported dispute over repertoire ended the association. Horowitz signed with Columbia Records but twelve years later returned to RCA.

According to one calculation, Horowitz made upwards of 150 recordings. There are discographies of his published recordings, of his studio recordings, of his live recordings and even an extensive discography of his unpublished recordings. The definitive discography has yet to be compiled. The 35 CDs included in the RCA Victor and Sony (CBS) "Horowitz Collections" may take care of the "official" recordings, but more "unofficial" discs are bound to be forthcoming. (For an in-depth discussion by Bryce Morrison of the RCA and Sony collections, see *Gramophone*, July 1994, pp. 84, 88.)

What are Horowitz's finest recordings? What performances best represent both pianist and musician? His first (there are two others) recording of the Rachmaninoff Concerto No. 3, made with Albert Coates and the London Symphony Orchestra in 1930 (see Discog.), gets very high marks. "It is propulsive, even savage, and he simply eats up the notes. There are none of the mannerisms of which he was later accused, and the slow movement emerges in a singing, natural kind of poetry." (Schonberg, *Horowitz*)

One writer believes that Horowitz's recording of the Liszt Sonata in B Minor, made in England in 1932, had an enormous impact on his colleagues. There is in the Liszt sonata "much of the scatterbrained personality of Liszt the poet, the piano virtuoso, and the romantic lover. It was this side of Liszt which Horowitz, with his magnificent bag of octaves, chords, arpeggios, and above all his wistful rubati, chose to present. The sonata has never been the same since, and neither have other pianists." (Lipman)

Other outstanding recorded performances include the Prokofiev Sonata No. 7 (1945), the Samuel Barber Sonata (1950) and the fine collection of Scarlatti sonatas dating from the 1960s (Sony, vol. 7). In the Prokofiev Sonata, with its angular melodies and forceful contrasts, Horowitz uses comparatively little pedal, resulting in fine, clear textures. The Samuel Barber Sonata was written for Horowitz, and his followers rank the Horowitz version as the finest.

Paradoxically enough, Horowitz, "the last Romantic," achieved some of his most delightful readings in a group of Scarlatti sonatas. Horowitz, the supreme pianist, does not attempt to imitate the harpsichord mystique, but his articulation is clear, pedaling is at a minimum and at almost every turn he respects the music's demands for discipline and order.

A 1989 appraisal of Horowitz recordings offers suggestions for a small selected discography: *Horowitz Live at Carnegie Hall*; *Horowitz in Moscow*; *Horowitz plays Liszt*; a Schumann album; *Portrait of Vladimir Horowitz*; *Favorite Chopin*; a Scriabin album; Rachmaninoff Concerto No. 3 with Coates and the London Symphony Orchestra. (*NYT*, 12 Nov 1989)

There are, of course, many other fine Horowitz recordings. His first Columbia recording, released 1 October 1962, included works by Chopin, Liszt, Rachmaninoff and Schumann. This, wrote one reviewer, was Horowitz's "finest record to date and . . . one of the finest piano records ever made." (*MA*, Oct 1962) The best-selling classical album of the year, it also won a Grammy award for the best recording of the year in the classical category. Grammy awards in 1963, 1964 and 1965 made Horowitz the first performer in recording history to be honored with four consecutive awards. Actually, over a 32-year period (1958–1990), his albums garnered a total of 27 Grammys.

A recent Sony CD titled *Discovered Treasures* features heretofore unreleased CBS performances—Chopin, Clementi, Liszt, Medtner, Scarlatti, Scriabin—from studio recordings made between 1962 and 1972. Most were originally recorded to be included on what are now famous records: i.e., the six Scarlatti sonatas were for the 1964 Scarlatti record; the Chopin "Raindrop" Prelude was meant for the spectacular all-Chopin record of 1971. They are indeed treasures from one of the artist's most productive periods, arguably his best years. For one reviewer, the six sonatas by Domenico Scarlatti are "brightly shining, flawless gems. . . . The four selections from Clementi's sonatas have a dramatic urgency and poise that could only be Horowitz." (*CS*, 10 Jan 1993)

Although another critic finds the Scarlatti sonatas "unnecessarily harsh and pointed," for him, the other selections show Horowitz as the great artist he was: "Nicolai Medtner's 'Fairy Tale' is a moving Christmas story in notes. Horowitz's acute timing and melodic inflection have never been sharper. . . . Scriabin's late and fiery etude from Op. 65 is another welcome addition to Horowitz's great performance legacy with this composer's music. And of the three Chopin selections, the A-flat Etude from the three 'new' ones is perhaps the most beautiful thing on the disc." (*W-SJ*, 13 Dec 1992)

Horowitz's Mozart recording—the Concerto in A Major, K. 488 (performed with the Orchestra of *La Scala*, conducted by Carlo Maria Giulini), and the Sonata in B-flat Major, K. 333—stirred up a critical storm. For one critic these are merely the "mannered, mincing Mozart recordings that the pianist made for Deutsche Grammophon a year or two before his death." (Page) From another critic: "The andante cantabile movement of the sonata is as close as the pianist comes to a truly lyrical reading. . . . But [he] consistently fails to make of these scores the effortless, inevitable flow of musical sounds and ideas that a convincing Mozart performance must be. Horowitz is simply too busy being Horowitz, too occupied with coaxing beautiful sounds and executing beautiful figures from his Steinway, to bow before Mozart's style." (*RT*, 6 Dec 1987)

But, wrote yet another critic, "This is very much Horowitz's record—and at times in the finale [Concerto] there is not too much of the orchestra, nor is there much sign of rapport between Horowitz and Giulini! Still, this is remarkable piano playing, quite unlike any other." (Pen/Gui, 1990, see Bibliog.)

SELECTED REFERENCES

Alder, Caine. "The Recordings of Vladimir Horowitz." *High Fidelity*, July 1973, pp. 48–52.
———. "The Unknown Recordings of Vladimir Horowitz." *High Fidelity*, Jan 1978, pp. 69–74.
Banowetz, Joseph. "Arrau, Horowitz, Serkin: A Walk Among Giants." *Piano Quarterly*, Fall 1979, pp. 23–30.
Brown, Steven. "Horowitz: Was He a Romantic Pianist." *Piano Quarterly*, Fall 1991, pp. 36–40.

Cardus, Neville. "Vladimir Horowitz." (An Appreciation) *Gramophone Record Review*, April 1957, pp. 440–441.

Chasins, Abram. "Vladimir Horowitz." *High Fidelity/Musical America*, Aug 1965, pp. 122, 131.

Chotzinoff, Samuel. "Vladimir Horowitz." In *A Little Nightmusic*. New York: Harper & Row, 1964, pp. 31–49.

Dubal, David. *Evenings with Horowitz*. New York: Birch Lane Press, 1991.

Dubal, David, ed. *Remembering Horowitz* (125 Pianists Recall a Legend). New York: Schirmer Books, 1993.

Epstein, Helen. "The Grand Eccentric Of The Concert Hall." *New York Times Magazine*, 8 Jan 1978, pp. 13–15, 46–47.

Gruen, John. "The Curse of Being Vladimir Horowitz." *New York Times*, 23 Nov 1975, sec. 11, pp. 1, 8.

Henahan, Donal. "The Fine Art of Going to Extremes." *New York Times*, 5 Oct 1975, sec. 2, p. 17.

Holcman, Jan. "An Interview with Horowitz." *Piano Teacher*, Sept–Oct 1960, pp. 4–7. Reprinted from *Saturday Review*, 30 April 1960.

"Horowitz on the Road." *Newsweek*, 2 Dec 1974, pp. 95–96.

Kennicott, Philip. "Have Piano, Will Travel." *Musical America*, Nov/Dec 1991, pp. 28–32.

Klein, Howard. "The Horowitz Method: 'Listen and sing'." *New York Times*, 9 May 1965, pp. 32-33, 82-83.

Kochevitsky, George. "Horowitz Remembered." *Piano Quarterly*, Winter 1989/90, pp. 36–48.

Kupferberg, Herbert. "Vladimir Horowitz." *High Fidelity/Musical America*, Jan 1978, pp. MA 8–9.

Lipatti, Dinu. "Vladimir Horowitz." In *Lipatti*, by Dragos Tanasescu & Grigore Bargauanu. London: Kahn & Averill, 1988, pp. 68-69.

Lipman, Samuel. "Horowitz: King of Pianists." In *Music After Modernism*. New York: Basic Books, Inc., 1979, pp. 138–149.

Mach, Elyse. "The New Horowitz." *Piano Quarterly*, Summer 1975, pp. 11–14.

Mays, Bruce. "A Salute to Horowitz." *Clavier*, Oct 1979, pp. 23–25.

McAlear, Robert. "The Fall and Rise of Vladimir Horowitz." *Music Magazine*, Jan/Feb 1988, pp. 6–10.

McLellan, Joseph. "The Horowitz Magnum Opus." (A portrait of Glenn Plaskin, a Horowitz biographer). *Washington Post*, 23 March 1983, sec. B, p. 1.

———. "Horowitz, Wizard Of the Keyboard." *Washington Post*, 6 Nov 1989, sec. D, pp. 1, 6.

Mohr, Franz. *My Life with the Great Pianists*. Grand Rapids: Baker Book House, 1992, pp. 19–47, 75–90.

Montparker, Carol. "Horowitz in Moscow." *Clavier*, July–Aug 1986, p. 33.

Morrison, Bryce. "Vladimir Horowitz." *Music and Musicians*, Aug 1975, pp. 32–33.

Obituary. *New York Daily News*, 6 Nov 1989, p. 3. *New York Post*, 6 Nov 1989, p. 2. *New York Times*, 6 Nov 1989, sec. 1, pp. 16–17. *Newsweek*, 20 Nov 1989, p. 81. *Washington Post*, 6 Nov 1989, sec. A, pp. 1, 24.

Page, Tim. "Roll Over Liszt." (An in-depth review of *Horowitz* by Harold C. Schonberg.) *The New Republic*, 30 Nov 1992, pp. 39–42.

Pfeiffer, John. "Manhattan Holiday." *High Fidelity*, Oct 1957, pp. 59–61, 194–196.

Plaskin, Glenn. *Horowitz*. New York: William Morrow & Company, 1983. Contains a discography compiled by Robert McAlear.

———. "A Lesson With Vladimir Horowitz." *Keyboard Classics*, March/April 1983, pp. 4–9.

———. "The Secret Career Of Horowitz." *New York Times Magazine*, 11 May 1980, pp. 95–99.

———. "Vladimir Horowitz." *Ovation*, March 1983, pp. 8–11, 36–37.

Saal, Hubert. "Lord of the Piano." *Newsweek*, 23 Jan 1978, pp. 62–63, 66–67.

Sachs, Harvey. "Vladimir Horowitz." In *Virtuoso* (Sac/Vir, see Bibliog.), pp. 165–175.

Schonberg, Harold C. "Books of The Times." (A review of Horowitz by Glenn Plaskin). *New York Times*, 10 March 1983, sec. 3, p. 18.

———. *Horowitz: His Life and Music*. New York: Simon & Schuster, 1992. Contains a discography compiled by Jon M. Samuels.

———. "Vladimir Horowitz." *Encore*, March 1987, pp. 1, 12.

———. "Vladimir Horowitz: Thunder, Lightning and Awe." *New York Times*, 12 Nov 1989, sec. 2, pp. 1, 32. Includes a selected discography.

Stearns, David Patrick. "Wanda's World." *Classical Pulse*, June/July 1994, p. 43. A review of the Video *Vladimir Horowitz: A Reminiscence*.

Taruskin, Richard. "Why Do They All Hate Horowitz?" *New York Times*, 28 Nov 1993, sec. 2, p. 31. Letters by Stuart Isacoff and Tim Page in rebuttal to this essay appeared in the 19 Dec 1993 issue.

"Vladimir Horowitz: October 1, 1904—November 5, 1989." *Piano Quarterly*, Winter 1989/90, pp. 36–48. A collection of tributes and memorials by friends and admirers.

Walsh, Michael. "The Prodigal Returns." *Time*, 5 May 1986, pp. 56–65.

See also Bibliography: Car/Del; Cha/Spe; Cur/Bio (1966); Dan/Con; Dow/Oli; Dub/Ref; Ewe/Li; Ewe/Mu; Ham/Lis; IWWM; Kai/Gre; Kau/Art; Mac/Gre; Moh/My; New/Gro; Sac/Vir; Sal/Fam; Sch/Glo; Sch/My; WWAM.

SELECTED REVIEWS

BaS: 27 Feb 1978. *CST*: 1 May 1978. *CT*: 30 April 1978; 18 April 1983. *GM*: 8 May 1933. *LAT*: 5 Nov 1974; 24 Feb 1976; 2 March 1976; 22 March 1977. *MA*: 3 March 1928; 10 March 1932; 25 March 1944. *MiT*: 21 May 1979; 19 Oct 1981. *MT*: 1 May 1927; Feb 1935; Dec 1951; July 1982. *NW*: 2 Dec 1974. *NYT*; 13 Jan 1928; 21 Feb 1928; 3 Nov 1928; 16 Nov 1929; 25 Feb 1930; 22 Jan 1931; 27 Feb 1932; 30 March 1933; 15 March 1935; 14 April 1935; 16 Feb 1940; 13 April 1940; 7 May 1940; 13 Jan 1953; 10 May 1965; 18 April 1966; 25 Nov 1968; 13 May 1974; 18

Nov 1974; 17 Nov 1975; 30 May 1976; 13 March 1978; 16 May 1983; 16 Dec 1985; 28 April 1986; 15 Dec 1986. *PP*: 10 Dec 1979. *SR*: 22 May 1965. *STL*: 23 May 1982. *Time*: 21 May 1965. *TL*: 11 Nov 1932; 29 May 1934; 1 March 1939; 31 May 1982. *WP*: 29 March 1982; 21 April 1986; 28 April 1986. *WS-N*: 3 June 1977.

SELECTED DISCOGRAPHY

Barber: Sonata, op. 26. Fauré: Nocturne in B Minor, op. 119. Kabalevsky: Sonata No. 3, op. 46. Poulenc: Presto in B-flat. Prokofiev: Sonata No. 7 in B-flat Major, op. 83; Toccata, op. 11. RCA Gold Seal 60377-2.

Brahms: Waltz in A Flat. Chopin: Barcarolle; Nocturne, op. 15, no. 2; Mazurka, op. 24, no. 4; Mazurka, op. 30, no. 4; Scherzo No. 3. Debussy: Serenade to the Doll. Fauré: Impromptu No. 5. Liszt: Hungarian Rhapsody No. 6; *Valse oubliée* No. 1. Liszt-Busoni: Etude No. 2 (after Paganini). Mendelssohn: Song Without Words, op. 62, no. 1. Schumann: Clara Wieck Variations; *Kinderscenen*. RCA Victor 09026-60463-2.

Discovered Treasures. Bach-Busoni: "*Ich ruf zu dir, Herr Jesu Christ.*" Chopin: Etude in E-flat Minor, op. 10, no. 6; Etude No. 1 in A-flat Major (*Trois nouvelles études*); Prelude in D-flat Major, op. 28, no. 15. Clementi: Adagio (Sonata in A Major, op. 50, no. 1); Adagio sostenuto in F Major (*Gradus ad Parnassum*, Book I, no. 14); Rondo (Sonata in E-flat Major, op. 12, no. 2); Rondo (Sonata in B-flat Major, op. 25, no. 3). Liszt: Consolation No. 2 in E Major. Medtner: Fairy Tale in A Major, op. 51, no. 3. Scarlatti: Sonatas in G Major (K. 547), B Minor (K. 197); F-sharp Minor (K. 25); D Minor (K. 52); G Major (K. 201); C Minor (K. 303). Scriabin: Etude, op. 65, no. 3; *Feuillet d'album*, op. 58. Sony Classical SK 48093 (CD).

Encores. Bizet-Horowitz: Variations on a Theme from "Carmen." Chopin: Polonaise in A-flat Major, op. 53. Debussy: Serenade to the Doll. Liszt: *Valse oubliée* no. 1. Liszt-Horowitz: Rakóczy March. Mendelssohn: *Scherzo a capriccio*: Presto; Songs Without Words, op. 62, no. 6, op. 67, no. 5, op. 85, no. 4. Mendelssohn-Liszt-Horowitz: Wedding March and Variations. Moszkowski: Etudes, op. 72, nos. 6 and 11; *Étincelles*, op. 36, no. 6. Rachmaninoff: Prelude in G Minor, op. 23, no. 5. Saint-Saëns-Liszt-Horowitz: *Danse macabre*. Schumann: *Träumerei*, op. 15, no. 7. Sousa-Horowitz: The Stars and Stripes Forever. RCA (Gold Seal) 7755-2.

Favorite Encores. Chopin: Etudes, op. 10, nos. 3, 5, 12; Polonaise in A-flat Major, op. 53. Debussy: Serenade to the Doll. Horowitz: Variations on Themes from Bizet's *Carmen*. Moszkowski: Etude in A-flat Major, op. 72, no. 1. Mozart: *Rondo alla Turca* (Sonata, K. 331). Rachmaninoff: *Etude-tableau* in C Major, op. 33, no. 2; Prelude in G-sharp Minor, op. 32, no. 12. Scarlatti: Sonata in E Major, K. 531; Sonata in A Major, K. 322. Schubert: Impromptu in G-flat Major, D. 899, no. 3. Schumann: Arabesque in C Major, op. 18; Toccata in C Major, op. 7; *Träumerei* (*Kinderscenen*). Scriabin: Etude in C-sharp Minor, op. 2, no. 1. Etude in D-sharp Minor, op. 8, no. 12. CBS MK 42305 (CD).

Horowitz Collection. RCA Victor Gold Seal 90926-61655-2 (22 CDs). Contains all of the pianist's recordings for RCA Victor.

Horowitz Live at Carnegie Hall. The Historic Concerts of 1965, 1966 and 1968. CBS M3K-44681 (3 CDs).

Horowitz plays Liszt. Ballade No. 2 in B Minor; Consolation No. 3; *Funérailles*; Mephisto Waltz No. 1; Sonata in B Minor (1977). RCA (Red Seal) 09026-61415-2.

The Last Recording. Chopin: Etudes, op. 25, nos. 1 and 5; *Fantaisie-Impromptu*, op. 66; Mazurka, op. 56, no. 3; Nocturnes, op. 55, no. 2, op. 62, no. 1. Haydn: Sonata in E-flat Major, Hob. XVI:49. Liszt: *Weinen, Klagen, Sorgen, Zagen*. Wagner-Liszt: *Isolde's Liebestod*. Sony Classical SK 45818.

The Legend: Recordings from the 1930s. Liszt: Sonata in B Minor. Rachmaninoff: Concerto No. 3 in D Minor, op. 30. Scarlatti: Sonata in G, K. 125. Fidelio 3465 (CD). Coates/London SO.

Schumann: *Arabeske*, op. 18 (1968); *Blumenstück*, op. 19 (1966); *Kinderscenen*, op. 15; *Kreisleriana*, op. 16 (1969); Toccata, op. 7 . CBS MK-42409 (CD).

Scriabin: Etudes, op. 2, no. 1, op. 8, nos. 2, 8, 10–12, op. 42, nos. 3–5; *Feuillet d'album*, op. 45, no. 1; *Poèmes*, op. 32, no. 1, op. 69, nos. 1 and 2; Sonata No. 9 in F Major, op. 68; Sonata No. 10, op. 70; *Ver la flamme*, op. 72. CBS MK-42411 (CD).

Sony Horowitz Edition. Sony 53456 (13 CDs). Contains all the approved Horowitz recordings made between 1962 and 1973 for Columbia/CBS.

Tchaikovsky: Concerto No. 1 in B-flat Minor, op. 23. Brahms: Concerto No. 2 in B-flat Major, op. 83. Toscanini/NBC SO (1941). RCA Victor Gold Seal Toscanini Collection 60319-2.

Vladimir Horowitz in Recital. Bizet-Horowitz: Carmen Fantasy. Chopin: Ballade in G Minor, op. 23; *Valse brillante*, op. 34, no. 2. Clementi: Sonata in C Major, op. 36, no. 3. Liszt: *Au bord d'une source*; *Valse oubliée*. Moszkowski: *Étincelles*. Rachmaninoff: Prelude in G-sharp Minor, op. 32, no. 12; *Etudes-Tableaux*, op. 33, no. 2, op. 33, no. 5, op. 39, no. 5, op. 39, no. 9; Sonata No. 2 in B-flat Minor, op. 36. Scarlatti: Sonatas in G Major (K. 55), A Major (K. 101), G Major (K. 260), F-sharp Major (K. 319), F Minor (K. 466). Schumann: *Arabeske*, op. 18; Sonata No. 3 in F Minor, op. 14; *Träumerei*. Music and Arts CD-666 (2 CDs).

VIDEO

Horowitz in Moscow. Chopin: Mazurkas, op. 7, no. 3, op. 30, no. 4; Polonaise in A-flat Major, op. 53. Liszt: *Sonetto del Petrarca* No. 104. Mozart: Sonata in C Major, K. 330. Moskowski: *Étincelles*. Rachmaninoff: *Polka de W. R.*; Preludes, op. 32, nos. 5 and 12. Scarlatti: Sonatas in B Minor (K. 87), E Major (K. 135), E Major (K. 380). Schubert: Impromptu in B Flat, D. 935, no. 3. Schubert/Liszt: *Soirées de Vienne* No. 6. Schumann: *Träumerei*, op. 15, no. 7. Scriabin: Etudes, op. 2, no. 1, op. 8, no. 12. MGM/UA Home Video MV401051.

Horowitz in Vienna. Chopin: Mazurka, op. 33, no. 4; Polonaise No. 6, op. 53. Liszt: Consolation No. 3. Moszkowski: *Étincelles* . Mozart: Rondo, K. 485; Sonata, K. 333. Schubert: Impromptu, D. 899, no. 3; *Moment musical*, D. 780, no. 3. Schubert-Liszt: Valse-Caprice No. 6. Schumann: *Kinderscenen*, op. 15. Polygram Music Video 072 221-3. NTSC.

Vladimir Horowitz: A Reminiscence. Part I: Vladimir Horowitz: A Reminiscence. Includes recently discovered footage from 1974. Part II: Chopin's Introduction and Rondo in E-flat Major, op. 16. Part III: From Horowitz in London. Scarlatti: Five Sonatas. Chopin: Waltz in A-flat Major, op. posth. 69, no. 1. Rachmaninoff: Sonata No. 2 in B-flat Minor, op. 36; *Polka de W. R.* Sony Classical SHV 53478. An extremely interesting and informative documentary.

HORSZOWSKI, MIECZYSLAW: b. L'vov, Poland, 23 June 1892; d. Philadelphia, Pennsylvania, 22 May 1993.

> Mr. Horszowski can convey more music in two or three gently shaped measures than an artillery of note-perfect pianists can drive home in an evening.
>
> Tim Page (*New York Times*, 13 April 1987)

In 1989 Mieczyslaw Horszowski reached the remarkable age of 97. Even more wondrous, he was still giving concerts (that season in New York, Chicago, Vienna, Lucerne) and still teaching (two students in his studio at the Curtis Institute). A concert pianist for more than 80 years, Horszowski's long and continuous musical life linked the world of 20th-century music back to the great composers and musicians of the past. In the historical chain of great musicians Horszowski, as his pupil Peter Serkin put it, represented "a thread of lineage, a sense of continuity." Indeed, Horszowski was the last active pupil of Leschetizky, the legendary pedagogue who had studied with Czerny, who in his day had studied with Beethoven. Horszowski's mother, his first teacher, had studied with Karol Mikuly, a pupil of Chopin. And as a child in L'vov, Horszowski had received a thorough scolding from an elderly lady for smudging some of the 32nd-note runs in the finale of Mozart's "Coronation" Concerto. She of course knew how they should sound, for she had studied with Mozart's youngest son Franz Xaver Mozart, a teacher in L'vov until 1838.

Furthermore, Horszowski could remember the live sound of great pianists of the past—Eugen d'Albert, Ferruccio Busoni, Teresa Carreño and Vladimir de Pachman. Over his long life span this gentle, wonderful musician became close friends with, and often played with, some of the greatest musicians of this century. In 1903 he met Artur Rubinstein, beginning a friendship that would endure for more than 70 years; and that same year he met Joseph Joachim, the 19th-century violinist for whom Brahms wrote his Violin Concerto.

Horszowski likewise treasured the memory of himself, only 13 years old at the time, playing for Gabriel Fauré in Paris; the memory of meeting (1906) Pablo Casals, and their lifelong musical association and friendship. Among his other cherished memories (think how many have been lost!) was performing under the baton of Maurice Ravel, playing privately for Paderewski and Granados and performing hours of chamber music with Szigeti, Casals and others.

Horszowski's mother had been a piano teacher before her marriage, and his father, possibly also a musician, owned a music store where he sold both pianos and music. Their son, not merely a mechanically skilled child but a true prodigy gifted with musical insight, began piano lessons with his mother at "half-past four," as he said, and soon was devoting seven hours a day to music. Before he was six years old he astounded conservatory professors by playing from memory and transposing Bach's Two-Part Inventions. Besides his mother's lessons, he studied with Henryk Melcer, a pupil of Leschetizky, and with Mieczyslaw Soltys at the L'vov Conservatory.

Horszowski was only seven years old when he began four years (1899–1903) of study with Leschetizky in Vienna. He made his recital debut in Vienna at age eight, in 1900, and his official orchestral debut in 1902, playing Beethoven's Concerto in C Major, op. 15, with the Warsaw Philharmonic Orchestra, conducted by Emil Mlynarski (father-in-law of Artur Rubinstein). At this young age Miecio—his childhood nickname—began concertizing. Accompanied by his mother, he toured in Europe (Vienna, Berlin, Leipzig, Geneva, Paris, Madrid, Portugal, Rome, Milan, Naples); he played for Queen Alexandra at Buckingham Palace; in 1906 he gave a recital at the Vatican for Pope Pius X (36 years later, in 1940, Horszowski played a Chopin recital in honor of Pope Pius XII); and in 1906 he also toured in Brazil and Uruguay.

By the time Horszowski made his American debut (30 Dec 1906) at Carnegie Hall, he was already, at age 14, a seasoned veteran of the concert hall. But in 1911, at age 19, he interrupted his concert career to study in Paris because, as he later explained, "there were so many things to learn that I did not know, in Bach, Mozart, and in areas other than music: literature, Latin, Greek." (Shear) He returned to the concert stage in 1913, and from 1914 to 1940 made his home in Milan, his choice because it was, he felt, a fine musical center (Toscanini was conducting at *La Scala*) and cultural city. All through the Milan years Horszowski toured extensively, mostly in Europe, in America (1926, 1927) and South America (1924, 1934, 1940). On tour in Brazil when World War II overran Europe, he went directly to the United States, not home to Milan, and in 1948 became an American citizen.

Changing continents made little difference. Horszowski's quiet career continued without a break. Among many noteworthy appearances are two performances with the NBC Symphony Orchestra, the first on 5 December 1943 (his New York concerto debut, he played Mozart's Concerto in B-flat Major, K. 595) and the second on 17 January 1953 (Martucci Concerto in B-flat Minor). Other memorable appearances include a gigantic cycle (12 recitals) encompassing, with minor exceptions, Beethoven's complete works for piano solo, presented at the New York YM-YWHA during the 1954–55 season; a cycle of all the Mozart piano sonatas played in four recitals at the YM-YWHA in 1960; a series of ten Mozart concertos performed at the Metropolitan Museum of Art in 1962; and another cycle of Mozart concertos, played with the *Musica Aeterna* Orchestra, Frederic Waldman conducting, presented in 1976.

Horszowski, who loved to play chamber music, often performed with musicians such as Heinrich Grunfeld, Joseph Szigeti, Alexander Schneider and especially with his friend Pablo Casals. Beginning in 1927 when he performed with Casals at the Beethoven Festival in Barcelona, Spain, these two compatible musicians played together as their schedules allowed, notably at the Casals Festivals (in Prades and in Puerto Rico) and the 1958 United Nations Day Concert (24 Oct), broadcast throughout the world. It should be pointed out that Horszowski, full of cherished memories and a wealth of musical experience, also greatly enjoyed playing chamber music with ensembles of young musicians. One of his most valuable contributions lies in his unique role as a bridge between the great traditions and musicians of the past and the young artists of today.

In 1976 he marked the 70th anniversary of his American debut with a recital at New York's Metropolitan Museum of Art. Reaching the venerable age of 90 slowed him down, but not much. Always a sensitive, musicianly pianist, he continued to play concerts in America and Europe, still taught at the Curtis Institute of Music and taught summer sessions in Europe. In 1986, at age 94, he marked the 80th anniversary of his American debut with a performance (at the Metropolitan Museum of Art) of the Mozart Piano Concerto in D Minor, K. 466, with Leon Fleisher conducting the Orchestra of St. Luke's. On 28 June 1987 the indomitable Horszowski celebrated his 95th birthday with a solo recital at London's Wigmore Hall. In December of that year he made his debut appearance in Japan at the inauguration of the Casals Hall in Tokyo. During the 1988–89 season he played in New York, Chicago, Vienna and Lucerne.

The truth is that Horszowski never "retired" from his beloved piano, although in the last years failing eyesight forced him to rely on repertoire firmly entrenched in his wonderful memory. He not only kept playing, reviews confirm that he played well: "Mr. Horszowski played the most satisfying piano recital [26 Feb 1989] this critic has heard all season—perhaps in several seasons. . . . As he approaches 100 (he will turn 97 in a few months), he only seems to improve." (*NYT*, 1 March 1989)

Why (and how) a few musicians can keep playing, and playing beautifully, at such an advanced age is truly a mystery. In Horszowski's case, he was most fortunate in that for the last decade of his life his precious, longevous musical gifts received invaluable protecting and nurturing from Bice (Costa) Horszowski, the young wife he married (July 1981) when he was 89 years old. They had been friends for a quarter of a century, since they met at her family home in Genoa, and she had sometimes been his teaching assistant. With her selfless support, Horszowski gave his last Carnegie Hall performance on 23 April 1990, exactly two months before his 98th birthday. On 31 October 1991 he gave his last recital at Philadelphia's Port of History Museum. He died on 22 May 1993, a month away from his 101st birthday.

Horszowski began teaching at the Curtis Institute in 1942 and continued there almost until the year of his death. He conducted master classes in Europe and America, and for many years was associated with Rudolf Serkin and Alexander Schneider at the Marlboro Festival and School in Vermont. In 1982 he spent the month of April as artist-in-residence at the State University of New York at Buffalo.

As a teacher, Horszowski tried to instill in his students (among them Murray Perahia and Peter Serkin) a high regard for both piano literature and for chamber music. His own teacher Leschetizky had kept him hard at work on the Etudes of Cramer, Czerny and Clementi, and he always believed *that* had been immensely helpful. But Horszowski realized that with the pressures of modern living students simply do not have the time for those studies. "Instead," he said, "I use Bach, Beethoven, Mozart, Mendelssohn and contemporary music for the development of technique and musicianship. Bartók and Hindemith are excellent for that purpose, especially Bartók. Their works are wonderful studies in rhythmic and polyphonic playing. Scale and arpeggio practice is, of course, a necessity and I recommend that they be played slowly for evenness of touch. Exercises can be made up from difficult passages in pieces." (Kammerer)

Peter Serkin, one of Horszowski's most renowned pupils, not only studied with him at Curtis but periodically coached with him after leaving that institution. At a 1986 interview, Serkin readily nominated Horszowski as his favorite performer. "I love his curiosity, his inquisitiveness. He's so *respectful* of the music in a genuine way. . . . A great performer, like him, respects the composer, the fundaments of Western classical music—and respects the audience, too. There is a responsibility in sharing a great work and helping the listener to hear it properly. It's a kind of playing that defies definition, that is completely of the moment. Playing has to be interesting, bold. Horszowski is always bold, he always makes new choices, but it comes out convincingly, as if it's the only way to do it." (*OV*, Jan 1986)

While most Leschetizky pupils became dazzling interpreters of the Romantic repertoire, Horszowski, like Artur Schnabel, another Leschetizky pupil, played the Baroque repertoire (Bach), the Classic repertoire (Mozart, Beethoven), as well as the lyrical Romantic composers (Schubert, Chopin, Liszt, Schumann) and the French impressionists (Ravel and Debussy).

Surprisingly, this refined classicist was also a pioneer in performing contemporary music. As a child Horszowski had played Tchaikovsky and Grieg, both of them at that time new composers. In 1923 he gave the first performance of Karol Szymanowski's Third Piano Concerto. On 11 January 1927 he played what he believed to be the first New York performance of the Stravinsky four-movement Serenade, prompting one reviewer to write that "the unfamiliar music, however sensitively performed, betrayed a characteristic bitterness of muted cacophony, without any clearly compensating boldness of melodic line." (*NYT*, 12 Jan 1927) About a month later a Horszowski recital (23 Feb 1927) included the first New York performance of Vincent d'Indy's *Thème varié, fugue et chanson*, composed in 1925. Although Horszowski played extremely well, the audience seemed only mildly interested; however, it is worth noting that Horszowski concluded that recital "with a varied and descriptive composition by Maurice Ravel, called 'Gaspard de la nuit'." (*NYT*, 24 Feb 1927)

Horszowski's Town Hall recital of 23 October 1948 included, according to one reviewer, "two works seldom, if ever, played here, Szymanowski's lengthy second Sonata and a new Sonatina No. 3 by Camargo Guarnieri." (*NYT*, 25 Oct 1948) And at his second appearance (17 Jan 1953) with Toscanini and the NBC Symphony Orchestra, Horszowski had played "a virtually unknown piano concerto" in B-flat Minor by Giuseppe Martucci. Still supporting contemporary music, on 27 September 1975 the 83-year-old Horszowski gave the first New York performance of Jonas Kokkonen's Five Bagatelles.

A performer for more than 85 years, Horszowski was music history personified, "and must be counted as one of the world's wonders." (*NYT*, 2 Feb 1986) The question, then, is why was he such a little-known wonder? One writer explains that while piano aficionados always admired Horszowski's lean, clear, unaffected playing, always dignified and graceful, the problem was that during his first 50 years of concertizing the public "favored flashier, more virtuosic performers, and he settled into a career just beyond the spotlight. Now that his quiet and elegant brand of playing has found more general favor, Mr. Horszowski is enjoying a late flowering of attention." (Kimmelman, "Horszowski's Quiet. . .")

Throughout his amazingly long career, critics consistently praised Horszowski for the purity of his approach, his unmannered and straightforward musicianship and his exquisite, subtle pianism. As long ago as his American debut (30 Dec 1906) one New York reviewer wrote: "In many ways his playing is excellent. It is graceful, fluent, fresh and, for a child of his age, of exceptional dynamic variation." (*MA*, 5 Jan 1907) Twenty years after that American debut a critic at one of Horszowski's London recitals noted "an understanding of his music so thorough that he has no need to resort to the least extravagance." (*STL*, 21 April 1926) And 40 years after his debut the brilliant critic-composer Virgil Thomson enthusiastically affirmed those earlier critiques: "Few pianists play with such beauty, such distinction, such unfailing seriousness of thought." First noting Horszowski's wonderful qualities: his beautiful sound, his grace ("the airy way he treats a melody and its ornaments") and his strength (physical, emotional, intellectual), Thomson concluded that, "the whole complex variation of tonal color, accent, and phraseology that goes to make up great piano playing is dominated by a grand line that sweeps through a piece, holds it firm and clear, makes it meaningful, keeps it a composition." (*NYHT*, 20 Oct 1949)

Some three decades after Thomson's glowing assessment, Horszowski's unfailing musicality still impressed critics, for though his age could hinder virtuosity, said one reviewer, his musicality "remains at the fore, defying circumstances." James Methuen-Campbell has written a discerning essay on Horszowski, and it is well worth quoting at length. "Horszowski may have been termed 'the least-known of the world's great pianists,' but his colleagues have always recognized his genius, and this because he is *par excellence* the musician's musician. . . . His readings of the classics, Bach, Mozart and Beethoven, have an authority that is undeniable, and this authority is embedded in an inner conviction that is the result of over eighty-five years' study. . . . Regarding Horszowski's Bach, he plays the music with a natural blending of buoyant rhythm and academic correctness, though there is no dryness. He understands how different textures can be applied to add richness to the music. Tonal and dynamic colourings are based on the imitation of vocal lines, the bowings of string instruments, and the sonorities of solos and tuttis. . . . He does not resort to the eccentricity of Gould, the rigidity of Tureck, nor the relentless energy of Andras Schiff. . . . He reveals details in the score that virtually all other pianists neglect—and yet he never accomplishes this in a way that disrupts the flow of music, as do so many others. . . . Suffice to say that he has a passionate integrity about music that always shines through his interpretations; an almost uncanny ability to reveal the core of a work that has remained with him from childhood till old age." (*MM*, June 1985, reprinted by permission)

A review of the concert (31 Jan 1986, Metropolitan Museum of Art) commemorating the 80th anniversary of Horszowski's American debut included the following: "The audience . . . was fortunate to be able to hear, in 1986, a live exponent of the 19th-century brand of leisurely and personal music-making. . . . His Mozart was tender, indulging every detail of phrasing. If one missed robustness in the forte passages, the pure grace Horszowski lent to the cantabile lines more than compensated for any lack of vigor. . . . Horszowski is somewhat of a miracle." (*CL*, April 1986)

Horszowski made numerous recordings during his long performing career, many of them with chamber-music ensembles. There are also some Bach concertos and Volume I of the Well-Tempered Clavier—the latter now reissued on CD. Vox has also reissued three memorable Beethoven sonata performances, recorded in 1951: Sonata in B-flat Major, op. 106; Sonata in E Major, op. 109; Sonata in C Minor, op. 111 (see Discog.). Greatly in evidence here is the pianist's musicianly, scrupulously objective adherence to the text: "Horszowski stresses the music's lyricism and intimacy over power and drama. He brings ravishing nuances to the first movement of Op. 109 yet remains brisk and unsentimental." (*KeCl*, Sept/Oct 1992) Also outstanding are the clarity of the fugue from Op. 106 and the entire concept of Op. 111.

One of Horszowski's most remarkable late studio recordings is the collection recorded by Elektra/Nonesuch between May 12 and 15, 1986 (see Discog.), a project arranged by, and funded through, a group of his former pupils to honor their teacher and preserve his artistry. A long article by Harris Goldsmith in *Opus* (Dec 1987) discusses each work of the recorded recital: the Mozart D Minor Fantasia, K. 397, which "unfolds with hypnotic, magisterial breadth"; the two Chopin Nocturnes (op. 5, no. 2; op. 27, no. 2), where the pianist "shows complete understanding of voice-leading and harmonic function"; the "humor, bold characterization" evident in Debussy's Children's Corner; and "the wonders of this pianism" in Beethoven's Sonata in A Major, op. 2, no. 2.

A second Nonesuch CD (79202-2, see Discog.), taped two years later, has two Mozart sonatas (K. 332, K. 576), a group of Chopin works, the Schumann *Arabeske*, op. 18, and *Kinderscenen*, op. 15. In his liner notes for this album, Joseph Horowitz succinctly evaluates the essence of Horszowski's performances, stating in part: "The present Horszowski performances of Mozart, Schumann, and Chopin are as unaffected as the man himself. The K. 332 and K. 576 Sonatas, as here recorded, register with child-like immediacy. At the same time, this is the most eventful Mozart playing imaginable, teeming with details of voicing and articulation, savoring every structural or harmonic surprise. Other pianists struggle to tailor Mozart to modern instruments, or to canons of aesthetic decorum. Horszowski's Mozart playing is distinctively unvarnished, unfettered, uninhibited." And another critic writes, "You may not think any pianist can still make Traumerei sound fresh and beautiful, but wait until you hear Horszowski's unaffected performance." As for the sonatas, "These Mozart performances are near-ideal demonstrations of how to play Mozart on the modern piano. Horszowski captures the essential lightness of spirit of these pieces very beautifully, yet never miniaturizes them." (*Fan*, May/June 1989)

At age 97, Horszowski made a third recording (1989)—a program of Bach (English Suite No. 5), two Chopin Nocturnes and the Beethoven Sonata in F Major, op. 10, no. 2. The difficult Bach Suite "is firmly shaped; contrapuntal lines are clearly balanced, and Horszowski maintains steady control of touch and tempo." In the two Chopin Nocturnes the pianist "eschews the robust melodic tone of Rubinstein and offers instead a paler, more intimate treatment in which his affection for the music is obvious." (*ARG*, July/Aug 1990) Another reviewer liked the Bach Suite for "the rich elaboration that helps project long phrases, and all sorts of smaller details." And although this critic found the Beethoven "a trifle blotchy, deliberate and over-pedalled," and the E Flat Chopin Nocturne "a bit ordinary and emotionally constrained," Horszowski's reading of Chopin's B-Major Nocturne was "touched by magic and unforgettably rendered." (*CLA*, Dec 1990)

There are some Horszowski recordings made from live performances. During the period 1962–1972 a number of Mozart concertos, played at the Metropolitan Museum of Art with Frederic Waldman and the *Musica Aeterna* Orchestra, were taped. Five of these have been issued on CD (see Discog.). The performances "are alive with all the spontaneous enthusiasm of music-making which involved no record companies, no editing and no public relations. . . . This is robustly individual Mozart playing." (Gram, March 1995)

His 1986 recital at the Prades Festival—a well-balanced program of Mozart, Debussy, Beethoven and Chopin—was taped and produced commercially. "The Debussy suite [Children's Corner] is played with exquisite refinement and charm, and a good deal of humor." In the Beethoven Sonata, op. 28, "the depth of poetic expression he evokes makes it a memorable experience." (*Fan*, May/June 1989)

In October 1987 Horszowski gave two recitals at the *Comédie des Champs-Elysées* in Paris which were recorded live and portions later put on one CD (*Thésis* 82008, see Discog.). One critic recommends this CD "for devoted Horszowski fanatics only." (*ARG*, July/Aug 1990) But, not unexpectedly, another reviewer is more kindly disposed, calling this "a very special disc," notably because of the rich chordal textures in the Bach-Liszt Prelude, the dynamic contrasts in the Beethoven and the sensitivity to musical line and overall structure in the Chopin. "The subtlety of his keyboard technique demonstrates that there is more to 'technique' than playing fast and loud." (*Fan*, Sept/Oct 1990)

In 1992 Pearl Records issued *A Centenary Celebration* (see Discog.), a two-CD collection of unpublished live recordings made between 1958 and 1983 and assembled from performances in Florence and Rome, in Buffalo and in New York's Hayden Planetarium. Again, one could point out the technical flaws and lack of fluency in rapid passages, but in the end they are not important. "One is not so much bowled over as won over, gradually and surely, by an intense, ir- refutable musicality. There's a rightness to his performances—a drama, direct- ness of expression, sense of scale, rhythmic suppleness and coloristic subtlety— that is vastly more persuasive than technical perfection." (Kimmelman, "A Pianist. . .")

If Mieczyslaw Horszowski was once a little-known wonder, he has come into his own full measure. Playing with splendid artistry into his nineties, his great age may have restrained virtuosity but his incredible vitality and pure musicality remained intact, challenging time and tradition.

SELECTED REFERENCES

Dyer, Richard. "Horszowski at 98: a pianist still pushing the bounds of his imagination." *Boston Globe*, 6 Nov 1990, pp. 53, 58.
Goldsmith, Harris. "Instrumentalist of the Year." *Musical America International Directory of the Performing Arts*. 1993, pp. 36–39.
Horowitz, Joseph. Liner notes, Elektra/Nonesuch recordings.
Horszowski, Mrs. M. Correspondence, 8 Nov 1989; 21 Nov 1989; 31 Oct 1993.
Jepson, Barbara. "In a Parting Glimpse, a Onetime Dazzler As Geriatric Marvel." *New York Times*, 29 May 1994, sec. 2, p. 30. A review of the pianist's final recording.
Kammerer, Rafael. "Horszowski: Pianist Of Uncompromising Standards and Integrity." *Musical America*, Dec 1960, pp. 97–98.
Kimmelman, Michael. "Horszowski's Quiet, Elegant Pianism." *New York Times*, 27 Sept 1987, p. 27. A review of recordings.
———. "A Pianist for the Centuries." *New York Times*, 20 Dec 1992, sec. 2, p. 29.
Methuen-Campbell, James. "Mieczyslaw Horszowski." *Music and Musicians*, June 1985, pp. 10–11.
———. "Mieczyslaw Horszowski." *Gramophone*, Dec 1993, pp. 91–92. An in-depth review of the available Horszowski recordings.
Montparker, Carol. "Mieczyslaw Horszowski—Musical Fountain of Youth." *Clavier*, Sept 1990, pp. 12–15.
"A New Musical Prodigy." *New York Times*, 10 Dec 1906, p. 2.
Obituary. *Chicago Tribune*, 24 May 1993, sec. 2, p. 7. *Los Angeles Times*, 25 May 1993, sec. A, p. 18. *New York Times*, 24 May 1993, sec. 4, p. 9. *The Times* (London), 25 May 1993, p. 19. *Washington Post*, 24 May 1993, sec. B, p. 4.

Page, Tim. "Horszowski, 94 and Still Playing." *Long Island Newsday*, 25 June 1987, sec. 2, pp. 9, 19.

Reich, Howard. "A past master." *Chicago Tribune*, 29 Jan 1989, sec. 13, pp. 14–16.

Schonberg, Harold C. "A Pianist Who Makes Longevity an Art." *New York Times*, 22 April 1990, sec. 2, p. 23.

Shear, Nancy. "Mieczyslaw Horszowski: Last of the Leschetizky Line." *Keyboard*, April 1983, pp. 32–34.

Valdes, Lesley. "A student of piano masters is, at 96, still a master himself." *Philadelphia Inquirer*, 11 Dec 1988, sec. G, pp. 1, 10.

Webster, Daniel. "Famous students celebrate Horszowski's centenary." *Philadelphia Inquirer*, 23 Sept 1991, sec. E, p. 3.

———. "He plays the piano, and history lives." *Philadelphia Inquirer*, 23 Jan 1985, sec. D, pp. 1, 9.

———. "A pianist plays his memories." *Philadelphia Inquirer*, 6 April 1991, sec. D, p. 3.

Zawadzinski, John G. "A Child Prodigy . . . 90 Years Later." *Los Angeles Times*, 28 Jan 1990, CAL, p. 56.

———. "97-Year-Old Pianist Doesn't Look Back." *Christian Science Monitor*, 13 April 1990, p. 10.

———. "Pianist Horszowski's music unburdened by his 93 years." *New York City Tribune*, 25 Jan 1985.

Zimmern, Helen. "The Coming of Mieceo Horszowski." *New York Times*, 30 Dec 1906, sec. 3, p. 2.

See also Bibliography: Ewe/Mu; New/Gro; Tho/Mus; WWAM.

SELECTED REVIEWS

BG: 6 Nov 1990. *CL*: April 1986. *CT*: 22 April 1987; 12 Feb 1989. *DT*: 1 Dec 1925. *GM*: 11 June 1985. *LAT*: 17 May 1977; 2 Feb 1990. *MA*: 5 Jan 1907. *MM*: Nov 1987. *NYDN*: 25 April 1990. *NYHT*: 20 Oct 1949. *NYP*: 29 Sept 1975; 13 April 1987. *NYT*: 31 Dec 1906; 24 Feb 1927; 10 Feb 1942; 21 Oct 1943; 25 Oct 1948; 10 Dec 1952; 18 Jan 1953; 9 Nov 1954; 20 Oct 1960; 20 Nov 1966; 29 Nov 1971;29 Sept 1975; 21 Nov 1976; 2 Feb 1986; 10 March 1986; 1 March 1989; 25 April 1990. *PI*: 25 Jan 1985; 4 Nov 1985; 14 May 1988; 16 Dec 1988; 25 April 1990; 2 Nov 1991. *STL*: 21 April 1926. *TL*: 3 July 1951; 11 June 1985; 7 June 1986; 12 June 1987. *WP*: 13 Oct 1984; 30 Sept 1985.

SELECTED DISCOGRAPHY

Bach, J. S.: English Suite No. 5 in E Minor, BWV 810. Beethoven: Sonata in F Major, op. 10, no. 2. Chopin: Nocturnes in E-flat Major, op. 9, no. 2, B Major, op. 32, no. 1. Elektra Nonesuch 9 79232-2.

Bach: *Well-Tempered Clavier*, Book One. Vanguard Classics OVC 8046/7 (2 CDs).

Beethoven: Sonata in A Major, op. 2, no. 2. Chopin: Nocturnes op. 15, no. 2, op. 27, no. 2. Debussy: Children's Corner. Mozart: Fantasia in D Minor, K. 397. Elektra/Nonesuch 9 79160-2.

Beethoven: Sonata in B-flat Major, op. 106; Sonata in E Major, op. 109; Sonata in C Minor, op. 111. Vox CDX2 5500 (2 CDs).

Chopin: Mazurkas in C Major, op. 24, no. 2, B Minor, op. 33, no. 4; Nocturne in B-flat Minor, op. 9, no. 1. Mozart: Sonata in F Major, K. 332; Sonata in D Major, K. 576. Schumann: *Arabeske*, op. 18; *Kinderscenen*, op. 15. Elektra/Nonesuch 9 79202-2.

Horszowski à Prades. Beethoven: Sonata in D Major, op. 28. Chopin: Impromptu op. 38. Debussy: Children's Corner. Mozart: Sonata in F Major, K. 332. *Lyrinx* LYR CD070.

Horszowski à Prades: Les Années Casals. Bach: Preludes and Fugues in F-sharp Minor, G Major, B Minor. Beethoven: Concerto No. 2 in B-flat Major, op. 19; Sonata in C Minor, op. 111. Brahms: Fantasy Pieces, op. 116. Mozart: Fantasy in C Minor, K. 475; Sonata in C Minor, K. 457. *Lyrinx* LYR 119/120 (2 CDs). Casals/London CM.

Horszowski en Concert. Bach: Prelude and Fugue in A Minor. Beethoven: Sonata in A Major, op. 2, no. 2. Chopin: Impromptu op. 36; Nocturne, op. 32, no. 1; Scherzo, op. 20. Schumann: *Rêverie*. Villa Lobos: *A Maré Enchen*; *Passa, passa gaviao*. *Thesis* THC 82008 (CD).

Mieczyslaw Horszowski. J. S. Bach: French Suite No. 6 in E Major, BWV 817. Chopin: Mazurka, op. 24, no. 4 in B-flat Minor; Preludes, op. 28, no. 13 in F-sharp Major, no. 15 in D-flat Major. Schumann: *Papillons*, op. 2. Electra Nonesuch 9 79264-2.

Mieczyslaw Horszowski: A Centenary Celebration. Bach, C. P. E.: Fantasia No. 2 in C Major. Bach, J. S.: Sarabande from Partita No. 2 in C Minor. Beethoven: Diabelli Variations, op. 120; Sonata in A-flat Major, op. 110. Chopin: Fantasy in F Minor, op. 49; Nouvelle Etude in F Minor; Polonaise in C Minor, op. 40, no. 1. Mozart: Variations, K. 455. Schubert: Sonata in C Minor, D. 958. Pearl GEMM CDS 9979 (2 CDs).

Mozart: Concerto in E-flat Major, K. 271; Concerto in A Major, K. 414; Concerto in C Major, K. 415; Concerto in E-flat Major, K. 449; Concerto in F Major, K. 459; Sonata in C Major, K. 545. Pearl GEMM CDS 9138. Waldman/*Musica Aeterna* Orchestra.

Mozart: Concerto in B-flat Major, K. 595. Sony Classical SMK 58984 (CD). Casals/Perpignan FO.

♩

JANIS, BYRON: b. McKeesport, Pennsylvania, 24 March 1928.

> When the piano does not sing it is the most boring instrument in the world.
>
> Byron Janis (Dubal, *Reflections from the Keyboard*)

When Byron Janis's Polish-Russian parents Samuel and Hattie (Horelick) Yankilevitch emigrated to America, they shortened the family name to Yanks. When Byron as a prodigy of ten played on the Magic Key radio program in New York, Samuel Chotzinoff and Milton Cross changed his name to Jannes. When he was 15, John Rosenfeld, critic for the *Dallas Morning News,* changed Jannes to Janis.

Work being scarce in McKeesport during the Depression, the Yanks family moved to Pittsburgh, where Samuel opened a sporting goods store. Since neither his hard-working father nor his devoted mother was musical, Byron Janis's talent went unnoticed until at age five he dumbfounded a kindergarten teacher by playing on his toy xylophone exactly the tune she had played on the piano. She pinned a note to his suspenders telling his parents of his remarkable skill, and they arranged piano lessons with Abraham Litow, who had been trained at the Moscow Conservatory. Within six months the six-year-old Janis played C. P. E. Bach's *Solfeggietto* on a Pittsburgh radio program, having been called upon to substitute for an ailing Litow pupil. A year later Janis's rapid advancement impelled Litow to arrange an audition with Josef and Rosina Lhévinne, also alumni of the Moscow Conservatory. In October 1935 Janis's ever-supportive parents took him to New York to play for the Lhévinnes, and the following spring he started lessons with them.

Just eight years old when he, his mother and sister Thelma moved to New York (his father stayed in Pittsburgh to run the store), Janis studied with the Lhévinnes for about a year, until their concert schedules made consistent lessons impossible. They first assigned him to Dorothea Anderson LaFollette, with the condition that he must play for them once a month as a progress check. About eight months later the Lhévinnes decided that he should study with their associate Adele Marcus, a teacher at the Chatham Square Music School. For six years Janis had two lessons a week with Marcus, and he credits her with laying the foundation of his musical understanding.

Adele Marcus also found an unofficial sponsor for Janis, having fore-sightedly arranged for him to play for Samuel Chotzinoff, music critic for the *New York Post*, music consultant for NBC radio and also founder of the Chatham Square Music School. Chotzinoff's support proved invaluable. He found a rent-free apartment for the Janises, obtained a scholarship for Byron at the private Columbia Grammar School and let him attend composition and har-mony classes at the Chatham Square Music School. Chotzinoff also told philan-thropist William Rosenwald about Byron, and Rosenwald agreed not only to pay for the music lessons but to provide a monthly allowance until Janis could sup-port himself. (Janis came to consider Samuel and Pauline [Jascha Heifetz's sis-ter] Chotzinoff as second parents, often staying with them in New York or at their country estate.)

When Adele Marcus accepted a teaching position at the Hockaday Music School in Dallas, Texas, the faithful Chotzinoff saw to it that the 14-year-old Janis continued his lessons with Marcus. For the next two winters Janis boarded with the Samuel Tallals family in Dallas and divided his summers between New York and Pittsburgh, where his mother and sister once again lived with his father.

At age nine Janis made his recital debut (15 Oct 1937) at Pittsburgh's Carnegie Hall. At age 10, through Chotzinoff's NBC connections, he played on the Magic Key radio program, the Sunday afternoon variety hour hosted by Alexander Woollcott. At age 15 he made his orchestral debut (12 Sept 1943) playing Rachmaninoff's Concerto No. 2 in C Minor with the NBC Symphony Orchestra, conducted by Frank Black. Janis played the same concerto when he made his hometown orchestral debut (20 Feb 1944) with the Pittsburgh Symphony Orchestra, conducted by Lorin Maazel, another musical prodigy, at that time just two weeks away from his 14th birthday. Vladimir Horowitz hap-pened to be in Pittsburgh on that day, heard Janis play and invited the teenager to play for him privately in New York. Before Janis could audition for Horowitz, he had to return to Dallas for lessons and also fulfill some playing engagements, including another appearance (9 June 1944) with the NBC Symphony Orchestra under Frank Black, this time a performance of the Beethoven Concerto No. 4 in G Major.

Then the 17-year-old Janis played for Horowitz and became his first pupil. For three years he had weekly lessons with Horowitz, the generous Rosenwalds paying $50 an hour for the sessions. To preserve lesson continuity,

Janis would go on tour with the Horowitzes and sometimes spend his summer vacations with them. Horowitz forbade him to play for other pianists on the grounds that conflicting advice would confuse him, but at the same time insisted that Janis must not imitate his own playing. Although he gave Janis very little in the way of structural or stylistic analysis, Horowitz made him acutely aware of the piano and its limitless possibilities. "I learned the most about piano playing from Horowitz," Janis told a 1984 interviewer. "I learned how to make the piano sing and how to use colors. I learned how to use the instrument to its maximum advantage." (*PP*, 15 April 1984)

Following Horowitz's advice, Janis postponed a Carnegie Hall debut, opting to build up self-confidence and acquire stage presence before making a New York debut. During the Horowitz years (1944–48) Janis made about 50 appearances, including two tours of smaller American cities and a long, tremendously successful tour (summer 1948) through Brazil, Uruguay and Argentina. Patience and hard work brought their reward. Janis's New York recital debut (Carnegie Hall, 29 Oct 1948) drew unstinting critical praise. And his performance (27 Jan 1949) of Gershwin's Concerto in F with the New York Philharmonic Orchestra, conducted by Leopold Stokowski, forced a grumbling Virgil Thomson, not too happy with the choice of music, to admit that Janis was "a whopping piano player both by technique and by temperament." (*NYHT*, 28 Jan 1949)

Janis was 20 when Horowitz stopped the lessons, telling him to go out into the world, make his own mistakes and say something personal. For a quarter of a century Janis did exactly that, pursuing a steady schedule of recitals, orchestral appearances and recording sessions in both Europe and the Americas. His first European tour (1952) began with five performances as soloist with the Amsterdam *Concertgebouw* Orchestra under Eduard van Beinum and included an appearance (21 June 1952) with the London Symphony Orchestra, conducted by Antal Dorati.

Janis was invited to launch American Festival Week at the Brussels World's Fair in July 1958. In 1961 both the Boston Symphony Orchestra and the Paris Conservatory Orchestra chose him to play the Liszt Concertos Nos. 1 and 2 as the climax of their celebrations of the 150th anniversary of Liszt's birth. And he was the first American pianist sent to Russia on the Soviet-American cultural exchange, an exciting tour (Oct–Nov 1960) that remains one of the special high points of his career. He played a total of 10 concerts (Moscow, Leningrad, Odessa, Minsk and Kiev), eliciting such a spectacular response that the Soviet Ministry of Culture invited him to return. Janis's second Russian tour (May–June 1962) began in Moscow with a staggering program: three concertos (Schumann in A Minor, Rachmaninoff No. 1 and Prokofiev No. 3) with the Moscow Philharmonic Orchestra, conducted by Kiril Kondrashin. Although Moscow audiences had had a surfeit of piano music (judges and contestants from the just completed International Tchaikovsky Competition were in the audience), Janis's tour de force performance brought forth a thunderous ovation.

That same year (1962) Mercury Records sent a crew to Russia to record Janis and the MPO, under Kondrashin, playing the Rachmaninoff Concerto No. 1 and Prokofiev Concerto No. 3, the first discs made by American engineers in

Russia. In 1963 Janis's recording of the Prokofiev won the *Grand Prix du Disque*. In 1965 the French government chose Janis as the first American pianist to become a Chevalier in the Order of Arts and Letters, an honor previously bestowed on only two other American-born artists, sculptor Alexander Calder and violinist Yehudi Menuhin.

By 1967 Janis was performing nearly 100 concerts a year, and in a typical season would maintain two recital programs and from five to eight concertos. In 1973, at age 45 and in the prime of his career, he faced the worst kind of trauma for a pianist. At a London recording session he noticed redness and swelling in the middle finger of his left hand. Diagnosed as psoriatic arthritis, within six months it had spread to all fingers and eventually caused the joints of nine fingers to fuse. Janis took a year off, but not wanting the arthritis to be an excuse for poor playing, he kept his condition secret. For 12 years only his family and a few close friends knew the truth. He learned to use what he had, adjusting his technique by changing his fingering and hand positioning. He practiced his usual five to six hours daily, sometimes in excruciating pain, but once on the concert platform the pain seemed to disappear in the joy of playing.

He managed about 50 concerts a year, preserving his own standards enough of the time to keep going and still pleasing audiences with his brilliant pyrotechnics and emotionalism. For example, at a Minneapolis recital (17 March 1975) of predominantly Chopin works Janis seemed to be able to do anything required of him technically: "The rigorous left-hand arpeggios of the famous 'Revolutionary' Etude, the double octaves of the Scherzo (op. 39), were delivered in fluent, clean fashion, as were all the other technical hurdles these pieces present." (*MiT*, 19 March 1975) But each year playing became more difficult, and the strain of keeping his secret and of always trying to find new ways to play took its toll.

Meanwhile Janis tried every kind of cure, from conventional treatments to faith healing and "a pin in my ear," willing to try anything because of the dread of not being able to play. By the summer of 1984 he was taking massive doses of drugs and had become physically ill and mentally depressed. He stopped concertizing and withdrew from social contacts. Making music was his life, and the thought that he might not be able to play terrified him. In desperation, he tried an experimental technique—transcranial electrostimulation therapy (TCET)—at the University of Texas Health Science Center at Houston, and responded extremely well. With the constant help of his wife, the painter Maria Cooper (m. 1966), who learned to give therapeutic massage, he returned to playing. In 1983–84 he gave a major round of performances, a year-long celebration of his 40-year career, including a performance (Aug 1983) at the White House for President Reagan; television appearances; concerts with the Philadelphia, Pittsburgh, Houston, Los Angeles and Chicago orchestras; a New York recital, a Paris recital and appearances at European festivals.

The arthritis is not cured, but Janis has learned to cope, so much so that at the recital (29 Nov 1988) celebrating the 40th anniversary of his Carnegie Hall debut, his playing often reminded one reviewer "of the dazzlingly facile and arrestingly individual young pianist first heard more than 30 years ago." (*NYT*, 1 Dec 1988) Janis finally spoke publicly about his arthritis at a White House concert on 28 February 1985. Since then he has served as a cultural ambassador for the National Arthritis Foundation, playing concerts across the United States to raise funds for the cause.

Janis has been teaching since 1962, both private students and master classes, and since 1987 has been on the faculty of the Manhattan School of Music. Like his teacher Horowitz, he rarely plays for his students. "Talent needs a very limited amount of teaching and a very careful approach," says Janis, "otherwise, all you get is a mimic, and that's what will happen ninety-eight percent of the time when you demonstrate a point at the piano." What is most important, he tells them, is to make the piano sing, for that is what makes an audience remember the playing. "Phrasing, the part of the piano that sings, the heart, the soul, the inner color, cannot be given from one artist to another." (Mac/Gre, see Bibliog.)

In October 1967 Count Paul de la Panouse allowed Janis to search through some uncatalogued music manuscripts and other materials at his 17th-century Chateau de Thoiry at Yvelines, near Paris. In a box tagged "old clothes" he found a folder marked "written and given by Frederic Chopin, 1833." It contained two previously unknown Chopin works, one a manuscript of the G-flat Major Waltz, op. 70, and the other manuscript one of only three known "originals" of the famous *Grande Valse brillante* in E-flat Major. Six years later while at Yale preparing for a series of master classes, Janis was invited to browse through the scores at the John Herrick Jackson Music Library. Among material bequeathed to Yale by Yale graduate B. Allen Rowland, Janis found two completely different versions (dated 1832) of these same waltzes. He has published the waltzes, with explanatory commentary. (Chopin/Janis)

Practicing has always been immensely important to Janis. His *Etude* article written many years ago reminds musicians that "the quality of your performance is shaped by the quality of your practicing" and describes what he calls "The Fine Art of Practicing." He discusses memory, refining difficult passage work, strengthening fingers, the importance of wrist, key attack, all with intelligence and clarity. (*Etude*, Oct 1949)

When asked by an interviewer to explain how he could project emotion in his playing while preserving total technical control, Janis explained that when he studies a new work he first plays it through, "excited both by its emotion and its architecture. Then I start pulling it apart, solving the technical points. During this process the emotion is gone. The technique gets in the way. Then I drop it completely for a time. When I come back to it I again find the emotion." (*CSM*, 9 Dec 1964)

It has been said that Janis can play just about anything authentically and beautifully, but the mainstays of his repertoire have been the large-scale dramatic works of the 19th and early 20th centuries, particularly the Romantic (Schubert, Schumann, Chopin) and post-Romantic (Prokofiev and Rachmaninoff) works. His big technique is especially suited to the tempestuous post-Romantic concertos, and he should perhaps thank his Russian genes for his innate preoccupation with tone color and emotional projection. Long before it became fashionable, Janis was an enthusiastic advocate of the exotic music of Louis Moreau Gottschalk.

Byron Janis is a sensitive musician, recognized for his keen understanding of musical content. At the same time, he owes much of his success to his sparkling, mercurial style, his innate ability to sway listeners by the sheer force of musical emotions; in other words, his gift for making the piano sing.

From the very start of his career Janis has drawn consistently fine reviews from some of America's most formidable critics. For example, this from a 1948 review: "Not for a long time has this writer heard such a talent allied with the musicianship, the feeling, the intelligence and artistic balance shown by the 20-year-old pianist Byron Janis." (*NYT*, 30 Oct 1948) Ten years later Janis's performance at the World's Fair in Brussels caused Belgian critics to marvel that an American had such "a remarkable technique, a romantic but strongly controlled melodiousness free from affectation and pathos." And this from a review of Janis's Carnegie Hall performance (6 April 1961) of the Liszt Piano Concertos Nos. 1 and 2 with the Boston Symphony Orchestra, Charles Munch conducting: "Few pianists have Janis's flair for the big bravura pieces of Tchaikovsky or Liszt. Last week's concert, studded with thunderous chords and octaves, zipperlike runs and occasionally a singing, tenoresque line, proved to be a wrist-breaking tour de force. . . . His piano sound positively glittered." (*Time*, 14 April 1961)

Louis Biancolli found Janis "a little titan as he romped through variation after variation [Rachmaninoff's Rhapsody on a Theme by Paganini]. It all seemed child's play, but what strength and study and ceaseless reappraisal must have gone into that glorious performance. Apart from the prodigious bravura, there was the mood of starlit reverie that haunts so much of this rhapsody. There, Byron Janis, like Rachmaninoff before him, tiptoed on gossamer." (*NYWT*, 12 Nov 1965)

On 3 August 1971, Janis and the Los Angeles Philharmonic Orchestra, Kazuyoshi Akiyama conducting, played Rachmaninoff's Concerto No. 3 at the Hollywood Bowl. "Technique never became an end in itself so well was it all controlled and integrated. But there was limitless endurance and ample power for the dramatic episodes and there were some particularly impressive moments." (*LAT*, 5 Aug 1971)

As the arthritis worsened, Janis's performances increasingly baffled the unknowing critics. Some found his playing fitful, inconsistent; others complained about his eccentricities and excesses, his sometimes uncomfortably hard and steely tone. "Byron Janis," wrote a puzzled Chicago critic, "has been responsible for some of the most memorable pianism this reviewer has experienced in the concert hall and also some of the most inexplicably poor . . . with inspired playing giving way to lackluster routine, occasionally within the same program." (*CT*, 20 Feb 1978)

But nothing could change Janis's innate flair and impeccable taste. On 7 March 1981 his first San Francisco recital in 11 years caused one reviewer to reminisce: "It was the Janis of old memories, displaying the fabled glassy tone, the tendency toward understatement rather than reveling in tubercular angst, and the sensitivity to rhythm and meter that projects the emotional intensity of the work." (*SFC,* 9 March 1981)

At his all-Chopin Carnegie Hall recital on 29 November 1988 Janis "tended to play as in the past, in brilliant lunges and bursts, relaxing only as if to build up energy for the next attack. The Valse Brillante in A-flat (Op. 34, No. 1) was, typically, deeply inward at one moment, a fireworks display the next. . . . Mr. Janis is still an artist worth paying attention to." (*NYT,* 1 Dec 1988)

Most of Janis's recordings date from the 1960s, divided between RCA and Mercury. His discography is not extensive, consisting of around two dozen items, some of which are long out of print. Both record producers have begun to reissue his most memorable performances on CD. The first of these, a Mercury CD, contains the two Liszt piano concertos and some short solo pieces by Liszt, Schumann, Falla and Guion (see Discog.). "This is exciting, high-strung, Horowitzian pianism that is tempered by unfailing good taste, tonal subtlety, and a true sense of Lisztian style." (*ARG,* March/April 1991)

Shortly thereafter Mercury reissued Janis's readings of the Schumann and Tchaikovsky (No. 1) concertos (see Discog.). Listening to these superb interpretations, one can only agree that "these Schumann and Tchaikovsky performances are an invaluable document of one of this country's finest pianistic products." (*ARG,* July/Aug 1991)

A third reissue into CD format, this time by RCA, makes available the second and third concertos of Rachmaninoff (see Discog.), music with which Janis was closely associated, music that he plays with great authority, music wherein his talents meld with those of the composer to produce two memorable musical monuments. The latest CD, Janis's performance of Mussorgsky's Pictures at an Exhibition, is not a reissue. Recorded in 1961, it remained in Mercury's vaults and was released for the first time in 1994!

SELECTED REFERENCES

Apone, Carl. "McKeesport's Byron Janis still captivates piano world." *Pittsburgh Press,* 15 April 1984, sec. J, pp. 1, 4.

Beigel, Greta. "The Aches and Pains of a Decade's Promising Pianists." *Los Angeles Times,* 30 Sept 1984, CAL, pp. 50–51. Browning, Fleisher, Janis.

Brooks, Muriel. "Chopin/Janis." *American Music Teacher,* April/May 1979, pp. 6–8.

Chopin/Janis. *The Most Dramatic Musical Discovery of the Age. Waltz in G-flat, Op. 70, No. 1 and Grande Valse brillante, Op. 18.* Envolve Books, Inc., 1978.

Emerson, Gordon. "Playing through pain." *New Haven Register,* 22 Sept 1985, sec E, p. 1.

Fein, Esther B. "After 28 Years, a Return to a Changed Moscow." *New York Times,* 23 Oct 1988, sec. 1, p. 57.

Fishman, Steve. "Rebuilding Bodies." *New York Times Magazine*, 16 April 1989, pp. 28–32.

Goldsmith, Barbara. "The First Thing I Had to Conquer Was Fear." *Parade Magazine*, 13 Oct 1985, pp. 4–6.

Goodman, Peter. "Byron Janis Plays through the Pain." *Long Island Newsday*, 27 Nov 1988.

Helm, Everett. "Byron Janis, 'Sacred Monster'." *Musical America*, Oct 1962, pp. 32, 46.

Janis, Byron. "The Fine Art of Practicing." (interview) *Etude*, Oct 1949, pp. 9–10.

Petersen, Clarence. "Byron Janis: Piano virtuosity still his forte." *Chicago Tribune*, 12 Jan 1984, sec. 5, p. 1.

Rogers, Harold. "Pianist Explains Power of Musical Emotion." *Christian Science Monitor*, 9 Dec 1964, p. 13.

Rosenberg, Donald. "Janis customizes his piano work to cope with arthritic restrictions." *Pittsburgh Press*, 5 Aug 1990.

"Triple Crown Pianist." *Time*, 25 May 1962, pp. 95–96.

See also Bibliography: Cur/Bio (1966); Dub/Ref; Ewe/Li2; Ewe/Mu; Mac/Gre; New GrA; Sal/Fam.

SELECTED REVIEWS

AR: 4 May 1981. *CaT*: 10 Feb 1982. *CST*: 20 Feb 1978. *CT*: 20 Feb 1978; 27 April 1982. *LAT*: 4 Feb 1961; 3 Aug 1961; 28 Jan 1965; 14 Dec 1967; 5 Aug 1971; 17 March 1975; 12 April 1976; 15 April 1978; 26 Nov 1980. *MA*: Feb 1963. *MiT*: 19 March 1975. *NYT*: 30 Oct 1948; 9 Dec 1958; 6 April 1961; 14 May 1962; 15 Feb 1971; 1 Dec 1988. *PEB*: 5 March 1976. *PP*: 22 Jan 1936; 19 Sept 1943; 9 June 1944; 8 July 1958; 4 Nov 1960; 16 April 1961; 21 April 1984. *PPG*: 15 Oct 1941; 25 March 1965. *SFC*: 9 March 1981. *TP*: 7 Jan 1983. *WE*: 19 Feb 1979.

SELECTED DISCOGRAPHY

Liszt: Concerto No. 1 in E-flat Major (Kondrashin/Moscow PO); Concerto No. 2 in A Major (Rozhdestvensky/Radio SO; *Sonetto del Petrarca* No. 104; *Valse oubliée No. 1*; Hungarian Rhapsody No. 6. Schumann: Romance No. 2; Novelette No. 1. Falla: Miller's Dance. Guion: The Harmonica Player. Mercury 432-002 (CD).

Liszt: *Totentanz*. Rachmaninoff: Isle of the Dead. Ravel: *Rapsodie espagnole*; *Pavane*. Weber: Invitation to the Dance. RCA Living Stereo 09026-61250-2. Reiner/Chicago SO.

Mussorgsky: Pictures at an Exhibition. Chopin: Etude in F Major; Waltz in A Minor. Mercury 434 346-2. Also includes the Mussorgsky-Ravel Pictures (Dorati/ Minneapolis SO).

Prokofiev: Concerto No. 3 in C Major, op. 26; Toccata. Rachmaninoff: Concerto No. 1 in F-sharp Minor, op. 1. Mendelssohn: Song without Words, op. 62, no. 1. Pinto: Three Scenes from Childhood. Schumann:

Variations on a Theme by Clara Wieck.   Mercury 434 333-2.
    Kondrashin/Moscow PO.
Rachmaninoff: Concerto No. 1 in F-sharp Minor, op. 1. Strauss: *Burleske*.
    Victrola VICS-1101. Reiner/Chicago SO.
Rachmaninoff: Concerto No. 2 in C Minor, op. 18 (Dorati/Minneapolis SO);
    Concerto No. 3 in D Minor, op. 30 (Dorati/London SO); Prelude in C-sharp
    Minor, op. 3, no. 2; Prelude in E-flat Major, op. 23, no. 6. Mercury 432
    759-2.
Rachmaninoff: Concerto No. 2 in C Minor, op. 18; Concerto No. 3 in D
    Minor, op. 30. RCA (Silver Seal) 60540-2. Munch/Boston SO.
Schumann: Concerto in A Minor, op. 54 (Skrowaczewski/Minneapolis SO).
    Tchaikovsky: Concerto No. 1 in B-flat Minor, op. 23 (Menges/London
    SO). Mercury 432-011-2.
Strauss: *Burleske*; Don Quixote. RCA 5734-2. Reiner/Chicago SO.

VIDEO

In the Steps of Chopin: A Portrait by Byron Janis. 58 minutes, color. Films
    for the Humanities FFH 898E.

JOHANNESEN, GRANT: b. Salt Lake City, Utah, 30 July 1921.

> I've had a career that was my own; I've never followed the stereotype of
> the same repertory all the time; I didn't play only the works you're sup-
> posed to play if you're going to make a career. And if I were starting
> all over again, I would do exactly the same thing.
>
> Grant Johannesen (*Musical America*, December 1986)

Blazing his independent trail through the piano repertoire has worked out splendidly for Grant Johannesen. One of America's most distinguished pianists, he
has for more than half a century dedicated his talents to the concept that "there is
a higher purpose to music-making than repeating the 50 most familiar pieces."
Throughout his career Johannesen has consistently performed a unique repertoire,
one that sets him apart from his colleagues. Instead of the "50 most familiar
pieces," he often will program seldom-played works by great composers; even
more unusual, just about every Johannesen program includes music from the
20th century, especially works by French and American composers. Why has he
set himself apart this way? Because, he says, making the public more aware of
unfamiliar works by great composers and neglected works of modern composers
"is a great and generating pleasure for me." (Johannesen, "Artist's Life")

His parents were H. Christian Johannesen and Josefa (Rogeberg)
Johannesen, Norwegian émigrés who married in Salt Lake City in 1910. They
gave Johannesen his first piano lessons at age five, with Cicely Adams. Five

years later he gave his first public recital. When he was 11 years old, Adams turned him over to Mabel Borg Jenkins, her own teacher, at the McCune School of Music and Art. Jenkins made him work hard and gave him a strong technical foundation.

The forward-thinking Jenkins also introduced him to a most unusual repertoire. While other young piano pupils of the time most likely were concentrating on the Chopin waltzes and the Brahms intermezzos, she had Johannesen playing modern works. In 1934 she returned from Europe with Poulenc's *Suite française*, and the 12-year-old Johannesen "gobbled it up." He played it on his first public recital as her student, along with Bartók's Sonatina, certainly not the standard musical diet for young piano pupils in the 1930s. His teacher, says Johannesen, "was something absolutely special. . . . She had her finger on modern music. I never knew anyone with the scale this woman had in her knowledge. . . . She just happened to have that kind of curiosity and was able to infect a young kid with it." (Mathews)

Johannesen made his orchestral debut at age 14, playing the Liszt Concerto No. 1 in E-flat Major with Reginald Beales conducting a WPA (Works Projects Administration) orchestra, the forerunner of the Utah Symphony Orchestra. He graduated from McCune in June 1940. That summer he began advanced studies with Robert Casadesus at St. George's School (wartime home of the American Conservatory at Fontainebleau) in Newport, Rhode Island; during 1941–44 he commuted from New York to Princeton, New Jersey, to continue working with Casadesus and to study theory with Roger Sessions; and he had two summers (1947–48, 1948–49) at Fontainebleau in France, again working with Casadesus and studying Beethoven, Stravinsky and Fauré with the illustrious Nadia Boulanger. In addition, Johannesen studied with Egon Petri on a fellowship at Cornell University.

Interestingly enough, Johannesen feels that the high points of his studies with Casadesus were not so much with French music but their sessions on Mozart, Chopin, Bach and Schumann. "The one great thing Casadesus had to offer," he says, "was a sense of the unity in a large work—the Liszt Sonata, the Schumann *Fantasy*, the *Hammerklavier*. He had a marvelous sense of what makes a piece a totality." (Finn)

Johannesen made his professional recital debut (17 April 1944) at New York's Times Hall. "The important thing to note about this young man's playing," said one reviewer, "is that he knows how to make the piano sound interesting all the time." (*NYHT*, 18 April 1944) He gave a second New York recital at Town Hall on 18 February 1945, and ever since has played regularly in New York. In 1949 he placed first at the Ostend *Concours Internationale* and made his first European tour (Belgium, Holland, France). In 1955 Johannesen was one of several soloists (Casadesus, Curzon, Hess) performing with Dimitri Mitropoulos and the New York Philharmonic-Symphony on their tour of Europe; and in 1965 he made an unplanned tour with George Szell and the Cleveland Orchestra. Leon Fleisher and John Browning had originally been engaged as soloists for this State Department–sponsored 11-week tour (Russia, Sweden, Poland, Germany, France, Czechoslovakia, England), but Fleisher's continuing problems with his right hand forced him to cancel only a week or so before departure, and Johannesen stepped in as his substitute.

Johannesen kept a diary ("Notes of an Instant Soloist") of that grueling tour. "We did 23 performances of the Mozart C Minor Concerto. . . . And Szell spoiled me completely for playing Mozart with any other conductor." (Blomster) Nevertheless, Johannesen confesses that, like some of his colleagues (notably pianist Ivan Moravec) he had to battle with the strong-minded Szell over matters of interpretation. "Not that I don't find his ideas fascinating, reasonable, and always pointed, but some interior voice nags at me to resist the attempts of this persuasive Pygmalion toward the alteration of my own conception, wrong though I may very well be." (Finn)

From the early 1950s to the early 1970s, Johannesen toured globally —North and South America, Russia, Australia, New Zealand, the Orient, South Africa, India, the Philippines and Europe (every March for the last 20 years, said Johannesen in 1979). Much admired for his intelligence and integrity, he "has been among the most respected American pianists, with a career that has proceeded on a remarkably even keel." (Kupferberg)

Johannesen is a man of broad cultural interests—music, art, theater. In the early lean years in New York he had to give piano lessons to support himself, but whenever possible he went to concerts (often multiple events in one day) or spent hours browsing through the city's museums. His love for the theater may come from his father, who used to read him Ibsen in the original Norwegian.

In 1958 Johannesen received the Harriet Cohen International Music Award, presented in London each year "for outstanding artistry and performance." In 1966 he received an honorary doctorate from the University of Utah and in 1974 a degree from the Cleveland Institute of Music. In 1985 the French government granted him the rank of *Chevalier des Arts et Lettres* because of his substantial contributions in the area of French music performance.

Helen Taylor Johannesen, his first wife, died in an automobile accident in 1950, when their son David was about four years old. In 1963 he married Zara Nelsova, the Canadian cellist. They were divorced 10 years later.

Johannesen taught out of necessity in the early days in New York, somewhat less as his performing career prospered. From 1960 to 1966 he taught at the summer music school at Aspen, Colorado, possibly, say some writers, because he was anxious to see how young pianists reacted to his out-of-step ideas about repertoire. As he puts it, "I feel that when I teach my own repertoire and then hear it back fresh from someone else's hands, it refreshes my own thinking. . . . It is wonderful to hear a really talented student approach a piece for the first time. It's like tapping a well. It brings up fresh ideas." (Finn)

As his touring schedule permitted, in the early 1970s he began teaching a few days at the Cleveland Institute of Music, an experience that convinced him that every pianist should teach as much as possible. Teaching, Johannesen tells interviewers, "reminds you of what you have to give. You don't get lazy about sharing your ideas. I've had a very rich experience with that." He became music director at the Cleveland Institute in 1973 and was president from 1977 through

1985, dividing his time between apartments in New York and Cleveland. He continues to teach a small group of advanced students at the Mannes School of Music in New York and also teaches at the Salzburg *Mozarteum* in the summers.

Johannesen's students get direct, concrete advice. He attempts to sharpen their technical skills by concentrating on, as he says, "things that people don't consider interesting, such as hand position. Pianists are losing the use of their right hands." He directs students to practice slowly (this drills the fingers) and softly (this makes the fingers sensitive to evenness on the keys), thus "the sheer sound of the piano does not overwhelm one and the music itself has a chance to come through." (Johannesen, "Listen to Yourself") It is his opinion that too much practicing can actually be harmful, that one can *play* the piano eight hours a day, but not really *practice* that long. Rather than overpracticing, he encourages students to explore other music, to go to museums and to learn as much as possible about literature, poetry and language.

Johannesen has always practiced what he teaches. He has, he says, "spent a lot of time looking at pictures." Languages fascinated him even as a teenager, and he is still intrigued by the relationships between linguistics and music. "He loves the pure sound of words and particularly poetry, and he can expound, for instance, on the connection between Schumann and the German romantic poets or Debussy and the French writers." (Milburn)

Above all, Johannesen wants his students to listen carefully to their own playing and to aim for "singing on the piano." They should, he says, spend some time "intoning musical lines with their peers." As for listening carefully, it is a habit that he feels can be acquired. If students find it difficult at first, they must keep trying. On the other hand, he prefers that students do *not* listen to other pianists' recordings of the works they have in progress. "The time that is spent on listening to records could be so much better applied to *thinking* of music on its *own* terms rather than being influenced by someone else's performance. As a teacher I do not encourage students to listen to records much, but rather try to stimulate them to develop, and then believe in their own approaches—no matter how awkward or halting the attempts." (Johannesen, "Prisms")

Grant Johannesen's substantial, eclectic repertoire stands out in today's concert world. He plays fewer of the familiar works of the great composers than do most concert pianists, and never plays what Virgil Thomson used to call "wow" music (for example, the flamboyant concertos of Rachmaninoff, Liszt and Tchaikovsky). Instead, Johannesen chooses less familiar works by these well-known composers.

And he has always done so. Some forty years ago, in a performance (23 Oct 1954) with Dimitri Mitropoulos and the New York Philharmonic-Society, Johannesen chose to play two rarely heard works: Schubert's "Wanderer" Fantasy in Liszt's arrangement for piano and orchestra, and Milhaud's *Le Carnaval d'Aix*. Almost 30 years later, he played an all-Beethoven program (13 Sept 1981) in New York and, true to form, "Mr. Johannesen was not about to offer a collection of Beethoven standards." He started off with two seldom-heard works—the G Minor Fantasy, op. 77, and the F-sharp Major Sonata, op. 78, and offset these rarities with one of Beethoven's "most cheery early works, the Sonata in E Flat (op. 31, no. 3)." He then played the six Bagatelles, op. 126, and the Sonata in A-flat Major, op. 110. (*NYT*, 14 Sept 1981)

All the more unusual, Johannesen plays a great deal of modern music, especially works by French and American composers. Even then he bypasses the more famous works of Debussy and Ravel, choosing instead less well-known works by other French composers (Poulenc, Fauré, Milhaud, Satie, Roussel, Dukas, Déodat de Séverac). As his programs reveal, he also plays many works by American composers (Copland, Gottschalk, Mennin, Thomson, Barber, Carpenter). He has given first performances of Peter Mennin's Partita, the Second Sonata of Robert Casadesus (dedicated to Johannesen), Milhaud's Hymn of Glorification and Juan José Castro's Suite of Tangos. In October 1984 Johannesen played the Carlos Chávez Piano Concerto with the Bavarian State Orchestra in Munich, Germany.

He maintains his repertoire by practicing about four hours a day, first warming up on scales and arpeggios, and then moving on to some Bach pieces, which he practices at any tempo and in all ways—legato, staccato, etc., (an excellent drill combining technique with musical thought). However, Johannesen points out that, "musically speaking . . . it is not fleetness of technique but refinements of technique which mark the master pianist."

Johannesen begins preparation by reading a work through in order to acquaint himself with the music, the composer's intentions and the problems. Once secure with the notes, he breaks the piece down into phrases, starting "from the indications, every least one of which must be scrupulously observed. . . . One works from the phrase, getting from it its full complement of meaning (always with the intentions of the composer), linking it to its fellows. One's ultimate interpretative success, however, depends as much on individual sympathies as it does on study." (*Etude*, June 1953)

Reviewers find Johannesen to be a highly intelligent, versatile, inquisitive pianist; a solid, satisfying pianist; a thinking musician, not a flamboyant virtuoso. All agree that he is an honest, thoughtful interpreter who puts his virtuoso technique at the service of the composer. In 1955 Louis Biancolli wrote: "Johannesen played Mozart in terms of Mozart, rather than in terms of Johannesen, and that went for Franck, Schumann, Fauré and Debussy." (Cur/Bio 1961, see Bibliog.) That still applies, even though some early critics felt that Johannesen's playing was "unimaginative, too bereft of intensity and color to avoid monotony of effect." (*NYT*, 19 Feb 1945)

Invariably reviewers mention Johannesen's superb training, distinctive technique and his diverting choice of repertoire. And they give his playing high marks for its large tone, clarity, rhythmic precision, strength, poetry and subtlety. "In his quiet way he can do things that would make virtuosos of bigger repute flinch." (*NYT*, 27 Nov 1962)

Being such a "quiet" pianist may be the reason for Johannesen's slow start. His first New York recital (17 April 1944) received polite compliments. "Johannesen appeared not only to have been well schooled, but to have assimilated his schooling with intelligence and integrity. He has a sane, forthright and well-calculated approach to the keyboard, and his renditions show a theoretical and structural perception." (*NYS*, 18 April 1944) Another reviewer likewise found Johannesen's interpretations to be carefully calculated and well-balanced; and also "shaped with intellect, as well as with feeling. The resulting performances are not cold; they are colored with practice and with work, rather than with spontaneous emotion." (*NYT*, 18 April 1944)

With his third New York recital (17 Nov 1946), Johannesen showed much improvement in his art. His tone, "which previously had taken on edge under stress, has grown admirably mellow and sensitive throughout its wide dynamic range. His work could now be praised not merely for its technical proficiency, but because of its new wealth of coloring and its surprising gain in interpretative skill." (*NYT*, 18 Nov 1946)

Johannesen kept on improving. His program of 19 December 1948 "put him in the front ranks of American pianists. . . . His Town Hall recital disclosed solid comprehension of musical values. He places artistry above technical virtuosity, and he has the fine technique, the musicianship and the spirit to sustain interest continuously." (*NYJA*, 20 Dec 1948) The *New York Times* critic at that same concert singled out Johannesen's mixing of traditional concert works with lesser-known compositions by famous composers. For example, he played the first New York performance of Poulenc's *Suite française*, Schumann's seldom-heard Intermezzos, op. 4, and a group of French pieces that included Debussy's *Etude pour les sonorités opposées*, *Etude pour les cinq doigts* and *Hommage à Rameau*; Fauré's Fifth Impromptu, op. 102; and Roussel's *Bourrée* (Suite, op. 14). Bach's Prelude and Fugue in A Minor, Mozart's Sonata in B-flat Major, K. 570, and Chopin's Ballade in F Minor made up the familiar portion of the mix.

The steadily maturing Johannesen developed into a superb pianist. After 18 years on the concert circuit he had become "a very important artist—an artist who has preserved his individuality and gone his own way. Of not too many can this be said." This review of Johannesen's Philharmonic Hall recital of 26 November 1962 includes: "He is disciplined technically as well as emotionally. He never lets himself go, and always there is a feeling of emotional reserve. But his is music-making in the best of taste, animated by a fine mind and a pair of hands that must be the envy of his colleagues." (*NYT*, 27 Nov 1962)

On another occasion (18 Nov 1969) he played Darius Milhaud's Concerto No. 1 in New York with the Little Orchestra Society, conducted by Thomas Scherman. Johannesen "played the concerto—by no means a simple work—with just the right mixture of classicism, fun, rhythmic finesse and clear finger work. This kind of elegance is invariably captured by Mr. Johannesen in the French literature from Fauré to today. Part of the trick is an avoidance of overstatement, another part is extreme clarity of line, and still another part is just the proper admixture of delicate color. Most satisfactory." (*NYT*, 19 Nov 1969)

On 14 January 1983, Johannesen played Fauré's Ballade, op. 19, and Fantaisie, op. 111, with the Ohio Chamber Orchestra, conducted by Dwight Oltman. The Ballade "was performed with a refined feeling for proportion and line. The music ebbed and flowed naturally, the wistful theme sang with unaffected nuance and the gentle finale melted with the deliciousness of Johannesen's warm tone and deep touch." (*CPD*, 15 Jan 1983)

Johannesen made a piano arrangement of several episodes from Poulenc's ballet *Les Animaux modèles* and played it on a New York recital (27 Oct 1976) devoted to all-French music—Dukas, Debussy, Fauré, Poulenc. "The pianist is probably Poulenc's outstanding interpreter today, and naturally he knows the Poulenc style inside out. These little sketches, so skillfully worked up by Mr. Johannesen, provide a charming set of miniatures." (*NYT*, 28 Oct 1976)

All three of Johannesen's New York recitals during the 1985–86 season were devoted to the music of Schumann and Fauré. He was joined in the first program by the venerable 83-year-old Gaby Casadesus, widow of Johannesen's beloved teacher. Together they played Fauré's *Dolly*, op. 56 (pianoforte duet). The second program highlighted Schumann's six *Intermezzi*, op. 4, plus the *Fantasiestücke*, op. 12, also a Fauré group including the Nocturne in C-sharp Minor, op. 74, Impromptu in F-sharp Minor, op. 102, and the Valse Caprice in G-flat Major, op. 59. At least one critic found this program enchanting. "Perhaps the most wonderful gift this distinguished artist imparts is the ability to project the rhythmic underpinnings of a work with extraordinary clarity and élan. . . . Johannesen's lyrical playing is a grand lesson in sensitive tone coloring and intelligent phrasing, but what impresses this listener over and again is his enormous and spontaneous-sounding control of the music's overall flow." (*MA*, May 1987)

Saint-Saëns's Concerto No. 5 in F Major, op. 103, described as "the most pictorial of all the concertos," is not often performed. Johannesen gave his audience the opportunity to hear and enjoy this most challenging work on 5 July 1991, when he played it with the Cleveland Orchestra, Louis Lane conducting, at the Blossom Music Center. "Johannesen, an American pianist with a flair for French style, shaped an elegant performance. In the first movement, he balanced playfulness and poetry, delicacy and weight. In the finale, he abandoned himself to the work's sparkling virtuosity." (*CPD*, 6 July 1991)

The "quiet virtues of a longtime pianist" were well in evidence when the 74-year-old Johannesen played a Carnegie Hall recital (18 Feb 1995) to commemorate the 50th anniversary of his New York debut. There were some technical mishaps, but throughout Johannesen "showed a deep intelligence and unmannered expressivity," and he gave elegant and commanding readings of a wide-ranging repertoire: Franck's *Prélude, Choral et Fugue*, Beethoven's Sonata in F-sharp Major, op. 78, Schubert's Sonata in B-flat Major, D. 960, Fauré's Ballade, op. 19, and Ravel's Five O'Clock Fantasy. At his best form in Schubert's great Sonata, Johannesen played "with an utterly natural grasp of phrase and cadence. This reading was supremely tasteful, an oasis of grace." Everything about this recital "made sense and sounded right." (*NYT*, 22 Feb 1995)

The catalogue of Grant Johannesen's recordings—for Vox, HMV, Pantheon and Golden Crest—reveals the wide range of his musicianship (see Discog.). Unfortunately much of this repertoire remains on LP, not having yet been transferred to CD. He has recorded works by Bach, Mozart, Beethoven, Schubert, Chopin and Schumann. In addition he displays a special affinity for the French repertoire and for contemporary American music.

A generous selection of Johannesen's French repertoire has recently been reissued in a 3-CD Vox Box (see Discog.). Compositions by Chabrier, Chausson, Debussy, d'Indy, Dukas, Fauré, Franck, Milhaud, Ravel, Roussel, Saint-Saëns and Sévérac make this a totally engaging collection. Johannesen's "artistry is secure in every important respect—in depth of understanding, technique, choice of tempos, control of tone and color. . . . In many of these selections he uses skillful fingering, pedalling and phrasing to produce a soft-edged tone that is lovely and entirely appropriate to the music; but he is also capable of brilliance when required." (Alexander Morin, *American Record Guide* [Sept/Oct 1994]. Reprinted by permission.)

A definitely "unserious" work is the Sports and Diversions (*Sports et Divertissements*) with text and music by Erik Satie. Johannesen plays the music and the eminent actress Mildred Natwick narrates the text in an English version by Virgil Thomson. All in all, a delightful, sometimes hilarious, experience.

Many of the compositions recorded by Johannesen are available nowhere else, a tribute to his penchant for the unusual and unhackneyed.

SELECTED REFERENCES

Blomster, Wes. "Grant Johannesen performs five concerts in a week for CMF." *Daily Camera*, 1 July 1990.

Crutchfield, Will. "Johannesen's 40 Years of Concerts." *New York Times*, 30 Sept 1984, sec. 2, p. 23.

Delacoma, Wynne. "Pianist Grant Johannesen promotes modern music." *Chicago Sun-Times*, 20 May 1988 (Weekend Plus), p. 25.

Finn, Robert. "Grant Johannesen: Renaissance Man." *Clavier*, Nov 1979, pp. 12–16.

Fruchter, Rena. "Distinguished Pianist to Play." *New York Times*, 4 Jan 1987, p. 22.

Henry, Derrick. "Grant Johannesen Finds Joy in Reclaiming Repertoire." *Atlanta Journal*, 5 March 1989, sec. K, p. 4.

Johannesen, Grant. "Artist's Life." *Keynote*, Sept 1984, p. 31.

―――. "The Lesson." *Piano Quarterly*, Fall 1982, pp. 24–26. A lesson with Robert Casadesus.

―――. "Listen to Yourself." *Etude*, June 1953, pp. 17, 60.

―――. "Prisms." (interview) *Piano Quarterly*, Summer 1979, pp. 10–12.

Kupferberg, Herbert. "Grant Johannesen." *Musical America*, Dec 1986, pp. 8–9, 42.

Marum, Lisa. "Grant Johannesen Champions The Lesser-Known Masters." *Ovation*, July 1989, pp. 33–34, 68.

Mathews, Anne. "Catching Up with Grant Johannesen." *Salt Lake City Tribune*, 18 March 1990.

Milburn, Frank, Jr. "Johannesen—His Pianism Mirrors Other Arts." *Musical America*, 15 Dec 1958, pp. 12–13.

See also Bibliography: Con/Bak; Cur/Bio (1961); Dub/Ref; WWAM.

SELECTED REVIEWS

ADN: 8 Dec 1985. *AR*: 7 Nov 1983; 26 Feb 1985. *CCC-T*: 15 Jan 1984; 16 Feb 1990. *CPD*: 15 Jan 1983; 3 Nov 1983; 3 Feb 1989; 6 July 1991. *CSM*: 12 Dec 1984. *DC*: 24 June 1983; 9 July 1990. *DDN*: 18 April 1991. *DP*: 22 Aug 1980. *GBPG*: 3 June 1990. *LAT*: 5 Nov 1984. *MA*: 1 Jan 1949; May 1987. *MoT*: 17 March 1988. *NYJA*: 20 Dec 1948. *NYP*: 3 Nov 1986. *NYS*: 18 April 1944. *NYT*: 18 April 1944; 19 Feb 1945; 18 Nov 1946; 20 Dec 1948; 25 Oct 1954; 27 Nov 1962; 23 Jan 1969; 19 Nov 1969; 29 Nov 1971; 28 Oct 1976; 14 Sept 1981; 23 Oct 1984; 3 Nov 1986; 28 Nov 1992; 22 Feb 1995. *OWH*: 11 Jan 1985. *PI*: 13 Nov 1984. *SFC*: 28 Feb 1957; 5 Nov 1984; 22 Sept 1986; 23 Jan 1989; 15 Oct 1990. *SFR*: 27 March 1985. *S-L*: 23 July 1990. *SLT*: 19 May 1969; 10 May 1981; 22 Feb 1987; 24 March 1990. *TL*: 23 June 1965. *WE*: 10 Feb 1985. *WP*: 15 Feb 1984; 14 March 1990; 30 May 1994.

SELECTED DISCOGRAPHY

American Encores from a Russian Tour. Bowles: 6 Preludes. Carpenter: Impromptu, July 1915. Gershwin: 3 Preludes. Gottschalk: *Souvenir de Porto Rico.* Menin: Canto and Toccata. Thomson: Ragtime-Bass. Golden Crest CR 4065.

Casadesus: Second Sonata. Milhaud: *L'Album de Madame Bovary.* Golden Crest CR 4060.

Chopin: Polonaises Nos. 1-4, 6, 8-10. Allegretto ACD-8043.

Fauré: Complete Piano Works. 6-Golden Crest CR 40348 (LP).

Four American Composers. Bergsma: Tangents. Copland: Piano Variations. Dello Joio: 2 Nocturnes. Harris: American Ballads. Golden Crest CRS 4111.

Grant Johannesen in Recital. Copland: Piano Variations. Debussy: *Masques*; *L'Isle joyeuse.* Schumann: Intermezzi, op. 4. Golden Crest CRSD-1

Grant Johannesen performs Rare Russian Repertoire. Prokofiev: Fragments; Sonata No. 7 in B-flat Major, op. 83. Rachmaninoff: Six Songs (trans. Wild). Stravinsky: Tango. Bonneville Classics CDD 3521.

Grant Johannesen plays French Music. Chabrier: *Ballabile*; *Bourrée fantasque*; Impromptu. Chausson: *Quelques danses.* Debussy: Children's Corner. D'Indy: *Chant de bruyères.* Dukas: Variations, Interlude and Finale on a Theme by Rameau. Fauré: Ballade in F-sharp Major, op. 19; Fantaisie in G Major, op. 111 (de Froment/Orch. of Radio Luxembourg); Impromptu in A-flat Major, op. 34; Impromptu in F-sharp Minor, op. 102; Nocturne in C-sharp Minor, op. 74. Franck: *Prélude, Choral et Fugue.* Milhaud: Four Romances; *Hymne de glorification.* Ravel: *Sérénade grotesque.* Roussel: *Bourrée* (Suite, op. 14); Three Pieces, op. 49. Saint-Saëns: *Bourrée* (Etude for left hand); Concerto No. 4 in C Minor, op. 44 (Kontarsky/Orch. of Radio Luxembourg). Satie: *Poudre d'or*; *Croquis et agaceries d'un gros bon-homme en bois*; *Préludes flasques pour un chien*. Sévérac: *Pippermint-Get*; *Sous les lauriers roses*. Vox Box CD3X3032 (3 CDs).

Grant Johannesen Recital. Fauré: Ballade in F-sharp Minor, op. 19a. Mozart: Variations on a Minuet by Duport, K. 573. Poulenc: *Thème varié*. Schumann: *Drei Fantasiestücke*, op. 111. Golden Crest CRS 4201.

Grieg: Ballade, op. 24. Poulenc: *Les Animaux modèles*. Tveitt: Haringol. Golden Crest CRDG-4207.

Grieg: Concerto in A Minor, op. 16. Vox/Turnabout PVT 7121 (CD). Abrava-nel/Utah SO.

The Mozart Family Album. Mozart, Franz Xavier Wolfgang: Concerto No. 2 in E-flat Major, op. 25; Mozart, Leopold: Sinfonia. Mozart, Wolfgang Amadeus: *Les Petits riens*. Centaur CRC 2062 (CD).

Poulenc: The Story of Babar the Elephant. Satie: Sports and Diversions (narrated by Mildred Natwick). Golden Crest CRS 4133.

About the Authors

JOHN GILLESPIE is Professor Emeritus, University of California, Santa Barbara, Music Department, where he taught courses in keyboard literature and American music. He is the Series Editor for Greenwood's Bio-Critical Sourcebooks on Musical Performance.

ANNA GILLESPIE and JOHN GILLESPIE have collaborated on and coauthored several books and anthologies.

ISBN 0-313-29695-2

EAN

9 780313 296956

HARDCOVER BAR CODE